T0305579

THE HANDBOOK OF
CHINA'S
FINANCIAL
SYSTEM

THE HANDBOOK OF
CHINA'S FINANCIAL SYSTEM

EDITED BY

**Marlene Amstad,
Guofeng Sun,
and Wei Xiong**

PRINCETON UNIVERSITY PRESS
PRINCETON AND OXFORD

Published by Princeton University Press
41 William Street, Princeton, New Jersey 08540
6 Oxford Street, Woodstock, Oxfordshire OX20 1TR

press.princeton.edu

Library of Congress Cataloging-in-Publication Data

Names: Amstad, Marlene, editor. | Sun, Guofeng, 1972– editor. | Xiong, Wei, 1971– editor.
Title: The handbook of China's financial system / Marlene Amstad,
Guofeng Sun, and Wei Xiong.
Description: Princeton : Princeton University Press, 2020. |
Includes bibliographical references and index.
Identifiers: LCCN 2020005408 (print) | LCCN 2020005409 (ebook) |
ISBN 9780691205731 (hardback) | ISBN 9780691205847 (ebook)
Subjects: LCSH: Banks and banking—China. | Monetary policy—China. |
Finance—China. | Capital market—China. | China—Economic policy—1976–2000. |
China—Economic policy—2000–
Classification: LCC HG3334 .H36 2020 (print) | LCC HG3334 (ebook) | DDC 332.10951—dc23
LC record available at https://lccn.loc.gov/2020005408
LC ebook record available at https://lccn.loc.gov/2020005409

British Library Cataloging-in-Publication Data is available

Editorial: Joe Jackson and Jacqueline Delaney
Jacket Design: Layla Mac Rory
Production: Erin Suydam
Publicity: Kate Farquhar-Thomson
Copyeditor: Mark Woodworth

This book has been composed in Palatino.

Printed on acid-free paper. ∞

Printed in the United States of America

1 3 5 7 9 10 8 6 4 2

CONTENTS

FOREWORD

Darrell Duffie

Over the past quarter century, China's economy has achieved growth exceeding that ever experienced in modern economic times by a large country over a comparatively long period. Because finance is so critical to economic performance, China's exceptional macroeconomic success would not have been possible without a financial system that was at least relatively effective, under the circumstances that applied during this period.

China's GDP growth rate, although still higher than that of all major developed-market economies, has fallen to less-spectacular levels. China is no longer starting from the extremely low base of total output that applied in the 1980s, from which it was possible for even moderate improvements in market efficiency to drive enormous increases in prosperity. Moreover, China faces serious economic challenges, including many extremely heavily indebted state-owned enterprises and a problematic trade dispute with the United States.

Although China's financial system has become more sophisticated and open in recent years, in order to support continued robust growth in the mid-to-long-term future, it will likely need to go through significant further improvements. As part of this, the country's macroeconomy will probably require more efficient allocation of capital (both debt and equity) to industries and enterprises, more effective reorganization or liquidation of overleveraged enterprises, and greater financial transparency. At the same time, though, many bright spots have recently been seen in China's financial sector. For example, its fintech sector is booming, with a vibrancy and sophistication that dominate fintech in all other major economies. Cross-border financial markets have recently become somewhat more open, which will improve access to capital and investment opportunities.

China's financial system has several key structural features that distinguish it from the financial systems of other major economies. First, the central government and local governments play much more significant roles in the allocation of capital. This is sometimes called "state-directed capitalism." Second, participation by domestic investors in foreign capital markets, as well as by foreign investors and other market participants in domestic capital markets, remains heavily restricted by regulation, although these restrictions are being eased over time. Finally, China's most important providers of financial services, by far, are a small number of very large banks. As of 2018, the four largest banks in the world, by assets, were all Chinese. In addition to providing around half of China's banking services, these giant banks are also leading intermediaries in other financial markets, including those for government bonds and "shadow banking" products. The corporate governance of these large banks is dominated by the central government, which owns a large share of each of them.

By comparison with other major global market areas, China's banks are also more important to its economy than are other forms of financial intermediaries. For example, the banks provide more credit to the nonfinancial sector of the economy than do banks in other major regions, especially the United States, although the trend in China is toward a greater role for bond markets.

In most other respects, however, the elements of China's financial system are similar to those of Europe and the United States. For example, other major players in China's financial markets include securities firms, which develop, underwrite, and provide market-making, brokerage, and investment-management services; insurance firms; the operators of exchanges, clearinghouses, securities depositories, payment and settlement systems, and other market infrastructure; and agency-based asset managers such as hedge funds, private-equity firms, venture-capital firms, and purveyors of mutual funds. Financial information providers include auditing firms, credit-rating agencies, and financial benchmark administrators.

The greatest challenge to China's financial system over the next quarter century is likely to be the significant indebtedness of China's state-owned enterprises (SOEs). Its SOEs alone have total corporate debt of about 115% of GDP, of which roughly 10% is "at risk," according to the Asian Development Bank. The fact that China's local and central governments have been so willing to "bail out" many SOEs that would otherwise default is an important weakness of China's economy. These bailouts have the effect of allowing SOE debts to continue to grow, to the point that they may one day need to be resolved with much greater economic costs than would apply if these firms were to be restructured in the near term. In the meantime, capital is being diverted from projects offering greater economic returns. Since roughly 2016, however, China's government has shown more willingness to allow SOEs to default, and the number of such bankruptcies increased significantly in 2018.

The problem of SOE indebtedness is linked to the heavy debt loads of local governments that were incurred through local government financing vehicles (LGFVs), a form of SOE. Under central government direction, the debts of LGFVs are gradually being regularized through debt swaps into official local government bonds and loans.

While the turmoil in China's stock markets that occurred in 2015 and early 2016 received major attention in the global media and caused a significant amount of anxiety about how the country's government involves itself in its financial markets, this was a temporary (albeit costly) distraction. The allocation of capital in primary capital markets, especially debt financing and debt restructuring, is a much bigger economic and social issue. The growth of debt in the nonfinancial sector since 2008 is unprecedented among all large nations.

China's financial policymakers face many other challenges, including how (and especially with what timing) to further open the country's capital markets to two-way global participation (a problem that includes the management of the price of China's currency, the renminbi) and how to regulate shadow banking and Internet finance. China has faced and overcome much greater challenges. I am optimistic.

The Handbook of China's Financial System, edited by Marlene Amstad, Guofeng Sun, and Wei Xiong, will prove to be an invaluable resource for students, researchers, and policymakers alike, who will benefit enormously from access to its in-depth analyses of structure and developments in China's financial system. The handbook covers its many elements, including commercial banking, central banking, equity markets, bond markets, asset management, the pension system, cross-border markets, venture capital, shadow banking, regulation, and the real estate market, among numerous other important topics. The authors of this handbook's chapters constitute a dream team of experts, drawn mainly from leading academic institutions as well as from China's official sector. Readers of this tremendous resource will greatly deepen their understanding of how the financial system works, better appreciate the challenges faced by China's financial regulators and other policymakers, and perhaps also learn more about how to participate profitably in the country's financial markets.

THE HANDBOOK OF
CHINA'S
FINANCIAL
SYSTEM

INTRODUCTION

Marlene Amstad, Guofeng Sun, and Wei Xiong

China's financial system has served indispensable roles in China's spectacular economic growth over the past 40 years. Given the size and growing complexity of the Chinese economy, China's financial system is likely to become even more important in mobilizing capital across the economy in the next stage of China's economic development. However, concerns are being expressed both inside and outside China about the potential instability in its financial system, with particular concerns about elevated real estate prices and debt levels. This handbook collects 17 chapters written by leading experts from academia, the policy community, and the financial industry to provide a holistic view of multiple sectors of China's financial system.

One may easily characterize that system as being large yet underdeveloped. This system builds around a dominant banking sector, a quickly growing bond market, and a widely followed stock market. Each of these markets is already among the largest in the global system, although not quite as developed as those in many advanced countries.

China's banking sector entails 5 of the 10 largest banks in the world. It remains the core of China's financial system and the key channel for implementing China's monetary policy. Chapter 1, **"Banking Institutions and Banking Regulations,"** by Guofeng Sun, documents the dominance of banking institutions in China's financial system. The loans made by banking institutions accounted for 92% of the Aggregate Financing to the Real Economy (AFRE) in 2002. While this ratio came down in recent years, it remained at a very high level of 76% in 2018. Even more impressively, banking institutions owned more than 97% of the total assets in China's financial system in 2018, reflecting the fact that banks not only make loans but also serve as the main sources of funding for the bond markets, for shadow banking products (such as trust loans and entrusted loans), and for even the asset management industry. This dominance is bolstered by the high saving rate of households and firms throughout China. Different from other countries, where savings are mostly absorbed by direct investment in bond and equity markets, in China the banking system captures a large share of these savings. This empowers the banking sector as the key channel for funding China's financial and monetary policies, as well as for developing other new financial sectors, particularly the bond market.

The bond market has experienced rapid growth in the past decade, with bond market capitalization over GDP growing from 35% in 2008 to over 95% in 2018. Albeit still far from the level of over 200% in the United States, the Chinese bond market in 2019 became the second largest bond market in the world with $13 trillion, only after the United States with $38 trillion and before Japan with $12 trillion. Despite its size, the bond market has remained in some respects underdeveloped, as documented in chapter 5, **"Chinese Bond Markets and Interbank Market,"** by Marlene Amstad and Zhiguo He. While a centralized exchange market exists to enable nonbank institutions and individuals to invest in bonds, it accounts only for a small share of the bond market. Interestingly, the biggest part, listing about 89% of all bonds outstanding at the end of 2018, is another segmented market—the interbank bond market, which mainly serves the investment needs of banking institutions. The dominance of this largely bank-driven interbank bond market deeply connects the bond market to China's banking reforms, and in particular to both its interest rate liberalization and the internalization of its currency, the RMB. Room for further development and market deepening also exists in the corporate bond market. Despite its rapid growth and large market size, China's corporate bond market shows little credit differentiation, as over 95% of the outstanding amount of nonfinancial credit bonds are covered in only three rating categories. This bond market has so far seen very few public defaults.

While the stock market contributes less to the AFRE than do the banking sector and even the bond market, it has grown into the second largest equity market in the world, with a total market capitalization of $8.7 trillion at the end of 2017, trailing only the U.S. equity market with $32 trillion and ahead of Japan with $6.2 trillion. Chapter 11, **"The Development of the Chinese Stock Market,"** by Franklin Allen, Jun "QJ" Qian, Chenyu Shan, and Julie Lei Zhu, reviews the development of China's stock market and summarizes its institutional arrangements and market performance. Differing from most of the other financial sectors, the stock market initially grew outside of the banking sector and has been dominated by individual investors in terms of trading, as characterized by its high annual turnover ratios of 161.6% and 264.5% in the Shanghai and Shenzhen Stock Exchanges, respectively, which far exceed the ratios of other major stock exchanges throughout the world. The high liquidity in the secondary market contrasts with that in the tightly regulated primary market. China is one of few markets with a performance-based IPO system, incentivizing Chinese firms to get listed abroad despite their already being in the country with the second largest equity market. This is again a testament to the need of further development, despite the achieved size. It should be noted that this need has supported the rise of the venture capital market.

It is probably less known that the past 10 years have seen a period of unprecedented successes for both China's emerging industries and the venture capital (VC) market, which have both grown to global significance. Chapter 15, **"China's Venture Capital Market,"** by Zhaojun Huang and Xuan Tian, compares Chinese VC activities with U.S. ones. While the VC world was dominated by experienced foreign VCs in the 1990s and early 2000s, its growth in recent years is currently being driven largely by domestic VCs. Despite the Chinese VC market's size as the second largest in the world in terms of deal value, this market has nevertheless not yet matured.

It is tempting to adopt the common framework developed for evaluating Western financial systems to evaluate the strength as well as the weakness of China's financial system. This system certainly faces some common problems, such as a booming real estate sector and a largely expanded shadow banking sector. Chapter 7, **"China's Real Estate Market,"** by Chang Liu and Wei Xiong, describes the dramatic and long-lasting real estate boom that has occurred across China and discusses the crucial links of this boom to households, local governments, firms, and banks. In 2003–2017, housing price indices in China's four so-called first-tier cities—Beijing, Shanghai, Guangzhou, and Shenzhen— grew from 7 to 11 times higher, and even in the so-called second- and third-tier cities it grew from 3 to 5 times higher. As housing sales today contribute to almost a fifth of China's GDP, and as real estate–related loans account for about a quarter of its banking assets, a crash in the real estate sector would have enormous consequences on the country's economy, with potential spillover effects to the rest of the world economy.

While the real estate boom in China is reminiscent of the U.S. housing bubble in 2006, it is important to recognize that the origin of China's real estate boom is substantially different. The U.S. housing bubble, which eventually led to the U.S. financial crisis in 2008, was driven by a credit expansion through shadow banking to households. In China, the real estate boom is instead deeply rooted in local governments, which rely heavily on land sales revenues as well as debt collateralized by real estate assets to fund local fiscal spending. Interestingly, the shadow banking sector in China played a key role in channeling debt to the so-called local government financing vehicles, which are firms set up by local governments to raise debt financing for local infrastructure projects.

China's financial system has undergone many reforms in the past four decades, yet in many respects it remains substantially different from those in a typical Western country. Many of these differences are rooted in the institutional foundation of China's financial system. It is particularly useful to recognize that the government has consciously used the financial system as a toolbox to implement government policies and to resolve financing issues it has encountered during the country's economic reforms, as discussed by a recent review by Song and Xiong (2018). This perspective explains why its financial system is still underdeveloped despite its enormous size. In particular, it explains banks' lending preferences to state-owned enterprises (SOEs)—a key feature of China's banking sector, as highlighted by the celebrated model of the Chinese economy by Song, Storesletten, and Zilibotti (2011)—and it further explains the advantages of SOEs in qualifying for public listing in China's stock market. This handbook covers these key pillars of the institutional framework through several chapters.

To systematically understand how China's financial system differs from other countries, it is illustrative to look into financial policies, particularly those related to infrastructure financing. Chapter 6, **"Macroeconomic Effects of China's Financial Policies,"** by Kaiji Chen and Tao Zha, summarizes how regime shifts in the government's active financial policies influenced the ways in which preferential credits were allocated to SOEs and the heavy sector, mostly through the banking sector. The transition of the economy is presented in three phases from an economy led by growth and reforms of SOEs (1978–1997) to one driven by investment in large and capital-intensive enterprises, termed "the heavy sector" (1998–2015), to what the Chinese government calls "a new normal economy" (2016 to the present). The crucial role played by the government and the financial sector alike in mobilizing resources is highlighted for infrastructure investment. Chapter 8, **"Infrastructure Financing,"** by Zhiwei Zhang and Yi Xiong, covers the financing of sustained high levels of investment in infrastructure, which has been a key factor in China's economic success over the past decades. The chapter elucidates the complex system of fiscal and financial arrangements by government, focusing on the important role played by quasi-fiscal entities such as local government financing vehicles (LGFVs), allowing them to mobilize resources far beyond budget constraints and thus creating substantial amount of quasi-fiscal debt, which has eventually led to a major macro problem in the Chinese economy today.

While the financial system provides key funding for the development of the economy, its powerful instruments, without proper regulations, may also exacerbate existing distortions, which are ample in China's transitional economy. Chapter 2, **"Monetary Policy Framework and Transmission Mechanisms,"** by Yiping Huang, Tingting Ge, and Chu Wang, discusses the broad direction for monetary policy evolution against the background of the Chinese economy's transition from a centrally planned system to a market economy. Different from the apparently more effective, price-based monetary policy frameworks that are based on targeting certain interest rates, China's monetary policy targets the quantity of money supply in the economy. This important policy choice reflects the inability of the People's Bank of China (PBC) to effectively influence market interest rates in a substantial portion of the economy, such as SOEs and local governments, which is still not fully driven by market forces. Chapter 3, **"Monetary Policy Instruments,"** by Tao Wang, details how the PBC in recent years has increased the use of price-based policy instruments. However, to date the key framework still relies more on quantity-based policy instruments and also on macro prudential and administrative measures.

With China's widely observed successes in reforming its state sector, it has also started to speed up its liberalization and internationalization processes of the financial sectors. However, the government has been cautious in liberalizing the financial system owing to its concerns about potential adverse effects. A recent theory of Xiong (2018) argues that the liberalization of debt financing by local governments during China's postcrisis stimulus in 2008–2010 served to fuel the agency problems between the central government and local officials, leading to the rapid rise of leverage levels across the country. This balancing act over several stages can be seen in liberalizing interest rates, as summarized in chapter 4, **"China's Interest Rate Liberalization,"** by Jun Ma and Xiaobei He. The process of interest rate liberalization is described as being a gradual sequence from domestic money and bond market, over onshore loan and deposit rates in foreign currencies, to liberalization of RMB lending and deposit rates.

Similarly, Chapter 9, **"RMB Internationalization,"** by Kai Guo, Ningxin Jiang, Fan Qi, and Yue Zhao, discusses the current state of RMB internationalization from the time of limited progress before the global financial crisis to the acceleration post the crisis that peaked in the RMB's inclusion into the Special Drawing Right (SDR) currency basket of the International Monetary Fund. These efforts aim at meeting market demands by removing unnecessary administrative barriers and constructing a complete chain of RMB cross-border flows, including currency swaps as well as improved infrastructure for cross-border RMB trading and settlement. Started four decades ago, the opening of the capital account had seen twists and turns. Chapter 10, **"China's Capital Account Liberalization,"** by Yanliang Miao and Tuo Deng, describes how the opening of the country's capital accounts has been slower and bumpier than one might have anticipated. Despite various government efforts, starting with the foreign direct investment (FDI) expansion from 1992, the Q Schemes (RQFII, QDII, QFII) related to the dual surplus after 1997 as well as the C Schemes (stock connect, bond connect) related to the liberalization and carry trades reversal, the current degree of openness is still mixed between being much freer for certain types of flows (FDI) while still being stringent for others.

Aside from already large markets, the Chinese financial system is also home to several markets and institutional setups, which are relatively new to the country or are currently limited in scale but quickly developing. This includes standards in corporate governance as well as accounting principles. Of increasing importance are also the pension system and the development of asset management industry. Finally, in specific sectors such as payments, the growth of the fintech industry has leapfrogged the traditional system in just a few years.

Corporate governance and financial reporting standards in China have seen integration toward international standards. Chapter 12, **"Corporate Governance in China,"** by Cong Wang, evaluates the various types of agency problems dominating in Chinese companies, including concentrated ownership structures that lead to agency conflicts manifested in different forms of minority shareholder expropriation. While internal governance concepts are modeled after those in Western countries, their effectiveness is questioned as they often lack company-specific monitoring and independent design of managerial compensation in SOEs. Market-oriented approaches such as shareholder activism and the market for corporate control are still dysfunctional because of short-term-focused investors and ownership concentration. Regulatory reforms, including the investigations and enforcement actions by the China Securities Regulatory Commission (CSRC), are expected to play a more important role in China's corporate governance system. High demand for accounting information in the market has triggered groundbreaking changes during recent decades. Chapter 13, **"The Accounting System in China,"** by Tianyu Zhang, introduces the legislative framework of China's accounting system and reviews its evolution. It also identifies the need for further improvement in spite of the accounting profession's transition to a new era in China.

Alongside the maturing Chinese financial markets, the asset management industry gains in importance. Chapter 14, **"Investment Funds in China,"** by Wenxi Jiang, reviews important facts about China's investment funds over the past 20 years. Despite its fast growth, the mutual fund sector remains relatively small, covering only 3% to 4% of the Chinese stock market capitalization, compared with about 30% in the United States. Interestingly, while China's mutual fund's average expense ratios of active and passive mutual funds seem higher than in the United States, China's active managed mutual funds' return net of fees does *not* appear to underperform the market or a risk-adjusted benchmark, thus being different from its U.S. counterpart.

As the Chinese population ages, reforming and improving the pension system is of utmost importance. Chapter 16, **"The Chinese Pension System,"** by Hanming Fang and Jin Feng, details the three layers of China's pension system. The public pension schemes aiming to provide basic social security to all residents reaches 65% of the population, while the employer-sponsored annuity programs voluntarily provided by employers account for less than 0.5% of all the firms in China. Meanwhile, household savings-based annuity insurance policies are still in their infancy. The chapter further discusses many open issues to study in all these areas, including the efficiency cost of China's fragmented social insurance system, fiscal implications in case of a growth slowdown, optimizing investment product characteristics, and impacts on the Chinese labor market.

Unexpectedly, the underdevelopment of China's financial system provides room for the country to leap over many developed countries in adopting frontier fintech innovations. In particular, mobile payment has found many wider applications in China than in any other countries. The two widely used mobile payment systems, Ali Pay and Wechat Pay, now anchor two ecosystems that offer a wide range of financial services, including payment, risk assessment, and credit, to a large pool of individuals and small firms that are otherwise underserved by traditional financial institutions. Chapter 17, **"Fintech Development,"** by Bohui Zhang, documents how China has emerged as a leader in fintech adoption rates, companies, and hubs.

China's financial system has undergone broad and fast changes over the past three decades and will continue to do so for the foreseeable future. Often the change occurs as many small steps, hampering the ability to see the bigger picture. Also, it's inevitable that events such as the pandemic in 2020 will leave its trace. This handbook aims to uncover the underlying long-term features of China's financial system and thus to offer a solid foundation to understand the changes that lie ahead.

Taken together, the chapters in this handbook can be used in universities and business schools as reading material for undergraduate or master-level courses. As a whole, it can be used as the main reading material for a course that specializes in the Chinese financial system. Its chapters can also be used separately as reading material for a broad range of courses, including ones that provide a general introduction to financial markets or to the Chinese economy as well as courses that cover specific economic and financial issues related to emerging economies. For finance practitioners and policymakers alike, this handbook offers a one-stop solution for an in-depth overview of the current state of China's financial markets and institutions. Furthermore, academics can use different chapters of the handbook as a reference to a wide range of economic and finance topics related to China process.

ACKNOWLEDGEMENTS

This Handbook started out as lecture notes and reading materials for the three editors' courses on the Chinese financial system. We thank students of our courses at Shenzhen Finance Institute; the Chinese University of Hong Kong, Shenzhen; and Princeton University for extensive discussions and feedback on early drafts made available on the Handbook webpage, www.chinafinancialsystem.com. We thank all the contributors for their tireless efforts throughout the process, and we thank Yating Yuan for invaluable research assistance. Finally, we thank Joe Jackson and Jacqueline Delany from Princeton University Press for their great efforts to make the publication of this Handbook possible, and Angela Piliouras from Westchester Publishing Services for a thorough editing and production process.

REFERENCES

Song, Zheng, Kjetil Storesletten, and Fabrizio Zilibotti (2011). "Growing Like China." *American Economic Review* 101(1): 196–233.

Song, Zheng, and Wei Xiong (2018). "Risks in China's Financial System." *Annual Review of Financial Economics* 10: 261–86.

Xiong, Wei (2018). "The Mandarin Model of Growth." Working paper, Princeton University.

PART 1

BANKING AND MONETARY POLICY

1

BANKING INSTITUTIONS
AND BANKING REGULATIONS

Guofeng Sun

China's financial sector has undergone dramatic changes over the last 40 years. Before the start of China's market-oriented reform in 1978, the sector consisted of a handful of institutions with extremely limited functions, whereas today it is home to some of the world's largest banks. The recovery and reconstruction of the Agriculture Bank of China (ABC), the Bank of China (BOC), and the China Construction Bank (CCB) in 1979 signaled the start of the reform of China's banking industry. The Industrial and Commercial Bank of China (ICBC) was founded in January 1984; shortly afterward, on April 1, 1987, the Bank of Communications (BCM) was restructured. ABC, BOC, CCB, and BCM existed before these reconstructions in different names or as subsidiaries of other institutions.

To understand China's financial sector, it is necessary to view it within the broad context of economic reform, which transformed China from a closed, stagnant, centrally planned, agrarian economy to an open, dynamic, market-oriented, industrial economy. Before the reforms, the financial sector was largely sidelined or even eliminated and played no role in the central-planning machinery other than that of cashier and accountancy; it gradually gained greater prominence as the market started to play a larger role in allocating resources as a result of China's market reforms (Yi, 2009). Today, China's banking industry is the synthesis of China's economic reforms and its historical legacy. Through a series of reforms, China's banking institutions have become some of the best in the world and dominate China's financial system (Yi and Guo, 2014).

This chapter gives an overview of the ongoing development of banking institutions and banking regulations in China, with a focus on the main characteristics, formation, and reform processes that have changed the sector since 1978. The first section introduces the main characteristics of the banking institutions, which are at the center of the financial system. The sector is highly concentrated in large, state-owned commercial banks. The second section describes the major types of China's banking institutions. The third section discusses the reforms of the state-owned commercial banks, and then reviews the recent reforms of the banking industry. The fourth section describes the regulators of China's banking industry—the People's Bank of China (PBC), the China Banking and Insurance Regulatory Commission (CBIRC), the Ministry of Finance (MOF), and the State Administration of Foreign Exchange (SAFE). The fifth section summarizes both what has been achieved through the implementation of regulations, including micro-prudential supervision initiatives and macro-prudential policies, and what remains to be done. The sixth section introduces China's shadow banking, detailing its composition, size, development, financial risk, monetary policy challenges, and recent regulations.

1. INTRODUCTION

1.1. Banking Institutions Dominate China's Financial System

Banking institutions make up most of China's financial system (Sun, 2015a). In the 40 years since the beginning of China's economic reform and opening-up policy, China's banking industry has made rapid progress and has now established its leading role in the world (table 1.1). In *The Banker*'s list of the 1,000 top banks in the world, 136 were Chinese. Among the top ten banks ranked by tier-one capital, China's banks and U.S. banks took four places each.

Banking institutions have consistently dominated China's financial system. The banking industry has been the major financial support for substantive economic development throughout the country.

The total assets of China's banking system are enormous; in fact, most of the assets in China's financial system are concentrated in the banking system (Demirgüç-Kunt and Levin, 2004). As shown in table 1.2, the banking industry owns more than 97% of the financial system's total assets.

In addition, the scale of the banking industry far exceeds the total financing of the bond and stock markets (Sun, 2015b). As demonstrated in table 1.3, in 2002, the loans by the banking industry accounted for more than 90% of the flow of Aggregate Financing to the Real Economy (AFRE)[1]. As it was developed, the banking industry has decreased its share of support to the real economy, but it remains very high—in 2018, it accounted for 65% of the flow of AFRE. There are two points worth noting. First, although the banking industry has decreased the amount of loans for AFRE, its asset management business, as listed in table 1.3, is rapidly growing. Second, the main source of funding for trust loans, a key component of the shadow banking, is still the banking industry.

1.2. High Concentration in Big Banks

In China's banking system, the five big state-owned commercial banks have always maintained their dominance. They are the Industrial and Commercial Bank of China, the Agriculture Bank of China, the Bank of China, the China Construction Bank, and the Bank of Communication.

These five state-owned commercial banks have the highest profits. In 2005 to 2016, their pretax profits increased 6.3 times, from 23.5 billion dollars to 171.7 billion dollars, for a compound annual growth rate of 19.8%. At the end of 2016, the total amount of profits of these five had exceeded the overall profits of seven global banks: Citigroup Inc.,

Table 1.1. Top 10 Banks in 2019 Ranked by *The Banker* (in USD million)

Rank	Bank	Country	Tier-one capital	Pretax profit	Total assets
1	ICBC	China	337,539.12	54,366.86	4,043,728.47
2	CCB	China	287,461.31	44,986.86	3,390,174.16
3	ABC	China	242,895.33	36,740.73	3,300,652.70
4	BOC	China	229,969.78	33,524.53	3,104,711.68
5	J.P. Morgan Chase	US	209,093.00	40,790.00	2,622,532.00
6	Bank of America	US	189,038.00	34,585.00	2,354,980.00
7	Wells Fargo	US	167,866.00	28,537.00	1,895,883.00
8	Citigroup	US	158,122.00	23,437.00	1,917,383.00
9	HSBC	UK	147,142.00	19,890.00	2,558,124.00
10	Mitsubishi UFJ	Japan	146,739.09	10,325.70	2,805,074.86

Source: The Banker, July 1, 2019.

Table 1.2. Structural Changes in the Total Assets of China's Financial System, 2003–2017 (in RMB billion)

Year	Banking institutions' total assets[a]	Nonbank financial institutions' total assets[b]	Percentage of total assets owned by banking institutions
2003	27,658	910	97
2004	31,599	873	97
2005	37,470	1,016	97
2006	43,950	1,059	98
2007	53,116	972	98
2008	63,152	1,180	98
2009	79,515	1,550	98
2010	95,305	2,090	98
2011	113,287	2,607	98
2012	133,622	3,230	98
2013	151,355	3,968	97
2014	172,336	5,012	97
2015	199,345	6,488	97
2016	232,253	7,931	97
2017	252,404	11,942	95

Source: CBIRC.

[a] Banking institutions' total assets are resources formed by past transactions or events of commercial banks, owned or controlled by commercial banks and expected to bring them economic benefits. The main resources are loans, investments (securities investment, cash assets investment, and fixed assets investment), leasing, foreign exchange trading, bill discounting, and so on, the most important being loans and investments. Loans include short-term, medium-term, long-term credit, and consumer loans.

[b] Nonbank financial institutions raise funds in the form of issuing stocks and bonds, accepting credit entrustment, providing insurance, and the like. They use the funds raised for long-term investment.

Table 1.3. Structure of China's AFRE,[a] 2003–2018

Year	AFRE (flow) (RMB billions)	RMB/foreign currency loans and bank's acceptance bill (%)	Entrust loans[b] (%)	Trust loans (%)	Corporate bonds (%)	Nonfinancial enterprises' domestic stock financing (%)	Other (%)
2002	2,011	92	1	0	2	3	2
2003	3,411	94	2	0	2	2	1
2004	2,863	83	11	0	2	2	2
2005	3,001	83	7	0	7	1	2
2006	4,270	81	6	2	5	4	2
2007	5,966	79	6	3	4	7	2
2008	6,980	75	6	5	8	5	2
2009	13,910	79	5	3	9	2	2
2010	14,019	77	6	3	8	4	2
2011	12,829	71	10	2	11	3	4
2012	15,763	65	8	8	14	2	3
2013	17,317	59	15	11	10	1	4
2014	16,457	61	15	3	15	3	3
2015	15,409	62	10	0	19	5	3
2016	17,802	56	12	5	17	7	3
2017	26,154	55	3	9	2	3	28
2018	22,492	65	-7	-3	12	2	32

Source: PBC.

[a] AFRE (flow) refers to amount of financing that a financial system provides to the real economy in a designated period.

[b] An entrusted loan is a lending arrangement organized by an agent bank between borrowers and lenders. In such a loan, the agent bank is considered the trustee and the company providing the funds is considered the trustor. The trustee is responsible for the collection of principal and any interest, for which it charges a handling fee, but it is not supposed to assume any of the loan risks.

Table 1.4. Composition of Profits of China's Banking Industry, 2019 Q1

Institution type	Net profits (RMB billions)	Percentage
Big commercial bank	294.5	51.53
Joint-stock commercial bank	120.2	21.03
City commercial bank	77.5	13.56
Private bank	1.9	0.33
Rural financial institution	72.3	12.65
Foreign bank	5.3	0.93
Total amount	571.5	100

Source: CBIRC.

Table 1.5. Structure of Total Assets of China's Banking Institutions, 2003–2018

Year	Assets of banking institutions (RMB billions)	Assets of five big commercial banks (RMB billions)	Percentage of assets owned by five big commercial banks (%)
2003	27,658	16,051	58.03
2004	31,599	17,982	56.91
2005	37,470	21,005	56.06
2006	43,950	24,236	55.15
2007	53,116	28,500	53.66
2008	63,152	32,575	51.58
2009	79,515	40,800	51.31
2010	95,305	46,894	49.2
2011	113,287	53,634	47.34
2012	133,622	60,040	44.93
2013	151,355	65,601	43.34
2014	172,336	71,014	41.21
2015	199,345	78,163	39.21
2016	232,253	86,598	37.29
2017	252,404	92,815	36.77
2018	268,240	98,353	36.67

Source: CBIRC.

HSBC, Bank of America, JP Morgan Chase, MUFG, Crédit Agricole Group, and Wells Fargo. As shown in table 1.4, in 2019 Q1, these five banks alone created profits of 294.5 billion yuan, accounting for 51.53% of the entire profits of China's banking industry.

At the end of 2018, the total assets of the financial institutions making up China's banking industry were 268,240 billion yuan. The percentages of the total assets owned by different types of financial institutions are shown in table 1.5: big commercial banks account for 36.7%, joint-stock commercial banks account for 17.5%, city commercial banks account for 12.8%, and rural area financial institutions account for 12.9%. With the start of the joint-stock reform in 2004, the total assets of joint-stock banks continue to rise. With the intensification of competition, the concentration of big commercial banks has been declining, which is 20.2% lower than the 56.91% in 2004. At the end of 2017, the total

Table 1.6. Composition of Employment in China's Banking Sector

Year	Banking institutions (thousands)	Big commercial banks (thousands)	Percentage of employees in big commercial banks
2010	2,990.7	1,545.1	51.66
2011	3,197.9	1,626.2	50.85
2012	3,362.1	1,666.0	49.55
2013	3,550.4	1,720.7	48.46
2014	3,763.4	1,764.6	46.89
2015	3,803.5	1,730.3	45.49
2016	4,090.2	1,676.6	40.99
2017	4,170.5	1,651.2	39.59

Source: China Financial Yearbook, 2018.

number of employees in the banking sector was 4.17 million, and 39.6% (1.65 million) worked for the big commercial banks (table 1.6).

2. BANKING INSTITUTIONS

At the end of 2017, China's banking industry consisted of 4,532 banking institutions with licenses, the number modestly rising in last several years (see figure 1.1), and included 5 state-owned commercial banks, 3 policy banks, 12 joint-stock commercial banks, 134 city commercial banks, 17 private banks, 965 rural area financial institutions, 1,262 rural cooperative banks, and a number of foreign subsidiary banks, assets management companies, money brokerage companies, and trust companies (see table 1.7).

2.1. State-Owned Commercial Banks

The largest five banks are majority-owned by the central government and focus on traditional financial intermediation between savers and borrowers. At the end of 2016, domestic deposits were the main funding source and accounted for around 80% of their total liability. At the same time, loans are the main investment channel for financing borrowers and account for 60% of total assets. Five big commercial banks have similar business models, which can be seen from their balance sheets. In terms of total assets, ICBC and CCB rank as the first two, with Bank of Communications ranking last (see table 1.8). The big banks strive to balance the goal of earning profits and expanding operations guided by the overall economic policy objectives of the State Council, the PBC, and other government agencies.

2.2. Policy Banks

In 1994, three policy banks—the China Development Bank (CDB), the Export-Import Bank of China (CEXIM), and the Agriculture Development Bank of China (ADBC)— were established in an effort to separate policy-related lending from commercial lending. Policy banks are wholly state owned, and each has a distinct mission.

The ADBC was established in 1994, with a registered capital of 57 billion yuan. It operates under the direct leadership of the State Council and is the only agricultural policy bank. Its main task is to raise funds, with national credit support and through market-oriented methods, to support farmers and the development of agriculture and rural

Table 1.7. Specific Structure Distribution of the Number of Banking Institutions, 2006–2017

Year	Total number of banking financial institutions	Large commercial banks	Policy banks	Joint-stock commercial banks	City commercial banks	Rural credit cooperatives	Rural commercial banks	Rural cooperative banks	Private banks
2006	19,797		3	12	113				
2007	8,877		3	12	124				
2008	5,634		3	12	136	4,965	22	163	
2009	3,857		3	12	143	3,056	43	196	
2010	3,769	5	3	12	147	2,646	85	223	
2011	3,800	5	3	12	144	2,265	212	190	
2012	3,747	5	3	12	144	1,927	337	147	
2013	3,949	5	3	12	145	1,803	468	122	
2014	4,089	5	3	12	133	1,596	665	89	
2015	4,261	5	3	12	133	1,373	859	71	5
2016	4,398	5	3	12	134	1,125	1,114	40	8
2017	4,532	5	3	12	134	965	1,262	33	17

Source: CBIRC.

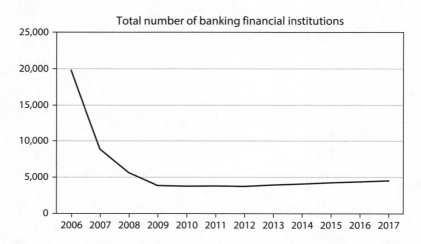

FIGURE 1.1. Trends in the number of banking financial institutions, 2006–2017. *Source:* CBIRC.

Table 1.8. Simplified Balance Sheet for the Five Big Banks, December 2018
(in RMB millions)

	ABC	BOC	BCM	CCB	ICBC
Total Assets	22,609,471	21,267,275	9,531,171	23,222,693	26,691,916
loans	11,461,542	11,515,764	4,854,228	13,365,430	14,600,596
corporate loans	6,514,383	7,347,598	3,218,601	6,497,678	8,019,984
personal loans	343,961	4,440,085	1,635,627	5,839,803	4,891,776
Investments	6,885,075	5,054,551	2,822	5,714,909	5,483,420
Cash & balance with other banks	109,728	1,144,937	163,646	836,676	1,628,820
Liabilities	20,934,684	19,541,878	8,825,863	21,231,099	24,560,708
Customer deposits	17,346,290	14,883,596	5,793,324	17,108,678	19,317,269
corporate deposits	6,559,082	7,932,413	3,944,098	8,667,322	10,270,329
personal deposits	9,791,974	6,442,470	1,776,488	7,771,165	8,207,406
deposits from others	995,234	508,713	72,738	670,191	839,534
Net worth	1,674,787	1,725,397	705,308	1,991,594	2,131,208

Source: Annual reports.

areas in accordance with the national strategy. Its management principle is to act as an agricultural bank that has clear and targeted functions, sufficient funds, proper control, strict inner discipline, safe operation, good service, and sustainability.

The CEXIM provides financial services to promote China's exports, particularly high-tech and new-tech products, and also to facilitate the import of technologically advanced machinery and equipment. The CEXIM is funded by the state and operates under the direct leadership of the State Council. The goal is to support the development of China's external commerce and outbound investment and to facilitate international economic cooperation.

At the end of 2018, it had 32 operating branches and a Hong Kong Representative Office in China. As for global presence, CEXIM operates the Paris Branch, Representative Office for Southern and Eastern Africa, St. Petersburg Representative Office, and Representative Office for Northern and Western Africa. The main areas supported by the CEXIM are the external economy, trade development and cross-border investment, "The Belt and the Road" construction, international cooperation on production capacity, a "going global" policy for small and medium business, and similar areas.

Established in 1994, the CDB is a policy financial institution under the direct leadership of the State Council. In December 2008, the CDB was reformed into the China Development Bank Corporation. In March 2015, the State Council explicitly positioned the CDB as a development finance institution. The registered capital of the CDB totals 421.248 billion yuan. According to CDB's website, it "is the world's largest development finance institution, and the largest Chinese bank for financing cooperation, long-term lending and bond issuance." It mainly provides strategic support for important medium- to long-term national economic initiatives by providing medium- to long-term financing.

2.3. Joint-Stock Commercial Banks

The most common path for private capital to infiltrate the banking sector is through joint-stock banks. In the mid-1980s, joint-stock commercial banks were created to advance the reforms of China's financial system and to provide an environment suitable for specialized banks to become commercial banks. Joint-stock banks are held by corporations, including non-state entities. For example, unlike the state-owned commercial banks, which are all controlled by the state, the China Minsheng Bank is the first commercial bank in mainland China to be founded by private capital (see table 1.9). Although it is not completely privately owned, the government holds a stake in it, one significantly smaller than in the big state-owned banks. Figure 1.2 shows the assets and liabilities of ten Chinese joint-stock commercial banks as of December 2018. The banks included are the Shanghai Pudong Development Bank (SPD), China Citic Bank (CITIC), China Everbright Bank (CEB), China Guangfa Bank (CGB), Industrial Bank (CIB), Huaxia Bank (HXB), China Merchants Bank (CMB), China Minsheng Bank (CMBC), Ping An Bank (PAB), and China Zheshang Bank (CZB).

2.4. Other Commercial Banks

2.4.1. Private Banks
The China Banking Regulatory Commission started a pilot program in 2014 to allow private capital to found banks, with an objective to provide better financial services to small and micro enterprises, rural area development, and small communities. This initiative aims to establish a scheme in which banks are responsible for their own risks. Private banks only serve enterprises in a designated geographic area. Private banks have a variety of business models, including small deposits and small loans (e.g., Ali Loan by Alibaba) and large deposits and small loans (e.g., WeBank by Tencent).

2.4.2. Private Banks: MYbank and WeBank
Established in southern China's tech hub of Shenzhen three years ago, WeBank is China's first online-only bank. WeBank focuses on providing small-scale consumer loans to "long-tail" clients (those who have less access to financial services due to location and

Table 1.9. Shareholder Status of China's State-Owned Commercial Banks and
China's Joint-Stock Commercial Banks, December 2018

2018	Largest shareholder	Largest shareholder proportion %	Top 10 shareholders proportion %
ICBC	Central Huijin Investment Co., Ltd.[a]	34.71	96.7
ABC	Central Huijin Investment Co., Ltd.	40.03	93.52
BOC	Central Huijin Investment Co., Ltd.	64.02	96.51
CCB	Central Huijin Investment Co., Ltd.	57.11	97.44
BCM	Ministry of Finance	26.53	78.52
CMBC	Hong Kong Securities Clearing Company Nominees Limited	18.92	59.58
CITIC	China CITIC Co., Ltd.	65.37	98.12
CEB	China Everbright Group	25.43	95.77
CMB	Hong Kong Securities Clearing Company Nominees Limited	18.03	66.32
SPD	Shanghai International Group Co., Ltd.	21.57	76.37
HXB	Shougang Group Co., Ltd.	20.28	73.25
PAB	Ping An Group	49.56	66.17
CGB	China Life Insurance Co., Ltd.	43.69	92.35
CZB	Hong Kong Securities Clearing Company Nominees Limited	24.33	77.07

Source: Annual reports.
[a] Central Huijin Investment, Ltd., is a state-owned investment company. Its major business is to hold equity investment in major domestic finance companies and to exercise shareholder rights accordingly. China Investment Corporation holds shares of Central Huijin Investment, Ltd.

limited collateral), as well as offering business turnover loans to small and micro-enterprises. A key advantage of WeBank is its ability to effectively gather data from more than one billion QQ and WeChat users, thanks to the participation of its major shareholder, Tencent. WeBank has also outlined a four-fold "ABCD" tech strategy, referring to AI (artificial intelligence), blockchain, cloud computing, and (big) data.

MYbank was established in June 2015 and claims to be the first bank in China whose core systems are situated in the cloud. This online lender says it uses its "internet and big data advantages to provide financial services to more small and micro enterprises," announcing at the time of its establishment that it would limit loans to

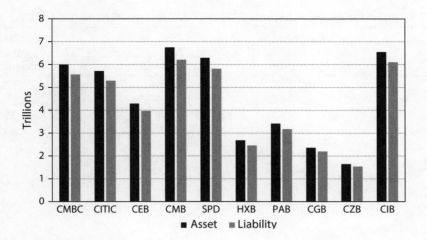

FIGURE 1.2. Assets and liabilities of 10 joint-stock commercial banks as of December 2018 (in RMB trillions). *Source:* Annual reports.

less than 5 million yuan. That online bank's core advantage lies in its popularity with small and micro e-commerce enterprises that make use of Alibaba platforms such as Taobao and Alipay.[2]

2.4.3. City Commercial Banks

Formerly, local governments wholly owned city commercial banks, but during the 2000s the banks were transformed into joint-stock banks in which the local governments became the main shareholders. City commercial banks are often chosen to handle local government-related accounts because they are deemed more capable of assessing local companies' creditworthiness. Due to one regulatory rule (namely, the Measures of the China Banking Regulatory Commission on the Administration concerning Cross-Region Development of City Commercial Banks, 2006), the establishment of branches of city commercial banks outside of the home city is restricted, to a certain extent, and therefore the number of branches is much fewer than that of joint-stock commercial banks.

2.4.4. Rural Area Financial Institutions

Examples of rural area financial institutions are rural credit cooperatives, village and township banks, rural commercial banks, and rural cooperative banks. In general, these provide services only to rural populations. Private capital accounts for 90% of the total capital in rural cooperatives and 70% of the capital in rural banks.

2.4.5. Foreign Banks

With the gradual outward development of China's economy, its banking industry has accelerated its opening-up policy in an effort to further promote the reform of the banking industry. As a result, many foreign banks have started to enter China's market at a large scale. Foreign banks typically focus on foreign companies as their main customers, and their market share in China's banking system remains very low, consistently below 3% (table 1.10).

Table 1.10. Assets of Foreign Banks Operating in China, 2003–2017

Year	Banks with foreign capital: Assets (RMB billions)	Banking institutions: Assets (RMB billions)	Percentage of banks with foreign capital
2003	416	27,658	1.50
2004	582	31,599	1.84
2005	715	37,470	1.91
2006	928	43,950	2.11
2007	1,253	53,116	2.36
2008	1,345	63,152	2.13
2009	1,349	79,515	1.70
2010	1,742	95,305	1.83
2011	2,154	113,287	1.90
2012	2,380	133,622	1.78
2013	2,563	151,355	1.69
2014	2,792	172,336	1.62
2015	2,681	199,345	1.34
2016	2,929	232,253	1.26
2017	3,244	252,404	1.29

Source: CBIRC.

3. BANKING REFORM

3.1. Background

In the late 1990s, as a result of the Asian financial crisis and management problems within the Chinese banks, substantial nonperforming loans accumulated in China's banking system, preventing the banks from making new loans. To deal with the challenges caused by that financial crisis, the Chinese government urgently needed both to recapitalize the state-owned banks and to lower the amount of the nonperforming loans.

Under these circumstances, the Chinese government had two options. The first option was to let the banks clear their own nonperforming assets and replenish capital by themselves; the second option was to perform "online repair" (在线修复). However, because of the excessive amount of nonperforming assets, the first option would have resulted in a long period during which the banks could not achieve the necessary regulatory standards, such as capital adequacy ratio, as only one example, and thus would not be able to provide the necessary loans for China's economy. Therefore, there was only one real option.

To ensure the continuation of economic growth and avoid a repetition of Japan's "lost decade" in the 1990s, the Chinese government took the second option—"online repair." This approach was based on the experience of the United States during the savings and loan crisis of the late 1980s. The Chinese government created a new scheme that distinguished "good" banks from "bad" ones. By carving out the nonperforming assets from "good banks" and concentrating the bad assets in "bad banks," the Chinese government ensured that the "good banks" could operate normally. This was the first round of China's banking system reform (Walter and Howie, 2011).

In 1998, the National People's Congress considered and then adopted a capital injection plan for the Big Four Banks—ICBC, ABC, BOC, and CCB. The People's Bank of China (PBC) lowered its reserve requirement ratio from 13% to 8%. The Big Four Banks used the released capital to buy RMB 270 billion special treasury bonds issued by the Ministry of Finance (MOF), and the MOF injected the money back into the banks as capital.

From 1998 to 1999, the Big Four Banks replenished capital and cleaned up their balance sheets through capital injection, nonperforming assets stripping, and other financial restructuring methods. At the same time, four asset management corporations—the China Great Wall, China Cinda, China Huarong, and China Orient—were created to absorb the bad assets of the Big Four Banks.

The four asset management companies then separated RMB 1,394 billion of nonperforming loans from the Big Four Banks and the China Development Bank (CDB), thereby lowering the nonperforming loan ratio of the Big Four Banks by an average of 10%.

Since 2001, China's regulators have gradually implemented a five-category asset classification method[3] for bank loans, and have also gradually lowered the business tax of commercial banks. However, the first round of reforms was mainly technical, as, for example, handling the nonperforming assets, enhancing internal management, and dealing with other matters without also addressing the in-depth systematic and mechanical issues.

3.2. Reform of the Big Banks in the 2003–2010 Period

The second round of bank reforms, which occurred between 2003 and 2010, was implemented in response to the reoccurrence of a large amount of nonperforming assets in the banking system. One reason for this reoccurrence was that the corporate governance structure had not been thoroughly reformed, so bad loans were continuously being created by banks after the first round of China's banking system reform in 1998. Another reason was that during the original reform in 1998, the banks did not fully report their real situation to the government.

Why did this happen? During the first round of reform, the government did not explicitly indicate that this bailout was the "last free lunch." At the time of the second round of reforms, the government stated that this was in fact their last opportunity to report the real situation. This round took the experience of the first round into consideration—so that, in addition to capital injections, the shareholding structure needed to be diversified. Improving the corporate governance structure was a major objective of the round. Because the previous capital injections to the banks were criticized for being based on internal circulation of capital, the government used foreign exchange reserves of the PBC for capital injection in the second round (Jiang and Zhan, 2019).

At the end of 2003, the central government chose the Bank of China (BOC) and China Construction Bank (CCB) as the pilot banks for the new shareholding system. Through the newly established Central Huijin Investment Co., USD $45 billion of China's foreign exchange reserve was injected into the BOC and CCB so that they could begin a new round of reform, along with starting the public listing process.

The second round of reforms occurred in four stages: financial restructuring and capital injection; establishing joint stock companies; introducing strategic investors; and launching IPOs.

The joint-stock reform of the wholly state-owned commercial banks started after the Chinese government approved the shareholding reforms of the BOC and CCB. The entire process ended in 2010, when the ABC dual-listed its shares on the stock exchanges of mainland China and Hong Kong (see table 1.11).

Table 1.11. Reform of the State-Owned Banks, 2003–2010

Year	Reform of the state-owned banks
2003	Chinese government approved the shareholding system reform of the BOC and CCB
2004	Restructuring of the BOC and CCB in accordance with the shareholding system reform
2005	CCB listed in HK; ICBC's shareholding system reform approved; BCM listed on H shares
2006	BOC listed on H and A shares; ICBC simultaneously listed on A and H shares
2007	CCB listed on A shares; BCM listed on A shares
2008	ABC joint-stock reform began
2009	ABC Limited founded
2010	ABC listed on both A and H shares

Collectively, these reforms fundamentally strengthened the financial condition of the banking sector. The internal control mechanism and risk management capability were also improved. For example, the total assets and loans balance increased significantly, while the NPL ratio from around 17.9% in 2003 dropped rapidly to around 1.8% (see figure 1.3). Accordingly, the capital adequacy rate increased and changed from a negative to a positive percentage. Although concerns were expressed about the health of the banks' balance sheets because of exposures to the real estate sector and to local government financing vehicles, stress tests showed that the major banks' capital buffer was strong enough to withstand significant shocks (IMF, 2011).

At the international level, the sector's market position and international competitiveness were improved significantly. The number of Chinese banks on the list of the top 1,000 big banks worldwide increased from 15 (in 2002) to 83 (in 2010). Both the profit levels and the market capitalization of the country's four state-owned banks reached the very top levels. The capital adequacy ratio, provision coverage ratio, and return on assets all reached historically high levels and surpassed those of other global banks.

3.3. Recent Progress

Recently, further progress has been made in China's banking industry reform efforts. In July 2015, USD $48 billion and USD $45 billion worth of foreign exchange reserves were injected into the China Development Bank (CDB) and Export-Import Bank of China (CEXIM), respectively, significantly improving their capital strength and risk control capability. That capital injection into the policy banks, along with the introduction of capital adequacy ratio requirements, has enhanced the capital restraint on policy banks.

In December 2015, the Postal Savings Bank (PSB) successfully attracted 10 domestic and foreign strategic investors, with a financing scale of RMB 45.1 billion, moving from a single shareholder to equity diversification. PSB was listed on H shares in September 2016 and on the domestic A-share market in December 2019. By introducing strategic investors and also diversifying its shareholders, PSB's reforms allowed it to improve its corporate governance structure.

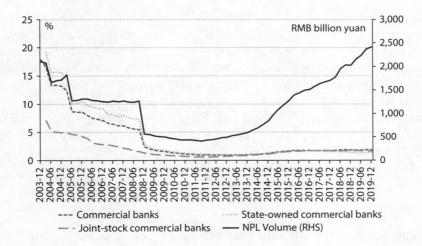

FIGURE 1.3. Trends of nonperforming loans, 2003–2019. *Source:* CBIRC.

In sum, the reform of China's commercial banks has made significant progress. From a micro perspective, China's commercial banks have created market-oriented business objectives and mechanisms and have improved both the internal risk control mechanisms and the mechanisms for constraining capital and costs. Through comprehensive operational transformation, China's commercial banks have become more international, with full information technology capacity. For the foreseeable future, however, these banks will face the challenge of continuing their reforms. Improving corporate governance, enhancing risk control capabilities, and elevating overall competitiveness continue to be the principal goals.

4. BANKING REGULATORS

In 2017, the Office of the Financial Stability and Development Committee under the State Council (hereinafter referred to as the Financial Committee) was located in the People's Bank of China. Its responsibilities include: promoting the implementation of the decision-making and deployment of financial work of the Central Committee of the Communist Party and the State Council; work arrangements of the Financial Committee; organizing drafting of major plans for the reform and development of the financial industry; putting forward major policy recommendations for the prevention and containment of systemic financial risks; maintenance of coordination mechanisms between central and local financial supervision, risk management, consumer protection, and information sharing; guiding the development and supervision of local financial reform; formulating accountability measures for financial management departments and local financial supervision; and undertaking supervision and accountability.[4] Under the leadership of the Financial Committee, China's banking regulatory system consists of five key entities: the PBC, CBIRC, MOF, SAFE, and CSRC.

4.1. PBC

Before 1978, the People's Bank of China (PBC) functioned as both the central bank of China and the sole commercial bank, functioning administratively under the leadership of the MOF. In the 1980s, four state-owned banks were established by parts of the PBC and became commercial banks. The PBC has a branch banking system in which each branch is responsible for the financial regulation and implementation of monetary policy within its jurisdiction. Since 2003, that supervisory function has been transferred to the China Banking Regulatory Commission. The main responsibilities of the PBC in the regulation of China's banking industry include setting monetary policy (such as determining benchmark interest rates); ensuring financial stability; managing the payment system; and regulating interbank lending, bond markets, gold markets, and foreign exchange markets. By the end of 2018, the PBC had 2,183 branches, one or more in roughly every city throughout the country, with 125,357 employees, and had established a sound regulatory system.

4.2. MOF

The Ministry of Finance (MOF) is the national executive agency of China's central government and was once the sole authority of China's financial sector. Its main functions include administering macroeconomic policies; preparing and administering the national budget; and handling fiscal policy, economic regulations, and government expenditures for the state. Although the direct management of financial institutions by the MOF has been reduced, it continues to hold some authority, either through equity holdings or by having a representative on the banks' governing boards.

4.3. CBIRC

The China Banking and Insurance Regulatory Commission (CBIRC) was established on April 8, 2018. It was previously known as the China Banking Regulatory Commission (CBRC) and the China Insurance Regulatory Commission (CIRC).

The CBRC was created in 2003 to conduct regulatory oversight of the country's banks. Its goal is to promote the lawful and stable operation of the banking industry and to maintain public confidence in the banking industry. The banking regulatory authorities, in accordance with laws and administrative regulations, formulate and publish regulations and rules for the supervision and administration of banking financial institutions and their business activities.

The CBRC's main functions include authorizing the establishment and business scope of banks in China, formulating and enforcing banking regulations, auditing and supervising all banking institutions, and compiling and publishing information on China's banking sector.

In January 2015, the CBRC carried out a reform of the regulatory framework, set up the Prudential Regulation Bureau, led the nonfield supervision work, and unified the rules and regulations of the Prudential Management of the banking industry.

4.4. SAFE

The State Administration of Foreign Exchange (SAFE) was established in 1979, and was administratively under the control of the State Council and the PBC. The foreign exchange management structure has been gradually improved over recent years.

Existing at the operational level of a commercial bank, SAFE is responsible for the supervision of the national foreign exchange market and the settlement and sale of foreign exchange. In addition, it is responsible for cultivating and developing the foreign exchange market and punishing acts that are against foreign exchange regulations.

4.5. CSRC

China Securities Regulatory Commission (CSRC) is a ministerial-level public institution directly under the State Council that performs a unified regulatory function, according to the relevant laws and regulations, and, with the State Council's authority over the securities and futures market of China, maintains an orderly securities and futures market order, and also ensures the legal operation of the capital market. Pursuant to the relevant laws and regulations, CSRC performs the following duties in the supervision and administration of the banking industry.

First, it supervises the issuance, listing, trading, custody, and settlement of stocks, convertible bonds, bonds of securities companies, and bonds and other securities under the charge of CSRC as assigned by the State Council; it also supervises the securities investment bonds, approves the listing of corporate bonds, and supervises the trading of the listed treasury bonds and corporate bonds. Second, it supervises the securities market behaviors of the listed companies and their shareholders who must fulfill the relevant obligations according to the relevant laws and regulations. Third, it supervises the direct or indirect issuance and listing of shares overseas by domestic enterprises, as well as the listing of convertible bonds by those companies listed overseas.

5. REGULATORY IMPLEMENTATION

In the early stages of reform, the regulation of China's commercial banks moved from single financial entity planning management to micro-prudential supervision. After the subprime crisis in 2007, to prevent systematic risk as well as to maintain the overall stability of the financial system, the regulation gradually moved toward a period of combining micro-prudential and macro-prudential supervision.

5.1. Micro-prudential Supervision

Since the state-owned banks separated from the PBC, banking regulation has been improved and has evolved through three stages toward micro-prudential supervision.

The first stage, from 1978 to 1992, was marked by administrative regulation and management of credit scale. Since January 1984, the PBC has solely functioned as a central bank. Credit funds management was implemented under a "unitary plan, divided funds, real credit and deposit, mutual finance" principle. Credit funds at each professional bank had to be included in the national comprehensive credit plan. This stage was in fact a planning phase, with the PBC in charge of balancing, appraising, and rectifying the credit funds.

In the second stage, from 1992 to 2006, with the establishment of the PBC, CSRC, CIRC, and CBRC,[5] and as commercial bank management was transferred to professional management, a prudential regulatory system gradually formed, which included risk management, funds regulation, and internal management. In the early phase, the management focused on asset-liability ratio management and loan-deposit ratio. Since 2000, risk management has shifted into three-risk management, which considers credit risk, market risk, and operation risk. With the implementation of the Basel New Capital Agreement, the idea of capital management was introduced into commercial bank management.[6]

After the establishment of the CBRC, a Chinese banking regulatory framework based on risk control was gradually instituted. First, a prudential regulatory framework for the banking industry based on capital supervision was set up to implement the prudential regulation of capital supervision and risk supervision by defining prudential regulatory indicators such as the capital adequacy ratio, asset quality, credit risk, and the risk of credit. At the same time, the reforms strengthened corporate governance mechanisms, internal control, and compliance risk management to further improve the legal framework for banking supervision.

Under the new regulatory framework, the governance structure of large commercial banks began to play a great role in banks' governance. The balance of nonperforming loans in commercial banks fell from 2.1 trillion yuan in 2003 to 1.3 trillion yuan in 2007, and nonperforming loans ratio fell from 17.9% in 2003 to 6.2% in 2007. The provisioning coverage ratio (拨备覆盖率 in Chinese, i.e., asset provisions divided by outstanding NPL volume) was raised from 19.7% in 2003 to 39.2% in 2007, and the proportion of bank asset with up to standard capital adequacy ratio was greatly improved from 0.6% in 2003 to 79% in 2007.

During the third stage, after the subprime crisis in 2007 and with the implementation of Basel III, the CBRC formed a new framework—"Chinese Basel III supervision." It used "dynamic capital, dynamic provision, leverage rate, and liquidity" as its four new regulatory tools.[7] The first-tier capital adequacy ratio of commercial banks was raised from 4% to 6%, with the capital adequacy ratio maintained at 8%. In addition, the CBRC extracted 2.5% retained capital and set a 1% additional capital requirement for systemically important banks. Furthermore, the CBRC introduced and revised the regulatory framework for the leverage ratio of commercial banks, in accordance with Basel III, which should be no less than 4%. At the current liquidity ratio supervision, the CBRC introduced a liquidity coverage rate and a net stable funding ratio. In this way, the micro-prudential supervision framework was gradually built (Wang, 2015).

In recent years, the Financial Sector Assessment Program (FSAP), which is conducted by the World Bank and International Monetary Fund, as well as by the Regulatory Consistency Assessment Programme (RCAP), which in turn is conducted by the Basel Committee on Banking Supervision (BCBS), both stated their high appreciation of China's banking regulatory rules and regulatory effectiveness.

5.2. Macro-Prudential Policy

In 2007, the subprime crisis broke out worldwide. Many countries became aware that the stability of individual micro-financial entities could no longer guarantee the stability of the entire financial system. Procyclicality exists in any micro-prudential policy, which could not avoid the systematic risk caused by the expansion of the banking industry, asset price bubbles, and excessive financial innovation. The crisis led to the implementation of the Basel III accords, after which China reevaluated its regulation policy framework and introduced a macro-prudential policy.[8] The establishment of the macro-prudential regulatory framework has shifted its emphasis from micro-regulation to prudential policies that balance micro and macro regulations so as to better recognize and prevent the outbreak of systematic risks and to relieve the spillover effect of financial crises (Sun, 2017a).

In 2010, the PBC implemented a macro-prudential regulation strategy.[9] The next year, a mechanism for the dynamic adjustment of differential reserves and consensus loan management was established to reduce systematic financial risk. In 2016, the mechanism was updated to Macro-Prudential Assessment (MPA), which is an important component of the macro-prudential regulatory framework. The MPA assesses seven aspects of the banking industry and financial institutions: capital and leverage, balance, liquidity, price fixing, quality of assets, risk of cross-border finance, and implementation of credit policy. The aim is to enhance self-regulation and self-restraint, which help with the prudent operation of financial institutions (Sun, 2017b). The MPA has been gradually improved; for example, in 2017, the PBC included underlying assets of wealth management products within the MPA to control shadow banking activities of commercial banks; in 2018, the MPA included interbank CDs in the evaluation of interbank liability to encourage financial institutions to enhance liquidity management, lower interbank business, and use stable funding sources to develop their business (Sun, 2018). In the future, more financial activities, financial markets, financial institutions, and financial infrastructures will be included in the macro-prudential policy.[10]

Since 2017, with the establishment of the two-pillar policy—that is, macro-prudential policy and monetary policy—the tasks of maintaining currency value stability and financial stability are far better integrated.[11] Under this new framework, the aim of monetary policy is clearer: to exercise macro control over monetary value stability and economic growth. Macro-prudential policy focuses on the stability of the financial system itself and on the control of systematic risk.

6. SHADOW BANKING

In recent years, China's shadow banking system has become an integral part of the financial system. Distinguished from advanced economies, China's shadow banking is dominated by commercial banks as a result of its bank-dominated financial system. Since 2017, financial regulators in China have strengthened regulation on shadow banking (Sun, 2019). This produced two benefits, which are ultimately beneficial to the long-term, stable growth of the Chinese economy. The first is to defuse financial risks embedded in the complex transaction structure of shadow banking. The second is to restrict the abnormal growth of money and credit through shadow banking. Loans and bond investments have a larger share in money and credit creation, which greatly enhances the effectiveness of monetary policy and limits unwanted fluctuation in money supply, as well as credit growth. Although shadow banking has shrunk, perhaps due to strengthened regulation, Chinese financial authorities have strived to continue to give accurate financial support to the real economy in the form of RMB loans and bond issuance, and have also rolled out several new policy tools to increase funding support to the agricultural sector, small and micro enterprises (SMEs), and the private sector, to give a few examples. As a result, the overall monetary and financial condition for the real economy has proven conducive for stable growth.

6.1. Composition of China's Shadow Banking

A key characteristic of shadow banking in China is that banks hide loans as alternative accounting subjects. From the perspective of banks' credit money creation, Chinese shadow banking can be divided into two categories: banks' shadow banking and traditional shadow banking. Both provide funding under the general shadow banking system, but only banks' shadow creates a new money supply, which is an intermediate objective of the monetary policy of the People's Bank of China. Sun (1996, 2001, 2017b) introduces the Loan Creates Deposit theory (LCD) with four types of market participants: monetary authorities, banks, nonbank financial institutions, and nonfinancial sectors (enterprise and resident). Only banks have the money-creation function. Banks increase customer deposits and create credit money while expanding their assets through loans, foreign exchange purchases, and corporate bond purchases. This process is constrained by restrictions on cash, clearing, and the required reserve by the monetary authorities and is also subject to restrictions on capital and credit policy.

The term "banks' shadow" refers to bank activities that provide funding for enterprises through the creation of credit money, but that circumvent regulatory restrictions and constraints on loan granting by adopting nonstandard accounting bookkeeping (Sun, 2019). Specifically, banks' shadow includes (1) assets channeled by other banks, such as the dual buyout of credit assets, the reverse repo of bills, interbank payment, purchases, and resales; and (2) activities channeled by nonbank financial institutions, such as the transfer of trust beneficial interests, credit-linked total return swap, oriented asset management plan of security brokers, and specific asset management fund plans. Banks' shadow is inherently identical to bank loans in the sense that it creates credit to fulfill the funding need of the real economy while expanding assets and creating money. However, it differs from bank loans in the sense that it is not listed as a loan in balance sheet items. Banks' shadow is mainly channeled through a third-party financial institution. Therefore, it exists in terms of interbank assets (on the asset side of the bank balance sheet), investment assets, or off-balance sheet items (e.g., off-balance sheet interbank assets that correspond to off-balance sheet wealth management products, or WMPs).

The term "traditional shadow banking," by contrast, refers to credit creation activities undertaken by nonbank financial institutions. It transfers money independently out of the banking system to provide funding for enterprises. As its credit creation mechanisms are analogous to those in advanced economies (e.g., money market funds and asset securitization), this category of China's shadow banking is called traditional shadow banking. The mode of traditional shadow banking is mainly through nonbank financial institutions' (e.g., trust companies, securities companies, finance companies, financial leasing companies, and microcredit companies), which transfer funds that are raised to the real economy borrowers (not a channel for banks) through trust loans, asset management plans, equipment leasing, mortgages, and credit loans. In this process, nonbank financial institutions act as credit intermediaries. The credit scale increases, but the quantity of money is unchanged, as credit is created by adjusting the distribution of money (i.e., money is transferred from investors to financiers).

Innovations of shadow banking activities in China stem from the bank-dominant financial system and its feature of regulatory constraints. First, shadow banking in China generates more shadow as a result of the binding capital adequacy requirements of commercial banks. Those additional credits were allocated to industries in which the government restricts the credit supply from banks. Second, although the leverage ratio restriction of commercial banks in China is not binding, the shadow banking practice also influences commercial banks' leverage. Note that the reclassification of loans as "other items" does not influence the leverage ratio of banks. Yet, by initiating new loans to "hide" under other accounting subjects, banks' shadow first expands its balance sheet and then reduces the risk weights of those assets. As a result, the leverage ratio first increases and then reduces. A similar pattern applies to the shadow banking activities that are moved off banks' balance sheets, such as entrusted loans. China's shadow banking system explicitly differs from shadow banking in advanced economies (e.g., Europe and America) in terms of its background, operation mechanism, and risk profile. The main funding source of shadow banking in advanced economies is mutual funds, with such underlying assets as subprime loans and other illiquid financial claims, and products mainly including asset securitization and repo. In advanced economies, shadow banking mainly pertains to the traditional shadow banking that performs credit money transferring. Contrarily, China's shadow banking system primarily pertains to banks' shadow, with credit money created through the expansion of liabilities with loan-like assets at its core.

6.2. Measuring China's Shadow Banking and Development Phase Illustration

Most research utilizes an aggregation approach to measure the scale of shadow banking; that is, it directly sums up the products or subcategories of shadow banking. This creates two issues. First, the different definitions or classifications of shadow banking lead to significant differences in measurement results. Second, the aggregation approach cannot avoid double counting or omission.

The author measures China's shadow banking by its two subcategories: banks' shadow and traditional shadow banking.

First, banks' shadow is measured by a deduction approach introduced by Sun and Jia (2015). Given the basic accounting principle that total debits must equal total credits for each transaction, the asset expansion of banks' shadow must equal the deposit size created in the subsequent phases. Sun and Jia measure banks' shadow from the banks' liability side by deducting all "nonshadow assets" (including traditional assets such as loans, foreign exchanges, and corporate bonds) from the possible liabilities.

Figure 1.4 shows not only the evolution of banks' shadow in China, but also the impacts of regulations on banks' active responses in switching between various channels of their shadows. According to the timeline of the global financial crisis and related regulations, the evolution of banks' shadow and its proportion in money creation can be divided into four stages.

During the first stage (January 2006 to October 2008), the scale of banks' shadow was quite stable, but its proportion in money creation decreased sharply. Before the subprime crisis, the gap between banks' deposit liabilities and traditional assets (mainly loans and foreign exchanges) was positive, with a scale of approximately RMB5 trillion to RMB7 trillion. However, this is irrelevant to banks' shadow, mainly due to the reform of state-owned banks before 2004, when banks bought bonds of asset management companies, massively wrote off nonperforming loans, and received capital injections of foreign exchange reserves. From 2006 onward, the gap remained stable and the proportion of banks' shadow in money creation decreased dramatically year after year, indicating that the main credit money creation channels were traditional bank loans and foreign exchange channels.

During the second stage (October 2008 to October 2011), the scale of banks' shadow and its proportion in money creation were both stable. The RMB4 trillion investment plan of the Chinese government greatly stimulated the asset expansion of banks, causing the gap between the deposit liabilities and traditional assets to increase from RMB3.48 trillion at the beginning of this period to RMB7.2 trillion in October 2011. Nevertheless, as the amount of credit money created by banks was also quite large, the proportion of the

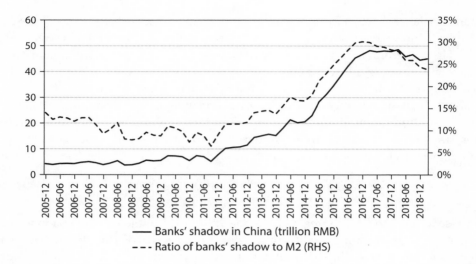

FIGURE 1.4. Size of banks' shadow in China. *Sources:* PBC and author's calculation.

gap in total money creation increased moderately, from 7.54% to 8.81%. This implies that during the aforementioned stage, the role of banks' shadow asset channel in banks' credit expansion did not change fundamentally. Furthermore, the main channels were still traditional loans and foreign exchange channels.

During the third stage (October 2011 to January 2017), both the scale of banks' shadow and its proportion in money creation increased. In the second quarter of 2010, the monetary authorities began to implement prudent monetary policies, introduced macroprudential policies characterized by capital constraints to strengthen regulations, and applied specific credit regulations to sectors with excess capacity (e.g., real estate). To circumvent the preceding regulations and capital restrictions, banks converted loan assets to banks' shadow through such tools as investment and interbank businesses, to meet the rigid financing needs of real estate developers and local government financing platforms. As shown in figure 1.4, from October 2011, the scale of banks' shadow continued to increase, hitting a record high of RMB47.86 trillion in January 2017; the corresponding proportion in money creation also increased to 30.37%.

Note that during this period, both the scale of banks' shadow and its proportion in money creation fluctuated. For example, the shrinkage in banks' shadow during the period June to December 2014 was mainly caused by reductions in banks' shadow business channeled through other banks, influenced by the "Notice about regulating interbank business of financial institutions" jointly issued by the PBC, China Banking Regulatory Commission (CBRC), China Securities Regulatory Commission (CSRC), China Insurance Regulatory Commission (CIRC), and State Administration of Foreign Exchange (SAFE). Until the end of December 2014, the size of banks' shadow had decreased from RMB21.31 trillion to RMB20.55 trillion, and the corresponding proportion decreased from 17.62% to 16.73%.

During the fourth stage (from January 2017 and after), the scale of banks' shadow became stable while its proportion of money creation began to decrease, mainly as a result of stricter regulations and other factors, such as the slowing down of economic

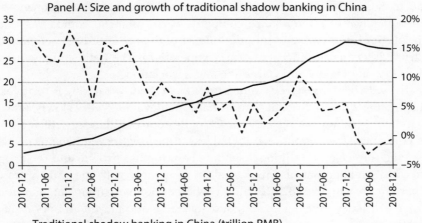

Panel A: Size and growth of traditional shadow banking in China

—— Traditional shadow banking in China (trillion RMB)
- - - Quarter-on-quarter growth rate of traditional shadow banking in China (RHS)

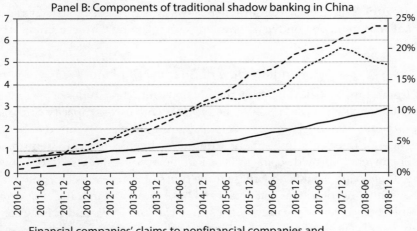

Panel B: Components of traditional shadow banking in China

—— Financial companies' claims to nonfinancial companies and
      households (trillion RMB)
- - Balance of finance lease contract (trillion RMB)
- - Balance of microfinance company loans (trillion RMB)
····· Balance of trust assets (excl. Bank-Trust cooperation mode, trillion RMB, RHS)

FIGURE 1.5. Measuring traditional shadow banking in China. *Sources:* PBC, China Leasing Union, and China Trustee Association.

growth and the increase in credit risk. China has tightened financial regulations since January 2017, when off-balance sheet products, such as trust and entrusted loans, were included in the Macro-Prudential Assessment (MPA) and local governments were prohibited from continuously expanding their debt. Nevertheless, the scale of banks' shadow is still quite high and may surge again, once either external environmental changes occur or banks continue to carry out financial innovation aimed at circumventing regulations.

Second, to measure the scale of traditional shadow banking, four components are considered: the balance of microfinance company loans, financial companies' claims to nonfinancial companies and residents, the balance of finance lease contracts, and the balance of trust assets (excluding bank-trust cooperation). The data sources include the PBC, China Leasing Union, and China Trustee Association.

Compared with banks' shadow, China's traditional shadow banking is relatively small (figure 1.5). Before 2010, traditional shadow banking developed very slowly, with a scale of less than RMB2 trillion, taking less than 2% of the total credit money created by banks, as nonbank financial institutions contributed less to meeting social financing needs. Since 2010, however, the scale of traditional shadow banking has grown, and the proportion of banks' credit creation has also increased. In September 2017, the scale of traditional shadow banking reached RMB28.32 trillion, whereas nonbank financial institutions enhanced their efficiency in using existing money stocks and played an important role in credit creation and meeting social financing demands.

Among the channels of traditional shadow banking, trust assets take the largest share, and their contraction led to a sharp drop in the scale of traditional shadow banking in 2015. This contraction of trust assets was a result of stricter regulations (e.g., capital requirements) on trust companies imposed by Chinese financial market regulators.

6.3. Funding Flow of Shadow Banking

Funding from China's shadow banking mainly flows into three types of borrowers: local government financing vehicles (LGFVs), enterprises with excess capacity, and real estate developers. Banks' shadow is essentially bank loans in names disguised either as interbank business or interbank investment. Commercial banks typically require shadow banking borrowers to provide collaterals as loan borrowers and also to bear higher interest rates than loans. That is how these three types of borrowers come into play. They usually have land inventories as collaterals and have the ability to transfer or take higher interest rates themselves. Some previous research claimed SMEs and private companies to be main beneficiaries of shadow banking. But these two things are what SMEs and private companies (non–real estate) lack, which makes them unqualified for shadow bank funding as well.

The following provides a typical funding flow of China's shadow banking. State banks may lend to nonbanking financial institutions, which then lend as entrusted loans to LGFVs, enterprises with overcapacity, and real estate developers. Trust companies are the main carriers of shadow fund flows. In China, the trust company license allows participation in money market business, capital market business, and alternative investments. Trust companies can lend to restricted or high-risk industries (e.g., real estate, LGFVs) and are subject to less scrutiny, as they only act on behalf of their beneficiaries.

6.4. Financial Risk from Shadow Banking

China's shadow banking system might induce the following financial risks.

First, it raises risk exposures. The debt liability of state-owned enterprises (SOEs) increases significantly, as illustrated by the rising corporate credit-to-GDP ratio; the total exposure to real estate sector increases, including direct investment exposure and ex-

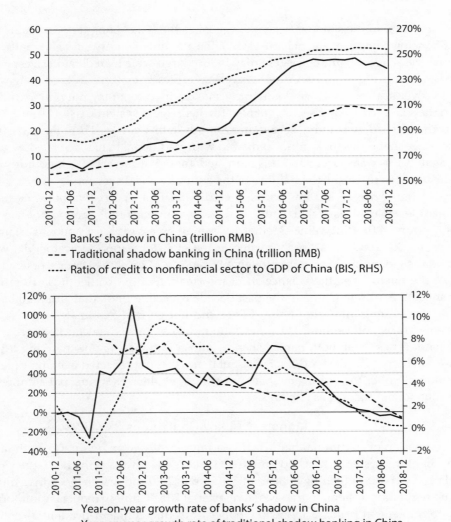

- —— Banks' shadow in China (trillion RMB)
- --- Traditional shadow banking in China (trillion RMB)
- ···· Ratio of credit to nonfinancial sector to GDP of China (BIS, RHS)

- —— Year-on-year growth rate of banks' shadow in China
- --- Year-on-year growth rate of traditional shadow banking in China
- ···· Year-on-year growth rate of credit to nonfinancial sector to GDP of China (RHS)

FIGURE 1.6. Shadow banking and credit-to-GDP ratio: Scale and growth. *Sources:* PBC and author's calculation. Credit-to-GDP ratio is from the Bank for International Settlements.

posure through collateral; and the risk exposure of local governments also increases due to LGFVs, which are an important source of credit.

The credit-to-GDP ratio is usually deemed to be an indicator of financial risk at the macro level. As shown in figure 1.6, the scale and growth of banks' shadow is more in line with the credit-to-GDP ratio than with traditional shadow banking.

Second, an unreliable supply of funds enhances financial risk. Maturity mismatch and rollover risk are critical issues in the Chinese shadow banking system. Most funding from shadow banking is short term and must be rolled over constantly. Moreover, the capital structure in the shadow system exaggerates the issue. Long-term capital is rare. Debt financing comprises the majority, while the amount of equity share is small.

Third, the shadow banking system may induce large-scale loan defaults. Despite the lack of any explicit guarantee, Chinese investors typically expect banks or the government to cover any losses. Once this trust is shaken, investors may not only panic and run on the shadow banking sector, but also further trigger systemic risk.

Fourth, the shadow banking system increases systematic risks. There are no real off-balance-sheet liabilities for banks. Compared with traditional banks, the shadow banking system is less transparent and less regulated, though it carries a high liquidity risk. Shadow banking threatens the stability of the entire financial system.

The relation between shadow banking credit and financial risk at both the macro and micro levels is investigated. Chinese shadow banking funds are mainly used for local government funding vehicles, enterprises with excess capacity, and real estate developers. Banks' shadow is closely related to the money creation indicator M2, while traditional shadow banking is less relevant, making M2 a less-accurate policy measure. At the micro level, the balance sheet information of 311 banks (including listed and nonlisted banks) in China in the past decade is used; it finds that although banks' shadow drives up banks' credit risk, banks did not properly estimate that risk and adopt enough risk prevention. The results are more obvious when checked across different bank types. First, both banks' shadow and traditional shadow banking lead to increases in banks' credit risk (NPL ratio), but that risk is not reflected in banks' internal estimation. Second, the risk from shadow banking challenges municipal commercial banks more than other types of banks.

6.5. Monetary Policy Challenges

Strict regulation of traditional banking is an important reason behind growth of the shadow banking system. The rapid growth of China's shadow banking has largely been stimulated by credit-tightening policies introduced in 2010 and driven by China's unique banking regulation system. In the second quarter of 2010, Chinese monetary authorities began to implement prudent monetary policy, introduced macro-prudential policies characterized by capital constraints to strengthen regulation, and applied specific credit regulations to sectors that have excess capacity (e.g., real estate). To circumvent regulations and meet the financing need in certain sectors, shadow banking activities rose sharply, posing threats to financial stability. Allen et al. (2019) argue that entrusted loans are essentially a market reaction to credit shortages. Zhu (2018) also suggests that China's shadow banking has been a long-existing phenomenon since the 1980s, one mainly used to circumvent government regulation and restrictions on credit supply.

Conversely, shadow banking demolishes the effects of monetary policies. The effectiveness of some regulatory policies and tools has been compromised or partially offset by the shadow banking system. For example, the Chinese government set credit limitations—such as limitations on loans from traditional banks and the equity ratio of developers—on the real estate sector to prevent housing bubbles, yet shadow banking provides alternative funding resources. A similar case holds for enterprises with excess capacity. Furthermore, the capital adequacy requirement for banks became less effective, as shadow banking activities enabled banks to move some assets off-balance sheet, such as entrusted and trust loans through bank-trust cooperation, as mentioned previously.

Chen, Ren, and Zha (2018) examine the impact of shadow banks on the effectiveness of monetary policy by considering a specific form of shadow banking: entrusted loans.

6.6. Recent Regulations of China's Shadow Banking

Financial regulators in China have been monitoring the evolution of shadow banking closely since 2009 or even earlier. The main regulator of Chinese shadow banking is the China Banking and Insurance Regulatory Commission (CBIRC, previously known as CBRC and CIRC), which coincides with the reality that Chinese shadow banking is more centric around banks than is traditional shadow banking channeled through other types of financial institutes. The PBC, CSRC, and SAFE also play roles in this regulation.

Financial regulators in China actually react in a very timely fashion to new forms of shadow banking. In the early stages of Chinese shadow banking, banks-trust cooperation acted as a dominant channel of shadow banking fund flow. The CBRC quickly set restrictions on off-balance sheet assets formed by bank-trust cooperative wealth management businesses, capped the balance of bank-trust cooperative financing at 30% of total bank-trust cooperation business, and required banks to move their off-balance sheet assets formed by bank-trust cooperative wealth management products back onto the balance sheet by the end of 2011.

Both the cash flow into and out of banks' shadow has been closely monitored by regulators. On the one hand, new regulations and guidance have been released every year upon the main funding source, WMPs. For example, in 2013, the CBRC sets limits on WMPs that invest in nonstandard credit, including entrusted loans, trust loans, bankers' acceptances, accounts receivables, and beneficiaries. On the other hand, a main channel of shadow banking funding—interbank refinancing, which emerged after the bank-trust restrictions of 2011—has been tracked and strictly regulated. For example, in 2014, the PBC, CBRC, CSRC, CIRC, and SAFE jointly issued a notice on regulating the interbank business, which includes interbank lending, interbank deposit, interbank borrowing, interbank agent payment, repo, and reverse repo. In 2017, CBRC announced that it considered negotiable certificates of deposit (NCDs) to be part of interbank lending and borrowing, and required banks to ensure that interbank liabilities restrictions are still satisfied. Specifically, interbank liabilities must not exceed one-third of total liabilities, and total interbank lending balance (including NCDs) must not exceed 50% of banks' tier-one capital.

China has tightened financial regulations since 2017, in several ways. First, the MPA has been erected; all off-balance sheet products, such as trust and entrusted loans, must be included in the MPA. Second, limitations on the scale of WMPs have been set; banks are forbidden from providing principal or interest guarantees on WMPs and must set separate accounts for each product. Third, the central government has prohibited local governments from continuously expanding their debt. Fourth, within the background of supply-side structural reform, funding support to enterprises with excess capacity and to real estate companies is still limited, with the limitations now expanding from loans to other financial products. Those regulations have slowed down the growth of the shadow banking sector.

On the one hand, these new financial regulations on shadow banking, including the so-called New Regulations on Asset Management Businesses, are mainly intended to defuse the excessive financial risk caused by shadow banking activities. The defusion of risk is ultimately beneficial to the long-term stable growth of the Chinese economy.

On the other hand, monetary policy has become more effective in controlling money and credit growth. These new regulations restrict the abnormal growth of money and credit through shadow banking. Loans and bond investments have assumed a larger share in money and credit creation, which in turn greatly enhances the effectiveness of monetary policy and limits an unwanted fluctuation in money supply as well as credit growth.

NOTES

1. Aggregate Financing to the Real Economy (AFRE) is the official name designated by the PBC to 社会融资规模 (in Chinese). In subsequent chapters and other discussions, Total Social Finance (TSF) is also widely used. In this book, these two terms refer to the same variable.
2. "AI Bank, MYbank, and WeBank Apply AI and Big Data to Online Lending," *China Banking News*, September 19, 2018. http://www.chinabankingnews.com/2018/09/19/aibank-mybank-webank-apply-ai-big-data-online-lending-china/.
3. The categories are Normal, Concern, Secondary, Suspicious, and Loss.
4. China Institutional Network, "Provisions of the People's Bank of China on Function Allocation, Internal Institutions and Staffing." http://www.gov.cn/zhengce/2019-02/02/content_5363338.htm.
5. The CSRC was established in 1992; the CIRC in 1998; the CBRC in 2003.
6. On February 23, 2004, the China Banking Regulatory Commission Order No. 2 (2004), Commercial Bank Capital Adequacy Ratio Regulation, was released.
7. In November 2010, the G20 Seoul Summit approved the Basel III Accords, which had been drafted by the Basel Committee to establish new standards for the supervision of capital and the liquidity of the banking industry. The member states were required to implement the new standard from 2013 and to reach it before 2019. On June 7, 2012, the China Banking Regulatory Commission Order No.1 (2012), Methods of Capital Management for Commercial Banks, was released.
8. The PBC's *China Monetary Policy Report of Quarter Three, 2009* first proposed to bring macro-prudential management into the macro-economic regulation framework.
9. Chapter 3 also provides detailed coverage of macro-prudential policy as a monetary policy instrument.
10. The PBC's *China Monetary Policy Report of Quarter Three, 2017* suggests that additional financial activities and financial markets will be brought into the macro-prudential supervision framework, and financial institutions will be guided both to manage liquidity and to maintain a stable, neutral moderate financial environment.
11. *China's Monetary Policy Report of Quarter Three, 2017*.

REFERENCES

Allen, Franklin, Yiming Qian, Guoqian Tu, and Frank Yu (2019). "Entrusted Loans: A Close Look at China's Shadow Banking System." *Journal of Financial Economics*, 133(1):18–41.
Chen, Kaiji, Jue Ren, and Tao Zha (2018). "The Nexus of Monetary Policy and Shadow Banking in China." *American Economic Review*, 108(12): 3891–3936.
Demirgüç-Kunt, Asli, and Ross Levin (2004). *Financial Structure and Economic Growth*. Cambridge, MA: MIT Press.
IMF (2011). "People's Republic of China: Financial System Stability Assessment." IMF Country Report, 11.
Jiang, Jianqing, and Xiangyang Zhan (2019). *History of Share Reform of Large Commercial Banks in China*. Beijing: China Financial Publishing Company, 171–222.
Sun, Guofeng (1996). "A Study on the Chinese Monetary Policy Transmission Mechanism." *Studies of International Finance*, 5: 63.
Sun, Guofeng (2001). "Money Creation and Bank Operation in the Credit Money System." *Economic Research Journal*, 2: 29–37.
Sun, Guofeng (2015a). *Reforms in China's Monetary Policy: A Frontbencher's Perspective*. New York: Palgrave Macmillan US.
Sun, Guofeng (2015b). *Financial Reforms in Modern China: A Frontbencher's Perspective*, New York: Palgrave Macmillan US.

Sun, Guofeng (2017a). "Understanding MPA: A Continuously Improved Macro-prudential Assessment System." *China Banking Industry,* (11): 44–47.

Sun, Guofeng (2017b). "Structural Liquidity Deficit and Monetary Policy Operating Framework." *Comparative Studies,* 91(4): 156–178.

Sun, Guofeng (2018). "Measuring Chinese Shadow Banking: Banks' Shadow and Traditional Shadow Banking." VoxChina, February 7. http://www.voxchina.org/show-3-65.html.

Sun, Guofeng (2019). "China's Shadow Banking: Bank's Shadow and Traditional Shadow Banking." BIS Working Papers, No. 822, November 8.

Sun, Guofeng, and Jia Junyi (2015). "Definition and Measurement of China's Shadow Banking: From the Perspective of Credit Money Creation." *Social Sciences in China,* 2015(11), 92–110. (English version available at http://voxchina.org/show-55-40.html).

Walter, Carl E., and Fraser J. T. Howie (2011). *Red Capitalism: The Fragile Financial Foundation of China's Extraordinary Rise.* Singapore: John Wiley & Sons, 24–30.

Wang, Zhaoxing (2015). "Reform of China's Micro and Macro Prudential Regulation." *China Finance* 5: 17–19.

Yi, Gang (2009). *On the Financial Reform of China.* Beijing: Commercial Press, 291–96.

Yi, Gang, and Kai Guo (2014)."Banking and Financial Institutions," in *Routledge Handbook of the Chinese Economy,* edited by Gregory C. Chow and Dwight H. Perkins. London: Routledge, 235–37.

Zhu, Xiaodong (2018). "The Varying Shadow of China's Banking System." University of Toronto working paper, no. 605, May.

2

MONETARY POLICY FRAMEWORK AND TRANSMISSION MECHANISMS

Yiping Huang, Tingting Ge, and Chu Wang

1. INTRODUCTION

On June 24, 2016, the then-governor of the People's Bank of China (PBC), Zhou Xiaoch-uan, delivered the 2016 Michel Camdessus Central Banking Lecture, titled "Managing Multi-Objective Monetary Policy: From the Perspective of Transitioning Chinese Econ-omy," at the International Monetary Fund (IMF) in Washington, DC. During the lecture, Governor Zhou observed that "as China has the features of both a large transition econ-omy and an emerging market economy, the central bank of China and its monetary pol-icy are yet to be well understood by the outside world" (Zhou, 2016). This is somewhat odd, given that China's monetary policy actions have become important factors influ-encing both the economy and the financial markets in not only China but also the rest of the world. So what makes it difficult for the outside world to understand China's mon-etary policy framework? What factors are unique in China's monetary policy? And what are the likely directions of its future evolution? These are among the questions that we intend to address in this chapter.

China's current monetary policy framework was built during the past four decades (Sun, 2015). When economic reforms started in late 1978, China had no properly func-tioning monetary policy, other than the central credit plan, which was a part of the over-all central plan. Today, China does have a comprehensive monetary policy framework, which contains almost all parts of typical monetary policies in advanced market econo-mies, such as the United States and the eurozone. It has a central bank, a Monetary Pol-icy Committee (MPC), a number of policy instruments, several intermediate targets, and some policy objectives. But in almost every respect, the Chinese monetary policy differs from those of advanced market economies: The PBC is not an independent cen-tral bank; the MPC plays only advisory roles at best; there are multiple policy objectives, including growth, employment, inflation, external account, reform, economic structure, household welfare, and financial stability; and the policy tools are mostly quantitative instruments, rather than price-based instruments like short-term market interest rates.

Both these similarities and differences are results of China's economic transition from the Soviet type of central planning to a market economy. While the general direction is for the economy to move toward a free market system, some features of the planned economy remain. For instance, the less efficient SOEs continue to survive in key economic sectors. They still enjoy some forms of soft-budget constraints, receiving explicit or implicit subsidies. As they are not subject to hard market discipline, direct quantitative controls are often more effective for them than indirect price instruments. But as the non-state sector, which responds to changes in interest rates more sensitively, becomes more dominant in the economy over time, the overall effectiveness of the price instruments and their transmission mechanism should improve significantly.

For the past four decades, the monetary policy framework has been evolving, following two key themes: one is migrating from direct control to indirect control, and the other from quantitative regulation to price regulation. Such evolution will most likely continue in the coming decades. It is possible that the Chinese monetary policy framework will converge, in many ways, to those of the advanced market economies. For instance, the PBC may over time gain more independence in monetary policymaking. The MPC may become a decision-making body. The list of policy objectives may be reduced to primarily focus on inflation. The PBC may also select a short-term market interest rate as its operational target. And the Taylor rule may take over the McCallum rule as the key decision-making mechanism. But it is also possible that, for quite a long time, the Chinese monetary policy framework will retain certain features different from those of the advanced market economies. For example, other economic ministries may continue to give input into the decision-making process, through the State Council, the MPC, or the newly established State Council Financial Stability and Development Committee (FSDC). The quantitative rule of the monetary policy may continue to play a role in China. This is likely not only because transition of the Chinese economy will take a long time but also because thoughts about the optimal model of monetary policy started to change after the global financial crisis.

In this chapter, we attempt to provide a brief introduction to China's monetary policy framework. In the next section, we discuss the broad direction for monetary policy evolution against the background of the transition of the Chinese economy from the centrally planned system to a market economy. Section 3 explains the policy framework by detailing the decision-making process, the policy objectives, the policy tools, and the intermediate targets. Section 4 examines the transmission mechanisms of China's monetary policy, by first summarizing the possible channels and then surveying empirical analyses of the Chinese case. Section 5 reviews identification of China's monetary policy rules, by focusing on the Taylor rule versus the McCallum rule. And the final section discusses the future of China's monetary policy framework by focusing on three important questions about the decision-making process, the number of policy objectives, and the key policy instruments.

2. TRANSITION OF THE MONETARY POLICY FRAMEWORK

China's first central bank, the *Household Bank,* was established in 1905 in the Qing Dynasty. Another central bank, the *Daqing Bank,* was set up in 1908 and three years later was restructured into the *Bank of China*. In 1924, the Nationalist Government created the

Central Bank, with its headquarters based in Shanghai and other branches around the country. The Communists established the PBC in 1948, which eventually became China's central bank after the founding of the People's Republic of China (PRC) in 1949, while the Nationalists' Central Bank moved to Taiwan.

Until 1935, those various central banks did not play all the roles of a modern central bank. This was mainly because China adopted the silver standard at that time, and there was no room for monetary policy. After the Paris International Monetary Conference in 1867, most of the major countries transitioned to the gold standard. China was the only one left on the silver standard. This resulted in abundant liquidity conditions and a weakening currency in the country, which contributed to economic prosperity and a financial market boom. After the Great Depression, however, China was forced off the silver standard, following the adoption of the *Silver Protection Act* by the United States Congress in 1934, and had to start a new monetary system of fiat money in 1935. That monetary system contained an important defect in its design, without a monetary anchor. And, as a result, skyrocketing inflation eventually destabilized the economy and even the overall society.

Since 1949, the PBC has been serving as the country's only central bank and, sometimes, also as a commercial bank. It played an important role in monetary policymaking and financial regulation. However, the actual functioning of the monetary policy has also changed significantly since the establishment of the PRC. The current monetary policy framework was largely built during the past four decades and is still in the process of transition. To understand why China's monetary policy framework exhibits certain special features, we must first understand the transition of the Chinese economy after 1978.

2.1. Economic Transition

The fact that China is a transition economy not only makes it more difficult for the outside world to understand its monetary policy, as pointed out by Governor Zhou (2016), but probably also affects the way its monetary policy's transmission mechanism works. China's transition from central planning to a market economy has been progressing for four decades, but this process has not yet been completed. The government adopted the gradualist "dual-track" reform approach, which, in essence, means continuous support to the state-owned enterprises (SOEs), while allowing the non-state sectors to expand quickly. In theory, after a certain period of reform, the proportion of the SOEs would fall to a low level, and thus by then the economy would be dominated by market forces. This reform approach was once characterized as "growing out of the plan" (Naughton, 1995).

Judging from economic growth and financial stability, this dual-track reform approach worked quite well (Huang and Wang, 2011). But it has an important drawback. Since the SOEs were generally less productive and profitable than the rapidly growing private firms and foreign-invested companies, they needed to be subsidized to survive (Huang, 2010). This implies that the "soft budget constraint" of the SOEs has to continue. As a result, while the proportion of the SOEs declined steadily, the macroeconomic conditions actually deteriorated in the 1990s, a period when the state sector as a whole made net losses, the fiscal system nearly collapsed, and the banks' average bad loan ratio skyrocketed. The government had to undertake several decisive steps to deal with these problems, including an aggressive privatization program for the SOEs, a fiscal reform policy segregating the areas of local and central government public finance, and a series of efforts to transform the technically insolvent commercial banks. In fact, the PBC played critical roles in designing and implementing some of the reform programs, especially the banking reform (He and Wang, 2012). After joining the World Trade Organization (WTO) at the end of 2001, China's macroeconomic performance improved significantly. Yet the problems of "soft budget constraint" and "government guarantees" continued.

Since the government does not have sufficient fiscal resources to subsidize the SOEs, it turned to the financial system by depressing banks' deposit and lending rates and also by influencing banks' credit allocation in favor of the SOEs. This was the root cause of the unique pattern of China's financial reform and development—strong on quantity but weak on quality (Huang et al., 2013; Huang and Wang, 2017). When China started economic reform in late 1978, it had only one important financial institution, the PBC, which accounted for 93% of the country's financial assets. In the following 40 years, China built a very comprehensive financial sector. As a proxy indicator of China's relative financial assets, M2/GDP ratio is around 210%, the highest in the world. China's big four commercial banks are currently ranked among the world's top 10. Market capitalization of China's stock market ranks second globally, while that of the debt market ranks third. In the meantime, the authorities still regularly guide bank interest rates, advise on credit allocation, intervene in exchange rate, control cross-border capital flows, and own majority shares of most of the large financial institutions.

Repressive financial policies are necessary for the dual-track reform approach and provide effective subsidies to the SOEs, through depressed lending rates and favored credit allocation. This implies that, while the entire economy moves rapidly toward the market system, some nonmarket behavior continues to prevail. For instance, the SOEs are probably less responsive to changes in interest rates than the private firms. Likewise, the local government finance vehicles (LGFVs), which borrowed massively from the banks and the markets after the recession of 2008, also enjoy certain degrees of government guarantees. As a result, the financial institutions also favor the SOEs and LGFVs in their fund allocation. If a bank's lending to a private firm becomes nonperforming, the responsible employee and the executive are often more harshly punished. Existence of such nonmarket behavior explains why quantity-based policy tools are still useful, alongside the price-based policy tools, and also why the lack of independence of the central bank might not be completely undesirable.

2.2. Changes in Monetary Policy

The history of the PRC's monetary policy may be divided into three periods: the period of credit plan in the central planned economy (1949–1978), the period of direct control based on management of total credit (1979–1997), and the period of indirect control of aggregate money and credit (1998–to date).

2.2.1. The Period of Central Credit Plan

In the early 20th century, China's financial sector was actually rather advanced. At that time, Shanghai was a major international financial center, with all types of financial institutions, including commercial banks, insurance companies, and stock markets. The financial system was also quite open and, at one point, more than a hundred foreign currencies were in circulation in the city's market. China's financial sector, however, collapsed during the wars in the 1930s and the 1940s. After 1949, financial institutions began to be reestablished or to recover. However, the PRC quickly nationalized all the financial institutions from 1952 on and shut down most of them from 1956 on, when the country started the moment of socialist transformation. The financial sector was effectively reduced to a mono-bank system, with the PBC affiliated with the Ministry of Finance (MOF).

Under the newly established central planning system, "bourgeois rights" were denunciated and commercial activities were regarded as useless. The most important economic working mechanism was the central plan, compiled by the State Planning Commission. The central credit plan was one part of the central plan. In fact, most of the financial intermediaries, operating under the investment plan, allocated long-term credit to priority sectors and to projects selected by the national and local governments. As the primary objective of the credit plan was to provide working capital for industry and commerce and also to meet the requirements of the five-year development plans and the annual investment plans, the PBC and financial intermediation played only limited roles in controlling changes in money in circulation (Montes-Negret, 1995).

2.2.2. The Period of Direct Credit Control
At the start of 1978, the PBC was separated out from the MOF to act as both the central bank and a commercial bank. Meanwhile, the authorities also moved quickly to reestablish the financial system, including commercial banks and insurance companies, from the end of the 1970s and stock markets from the early 1990s. At the start of 1984, the original PBC was split into two institutions, with the commercial activities moved to the newly established Industrial and Commercial Bank of China (ICBC) and the remaining activities forming the new central bank, the PBC. The new PBC became a key player in monetary policymaking and financial regulation, although it functions under direct instruction and supervision of the State Council.

In the meantime, the central credit plan evolved over time to suit the new financial and economic environment. The PBC formulated a direct regulatory framework for management of bank credit, applying quotas for credit and cash. The central bank selected bank credit as its main intermediate policy target, in large part because of the administrative control it exercised over a highly concentrated banking sector (Yi, 1994). Gradually, the credit plan replaced the weakening fiscal tools at the central government's disposal and became a vehicle for channeling subsidies to the SOEs. The PBC dictated not only targets for annual growth of total bank credit but also allocation of credit to provinces and industries. In the meantime, the PBC also started to experiment with new methods of monetary policy, including compiling a money supply plan from 1987 and the aggregate social credit plan from 1989, to strengthen the monitoring and forecast of bank credit.

2.2.3. The Period of Indirect Control of Money and Credit
In early 1995, the National People's Congress passed The People's Bank of China Law of the People's Republic of China (the PBC Law). According to this Law, the PBC's responsibilities are, under the leadership of the State Council, to make and implement monetary policy, to prevent and resolve financial risks, and to maintain financial stability. One of the most important moves that the PBC undertook was to abolish the direct controls over bank credit at the start of 1998. Although the central bank still announced annual

credit plans, it established an indirect management framework for money and credit, using mainly a set of new tools such as open market operations (OMOs), the reserve requirement ratio (RRR), central bank lending, and rediscount windows to regulate aggregate money supply and bank credit. Later on, the PBC created a number of new policy facilities for managing short-term liquidity conditions. As the relevance of M2 and new bank loans declines, the central bank compiled a new indicator, Aggregate Financing to the Real Economy (AFRE), to gauge the financial sector's support to the real sector.

During this period, the PBC gradually focused more on interest rate instruments. On the one hand, it pushed ahead the interest rates liberalization and granted commercial banks greater degrees of freedom in setting their deposit and lending rates by widening the allowed bands. By the end of 2015, the PBC had abolished all the restrictions on commercial banks' interest rates. On the other hand, the central bank also paid more attention to the short-term market interest rates. In 2007, it rebuilt a new interbank market, the Shanghai Interbank Offered Rate (SHIBOR), which became an important parameter for measuring liquidity conditions in the interbank market. It seems that the next step would be for the PBC to select a short-term interest rate as either the key monetary policy tool or the operational target.

Several new features are also emerging, especially after the global financial crisis (Guo and Schipke, 2014; Zhang, 2018). And changes in China's monetary policy framework during the reform period may be summarized by two consistent themes: one is *the transition from direct to indirect controls*, and the other is *the transition from quantitative to price regulations*.

3. HOW DOES THE MONETARY POLICY WORK IN CHINA?

3.1. The Decision-making Process

The first thing to notice about the actual working mechanism of China's monetary policy is that the PBC is not an independent central bank. Instead, as of March 2018, the PBC is one of the 26 State Council's ministries. The PBC Law states explicitly that the PBC makes and implements monetary policy under the leadership of the State Council. The PBC Law also requires that the PBC regularly report to the National People's Congress on conditions of monetary policy and financial industry. Additionally, the *PBC Law* stipulates that the PBC set up the MPC, which should play important roles in macroeconomic regulation and also in making and adjusting monetary policies. In reality, however, the MPC, which is chaired by the PBC governor and joined by senior officials of various economic ministries and agencies as well as several academic experts, plays at most advisory roles in the formulation of monetary policies.

There is no official documentation of the formal process of China's monetary policy-making. But it probably works as follows. First, at the beginning of the year, the State Council decides on key economic policy targets, including a GDP growth rate and an inflation rate, which are approved by the National People's Congress. Second, when key economic indicators deviate from their respective targets, the PBC prepares proposed plans for monetary policy actions and submits them to the State Council. And, third, the State Council reviews the recommendations and makes the final decision. If the proposals are approved, then the PBC announces these policy actions and implements

The monetary policy framework

Operational instruments	Operational targets	Intermediate targets	Policy objectives
• Quantity-based instruments. (e.g., RRR, CBBs, central bank lending, OMOs, etc.) • Price-based instruments (e.g., banks' base deposit and lending rates) • Window-guidance	• Nonborrowed reserves • Borrowed reserves • Short-term money market rate • Monetary base	• Money supply (narrow money supply M1 and broad money supply M2) • Bank credit (and also the total social financing) • Market interest rate (such as SHIBOR)	• Rapid economic growth • Full employment • Low and stable inflation • Balanced external account

FIGURE 2.1. China's monetary policy framework. *Source*: Compiled by the authors.

them accordingly. This process is mainly applicable to important policy instruments such as interest rates and RRR. The PBC enjoys a certain degree of effective autonomy on other policy actions, such as OMOs.

The Chinese monetary policy stances are often described as "tightening," "prudent," and "easing" (McMahon et al., 2018). Sometimes, a "prudent" stance may be further clarified as "prudent with a tightening bias," "prudent neutral," or "prudent with an easing bias," The term "prudent" for describing monetary policy bias is quite unique in China, probably because the PBC is not an independent monetary policymaker. Here, "prudent" means a narrow range around a "neutral" policy. Therefore, when the PBC states that its monetary policy bias is "prudent," it could refer to "neutral," "slightly tightening," or "slightly easing."

China's overall monetary policy framework looks quite similar to those in advanced market economies—the PBC applies a wide range of policy instruments to achieve the policy objectives, through several intermediate targets (figure 2.1).

3.2. Policy Objectives

Monetary policy objectives are the central bank's mandate. In most advanced market economies, the central banks often have a very simple objective of maintaining price stability. In China, the PBC Law also stipulates that "the objective of the monetary policy shall be to maintain stability of the value of the currency and thereby promote economic growth."[1] But in reality, "the annual objectives of the PBC mandated by the Chinese government have been maintaining price stability, boosting economic growth, promoting employment, and broadly maintaining balance of payments" (Zhou, 2016). For instance, an important reason why China has multiple monetary policy objectives can be attributed to its feature of being both a transitional and an emerging market economy. Balance of payments largely affect the central bank's monetary policy, money supply, and price stability objectives. Therefore, the PBC must pay attention to balance of payments, and accordingly needs to assume roles such as managing the exchange rate, the foreign exchange market, the foreign exchange reserves, the gold reserves, and the balance of payments statistics.

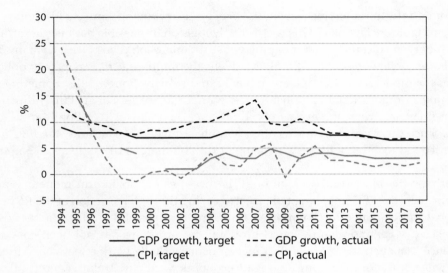

FIGURE 2.2. GDP growth rate and inflation rate: Target and actual. *Sources:* National Development and Reform Commission, National Bureau of Statistics, authors' calculation.

Governor Zhou has also pointed out that, despite the multipolicy objectives, the PBC always takes monetary policy as the foremost fighting line for maintaining stability of the general price level. This implies that *inflation* is actually the most important policy objective for the PBC's monetary policy, which is in line with practices of many other central banks as well as recommendations by some scholars. Goodfriend and Prasad (2006), for instance, suggested that anchoring monetary policy with an explicit inflation target would be the most reliable way for the PBC to tie down inflation expectations, and thereby to enable monetary policy to make the best contribution to macroeconomic and financial stability as well as to economic growth. In the meantime, Mehran et al. (1996) believed that price stability is the prominent target for the PBC, as most Chinese officials recognize that, in the long run, rapid economic growth can be achieved only if price stability persists. Figure 2.2 illustrates the yearly targets for GDP growth and CPI and their actual evolvements over time in China since the early 1990s, where the targets are often announced in the Government Work Report.

The nominal *exchange rate* has been serving as the main nominal anchor of China's monetary policy for the past decade. China had a fixed exchange rate regime when economic reform started in 1978. In the following years, renminbi devalued continuously until the beginning of 1994, when the PBC introduced the managed float exchange rate system for renminbi. After a period of fixed exchange rate between 1997 and 2005, renminbi shifted toward a new managed floating exchange rate regime with reference to a basket of currencies. The PBC has explicitly stated its desire to increase exchange rate flexibility, while several senior PBC officials point to "clean float" as a goal for exchange rate policy reform. If this is indeed the plan, then the central bank probably will need to find a new nominal anchor, preferably the inflation rate.

However, sometimes policymakers hope that the monetary policy could play even more roles. The 2017 PBC Work Conference, for instance, called for the monetary policy to balance among different policy objectives—stabilizing economic growth, promoting economic reform, adjusting economic structure, improving household welfare, and preventing financial risks.[2] This is effectively mission impossible because, according to the Tinbergen rule, the number of policy instruments should be at least as many as the number of policy objectives.[3] Or alternatively, the multi-objective monetary policy requires the monetary policymakers to have extraordinary policy skills. Sometimes, the PBC takes on additional responsibilities, without a choice. For instance, during the Asian financial crisis, the average NPL ratio reached above 30% (Bonin and Huang, 2001). Since the fiscal system was already quite stretched at that time, the PBC had to step forward to assist with restructuring of the commercial banks to avoid a systemic collapse.

Perhaps the most controversial of all is the so-called structural monetary policy. For instance, the PBC implemented targeted easing through reduction of the RRRs only for local banks in an effort to improve financing for the small- and medium-sized enterprises (SMEs) and also the rural economy. So far, there has not been convincing evidence that such structural policy mechanisms actually work effectively. Monetary policy is mainly for managing aggregate economic variables. If the agricultural sector does not receive enough funding, for example, it is most likely either because that sector could not meet the risk assessment criteria or because the regulated interest rates were too low to cover the associated risk. The better strategies should be to increase competition of financial institutions in the rural area, to innovate on risk assessment methods, and to liberalize the restrictions on lending rates. Simply releasing more funds to the rural banks would not work, because most of the rural banks already have surplus funds.

In summary, the key objective for China's monetary policy is to maintain price stability and therefore promote economic growth. But as the monetary policy is decided by the State Council, not the central bank alone, it is not surprising that monetary policy is also often required to pay attention to certain other policy objectives, such as economic structure, household welfare, and financial stability. This could, in turn, have an impact on monetary policy. For instance, the Chinese monetary policy shows a tendency of greater willingness to ease rather than to tighten. This could compromise the monetary policy's discipline and might have contributed, at least partially, to the high leverage ratio in China today.

3.3. Intermediate Targets

In order to achieve the monetary policy objectives, the PBC regulates a number of intermediate targets, including money supply (narrow money supply M1 and broad money supply M2), bank credit (and increasingly also the aggregate financing to the real economy), and market interest rate (such as SHIBOR and, sometimes, bond yields). The relative importance of quantity-based and price-based intermediate targets changed over time, while the relevance of the intermediate indicators to monetary policy objectives also evolved over time. For instance, in the past, the correlations between M2 growth and bank credit (figure 2.3), on the one side, and GDP growth and inflation, on the other side, were quite high. This relationship almost broke down recently.

After abolition of the mandatory credit plan in 1998, bank credit and money supply became the two most important intermediate targets for the PBC's monetary policy. The

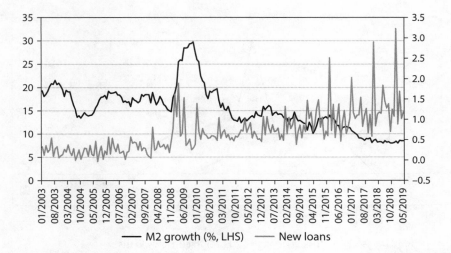

FIGURE 2.3. Growth of M2 and amount of newly increased loans (in RMB trillions). *Sources:* PBC, authors' calculation.

Premier often specifically outlines targets for *newly increased bank loans* and *broad money supply M2* in the Government Work Report (GWR), submitted to the National People's Congress at the beginning of the year, although no more-specific targets for M2 were proposed in the GWR for 2018 and 2019. This is probably because the Chinese financial system is dominated by commercial banks. Bank loan and money supply pretty much reflect financing conditions of the economy. Various economic studies confirmed the high relevance of these quantitative intermediate targets to the monetary policy objectives, particularly inflation and growth (Xia and Liao, 2001; Xie, 2004; Yu, 2001). In addition to the Government Work Report, the PBC also regularly refers to M2 growth and bank loans as important monetary policy concepts.

In recent years, however, the correlations between these quantitative intermediate targets and monetary policy objectives declined visibly. This is probably because non-banking financing grew rapidly. In addition to the government's efforts to promote development of multi-layer capital markets, banks' off-balance-sheet transactions, or the shadow banking businesses, also expanded quickly. Economists estimated that the total size of such shadow banking activities ranges between 50 and 90 trillion yuan, compared to the total outstanding loans of the banking sector of 120 trillion yuan at the end of 2017. As bank credit became a smaller portion of total finance, its relevance to monetary policy objectives declined. From 2011, the PBC introduced a new indicator, Aggregate Financing to the Real Economy (AFRE), which covers renminbi and foreign currency loans, trusted loans, undiscounted banks' acceptance bills, corporate bonds, nonfinancial institutions' domestic equity financing, and others. While the construction and calculation methods are still subject to change, AFRE has become a more important intermediate target, at least partially replacing the newly increased bank loans. According to figure 2.4, we can find that the newly increased bank loans are only one of the several components of AFRE and that its share has been relatively declining, especially since 2008.

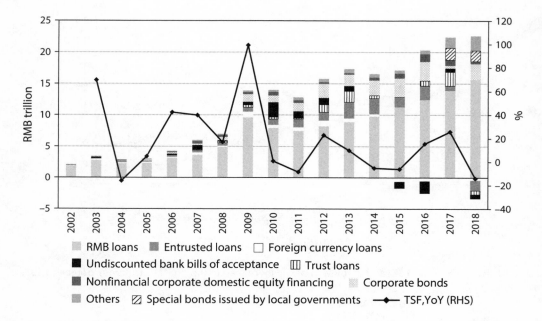

FIGURE 2.4. Components of new issued total social financing. *Source:* PBC, authors' calculation.

Over time, the PBC also started to pay attention to market interest rate. In 1996, it established a new interbank rate, China Interbank Offered Rate (CHIBOR), which was the weighted average of borrowing rates among banks. And, in 2007, the PBC rebuilt it into a new Shanghai Interbank Offered Rate (SHIBOR), to improve the representativeness and liquidity conditions of the instrument. While, initially, this market was intended to allow participants to trade short-term liquidity, soon this became an important platform for the PBC to conduct OMOs. Moreover, SHIBOR also behaves as an important indicator of market liquidity condition, which may serve as an intermediate target (e.g., 7-day SHIBOR, 7-day repo rate) (figure 2.5). In this process, the PBC emphasized the gradual use of price-based policy tools such as interest rates to adjust the level and structure of market rates. Of course, the usefulness of such price-based instruments is also constrained by institutional factors. For instance, the big five banks, which account for two-thirds of total assets and liabilities of the Chinese banking sector, are often less interest rate–elastic (Prasad and Zhang, 2014).

3.4. Policy Instruments

The PBC's policy tools fall into several categories, including quantity-based instruments, price-based instruments, and prudential and regulatory instruments, as well as administrative instruments.[4] *Quantity-based instruments* include RRR, Central Bank Bills (CBBs), central bank lending, rediscount window, OMOs, and so on. Among these, the RRR is probably the best-known policy tool. Frequent adjustments to RRR started around 2005–2006 as sterilization policy actions. Before that, the PBC sold CBBs, which first became a policy tool in 1993, to absorb renminbi liquidity released passively when accumulating foreign exchange reserves. Soon, however, the amount of the CBBs exceeded the size of

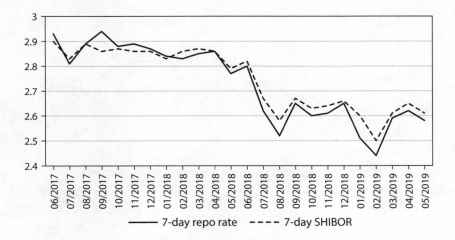

FIGURE 2.5. 7-day SHIBOR and 7-day repo rate. *Source:* CEIC database, authors' calculation.

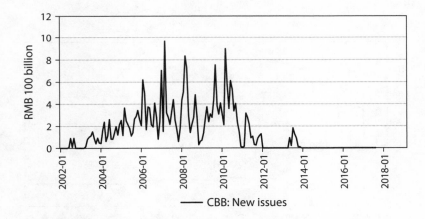

FIGURE 2.6. New issued central bank bills. *Source:* China Bond Data, authors' calculation.

the government bonds, and the transaction costs of managing an ever-growing CBBs market became increasingly high (figure 2.6).

Then the PBC turned to RRR as a liquidity management policy tool. And in 2011, the official RRRs reached the peaks of 21.5% for large financial institutions and 19.5% for small- and medium-sized financial institutions (figure 2.7). Soon after that, however, the PBC became more reluctant, and reduced RRR for three possible reasons. One, cutting RRR would send a very strong message of aggressive monetary policy easing to the market, while in reality the purpose could simply be to stabilize the liquidity condition. Two, knowing that the State Council is more willing to approve cutting RRR than to approve hiking RRR, the PBC takes extra caution when recommending a cut to RRR. And, three, compared to some other options such as CBBs, RRR is a more cost-effective method for absorbing liquidity, which directly changes banks' ability to multiply base money through credit creation.[5] Beginning in 2013, the PBC started to

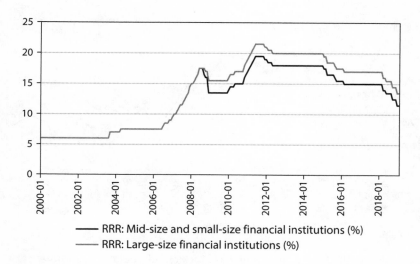

FIGURE 2.7. RRRs vary among financial institutions of different sizes. *Source:* PBC, authors' calculation.

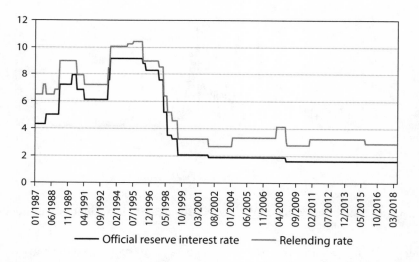

FIGURE 2.8. Interest rates for official reserves and for central bank relending. *Source:* PBC, authors' calculation.

create another new set of monetary policy tools, such as the standing lending facility (SLF), medium-term lending facility (MLF), short-term liquidity operations (SLOs), targeted medium-term lending facility (TMLF), and others. These are tools mainly for injecting liquidity into the banking sector. Most recently, in January 2019, the PBC also announced the creation of the central banks swap (CBS), aimed at supporting commercial banks' perpetual bond sales.

The *price-based instruments* include not only banks' base deposit and lending rates, which became important policy tools in 1983, but also the required reserve rate and the relending rate (figure 2.8).[6] This is very different from the practice of the central banks in other countries where market interest rates are indirectly influenced. This worked quite well for some time, probably because banks were the dominant players in the financial system. Economic activities are sensitively affected by banks' deposit and lending rates. Initially, the banks had to strictly follow the interest rates set by the PBC. Over time, however, the PBC allowed the commercial banks to set their deposit and lending rates within certain ranges around the base rates. At the end of 2015, the PBC lifted the last ceiling restriction on the deposit rate. In theory, the banks become completely free in setting deposit and lending rates. However, as was pointed out by the PBC, the process of interest rate liberalization in China had not been completed. Further significant improvements are still needed in financial institutions' risk pricing capability and in the financial sector's interest rate transmission mechanism.

Window guidance is an unspoken but very powerful policy tool. Literally, it means that the central bank orally advises financial institutions in their decisions on interest rates and the quantity and allocation of credit. Window guidance is a legacy of the central planning system. In a transitional economy like China, even though window guidance is only an advisory act, it could be quite effective, especially for those state-owned commercial banks.

4. THE TRANSMISSION MECHANISMS OF CHINA'S MONETARY POLICY

So the PBC has all the key components of a monetary policy framework—policy objectives, intermediate targets, and policy instruments. But can China's monetary policy work properly? Answers to this question boil down to the effectiveness of the policy transmission mechanism. This mechanism of the monetary policy concerns how policy actions affect the policy targets:

Policy instruments → operational targets → intermediate targets → ultimate goals

Alternatively, the transmission mechanism may also be viewed as follows:

Central bank → financial institutions/financial markets → enterprises/households → national income/national price

After the central bank adjusts the policy instruments, monetary aggregates and interest rates change accordingly. These affect the lending activities of commercial banks and conditions of financial markets. These are then transmitted to the real economy, such as investment and consumption, which in turn determine price and output of the whole economy. In any case, the effectiveness of the transmission mechanism of monetary policy depends on proper functioning of both the financial and the real sectors. Failure in any segment of the above process will weaken the efficiency of monetary policy transmission.

4.1. Possible Transmission Channels

The literature has specified several possible channels for transmission of the monetary policy. According to the overview given by Mishkin (1996), there exist not only a traditional interest rate channel, but also asset price channels and credit channels. Additionally, there also exists an "expectations channel," which emphasizes the central bank's ability to influence expectations of economic agents and thus to affect economic outcomes

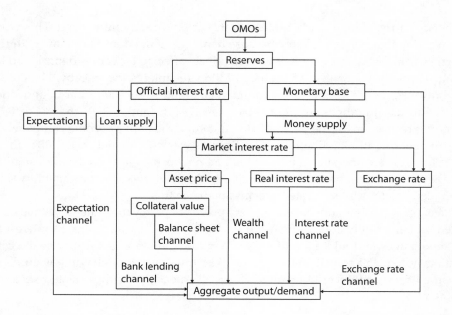

FIGURE 2.9. Summary of monetary policy transmission channels in previous literature. *Source:* Kuttner and Mosser (2002), recompiled by the authors.

through its communication with the market (Evans et al., 2001; Woodford, 2005; Geraats, 2009). Based on chart from Kuttner and Mosser (2002), figure 2.9 is compiled to illustrate most of the channels discussed in the literature.

The *interest rate channel* is probably the most common monetary policy transmission mechanism that has been featured in the literature for more than 70 years. In accordance with the Keynesian IS-LM model, it refers to the policy transmission via capital user-cost adjustment (Taylor, 1993, 1995, 2000; Bernanke and Blinder, 1992; Mishkin, 1995).

The *asset price channels* emphasize the critical role of asset prices in transmitting monetary effects to the real economy, including the exchange rate channel and the wealth channel. The *exchange rate channel* transmits monetary policy changes in open economies to changes in the exchange rate. The *wealth channel* describes how interest changes affect consumption profile through equity price, bond price, or housing price changes over time (Ando and Modigliani, 1963).

The *credit channel* has attracted considerable attention, which was built on breakthroughs in the economics of imperfect information such as agency problems in the 1970s. The credit channel can be further split into the *bank lending channel* (narrow credit channel) and the *balance-sheet channel* (broad credit channel). The bank lending channel is based on the view that banks have a special role in the financial markets, because they are well suited to deal with asymmetric information problems in the credit market (Mishkin, 1996; Kashyap and Stein, 2000). The balance-sheet channel assumes that changes in the external finance premium amplify the direct effects of monetary policy on interest rates (Bernanke and Gertler, 1995).

4.2. Empirical Assessment of the Chinese Case

The functioning of the transmission channels discussed above is summarized mainly from the viewpoint of experiences in the advanced market economies. But as we speculated earlier, the special transition features of the Chinese economy may affect the transmission mechanisms of the monetary policy. Here we attempt to depict the way the transmission channels work by reviewing the related empirical literature. While the empirical analyses reveal quite mixed findings on almost all fronts, the general patterns are that the interest rate channel was quite weak in the earlier years but grew much stronger in recent years; that the credit channel is quite effective, relatively speaking; that functioning of the wealth channel is unclear, as monetary policy has distinct effects on asset prices but asset prices do not have stable impacts on consumption; and that the exchange rate channel is also not stable.

In advanced market economies, interest rates are probably the most important parameters for monetary policy and financial markets. Central banks often choose short-term market interest rates as either policy tools or operational targets. In China, however, the PBC does not directly adjust or target at the short-term market rates, although it started to pay greater attention to those rates in recent years. Early economic studies find interest rates having a modest role in the Chinese economy and a weak linkage between interest rates and real sector activities. For instance, studies by Laurens and Maino (2007) and Koivu (2009) confirm that the interest rate channel does not function properly. Possible explanations for this phenomenon include the repressive financial policies: Banks' credit allocation favors large SOEs, which still exhibit certain degrees of "soft budget constraint." The main borrowers are less sensitive to changes in interest rates, while the interest rate sensitive sectors, such as private firms, are either discriminated against or altogether excluded from formal financial services.

However, this situation is gradually changing, as interest rate liberalization and other market-based reforms continue to be pushed ahead. In recent years the non-state sectors have accounted for more than half of total outstanding bank loans. Even the SOEs also gradually become more responsible to financial prices, as a result of intensified competition pressures and hardening financial disciplines. The PBC also started to rely more on market forces in conducting its monetary policy. It gradually relaxed the rigid controls over banks' interest rates and now attaches less importance to quantitative intermediate targets. More attention has also been paid to short-term interest rates. In the 2017 Q3 Monetary Policy Executive Report, the PBC recognized the ability of DR007, the short-term money market interest rate, in reflecting banking system liquidity conditions. In 2018, the PBC reiterated its commitment to further improve the central bank's credibility and transparency. By providing more timely information, the PBC would strengthen its policy interpretation and information disclosure, deliver its policy intentions, and reasonably guide market expectations (PBC, 2018; McMahon et al., 2018). Recent studies using more recent economic data have discovered that changes in interest rates result in considerable impacts on economic activities and inflation in China (see Fernald et al., 2014; Zha and Chen, 2017; Ge, 2019). This suggests that the transmission mechanism of China's monetary policy started to converge to that of the advanced market economies.[7]

The credit channels are very important mechanisms for the Chinese monetary policy. The PBC first introduced the "credit policy" framework in 1986, calling it the credit growth quota system, with a goal of bringing bank lending under control. At that time, loan quota was a compulsory requirement for banks, which was initially derived from the central planning policy. From January 1998, the advisory quota, implemented through a number of indirect policy tools plus window guidance, replaced the credit growth quota system. Economic analyses reveal mixed findings as they attempt to test the existence of the bank lending channel by focusing on the correlations among aggregate output, bank credit, and monetary policy indicators. By examining the relationships among monetary aggregates (M1 and M2), credit aggregate, and GDP, Sun (2004) finds that it is the money channel rather than the credit channel that plays a prominent role in China's monetary policy transmission. However, the Granger causality test for their empirical outcome is ambiguous, and clear conclusions are difficult to ascertain unless the data can be described by a simple two-dimensional system.

Sheng and Wu (2008) and Zhou and Jiang (2002) also emphasize the importance of the credit channel in monetary policy transmission. Sun et al. (2010) also confirm the existence of the bank lending channel with a VAR/VECM model, finding that bank lending is negatively related to RRRs and lending rate in the long term. Gunji and Yuan (2010) use bank-level data to investigate whether the impact of monetary policy on bank lending is dependent on bank-level characteristics in China. The results show that such impact is weaker for banks of larger size or lower levels of liquidity, and that banks' responses to monetary policy do not necessarily vary in accordance with the level of their capital. Nguyen and Boateng (2013) examine the bank lending channel in the case of involuntary excess reserves in China; they find that banks with larger involuntary excess reserves are less responsive to the monetary policy interest rate change, which in turn makes the monetary policy less effective. Another comparative analysis, by Li and Lee (2015), also reveals that foreign banks are less responsive than Chinese banks to monetary policy in China.

Given China's persistent high savings rate, it is possible that Chinese households' saving and consumption behaviors are not particularly sensitive to changes in interest rates. That, in turn, could reduce the effectiveness of the wealth channel of the Chinese monetary policy. Koivu (2012) studies the wealth channel by examining both the linkage from monetary policy to asset prices and the linkage from asset prices to consumption. The first linkage is found to exist—that is, monetary policy does affect asset prices. However, the author could not verify the second linkage, which implies that the wealth channel remains weak in China. Many studies of the wealth channel focus on roles of China's bond market. The study by Zhang and Huang (2017) confirms the role of bond price in transmitting the monetary policy change to the real-sector activities. They find that monetary policy is effective in managing fluctuation of bond market yields and that short-term bond yields have remarkable and significant impacts on both output and price variables of the economy. Their study also reveals the much more limited roles of long-term bond yields. These results suggest that both households and entrepreneurs are taking interest rates more seriously when making consumption and investment decisions.

Since January 1994, China has been implementing the managed floating regime for renminbi exchange rate, with the exception of the period between mid-1997 and mid-2005, when renminbi was effectively fixed to the U.S. dollar. But, in general, "floating" has always been very limited. As China still maintains certain degrees of capital account controls, there is still some room left for the PBC to maneuver the independence of monetary policy. The trends are that China's exchange rate regime becomes more flexible and that its capital account becomes more open, although whether this will lead to more independent monetary policy remains to be seen. If the Mundell Trilemma prevails, then a more flexible exchange rate should lead to a more independent monetary policy. However, according to Rey (2015), the global financial cycle constrains monetary policies regardless of the exchange rate regime when the capital account is freely mobile. So if the Rey Dilemma overrules the trilemma, then more-open capital accounts should cause less independent monetary policy. A parallel policy effort is to internationalize renminbi, especially dating from 2009. This effort, alongside China's growing weight in the world economy, lifted the ranking of renminbi in international payment and created a huge offshore RMB market (He et al., 2017).

When it comes to the exchange rate channel, it can be split into two parts. The first part is transmission from monetary policy to exchange rate, and the second part is transmission from exchange rate to the real economy. The latter part functions relatively effectively, with strong evidence provided by several empirical studies (for example, Lv, 2007). The former part remains a problem. For example, Zhang and Huang (2011) find that monetary policy is not a driving force for exchange rate volatility. This odd phenomenon could be caused by two possible reasons. First, the exchange rate regime remains quite rigid, and it does not sensitively respond to changes in monetary policy. Second, variation of exchange rate is determined by many factors in addition to monetary policy, such as external economic environment, trends of economic growth, and others. But in any case, as the exchange rate becomes more flexible, interest rate becomes more market-determined, and market participants respond more sensitively to price signals, then the exchange rate channel of monetary policy transmission mechanism should work more smoothly and more effectively.

5. IDENTIFICATION OF THE MONETARY POLICY RULE

5.1. Review of Related Literature

Economic research on monetary policy rules experienced a quiet period following publication of a seminal study by Sargent and Wallace (1975), which argued that monetary policy can be ineffective under rational expectations, until the late 1980s. One of the active strands in the literature begins with Taylor (1993). He proposed a rule illustrating how central banks should raise the nominal target interest rate when the expected inflation is higher than the desired target level and when the actual output level is higher than the natural output. Economists around the world have since estimated empirically the Taylor rule and its variations for the United States and many other countries.

In contrast, the McCallum rule is a rule for growth of money supply (McCallum, 1988). The original McCallum rule describes growth of money supply as a function of real GDP growth and money velocity. More recent studies, such as Esanov et al. (2005), revise the McCallum rule so that money supply growth also targets both the expected inflation rate gap and the output gap, parallel to the Taylor rule. The revised McCallum rule describes how central banks should reduce money supply when the expected inflation is higher than the desired target level and when the actual output level is higher than the natural output. In both academic and policy circles, the McCallum rule is much less prominent than the Taylor rule, primarily because nowadays central banks in advanced market economies mainly focus on interest rate rather than monetary base.

Empirical studies to identify monetary policy rules are chiefly based on vector autoregressive (VAR) models. For example, Sims (1992) developed the VAR model and showed that impulse responses of prices and output to interest rate shocks share some consistency, while Bagliano and Favero (1998) find that the inclusion of long-term interest rates can not only reveal the contemporaneous reaction of the federal fund rate, but can also improve the precision of estimated structural responses to monetary policy shock. However, Evans and Kuttner (1998) also question VAR accuracy in predicting changes in monetary policy and suggest that more research along these lines would be warranted.

5.2. The Chinese Case

A number of studies have evaluated China's monetary policy in terms of simple policy rules, although one should not assume that all aspects of policy could be summarized by such a simple rule or that the central bank would mechanically follow a rule. Nevertheless, adoption of a policy rule could make it easier for the central bank to evaluate various policy options and to communicate with the market. It could, in turn, make it easier for the public to better understand the central bank's policy objectives and judge the performance. Thus time-inconsistency problems in the case of discretionary policy can be avoided.

In practical policy discussions, numerous controversies and confusions abound about whether the interest rate or the money supply is more appropriate as an intermediate target for China's monetary policy. Empirical findings on whether the Taylor rule or the McCallum rule better characterizes China's monetary policy rules are also inconclusive. The McCallum rule focuses on illustrating the growth of money supply as a function of targeted nominal GDP growth, corrected for changes in money velocity. However, the Taylor rule emphasizes the effective signaling of short-term interest rates.

Xie and Luo (2002) conducted an empirical analysis of China's monetary policy under the Taylor rule framework with historical analysis and the reaction function method. They found that the Taylor rule can still capture the monetary policy stances and provide a benchmark for China's monetary policy rule, despite distortions remaining in the interest rates and the financial markets. The Taylor rule can also strengthen the stability of China's monetary policy rule and help implement forward-looking monetary policy by transparency enhancement. Nevertheless, given the prominent role of money supply in China's monetary policy, a McCallum monetary policy rule could seem more appropriate for the country. Counterfactual simulation results by Sun et al. (2012) evaluated the feasibility of the McCallum rule and its advantages in reducing the nominal GDP fluctuations. They advocated that the PBC adopt the McCallum rule as the illustrative benchmark, instead of strictly following the simple McCallum rule in a "mechanical-looking" form.

More recently, Sun (2015) showed that the PBC's policy rule cannot be represented by either a money growth rule or an interest rate rule, and therefore that the best characterization is a mixture of both. Wu and Lian (2016) confirmed that a hybrid rule taking into account information about money growth and about interest rate change is a welfare-optimization choice. Studies such as that of Zha and Chen (2017) also exerted efforts to evaluate China's forward-looking monetary policy rules from a regime-switching perspective. Those authors also confirmed the asymmetric characteristics of China's monetary policy transmission in an endogenous-switching nonlinear structural vector autoregression (SVAR) framework. They find that the forward-looking rule is more consistent with the PBC's actions, and it can not only improve the transparency and accountability but also stabilize public expectations.

6. FUTURE DIRECTIONS OF THE POLICY FRAMEWORK

Since 1978, the PBC and its monetary policy has experienced significant transformation. The PBC, which originally acted as both the central bank and a commercial bank, became the specialized central bank responsible for monetary policy and financial stability in January 1984. Its monetary policy also evolved over time, following two key themes: from direct to indirect controls and from quantitative to price regulations.

In many ways, however, China's monetary policy framework still looks distinctively different from those of advanced market economies. First, the PBC is not an independent central bank. It is a ministry-level agency under the State Council, which makes final decisions on monetary policy. Second, although the PBC Law stipulates that the objective of monetary policy is to maintain stability of the value of the currency and thereby to promote economic growth, in practice monetary policymakers have to consider a long list of policy objectives, including economic growth, employment, inflation, external account, reform policy, economic structure, household welfare, and financial stability. Third, the majority of the policy instruments in the PBC's toolkit are quantitative, such as RRR, rediscount window, central bank lending, and other liquidity management instruments. Although the PBC also adjusts interest rates from time to time, these are banks' base deposit and lending rates, not the short-term market interest rates that other central banks often target. Fourth, not all the transmission mechanisms of the monetary policy work smoothly. In general, the credit channel works reasonably well, and the effectiveness of the interest rate channel improved recently, although the wealth channel and the exchange rate channel still do not function properly. And, finally, the McCallum rule (quantitative rule) better characterizes China's monetary policy at the moment than does the Taylor rule (price rule). Currently, central banks of most advanced market economies follow the Taylor rule.

The unique features of China's monetary policy framework are a result of its ongoing transition from a central planned system to a market system. In both the real economy and the financial sector, certain agents, such as the SOEs and LGFVs, are still protected by the government, implicitly or explicitly, and are not fully subject to market disciplines. State-owned commercial banks are also not pure commercial entities. They do not always respond sensitively to changes in interest rates. This is why quantitative measures sometimes work better than price instruments.

Yet China's monetary policy framework is still in mid-transition. As its economy moves closer to the free market system, its monetary policy framework may also converge with frameworks of the advanced market economies. In the meantime, we may ask three questions in order to gauge the future direction of the country's monetary policy framework.

6.1. Should the PBC Become an Independent Central Bank?

Monetary policymaking requires specialized skills. International experiences confirm that higher degrees of independence of the central banks are often associated with lower and more stable inflation rates. This means that independence helps a central bank better pursue its policy objectives. The fact that China's monetary policy is made by the State Council, not the PBC, has several benefits under the current economic and market conditions. One, it could strengthen coordination between monetary, fiscal, and other economies policies. And, two, it could also improve effectiveness of some policy measures, especially the impacts of the quantitative instruments on the SOEs and LGFVs. But it also has important drawbacks. The decision process often is too long. As it could easily miss the best time-window to act, monetary policy often becomes a lagging, not a leading, policy instrument. And senior policymakers at the State Council have other policy priorities, in addition to price stability. This is probably why China's monetary policy shows a consistent tendency of being easy to loosen but difficult to tighten. Therefore, making the PBC an independent central bank would have obvious benefits.

But this does not necessarily mean that the PBC should immediately become fully independent. After the latest global financial crisis, central banks and governments of many countries started to work together on some policy initiatives. In the United States, for instance, the Federal Reserve Bank and the Department of the Treasury cooperated in rescuing the failing financial system and fighting against economic recession. The Chinese experiences during the reform period also suggest that, while some division of labor is useful, at times collaboration might also become useful. For instance, in the wake of the Asian financial crisis, the PBC worked closely with the government to transform the commercial banks. Without that support, the majority of the banking sector would probably have collapsed. All these means that, while it is clear that a higher degree of independence for the PBC should be beneficial, some channels for cooperation between the central bank and the government may still be preferable.

6.2. Should the Monetary Policy Reduce the Number of Its Objectives?

The Tinbergen rule tells us that the number of policy objectives should be equal to or less than the number of independent policy tools. It is difficult for a monetary policy that is simultaneously pursuing four or even eight policy objectives to obtain an equilibrium solution, which, even if one were obtained, would be unstable. To be sure, monetary policymakers should pay attention to important issues such as household welfare and financial stability. But other policy objectives should be implemented for other types of policy instruments, such as macro-prudential regulations for safeguarding financial stability, and income and social security policies for household welfare. Most important, Chinese monetary policymakers should probably give up the idea of "structural monetary policy," meaning the application of monetary policy to improve economic structure. Again, this is almost impossible to achieve, as monetary policy is an aggregate instrument. It is probably best to realize what is specified by the PBC Law—the objective of the monetary policy is to maintain the stability of the value of the currency and, thereby, to promote economic growth.

In the United States, the Federal Reserve Bank learned an important lesson from the global financial crisis. Under Chairman Alan Greenspan, the Fed maintained quite loose monetary policy conditions. At the time, it appeared to work pretty well, as the U.S. economy was growing very strongly while the inflation rate was low and stable. However, the loose monetary policy boosted the asset prices and caused the housing bubble. The lesson is that if monetary policymakers do not pay attention to conditions of the asset markets, that might lead to undesirable consequences. This is why, after the global financial crisis was past, central banks around the world started to explore ways to incorporate financial stability into their objective functions.

6.3. Should a Short-Term Market Interest Rate Become the Key Operational Target?

The PBC has already removed all the around the commercial banks' deposit and lending rates. This should pave the way for the central bank to eventually focus on short-term market rates as its policy tool or operational target. In the past, the PBC mainly used money supply and bank credit as the intermediate targets. In recent years, the central bank even introduced the new target of aggregate financing to the real economy (AFRE). Quantitative targets suffer from two main problems. The first is that it is difficult to be accurate. The second is that, as economic and financial structures change over time, the correlation declines rapidly between these quantitative targets, such as M2 and AFRE, and policy objectives, such as inflation and GDP growth. The PBC likely has not yet decided on which short-term market rate to serve as an operational target. Previously, the market thought the seven-day SHIBOR (SHIBOR007) could be a potential candidate. But it looks like the PBC is shifting its focus toward the seven-day repo rate (DR007), with an interest rate corridor defined by the MLF interest rate as the ceiling and the interest rate of extra reserve as the floor.

In the meantime, however, the transition of the Chinese economy will continue for quite a long time. Some of the nonmarket behaviors may also continue. For market participants like SOEs and LGFVs, interest rate instruments would not be particularly effective. Therefore, some types of quantitative instruments might still be needed, going forward.

Once, we believed strongly that the future model for the PBC would be very similar to that of the Fed of the United States or the European Central Bank (ECB) of the eurozone—that is, an independent central bank with a simple policy objective and a key short-term policy rate. These are probably still the right directions for the Chinese central bank to go. Yet the PBC might not look like the Fed or the ECB anytime soon. China has a transition economy as well as an emerging market economy. This implies that the transition of the PBC should be gradual, because the lack of central bank independence, the multiple objectives of the monetary policy, and a combination of both quantitative and price policy instruments are actually beneficial for the economy. And, more important, even the Fed and the ECB may be asked if some modifications to their current models might be desirable, especially in areas of policy cooperation with the government as well as policy objectives in terms of financial stability. If the latter is true, then the PBC will probably move toward the Fed or the ECB models but will never look exactly like them.

NOTES

1. *The People's Bank of China Law of the People's Republic of China.* http://www.npc.gov.cn/wxzl/wxzl /2000-12/05/content_4637.htm.
2. Yang Zhao, "Prudent Neutral Monetary Policy Should Focus on Strengthening Guidance of Expectations," *Financial Times*, January 9 (in Chinese). http://www.financialnews.com.cn/pl/cj /201701/t20170109_110799.html.
3. The Tinbergen rule also requires that these policy instruments be independent from each other.
4. For a more detailed description of these instruments, please refer to chapter 3.

5. For more extensive discussion, please refer to section 1 of chapter 3.
6. For a more detailed discussion of these price-based policy interest, please refer to section 2 of chapter 3.
7. Evolution of the transmission mechanism of interest rate in China is discussed in more detail in chapter 4.

REFERENCES

Ando, A., and F. Modigliani (1963). "The 'Life Cycle' Hypothesis of Saving: Aggregate Implications and Tests." *American Economic Review* 53(1): 55–84.

Bagliano, F. C., and C. A. Favero (1998). "Measuring Monetary Policy with VAR Models: An Evaluation." *European Economic Review* 42(6): 1069–1112.

Bernanke, B. S., and A. S. Blinder (1992). "The Federal Funds Rate and the Channels of Monetary Transmission." *American Economic Review* 82(4): 901–21.

Bernanke, B. S., and M. Gertler (1995). "Inside the Black Box: The Credit Channel of Monetary Policy Transmission." *Journal of Economic Perspectives* 9(4): 27–48.

Bonin, J. P., and Y. Huang (2001). "Dealing with the Bad Loans of the Chinese Banks." *Journal of Asian Economics* 12(2): 197–214.

Esanov, A., C. Merkl, and L. V. de Souza (2005). "Monetary Policy Rules for Russia." *Journal of Comparative Economics* 33(3): 484–99.

Evans, G. W., S. Honkapohja, and R. Marimon (2001). "Convergence in Monetary Inflation Models with Heterogeneous Learning Rules." *Macroeconomic Dynamics* 5(1): 1–31.

Evans, C., and Kuttner, K. N. (1998). Can VARs Describe Monetary Policy? (vol. 9812). Federal Reserve Bank of New York.

Fernald, J. G., M. M. Spiegel, and E. T. Swanson (2014). "Monetary Policy Effectiveness in China: Evidence from a FAVAR Model." *Journal of International Money and Finance* 49: 83–103.

Ge, T. (2019). "Time-Varying Transmission Efficiency of China's Monetary Policy." *China Economic Journal* 12(1): 32–51.

Geraats, P. M. (2009). "Trends in Monetary Policy Transparency." *International Finance*, 12(2): 235–68.

Goodfriend, M., and E. Prasad (2006). "A Framework for Independent Monetary Policy in China." IMF Working Paper No. 06/111, May.

Gunji, H., and Y. Yuan, Y. (2010). "Bank Profitability and the Bank Lending Channel: Evidence from China." *Journal of Asian Economics*, 21(2): 129–41.

Guo, K., and A. Schipke (2014). "New Issues in Monetary Policy: International Experience and Relevance for China." PBC and IMF Joint Conference, International Monetary Fund, March 27.

He, D., and H. Wang (2012). "Dual-Track Interest Rates and the Conduct of Monetary Policy in China." *China Economic Review* 23(4): 928–47.

He, Q., I. Korhonen, and Z. Qian (2017). "Monetary Policy Transmission with Two Exchange Rates and a Single Currency: The Chinese Experience." BOFIT Discussion Papers, No. 14/2017, Bank of Finland, Institute for Economies in Transition

Huang, Y. (2010). "Dissecting the China Puzzle: Asymmetric Liberalization and Cost Distortion." *Asian Economic Policy Review* 5(2): 281–95.

Huang, Y., and Wang, X. (2011). "Does Financial Repression Inhibit or Facilitate Economic Growth?: A Case Study of China's Reform Experience." *Oxford Bulletin of Economics and Statistics* 73(6): 833–55.

Huang, Y., and X. Wang (2017). "Building an Efficient Financial System in China: A Need for Stronger Market Disciplines." *Asian Economic Policy Review* 12(2): 188–205.

Huang, Y., X. Wang, B. Wang, and N. Lin (2013). "Financial Reform in China: Progress and Challenges," in *How Finance Is Shaping Economies of China, Japan and Korea*, edited by Y. Park and H. Patrick. New York: Columbia University Press, 44–142.

Kashyap, A. K., and J. C. Stein (2000). "What Do a Million Observations on Banks Say about the Transmission of Monetary Policy?" *American Economic Review* 90(3): 407–28.

Koivu, T. (2009). "Has the Chinese Economy Become More Sensitive to Interest Rates?: Studying Credit Demand in China." *China Economic Review* 20(3): 455–70.

Koivu, T. (2012). "Monetary Policy, Asset Prices, and Consumption in China." *Economic Systems* 36(2): 307–25.

Kuttner, K. N., and P. C. Mosser (2002). "The Monetary Transmission Mechanism: Some Answers and Further Questions." *Federal Reserve Bank of New York Economic Policy Review* 8(1): 15–26.

Laurens, M. B., and M. R. Maino (2007). "China: Strengthening Monetary Policy Implementation." IMF Working Paper No. 07-14, January.

Li, N., and Y. Lee (2015). "The Bank-Lending Channel of Monetary Policy Transmission in China: A Comparison between Chinese and Foreign Banks." *Korea and the World Economy* 16: 167–93.

Lv, J. (2007). "Empirical Analysis of RMB Pass-through to Domestic Prices." *Studies of International Finance* 8: 53–61.

McCallum, B. T. (1988, January). "Robustness Properties of a Rule for Monetary Policy." In Carnegie-Rochester Conference Series on Public Policy, vol. 29: 173–203. North-Holland.

McMahon, M., M. A. Schipke, and X. Li (2018). "China's Monetary Policy Communication: Frameworks, Impact, and Recommendations." IMF Working Paper No. 18/244, May.

Mehran, H., B. Laurens, M. Quintyn, and T. Nordman (1996). "Monetary and Exchange System Reforms in China: An Experiment in Gradualism." IMF Occasional Papers 141, September.

Mishkin, F. S. (1995). "Symposium on the Monetary Transmission Mechanism." *Journal of Economic Perspectives* 9(4), 3–10.

Mishkin, F. S. (1996). "The Channels of Monetary Transmission: Lessons for Monetary Policy" (No. w5464). National Bureau of Economic Research.

Montes-Negret, F. (1995). "China's Credit Plan: An Overview." *Oxford Review of Economic Policy* 11(4): 25–42.

Naughton, B. (1995). *Growing Out of the Plan: Chinese Economic Reform 1978–93*. Cambridge, U.K.: Cambridge University Press.

Nguyen, V. H. T., and A. Boateng, A. (2013). "The Impact of Excess Reserves beyond Precautionary Levels on Bank Lending Channels in China." *Journal of International Financial Markets, Institutions, and Money* 26: 358–77.

People's Bank of China (PBC) (2018). "Information Disclosure and Transparency" (in Chinese). Beijing: PBC, May 23. http://www.pbc.gov.cn/zhengwugongkai/127924/128038/128109/3544192/index.html.

Prasad, E., and B. Zhang (2014). "Monetary Policy in China," in *The Oxford Companion to the Economics of China*, edited by Shenggen Fan, Ravi Kanbur, Shang-Jin Wei, and Xiaobo Zhang. Oxford: Oxford University Press, 194–99.

Rey, H. (2015). "Dilemma not Trilemma: The Global Financial Cycle and Monetary Policy Independence" (No. w21162). National Bureau of Economic Research.

Sargent, T. J., and N. Wallace (1975). "'Rational' Expectations, the Optimal Monetary Instrument, and the Optimal Money Supply Rule." *Journal of Political Economy* 83(2): 241–54.

Sheng, S., and P. Wu (2008). "The Binary Transmission Mechanism of China's Monetary Policy—A Research on the 'Two Intermediaries, Two Targets' Model." *Economic Research Journal* 10: 37–51.

Sims, C. A. (1992). "Interpreting the Macroeconomic Time Series Facts: The Effects of Monetary Policy." *European Economic Review* 36(5): 975–1000.

Sun, G. (2015). *Reforms in China's Monetary Policy: A Frontbencher's Perspective*. Basingstoke and New York: Palgrave Macmillan.

Sun, L., J. L. Ford, and D. G. Dickinson (2010). "Bank Loans and the Effects of Monetary Policy in China: A VAR/VECM Approach." *China Economic Review* 21(1): 65–97.

Sun, M. (2004). "An Empirical Analysis of the Transmission Mechanism of Monetary Policy in China." *The Study of Finance and Economics* 30(3): 19–30.

Sun, S., C. Gan, and B. Hu (2010). "Bank Lending Channel in China's Monetary Policy Transmission Mechanism: A VECM Approach." *Investment Management and Financial Innovations* 7(2): 59–71.

Sun, S., C. Gan, and B. Hu (2012). "Evaluating McCallum Rule as a Policy Guideline for China." *Journal of the Asia Pacific Economy* 17(3): 527–45.

Taylor, J. B. (1993). "Discretion Versus Policy Rules in Practice." In *Carnegie-Rochester Conference Series on Public Policy* 39 (December): 195–214. North-Holland.

Taylor, J. B. (1995). "The Monetary Transmission Mechanism: An Empirical Framework." *Journal of Economic Perspectives* 9(4): 11–26.

Taylor, J. B. (2000). "Alternative Views of the Money Transmission Mechanism: What Difference Do They Make for Monetary Policy?" *Oxford Review of Economic Policy* 16(4), 60–73.

Wang, T., and H. Hu (2011). *The China Monetary Policy Handbook* (2d ed.). *Asian Economic Perspectives*, February. UBS Investment Research.

Woodford, M. (2005). "Central Bank Communication and Policy Effectiveness" (No. w11898). National Bureau of Economic Research.

Wu, G., and F. Lian (2016). "The Transition of China's Monetary Policy: Exploration on a Mixture of Quantity Rule and Price Rule." *Journal of World Economy* 39(3): 3–25.

Xia, B., and Q. Liao (2001). "Money Supply Is No Longer Suitable to Serve as Intermediary Target of China's Current Monetary Policy." *Journal of Economic Research* 8: 33–43.

Xie, P. (2004). "China's Monetary Policy: 1998–2002." Stanford Center for International Development, Working Paper No. 217.

Xie, P., and X. Luo (2002). "Taylor Rule and Its Empirical Test in China's Monetary Policy." *Economic Research Journal* 3: 3–12.

Yi, G. (1994). *Money, Banking, and Financial Markets in China*. Boulder: Westview Press.

Yu, Y. (2001). "A Review of China's Macroeconomic Development and Policies in the 1990s." Beijing: Chinese Academy of Social Sciences, June. www.iwep.org.cn.

Zha, T., and K. Chen (2017). "The Asymmetric Transmission of China's Monetary Policy," *2017 Meeting Papers*, 516. Society for Economic Dynamics. https://economicdynamics.org/meetpapers/2017/paper_516.pdf.

Zhang, H., and H. Huang (2017). "An Empirical Study of the Asset Price Channel of Monetary Policy Transmission in China." *Emerging Markets Finance and Trade* 53(6): 1278–88.

Zhang, H., and Z. Huang (2011). "A Study of the Exchange Rate Transmission Channel of China's Monetary Policy." *Economic Perspectives* 8: 53–57.

Zhang X. (2018). "Past and Present of China's Monetary Policy Framework, " in *Views of China Finance 40 on Past 40 Years*, edited by Chen Yuan and Huang Yiping. Beijing: CITIC Press Group.

Zhou, Y., and Z. Jiang (2002). "Monetary Channel, Credit Channel and the Effectiveness of Monetary Policy." *Journal of Finance* 9: 34–43

Zhou, Xiaochuan. (2016). "Managing Multi-Objective Monetary Policy: From the Perspective of Transitioning Chinese Economy." *2016 Michel Camdessus Central Banking Lecture*, International Monetary Fund, Washington, DC, June 24, 2016.

3

MONETARY POLICY INSTRUMENTS

Tao Wang

China's monetary policy has multiple objectives, including growth and employment, price and currency stability, external balance, financial stability, and, in recent years, facilitating structural changes. Although the People's Bank of China has been increasing the use of price-based policy instruments, to date it still relies more on quantitative policy instruments and on macro-prudential and administrative measures. The key framework is still managing the quantity of base money supply and also controlling credit growth to help achieve its desired broad money growth and also, in recent years, its credit (total social financing) growth, although price-based instruments and other parts have since been added to the framework.

The PBC can manage base money supply either by purchasing (or selling) foreign exchange or domestic assets from commercial banks, or by changing the required amount of deposits that commercial banks either hold at the central bank (reserve requirement) or use other liquidity facilities. China also employs a mix of administrative controls and prudential regulations to manage credit growth, so as to affect the broad money growth, which, when combined with the impact of financial liberalization (shadow credit development), helps to explain the weakening relationship between China's base money supply and its broad money aggregates (figure 3.1). The PBC uses policy and quasi-policy rates to influence bond market and credit market rates and credit extension, with the help of prudential and administrative measures.

1. QUANTITY-BASED INSTRUMENTS

Unlike typical central banks in developed and many emerging markets, the People's Bank of China relies mainly on quantitative means to manage its monetary policy. Until 2018, the PBC set a specific monetary aggregate (M2) target each year. To achieve this target, the PBC provides "high-powered" liquidity (base money) to commercial banks under the "fractional-reserve banking system," as is done in most developed economies; banks in turn create new loans and deposits via the money multiplier (Wang and Hu, 2011).

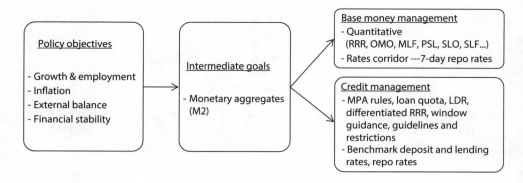

FIGURE 3.1. Monetary policy objectives and instruments. *Sources:* CEIC, authors' calculation.

Asset	Liability
Foreign asset	Reserve money
Of which foreign exchange asset	Currency issue
Domestic asset	Deposits of other financial institutions
Claims on government	Central bank bond issue
Claims on other financial institutions	Deposits of government
Claims on nonfinancial institutions	Own capital
Other	Other

FIGURE 3.2. The PBC's balance sheet. *Sources:* CEIC, author's calculation.

The PBC can adjust the quantity of base money supply by adjusting either side of its balance sheet. Figure 3.2 is an example of the PBC balance sheet. The asset side has foreign assets such as foreign exchange and gold, and domestic assets such as lending to domestic banks and the government (government bonds). The liability side includes reserve money—cash issuance and deposits that commercial banks hold at the central bank—and the central bank's bond issuance. The PBC can manage base money supply by buying or selling foreign exchange or domestic assets (such as treasury bills, repo/reverse repo, and various liquidity facilities) from commercial banks, changing the required amount of deposits that such banks hold at the central bank (reserve requirement), or either issuing or redeeming central bank bills (figures 3.2 and 3.3). Between 2001 and 2017, the PBC's main tools of managing base money supply varied in response to foreign exchange (FX) flows.

1.1. Base Money Supply and FX Assets Management

Foreign exchange movement is closely related to China's base money supply management, and it has a profound influence on the use of various monetary instruments. Before 2007, China had "compulsory foreign exchange settlement," which means that exporters are required to sell their FX proceeds to banks. Because currency stability is an important mandate of the PBC, the central bank is obliged to purchase foreign exchange from commercial banks with renminbi, although the process passively increases base

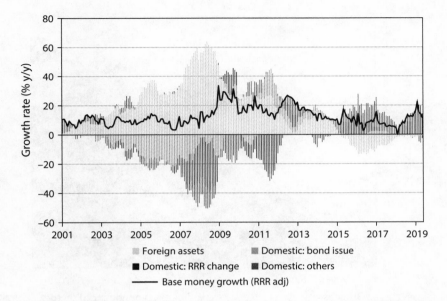

FIGURE 3.3. Contributors to base money growth. *Sources:* CEIC, UBS estimate.

money supply. When FX flows out, the PBC has to sell USD to keep RMB stable, thereby passively reducing base money supply.

During much of the period between 2002 and 2014, China saw large FX inflows from current account surpluses and, in some years, even financial account surpluses. PBC's accumulation of FX reserves while keeping the RMB exchange rate stable released RMB liquidity. Base money targeting was effectively achieved by adjusting the degree of sterilization of FX inflows, through either open-market operations or hikes in RRR (reserve requirement ratios). As FX inflows stagnated or reversed, base money targeting gradually moved to replenish the liquidity by either cutting RRRs or expanding PBC domestic asset holdings (figure 3.4).

1.2. Base Money Supply and RRR

As in a typical fractional-reserve banking system, Chinese banks are required to hold a portion of their deposits with the central bank as required reserves. Because banks cannot use this portion of liquidity held at the central bank, and because they receive only a minimum remuneration (1.62% for much of the past decade), RRR is considered a cost (and a tax) on those banks. Reserve requirement ratio (RRR) is typically considered a heavy-handed monetary instrument since it changes banks' ability to multiply base money through credit extension.

In China, RRR adjustments rarely took place until 2006, when the PBC started to use it as a liquidity management tool to sterilize the persistently large FX inflows. Between June 2006 and June 2008, PBC raised banks' RRR from 7.5% to 17.5% as a cheaper alternative to central bank bills (C-bills) to freeze liquidity generated by rapid FX reserves accumulation. The RRR was further raised to a record 21% (21.5% for large banks) in Q2 2011 before it was gradually lowered to release liquidity as it was being drained by

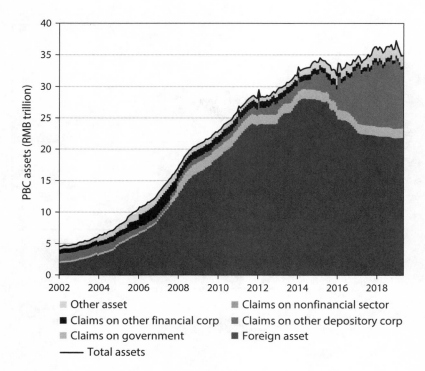

FIGURE 3.4. PBC balance sheet expansion was mainly driven by foreign assets until 2014. *Sources:* CEIC, UBS estimate.

declining FX reserves. RRR adjustment was hence a very important tool for the PBC to adjust its base money liquidity supply in the system. High RRRs since 2008 have placed a heavy cost on banks, which was one of the reasons why banks were incentivized to develop off-balance sheet wealth management products.

Despite the fact that RRR has been used as a liquidity management tool to offset the flows of FX reserves in China, it still carries a strong signaling effect as far as markets and banks are concerned. Between 2015 and 2018, the PBC remained reluctant to unwind earlier RRR hikes for fear of sending too strong an easing signal at a time when the government was concerned about property bubbles and rising leverage. Instead, the PBC developed a new set of liquidity facilities to maintain adequate base money supply amid stagnating or even falling FX reserves. Temporary instruments with effects similar to those of an RRR cut, such as TLF (Temporary Liquidity Facility) and CRA (Contingent Reserve Arrangement), were used during the Chinese New Year period in 2017 and 2018, respectively, to help manage peak season liquidity demand.

The reluctance to wind down RRRs started to change in April 2018, when the PBC cut RRR by 100 bps to release approximately RMB 1.3 trillion in liquidity, of which 900 bn was used to "swap out" maturing medium-term lending facilities (MLFs). This was followed by three other cuts in 2018 and one in 2019, releasing net liquidity of >RMB 3.1 trillion after swapping matured MLFs, some of which were intended for encouraging lending to SMEs.

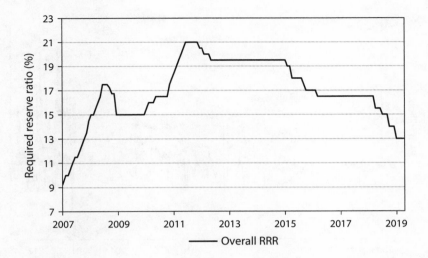

FIGURE 3.5. RRR was used to freeze FX-related liquidity. *Sources:* CEIC, UBS estimate.

As of March 2019, RRR for Chinese big banks was still at 13.5% (or 13%/12% for those with "inclusive finance" of more than 1.5%/10%) and approximately 11.5% for small and medium banks (or 11%/10% for those with "inclusive finance" of more than 1.5%/10%). Since RRR was a special sterilization tool devised during a special period, and against the background of slowing/reversing FX inflow, there is still room for significant RRR cuts to replace some maturing MLFs, provide cheaper liquidity to banks, and reduce distortions in the market (figure 3.5).

1.3. Open Market Operations

Open market operation (OMO) in RMB started in 1996 by the People's Bank of China. The PBC carries out OMOs with primary dealers (49 institutions as of 2019, including 46 banks/policy banks, two security companies, and one bond insurance company) in the interbank market to manage liquidity conditions. OMO are composed of the following types of transactions: repurchase agreements (repo), outright bonds transactions, central bank bills, short-term liquidity operations (SLO), and central government treasury cash management operation (figure 3.6).

1.3.1. Repurchase Agreements
Repurchase agreements (repo) can be divided into repos and reverse repos. In repo transactions, the PBC sells securities to primary dealers and agrees to buy them back on a specific future date, thus withdrawing liquidity from the market during the period. In reverse repo transactions, the PBC buys securities from primary dealers and agrees to sell them back on a specific future date, thus injecting liquidity during the period.

1.3.2. Outright Bond Transactions
Outright bond transactions are conducted by the PBC to directly buy or sell bonds from the secondary market. The former will increase the base money liquidity, and vice versa. It was only used in 2002 and has not been used since.

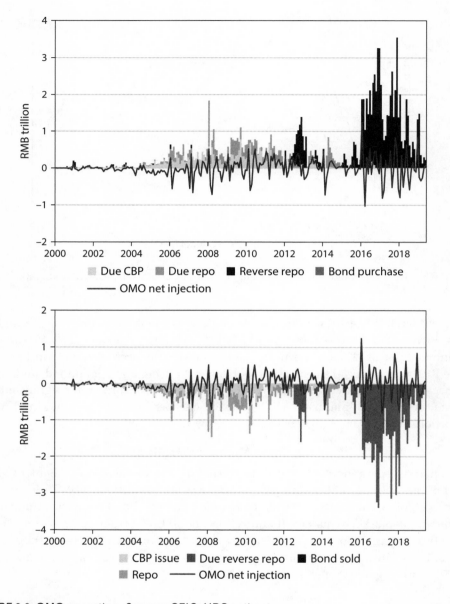

FIGURE 3.6. OMO operation. *Sources:* CEIC, UBS estimate.

1.3.3. Central Bank Bill

A central bank bill (CB) is a debt instrument issued by the central bank to commercial banks to adjust the excess reserves of commercial banks in the short term. Main maturities of CBs were 3-month and 12-month, although some CBs with longer duration were issued in the past. When the PBC issues central bank bills, excess reserves in the interbank market are reduced, and when those CBs mature, excess reserves are returned to the banks.

Starting in 2002, as foreign exchange assets grew rapidly, the PBC had to manage base money supply by adjusting the magnitude of "sterilization" of the FX inflows. An obvious way to sterilize an increase in FX assets is to reduce domestic assets—by selling the PBC's holding of government bonds, for example. However, the PBC held very few government bonds. Instead, it started to issue CBs to mop up liquidity. Central bank bills were used as a fertilization instrument between 2002 and 2013 and stopped after that when FX inflows declined or reversed. Currently no central bank bills are outstanding.

1.3.4. SLO

Created in January 2013, Short-Term Liquidity Operations (SLO) were originally designed to be a contingent facility to meet temporary liquidity needs, when OMO was only carried out on each working Tuesday and Thursday. Liquidity provided by SLO is usually very short-term (less than seven days) and is offered only to major national banks and policy banks. Since OMO became a daily operation from February 2016 onward, SLO has ceased to be used.

1.3.5. Central Treasury Cash Management Operation

Treasury cash refers to the Treasury's demand deposit in the central bank's vault. PBC can deposit it with commercial banks through an auction process, thus releasing base money during the period of the deposit. The maturities of Treasury deposits are usually 3/6/9 months, while the rates are decided jointly by PBC and commercial banks, depending on prevailing market conditions at the time of the auction. Since 2010, the average total amount of treasury cash auction is relatively stable at RMB ~500 billion each year, small compared with other liquidity facilities.

1.4. Liquidity Facilities

Since 2013, the central bank has created various liquidity facilities, including pledged supplementary lending (PSL), medium-term lending facility (MLF), and standing lending facility (SLF) to expand its domestic asset part of the balance sheet while net FX asset flows slowed or reversed. In the beginning of both 2017 and 2018, the PBC also created Temporary Lending Facility (TLF) and Contingent Reserve Arrangement (CRA), respectively, to meet large seasonal liquidity demand during the Chinese New Year season. While these facilities have done a reasonable job in expanding the PBC's balance sheet and providing base money supply, they have been accompanied by frequent bouts of market rate volatility, since banks have often been left guessing about the timing, quantity, and rates of such provisions (table 3.1).

1.4.1. PSL

Pledged Supplementary Lending (PSL) provides collateralized lending facilities to banks (only three policy banks are eligible at this stage) to support their lending to the real economy. It is effectively a new version of the PBC's traditional on-lending (or relending) program (Wang et al, 2014). The latter requires no collateral although PSL does. In principle, PSL could better protect the PBC from potential credit losses. Moreover, it allows the PBC to better calibrate the size and scope of its liquidity injection operations, by fine-tuning which assets may or may not qualify as collateral (such as high-rating bonds and other high-quality credit instruments) and which discount ratios should be applied.

In practice, PSL has been used mainly to fund policy banks' special loans for shantytown renovation, which in turn support local governments' shantytown projects or

Table 3.1. Overview of China's Liquidity Provisioning Facilities Tools

		Time of introduction	Purpose	Target banks	Tenor	Collateral required	Balance in April 2019	Latest rates (as of April 2019)
SLF	Standing lending facility	Early 2013	A facility to meet unusually large liquidity demand	All banks	1 day–1 month	High-quality bonds and credit assets	14 bn	O/N: 3.4% 7d: 3.55% 1M: 3.9%
PSL	Pledged supplementary lending	April 2014	A collateralized form of on-lending facility	So far only policy banks (CDB)	Normally >3 years	Adjustable by the PBC	3,541 bn	2.75%
MLF	Medium-term lending Facility	September 2014	To supply base money over the medium term	Qualified commercial banks and policy banks	3–12 months	High-quality bonds	3,560 bn	3M: 2.75% 6M:3.05% 12M: 3.3%
TMLF	Targeted medium-term lending facility	December 2018	To supply base money over the medium term (3 years) to provide liquidity to private sector and SMEs	Qualified commercial banks and policy banks	3 years (12M, can be rolled over twice upon request)	High-quality bonds	525 bn	12M: 3.15%
TLF	Temporary lending facility	January 2017	Temporary supply of base money	Five biggest state-owned commercial banks	28 days	No collateral needed		
CRA	Contingent reserve arrangement	January 2018	Temporary supply of base money	National commercial banks	30 days	No collateral needed		

Sources: CEIC, author's calculation.

monetary subsidies for such settlements. While PSL is designed to provide cheaper funding to policy banks to help fund the government's special objectives, it also can affect base money supply.

1.4.2. MLF

Against the backdrop of decreasing FX inflows, the PBC created the medium-term lending facility (MLF) in September 2014, as a new instrument to replenish base money supply. Financial institutions (such as commercial banks and policy banks) that are compliant with macro-prudential requirements can pledge high-quality assets to the PBC, in exchange for MLF. MLF's duration ranges from 3 to 12 months. Originally, qualified collaterals for MLF include government bonds, central bank bills, policy bank financial bonds, and high-grade credit bonds. In June 2018, the PBC expanded acceptable collaterals to include (1) AA-rated financial bonds that were issued to support small or micro enterprises, the green economy, or agricultural development; (2) AA-rated corporate bonds; (3) high-quality loans to SMEs; and (4) green loans.

In December 2018, the PBC further created Targeted MLF (TMLF), which allows banks to roll over matured 12M MLF by two additional years, with a discount rate lower than that for ordinary MLF by 15bps. Banks may request to roll over when the 12M MLF matures, and PBC will decide whether to approve based on the credential of the requesting bank and how much liquidity has been provided to the real economy, in particular, SMEs and private sector. The first operation was conducted in January 2019, totaling RMB 257.5 billion, with an interest rate of 3.15%.

While MLF has played an important role in recent years in expanding PBC's domestic assets and providing base money supply, the liquidity that MLF provides is not as "permanent" as RRR cuts, and as a result banks have often been left guessing about the timing, quantity, and rates of such provisions. As the PBC brings RRR back into its liquidity operation toolkit, outstanding MLFs can be partly and gradually phased out. That said, compared with RRR, MLF can be a more flexible solution and will likely continue to exist for some time.

1.4.3. SLF

Created by the PBC at the beginning of 2013, Standing Lending Facility (SLF) is designed to act as a routine liquidity supply channel of the PBC to meet the large liquidity demands of financial institutions. It targets mainly policy banks and national commercial banks with durations varying from one to three months. Collaterals are needed; eligible collaterals include high credit rating bonds and high-quality credit assets.

2. PRICE-BASED INSTRUMENTS

China's monetary policy framework has evolved in recent years, with interest rates playing an increasing role (Zhang 2015). Interest rate liberalization has been carried out since the late 1990s, culminating in the PBC's officially abolishing deposit rate ceilings in 2015 (table 3.2). However, although bank deposit and lending rates were officially fully liberalized, in reality the central bank still publishes benchmark rates and sets soft ceilings on bank deposit rates as of 2019.

Table 3.2. Major Steps of China's Interest Rate Liberalization

Year	Rates involved	Events
1996	Interbank offered rates	Interbank offered rates (CHIBOR) were liberalized.
1997	Interbank repo rates/bonds trading rates	Interbank repo rates and bonds trading rates were liberalized.
1998	Discount/rediscount rates	Discount/rediscount rates were liberalized.
1998–1999	Policy Bank/treasury bonds issuance rates	Auction was adopted in policy bank and treasury bonds issuance.
1998–1999	Lending rates	Floating ranges for lending rates were broadened three times.
2004	Lending/deposit rates	Floating ceiling for lending rates was canceled, floating floor for lending rates was broadened to 0.9x; deposit rates were allowed to float without floors.
2005	Interbank deposit rates	Interbank deposit rates were liberalized.
2012	Lending/deposit rates	Floating floor for lending rates was broadened to 0.7x.
2012		Floating ceiling for deposit rates was broadened to 1.1x.
2013	Lending rates	Floating floor for lending rates was canceled.
2014	Deposit rates	Floating ceiling for deposit rates was broadened to 1.2x.
2014	MLF	MLF was created, the operation rate of which later became an important monetary policy indicator.
2015	Deposit rates	Floating ceiling for deposit rates was canceled.
2015	Deposit insurance	Deposit insurance was introduced.
2014–2017	Interest rate corridor	Interest rate corridor was introduced and improved.

Sources: PBC, author's estimate.

As financial liberalization led to increased disintermediation away from bank loans and deposits, the PBC began to monitor and even influence interbank rates in its base money supply adjustments, and eventually settled on using the interbank seven-day repo rate as a reference rate in the interbank money market. In recent years, the PBC started operating an interest rate corridor to anchor the seven-day repo as a quasi-policy rate, using the remuneration on banks' excess reserves as the lower bound and SLF rates as the upper bound. Meanwhile, the PBC has also worked to improve the yield curve to affect both the transformation of monetary policy rates to bond market rates and the pricing effectiveness of direct financing through the bond market (Sun 2016). Table 3.3 provides a summary of key interest rates in China's monetary policy framework.

Table 3.3. Summary of China's Interest Rates

Types of rates	What they are	Latest level	Controlled/ free	Importance
PBC policy rate:				
Benchmark deposit/ lending rate	Rates that commercial banks pay their depositors and lend at to their borrowers	1.5 (1 yr, floating ceiling canceled in Oct 2015); 4.35 (1 yr, floating floor canceled in July 2013)	Controlled	Important
OMO rates	Yields on the PBC's open market operation	2.55 (7 day); 2.7 (14 day); 2.85 (28 day)	Semi-controlled	Important
Liquidity provision instruments rates	Yields on liquidity instruments such as SLF, MLF, SLO, PSL	SLF: 3.55 (7 day); 3.7 (14 day); MLF: 3.05 (6M); 3.3 (1 yr); SLO: 2.25; PSL: 2.75; TLF: Similar to 28d OMO rate TMLF: 15bps lower than MLF (1 yr)	Semi-controlled	Important
Required reserve rate	Rate of remuneration on required and excess reserves	1.62 for required reserves 0.72 for excess reserves	Controlled	Important
On lending rate	Rate at which the PBC provides refinancing liquidity to financial institutions	3.85 (1 yr)	Controlled	Rarely used
Rediscount rate	Rate at which commercial banks rediscount to the PBC to get liquidity	2.25	Controlled	Rarely used
PBC bill yields	Yields on PBC bills used for sterilization	3.5 (3-yr issuance rate in November 2013)	Semi controlled	Rarely used for now

(continued)

Table 3.3. (continued)

Types of rates	What they are	Latest level	Controlled/ free	Importance
Money market rates:				
SHIBOR	Average fixing of participating banks' offered rate	2.3 (7 day); 2.9 (3 month)	Free	Important
Interbank repo rate	Rate of interbank repo transactions	R007: 2.4 (7 day); DR007: 2.4 (7 day)	Free	Important
CD rates	Rate of bank CDs	3.0 (3 month, AAA)	Free	Important
CHIBOR	Trade-weighted interbank rates	3.2 (7 day)	Free	Somewhat
Bond yields:				
Rates Bond yields	Yield on rates bonds	3.4 (10-yr CGB); 3.8 (10-yr NDB)	Free	Important
Credit Bond yields	Yield on credit bonds	4.5 (AA+ 5 yr)	Free	Somewhat
WPMs rates:				
Wealth management product rate	Expected rate of banks' wealth management product	4.9 (3 month); 4.9 (6 month)	Free	Important
Lend rates:				
Banker's acceptance bill rate	Rates to discount banker's acceptance bill	2.5 (6 month)	Free	Somewhat
LPR rate	Loan prime rate, commercial banks loan rate provided to their best customers	4.3 (1 yr)	Free	Somewhat
Private lending rate	Local private financing interest rates	14.5 (Wenzhou, 1 yr)	Free	Not really

Sources: Wind database, author's calculation as of April 2019.

Note: R007 is the average seven-day repo rate traded for both credit and rates bonds by all institutions, including highly leveraged non-FIs that typically use credit bonds collateral, which are more vulnerable during periods of liquidity tightening. DR007 is an alternative rate for the average seven-day repos traded only by depository institutions in the interbank market, all of which are backed by rates bond collaterals that are relatively less vulnerable to liquidity tightening, thus

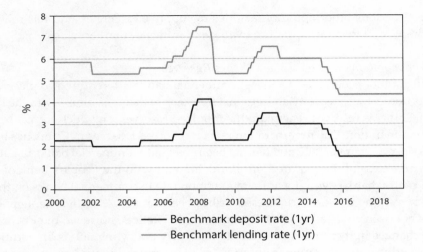

FIGURE 3.7. Banks' benchmark deposit and lending rates. *Sources:* CEIC, PBC.

2.1. PBC Policy Rates

2.1.1. Benchmark Rates

Commercial banks' benchmark lending and deposits rates (figure 3.7) have been the most talked-about interest rates in China; they have been directly controlled by the PBC, and the headline news on rate hikes/cuts until recently referred to their adjustments. Officially, China's interest rate liberalization was complete as of 2015 (table 3.2). In reality, banks still priced off the benchmark deposit and lending rates set by the PBC as of mid 2019, and have had limited scope to raise deposit rates on their own (Wang and Hu, 2014). This control on deposit rates is another reason why both households and corporates have shifted to various wealth management products, money market funds, and negotiable certificates of deposit (NCDs) in recent years. As tighter asset management product (AMP) rules are implemented and some shadow bank products unwind, allowing deposit rates to gradually rise would attract some savings back into bank deposits, helping to bring shadow bank assets back onto banks' balance sheets. The PBC's move to allow higher bank CD rates in April 2018 was a step in this direction, and similar moves are expected to continue over time. An actual full liberalization of deposit rates may have to wait for the establishment of China's financial institution resolution mechanism and an enhanced monetary policy framework.

2.1.2. On-Lending Rate and Rediscount Rate

The PBC quotes a range of benchmark policy rates on direct monetary operations, including a policy lending and discount rate. The PBC's lending and rediscount windows were important sources of base money supply during the 1990s; however, since the early 2000s, they have ceased to be major liquidity channels. In recent years, they mainly act as a channel to support commercial banks' lending to rural and small businesses, and these rates haven't been changed between 2010 and 2019. This is because, amid the excess liquidity before 2014, banks do not need to come to the PBC to borrow and hence are not affected by those lending rates. While as FX inflows slowed later on, the PBC has developed various other liquidity facilities to supply base money and has relied on a more complex interest rate structure to guide or influence market rates.

2.1.3. Remuneration on Required and Excess Reserves

As in most other economies, Chinese commercial banks are required to place a minimum portion of their deposit liabilities that they owe to their customers with the People's Bank of China as reserves. These are the required reserves, on which the central bank pays a remuneration. The remuneration rate on required reserves in China has been set at 1.62% since September 2012 and has not been changed. Commercial banks usually hold reserves in excess of the required minimum amount with the People's Bank of China, and the central bank pays a (lower) remuneration rate to commercial banks on these excess reserves. The rate on excess reserves has been set at 0.72% since September 2012 and has not been changed as of 2019. In rare circumstances, however, the PBC can also use the changes in these rates to signal its monetary policy intentions. In addition, the PBC also adjusts the remuneration rates in its macro-prudential assessment (MPA) framework—for example, if a bank is graded poorly in MPA, the PBC will apply a 0.7–0.9 coefficient to that bank's remuneration rate on its reserves at the PBC (Zhang, 2017).

2.1.4. PBC's OMO/Liquidity Facility Rate

The PBC's OMO includes three types of operations: repo/reverse repo, outright bond transaction, and central bank bills. Since February 2016, the PBC has conducted OMO on a daily basis, and the seven-day reverse repo rate has effectively become the quasi-policy rate, serving as a benchmark for the money market. Rates for various liquidity facilities such as SLO and MLF are correlated with the seven-day reverse repo rate, while rates for PSL are more independent, relatively low, and stable, since PSL is used to fund the loans for shantytown projects (figure 3.8).

After a major interbank market liquidity crunch in mid-2013, the PBC started to implement an interest rate corridor in early 2014 so as to anchor the seven-day repo as a quasi-policy rate. The lower bound of the corridor is the remuneration on banks' excess reserves, while the SLF rate is the upper bound (figure 3.9).

2.2. Money Market Rates

Money market interest rates are key links between policy rates and market interest rates. China's money market was launched in 1996 with the establishment of the China National Interbank Funding Center. Money market rates are essentially free market rates, driven mainly by interbank trading as well as by underlying supply and demand conditions. As money market expanded and various short-term financial instruments or facilities are developed over time, the PBC also influences the market interest rate and indirectly manages the interest rate curve.

China's money market interest rates include various short-term rates such as interbank lending rates, repo rates, and rates for short-term bonds, including Treasury bills, interbank CDs, and commercial papers (figure 3.10).

- **Repo rate.** In recent years, the interbank repo market has far outsized the CHIBOR market in turnover and liquidity, and repo rates such as DR007 (which is traded only by depository institutions in the interbank market using rates bonds collateral) and R007 (which is traded by all financial institutions in the interbank

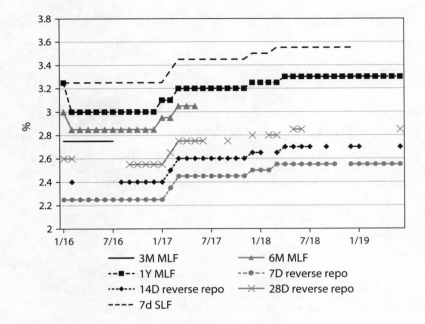

FIGURE 3.8. PBC's OMO/Liquidity facility rate. *Sources:* CEIC, PBC.

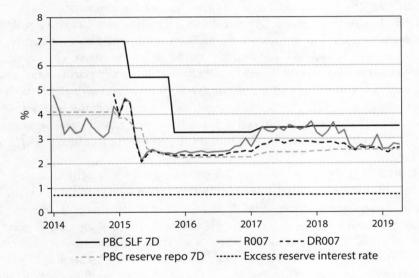

FIGURE 3.9. PBC's interest rates corridor. *Sources:* CEIC, PBC.

market using all kinds of bonds collateral) have replaced CHIBOR to be the most important short-term money market rate. Owing to higher risks associated with highly leveraged nonbank financial institutions (included in R007 but not DR007) that typically use credit bonds collateral—which are more vulnerable during periods of liquidity tightening—R007 tend to be higher and more volatile than DR007, especially toward month's-end. Market sees the seven-day repo

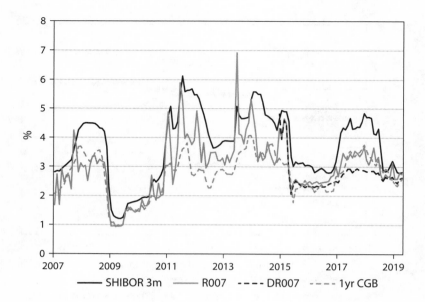

FIGURE 3.10. Money market rates and short bond yield. *Source:* CEIC.

and three-month SHIBOR rates as the best indicators of interbank market liquidity and benchmarks for pricing other financial instruments.

- **CHIBOR.** China Interbank Offered Rate (CHIBOR) was introduced in 1996, together with the establishment of the National Interbank Funding Center. CHIBOR rates are based on daily trading results of the interbank lending transaction. However, because of limited transaction volume and participants, and the very short nature of lending transactions (~90% are only one day), CHIBOR rates were not representative of liquidity conditions in the interbank market. As a result, in 2007 the PBC introduced a Shanghai-based market maker system, or SHIBOR, to achieve a more-stable market, especially for transactions of 90 days or longer.

- **SHIBOR.** SHIBOR rates are set in a similar way to LIBOR, with the rates calculated as arithmetic averages of the fixing of offered rates at 11:30 A.M. of each business day by participating banks, with tenors (maturity dates) varying from one day to one year. For much of the past decade, SHIBOR also has limited representativeness, as it is a quoted price rather than one based on actual transactions. However, with the fast development of interbank CDs after 2015, SHIBOR rates have gained more importance and become more representative of the interbank market, as the issuance rates of CDs are priced off SHIBOR.

- **Short-term bond yields.** With the development of China's bond market and money market funds, the amount of short-term bonds also increased, such as interbank CDs, commercial papers, and Treasury bills. As a result, the importance of short-term bonds yields also increased. This is especially true for interbank CDs, which amount to RMB 8.8 trillion outstanding and account for 11% of the total bonds outstanding as of early 2019, and serve an important sources of funding for commercial banks.

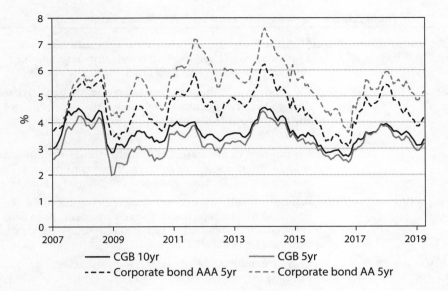

FIGURE 3.11. Long-term bond yields. *Sources:* CEIC, author's calculation.

2.3. Bond Yields

In developed countries, bond yields play an important role in determining the overall cost of capital and in passing inflation expectations through to the rest of the economy. In China, bond yields have become increasingly vital, given the rapid development of the bond market in recent years. The total size of credit bonds and rates bonds were at RMB 88 trillion as of March 2019, or 38% of total credit, up from 27% only 10 years ago. On the long end of the curve, bond market movement is still mostly driven by rate bonds (figure 3.11).

- **Mid- to long-term rate bond yields.** All rate bonds (including treasury bonds, financial bonds, and provincial government bonds) are now freely traded in the market. Yields are determined by a complex set of information, including liquidity conditions, expectations on inflation and economic outlook, and investors' preferences. PBC has limited control or influence over the entire yield curve, though it can influence or even manage the front end of the curve by adjusting base money supply and interbank policy rates.

- **Mid- to long-term credit bond yields.** PBC has even less control over credit bond yields. Credit bond yields are positively correlated with yields of rate bonds, as most SOE bonds still enjoy some degree of implicit guarantees. The credit risk of investment-grade credit bonds has become a reflection of market liquidity risk. For high-yield (HY) credit bonds, spreads have widened and become more varied with the development of the credit market and more defaults. The PBC can only influence credit bond yields through the rate bond market or by influencing general interbank liquidities. In addition, most credit bonds, especially HY bonds, are held by nonbank financial institutions, while the PBC mostly deals with large state-owned banks.

Table 3.4. Seven Areas Focused by PMA Assessment Rules

Areas	Focus
Capital and leverage	Expands broad capital credit constraints on financial institutions' assets and liabilities
Assets and liabilities	Determines whether the generalized credit growth exceeds certain thresholds, and also includes the requirements for the robustness of the financial institution's liability structure
Liquidity	Encourages financial institutions to strengthen liquidity management, use stable sources of funds to develop businesses, and improve the level of reserve management
Pricing behavior	Assesses whether the interest rate pricing behavior of financial institutions meets the requirements of market competition order, and in particular assesses the irrational interest rate pricing behavior
Quality of assets	Concerns mainly the abnormal worsening in asset quality of financial institutions
Cross-border financing risks	Adapts to the frequent flow of funds across borders and the growth of cross-border lending, and takes precautions to strengthen risk monitoring and prevention
Implementation of credit policies	Encourages financial institutions to support the key areas and weaknesses of the national economy, and constantly optimizes the credit structure

Source: PBC.

3. PRUDENTIAL AND REGULATORY INSTRUMENTS

3.1. Macro-Prudential Assessment Rules

The term "macro-prudential policy" usually refers to a set of macro policies, also called prudential tools, that are used to reduce systematic financial risks. These tools typically include "countercyclical capital buffers and provisions, sectoral capital requirements, measures to contain liquidity and foreign exchange (FX) mismatches, and caps on loan-to-value (LTV) and debt-to-income (DTI) ratios" (IMF 2013). Macro-prudential policy can also "seek to affect the design of products offered to borrowers in retail markets, and the functioning and institutional underpinnings of wholesale markets" (IMF 2013). It can also include monetary policy tools (e.g., reserves requirements) as well as fiscal and competition policies.

While China's bank regulator does carry out aspects of macro-prudential policies such as capital buffers, the central bank has a very specific definition about macro-prudential policy. The PBC introduced a macro-prudential assessment (MPA) framework at the beginning of 2016. This is, in effect, a refined and more systematic version of the earlier "dynamic reserve requirement adjustments" (which linked each bank's required reserve ratio with indicators of financial soundness such as capital adequacy ratio and asset quality). The MPA monitors seven categories of financial stability indicators on a bank-by-bank basis (table 3.4), aiming to influence each bank's loan and other credit expansion with the use of differentiated reserve requirements and remuneration on the reserves of that bank (Zhang 2017, Sun 2019). Financial institutions are classified as A/B/C types of institutions according to their scores in the MPA assessment, and required reserve rates and other policy support/punishment (such as liquidity access) are decided based on the MPA scoring.

The PBC has constantly tweaked the indicators in the MPA to better reflect monetary policy intentions, with adjustments between 2016 and 2018 aimed at containing the growth of banks' off-balance sheet and interbank assets. In December 2016, the PBC officially announced the inclusion of off-balance WMPs into MPA, which caused market jitters back then. In August 2017, the PBC announced the inclusion of interbank CDs into MPAs from Q1 2018 onward for banks with total assets greater than RMB500 billion. The PBC also announced in May 2018 that this rule will be further broadened to include all banks starting from Q1 2019.

The PBC considers the MPA framework an important part of its monetary policy mix. As China's monetary policy framework transitions gradually to one that is more price-based and market-based, MPA will likely remain an important tool in the meantime.

3.2. Prudential Banking Regulations

China often uses adjustments to prudential regulations to aid monetary policy management. In addition to the MPA framework described above, Chinese authorities, including the PBC and various regulators under the State Council, also use prudential regulations such as loan-to-deposit ratio (LDR), capital or loan provision requirements, down payment requirement for mortgage loans, and treatment of banks' off-balance sheet assets to help achieve the prevailing monetary policy stance.

Between 2016 and 2018, the China Banking Regulatory Commission (CBRC) and other regulators issued many new directives aimed at curtailing overall financial sector leverage and shadow credit expansion (table 3.5). The tighter financial regulations have proven to be effective in tightening shadow credit channels such as trust, entrust loans, and nonstandard assets. WMPs and interfinancial institutions leverage unwinding tightened credit market liquidity and pushed up rates, resulting in a drop in shadow credit as well as in corporate and local government bond issuance (figure 3.12). Meanwhile, the tightening of shadow credit channels reduced credit to local governments and developers alike. Despite robust growth in bank loans, overall credit growth slowed between 2017 and 2019 (figure 3.13).

3.3. FX and Capital Control Rules

Although China has gradually moved to open capital account and increase exchange rate flexibility in the past decade, both are still closely managed. Managing exchange rate expectations and cross-border capital flows has at times served as a useful tool for monetary policy management. For example, in 2016, when RMB depreciation pressure intensified and expectations of depreciation became increasingly entrenched, the central bank introduced a "countercyclical factor" into its daily fixing formula to blunt the momentum-driven RMB formation mechanism. That helped to stabilize market expectation. The PBC also implemented existing capital controls more forcefully and closed some earlier de facto opening channels, which significantly reduced net capital outflows. Both actions helped to insulate domestic monetary policy from external pressures. Because capital controls generally lose their effectiveness over the long run, sooner or later China will still need to let its exchange rate adjust, restructure its debt, and ensure that structural reforms are implemented so as to preserve or even improve the effectiveness of its monetary policy.

Table 3.5. A Non-Exhaustive List of Regulatory/Supervisory Tightening Measures

Time of issuance (year/month)	Regulatory documents/Activities
2016.3–2016.9	• CBRC Document 58 on Strengthening Trust Company Risk Administration • CSRC seeks comments on Document 29 to tighten regulations on subsidiaries of fund management companies (published in December 2016) • CSRC tightens regulatory standards for corporate bond issuance of LGFV and real estate companies
2017 Q1	The PBC started to include off-balance sheet WMPs in its MPA framework, and is reportedly taking the lead in a unified regulation on asset management businesses.
2017.4–5	• CBRC issued multiple documents (CBRC Office's Document 45, 46, 53, and CBRC's Document 4–7, "3-3-4 supervisions") to tighten supervisions and regulations, especially in banks' interfinancial institution business. • CIRC's circulation on further tightening risk controls in insurance industries. • CSRC prohibited security companies from increasing the scale of their quasi-deposit "fund pool products." • CSRC issued new regulations on stock selling by major shareholders and senior management of listed companies.
2017.4–6	MOF issued documents (document 50, 62, 87) to further tighten local government financing behaviors.
2017.11	• Regulators released draft AMP rules, aimed at reducing regulatory arbitrage, protecting investors, and reducing systemic financial risks. The rules set stricter limits on disclosure, leverage, provision, and investment in nonstandard assets (NSAs). They also prohibit guaranteed payment, pooled accounts, multiple layering, and channel businesses.
2018.1	• The PBC and other three financial regulatory commissions jointly issued a Notice on Regulating the Bond Transactions of Bond Market Participants (Notice 302), identifying irregular trading practices in bond markets and requiring off-balance sheet bond holding to be recorded in the balance sheet. • The PBC reportedly gave guidance on NCD quotas and effectively set a cap on commercial lenders' NCD issuance. • CBRC issued Measures for Managing Large-Amount Risk of Commercial Banks (Draft for Comment), specifying requirements to enhance control over large-amount risk. • CBRC issued Administrative Measures for Entrusted Loans of Commercial Banks, strengthening regulatory supervision over the entrusted loan business. • Entrust loans investments by AMP products of securities companies, security companies, and private funds are all prohibited. • The CBRC issued Document 4 on Further Remedying Irregularities in the Banking Sector, focusing on rectifying problems found in previous inspections.

Table 3.5. (continued)

Time of issuance (year/month)	Regulatory documents/Activities
2018.2	• NDRC and Ministry of Finance issued a notice on further strengthening the use of corporate bonds to serve the real economy and strictly prevent local government debt risks (Notice 194). According to the notice, in their bond declarations, companies shall take the initiative to publicly declare that they will not assume the function of government financing, and that the bond issue does not involve the addition of local government debt. The notice also requires strict evaluation of the scope of application of the PPP model, prudent assessment of debt issue risks of government-funded and viability gap-funded PPP projects, and strict prohibition of using the PPP model for illegal or indirect debt financing.
2018.4	• The revised and the final versions of AMP rules were released, which set a longer transition period for noncompliant products but remained true to the key principles of the earlier draft. AMPs must be managed on a NAV basis without implied guarantees, and are restricted in investment into nonstandard debt assets.
2018.5	• China introduced measures to manage large risk exposure of commercial banks, including rules on maximum exposure to interbank/noninterbank customers and cross-FI products.
	• The CBIRC unveiled measures for management of the liquidity risk of commercial banks.
2018.6	• The CBIRC released provisional measures on joint credit mechanisms for banking financial institutions, whereby banks jointly decide the total size of credit lines and monitor the use of credit.
2018.7	• The PBC released a notice regarding the new AMP rule, giving some extra leeway in the grace period and specifying that publicly offered products may invest in nonstandard debt assets. The CBIRC and CSRC released related draft regulation.
2018.9	• The PBC and CSRC jointly issued guidelines (Announcement No. 14 of 2018) for unified vetting of ratings agencies in both the interbank and the exchange-traded markets.
2018.1	• The CBIRC issued a consultation draft on administrative measures for commercial banks' wealth management subsidiaries, requiring that the publicly offered WMPs of banks' wealth management subsidiaries mainly invest in standardized debt assets and shares listed on the stock exchange; the shares issued by a single listed company held by open-ended publicly offered WMPs shall not exceed 15% of the company's tradable shares; and the outstanding balance of nonstandardized debt assets held by WMPs shall not exceed 35% of the net assets of the WMPs at any point in time.
2018.11	• The PBC, CBIRC, and CSRC jointly issued Guidance on Improving the Supervision of Systemically Important Financial Institutions.
2019.1	• To support banks issuing perpetual bonds to replenish capital, the PBC set up a central bank bill swap (CBS), allowing primary dealers engaged in open-market operations to swap the perpetual bonds they hold for central bank bills.

Sources: Media, government websites.

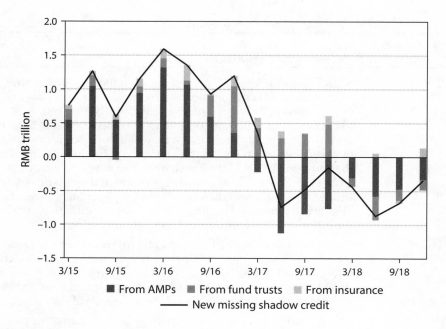

FIGURE 3.12. New shadow credit declined. *Sources:* CEIC, UBS estimate.

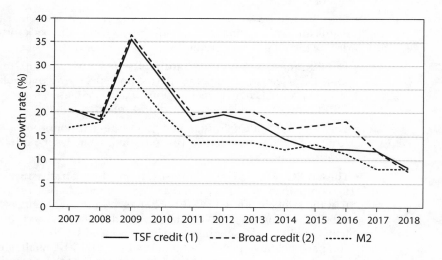

FIGURE 3.13. Broad credit growth versus M2 and TSF. *Sources:* CEIC, UBS estimate. *Notes*: (1) TSF credit is official TSF, excluding equity/ABS/loan write-off/special local government bond; (2) Broad credit includes TSF credit above, total local government bond, and missing shadow credit.

4. ADMINISTRATIVE INSTRUMENTS

China also uses administrative controls to directly manage credit growth, which also affect broad money growth. These measures include the government's sector-specific credit policies or restrictions, credit quotas, and window guidance, some of which are not implemented by the central bank. These credit policies and controls, combined with the impact of financial liberalization (shadow credit development), help to explain the weakening relationship between China's base money supply and broad money aggregates (Wang et al., 2017).

4.1. Credit Quota

A legacy from the planning era that still plays a role in China's monetary policy framework, albeit a much diminished one, is credit quota. Before 1998, the government (through the PBC) gave out strict lending plans to individual banks (that is, the big four). Since then, the lending targets have become softer over time, usually providing only guidance. However, during periods when bank lending was growing too fast, such as in late 2003, late 2007, and early 2010, the authorities took more aggressive actions, including forcing banks to call back loans (2003–2004), virtually freezing new lending (end of 2007), and imposing quarterly and even monthly lending quotas (early 2008, and 2010).

Usually, the PBC agrees with the State Council on an annual broad money (M2) growth target, which is usually announced during the National People's Congress meetings in March each year. The PBC then backs out total new bank loans for each year that are consistent with the M2 growth target, and gives banks their individual guidelines for loans. In recent years, however, as bond market and shadow credit grew rapidly, such detailed but narrowly defined credit as RMB loans no longer capture overall credit supply, so the relationship between RMB loan growth and broad money growth has weakened. The PBC created the "total social financing" (TSF) concept to capture overall credit to the nonfinancial sectors in the economy by the financial system, including in it bank lending to the nonfinancial sectors, corporate bonds and off-balance sheet bank credit such as trust and entrust loans as well as undiscounted bills, but not including local government bonds and nonstandard debt assets (although this concept was later amended to first include local government bonds in 2019 and central government bonds in 2020). In 2016 and 2017, the PBC agreed with the State Council on an annual TSF growth target, but this was discontinued in 2018.

4.2. Sector-Specific Credit Policies and Restrictions

Although aiding structural adjustments in the economy is not officially written by the PBC as one of its monetary policy objectives, it has often been cited by the government as such. Depending on the government's objective in promoting or restricting certain sectors, credit policies or restrictions are called on to play a corresponding role. For example, over the past two decades, the property sector has often been on the receiving end of credit restrictions (occasionally also getting credit relaxation). In such instances, banks are told either to restrict lending to property developers alone or to limit mortgage lending. Similar credit restrictions have been imposed on excess capacity sectors and sectors that are energy intensive or are highly polluting. Rural sectors and SMEs, by contrast, are often designated as the recipients of supportive credit policies—the PBC requires lower reserves or often cuts RRR to mandate greater lending to these sectors. Another example is shantytown renovations—the central bank issued PSL liquidity to policy banks to help finance this government initiative, relaxing money and credit supply in the process.

4.3. Window Guidance

The term "window guidance" refers to the central bank's move to influence commercial banks' credit behavior through advice and suggestions, usually only known to the recipient institutions but not to the general public as it is not disclosed by the PBC. Although window guidance is not a binding order but instead a form of moral suasion, financial institutions generally oblige the PBC. As a result, window guidance can be quick and effective. That said, with interest rate liberalization and the rapid development of the credit market, and under the PBC's complex MPA rules, window guidance has become less effective in managing individual banks' credit growth.

REFERENCES

Asian Development Bank (2012). People's Republic of China Bond Market Guide, ASEAN+3 Bond Market Guide. Asian Development Bank. http://hdl.handle.net/11540/927.

IMF (2013). "Key Aspects of Macroprudential Policies." IMF Policy Paper, June 10.

People's Bank of China (2010). "Central Bank Instruments to Deal with the Crisis—from the Perspective of the People's Bank of China." BIS Working Papers, No. 54. https://www.bis.org/publ/bppdf/bispap54h.pdf.

Sun, Guofeng (2016). "The Transition of Monetary Policy Framework and China's Financial Market Outlook." *Tsinghua Finance Review* 1: 30–33.

Sun, Guofeng (2019). "Monetary Policy Review and Outlook." *China Finance* 2.

Wang, Tao (2014). "The Unbearable Weight on Monetary Policy." UBS Investment Research, June 10.

Wang, Tao, Lan Chen, Donna Kwok, Ning Zhang, and Jennifer Zhong (2017). "Understanding China (Part III)—the Monetary Maze." UBS Investment Research, January 25.

Wang, Tao, and Harrison Hu (2011). *The China Monetary Policy Handbook* (2nd edition). UBS Investment Research, February 19.

Wang, Tao, and Harrison Hu (2014). "How Much Will Interest Rates Rise in China and How Does That Matter?" UBS Investment Research, January 10.

Wang, Tao, Donna Kwok, and Harrison Hu (2015). "Questions about China's Monetary Easing." UBS Investment Research, May 5.

Wang, Tao, Donna Kwok, Harrison Hu, and Ning Zhang (2014). "PSL: Form or Substance?" UBS Investment Research, July 24.

Zhang, Xiaohui (2015). "Monetary Policy under the New Normal." *China Finance* 2: 22–25.

Zhang, Xiaohui (2017). "Exploring Macro Prudential Policies in China." *China Finance* 11: 20–22.

4

CHINA'S INTEREST RATE LIBERALIZATION

Jun Ma and Xiaobei He

1. INTRODUCTION

Before the mid-1990s, most financial resources—especially bank loans—in China were allocated by governments or according to state plans, while deposit and lending rates were all set by the central bank. However, as the market elements of the economy expanded, it became increasingly clear that central allocations of financial resources resulted in serious inefficiencies. For instance, thriving financial institutions and private companies found it difficult to acquire enough financial resources, while inefficient companies with better political connections usually had easy access to loans. Since planned financial resource allocations were incompatible with the market-oriented shift in China's economic structure, China commenced its interest rate liberalization in mid-1990s as part of the process for developing a market-based allocation mechanism for financial resources. In this chapter, the so-called narrowly defined interest rate liberalization refers to a process in which the central bank lifts the controls or restrictions on interest rates. The "broadly defined" interest rate liberalization includes a series of supplementary reform measures, such as enabling financial markets and financial institutions to conduct market-based pricing, introducing market-based interest rate products, establishing the monetary policy framework under which policy rates can be adjusted to influence market interest rates, and improving the transmission mechanism of interest rates.

During the 20 years between the mid-1990s and 2015, the PBC took many "mini" steps in liberalizing interest rates, starting with rates in the fixed income market, followed by rates for bank lending and finally deposits. By 2015, most administrative restrictions (ceilings and floors) on deposit and lending rates had been lifted. By then, China had completed its "narrowly defined" interest rate liberalization. The gradual process of that liberalization was a smooth one and did not cause either financial instability or macroeconomic instability

However, policy interest rates and price-based monetary policy transmission mechanisms in China are yet to be fully developed. During the current transition period, a unique "dual-track" system continues to feature the Chinese financial system: The benchmark interest rates (deposit and lending rates) published by the PBC remain the anchor for interest rate pricing of deposits and loans in the banking sector, while the interest rates in money markets and bond markets are fully market-determined. To complete the "broadly defined" interest rate liberalization,[1] the PBC should ultimately abolish the benchmark rates, replacing them with a market-based short-term interest rate as the policy rate.

This chapter first describes China's progress in liberalizing interest rates and examines its impacts on the economy. It then presents the challenges faced by interest rate transmissions in China and presents our recommendations on reforming the monetary policy framework (Ma and Guan, 2018).

2. PRECONDITIONS AND SEQUENCE

2.1. Preconditions and Driving Forces

International experiences show that successful interest rate liberalization processes share some common traits. First, successful liberalization of interest rates—a process that does not necessarily lead to excessive financial market volatility or a financial crisis—requires a stable macroeconomic environment. Second, during the deregulation process, gaps between controlled interest rates and market rates should be small to avoid a surge in rates after liberalization. Third, most successful efforts to liberalize interest rates have been gradual. Fourth, an interest and credit risk management system should be in place to prevent excessive risk-taking among financial institutions after interest rates have been liberalized.

In China, the liberalization of interest rates began in the money market and bond market in 1996. Since then, preconditions for interest rate liberalization became more mature throughout the country, and interest rate liberalization began in the banking system. These preconditions include the following:

1. The Chinese government's fiscal capacity improved greatly after it implemented a tax reform in 1994. With the strengthening of revenue capacity, the government's reliance on bank funding for public investments with suppressed interest rates has declined.
2. As China continued to develop its financial markets, the financing options for companies expanded from bank loans only to also include equity and bond markets. The necessity then diminished for using loan quotas and interest rate controls (note that these two features of a "credit rationing regime" go together) to ensure the availability of bank loans to some "priority" firms or projects.
3. By 2000, China had adopted the Basel Accord in its banking sector supervision. The introduction of a comprehensive regulatory system such as that helped to mitigate problems associated with adverse selections and moral hazard behaviors of financial institutions that could intensify after interest rate liberalization.

4. The nonperforming loan (NPL) ratio came down from a very high level in early 2000 of nearly 40%. The high NPL ratio was one of the reasons for interest rate controls (including floors on lending rates and ceilings on deposit rates), since it ensured sufficient net interest margins (NIM) for banks to remain profitable and absorb loan losses. As the NPL ratio fell, the need for maintaining a high NIM via interest controls also diminished (see chapter 1 of this handbook).

5. China introduced deposit insurance in 2015. The establishment of a deposit insurance scheme was seen as an important premise for the final stage of interest rate liberalization, because it reduces risks of bank runs and contagious bank failures, even if some banks may engage in risky lending businesses after interest rate liberalization.

6. The establishment of the Self-Regulatory Pricing Mechanism of Market Interest Rate in China in 2013 laid a foundation for mitigating financial risks typically associated with overcompetition among banks after interest rate liberalization. The international experiences show that the self-regulatory mechanism of the banking sector plays an important role in financial regulation. In October 2013, the centralized pricing mechanism for the loan prime rate (LPR) was officially put into operation, which later became the new benchmark for pricing loans.

Apart from these preconditions, a number of additional driving forces affected China's interest rate liberalization. First, interest rate controls in the banking sector had led to a surge in shadow banking activities. For example, the outstanding amount of wealth management products rose from virtually nil in 2007 to 22.5 trillion yuan in 2016. To ensure smooth functioning of the banking system, there was a pressing need to relax restrictions on deposit rates. Second, the development of the bond market also drives the liberalization of loan interest rates. Different from loans, which were still subject to interest rate controls, interest rates on bonds were determined by market forces. Since 2005, various fixed income financing instruments, including commercial papers and corporate bonds, have provided the corporate sector with more options for financing their investments. If bank lending were still subject to quotas, and loan rates were still controlled, banks would "lose businesses" to the bond market.

2.2. The Sequence of "Narrowly Defined" Interest Rate Liberalization

Interest rate liberalization in China is generally aligned with foreign experiences. The PBC first relaxed restrictions on interest rates in money markets and bond markets. Liberalization of interest rates on bank lending rates and deposit rates were gradually implemented later. The timeline of interest rate liberalization is listed in table 4.1. China's interest rate liberalization process was marked by three features: (1) restrictions on lending rates were lifted before those on deposit rates; (2) controls on long-term interest rates were removed before those on short-term rates; and (3) onshore foreign interest rates were liberalized earlier than domestic interest rates. This gradual approach provides banks with enough time to adapt to a competitive environment in which they need to operate on a commercial basis.

The remaining section provides detailed accounts on China's interest rate liberalization.

Table 4.1. Timeline of Interest Rate Liberalization

Year	Events
1996	Removed the ceiling on interbank lending rate
1997	Introduced market-based repurchase agreements (repo)
1998–1999	Introduced auction to policy bank and treasury bonds issuance
2000	Removed restrictions on FX lending rates and large-account FX deposit rates
2003	Removed interest rate floors on small-account FX deposits
2004	Removed the ceilings on lending rates; Expanded the floating floors for lending rates to 90% of the benchmark rate; Removed the floors on deposit rates; Removed interest rate ceilings on small-account FX deposits with maturity above 1 year
2012	Expanded the floating range for lending rates to 70% of the benchmark rate; Expanded the floating range for deposit rates to 110% of the benchmark rate
2013	Removed the lending rate floors on all loan facilities except for mortgage
2014	Expanded the floating range for deposit rates to 120% of the benchmark rate
2015	Launched the bank deposit insurance scheme; Expanded the floating range for deposit rates to 150% of the benchmark; Removed the ceiling for deposit rates
2019	Linked loan prime rates (LPR) to medium-term lending facility (MLF); Required banks to price outstanding loans based on LPR

Source: PBC.

2.2.1. Liberalization of Interest Rates in the Money Market and Bond Market

The interbank lending rates were the first to be liberalized. In 1980s, the Chinese government decided that investment projects, which formerly were financed directly from fiscal budgets, would also be financed by bank loans. This policy stimulated rapid growth of the interbank borrowing and lending, as banks with surplus funds could now lend to other banks. Initially, the PBC imposed ceilings on interbank lending rates with the intention to limit borrowing for risky projects. In June 1996, it removed the ceilings and announced that interbank lending rates would be determined by market forces, with a view to enhancing the efficiency for resource allocation on the margin, noting that the majority of the funds for bank lending were from deposits (and lending rates and deposit rates were still subject to controls and remain so today).

Thereafter, interbank markets went through a period of rapid growth. In June 1997, market-based repurchase agreements (repo), through which banks could use bonds as collateral in exchange for short-term funding, were introduced. During 1998–1999, the regulators allowed market-based pricing of policy financial bonds (bonds issued by policy banks) and government bonds via auctions. Market-based pricing in the primary market also stimulated transactions in the secondary markets, leading to a rapid development of China's bond markets.

2.2.2. Liberalization of Foreign Exchange (FX) Loan and Deposit Rates

As part of its agreement in joining the World Trade Organization (WTO) in 2001, China committed to permit foreign financial institutions to enter its domestic market. To prepare for the WTO entry, the PBC decided to liberalize onshore foreign currency interest rates, which could prepare domestic commercial banks to adapt to the incoming competition from foreign banks. In addition, liberalization of onshore interest rates on loans and deposits in foreign currencies also helped stabilize cross-border capital flows (note that before the liberalization, the controlled onshore FX interest rates were lower than offshore rates for the same currencies).

In September 2000, the PBC removed restrictions on onshore FX lending rates and also on onshore FX deposit rates for large accounts (USD $3 million or more). In July 2003, the PBC removed restrictions of onshore FX deposits for small accounts except for four currencies (U.S. dollar, euro, Hong Kong dollar, and Japanese yen). In November of that year, interest rate floors on all small FX deposits were removed. In 2004, interest rate ceilings on small FX deposits with maturity above one year were removed. Following an experiment in the Shanghai Pilot Free Trade Zone, in 2015 the PBC decided to remove all remaining controls for onshore FX deposit and lending.

2.2.3. Liberalization of RMB Lending Rates

The liberalization of RMB lending rates had taken longer than those on foreign currency loans because the PBC was concerned that, without a sophisticated regulatory system, excessive competition among banks might lead to financial instability. Moreover, since state-owned banks used to be obligated to provide low-cost financing to support "strategic" industries, state-owned enterprises and other beneficiaries of interest rate controls were resistant to the liberalization of lending rates.

The first attempt to deregulating the RMB lending rates was made in 1987, when the PBC allowed banks to float their RMB lending rates by up to 20% above the benchmark rates. However, as the economy weakened in 1996, this floating range was cut from 20% to 10% to "reduce the burden on enterprises."

Since the outbreak of the Asian financial crisis in 1997, China's domestic economy also faced serious recessionary pressure. Under controlled lending rates, banks were unwilling to lend to small and medium-sized enterprises (SMEs), which were viewed as increasingly risky during the crisis. As a result, SMEs, which were major employers in the economy, suffered from a significant decline in financing. To encourage bank lending to SMEs, the PBC expanded a floating range of RMB lending rates to small enterprises from 10% to 20% in 1998 and further to 30% above the benchmark rates in 1999. Meanwhile, the floating range of lending rates to large enterprises remained at 10%, although loan rates to 512 super-large state-owned enterprises were still subject to the benchmarks.

After several rounds of adjustments to the floating range of RMB lending rates, in October 2004 the PBC finally removed the ceilings on all RMB lending rates,[2] although the floor of lending rates remained at 90% of the benchmark rate. Although this practice on lending rate ceiling did not apply to urban and rural credit cooperatives, their corresponding upward floating range was expanded to 2.3 times the benchmark loan rate. In

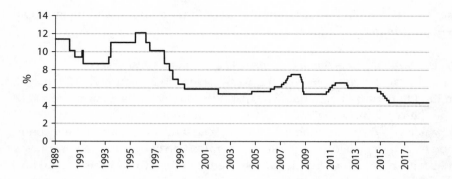

FIGURE 4.1. Benchmark lending rate (6m–1y). *Source:* CEIC.

2012, the PBC lowered the lending rate floor to 70% of the benchmark rate and in July 2013 subsequently removed the remaining lending rate floors and ceilings on all loan facilities (of all financial institutions, including rural credit cooperatives) except household mortgage loans. At that point, the majority of RMB lending rates had been fully liberalized. The benchmark lending rates are shown in Figure 4.1.

In 2019, the PBC took another step toward interest rate liberalization by linking the loan prime rates (LPR) to medium-term lending facility (MLF) and asking banks to price outstanding loans based on LPR. By doing so, the PBC aims to improve the transmission mechanism from a "semiofficial policy rate" (i.e., the MLF rate) to banks' lending rates, although the MLF rate has not yet been officially recognized as the policy rate.

2.2.4. Liberalization of RMB Deposit Rates

According to international experiences, liberalization of deposit rates is the most critical yet the riskiest stage, as it may provoke hostile competition among banks and cause financial instability. Therefore, the process of deposit rate liberalization in China was the last to be carried out and was implemented in a very gradual and prudent way.

Controls on deposit rates could be deleterious to the economy since they cause economic distortions and inefficient allocation of resources. Owing to such restrictions, the real deposit rates—that is, the nominal deposit rates, minus inflation—often fell into negative territories when the economy headed into periods of high growth and high inflation. While high-income individuals tended to have more investment opportunities apart from bank deposits, negative real deposit rates implicitly taxed the low-income population, resulting in a widening in income inequality. In addition, negative real rates also spurred speculation in property markets and commodities as investors sought higher returns on assets, causing bubbles in these markets.

In October 1999, the PBC allowed financial institutions to set interest rates on large-denomination deposit agreements on a market basis as the first attempt to liberalize deposit rates. At the same time, it introduced a floating range for other deposit rates. In 2004, the PBC removed the deposit rate floor and used the benchmark deposit rate as the ceiling of deposit rates. It then waited until 2012 (partly to avoid liberalization during periods of economic overheating) to allow banks to float deposit rates upward by

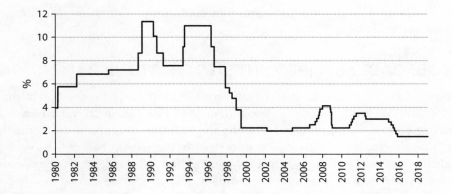

FIGURE 4.2. Benchmark deposit rate (1y). *Source:* CEIC.

10% of the benchmark rate while lowering benchmark deposit rates. In late 2014, China's monetary policy entered another easing cycle and the liberalization of deposit rates accelerated. During that period, the central bank expanded the floating range from 10% to 20% above the benchmark rate.

The PBC officially launched the bank deposit insurance scheme on May 1, 2015, considering it to be a precondition for the final move on deposit rate deregulation. The PBC then lowered benchmark interest rates four times consecutively—mainly due to the economic deceleration and deflation—and expanded the upward floating range of deposit rates to 1.5 times the benchmark set in 2015. In October 2015, the PBC made its fifth cut in benchmark interest rates in that year and simultaneously announced the final removal of the deposit rate ceiling (figure 4.2). This decision marked the completion of the "narrowly defined" interest rate liberalization process.

2.2.5. Lessons from China's Interest Rate Liberalization

A few lessons can be learned from China's gradual approach to liberalizing its interest rates. First, the development of the bond market was instrumental in creating the momentum for deposit and lending rate liberalization, as bond financing competed with bank lending and put pressure on policymakers and banks alike to accept market rates. Second, the timing of the liberalization measures was selected to coincide with periods of lower inflation and lower upward pressure on market rates. This helped avoid a surge in interest rates after deregulation. Third, many actions on liberalizing the interest rates were announced in conjunction with benchmark rate cuts or cuts in the reserve requirement ratios. Sufficient liquidity in the banking system as a result of these measures also kept interest rates stable after the interest rate ceilings were lifted. Fourth, a deposit insurance scheme and prudential regulations were introduced during the process of the interest rate deregulation, to prevent the risks associated with excessive price competition among banks.

Overall, the gradual process of China's interest liberalization was a smooth one. It significantly improved the efficiency of resource allocation and allowed many small and medium-sized companies to gain access to bank credit, but did not cause macroeconomic instability (e.g., a spike in interest rates) or excessive price competition among banks and bank failures, as seen in some Latin America countries during their own interest rate liberalization processes.

3. "BROADLY DEFINED" INTEREST RATE LIBERALIZATION

The removal of the ceiling on deposit rates in 2015 marked the completion of the Chinese banking system's "narrowly defined" interest rate liberalization. Yet, we regard this as the first half of the journey in achieving the ultimate objective of the "broadly defined" interest rate liberalization. The next steps in the second half of the interest rate liberalization should include the establishment of both a short-term policy rate and an effective interest rate transmission mechanism. The policy rate should enable policymakers to communicate their monetary stance to the economic agents, while the interest rate transmission mechanism should help the central bank to influence the market rates (e.g., deposit and lending rates as well as bond yields) and thus the real economy (investment and consumer behaviors) by changing the policy rate. Ideally, the policy rate should be determined by the PBC (rather than by the nontransparent decision-making process within the government), and once the policy rate changes, market rates should follow immediately in the right direction.

In this section we review the efforts made by the PBC over the past years in establishing short-term policy rates and stabilizing these rates by creating an interest rate corridor. It then analyzes the effectiveness of interest rate transmission in China, and the challenges faced by the PBC.

3.1. Policy Rate and Interest Rate Corridor

Almost every central bank in developed economies chooses a certain short-term market interest rate as an intermediate target—namely the policy rate—for monetary policy, and it also conducts open market operations to ensure that interbank market rates with the same maturity are close to this policy rate (Niu, Zhang, and Zhang, 2017). Examples of policy rates include the Fed Funds Rate for the Federal Reserve Bank in the United States, and the refinance rate for the European Central Bank.

Over the past 10 years, the PBC has stated many times that it would reform the monetary policy framework by moving toward a price-based system from one that is quantity-based. That means that it would gradually abandon the use of quantity targets (e.g., M2 and loan growth targets) and would rely more on interest rate tools to manage the business cycle. For the price-based system to work, the central bank would need to identify a suitable short-term market rate as a policy instrument.

The interbank seven-day repo rate (R007), which measures the weighted average seven-day repo rates of all transactions in the interbank market, has in recent years become a candidate for such a policy rate. In 2016, the interbank repo market with bonds as collaterals achieved a total trading volume of 601.3 trillion yuan, while the interbank lending market only recorded 95.9 trillion yuan. However, as the calculation of R007 involves transactions from nonbank financial institutions and those with collaterals other than government bonds, R007 is distorted by "noises" or volatilities caused by counterparty risks and credit qualities of collaterals. In December 2014, the PBC introduced an enhanced fixing indicator named DR007, which is the weighted average seven-day repo rates of transactions between depository institutions with risk-free collaterals, to exclude these "noises."

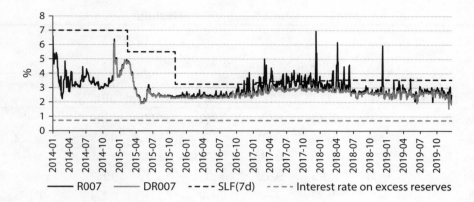

FIGURE 4.3. Interest rate corridor. *Source:* CEIC.

While SHIBOR (overnight), R007, and DR007 are candidates for the official policy rate, these rates are not commonly used in pricing bank loans and deposits. Financial institutions continue to rely on official benchmark lending and deposit rates as the basis for pricing loans and deposits. One reason is that these market rates were too volatile as a benchmark for longer-term assets. For example, the volatility of R007 during 2012–2014, measured by the coefficient of variation, was three to five times the volatility of both the U.S. Fed Funds Rates and the Euro Interbank Offered Rate in normal times.

To mitigate excessive volatilities in short-term market rates and to incubate a market-accepted policy rate, the PBC introduced an implicit interest rate corridor system. Interest rate corridors are widely used by central banks in advanced economies, including the European Central Bank, the Bank of Canada, and many others. This system features two standing facilities that form the upper bound and lower bound of short-term market rates. A credible interest rate corridor can stabilize market expectation of interest rates and eliminate hoarding behavior for liquidity at a time of market stress, thus reducing the volatility of money market interest rates.

The PBC introduced such an implicit corridor in 2015, with the standing lending facility (SLF) rate as the upper bound and the interest rate on excess reserves as the lower bound. By "implicit," we mean that the PBC did not officially call this attempt a corridor but instead stated that it aimed at "stabilizing short-term interest rates." Since then, open market operations and other monetary policy instruments such as SLF were implemented to keep market rates within the upper and lower bounds. Thanks to the corridor system, the volatility of short-term interest rates in China, measured by the coefficient of variations of R007, declined significantly between 2015 and 2016, to levels close to those in developed markets (figure 4.3).

3.2. Effectiveness of Interest Rate Transmission

As mentioned above, the PBC has indicated three candidates for policy interest rates over the past few years: SHIBOR (overnight), R007, and DR007. We conducted an empirical analysis to examine the effectiveness of interest rate transmission from these rates to longer-term bond yields and lending rates.

Table 4.2. OLS Estimation Results

Policy rates (short-term)	Government bond rates (medium to long-term)						Loan rates (medium to long-term)
	6M	1Y	2Y	3Y	5Y	10Y	Average lending rates
DR007	0.590	0.568	0.456	0.363	0.327	0.260	—
R007	0.813	0.756	0.618	0.458	0.288	0.155	0.172
Shibor	0.772	0.720	0.580	0.422	0.257	0.132	0.160
US	0.935	0.813	0.637	0.535	0.403	0.283	0.473
Korea	—	0.983	—	0.930	0.867	0.774	0.533
India	—	0.947	0.697	0.545	0.419	0.386	1.373

Sources: PBC, IMF, and the authors' estimates.

Notes: For the short-term policy rates, the authors used federal funds rate (January 1982–December 2008), Koribor (July 2004–July 2017), and Indian 7D repo rates (April 2001–July 2017) for the cases of the United States, Korea, and India, respectively. Note that the period chosen for the United States is to exclude the period after the launch of quantitative easing, which may alter the correlations between short-term and long-term rates. For the estimation for the bond market, monthly data was used. For the estimation for the lending market, quarterly data was used, including the weighted average of loan rates published by the PBC (Q3 2008–Q2 2017) for the case of China; and average lending rates published by the IMF for the United States (Q1 1982–Q4 2008), Korea (Q2 2004–Q4 2016), and India (Q2 2001–Q4 2016). Because DR007 was launched in 2014, DR007 was dropped for the estimation for the lending market.

We developed a simple regression model to estimate the correlations between our policy rate candidates and medium- and longer-term bond yields and bank lending and deposit rates. The models are specified as:

$$R_t^L = \alpha + \beta R_t^S + \gamma R_t^{bm} + \delta rrr_t + \epsilon_t \qquad (1)$$

where R_t^L is a medium- and longer-term bond yield and banks' lending rates and R_t^S is our short-term policy rate candidates; β measures conditional correlations between policy rates and bond yields/bank rates; R_t^{bm} is the benchmark lending rates; and rrr_t is the reserve requirement ratio (RRR) of banks. By controlling the benchmark rates and the RRR, we attempt to isolate the impact of a change in the policy rates on bond yields/bank rates.

Results from these analyses (shown in table 4.2) provide us with some interesting insights. First, among three potential candidates, R007 have the strongest correlations with medium- and longer-term bond yields. Second, the effectiveness of transmission (measured by β) is higher via the bond market than via the banking system. Third, the effectiveness of transmission in the Chinese loan market is less than half of that in the United States, Korea, and India (see chapter 3 of Ma and Guan, 2018). These findings are consistent with existing literature (Ma and Ji, 2016).

3.3. Barriers to Interest Rate Transmission

Without an effectiveness transmission mechanism, it is hard to justify the reform of the monetary policy framework from a "quantity-based" to a "price-based" system. That is, if a policy rate is used to replace M2 growth as the intermediate target but a change in the policy rate is unable to affect other rates, the entire monetary policy operation would become impotent in influencing the real economy. It is therefore critical to identify the barriers to interest rate transmission and to address these barriers. This section discusses five barriers to interest rate transmission in the banking system.

1. *The existence of benchmark rates prevents banks from adopting market-based pricing mechanism.*

   While the PBC has intended to introduce a policy rate, it continues to announce "benchmark deposit and lending rates for banks" for various maturities. Banks' deposit and loan pricing still relies heavily on these benchmark rates, typically in a formula of benchmark +/– points. As the central bank has yet to announce a timetable for abolishing the benchmark rates, the very low frequency of benchmark rate adjustments and a much higher frequency of short-term rate movements (including the three policy rate candidates) have caused market confusions on which rates were indeed representing policy stance.

2. *Soft budget constraints on state-owned enterprises (SOEs) reduces market sensitivity of interest rates.*

   Many SOEs and local government financing vehicles LGFVs are not very sensitive to interest rates in their financing decisions, due to soft budget constraints (SBCs). The sources of SBCs include implicit guarantees, political incentives to see expansion in size (rather than profits), as well as noncommercial functions imposed by the government. If these borrowers are not sensitive to interest rates, then rate hikes would have little impact on their borrowing, which would hamper monetary policy transmission. We note that this SBC problem has eased a bit in recent years for LGFVs as bond issuers.

3. *Large banks have limited incentives to float deposit rates.*

   Although restrictions on deposit rates have been removed, large commercial banks have limited interest in competing for deposits. Term deposit rates from five major state-owned commercial banks are still identical, while most smaller banks offer deposit rates that are 15 to 25 basis points above those offered by the big five state-owned banks. The principal reasons for such a phenomenon are, first, that state-owned banks still dominate the deposit market and, second, that major state-owned banks often face political pressure to keep interest rates stable.

4. *Wealth management products distort risk-free interest rates.*

   Although rapid development of the wealth management products (WMPs) since 2008 have served as a driving force of interest rate liberalization in China, it has also caused distortions to the money market. Banks and nonbank financial institutions alike have engaged heavily in WMPs, which are not shown on banks' balance sheets, are not included in calculation of capital adequacy ratios or liquidity coverage ratios, and are not subject to reserve requirement and loan-loss provisions. Owing to the very low regulatory costs, WMPs usually offer investors much higher returns than deposits. Although WMPs do not have explicit guarantees from banks, when sold by banks they appear to be risk-free in the public perception, and thus they put upward pressure on bank deposit rates. This problem weakens or distorts the role of monetary policy (especially the policy rates) in influencing market interest rates.

5. *Weak coordination between regulatory policies and monetary policies.*
   Apart from monetary policies, regulatory policies from the central bank and other regulatory authorities also affect interbank interest rates. For instance, the China Banking Regulatory Commission announced a number of new regulatory guidelines, which covered banks' governance of interbank activities and other investment businesses, between March and April in 2017. These actions triggered a spike in the money market (e.g., R007 shot up more than 150 basis points within two weeks). The reserve requirement ratio, which has been quite high in China relative to international standards, also impedes the transmission mechanism of monetary policy (Ma and Wang, 2014).

4. REFORM OF THE MONETARY POLICY FRAMEWORK

Between the mid-1990s and 2015, China succeeded in using a gradual approach to re-regulate interest rate controls without causing macroeconomic instability. The deregulation significantly improved efficiencies in allocation of financial resources and also reduced distortions caused by interest rate controls. However, the "broadly defined" interest rate liberalization remains an unfinished agenda. We believe that the final goal of interest rate liberalization requires that the monetary policy framework transition from a quantity-based to a price-based one. The PBC also needs to clarify the official policy rate, which would allow for efficient policy transmissions. In this section, we discuss issues associated with China's current policy framework, with a focus on problems related to the absence of central bank independence, and develop a medium-term roadmap for reforming the monetary policy framework.

4.1. Issues with the Current Monetary Policy Framework

The following sections lay out several key problems that limit the effective functioning of China's monetary policies, including interest rate transmission. Most of these problems are somewhat related to the PBC's lack of independence in monetary policy decision-making.

4.1.1. Too Many Policy Objectives

According to the Law of the People's Republic of China on the People's Bank of China, the PBC is responsible for both maintaining stability of the currency value and promoting economic growth. In reality, the PBC is obligated to support almost all economic objectives of the State Council. Apart from conventional economic objectives of a central bank, such as stabilizing inflation, ensuring employment, and maintaining financial stability, the PBC is also required to support government objectives such as achieving GDP growth targets, supporting strategically industries, meeting the balance of payment targets (including "basic stability of the exchange rate" and stability of FX reserves), and so on.

Although these objectives are not explicit in the law, the PBC needs to fulfill them, since the State Council (to which the PBC reports) has the final power on monetary policy decisions. Historically, key monetary policy decisions, such as money supply (M2) targets, benchmark deposit and lending rates, and reserve requirement ratios were all made by the State Council. Consequently, many government agencies and stakeholders will attempt to steer monetary policies that are in their favor through the State Council, often leading to pressures for excessive monetary expansion and a rising leverage ratio in the economy.

4.1.2. Absence of an Intermediate Monetary Target

Historically, China used M2 growth as an intermediate target for monetary policy, as the Premier's annual government work report (presented to and approved by the National People's Congress each March) included a specific growth rate as the target for M2 growth. In March 2018, the Annual Government Work Report no longer contained a target for M2 growth. This sent an important signal that monetary policy would shift toward a framework that centers on the use of price instruments, rather than quantity targets and instruments. The abolishment of the M2 target is justified by the weakening of the correlation between M2 and real economic indicators (such as GDP growth and inflation). However, a key problem is that when the monetary aggregate target is abolished, there is no specific price (interest rate) target for monetary policy operations. The absence of a monetary intermediate target may create difficulties for the PBC to communicate with the market on whether the monetary stance is tight or loose, since there is no longer any reference point for policy neutrality.

4.1.3. Too Many Policy Instruments

In addition to traditional policy instruments such as benchmark interest rates and reserve requirement ratio, over the past several years the PBC has introduced a series of new policy tools, including repurchase agreements, SLF, MLF (medium-term lending facility), and relending and rediscount facilities. Such tools provide the central bank with flexibility, because the use of them, which are labeled as technical instruments for adjusting liquidity, no longer requires State Council permission. In a sense, these instruments were "by-products" of the lack of central bank independence. Yet, because most of these instruments carry some policy implications, the frequent use of these instruments, which sometimes are inconsistent among themselves, send confusing signals to the market.

4.1.4. Complex Policymaking Mechanism

China has never clarified its process of monetary policy making, partly owing to the need to balance many policy objectives, the involvement of many parties, and the growing number of policy instruments. Market participants therefore often have a hard time deducing the implication of a given policy action. When certain monetary actions are taken, market participants sometimes debate such elementary matters as whether such actions are "expansionary" or "contractionary." These confusions in terms of monetary policy stance, as seen in China, rarely occur among central banks globally. It occurs in China mainly because of its complex monetary policymaking mechanism.

4.1.5. Limited Use of Forward Guidance

Forward guidance has evolved to be an important policy tool in recent decades among central banks in developed countries, owing to its effectiveness in influencing market expectations of future interest rates as well as its very low cost. However, since the PBC is not the final decision maker on key monetary policies, it is unable to credibly commit to a certain future monetary policy trajectory or decision-making rule; the PBC's statements usually contain ambiguous words like "appropriate" or "reasonable." As a result, the PBC has not proactively used communications as a monetary policy tool. Most of the communications by senior PBC officials with the market have been reactive in nature—for example, to correct market misperceptions or to boost confidence when the market starts to panic.

4.2. Roadmap toward a New Monetary Policy Framework

Interest rate deregulation has provided an important basis for China to move toward a "price-based" monetary policy framework, under which the adjustment of the policy rate may effectively influence the market rates (banks' deposit and lending rates, as well as bond yields), thereby achieving the goal of smoothing business cycles—which is to ensure price stability and support full employment. However, as a result of problems identified above, the current monetary policy framework, which is in a transition stage, is still far from ideal. Based on our research and a number of analytical studies, we suggest the following roadmap for China's monetary policy framework reform.

4.2.1. Goals of the Reform

1. Establish a legal framework to ensure the independence of monetary policy-making by the central bank.
2. Clarify that the new intermediate target for monetary policy (i.e., the policy rate) is a specific short-term rate, and abolish all the benchmark deposit and lending rates.
3. Clarify that there is only one policy rate; other monetary policy tools (such as SLF, MLF, etc.) should apply only under specific circumstances and do not carry the significance of a policy rate.
4. Establish a formal interest rate corridor whose ceiling and floor shall move accordingly when the policy rate is changed.
5. Establish an efficient transmission mechanism of policy rate to longer-term interest rates.
6. Improve the coordination between monetary policies and regulatory policies.

4.2.2. Specific Reforms

To achieve the goals laid out above, many specific reform steps need to be taken. Suggested key steps are as follows:

1. Amend the *Law of the People's Bank of China* to clarify that final policy objectives of the monetary policy will be limited to three items: ensuring price stability, supporting full employment, and achieving financial stability; and also to grant the PBC's Monetary Policy Committee (MPC) autonomy and full in-

dependence in making key monetary policy decisions, which is essential in the modern macroeconomic policy framework, as documented by Cukierman 2008. Specifically, give the mandate of policy rate decisions to the MPC, with a predetermined schedule for its meetings.

2. Announce the abolishment of the benchmark deposit and lending rates, the establishment of a short-term interest rate as a policy rate, and the establishment of a formal interest rate corridor. Expand the list of eligible collaterals for borrowing from SLF to enhance the credibility of the corridor; allow market-making securities firms to access SLF.

3. Enhance the transparency of monetary policymaking, and establish forward guidance as a formal policy tool. Apart from regular press releases, the PBC should also conduct press conferences to establish direct communications; enhance foreign accessibility to the PBC's content by translating at least one-fifth of the main contents on the PBC website to English; improve global exposure by conducting road shows on macroeconomic and monetary policy internationally; and strengthen the capability of working papers in guiding market expectations.

4. Remove the statement of "maintaining basic stability of the exchange rate" from all policy addresses—that is, abandon the exchange rate objective in monetary policy making.

5. Remove regulatory loopholes for wealth management products to avoid regulatory arbitrary actions and to minimize their distortions to risk-free interest rates.

6. Avoid the excessive use of quantity-based measures in macroprudential regulations, such as imposition of loan quotas.

7. Cut the reserve requirement ratios to enhance the efficiency of interest rate transmission.

8. Improve management of treasury balance to minimize its impacts on market liquidity and short-term interest rates. This can be achieved by diversifying the timing of the receipt of tax payments, and by improving the forecast of fiscal balance.

9. Develop interest rate derivative markets, including bond futures and interest rate swaps.

10. Further improve market access for foreign investors to China's bond markets.

11. Improve the credit rating systems by harmonizing domestic and international credit rating standards.

NOTES

This chapter draws heavily on Ma and Guan (2018), which reviewed in greater detail the history of China's interest rate liberalization and developed a reform proposal for China's monetary policy framework. The authors would like to thank Chan Seeyu for help in editing this article.

1. After the monetary policy committee's third-quarter meeting in September 2019, the PBC issued a statement saying it would deepen interest rate liberalization, improve the loan prime rate (LPR) regime, and promote its use in practice.

2. That ceiling still applies to all financial institutions except for urban and rural credit cooperatives, which are financial institutions providing basic financial services to rural areas.

REFERENCES

Cukierman, A. (2008). "Central Bank Independence and Monetary Policymaking Institutions—Past, Present and Future." *European Journal of Political Economy* 24(4): 722–36.

Ma, J., and T. Guan (2018). *Interest Rate Liberalization and Reform of Monetary Policy Framework.* Beijing: China Financial Publishing House.

Ma, J., and M. Ji (2016). *Interest Rate Transmission Mechanism in New Monetary Policy Framework.* Beijing: China Financial Publishing House.

Ma, J., and H. Wang (2014). "Theoretical Model on Policy Interest Rate Transmission Mechanism." *Journal of Financial Research* 414(12): 1–22.

Niu, M., L. Zhang, and X. Zhang (2017). "Interest Rate Corridor, Interest Rate Stability and Cost of Regulation." *Journal of Financial Research* 445(7): 16–28.

PART 2

BOND AND MONEY MARKETS

5

CHINESE BOND MARKETS AND INTERBANK MARKET

Marlene Amstad and Zhiguo He

1. OVERVIEW OF CHINESE BOND MARKETS

Over the past 20 years, especially the past decade, China has taken enormous strides to develop its bond market as an integral step in its financial reform, along with its tremendous effort in interest rate liberalization and internalization of its currency, the RMB.

Figure 5.1, Panel A, depicts the growth of Chinese bond market capitalization scaled by GDP in the past decade; we observe that bond market capitalization over GDP rises from 35% in 2008 to more than 98% in 2019. For comparison, bond market capitalization over GDP in the United States stays slightly above 200% during the same time period. Relative to stock market capitalization, the Chinese bond market has also experienced a steadily increasing trend, reaching 164% in 2019, which exceeded the U.S. level of 120%.[1]

For historical reasons, two distinct and largely segmented markets exist in today's Chinese bond markets: an over-the-counter interbank market, and a centralized exchange market. The interbank bond market in China resembles the interbank market observed in developed countries like the United States, while the exchange bond market in China is part of the stock exchanges in Shanghai and Shenzhen. Section 4.2 of this chapter offers a brief history of the development and evolution of these two bond markets. The interbank market is the more dominant of these two markets; at the end of 2019, about 89% of the total bonds outstanding in China were in the interbank market, while the remaining 11% were in the exchange.[2] Various fixed income securities are issued and traded on these two bond markets, with many multilayer regulatory bodies interacting with each other in an intricate way.

We first elaborate on the two bond markets in section 2, together with various bond instruments traded there. Section 3 provides a brief history of Chinese bond markets, while section 4 highlights their inherent connection with the banking system, together with the internalization of Chinese bond markets in the near future. Section 5 covers the credit ratings and rating agencies, then section 6 offers an account of ever-rising

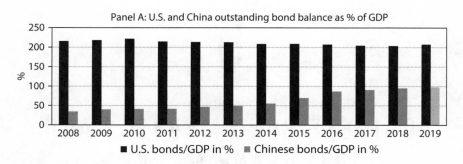

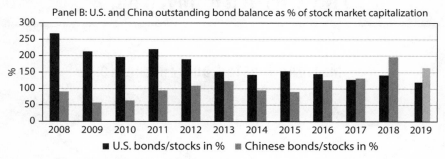

FIGURE 5.1. A comparison of U.S. and China bond market growth. *Data sources:* China, Wind Bond Overview; United States, SIFMA U.S. Bond Market Issuance and Outstanding (www .sifma.org/resources/research/us-bond-market-issuance-and-outstanding/); GDP: China, Wind database; United States, FRED Economic Data (https://fred.stlouisfed.org/series/GDP). The authors use nominal GDP because outstanding numbers are market value of bonds (also nominal). Stock market capitalization: China, Shanghai Stock Exchange (SSE) + Shenzhen Stock Exchange (SZSE) from Wind Stock Market Overview; United States, World Bank Database (https://data.worldbank.org/indicator/CM.MKT.LCAP.CD). *Note:* All numbers are as of the end of each year.

default incidents in China starting in 2014. Finally, we provide some data sources for an in-depth study of the Chinese bond market in section 7.

2. BOND MARKETS AND BOND TYPES

In this section, we first go over the details of the two segmented Chinese bond markets—namely, the interbank market and the exchange market. After explaining the various bond security types traded in Chinese bond markets, we provide a comparison of these two bond markets.

2.1. Segmented Bond Markets

2.1.1. The Interbank Market (银行间市场)

The interbank bond market, often referred to as the China Interbank Market (CIBM, 中国银行间债券市场), was established in 1997 and has become the dominant market for bond issuance and trading in China. Besides spot and repurchase transactions, swaps and

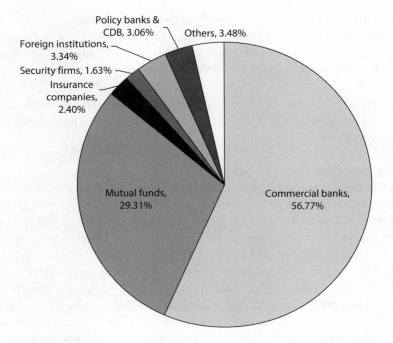

FIGURE 5.2. Chinese interbank market investor structure, 2019. *Data sources:* CCDC: http://www .chinabond.com.cn/Channel/19012917?BBND=2017&BBYF=12&sPageType=2#; SHCH: http:// www.shclearing.com/sjtj/tjyb/. *Note:* SHCH only reports investor structure information for major bond securities. As a result, the aggregated investment amount is lower than the total outstanding balance. The authors adjusted the outstanding balance for each investor while maintaining their corresponding shares. The numbers are as of 12/31/2019.

futures are also actively traded by participants in the interbank market. The value of outstanding bonds in the interbank market reached 86 trillion RMB at the end of 2019, with an annual issuance of 42 trillion RMB in the same year.

As a wholesale market, the interbank market restricts participation to various qualified institutional investors, including commercial banks, mutual funds, insurance companies, and security firms. As shown in figure 5.2, commercial banks (e.g., state-owned commercial banks, joint-stock commercial banks, and urban and rural commercial banks) form the largest group of institutional investors, holding about 57% of the outstanding bonds in the interbank market in 2019. The second largest group is mutual funds, broadly defined to include the fast-growing asset management industry, evolving in part by the rise of wealth management products after 2012; they held about 29% of outstanding bonds in the interbank market. Security firms, insurance companies, and foreign institutions are the next; these three groups of institutional investors formed a market share of 7% in the interbank market.

The main regulator of the interbank market is the People's Bank of China (PBC, 中国人民银行), the central bank in China. Participants in the interbank market trade via the China Foreign Exchange Trade System (CFETS, 外汇交易中心), and all participating institutions are required to open their accounts with China Central Depository & Clearing Co. Ltd (CCDC, 中债登), a leading depository and clearing house in China. After the terms of trades are finalized through bilateral bargaining, CFETS records these transactions and CCDC offers exclusive custodial and clearing services in the interbank market. This monopolistic position came to an end after the establishment of Shanghai Clearing House (SHCH, 上清所) in November 2009. Led by the PBC, SHCH competes with CCDC by offering clearing services for products like medium-term notes, commercial papers, and private placement notes.

2.1.2. The Exchange Market (交易所市场)

The exchange market for the Chinese bond market is part of the two stock exchanges located in Shanghai and Shenzhen, which were established around 1991 in the wake of state-owned enterprise (SOE, 国有企业) and financial reform. In August 1995, the exchange-based bond market was designated as the only legitimate bond market in China. This dominant position came to an end in May 1997 when the PBC, which worried about the overheated Chinese stock market fueled by bond repo financing, ordered all commercial banks to switch to the newly established interbank market on June 1997 (see section 4.2 for more details). Despite this setback, the exchange market has been keeping pace with the rapid growth of the ever-complicated Chinese financial system. At the end of 2019, the value of outstanding bonds in the exchange market reached 11 trillion RMB, with an annual issuance of 3.7 trillion RMB in 2019.

The regulator of the exchange bond market is the China Securities Regulatory Commission (CSRC, 证监会), the powerful agency that oversees the Chinese stock markets. The participants in the exchange bond market include both institutional players and high net-worth retail investors, with only spot and repurchase transactions available. Electronic order books aggregate all bids from investors, and matched trades are settled via China Security Depository & Clearing Co. Ltd (CSDC, 中证登).

2.2. Bond Types

We classify the fixed-income securities in Chinese bond market into three broad categories based on issuing entities: government bonds, financial bonds, and corporate bonds (the latter of which are issued by nonfinancial sectors). There is also another widely used classification among practitioners in China, which groups financial bonds and corporate bonds together as the so-called credit bonds. Note that, in Chinese bond markets, the issuers are primarily the government or entities it owns directly (e.g., SOEs and most commercial banks).

Consistent with international practice, overall speaking, the creditworthiness of these bond instruments is decreasing across these three broad categories. Although corporate bonds in some international contexts also include long-term bonds issued by financial institutions, we specifically separate out bonds issued by financial institutions, given that almost all entities in the Chinese financial sector are state owned. Figure 5.3 compares the outstanding bonds in China and the United States from 2008 to 2019 by these three categories. We observe relatively a large fraction of government bonds (U.S. Treasury) in the U.S. bond market, but the weight of financial bonds and corporate bonds are similar. Figure 5.4 depicts the composition of three types of bonds in the interbank market and exchange market in China, respectively, in 2019.

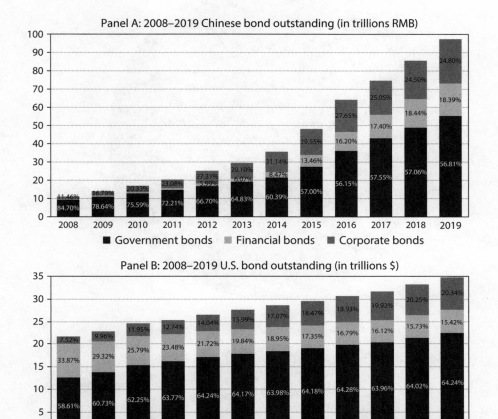

Panel A: 2008–2019 Chinese bond outstanding (in trillions RMB)

Panel B: 2008–2019 U.S. bond outstanding (in trillions $)

FIGURE 5.3. Outstanding bond balance in Chinese and U.S., 2008–2019. *Data sources:* China: Wind Bond Overview. The authors reorganize bond types into the three categories as in section 2.2, year by year; United States, Government/Nongovernment Bonds: SIFMA U.S. Bond Market Issuance and Outstanding (see figure 5.1 footnote)*;* Financial bonds: Financial Accounts of the United States (https://www.federalreserve.gov/releases/z1/current/); Domestic Financial Assets (L.108): Financial Bonds = Open Market Paper + Corporate and Foreign Bonds; Corporate Bonds = Nongovernment Bonds (from SIFMA) – Financial Bonds (from the Fed). *Note:* The authors exclude mortgage-related (agency- and GSE-backed) securities, which are a significant part of the U.S. bond market, in calculating the composition of U.S. bonds, because there are no comparable mortgage-related securities in Chinese bond markets. All numbers are as of the end of each year.

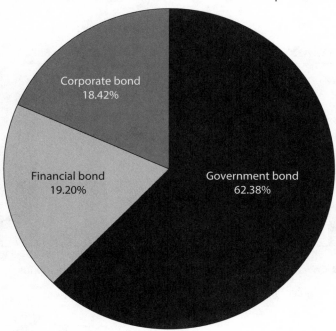

Panel A: 2019 Chinese interbank market bond composition

Corporate bond
18.42%

Financial bond
19.20%

Government bond
62.38%

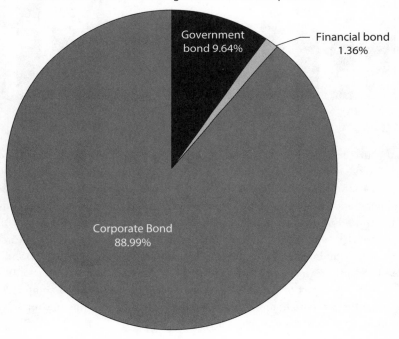

Panel B: 2019 Chinese exchange market bond composition

Government
bond 9.64%

Financial bond
1.36%

Corporate Bond
88.99%

FIGURE 5.4. Composition of bonds in Chinese interbank and exchange market, 2019. *Data sources:* Interbank, China Central Depository & Clearing (CCDC)+Shanghai Clearing House (SHCH); CCDC, http://www.chinabond.com.cn/Channel/19012917?BBND=2017&BBYF=12&sPageType =2#;SHCH, http://www.shclearing.com/sjtj/tjyb/); Exchange, China Securities Depository and Clearing Corp. (CSDC) (http://www.chinaclear.cn/zdjs/tjyb1/center_tjbg.shtml). *Note:* For CCDC, the authors only include bonds in the interbank market, the OTC market, and the Free Trade Zone market that are in custody of CCDC (i.e., excluding those bonds that dual-listed in the exchange market). All numbers are as of 12/31/2019.

We now turn to details of these bond types. Table 5.1 gives two snapshots of the outstanding balances of these bonds, by type, in Chinese bond markets in 2008 and 2019; and table 5.2 (see section 2.3, "Bond Liquidity") gives the outstanding balance and issuance amount by bond types in 2019.

2.2.1. Government Bonds (政府债)

Treasury Bonds (国债)

The Ministry of Finance issues treasury bonds, which are backed by the fiscal revenue collected by the central government of China and represent the creditworthiness of China as a sovereign nation. There are mainly two types of treasury bonds: book-entry treasury bonds that can be traded and transferred in the market, and certificate treasury bonds, which cannot be traded and hence are mainly used as a savings vehicle. As one of the PBC's key instruments for implementing its monetary policy through open market operations, treasury bonds are one of the most important financial products in today's Chinese financial market, enjoying relatively large issuance and trading volumes with significant secondary market liquidity. At the end of 2019, the treasury bonds reached 17 trillion RMB, which is about 17% of the Chinese bond market. This is rather small relative to the importance of U.S. Treasuries in the U.S. bond market (48%).

Nowadays, a market mechanism by which participating financial institutions (mainly commercial banks) bid competitively determines the interest rates offered on treasury bonds. We will come back to this issue in section 4.1.

Municipal Bonds (地方政府债)

Local governments in China issue municipal bonds. The market for such bonds almost did not exist until the 2009 four-trillion-yuan stimulus plan put forth by Beijing in the wake of the 2007–2008 global financial crisis. The outstanding municipal bonds grew steadily but rather slowly over the next five years, only to dramatically burst in issuance volume in 2015. As explained later in section 4.3, this is the outcome of a sequence of noticeable regulatory tightening from Beijing to rein in the ever-growing local government debt problem in the second half of 2014, especially the tone-setting guideline "Article 43." As a result, in 2015 local governments issued 2.8 trillion RMB municipal bonds, of which 2 trillion was used to swap the debt initially raised by local government financing vehicles (LGFVs, 地方政府融资平台). We will discuss the bonds issued by LGFVs (which are not municipal bonds) in section 2.2.3.

At the end of 2019, the outstanding municipal bonds reached 21 trillion RMB, with a value-weighted average maturity of 7.4 years at issuance. Because municipal bonds are assigned a zero risk weight, most municipal bonds in China are held by commercial banks (88% at the end of 2019).

Policy Bank Bonds (政策银行债)

China today has three policy banks: China Development Bank, Export-Import Bank of China, and Agricultural Development Bank of China. They were established in 1994 to take over the government-directed lending functions from state-owned commercial banks, and are responsible for financing economic and trade development as well as state-invested projects. Policy bank bonds are issued by these three policy banks, which

Table 5.1. Outstanding Bond Balance in Chinese Bond Markets, 2008 and 2019

2008	Market	Outstanding (number)	Outstanding (%)	Outstanding (RMB billions)	Outstanding (% RMB)
Total		**1,211**	**100.00**	**11,066.91**	**100.00**
Government bonds	**Interbank, Exchange, OTC**	**408**	**33.69**	**9,373.55**	**84.70**
Treasury bonds	Interbank, Exchange, OTC	149	12.30	5,478.32	49.50
Policy bank bonds	Interbank, Exchange	234	19.32	3,698.33	33.42
Other government bonds	Interbank, Exchange	25	2.06	196.90	1.78
Financial bonds	**Interbank**	**109**	**9.00**	**424.94**	**3.84**
Other financial bonds	Interbank	109	9.00	424.94	3.84
Corporate bonds	**Interbank, Exchange**	**694**	**57.31**	**1,268.42**	**11.46**
Enterprise bonds	Interbank, Exchange	272	22.46	485.37	4.39
Exchange-traded corporate bonds	Exchange	20	1.65	40.00	0.36
Medium-term notes	Interbank	39	3.22	167.20	1.51
Commercial papers	Interbank	256	21.14	419.31	3.79
Asset-backed securities	Interbank	68	5.62	49.26	0.45
Others	Exchange	39	3.22	107.29	0.97

2019	Market	Outstanding (number)	Outstanding (%)	Outstanding (RMB billions)	Outstanding (% RMB)
Total		**49,432**	**100.00**	**97,107.41**	**100.00**
Government bonds	**Interbank, Exchange, OTC**	**5,620**	**11.37**	**55,169.23**	**56.81**
Treasury bonds	Interbank, Exchange, OTC	281	0.57	16,650.53	17.15
Municipal bonds	Interbank, Exchange	4,874	9.86	21,118.29	21.75
Policy bank bonds	Interbank, Exchange	300	0.61	15,705.90	16.17
Other government bonds	Interbank, Exchange	165	0.33	1,694.50	1.74

Financial Bonds	**Interbank**	**17,243**	**34.88**	**17,856.77**	**18.39**
Negotiable certificates of deposit	Interbank	15,553	31.46	10,723.69	11.04
Other financial bonds	Interbank	1,690	3.42	7,133.09	7.35
Corporate bonds	**Interbank, Exchange**	**26,569**	**53.75**	**24,081.40**	**24.80**
Enterprise bonds	Interbank, Exchange	2,555	5.17	2,379.83	2.45
Exchange-traded corporate bonds	Exchange	6,564	13.28	6,903.90	7.11
Medium-term notes	Interbank	5,185	10.49	6,582.90	6.78
Commercial papers	Interbank	2,068	4.18	1,988.42	2.05
Asset-backed securities	Interbank	7,111	14.39	3,577.56	3.68
Private placement notes	Interbank	2,655	5.37	2,019.90	2.08
Other corporate bonds	Exchange	431	0.87	628.90	0.65

Source: Wind bond overview.

Note: The authors reorganize the original dataset based on the three bond categories in section 2.2: government, financial, and corporate. All numbers are as of 12/31/2008 and 12/31/2019.

Table 5.2. Chinese Bond Issuance, Outstanding and Spot Transaction Volume by Types, 2019

2019	Market	Issuance (billions RMB)	Issuance (%)	Outstanding (billions RMB)	Outstanding (%)	Transaction volume (billions RMB)	Turnover
Total	**Interbank, Exchange, OTC**	**45,185.50**	**100.00**	**97,107.41**	**100.00**	**213,490.09**	**2.34**
Government bonds	**Interbank, Exchange, OTC**	**12,547.24**	**27.77**	**55,169.23**	**56.81**	**136,115.97**	**2.62**
Treasury bonds	Interbank, Exchange, OTC	4,164.10	9.22	16,650.53	17.15	34,461.77	2.19
Municipal bonds	Interbank, Exchange	4,362.43	9.65	21,118.29	21.75	9,774.72	0.50
Policy bank bonds	Interbank, Exchange	3,823.71	8.46	15,705.90	16.17	90,171.04	6.01
Other government bonds	Interbank, Exchange	197.00	0.44	1,694.50	1.74	1,708.43	1.03
Financial bonds	**Interbank**	**20,729.32**	**45.88**	**17,856.77**	**18.39**	**53,935.14**	**3.21**
Negotiable certificates of deposit	Interbank	17,951.39	39.73	10,723.69	11.04	49,870.75	4.85
Other financial bonds	Interbank	2,777.93	6.15	7,133.09	7.35	4,064.39	0.62
Corporate bonds	**Interbank, Exchange**	**11,908.94**	**26.36**	**24,081.40**	**24.80**	**23,438.99**	**1.04**
Enterprise bonds	Interbank, Exchange	362.44	0.80	2,379.83	2.45	1,390.00	0.56
Exchange-traded corporate bonds	Exchange	2,543.86	5.63	6,903.90	7.11	649.37	0.10
Medium-term notes	Interbank	2,030.81	4.49	6,582.90	6.78	9,209.50	1.51
Commercial papers	Interbank	3,625.42	8.02	1,988.42	2.05	8,333.22	4.26
Asset-backed securities	Interbank	2,362.87	5.23	3,577.56	3.68	777.39	0.25
Private placement notes	Interbank	618.10	1.37	2,019.90	2.08	1,516.09	0.76
Other corporate bonds	Exchange	365.43	0.81	628.90	0.65	1,563.42	3.00

Source: Wind bond overview and Wind bond secondary market statistics.
Notes: The authors reorganize the original dataset based on the three bond categories in section 2.2: government, financial, and corporate. Transaction amounts are reported for spot transactions. RMB volume and turnover are calculated as spot transaction amount divided by average beginning and ending balance. All numbers are as of 12/31/2019.

are essentially backed by the central government, and hence considered to be quasi-sovereign bonds and risk-free (i.e., they receive zero risk weight if held by commercial banks).

At the end of 2019, there were 16 trillion RMB policy bank bonds outstanding, similar to the amount of outstanding treasury bonds issued by the Ministry of Finance. The weighted average of maturity at issuance is 8.1 years, and two major institutional holders are national commercial banks and mutual funds.

It is important to highlight that 55% of policy bank bonds are issued by China Development Bank (CDB, 国家开发银行). Thanks to its depth and sheer size, the CDB bond has achieved superb secondary market liquidity (even better than treasury bonds in some particular measures). In addition, from the perspective of most institutional investors, CDB bonds receive the same tax treatment as other fixed-income securities. As a result, CDB bonds are widely accepted as the risk-free benchmark in practice (as opposed to treasury bonds).

Other Government Bonds
Additional types of government bonds include central bank bills and other bonds with government support. They have been negligible in recent years.

2.2.2. Financial Bonds (金融债)
We classify all bonds issued by financial institutions, including commercial banks, insurance companies, and security firms, as "financial bonds." The financial sector, which is considered to be in a commanding heights industry, still remains state-owned and often operates with implicit government guarantees. As a result, financial bonds are considered to have a better risk profile than corporate bonds issued by nonfinancial firms. This better risk profile is reflected in a higher rating distribution received by financial bonds (see figure 5.7 in section 5.2); there is little difference in yield spreads between financial and nonfinancial bonds given the same rating class.

Negotiable Certificates of Deposit (NCDs, 同业存单)
As a money market instrument, an NCD is a certificate of fixed-term deposit issued by depository institutions in the interbank market. It is often also referred to as an interbank CD, or just a CD. As shown in table 5.1, there were no NCDs in 2008. Yet the NCD market grew rapidly since its inception in December 2013, reaching 10.7 trillion RMB at the end of 2019, thanks to its high credit quality (guaranteed by issuing banks), excellent secondary market liquidity, and reasonable premium over risk-free benchmark offered by government bonds. The NCD rates track closely with Shanghai Interbank Offered Rate (SHIBOR, 上海银行间同业拆放利率), with a premium of 80 basis points (bps) over CDB bonds in 2019.

The typical issuers of NCDs are relatively smaller joint-stock commercial banks and urban commercial banks, while the buyers of NCDs are large state-owned banks (e.g., the Big Five) or their wealth management products (WMPs, 理财产品), as large state-owned banks enjoy cheap funding sources from either retail deposits or various central bank facilities.[3] Besides large state-owned commercial banks, rural commercial banks, money market funds and mutual funds (broadly defined to include asset management plans funded by wealth management products) have also been investing in NCDs for favorable returns.

The recent turmoil during the summer of 2019 in the NCD market, which triggered the spate of regional bank bailouts (Baoshang Bank, Bank of Jinzhou, Hengfeng Bank), caught worldwide attention. As mentioned in He (2020), the running theme of China's financial market development in the past decade has been "underdeveloped financial markets with overdeveloped financial products." This fundamental tension has caused unbalanced growth in some areas, which will sometimes lead to the bursting of a market bubble. This time, the burst was in the NCD market in China, and the underlying economic mechanism was almost identical to the wholesale funding turmoil preceding the collapse of Lehman Brothers during the 2007–2008 global financial crisis. For more details, see He (2020).

Other Financial Bonds

For options besides NCDs, investors can also invest in senior or subordinate bonds issued by commercial banks (large state-owned banks, joint-stock banks, and urban and rural commercial banks), insurance companies, security firms, and other financial institutions. These financial bonds contribute to a relatively small part of the Chinese bond market (about 7% of the market at the end of 2019).

2.2.3. Corporate Bonds (产业债)

The category of corporate bonds broadly covers all fixed-income securities issued by nonfinancial firms in China, including asset-backed securities and other convertible securities.

Enterprise Bonds (企业债)

Emerging as early as the first half of the 1980s, enterprise bonds are an important financial instrument used by nonfinancial firms in China as an alternative to bank loans. After the interbank market was established in 1997, it became the sole market where enterprise bonds were issued and traded, as back then enterprise bonds were mainly issued by SOEs, which were not publicly listed in stock exchanges. In 2005, the exchange market started to compete for businesses, and issuing entities could choose to sell their bonds in both markets. As a result, about 82% of enterprise bonds became dual listed at the end of 2019. Both Wang et al. (2015) and Chen et al. (2018) study dual-listed enterprise bonds.

For historical reasons, the issuance of enterprise bonds has always been regulated by the National Development and Reform Commission (NDRC, 国家发展改革委员会), a powerful government agency that oversees SOE reform and is relatively remote from both PBC and CSRC. The outstanding value of enterprise bonds reached 2.4 trillion RMB at the end of 2019, and their investors are mainly commercial banks and mutual funds.

One important component of enterprise bonds is municipal corporate bonds (MCBs, 城投债), which at the end of 2019 consisted of 72% of enterprise bonds outstanding.[4] MCBs are bonds issued by LGFVs, which are state-owned enterprises, to support infrastructure investment at both the provincial and the city level. They are one of the perfect examples of the mixture between planning and market in today's Chinese economy: They have the implicit backing of the corresponding local government (hence the name *municipal*), but in a strict legal sense they are issued by LGFV entities just like other regular corporations (hence *corporate*).

Exchange-Traded Corporate Bonds (公司债)

The category of exchange-traded corporate bonds consists of corporate bonds issued in the exchange market and regulated by the CSRC. When first launched in 2007, exchange-traded corporate bonds could only be issued by publicly listed companies. In 2015, the CSRC expanded the eligible list of issuing entities in a significant way by allowing all firms registered as "corporations" to issue these bonds. In addition, the CSRC also loosened the bond-issuance criterion, and gave the green light to both public issuance as well as private placement. Since then, exchange-traded corporate bonds have grown rapidly, reaching 7 trillion RMB at the end of 2019.

Medium-Term Notes (中期票据)

Issued in the interbank market, since 2008 medium-term notes have mainly been used by large SOEs as well as prominent private enterprises. The typical debt maturity at issuance is between 3 and 5 years, but also can go as high as 10 years. At the end of 2019, the outstanding bond value of medium-term notes reached 6.6 trillion RMB.

Commercial Papers (Including Super Commercial Paper, 短融及超短融)

Issued in the interbank market, commercial papers are short-term (generally below one year) financing instruments mainly used by large SOEs as well as prominent private enterprises. For commercial papers, the typical debt maturity at issuance is less than one year, while for super commercial papers, it is about 270 days. Commercial papers were launched in 2005, and at the end of 2019, the outstanding bond value had reached 2 trillion RMB.

Asset-Backed Securities (ABS, 资产支持证券)

First launched in 2005 and growing by about 48% per year since then, ABS can be issued and traded in both interbank and exchange markets. As a nascent financial product, ABS is the financing engine behind peer-to-peer lending platforms, a burgeoning sector that experienced astonishing growth (for example, the microfinancing arm under Ant Financial Services Group) but recently hit heavy headwinds from a dramatic regulatory tightening in 2019. It is also common for commercial banks to issue ABS backed by consumer or industrial loans, which essentially moves their on-balance-sheet assets to off-balance-sheet. In 2019, the outstanding value of asset-backed securities reached 3.6 trillion RMB, which was about 15% of corporate bonds and 3.7% of all bonds.

Private Placement Notes (PPN, 定向工具)

Launched in 2011, PPN represents one of the financial innovations by the interbank market and essentially is a mixture of private debt and public bonds. Nonfinancial firms can issue PPNs to a relatively small number of select institutional investors, which then may transfer these notes among themselves before their maturity in the interbank market. Relative to other more-standard publicly placed bonds, PPNs face much less stringent requirements of information disclosure, as the issuers can even negotiate the particular method of information disclosure with a small number of select investors. This significantly alleviates the concern of information leakage for those small to medium enterprises, especially for startups in the technology sector. After several years of rapid growth, the outstanding value of PPN reached 2 trillion RMB at the end of 2019, which is about 2% of the market.

Table 5.3. China's Corporate Bond Market Liquidity

	China: Interbank	China: Exchange	United States
ZDays	0.88856	0.81326	0.78820
ZDays-w/trade	0.88768	0.79798	0.70940
Turnover	0.01212	0.00099	0.00150
Amihud	0.00016	2.54233	0.48810

Notes: This table, which is taken from Panel A of table A.1 in Chen et al. (2018), reports various measures of China's corporate bond market liquidity and its comparison with the U.S. bond market. ZDays is the time series average of the fraction of bonds that do not trade on a given day. ZDays-w/trade is the time series average of the fraction of bonds that do not trade on a given day, excluding bonds that have no single trade over the sample period. Turnover is the average daily turnover across all bond-day observations where a zero is recorded on days without trade. Amihud is the average Amihud (2002) measure across all bonds, where a bond's Amihud measure is estimated using its all non-zero daily trading observations and multiplied by 10^6. The sample period is 1/1/2012–12/31/2017 for China's two markets; the sample period is 1/1/2010–12/31/2014 for the U.S. market; liquidity measures are from Anderson and Stulz (2017).

Other Corporate Bonds

Other bond products include international institution bonds (国际机构债) and railway bonds. They made up only some 0.7% of the outstanding bond value in 2019.

2.3. Bond Market Liquidity

The last two columns in table 5.2 give the annual secondary market trading volume and the turnover (trading volume over the average outstanding balance) of each bond during 2019. Among all the categories, financial bonds have the highest turnover of about 3.2; government bonds rank second with a turnover of 2.6; corporate bonds have the lowest turnover at about 1.

Chinese government bonds are far less liquid than U.S. Treasuries; the latter is perhaps the most liquid financial instrument in the world, with an annual turnover of about 9.3 in 2019. The lack of market liquidity for Chinese government bonds is often blamed for hindering efficient price discovery, thereby potentially hurting the effective monetary policy conducted by the PBC.

Chinese corporate bonds are significantly less liquid than Chinese stocks, with an annual turnover of about three in 2019.[5] For a comprehensive study on the liquidity of Chinese corporate bonds and its evolution in response to Beijing's relentless interventions in the last decade, see Mo and Subrahmanyam (2019). This lack of corporate bonds' market liquidity is a universal phenomenon that holds in other developed financial markets like in the United States and Europe, perhaps because natural corporate bond investors such as insurance companies typically keep their holdings until maturity. By calculating the widely used liquidity measures between the two bond markets in China and the one in the United States, table 5.3 shows an overall similarity of the corporate bond market liquidity across these two economies.

Given the unique two-market system in Chinse bond markets, it is interesting to compare the market liquidity between the interbank and exchange markets. Figure 5.5, taken from Chen et al. (2018), plots the number of trades and RMB volumes of corporate bonds in these two markets, respectively. Compared to the interbank market, there is

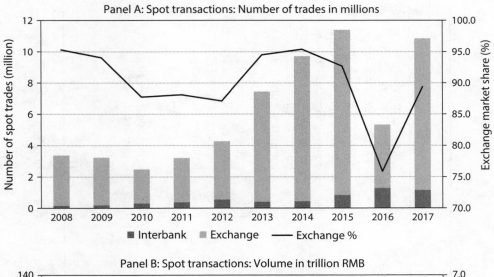

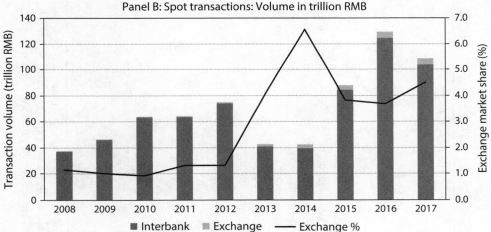

FIGURE 5.5. China's interbank and exchange market spot transactions. *Notes:* These figures plot China's interbank and exchange market spot transaction RMB volume 2008–2017. Panel A plots the number of trades for spot transactions in these two markets. Panel B plots spot transaction RMB volume of all bonds on the interbank and exchange markets. Data on the interbank-market transactions are from the China Foreign Exchange Trade System; data on the exchange-market transactions are from the Statistics Annuals of Shanghai exchange and the Shenzhen exchange.

significantly more trading activity in terms of number of trades in the exchange market (90% in terms of number of trades, shown in Panel A), but the volume weighted by trading size is minuscule (5% in terms of RMB volumes, shown in Panel B). This is consistent with table 5.3, and reflects the fact that retail investors speculate in the exchange market heavily, while in the interbank market various sophisticated financial institutions only trade when they need to. In summary, the interbank market is deeper but lacks immediacy, relative to the exchange market.

Table 5.4. Chinese Interbank and Exchange Market Comparison, 2019

	Interbank market		Exchange market
	CCDC	*SHCH*	*Exchange*
Depository institution	China Central Depository & Clearing Co. Ltd (CCDC)	Shanghai Clearing House (SHCH)	China Security Depository & Clearing Co. Ltd (CSDC), Shanghai Stock Exchange, Shenzhen Stock Exchange
Products	Treasury bonds, municipal bonds, policy bank bonds, central bank bills, enterprise bonds, medium-term notes, commercial bank bonds	Commercial papers, medium-term notes, NCDs, asset-backed securities, etc.	Treasury bonds, municipal bonds, policy bank bonds, enterprise bonds, exchange-traded corporate bonds, convertible bonds, etc.
Investors	Commercial banks, rural credit cooperatives, security firms, insurance companies, mutual funds, foreign institutions, etc.		Security firms, insurance companies, mutual funds, finance companies, individuals, enterprises, QFIIs (excluding commercial banks)
Trade type	Spot, repurchase, forward, swap, etc.		Spot, repurchase
Regulator	People's Bank of China (PBC)		China Securities Regulatory Commission
Outstanding balance (in trillion RMB)	63.63	22.54	10.94
Amount in %	66	23	11

Source: Market Overview: 2015 Chinese Bond Market Institutional Investor Manual, Guotai Junan Securities.

Notes: Outstanding balance, CCDC: http://www.chinabond.com.cn/Channel/19012917?BBND=2017&BBYF=12&sPageType=2#; SHCH: http://www.shclearing.com/sjtj/tjyb/; Exchange, CSDC: http://www.chinaclear.cn/zdjs/tjyb1/center_tjbg.shtml. All numbers are as of 12/31/2019.

2.4. Summary

Table 5.4 summarizes the comparison between the interbank and exchange markets, with a detailed list of various bond products traded there. Although largely segmented, these two markets overlap in several key bond products, mainly government bonds and enterprise bonds. Starting in 2015, the exchange market opened its access to enterprise bonds, which had previously been issued and traded only in the interbank market. Chen et al. (2018) provide an analysis on the market segmentation of dual-listed enterprise bonds, whose cross-market arbitrage is severely hindered by the transfer of depository, which is a time-consuming process.[6]

The market segmentation is also reflected in the distinct regulators for these two bond markets. The government agency that oversees the exchange market is CSRC, the powerful watchdog for the Chinese stock market. In contrast, the interbank market is overseen by the central bank PBC, which is the de facto gatekeeper of this market. Under the guidance of the PBC, the National Association of Financial Market Institutional Investors (NAFMII, 银行间交易者协会) is a self-regulatory organization established in October 2007 to formulate rules governing institutional participants in the interbank market. Regulatory competition among various government agencies is a recurrent theme commonly seen in the development of the Chinese financial system. For reference, table 5.5 provides a complete list of regulators specializing in each detailed bond product. One notable regulator besides the two mentioned above is the NDRC, which is in charge of the issuance of enterprise bonds; recently, it has played a greater role in regulating and approving local government debts, including municipal bonds (issued by local governments directly) and municipal corporate bonds (issued by LGFVs).

The coexistence of both an over-the-counter-based interbank market and an exchange-based bond market is an important feature that is unique to Chinese bond markets. For historical reasons, these two markets have been developed in a relatively independent fashion. Despite the recent effort made by the NDRC to integrate these two markets, which gives rise to dual-listed enterprise bonds (Chen et al., 2018), these two bond markets' coexistence is expected to last for quite a long time in China.

3. BRIEF HISTORY OF CHINESE BOND MARKETS

This section offers a brief account of how the bond market in China has evolved into what it looks like now. The thread that connects all the milestone events in its development is the segmented market system described in section 2.1: the exchange market and the interbank market.

3.1. Physical Bond Counter Market

The development of Chinese bond markets in the modern era started from the resumption of treasury bond issuance by the Ministry of Finance in 1981.[7] Besides the government, a few enterprises as well as financial institutions also conducted debt financing from either their own employees or outside investors. These nonbank-loan debt instruments became legal "enterprise bonds" after the release of "Regulatory Guidelines of Enterprise Bonds" by the State Council in 1987. The secondary market for bond trading followed, and in 1988, the Ministry of Finance carried out a pilot project for treasury bond circulation and transfer in 61 cities. Through this program, individual investors could

Market type		Regulator
Interbank bond market		PBC
Exchange bond market		CSRC

Bond Type		Regulator
Government bonds	Treasury bonds	PBC, MOF, CSRC
	Central Bank bills, Policy Bank bonds	PBC
Financial bonds	Special financial bonds	PBC
	commercial bank bonds, nonbank financial bonds	CBRC, PBC
	securities firm bonds, securities firms commercial papers	PBC, CSRC
Corporate bonds	Commercial papers, medium-term notes, private placement notes	NAFMII
	Asset-backed securities	CBRC, PBC
	Enterprise bonds	BC, CSRC
	International institution bonds	PBC, MOF, NDRC, CSRC
	Convertible bonds	PBC, CSRC
	Exchange-traded corporate bonds	CSRC
	Privately placed small and medium enterprise notes	Shanghai and Shenzhen Stock Exchange

Source: China's domestic bond market: "The Next Financing Engine," Goldman Sachs Global Market Research, 2015.

Notes: CBRC: China Banking Regulatory Commission (中国 银行业监督管理委员会); CSRC: China Securities Regulatory Commission (中国证券监督管理委员会); MOF: Ministry of Finance (中华人民共和国财政部); NAFMII: National Association of Financial Market Institutional Investors (中国银行间市场交易商协会); NDRC: National Development & Reform Commission (国家发展和改革委员会); PBC: People's Bank of China (中国人民银行).

buy and sell treasury bonds at bank counters as well as regional trading centers. Trading was done mostly in the form of physical bonds, hence it was called a "physical bond counter market" (Sun, 2015).

3.2. The Exchange Market Era

Many deficiencies emerged during the early 1990s in this physical bond counter market. Among them, the most critical was the lack of a uniform bond custody system. Fake treasury bonds were common, as it was extremely difficult for decentralized custody systems to verify the authenticity of the physical paper bonds.

The centralized exchange market, with electronic "book-entry" treasury bonds, was considered to be the solution to this problem. Established in December 1991, the Shanghai Stock Exchange provided uniform bond custody service across the country, and the government was explicit in supporting the development of this exchange bond market.[8] In August 1995, the government officially announced that stock exchanges, including both the Shanghai and the Shenzhen stock exchanges, were the sole legitimate bond market in China. This greatly improved the liquidity and functioning of the secondary market on these two exchanges, and an exchange-based bond market system took shape by the following year.

Before long, another dramatic turn pushed the interbank market onto the stage. It should be noted that the two exchanges in China were developed mainly for equity financing and stock trading. During the first half of 1997, the Chinese stock market experienced an unprecedented boom, witnessing the Shanghai A-share index rising from 1,000 in early 1997 to above 1,500 in May 1997. Secondary bond market activities, which involve commercial banks and individual investors, contributed to this speculation-driven stock market surge. Essentially, bond repo transactions in the exchange market allowed investors to use bonds as collateral to obtain debt financing from banks, which in turn was channeled toward the stock market to fuel its rally.

3.3. The Rise of the Interbank Market

Worried about the large amount of bank funds flowing into the overheated stock market, on June 1997 the PBC ordered all commercial banks to withdraw from exchanges and to switch to the newly established interbank market. The PBC also mandated that all commercial banks move their treasury bonds, central bank bills, and financial bonds issued by policy banks into the interbank market under the custody of CCDC.

This PBC-led event marked the beginning of the dramatic growth of the interbank bond market. Over the intervening 20 years, the "wholesale" interbank market, standing in contrast to the more-or-less "retail" exchange market, has become the dominating pillar of Chinese bond markets. The participants were initially restricted to only 16 head offices of commercial banks in 1997; by the end of 2000, a total of 693 financial institutions, including insurance companies, urban and rural commercial banks, and security firms, had become members of the interbank market.

In February 2014, facing the rapid rise of the "shadow banking business," the PBC allowed 16 large commercial banks to invest their own WMPs in the interbank market. In May 2016, direct access to the interbank market was further granted to all qualified institutional investors, including WMPs, investment funds, and trust companies. The total number of the interbank market members reached 7,027 by December 2019, and these financial institutions cover virtually the entirety of China's financial system nowadays.

3.4. Bond Markets and the Growth of the Chinese Economy

The rapid and steady development of the Chinese bond market offers great benefit for various economic agents in Chinese economy, for several reasons. First, the interbank market has become the primary place for the Ministry of Finance and government-backed entities like policy banks to issue bonds to finance their activities. Second, it helps the central bank, the PBC, to implement its open market operations and other monetary policies. For instance, in April 2003 the PBC conducted the first formal open market operation in the interbank market, by issuing central bank bills valued at 5 billion RMB with a maturity of six months. This topic will be taken up again in section 4.1.

But the Chinese bond market plays perhaps an equally important role by channeling household savings toward the real sector, which was critical for the Chinese economy to achieve its astonishing growth over the last three decades. Various forms of debt instruments have been developed in both markets. In the interbank market, commercial papers—a form of short-term, high-quality enterprise bonds with a typical maturity of less than one year—emerged in May 2005; medium-term notes with a typical maturity of five years saw their debut in April 2008. As far as instruments besides enterprise bonds are concerned, the first asset-backed securities were issued in the interbank market in December 2005; the first municipal bonds were issued by local governments via the Ministry of Finance in April 2009. On the exchange market, listed companies first issued exchange-traded corporate bonds in 2007, and in 2015 the CSRC expanded the eligible list of corporate bond issuers to all incorporated companies (as opposed to only listed ones). All these reform activities gave a significant boost to the development of the corporate bonds market throughout China.

4. ISSUES AND RECENT TRENDS OF CHINESE BOND MARKETS

This section will first point out that a full market mechanism has yet to be achieved by Chinese bond markets. It will then highlight the predominance of commercial banks in China's bond markets; that also explains why the Chinese bond markets are deeply intertwined with the shadow banking system in the country. Finally, it will discuss the recent trend since late 2017 in authorities' hardline stance on deleveraging and restraining shadow banking activities, together with opening up Chinese onshore bond markets to international investors.

4.1. Interest Rate Determination and Monetary Policy Transmission

The risk-free benchmark interest rates and the associated term structure, which are implied by the prices of all government bonds with various maturities, "anchor" the pricing of all financial assets in modern financial markets. Like in other modern financial markets such as in the United States, interest rates of newly issued Chinese government bonds are determined via competitive bidding of participating financial institutions (mainly commercial banks and securities firms) in the primary market; those institutions then can trade among each other in the secondary market. Today, it is fair to say that market mechanisms are fully at work in Chinese Treasury auctioning markets after more than two decades of successful and continuous development.

Figure 5.6 plots the yields for treasury bonds and CDB bonds for 1-year and 10-year maturities, respectively. These four series of interest rates have moved mostly in parallel and varied between 1.5% and 6% since 2012, with slightly lower yields for treasury bonds (than CDB bonds) because of their tax advantage. Overall, in the past half-decade, the term structure of interest rates in China has been upward-sloping; steadily falling interest rates over the period of 2013–2016 made this episode the "bull market" for Chinese bond traders.

Despite the rapid growth in the size of the bond market, though, it is well recognized among policymakers and practitioners alike that Chinese bond markets are still underdeveloped in many key dimensions. Compared to the deep and liquid market for U.S. Treasuries, the market for Chinese government bonds still lacks sufficient liquidity, and is often blamed for hindering efficient price discovery. The latter role is key to an effective PBC-led monetary policy that might better stabilize the Chinese economy.

Several institutional reasons may be suggested for the steady but somewhat slow development of the Chinese government bond market toward a full market mechanism. A well-functioning primary and secondary market for risk-free rate determination is an integral part of interest rate liberalization, which started in the late 1980s and saw its formal completion when the PBC finally lifted the banks' deposit rate cap and rolled out the deposit insur-

FIGURE 5.6. Treasury and CDB yield curve in different maturities. *Source:* Wind database bond yield analysis.

ance scheme in 2015. Second, the "12th five-year plan" in 2011 made it clear that future monetary policies should put more emphasis on market-driven, price-targeted tools (e.g., repos with the PBC, and various Standing Lending Facilities), although quantity-targeted tools (e.g., M2 growth, total bank credit) and "guidance rates" frequently published by the PBC still remain the most effective measures taken by Chinese monetary authorities. Third, from a market design perspective, an entry barrier exists for the primary market, which limits participation in the auctioning of government bonds to qualified financial institutions. Most market-makers, who serve the secondary market in the interbank market, are commercial banks with an unpleasantly high degree of homogeneity in trading strategies and funding sources. Finally, the above-mentioned segmentation between the interbank and exchange markets, with its potential violation of the "law of one price," hurts price discovery as well as the liquidity of the Chinese government bond market itself.

4.2. The Role of Banks and Shadow Banking

Another distinct feature that seems to be inconsistent with the fast development of the Chinese bond market is that the participants remain highly concentrated in one particular type of financial institution: commercial banks. As explained in section 3.3, the Chinese interbank bond market has been closely intertwined with the banking system ever since the establishment of the bond market in 1997, when commercial banks were mandated by the PBC to be the first participants of bond issuance and trading.

It is crucial to recognize that official statistics continue to significantly underestimate the dominance of commercial banks in the Chinese bond market. It is well known among practitioners and regulators that in China, commercial banks participate in the bond market via two channels: the direct on-balance-sheet channel, through which each bank's so-called financial market division buys and sells bonds (and engages in even arbitrage trades) in the interbank market; and the indirect off-balance-sheet channel, where each bank's asset management division sets up some wealth management plans (just like special purpose vehicles in the U.S. market) financed by WMPs to invest in both interbank and exchange markets. The dominating share of commercial banks (57%) of the interbank bond market shown in figure 5.2 only counts the first channel.

This perspective suggests that in China's financial system, corporate bonds, to a significant extent, can be considered to be another form of disguised bank financing. Facilitated by increasingly sophisticated shadow banking activities, the transfer of on-balance-sheet loans (inside the traditional banking system) to off-balance-sheet assets outside (say, corporate bonds) is commonly observed, especially when banks have faced tightened regulation on the overheated real estate sector and LGFV financing. This is why practitioners often argue that, unlike in other developed countries, in China shadow banking is literally just the "shadow" of commercial banks.

Consider the example of WMPs, which are the biggest component of shadow banking in China and the most important vehicle to connect back to the banking system. Every year, starting in 2014, the China Banking Wealth Management Registration System has released its annual report on WMPs, which gives an official account on the role they play in the contemporary Chinese financial system. According to these reports, a majority of WMPs are invested in the bond market, with the percentage estimated to have been 44% in 2016 and 42% in 2017.

In fact, many industry reports corroborate this view. Ehlers et al. (2018) estimate that 38% of the net issuance of all bonds was funded via bank-issued WMPs in 2014; the funding percentages were 35% and 31% in 2015 and 2016, respectively. In a more recent study, Lei et al. (2018) find that 7 trillion out of 18 trillion outstanding corporate bonds' balances are funded by WMPs; and as explained in note 8 in this chapter, these numbers are likely to be biased downward. Overall, evidence suggests that the bond market is an integrated part of bank-dominated shadow banking in China.

Chen et al. (2018) argue that China's shadow banking problem is connected to its local government debt problem, which is further rooted in the 4 trillion stimulus rolled out in 2009. They document that within three to five years after the 2009 stimulus plan, LGFVs needed to refinance their maturing bank loans or fund ongoing infrastructure projects. However, soon after the mid-2010s, indebted LGFVs were squeezed by tightening credit standards from traditional banks. As a result, these LGFVs then started issuing municipal corporate bonds (MCBs, as explained in section 3.3) in the interbank market. The majority of these MCBs were bought by WMPs, which were sold and implicitly guaranteed by commercial banks.[9]

There is another important channel through which commercial banks facilitate industrial firms to issue bonds in the interbank market and hence become exposed to default risk. In China, commercial banks often engage in guarantee provisions on corporate bonds, though it is hard to estimate the severity of this risk exposure.

To illustrate this point, consider the interesting case of the scandal of Cosun bonds (侨兴债事件), which involves financial innovations, shadow banking, and likely some malfunctioning of the commercial banking system itself. In December 2016, the Cosun Group, a privately owned telecommunication company in Guangdong, defaulted on a series of its private placement notes issued two years earlier.[10] Shocked by the default news, retail investors went to Zheshang Insurance, the insurance company that had provided insurance on this credit event. But Zheshang immediately made a public announcement stating that China Guangfa Bank, one of the earliest-incorporated joint-stock commercial banks, had promised some guarantee provision to repay it at the bond issuance but later reneged on its promise. It turned out the Huizhou branch of China Guangfa Bank provided a counterfeit letter of guarantee for this bond issuance;[11] that guarantee helped Cosun to issue these bonds, only to roll over Cosun's maturing loans extended by the Huizhou branch itself several years ago.

4.3. Regulatory Tightening Starting in 2017

The Chinese government is well aware of these so-called shadow-of-bank activities that essentially tie the commercial banking sector to financial products offered in the interbank market. The dramatic regulatory change started in 2017 is still expected to reshape the Chinese financial market in a profound way, bringing a sea change in the interbank market. Under this new framework, WMPs will be put under the scrutiny of the PBC for the first time and factored into its calculations on prudence, capital adequacy, and loan growth guidelines. Another equally important regulatory tightening concerns the rules of new asset management plans, first proposed in November 2017 and released in April 2018 (though still yet to be finalized). The new rules aim to prohibit implicit guarantees and multilayer structures, the two important ingredients that had contributed to excessively high leverage in China's shadow banking system over the past decade.

Not surprisingly, in 2017, in response to policy tightening, the Chinese bond market experienced a dramatic downward adjustment. The annual increment of the value of outstanding bonds, adding together the interbank and the exchange markets, experienced about a 35% drop, decreasing from 16 trillion RMB in 2016 to 10 trillion RMB the following year. This topic will be addressed again in section 6.2, together with the recent insurgence of corporate default in the Chinese bond market.

Looking forward, the authors believe that Beijing's recent efforts in streamlining and tightening regulations in the ever-complicated Chinese financial market are well justified. Although it is inevitably painful for market participants in the short run, a transparent regulatory environment is tremendously important for building a healthy and sophisticated bond market in a modern financial system in which market participants fully understand the consequences of their own decisions, including issuance, underwriting, trading, and investment.

4.4. Internalization of the Chinese Bond Market

Despite the fact that the Chinese bond market has developed to be the third largest in the world, foreign participation in it is minuscule. At the end of 2019, the total foreign holdings of Chinese bonds reached 3.2 trillion RMB, or approximately only 3.3% of bond market capitalization.[12]

Historically, to gain access to Chinese bond markets, offshore investors were required to go through several quota-based foreign investment programs. One of them is the Qualified Foreign Institutional Investor (QFII, 合格境外机构投资者) program, which was launched in 2002 and regulated by the State Administration of Foreign Exchange (SAFE, 国家外汇管理局, a powerful arm of the PBC), which monitors the remittance and repatriation of funds across the border. Initially QFIIs could only invest in the exchange bond market; since March 2013, they have been allowed to gain access to the much bigger interbank market.

Another closed related program is the Renminbi Qualified Foreign Institutional Investor (RQFII, 人民币合格境外机构投资者) program. This program allows domestic financial institutions to establish RMB denominated funds in Hong Kong, attracting offshore RMB that are in the hands of oversea investors back to the onshore bond market. At the end of 2019, the total quota combining QFII and RQFII was about 1.47 trillion RMB, though the actual usage was just 0.09 trillion RMB (of which about 10% was invested in bonds while the rest was in equities).[13]

As a milestone effort in the internalization of the RMB, Beijing launched the PBC bond direct-access program in 2010. Based on a case-by-case approval system, this program attracted offshore institutional investors (e.g., foreign central banks and offshore RMB clearing banks) to the Chinese interbank bond market. In July 2015, the PBC further eased regulation by allowing institutions with long-term investment mandates—such as foreign central banks and sovereign wealth funds—to participate in the interbank market without quota limits. More important, these qualified institutions can follow a registration system, rather than a preapproval system, to participate in the interbank market. In February 2016, similar access was granted to a much wider range of institutional investors, including commercial lenders, insurance companies, securities firms, and asset managers (excluding short-term or "speculative" investors). One year later, in February 2017, the SAFE was giving overseas investors access to its foreign-exchange derivatives market to allow hedging of bond positions, a crucial step in attracting foreign inflows.

In a separate and mostly independent effort, motivated by the success of Stock Connect, which started in November 2014, China launched Bond Connect (债券通) in July 2017. Like Stock Connect, Bond Connect is a mutual market access scheme that enables investors from mainland China and overseas to trade in each other's bond markets, through connections between the related mainland and Hong Kong financial infrastructure institutions. Thanks to Hong Kong's being a leading world-class financial center, foreign investors offered a warm welcome to Bond Connect: The rise of foreign ownership of mainland bonds in July and August 2017 was almost double the pace of the prior year.

No doubt the sophistication and development of mainland bond markets are crucial for advancing RMB internalization, one of the policy goals that has been a top priority for the Chinese government. Looking forward, given Beijing's strong intention to push forward the liberalization of the mainland bond market, a more and more relaxed regulatory environment can be expected in which foreign investors can participate. Likewise, today overseas investors are flocking to China's mainland bond market for its strong value and potentially tremendous opportunity. This process is likely to be expedited by the decision of Bloomberg L.P., which announced that, starting in April 2019, it will add over 300 of China's government bonds to the Bloomberg Barclay's Global Aggregate Bond Index. Of course, this progress might be interrupted by concerns about capital flight in the wake of a potentially significant slowdown of the Chinese economy.

5. BOND RATINGS AND RATING AGENCIES

A key characteristic of bonds is their credit risk as reflected in ratings. Rating agencies are vital in any financial market. While rating symbols used in China closely follow global standards, the rating scale itself differs. Currently, China has only three de facto rating categories. This section illustrates and discusses the skewed rating distribution. Reasons for this observation include low default rates, an ongoing trend of more upgrades than downgrades, implicit guarantees, regulatory requirements, and fierce competition among the domestic rating agencies, which differ little in their ratings assessments. The previous section introduced three different bond types. As ratings for government bonds are always AAA rated, this section focuses on "credit bonds," including financial and corporate bonds.[14]

5.1. China's Credit Rating Scale

China's domestic rating scale includes nine long-term grades (AAA, AA, A, BBB, BB, B, CCC, CC, and C) and six short-term grades (A-1, A-2, A-3, B, C, and D) as officially set by the PBC. This is in line with international standards as set by the three globally dominant U.S.-based rating agencies, Moody's, Standard & Poor's, and Fitch. However, two main differences may be observed in the rating scale used by Chinese versus global rating agencies. First, the definition of investment grade differs. In China, AA is generally seen as the lowest investment-grade level, while this is BBB in global ratings. Despite the higher threshold, the issuance of noninvestment grade bonds is much scarcer in China. Second, China's domestic rating scale includes an additional, informal rating grade: the "AAA+" or "super AAA" category provided by investors. These AAA+ issuers keep an official and legally relevant rating of AAA provided by rating agencies. However, the AAA+ issuers enjoy a higher weighting in valuation indices, reflecting lower default probability assigned by investors that expect these corporates bonds to essentially have a credit risk similar to government bonds. While there is no official list of AAA+ issuers, there were at least 10 central government–owned issuers since 2017 in this category (see table 5.6); their corresponding international ratings as per end of 2019 are also given for comparison.

5.2. Distribution of Credit Ratings

The distribution of the Chinese ratings is widely known to be skewed to the upside (Kennedy, 2008, Poon and Chan, 2008, Standard Chartered, 2017; and more recently, Deng and Qiao, 2019). Despite the large market size (about 2,000 corporate issuers) by global standards, over 97% of the outstanding amount of nonfinancial corporate bonds are rated in only three categories (figure 5.7, Panel A).[15] By the end of 2019, 58% of the corporate bonds outstanding in China enjoyed an AAA rating, versus about 1% in the U.S. corporate bond market; 21% were AA+, another 17% were AA rated, and only 2% were rated as AA– and below and therefore were noninvestment grade; 1% of the outstanding amount of corporate bonds are not rated. For financial bonds, the shares are AAA 88%, AA+ 9%, AA 2.5%, and AA– and below are 0.4% of the outstanding amount of corporate bonds respectively, reflecting the explicit government guarantees. The high share of AAA-rated corporate bonds in value terms is partly explained by large amounts of bond issuance of just a few issuers who are mostly linked to government. Of the top 10 issuers (see table 5.7), all of them are either Central or Local SOEs. However, clustering in only three categories also holds in terms of the number of issuers. Of the Chinese nonfinancial corporate issuers, 17% hold an AAA rating, 22% an AA+ rating, and 44% an AA. About 5% of corporate bonds are private placement where credit ratings are not mandatory. Only 11% hold a noninvestment grade rating of AA– and below (figure 5.7, Panel B). Consequently, China currently has essentially no high-yield or speculative-grade bond market.

The tilted distribution is the source of some disagreement. On the one hand, the low credit risk differentiation is generally seen as a hindrance to the development of the

Table 5.6. China's Super-AAA ("AAA+") Issuers

"AAA+" issuers	Chinese full name	International issuer rating (S&P/ Moody's/Fitch)	Outstanding (in billion RMB)
China Railway Corp	中国国家铁路集团有限公司	NR	1,610.50
China National Petroleum Corp	中国石油天然气集团有限公司	A+/A1/AA	204.96
China Petrochemical Group	中国石油化工股份有限公司	A+/A1	20.00
China National Offshore Oil Corp	中国海洋石油集团有限公司	A+/A1	–
China Telecom Corp	中国电信股份有限公司	NR	25.00
China Unicom Corp	中国联合网络通信有限公司	NR	13.00
China Mobile Group	中国移动通信集团有限公司	A+/A1	–
State Grid	国家电网有限公司	A+/A1/A+	227.00
China Southern Power Grid	中国南方电网有限责任公司	A+/A1/A+	136.00
China Three Gorges Corp	中国长江三峡集团有限公司	A/A1/A+	99.00

Source: Outstanding numbers are from Wind Database Credit Bond Research. International Issuer Ratings are from S&P, Moody's, and Fitch databases, respectively.
Notes: While there is no official list of AAA+ issuers, there were at least 10 central government-owned issuers since 2017 in this category. Their international ratings as per end of 2019 are also given for comparison. S&P: https://www.standardandpoors.com/en_US/web/guest/home; Moody's: https://www.moodys.com/; Fitch: https://www.fitchratings.com/site/home. Included are all bond types along with corporate bonds. This treatment only significantly affects China Railway Corp, because some bonds it issues are categorized as "bonds with government support (政府支持机构债)," which fall under the government bond category based on authors' definition. Outstanding numbers are as of 12/31/2019.

bond market. For domestic investors, the absence of more-granular credit risk opportunities and the lack of a speculative, high-yield market might lower the attractiveness of the bond market, particularly relative to the stock market. For international investors, the low guidance offered by the current rating distribution is often given as one reason why they currently take up only a small part of the investor base in the Chinese bond market, despite a steady loosening of investment restrictions (section 4.4). On the other hand, implicit guarantees entailed in the credit assessments of a good part of corporate issuers with links to government may partly justify a higher rating.[16]

5.3. Low Default Rate, Implicit Guarantees, and Rating Migration

5.3.1. Low Default Rate

One main reason for the high credit ratings is the very short and limited history of defaults in China. The first onshore public bond default occurred only in 2014. The amount that defaulted in the Chinese bond market was only 1.34 billion RMB in 2014,

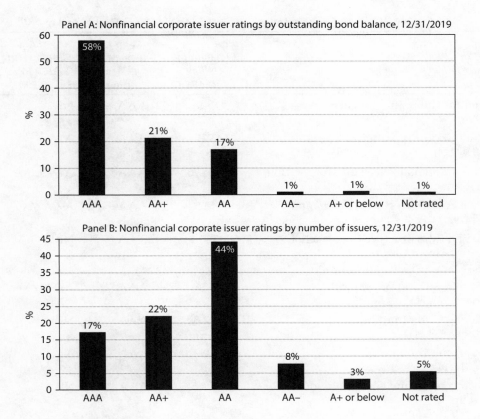

FIGURE 5.7. Rating distribution by outstanding bond balance and number of issuers, 2019. *Source:* Wind database. *Notes:* The authors sum up the outstanding bond amounts and count the number of issuers for each rating class using all corporate bonds available on 12/31/2019 (see table 5.1 for authors' definition of corporate bond categories). Excluded are all asset-backed securities (ABS, 资产支持证券) in the corporate bond category. Since the "issuer" performs an "underwriter" role to these ABS securities, the issuer ratings do not represent the creditworthiness of the security.

reached 34.7 billion RMB in 2017. The amount of defaults jumped to a new high of 145 billion RMB in 2019 (figure 5.8, Panel A, discussed in section 6.1). This surge in corporate defaults was triggered by challenging refinancing conditions and increasing redemptions (mentioned in section 4.3) caused by tightened regulation starting at the end of 2017. However, from the first default in 2014 until the end of 2019, these defaults represented only 0.3% of the overall outstanding amount, suggesting a rather small default probability relative to global counterparts. See more details on corporate bond defaults in section 6.

5.3.2. Rating Migration
As the number and amount of defaults start to increase, though at quite low levels, one might expect that this trend slowly but steadily would soften the skewness of the ratings distribution. However, the opposite has been the case so far. From the first default in 2014 until 2019, there were about 12 times more upgrades than downgrades (table 5.8).

Table 5.7. Top 10 Corporate Issuers in China Onshore Bond Market

Issuer	Outstanding (billion RMB)	Domestic issuer rating	International issuer rating (S&P, Moody's, Fitch)
Central Huijin Investment (中央汇金投资)	307	AAA	NR
State Grid Corporation of China (国家电网)	227	AAA	A1/A+
China National Petroleum Corporation (中石油)	204.96	AAA	A+/A1/AA
State Power Investment Corporation (国家电力投资公司)	181.94	AAA	A–/A2/A
Tianjin Infrastructure Construction & Investment Group (天津城市基础设施建设投资集团)	160.4	AAA	NR
China Southern Power Grid (中国南方电网)	136	AAA	A+/A1/A+
Datong Coal Mine Group (大同煤矿集团)	122.82	AAA	NR
Shougang Group (首钢集团)	106.5	AAA	A–
Shaanxi Coal and Chemical Industry Group (陕西煤业化工)	104.5	AAA	NR
China Three Gorges Corp (中国长江三峡)	99	AAA	A/A1/A+

Source: Outstanding numbers and domestic ratings are from Wind bond database. International issuer ratings are from S&P, Moody's, and Fitch databases, respectively.
Notes: S&P: https://www.standardandpoors.com/en_US/web/guest/home; Moody's: https://www.moodys.com/; Fitch: https://www.fitchratings.com/site/home. Outstanding numbers are as of 12/31/2019.

Of the 1,863 bond issuers, 887 received rating upgrades, only 71 were downgraded, and the vast majority of 905 remained at the same rating level over those four years until the end of 2019. The biggest rating migration occurred for the AA-rated bonds where over 81% were upgraded and only 4.6% were downgraded. Of the large share of AAA-rated bonds, only 2.4% were downgraded. The mismatch between increased defaults and an ongoing trend of an upward bias in rating changes lets many commentators doubt whether the upgrades are backed by improvement in credit fundamentals. Alternatively, they suggest that this phenomenon is related to the fierce competition among the many Chinese rating agencies that we cover in section 5.5.

Rating migrations are also discussed in the context of their timing, which is sometimes seen as too late or too hesitant, despite signs of weakening cash flow and earnings. As illustrated by the examples given in section 6, rating changes in the cases of bonds that later eventually defaulted often occur alongside announcements and media

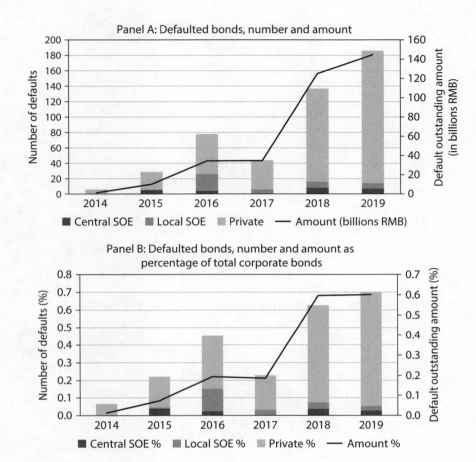

FIGURE 5.8. Number and amount of defaults by year. *Source:* Wind database credit bond research (Defaulted Bond Summary Table and Issuers First Default Table). *Notes:* The authors report the number and the amount of defaulted bonds, both in amounts (Panel A) and percentage (Panel B, relative to all corporate bonds). They count the principal value of defaulted bonds only (excluding interests). They keep only one record for duplicate events caused by defaulted dual-listed bonds, except Jiangquan and Hongchang Gas (for these two issuers, the two records on the same date are separate default events: one for principal, the other for interest). Private firms include all firms in the sample that are *not* SOEs. All numbers are as of the end of each year.

reports of financial distress. This somewhat limits the use of ratings as an early warning system for investors.

5.3.3. Implicit Guarantees

The low default rate and trends in rating migration are often related to implicit guarantees. While it is difficult to quantify the amount of defaults that are prevented by government support, in some cases ratings are obviously adjusted because of an expected, although not legally binding, moral commitment of the Chinese government. As an example we refer to the bonds issued by the four asset management companies (AMCs, 资产管理公司) that were established in 1999 to purchase a total of 2.4 trillion RMB in

Table 5.8. Upgrades Dwarf Downgrades in China's Onshore Bond Market

		Ratings as of 12/31/2019					# of Issuers	Upgrades (%)	Downgrades (%)	Maintain (%)
		AAA	AA+	AA	AA−	A+ or below				
Ratings as of 1/1/2014	AAA	249	4	0	1	1	255		2.35	97.65
	AA+	199	153	8	1	6	367	54.22	4.09	41.69
	AA	57	362	453	15	22	909	46.09	4.07	49.83
	AA−	6	39	184	42	13	284	80.63	4.58	14.79
	A+ or below	0	9	22	9	8	48	83.33		16.67
		511	567	667	68	50	1863			

Source: Wind database.

Notes: This rating migration matrix consists only of issuers with ratings on 1/1/2014 and 12/31/2019, excluding not-rated issuers. More specifically, the authors begin with a full list of corporate bonds available on 12/31/2019 with their respective issuer ratings. Each issuer's ratings are matched on 1/1/2014 and 12/31/2019. With the two ratings for each issuer, they are then assigned to their corresponding cells in the rating migration matrix.

nonperforming loans from commercial banks. The rating agencies classified the AMC bonds not as speculative, but as part of the highly rated Chinese sovereign debt, expecting the Ministry of Finance to intervene in case of default. Although implicit guarantees are not a uniquely Chinese feature, as the case of Fannie Mae and Freddie Mac in the United States illustrates, the degree of implicit guarantees is likely more severe in China as a result of more widespread or closer links of corporations to the government.

5.4. Regulatory Framework

The regulatory framework is another important factor that supports clustering in only the three highest rating classes.

5.4.1. Rating Requirements

For corporate bonds to be qualified for public issuance, minimum ratings are mandatory, but in most cases only one rating is required. This makes it often the main motivation for issuers to buy a rating and invites rating-shopping. The specific regulatory requirements vary with the bond type and are set by the respective regulator. For instance, in the interbank market, NAFMII asks for commercial paper and medium-term note issuers to be rated AA- or above.[17] For exchange-traded corporate bonds that are issued to retail and qualified investors, they generally need an AAA rating, except for issuers in the property sector where a rating of AA or above is sufficient. However, the CSRC has removed the rating requirements for corporate bonds that are issued only to qualified investors. Also, the NDRC has its own rating requirement for enterprise bonds. Guarantees are only required for LGFVs with debt-to-assets ratios of 65% or above. No guarantee is needed in the cases of an AAA-rated issuer of an enterprise bond with ratios below 85% or an AA+-rated enterprise bond issuer with ratios below 80%.

5.4.2. Repo Eligibility and Haircuts

The possibility to use a bond as collateral in a repo transaction, which is essentially collateralized borrowing, is an additional value to bondholders. The greater the "haircuts," the lower the capacity of collateralized borrowing. Bond issuers may therefore be hesitant to issue bonds that lack this property. The repo eligibility of corporate bonds is limited, as they are generally only accepted by nonbank financial institutions while banks accept only government bonds. Further, money market funds, as key players in the liquidity provision, are allowed to accept only bonds rated AA+ or higher as repo collateral.

The repo eligibility on the exchange market is even more restricted owing to its centralized nature. In this market, investors conduct repo transactions against the CSDC, which serves as the Centralized Counter-Party (CCP, 中央对手方) and sets bond-specific haircuts. Chen et al. (2018) document that haircuts are almost entirely determined by bond ratings, and explore the December 2014 policy shock when the CSDC suspended the repo eligibility for enterprise bonds with ratings below AAA. Later in 2017, the CSDC tightened the required minimum rating from AA to AAA for exchange-traded corporate bonds.

Overall, the regulatory framework offers clear incentives to issue ratings only in the very high-rated categories. It seems unlikely for bond issuances to receive a broader range of credit categories without at least some further loosening of the regulatory restrictions in that respect.

Table 5.9. China's Domestic Credit Rating Agencies

Agency	Market Share				NAFMII	CSRC	NDRC	CIRC
	Bond outstanding (in billion RMB)	Number of issuers	Bond outstanding (%)	Number of issuers (%)				
China Chengxin Securities Rating (中诚信证券)	2755.14	395	36.45	26.42		x		x
China Chenxin International Rating (中诚信国际)	12325.07	906			x		x	x
China United Rating (联合信用)	1481.90	336	26.86	19.59		x	x	x
China Lianhe Rating (联合资信)	9628.47	629			x		x	x
Dagong Global Credit Rating (大公国际)	2685.31	267	6.49	5.42	x	x	x	x
Shanghai Brilliance Credit Rating (上海新世纪)	4726.26	600	11.43	12.18	x	x	x	x
Pengyuan Credit rating (鹏元资信)	694.40	576	1.68	11.70		x	x	x
Golden Credit Rating (东方金诚)	2502.04	472	6.05	9.58	x	x	x	x
China Bond Rating Corporation (中债资信)	4569.07	744	11.05	15.11	x		x	x
Total	41367.65	4925	100.00	100.00				

Source: Wind Database Credit Bond Research.
Note: All numbers are as of 12/31/2019.

5.5. Rating Agencies

The specific structure of the rating agency industry in China is a further reason for the upward-skewed ratings in China. After a brief historical review, we discuss the increasing diversification by nationality, the incentive model of rating agencies, and possible impacts on the rating distribution.

5.5.1. A Brief Historical Review and Licensing

An early form of rating agencies was already established in 1987 when the State Council issued "Regulatory Guidelines of Enterprise Bonds," which introduced ratings in their guidance of bond issuance. At first, ratings were offered by credit rating departments in provincial branches of the PBC. Later several independent rating agencies were launched, in some cases as spin-offs of the previous rating departments. The PBC regulations on the types of bonds and loans requiring a rating became mandatory from 1993 onward, further fueling the offering of rating services. To ensure quality and consistency in the rating agency industry, since 1997 the PBC has demanded that corporate bonds must have at least one rating from a PBC-approved agency. It also has limited the number of qualified rating agencies to nine. In 2006, the CSRC followed with a formalized licensing process for credit rating agencies covering bonds regulated by the CSRC. Today, each of the three regulators covering corporate bonds (NAFMII, NDRC, CSRC) issues separate lists of qualified agencies for rating bonds under their respective program. Consequently, a rating agency usually needs to get approval from more than one regulator, depending on which types of bonds they are providing rating services for (table 5.9).[18] Recognizing the fragmented accreditation process for rating agencies, in 2014 the State Council started to issue notes that simplify and at least partially deregulate the accreditation of domestic agencies.

5.5.2. Nine Approved Rating Agencies

The international rating agency industry is famously dominated by three U.S.-based agencies: Moody's, Standard & Poor's (S&P), and Fitch. About 95% of all globally outstanding ratings are currently provided by these so-called Big Three.[19] China has a relatively large number with nine recognized domestic credit rating agencies (table 5.9 provides an overview on market share and accreditation). However, six agencies (or four, counting the sub-institutes as one) dominate with a market share of 81% of the outstanding bond issuance in China: Chengxin (Chengxin Securities Rating and Chengxin International Rating), Lianhe (China United Rating and China Lianhe Rating), Dagong Global Credit Rating, and Shanghai Brilliance Investor Service. Both Chengxin and Lianhe have a domestic agency licensed by the CSRC to offer ratings in the exchange market, and also have a separate joint venture, licensed by the PBC, with a minority ownership of an international rating agency to offer ratings in the interbank market. The fully domestically owned Chengxin Securities Rating, China United Rating, and Dagong were founded in 1992, 2002, and 1994, respectively. Chengxin International Rating was established in 2006, and 49% of its shares are owned by Moody's; Lianhe Rating was established in 2007, and 49% of its shares are owned by Fitch. S&P has had a partnership with Shanghai Brilliance Investor Service since 2008. It is worth emphasizing that all the joint-ventured rating agencies mentioned above operate completely separately from their corresponding international global rating agency, which takes no active role in the joint ventures.

Throughout this time, the global rating agencies could have only minority stakes in joint-venture operations. Further, they were not accredited to issue "national ratings," or ratings of Chinese firms issuing bonds onshore. Instead, the global agencies assign "international ratings" for Chinese firms issuing bonds offshore. In July 2017, the PBC announced liberalization steps on both accounts. Global rating agencies will be allowed to register for rating services in the China interbank bond market and to own a majority stake in an accredited agency, provided that the agency meets some criteria in terms of market experience and corporate governance.

Aside from the five major agencies (China Chengxin Securities Rating, China Chenxin International Rating, China United Rating, China Lianhe Rating and Dagong Global Credit Rating) mentioned above, there are four domestically owned accredited agencies with a relatively small market share. Shanghai-based Shanghai Brilliance was founded in 1992, Pengyuan Credit Rating based in Shenzhen in 1993, Golden Credit Rating International based in Beijing in 2005 (often labeled as "Orient" in the market), and China Bond Rating Corporation in Beijing in 2010. China Bond Rating Corporation is the only agency operating under an investor-pays model, a topic that is covered in the next section.

5.5.3. Little Differentiation of Rating Agencies

While, in the early days of rating agencies in China, a standardized procedure was found missing, today the rating industry is seen as too homogenous. Rating methodologies, including the specific factors and weights that are used to determine default probabilities, may only differ slightly. Also, rating decisions across domestic agencies offer little variation and are also similar in timing. None of the domestic agencies has gained a clear advantage in reputation or market leadership. Consequently, the rating industry in China is highly competitive, with similar fee structures. For agencies, the incentive to proactively downgrade an issuer is low. The problem worsens as bond issuers often aim for just one rating in order to fulfill regulatory requirements. This is obviously only the case under the issuer-pays model, which is the international standard and the model for eight of the nine officially approved Chinese agencies. Recognizing the challenging incentive structure, in 2010 the NAFMII installed an agency China Bond Rating Corporation (CBR, 中债资信) that operates under the investor-pays model. On average, the CBR offers a stricter rating scale, with ratings two to three notches below those given by the issuer-pays model.

Little difference is noticeable in rating assignments between the joint ventures and the fully domestically owned agencies. It remains to be seen to what extent the recently allowed entrance of foreign rating agencies will change the upward bias in ratings. Comparing ratings from domestic versus global agencies, Jiang and Packer (2017) find the latter to be six to seven notches lower on average. Furthermore, they find differences in underlying drivers. Domestic agencies weigh size more positively in the risk assessment, while global agencies weigh profitability and state ownership more positively and leverage more negatively. These findings can only serve as an indication, since currently the sample of bonds rated by both domestic and global agencies is limited. Moreover, as long as a single domestic rating fulfills the regulatory requirements, the appetite of domestic issuers to buy an additional global rating remains unclear. This status quo might change, however, once Chinese issuers see value in broadening their investor base and tapping the large but still underutilized pool of foreign investors, particularly institutional ones.

5.6. Outlook

The large and increasing Chinese bond market contrasts with its low diversification in credit risk as measured by ratings. This chapter has mentioned a series of contributing factors. Therefore, a change might not be imminent for the ratings provided by the approved agencies covered here, though shortcomings of the current narrow and upward-skewed rating distribution are obvious. Consequently, there is a strong appetite for alternative rating procedures, especially due to rising interest from overseas investors. A straightforward approach already used by some market participants is to complement the third-party rating agencies with market-implied credit ratings, which are determined by comparing the bond's secondary market value against valuation indices. Along these lines, in October 2017, the CCDC announced a plan to offer market-based ratings, using available information through their oligopolistic custodian and clearing services. We can expect more market-driven initiatives of this kind.

6. CREDIT SPREADS AND DEFAULTS IN THE CHINESE BOND MARKET

Ever since early 2014, China has witnessed a wave of credit events, which quickly peaked in 2016, mainly driven by the tightened liquidity and a deepening financial deleveraging campaign. Despite the comparatively tiny amount of defaulted bonds relative to the entire market, the jitters aroused by the default shocks have expanded far beyond the bond market—even to the entire Chinese financial system and the macro economy. Investors' expectations of an implicit government guarantee gradually broke down; financial institutions ceased taking it for granted that corporate bonds are absolutely safe and began to put more and more emphasis on the credit risks underneath the firms.

6.1. Bond Defaults in China: A Summary

The unprecedented bond default event of "11 Chaori Bond" that occurred on March 5, 2014, marked the elimination of an implicit government guarantee, thus opening a new era of the Chinese bond market. The issuer, Shanghai Chaori Technologies Inc., failed to pay its interests in full in the exchange market, constituting the first-ever default in Chinse bond markets. Section 6.3 reviews several landmark default cases in the Chinese bond market, and discusses recent progress in bankruptcy rulings in the country.

As of December 31, 2019, there have been 419 defaulted bonds, involving 154 issuers in total. Panel B of figure 5.8 plots the distribution of these default events since 2014, as a fraction of the entire corporate bond market in China, based on the Wind database. A total of 128 private firms have defaulted, constituting the majority of the issuers sunk in defaults. For state-owned firms, there were 16 defaulting SOEs owned by local governments, while only 10 were central SOEs. Industry-wise, before 2017, defaults were concentrated in those overcapacity "old economy" sectors like coal, steel, and commodity-related industries; but in 2018, the fraction of defaulting firms in the "new economy" rises. Finally, the percentage of total RMB value amount of defaulted bonds remains quite low, standing at 0.6% in its peak year of 2019. In contrast, the global counterpart during 2008–2017 was 1.8%, according to a recent report by Moody's.[20]

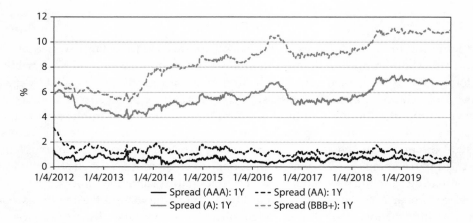

FIGURE 5.9. Credit spreads of enterprise bonds in China across ratings. *Source:* Wind database bond yield analysis. *Note:* This figure depicts the one-year credit spreads of bonds with different ratings (AAA, AA, A, BBB+) from the start of 2012 to 2019. Credit spread is the bond yield minus the corresponding CDB spot yield for each rating.

6.2. Defaults, Bond Ratings, and Credit Spreads

Credit ratings should reflect the bonds' default probabilities. Before 2014, ratings were not that indicative in China, as a result of the widely perceived "implicit government guarantee" among bond investors. The uptick of bond defaults in recent years brings investors' attention back to ratings. Figure 5.9 plots the credit spreads of enterprise bonds, which are defined as the bond yield minus the matched CDB yield, across all ratings classes since 2012. The credit spreads of lower-rated enterprise bonds (A and BBB+) experienced a clear upward trend since early 2014, dipped a bit in 2017, but soared again in early 2018.

Typically, both bond-level and issuer-level ratings are downgraded before the default event, following negative public announcements by firms. This partly explains the dispersion of credit spreads across ratings in figure 5.9. For example, before the default of "16 Katie Bond" on June 1, 2018, the bond rating status was adjusted to "Negative" on September 1, 2017, and the issuer, Sunshine Katie Co., Ltd., was downgraded by Pengyuan (one of the rating agencies) to "BBB" and put in the "credit risk" watch list on May 8, 2018.

The evolution of the credit spreads and their dispersions shown in figure 5.9 reflect not only the perceived default probabilities across various rating classes, but also the credit conditions of the bond market as a whole. The surge of bond defaults in the Chinese bond market, continually tightening credit, and the overall policy environment in combination with investors' jitters have all contributed to the spiking credit spreads.

The ever-growing default incidents in recent years have ignited investors' concerns about credit risks, though in the authors' perspective these temporary market disruptions are inevitable pains that China has to go through to reach a more market-oriented financial market. For instance, credit risk mitigation agreement (CRMA) and credit risk mitigation warrant (CRMW), which are essentially credit default swaps (CDS) derivative products and were initially introduced in 2010, gained their popularity following the recent wave of corporate defaults. Moreover, tightened regulations by Beijing, starting in late 2017, on wealth management plans, together with the government-led deleveraging campaign, further curbed the inflow of funds toward corporate bonds, especially those lower-rated ones on the edge of defaulting. This worsens their default probability and, in turn, makes institutional investors even more cautious in purchasing the bonds newly issued by these firms. This type of negative rollover spiral caused by market liquidity dry-up is responsible for the explosion of bond defaults in early 2018.[21]

6.3. Bond Default Cases, Bankruptcy, and Post-Default Recovery

This section discusses several recent prominent bond default cases in China.[22] These cases also illustrate the underdeveloped legal environment in China, as well as the uncertain bankruptcy litigation procedures that bond investors face when seeking recovery of their defaulted bonds.

Before delving into these detailed default cases, this section provides a bit of background on China's bankruptcy laws. A well-functioning bankruptcy law, including terms for restructuring and reorganization, is vitally important to business owners and investors. There are three types of bankruptcy proceedings: liquidation, settlement, and reorganization. China introduced the Enterprise Bankruptcy Law in 1986, although it was the 2006 reform that led the country on a path toward convergence with international practice, as this reform included reorganization proceedings that are similar in nature to those of Western bankruptcies and restructurings.

Despite these positive changes, many concerns about implementation of the bankruptcy code remain nowadays, owing to a lack of legal infrastructure, disparate court systems, and potentially ongoing moral hazard issues particularly related to SOEs. Besides, key differences remain between China and U.S. or U.K. bankruptcy proceedings, including a lack of debt-in-possession financing in China and the inability of creditors to propose a plan of reorganization.

6.3.1. Shanghai Chaori Solar (上海超日)

On March 4, 2014, Shanghai Chaori Solar, a privately held solar equipment producer, announced that it would not meet interest payments on its 1 billion RMB bond issued in the exchange market. This was the first case of a publicly issued bond default in China. Despite the small bond size, this event was still a big deal to market participants because until that point it seemed as though the government would support struggling companies to keep defaults from occurring.

What happened in the end? In October 2014, a number of state-owned entities, mostly asset management companies (including China Great Wall Asset Management), worked together to provide loans and guarantees to Shanghai Chaori Solar. With this help, Shanghai Chaori Solar fully repaid its past-due principal and interest. This led analysts to say that this action was "good for investors but bad for credit pricing," as many practitioners argue that real credit defaults in China would reduce the guise of moral hazard in the economy and therefore lead the country to develop a healthier credit market.

6.3.2. Baoding Tianwei (保定天威)

On April 21, 2015, Baoding Tianwei missed an interest payment on its 1.5 billion RMB medium-term note. While this was the third onshore default in 13 months, the Baoding default was meaningful in that it was the first for a 100% state-owned enterprise. Baoding

Tianwei had been established in 1995 as a unit of China South Industries Group, a military and defense company wholly owned by the State-Owned Assets Supervision and Administration Commission (SASAC, 国资委). As such, the default of Baoding on 1.5 billion RMB of bonds (and later up to 4.5 billion RMB) was a meaningful shift in the government's stance toward SOEs. With over 90% of corporate bonds outstanding issued by SOEs, this was an important event in China's history. While the company's issues have yet to be resolved, it has since defaulted on additional debt outstanding and formally filed for bankruptcy. Jin et al. (2018) have studied this historical event to estimate the value of an implicit guarantee in the Chinese bond market.

6.3.3. Sichuan Coal Industry Group (川煤集团)
A local SOE called Sichuan Coal Industry Group defaulted on its 1.05 billion RMB bond principal in June 2016. The local government quickly stepped in and provided emergency financing to the company, which was then able to pay back bondholders in full. The company repaid investors with entrusted loans from the state-owned Sichuan Provincial Investment Group, which in turn obtained loans from the Bank of Communications and other state-owned banks. Then, in December 2016, only five months after paying bondholders in full, Sichuan Coal defaulted again, as its operating metrics could nowhere near support its debt load. The government's intervention in June and July 2016 had only "thrown good money after bad." This example highlights the uncertain process with which different defaults have been handled in China.

6.3.4. Guangxi Non-Ferrous Metal (广西有色)
Another SOE bond default involves Guangxi Non-Ferrous Metal (GNFM), which is owned by the Guangxi provincial government. This case is unique because of the sheer size of GNFM's capital structure, which includes 14.5 billion RMB in debt outstanding. Also, after GNFM failed to propose a reorganization plan within six months after a court order, the restructuring period was brought to a close and the company declared bankruptcy; GNFM became the first interbank bond issuer to declare bankruptcy.

The failure of the plan of the reorganization was said to stem from the actions of the court-appointed administrator, who did not properly take creditor demands into account when forming the plan. In reaction to the proposed plan, one lawyer said, "Bankruptcy law in China is not aligned with the interests of the creditors, and the fact that the administrators are always appointed by a court raises the suspicion that there is government intervention."[23] But one has to see the positive side of this case, in which the Chinese government did not intervene to provide financing to GNFM or have government-backed asset management companies do so. This shows that the "implicit guarantee" is fading away and the Chinese government is letting the Enterprise Bankruptcy Law and the markets determine the fate of an increasing number of private enterprises and SOEs.[24]

6.3.5. Dongbei Steel (东特钢)
In a precedent-setting case for the Chinese bond market, Dongbei Steel agreed to a restructuring plan in 2017 to settle with its outstanding creditors. Dongbei Special Steel Group, a company that is majority owned by the Liaoning provincial government, defaulted on its 0.8 billion RMB commercial papers in March 2016. In August 2017, credi-

tors mostly agreed to "haircuts" in order to settle the first restructuring of an onshore bond default in China. The plan, which involves restructuring of 45.6 billion RMB, called for the following:

- Creditors owed less than 500,000 RMB are repaid in full.[25]
- Nonfinancial creditors and bondholders that are owed more than 500,000 RMB could elect for a one-time cash payment of 22.09% of the amount owed or have their bonds converted into equity.
- Financial creditors owed more than 500,000 RMB could have their amount owed converted to equity.
- Two strategic investors would inject a combined 5.5 billion RMB into the company in exchange for a 53% equity stake in the company. Creditors convert into the remaining 47% of the equity.

As the first market-led restructuring, Dongbei presented an important test case for future progress in corporate bankruptcy procedures. It set precedents akin to restructurings in the United States and the United Kingdom. While this could increase overall default rates in China, it could greatly improve economic efficiency and overall dynamism throughout the country.[26]

This section concludes by highlighting that "government-led/-coordinated solutions," especially by local governments, are one of the most prominent Chinese characteristics when dealing with defaulted bonds. For either economic or political reasons, or usually both, Chinese local governments often rescue failing firms by either issuing relevant guidance documents, or pushing other healthy local SOEs or financial institutions to inject capital. However, local governments do not have unlimited resources. The wave of breaking "implicit guarantees" should help local authorities to escape from the notion of unconditionally rescuing "zombie" firms, and should alleviate the notorious soft-budget-constraints problem that still looms in China's economic and financial reform practices today.

7. DATA SOURCES ON CHINESE BOND MARKETS

This section briefly summarizes commonly used data sources for conducting research on China's interbank market. The data on the exchange market can be obtained directly from the stock exchanges.

7.1. Data from Wind

Wind Information Co. (Wind, 万得) consolidates various data sources and offers comprehensive data access for interbank bond market data. At the bond level, Wind provides data on individual bonds' characteristics and time series of daily trading. Variables of bond characteristics include bond-issuance information, the issuer's financial statement information, and so on. Variables of daily trading include close clean price, dollar trading amount, and the like. In addition, data on yield-to-maturity based on secondary market transactions calculated by the CSDC (available from www.ChinaBond.com.cn) can also be downloaded through Wind. At the market level, Wind aggregates individual bonds' issuance and trading information by bond category, maturity, region, rating, and so forth. Wind also collects information on depository market and investor composition for various bond types. Besides gathering data on bond characteristics and trading, Wind has several special statistics on interbank market, such as bond credit risk analysis, convertible bonds, overseas bonds, open market operations, asset-backed securities, and interest rate swaps, among others.

7.2. China Foreign Exchange Trading System

The secondary market bond trading in the interbank market is conducted through the China Foreign Exchange Trading System (CFETS). It provides several standard bond data products for practitioners and academic researchers, including bond transaction data aggregated at daily frequency, effective bond quote data as of the end of each trading day, and interbank market spot and repo transactions aggregated at the institutional category level at daily, monthly, and quarterly frequencies, and so on. Among all standard products, the daily bond quote data and transaction by category data are proprietarily provided by the CFETS and not available from other data vendors. In addition, customized data service is possible for academic research on receipt of a written research proposal.

7.3. PBC Statistic Reports

The People's Bank of China releases various statistic reports covering the interbank market, including Financial Market Statistics, Financial Statistics Data Report, China Financial Stability Report, and similar reports. Most PBC statistics are also available from Wind and can be directly downloaded from the PBC website (under the Department of Statistics). Some reports, such as the China Financial Stability Report, are only available in hard copy.

7.4. Issues in Using the Interbank Market Data

Bond data quality of commercial vendors in China is on average lower than those in the U.S. market (e.g., in the TRACE dataset). Owing to the complexity of the interbank market, sometimes the same variables provided by two different data sources can be inconsistent. Researchers have to dig into details of the original data description files and regulatory documents to pick the right one. Finally, researchers should pay special attention to noticeable changes in time-series variables, as the measurement of statistics changes more frequently in China than developed countries, due to volatile policy and regulatory guidelines.

NOTES

The authors thank Tianshu Lyu (Research Professional at Fama-Miller Center) for excellent research assistance in preparing this chapter; Chang Ge for assistance with preparing section 5; Andrew Levin, who contributed to section 6.3; and Zhuo Chen (Tsinghua University), Kai Guo (People's Bank of China), Jinyu Liu (University of International Business and Economics), and Rengming Xie (CITIC, China) for many useful comments and discussions. Zhiguo He acknowledges financial support from the Macro Financial Research program's China Initiative at the University of Chicago.

1. In 2018, the ratio of bond-to-stock in China experienced a noticeable uptick, to reach 197%, due to the sluggish Chinese stock market in that year.
2. Besides these two major bond markets, there is also a counter trading system through which retail investors trade bonds with commercial banks at their bank counters. This retail over-the-counter market can be considered a natural extension of the interbank market.

3. The Big Five banks: Bank of China, Construction Bank of China, Commercial and Industrial Bank of China, and Agricultural Bank of China (these banks are often called the Big Four) and the Bank of Communications. The issuance of NCDs, especially for rural commercial banks, was severely curtailed by the recent macro-prudential assessment regulatory tightening starting in May 2017.

4. In other papers, these bonds have also been called urban investment construction bonds, or chengtou bonds, the transliteration of its Chinese name. Bai and Zhou (2018) offer the first comprehensive study on the pricing of MCBs, and Liu et al. (2017) investigate the role of implicit local government guarantees for these bonds.

5. Chinese stock markets have a higher turnover rate than U.S. stock markets, as the investor base in Chinese stock markets is mostly retail driven instead of being composed of institutional investors.

6. Suppose investors would like to sell their interbank holdings to the exchange market, perhaps for a better exchange price. According to Chen et al. (2018), investors need to apply for transfer of depository from the interbank market (the CCDC) to the exchange (the CSDC), which in 2014 took about three or four business days. The other way around, from exchange to interbank, took slightly longer (about four to six business days). The transfer of depository has become quicker in recent years, but still takes a few days.

7. Without market-based mechanisms at play, allocations of treasuries at that time were based on apportionment via administrative channels.

8. These initiatives include the pilot program of convertible bonds and the short-lived episode of treasury futures trading on the exchange. The Shanghai Stock Exchange introduced treasury futures contracts in December 1992, but terminated them in May 1995 after the infamous scandal known as "The Event of Treasury Futures Contract 327." The treasury futures market in the exchange was resumed in September 2013.

9. Chen et al. (2018) find that about 60% of investments in MCBs were by WMPs at the end of 2016. This number is likely to represent an underestimation of the extent to which MCBs rely on WMPs with the ultimate endorsement of banks. Before the 2017 regulation tightening China's shadow banking activities, it was popular for WMP managers to invest in asset management plans (or even several layers of such plans, like CDO square in the U.S. market before the 2007–2008 financial crisis), which then eventually invest in MCBs. The official statistics ignore this indirect exposure of WMPs in MCB (hence introducing a downward bias of the authors' estimate). According to practitioners in this market, the rough estimate of the true exposure is that sometime in 2016, about 70% of investment in MCBs was by WMPs.

10. These notes were placed in a local-government owned (Guangdong) exchange market but sold through some peer-to-peer platform to retail investors, with the help of financial innovation. Recall that strictly a select group of sophisticated institutional investors is only allowed to invest in PPNs. However, it turned out that many retail investors were buying pieces of PPNs issued by Cosun Group, as a result of the financial innovation of a certain peer-to-peer lending platform.

11. After the credit event, Zheshang Insurance released documents carrying Guangfa Bank's official seals, showing that the bank's Huizhou branch had promised the guarantee. However, the headquarters of Guangfa Bank claimed that the guarantee documents presented by Zheshang Insurance, together with official seals and personal seals, were "all fake." See Shu Zhang and Ryan Woo, "China Imposes Record Fine on Guangfa Bank over Guarantees for Defaulted Bonds." Reuters, December 8, 2017.

12. On the other way around, many Chinese firms have actively sought overseas funding sources by issuing foreign-currency denominated bonds (Huang et al., 2018).

13. Unfortunately, data exists only for stock investments for QFII. Therefore the total investment of QFII and RQFII is estimated at 90% invested in stock and 10% in bonds, assuming the same investment structure for RQFII.

14. "Nonfinancial credit bonds" and "corporate bonds" are used as synonyms in this section.

15. Our sample of corporate issuers includes LGFVs (see section 2.2.3), through which local governments carry out their infrastructure projects (especially during the 2009 stimulus package; see Chen et al., 2020). These firms often have explicit or implicit guarantee from local governments. As a result, the rating distribution documented here is more upward-skewed compared to Deng and Qiao (2019), who excluded LGFVs from their sample.

16. This is similar to the case of "stand-alone" versus "support" ratings assigned to some international banks, which enjoy a lower default risk and higher all-in rating owing to government support schemes.

17. For supercommercial papers, two ratings from different agencies are mandatory, with one being AA or above.
18. Further, the China Insurance Regulatory Commission, the regulator of the insurance sector (which was merged with the China Banking Regulatory Commission in early 2018), once issued a list of recognized agencies for fixed income investments of domestic insurance companies.
19. The global agencies made earlier attempts to enter the Chinese rating industry but at the time decided to disinvest. Fitch had a joint venture with Chengxin from 1999 to 2003 and Moody's a cooperative agreement with Dagong from 1999 to 2002.
20. This estimation is derived from "Annual Default Study: Corporate Default and Recovery Rates, 1920–2017" by Moody's, which covers the credit histories of more than 25,000 corporate issuers that had long-term rated bonds between 1920 and 2017.
21. Companies that defaulted in 2018 had much stronger balance sheets than those that defaulted in 2016–2017, in terms of simple financial ratios like book leverage and interest coverage as cited from an industry report by China International Trust Investment Corporation (CITIC) Securities.
22. We appreciate Andrew Levin's contribution to this section and have heavily drawn from his term paper for the MBA class "Chinese Economy and Financial Market" at Chicago Booth that Zhiguo He taught in the winter quarter of 2018.
23. Zhang Yu and Dong Tongjian, "Guangxi Nonferrous' Creditors Veto Insolvency Plan," *Caixin,* November 2, 2016. The lawyer was reacting to a plan of reorganization that would have seen creditors receive under 20% recoveries and a large amount of equity in lieu of their claims. Instead, the firm was placed in involuntary liquidation, being forced to start selling everything from equity ownership of subsidiaries to even office supplies and desk chairs.
24. "Guangxi Nonferrous Metals is China's first interbank bankruptcy," *South China Morning Post*, September 20, 2016.
25. The maximum cutoff of 500,000 RMB to receive full repayment is likely due to the deposit insurance in China implemented in 2015, which likewise sets a limit of 500,000 RMB. Perhaps more importantly, it reduced the number of claimants drastically, paving an easier path toward resolution.
26. Goldman Sachs Research, August 10, 2017.

REFERENCES

Amihud, Yakov (2002). "Illiquidity and Stock Returns: Cross-Section and Time-Series Effects." *Journal of Financial Markets* 5(1): 31–56.

Anderson, Mike, and René M. Stulz (2017). "Is Post-Crisis Bond Liquidity Lower?" (No. w23317). National Bureau of Economic Research.

Asian Development Bank (2012). People's Republic of China Bond Market Guide, ASEAN+3 Bond Market Guide. Asian Development Bank. http://hdl.handle.net/11540/927.

Bai, Jennie, and Hao Zhou (2018). "The Funding Cost of Chinese Local Government Debt." Working paper, George Washington University.

Chen, Hui, Zhuo Chen, Zhiguo He, Jinyu Liu, and Rengmin Xie (2018). "Pledgeability and Asset Prices: Evidence from the Chinese Corporate Bond Markets." Working paper, Chicago Booth.

Chen, Zhuo, Zhiguo He, and Chun Liu (2020). "The Financing of Local Government in China: Stimulus Loan Wanes and Shadow Banking Waxes." *Journal of Financial Economics* 137(1): 42–71

Deng, Kaihua, and Guannan Qiao (2019). "Double-A Failure." Working paper, Renmin University of China.

Ehlers, Torsten, Steven Kong, and Feng Zhu (2018). "Mapping Shadow Banking in China: Structure and Dynamics." BIS Working Papers, No. 701, February 12.

He, Zhiguo (2020). "Assessing China's Capital Requirement and Systemic Challenges." Testimony at U.S.-China Economic and Security Review Commission (USCC) Hearing on "China's Quest for Capital: Motivations, Methods, and Implications," January 23, Washington, DC.

Huang, Yi, Ugo Panizza, and Richard Portes (2018). "Corporate Foreign Bond Issuance and Interfirm Loans in China" (No. 24513). National Bureau of Economic Research.

Jiang, Xianfeng, and Frank Packer (2017). "Credit Ratings of Domestic and Global Agencies: What Drives the Differences in China and How Are They Priced?" BIS Working Papers, No. 648, June 28.

Jin, Shuang, Wei Wang, and Zhang Zilong (2018). "The Value and Real Effects of Implicit Guarantees." https://af.polyu.edu.hk/media/6534/jwz_bonddefaults_20170524.pdf.

Kennedy, Scott (2008). "China's Emerging Credit Rating Industry: The Official Foundations of Private Authority." *China Quarterly* 193: 65–83.

Lei, Katherine, George Cai, Stephen Tsui, Jemmy Huang, Haibin Zhu, Marvin Chen, and Soo Chong Lim (2018). "China Financials: Embracing a Rise in Corporate Bond Defaults." J. P. Morgan Asia Pacific Corporate Research.

Liu, Laura Xiaolei, Yuanzhen Lyu, and Fan Yu (2017). "Implicit Government Guarantee and the Pricing of Chinese LGFV Debt." Claremont McKenna College Robert Day School of Economics and Finance Research Paper No. 292294, February. Claremont, CA.

Mo, Jingyuan, and Marti Subrahmanyam (2019). "Policy Interventions, Liquidity, and Clientele Effects in the Chinese Corporate Credit Bond Market." Working paper, Stern School, New York University.

Poon, Winnie, and Kam C. Chan (2008). "An Empirical Examination of the Informational Content of Credit Ratings in China." *Journal of Business Research* 61(7): 790–97.

Standard Chartered (2017). "China's Credit Rating Framework." Global research report.

Sun, Guofeng (2015). *Reforms in China's Monetary Policy: A Frontbencher's Perspective.* New York: Palgrave Macmillan.

Wang, Shujing, Kuo-chiang Wei, and Ninghua Zhong (2015). "One Bond, Two Prices: The Demand Effect of Yield-Chasing Retail Investors." Conference paper, Asian Finance Association Annual Meeting, June 29 to July 1, Changsha, China.

PART 3

FINANCIAL SYSTEM AND THE REAL ECONOMY

6

MACROECONOMIC EFFECTS OF CHINA'S FINANCIAL POLICIES

Kaiji Chen and Tao Zha

1. INTRODUCTION

Since the beginning of China's economic reforms in 1978, the Chinese economy has undergone three major phases. The first phase (1978–1997) marks an economy led by growth and reforms of state-owned enterprises (SOEs). The economy in the second phase (1998–2015) was driven by investment in large and capital-intensive enterprises, which form what is called "the heavy sector." The heavy sector includes both SOEs and private-owned enterprises (POEs). In recent years (2016 to the present), observers have witnessed a transition to what the Chinese government calls "a new normal economy." All three phases have been shaped by particular government policies. This chapter focuses on the macroeconomic effects of financial policies throughout these phases and provides *stylized facts* to substantiate our analysis.[1]

Financial policies in China can be defined as *a set of credit policy, monetary policy, and regulatory policy*. Credit policy played an essential role in driving the SOE-led economy. Such a policy consists of a number of administrative tools, such as loan quotas and window guidance to limiting credits to specific sectors or industries. For the investment-driven economy, monetary policy, coupled with credit policy, played a crucial role in promoting overall economic growth. Monetary policy was particularly potent in combating the 2008 financial crisis in the short run, but with the cost of a high debt burden in the long run (measured by the debt-to-GDP ratio). Most of the stimulus was channeled to real estate and infrastructure, which formed a large portion of the heavy sector.

Since China's massive monetary stimulus of its economy in 2009, the effectiveness of its monetary policy has been eclipsed by the rise of shadow banking, owing to lax regulatory policy. In recent years since 2016, improvements have been made in coordination between monetary and regulatory policies within the framework of Macro-Prudential Assessment (MPA). In particular, the Chinese government has placed a number of unifying rules on asset management across several financial sectors (e.g., across formal banking and shadow banking).

The impacts of China's financial policies work through transmission channels different from those in developed economies. Bank credits have always played a special role in promoting the country's economic growth. And the government has always given preferential credits to certain firms or industries, although the preference has shifted through the three different phases.

In the SOE-led economy, credit preference was given to SOEs. As a result, SOEs, especially those in the light sector (e.g., the textile industry), suffered from problems with excess capacity and overleverage. Most of these SOEs were small and medium-sized. In the late 1990s, reforms were focused on SOEs by reducing overcapacity of small and medium-sized SOEs.[2] In Chinese this movement is called "Grasp the large and let go of the small." Reforms in the banking sector also focused on granting nonperforming loans to SOEs with overcapacity.

In the investment-driven economy, preferential credits were given to the heavy sector (e.g., real estate and infrastructure). During this phase, most industries in the heavy sector were favored by the Chinese government as part of the government's industrialization policy to promote that heavy sector. Two commonly discussed phases occur during the investment-driven period: the privatization-driven phase (a transition of a large number of SOEs to POEs) and the export-driven phase. During the transition from SOEs to POEs, most medium-term and long-term bank loans were directed to capital-intensive firms (often large firms), no matter whether these firms were POEs or surviving SOEs. The growth decomposition described in this chapter shows that while the efficiency gain measured by the contribution of total factor productivity (TFP) growth to GDP growth was far from trivial, capital's deepening through investment in both SOEs and POEs was a dominant factor, since the government's financial policies were designed to promote the capital-intensive (heavy) sector. For this reason, this chapter does not emphasize the privatization-driven phase during the investment-driven period.

After joining the World Trade Organization (WTO) in 2001, China experienced what is called "the export-driven phase," in which exports exploded. One might believe that the rapid rise of investment in the export-drive phase was directly driven by the growth of exports. As Huang et al. (2015) find, however, the capital intensity of the export sector declined as exports grew, suggesting that the major channel for exports to contribute to GDP growth is via the TFP increase, not through capital deepening.

This chapter documents that capital deepening was the most important source of GDP growth in China between 1998 and 2016. Emphasizing the driving engine of investment during this period by no means rules out the important role that either exports or the transition from SOEs to POEs played in GDP growth via the TFP increase. In fact, TFP contributed to about 32% of China's GDP growth during the investment-led period and played a more important role in the early stage of the investment-led economy.

The asymmetric credit allocation in favor of the heavy sector was exacerbated during the stimulus period (2009–2010). The main consequence was overstock in the real estate sector, overcapacity in industries supporting real estate, and overleverage in both real and financial sectors. Reforms in this economy, different from those in the SOE-led economy, focused on destocking the real estate, deleveraging certain overcapacity firms (e.g., steel, cement, and glass), and also deleveraging the financial sector.

While these reforms continue in the "new normal" economy, China faces new challenges. In particular, financial reforms have unintended consequences. For example, financial deleveraging has reduced bank credits to nonbank financial institutions and thus also reduced shadow banking loans to POEs. At the same time, the default rates of POEs and therefore of systemic risks have increased. SOEs in upstream industries, however, have continued to receive preferential credits and so remain unproductive and monopolistic. Implicit guarantees by local governments to such "zombie" firms make difficult the deleveraging of corporate debts.

The rest of the chapter is organized as follows. Section 2 provides the institutional background of China's financial policies. Section 3 analyzes the macroeconomic impacts of financial policies on the SOE-led economy, on the investment-driven economy, and on the new normal economy. Section 4 concludes the chapter.

2. INSTITUTIONAL BACKGROUND OF FINANCIAL POLICIES

2.1. Review of Financial Policies

As defined in the introduction, China's financial policies consist of credit policy, monetary policy, and regulatory policy. This section reviews these policies' interactions in the context of their impacts on the macroeconomy.

2.1.1. Credit Policy

First under discussion, credit policy was carried out mainly through administrative means. In 1984, the aggregate credit volume was chosen to be the intermediate target of monetary policy. Credit quotas were allocated to the banking system that consisted of the four major banks: Bank of China, China Industrial and Commercial Bank of China, China Construction Bank, and Agricultural Bank of China. Local governments played an integral part in allocating these credits through these banks' local branches. The limited coordination among local governments, however, made it impossible to control the aggregate volume of bank credits and therefore their allocations' efficiency. In 1998, the control of credit volumes as the intermediate target of monetary policy was eventually abolished.

From 1998 to 2017, the People's Bank of China (PBC) used a target of growth rates of M2 supply as an effective way to control aggregate bank loans and to promote an investment-driven economy. Credit policy, via window guidance and loan quotas, was also centralized to be in line with the growth of M2 supply. The PBC utilized window guidance to control the total volume of bank credits and also to redirect loans to the targeted industries (e.g., agriculture and small and medium-sized enterprises). Such loans were made regardless of prevailing interest rates. In line with M2 growth, the PBC planned the aggregate credit supply for the coming year at the end of each year and then negotiated with individual commercial banks to redirect credits to targeted industries when necessary during the coming year.

2.1.2. Monetary Policy

Before 1993, the PBC directly controlled the bank credit supply and its allocations often at local levels. In 1993, for the first time, it announced to the public the index of monetary supply; in 1996, it began a transition to using the money supply as an instrument for monetary policy at the national level. In 1998 the PBC announced that M2 supply was

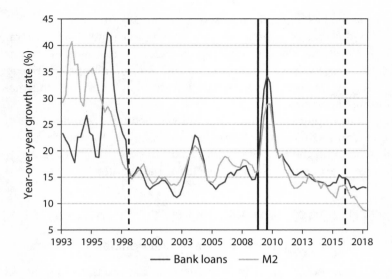

FIGURE 6.1. Year-over-year growth of M2 supply and bank loans. *Source:* Chen et al. (2017). *Note:* The black vertical bars mark the 2009 stimulus period. The first dashed vertical line divides the SOE-led economy and the investment-driven economy. The second dashed vertical line divides the investment-driven economy and the new normal economy.

the sole policy target. In May of that year, open market operations were initiated. From then to the end of 2017, China adhered to this quantity-based monetary policy framework, especially during the entire period of the investment-driven economy.

Monetary policy during the period of the new normal economy has undergone a gradual transition from the quantity-based framework to the interest rate–based framework. The discussion of this transition was initiated in the Thirteenth Five-Year Plan for "Economic and Social Development," held in 2016. In addition to its discussion of monetary policy, the plan outlined a new normal economy that features financial reforms along with a promotion of consumption growth to be supported by monetary policy. In 2018Q1, for the first time since 1998, the M2 growth target was no longer among the government's key economic objects.

Figure 6.1 shows the time series of year-over-year growth rates of M2 supply and aggregate bank loans. The rectangular bars mark the 2009 monetary stimulus period (2009Q1–Q3).[3] There are two vertical lines. The first line marks the beginning of 1998 and the second line the beginning of 2016. Clearly, the M2 supply and bank loans do not co-move in the SEO-led economy (the graph to the left of the first vertical line in figure 6.1), confirming that credit policy in this period was ineffective as an aggregate macroeconomic policy. In the second phase, the M2 supply and bank loans co-move (the graph between the two vertical lines in the figure), implying that monetary policy was effective in controlling aggregate bank loans. In the third phase, the small divergence between M2 growth and bank-loan growth (the graph to the right of the second vertical line in the figure) is driven mostly by reduction of bank credits to nonbanking financial companies (NFCs), which, in turn, reduced their bank deposits through the financial deleveraging. Bank loans to the real economy, however, remained stable during this period.

2.1.3. Regulatory Policy

Along with the other two policies, regulatory policy also went through the three phases. In the first phase, in which the state banks were fully owned and managed by the government, administrative tools were used to control bank credit advancements while the system for regulation and supervision on NFCs was immature and loose.

In the second phase, the loan-to-deposit ratio (LDR) regulation became one of the most important components of regulatory policy; it requires a commercial bank to keep the ratio of its loans to its deposits under 75%. The LDR regulation was established in 1994, but it was not credibly enforced until the late 2000s. The second most important component of regulatory policy is the restriction of advancement of bank credits to certain risky industries, a policy that is often called in Chinese the "safe loan regulation." In 2006, the State Council, concerned with China's real estate and many overcapacity industries, issued a notice to accelerate the restructuring process of these risky industries. In 2010, the PBC and the Chinese Banking Regulatory Commission (CBRC) jointly issued another notice to reinforce the 2006 notice issued by the State Council, making it operational to prohibit commercial banks from originating new bank loans to these industries. Although these regulatory actions prevented newly originated traditional bank loans from flowing to the risky industries, lax regulatory policy on shadow banking activities, combined with monetary policy tightening after the massive 2009 monetary stimulus, created the shadow banking boom and dampened the effectiveness of monetary policy in affecting the aggregate bank credit as a sum of traditional and shadow banking credits.

To achieve financial stability, deleveraging has become a priority for the financial policies in the third phase. In December 2016, deleveraging corporate debts was a major discussion for the Central Economic Work Conference. In March 2017, the Report on the Work of the Government (RWG) made it a priority to deleverage overcapacity firms that supported the real estate. In July 2017, the National Financial Work Conference reiterated this priority. In December of that year, the RWG no longer specified the M2 growth target for 2018, marking a gradual transition from quantity-based monetary policy to an interest rate–based monetary policy. In April 2018, the first meeting of the Central Financial Commission emphasized the importance of deleveraging zombie firms associated with local government debts.

Since 2016, the central government has adopted the MPA system both to ensure the financial stability and to enable cooperation between monetary and regulatory policies. Put in place were various regulations on specific banking assets and liabilities (e.g., interbank CDs) and on shadow banking products (e.g., entrusted loans and wealth management products). More important are a number of unifying rules enacted by the government on asset management across different financial sectors (e.g., across formal banking and shadow banking).[4]

2.2. The Nexus between GDP Growth and Financial Policies

2.2.1. The SOE-Led Economy

In 1978, economic reforms to be made with the so-called opening-up policy were initiated by the Third Plenary Session of the Eleventh Central Committee of the Communist Party. In 1984, decentralization took place, giving the local governments a stronger managerial power. In 1987, economic development was the central theme as well as the bottom line of the Thirteenth Central Committee of the Communist Party. In 1992, Deng Xiaoping advanced further economic reforms throughout the country. In 1994, the government implemented tax reforms with the tax-sharing system.

The year 1984 was a pivotal point for GDP growth. Since then, promoting local GDP growth has become the major task of local government officials, because their performance has always been based on local economic growth.[5] The external financing of SOEs, moreover, switched from direct credit allocations to bank loans in 1984. By relaxing credit quotas on state banks, credit policy was aimed at promoting growth of SOEs in each province, city, and district. Administrative tools were used to control credit advancements to SOEs and helped to close, restructure, or merge small and medium-sized SOEs that experienced large profit losses. Since SOEs were prevalent in every industry (in both heavy and light sectors), such credit policy influenced investment and consumption simultaneously.

The central government's preferential credit policy toward SOEs was channeled through local governments. Local governments often directed local branches of state banks to advance credits to SOEs beyond credit quotas (the so-called soft budget constraints). Pressures exerted by local governments on local branches of state banks to increase credits to local SOEs resulted in pressures from local branches on their headquarters to loosen credit quotas, which in turn forced the PBC to eventually raise the aggregate credit volume (in Chinese this is called the "reverse loan quota transmission").

Apart from banking lending, Brandt and Zhu (2007) show that during this phase, NFCs, including the rural credit cooperatives, urban credit cooperatives, and trust and investment corporations, emerged to be important sources of financing. Unlike state banks, NFCs were usually controlled or owned by local cooperatives, so their lending largely fell outside the government's credit plan. Lending from NFCs contributed 20% to 25% to the total source of funds.

2.2.2. The Investment-Driven Economy

In the investment-driven economy phase, the central government laid out multiple policy objectives, including (real) GDP growth, inflation, employment, foreign exchange rate, social stability, and environment. Out of these objectives, only two economic targets are of primary importance: GDP growth and consumer price index (CPI) inflation. Since 1988, the GDP growth target has been specified in the State Council's Report on the Work of Government (RWG). This is the overriding objective among all policy objectives. From 1999 to 2017, the M2 growth target was also specified in the RWG, along with the GDP growth target. The PBC is not an independent institution in making monetary policy. The State Council and other government units exerted considerable and often-dominant influences on the official target of M2 growth.

Two sets of tools were used to meet M2 growth as well as the growth of bank loans. The first set consists of monetary policy tools such as the benchmark reserve requirement ratio and open market operations that were used to meet the M2 growth target. The second set involves tools such as differential reserve requirements for different commercial banks, credit quotas (implicit and explicit), and "window guidance" that were used to make growth of bank loans closely in line with growth of M2 supply (the graph between the two vertical lines in figure 6.1).

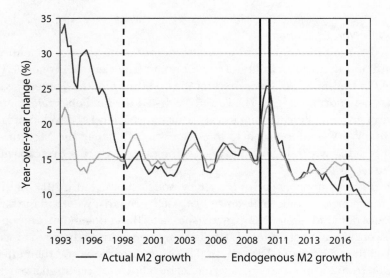

FIGURE 6.2. M2 growth and its systematic component. *Source:* Chen et al. (2018).

Chen et al. (2018) develop and estimate a quantity-based monetary policy rule based on China's institutional facts. Under this rule, monetary policy endogenously switches between two regimes, according to whether actual GDP growth is above or below the targeted GDP growth. In the normal situation where GDP growth is above the target, M2 growth responds positively to the gap between actual and targeted GDP growth rates. By contrast, in a shortfall state where the actual GDP growth is below the targeted GDP growth, monetary policy takes an unusually aggressive response to stem the shortfall needed to meet the GDP growth target.

For the most part, quantity-based monetary policy in the investment-driven economy followed its systematic response to output and inflation targets (the graph between the two vertical lines in figure 6.2). *Counterfactual* paths of M2 growth and its endogenous component are computed in the period of the SOE-led economy. These counterfactual paths, shown in the graph to the left of the first vertical line in that figure, reveal that in contrast to the investment-driven economy, monetary policy in the SOE-led economy would not have followed its systematic rule had it been implemented in this period. These results confirm that credit policy, not quantity-based monetary policy, was the main driver of monetary and credit aggregates in the SOE-led economy.

Unlike in the SOE-led economy, in which the government provided preferential credits to SOEs across both heavy and light sectors, most preferential credits in this phase were channeled to the heavy sector in order to stimulate investment as a way to meet the overriding GDP growth target. The heavy sector includes both SOEs and large POEs that are capital intensive. The government's objective of targeting GDP growth is asymmetric: The GDP growth target has been a lower bound for growth. Monetary policy was carried out to support GDP growth and at the same time control CPI inflation through effective ways of influencing bank loans (see various monetary policy reports, or MPRs). This is one of the main features in the investment-driven economy.

2.2.3. The New Normal Economy

In recent years, the Chinese central government strived to achieve a balance between GDP growth and financial stability of the economy. The Central Economic Work Conference, held in December 2014, declared for the first time that the Chinese economy had entered the "new normal stage." The 2015 RWG listed the dual objective: maintaining a healthy rate of growth while moving toward a sustainable level of development. The Central Economic Work Conference, held in December 2015, called for "structural reforms on the supply side," which included deleveraging debts, reducing overcapacity, and destocking the real estate.

This effort shows up as negative monetary policy shocks since 2014 (figure 6.2). According to the monetary policy rule since 1998, GDP growth lower than the target in this episode would demand higher M2 growth (shown as the endogenous component in that figure). The consideration of financial stability, however, induced the government to lower M2 growth at the sacrifice of GDP growth. These considerations and their effects, which are abstracted from the monetary policy rule set out above, are captured as negative monetary policy shocks (i.e., the difference between the solid and the dashed-x lines to the right of the second vertical line in figure 6.2).

3. MACROECONOMIC EFFECTS OF FINANCIAL POLICIES

The effects of financial policies on the macroeconomy are now to be analyzed. As figure 6.3 shows, GDP growth experienced expansion and slowdown in both the SOE-led economy and investment-driven economies. And financial policies affected trends as well as cycles of China's macroeconomy. This section first documents key patterns of trends and cycles for each economy and then analyzes the role of financial policies in driving those trends and cycles.

3.1. The Effects of Credit Policy on the SOE-Led Economy, 1978–1997

In the state-owned enterprise-led economy, SOEs permeated throughout the whole economy, including all the industries and across the light and heavy sectors. Credit policy was the main policy tool in allocating credit quotas to the banking system that channeled most of its loans to SOEs. Bank loans to various SOEs were both long-term and short-term.

The transmission of credit policy to the SOE-led economy is discussed by Chen and Zha (2019) and now summarized in figure 6.4. State banks provided preferential credits to SOEs in both heavy and light sectors. This is the most important aspect of credit policy in this economy. Under the central government's pro-growth policy and local governments' GDP growth tournament, SOEs in both sectors obtained implicit government guarantees of their bank credits. With these financial guarantees, state banks were willing to advance credits to SOEs in both sectors and across all industries.

Credit policy was essential to promoting both investment and consumption for the 1978–1997 phase. Since the data on consumption is fragmentary, we focus on an analysis of investment with the understanding that consumption and investment co-moved in this phase. Figure 6.5 shows that fixed asset investment (FAI) and bank loans to FAI moved hand in hand. Throughout the 1978–1997 period, the share of SOEs in FAI remained high (figure 6.6), while the share of SOEs in credit allocations to investment also

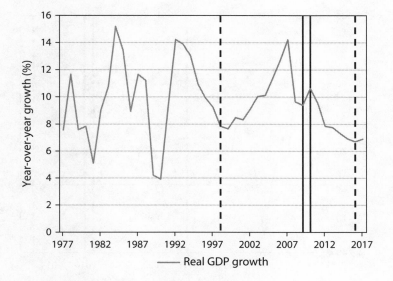

FIGURE 6.3. GDP growth (annual data). *Source:* CEIC.

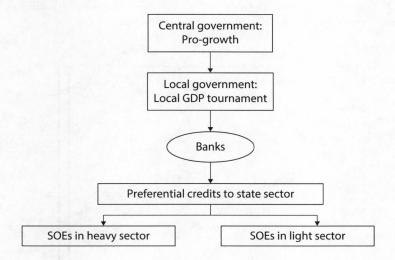

FIGURE 6.4. Transmission of credit policy to the SOE-led economy.

remained at a very high level (figure 6.7). According to Brandt and Zhu (2007), in most years during this phase, 80% to 85% of total credits were extended to SOEs through state banks in the form of either working capital or fixed investment loans. This observation reflected the central government's commitment to workers and job growth in SOEs while fiscal resources in local governments declined. The shares of SOEs in FAI and its loan volume were much higher in the period before 1998 than in the post-1997 period. High shares imply that SOEs, which enjoyed preferential bank credits, are a driving force of the aggregate investment fluctuation.

Two notable effects can be noted about China's macro economy of such preferential credit policy toward SOEs. First, the fluctuation of (real) GDP was driven by the fluctuations

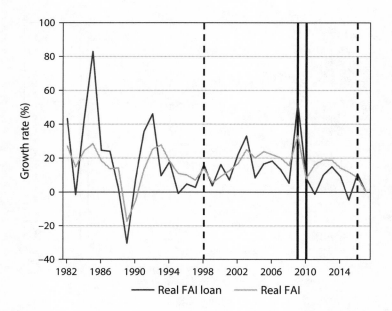

FIGURE 6.5. Year-over-year growth rates of FAI and bank loans to FAI. *Sources:* CEIC and authors' calculation.

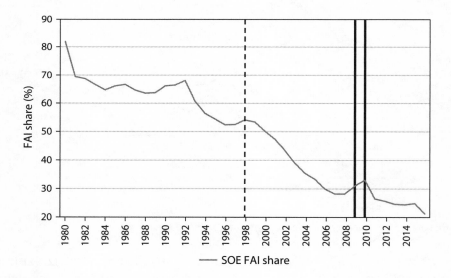

FIGURE 6.6. Share of SOEs in FAI (compiled from the aggregate data). *Sources:* CEIC and authors' calculation.

of both investment and consumption (the graphs to the left of the first vertical line in figure 6.8). Second, the correlation between investment and consumption growth rates during 1978–1997 was as high as 0.80, a correlation that is statistically significant. Table 6.1 reports this correlation, along with its p-value based on the Hodrick-Prescott (HP) filtered log annual series. In contrast to the investment-driven economy, as is discussed

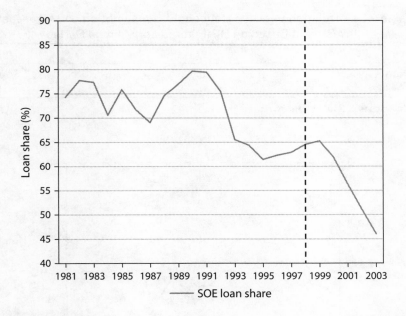

FIGURE 6.7. Share of SOEs in bank loans to investment. *Sources:* CEIC, Chen and Zha (2019). *Note:* This series was discontinued by China's National Bureau of Statistics.

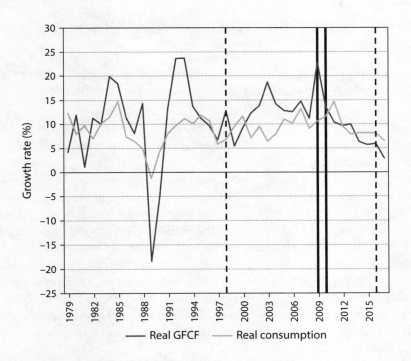

FIGURE 6.8. Year-over-year growth of aggregate investment and household consumption. *Sources:* CEIC and authors' calculation. *Note:* Aggregate investment is measured by gross fixed capital formation (GFCF).

Table 6.1. Correlation between Household Consumption and Aggregate
Investment Based on HP-Filtered Log Annual Series

	1979–1997	1998–2015
Correlation	0.8062	−0.3500
p-value	0	0.1545

Note: Each series is deflated by its own price index.

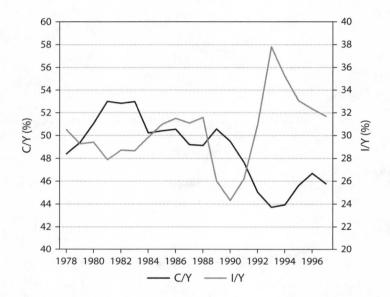

FIGURE 6.9. Ratios of investment and consumption to GDP. *Source:* CEIC. *Note*: "C" represents household consumption, "I" gross fixed capital formation, and "Y" GDP.

later, there was no secular pattern of an increasing investment-to-output ratio, and this ratio was very volatile (figure 6.9).

Other important facts of the SOE-led economy are the stationary ratio of gross output in the heavy sector to that in the light sector (figure 6.10) and the stationary ratio of gross fixed assets in the heavy sector to those in the light sector (figure 6.11). These observations were an outcome of credit policy in the SOE-led economy that was engineered to support SOEs across all sectors, not just the heavy sector. For instance, a large quantity of bank credits were channeled to the industries producing consumer durables. Many bank credits were allocated to SOEs producing watches, bicycles, and sewing machines in 1978–1982; color televisions and refrigerators in 1983–1988; and automobiles in 1992–1997. Thus, one prominent feature of the SOE-led economy can be observed: that investment and consumption co-move. As a result, the labor share of income was also stable prior to 1998 (figure 6.12).

The observation that credit policy fueled the demand for both investment and consumption in the 1978–1997 phase is also supported by the pattern of fluctuations for the two measures of inflation rate, as shown by figure 6.13 and by their summary statistics

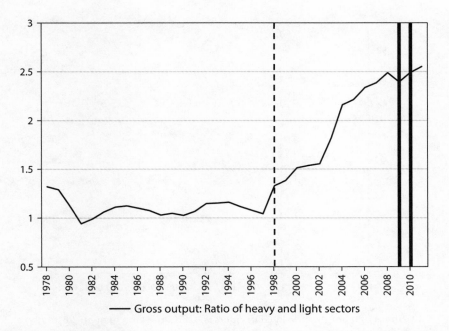

FIGURE 6.10. Ratio of gross output in the heavy sector to that in the light sector. *Source:* Chang et al. (2015).

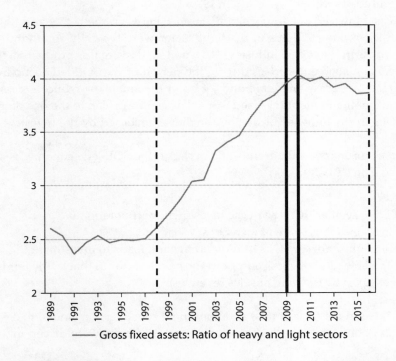

FIGURE 6.11. Ratio of gross fixed assets in the heavy sector to that in the light sector. *Sources:* CEIC and authors' calculation.

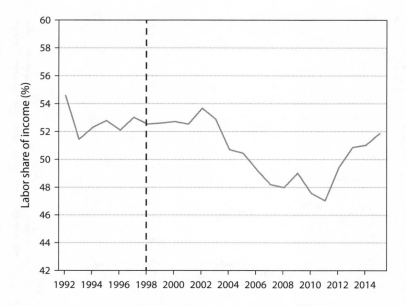

FIGURE 6.12. Share of labor income in GDP. *Sources:* CEIC and Chang et al. (2015).

reported in table 6.2. According to that, the produce price index (PPI) volatility was similar in magnitude to the CPI volatility in 1978–1997.

There was, however, one important difference between the heavy and light sectors in the SOE-led economy. SOEs in the light sector were typically small and medium-sized (e.g., firms in the textile industry). As small SOEs were less productive than large ones, reforms on such enterprises during the period of the SOE-led economy emphasized the task of "'grasp the large and let go of the small" to reduce excess capacity problems in small and medium-sized SOEs. These reforms led to the rise of many productive POEs in the light sector during the phase governed by the investment-driven economy.

Below are summarized the trends and cycles in the SOE-led economy, as discussed in Chen and Zha (2019).

- Trends:
  - » (T1) No secular increase in the investment-output ratio
  - » (T2) Stable labor share of income
  - » (T3) High shares of SOEs in FAI and in bank loans to investment
  - » (T4) Stable ratio of gross output in the heavy sector to that in the light sector (measured by the ratio of sales revenues)
- Cycles:
  - » (C1) Aggregate investment and household consumption tended to co-move
  - » (C2) Booms and busts of investment and its credits were driven mainly by SOEs
  - » (C3) The volatility of produce price index (PPI) inflation had a magnitude similar to the volatility of CPI inflation

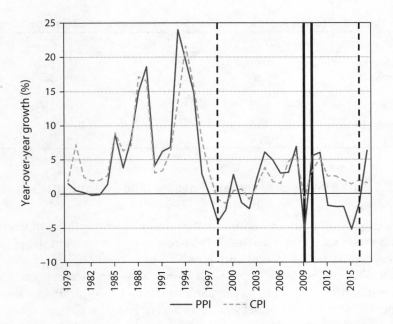

FIGURE 6.13. Inflation rates of PPI and CPI. *Sources:* CEIC and authors' calculation.

Table 6.2. Standard Deviations of CPI and PPI Inflation Rates

	1978–1997	*1998–2015*
CPI inflation	0.0618	0.0202
PPI inflation	0.0695	0.0397
Difference	0.0077	0.0195
p-value	0.6235	0.0083

These trend and cycle patterns observed in the data for the SOE-led economy can be explained by the theoretical framework of Chen and Zha (2019). The economy contains two sectors, heavy and light, differentiated by the capital intensity. The crucial model ingredient is that the government's implicit guarantees to SOEs, represented by its net worth, are symmetric across both light and heavy sectors. SOEs in the heavy sector do not face the borrowing constraint because the banks are not commercialized and, being of the government, are willing to make intertemporal (long-term) investment loans without conditions. Loans to SOEs in the light sector are of short term to fund working capital for paying labor wages and other factor inputs. Such loans are harder to be fully pledged than investment loans to the heavy sector. Thus, the light sector faces the binding collateral constraint governed by a fraction of their assets. As the government net worth increases, the collateral constraint of the light sector is relaxed, which increases its factor demand. This, in turn, increases the demand for capital investment of the heavy sector due to the imperfect substitutability between these two sectors. Accordingly, the ratio of gross output in the heavy sector to that in the light sector was stationary.

Table 6.3. Growth Accounting According to Long and Herrera (2016)

Growth (%)	1978–1997	1998–2015	2016	2017
GDP per worker	6.67	8.36	6.26	6.55
Due to capital intensity	2.89	5.71	4.55	4.11
Due to TFP	3.78	2.65	1.71	2.45
Contribution by investment	43.4	68.3	72.7	62.7

3.2. The Effects of Monetary Policy on the Investment-Driven Economy, 1998–2015

The period 1998–2015 marks an economy that was *qualitatively different* from the SOE-led economy. The most conspicuous difference was a change from the government's direct credit control policy to explicitly targeting growth of M2 supply as an effective way to control aggregate bank loans. Such monetary policy was designed to provide adequate and accurate liquidity to the banking system to support investment in the heavy sector, which includes both large SOEs and large POEs. Consequently, the share of SOEs in FAI declined steadily in 1998–2015 until it hovered below 20% (figure 6.8). Since monetary policy was used to support investment in the heavy sector, the share of SOEs in total bank loans to investment declined steadily after 1998 (figure 6.9).

The most striking facet of the investment-driven economy is that GDP growth was driven mostly by investment (so-called capital deepening). To illustrate this feature, growth decompositions can be calculated from the following production function:

$$Y_t = \text{TFP}_t \, K_t^{\alpha} \, N_t^{1-\alpha},$$

where Y represents output, TFP total factor productivity, K capital, N labor (employed workers), and α the share of capital income in total income. The decomposition of growth per worker is:

$$\Delta\log \frac{Y_t}{N_t} = \Delta\log\text{TFP}_t + \alpha \, \Delta\log \frac{K_t}{N_t},$$

where the second term on the right-hand side of the equation represents the contribution from capital intensity (capital per worker), or investment.[6]

Tables 6.3 and 6.4 report the growth accounting according to the above decomposition formula. The computation uses the value of the capital share set at 0.5 as in the literature. For the approach of Bai et al. (2006), the data of gross fixed capital formation for "structures and buildings" and "machinery and equipment" goes back only to 1981. The investment price data for these two categories extends only to 1990. The values reported under the column with the heading 1978–1997 in table 6.4, marked by the symbol *, are for the period 1990–1997. For 2017, the approach of Bai et al. (2006) requires gross investment price inflation in 2018 to be available, which was not accessible when this chapter was written.

Both tables show that TFP was a driving force for growth of GDP per worker in the SOE-led economy, although investment played a dominant role in driving GDP growth in the investment-driven economy. This finding is consistent with an independent study by Lagakos (2018). As a result, we see that the ratio of investment to GDP has increased steadily since 1998 (figure 6.14).

Table 6.4. Growth Accounting According to Bai et al. (2006)

Growth (%)	1978–1997	1998–2015	2016	2017
GDP per worker	7.05*	8.36	6.26	N/A
Due to capital	2.48*	5.61	4.69	N/A
Due to TFP	4.57*	2.75	1.57	N/A
Contribution by investment	35.1*	67.1	74.9	N/A

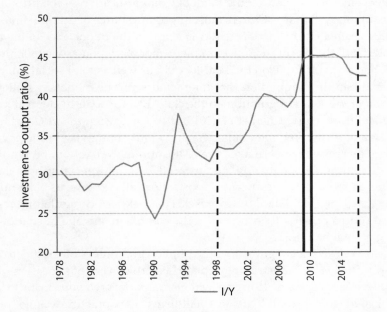

FIGURE 6.14. Secular pattern of the investment-to-GDP ratio, where I is measured by GFCF and Y is measured by aggregate value added. *Source:* CEIC.

The investment-driven economy experienced three distinct episodes: the "golden decade" (1998–2008), the stimulus period (2009), and the post-stimulus period (2010–2015). Along with preferential credit policy toward the heavy sector, both monetary and regulatory policies during these three episodes have distinctive features. The roles of financial policies in each of these three episodes are discussed next.

3.2.1. The Golden Decade

The government's early planning for the investment-driven economy was crucial for the success in the whole period. In 1995, China enacted the People's Bank of China law and other banking laws with decentralization of the banking system, which ironically led to the concentration of *large loans to large firms.*[7] In March 1996, the Eighth National People's Congress of China laid out a first five-year strategic plan to develop infrastructure, real estate, basic industries (metal products, automobile, and high-tech machinery), and other heavy-sector industries (such as petroleum and telecommunication). By 1998 the government completed the process of privatizing SOEs ("grasp the large and let go of the small") and began a privatization of the housing market. Before 2003, most houses were transacted below their market values (called affordable housing). In that year, however, affordable housing was largely abolished. Instead, the government encouraged the transactions of houses at their market value. These houses are called in Chinese "commodity houses." In 2000, real estate and auto industries were chosen to be the pillar industries by the government for its strategic plan. In 2001, China joined the World Trade Organization, which marked an important advancement in China's openness to the world economy and its trade liberalization.

In 2002, the four state banks became commercialized and thereafter many new commercial banks emerged, including the Bank of Communications—the fifth largest state bank. The banking system was China's most important source of external financing until the late 2000s when a rise of shadow banking eclipsed the importance of the traditional banking role. Until the rise of shadow banking, a monetary policy of explicitly targeting M2 growth had been effective on total bank credit as well as total social financing.

One crucial banking regulation that interacted with the monetary policy to affect the total bank credit was a regulation on the ceiling of the loan-to-deposit ratio (LDR). In a theoretical framework, Chen et al. (2018) show that when the PBC tightens monetary policy via open market operations, the probability of deposit withdrawals by primary dealers increases, which makes the LDR ratio more likely to be binding under the LDR regulation. Consequently, commercial banks, especially non-state banks, have to incur extra costs to recoup the deposit shortfalls (known as "last-minute rush costs," or 冲时点 [Cong Shi Dian] in Chinese). These expected regulatory costs reduce the effective return of bank lending and induce banks to engage in shadow banking by reducing formal banking.

As figure 6.15 shows, local governments' implicit guarantees on credits to real estate and its supporting heavy industries played a crucial role in credit allocations during the golden decade. When assessing loan applications, banks favored large loans to large firms and were biased against small loans to small firms. This practice was not only due to the asymmetric information problem facing small firms when banks assessed loan applications, but also a result of large firms in the heavy sector gaining implicit guarantees from local governments (Jiang et al., 2006). In short, banks favored lending to large firms or industries in the heavy sector targeted by the state (e.g., real estate and infrastructure). Compared to small firms, large firms produced more sales, provided more tax revenues, and helped boost the GDP of the local economy—the latter being the most important criterion for the political benefits of local government officials.

As financial policies switched from a reliance on credit policy in the SOE-led economy to an emphasis on quantity-based monetary policy in the investment-driven economy, this new economic regime also changed its characteristics. Because the government's monetary and credit policies focused on investment in the heavy sector during 1998–2015, the relationship between investment and consumption broke down. That is, the correlation between growth rates of investment and consumption changed from 0.80 in the SOE-led economy to being statistically insignificant in the investment-driven economy (table 6.1 and figure 6.5). And the correlation between investment and labor income was also close to zero (0.026 with the p-value 0.919). The promotion of investment at the sacrifice of consumption caused PPI inflation to be more volatile than CPI inflation (table 6.2 and figure 6.13) and the labor share of income to decline (figure 6.12).[8]

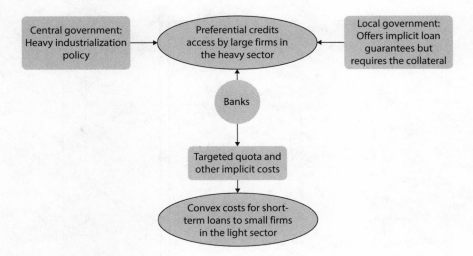

FIGURE 6.15. Transmission of monetary/credit policy in the investment-driven economy.

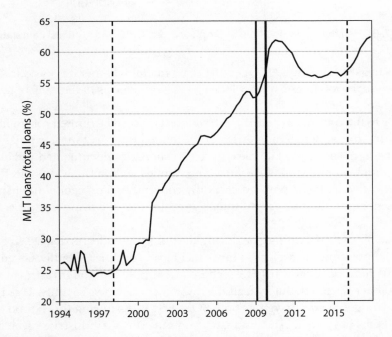

FIGURE 6.16. Share of medium and long-term (MLT) loans in total bank loans outstanding. *Sources:* CEIC and authors' calculation.

Investment during the golden decade was fueled by long-term bank credits, at the sacrifice of short-term bank credits to working capital in the light sector (figure 6.16). In other words, the increase in bank credits under the expansionary monetary policy was channeled disproportionally into long-term bank credits to finance investment. Accordingly, the correlation between short-term and long-term bank loans in the investment-driven

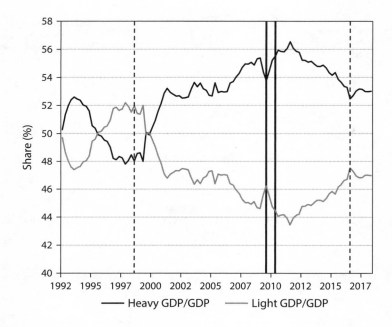

FIGURE 6.17. GDP in the heavy and light sectors. *Sources:* CEIC and authors' calculation.

economy is negative during 1998 Q1–2015 Q4, no matter whether it is measured in terms of year-over-year growth rate of new loans (−0.37) or in terms of the level of new loan as a percentage of GDP (−0.29).

Contrary to the common belief, the external sector played a limited role in investment growth during the golden decade. After China joined the WTO, most exports were produced in the light sector (e.g., textiles, toys, and shoes), as documented in Huang et al. (2015). In a number of newly industrialized economies in Asia (such as South Korea, Singapore, and Taiwan), the export-led economy concentrated on capital-intensive goods. Rapid investment in China's capital-intensive sector (i.e., the heavy sector) was not led by its exports.[9]

SOEs also played a declining role during the golden decade. As discussed earlier, the SOE share in investment as well as in investment loans declined steadily. Given the same preferential credit policy toward SOEs, these facts imply that the investment-to-output ratio would have declined. But instead the investment rate rose steadily. This is because the investment boom was driven by both SOEs and POEs during this period. In particular, large POEs in the real estate industry and other heavy industries received preferential bank credits to finance their investment.[10] In 2002, for instance, 65% of all firms were POEs in number, and the POE share of gross industrial output in total gross industrial output was 55%. In 2004Q1, the FAI growth rate in urban areas was 42.8% (80.7% for POEs vs. only 22.3% for SOEs).[11]

The preferential credit policy to firms in the heavy sector leads to the fact that gross output in that sector increased much faster than it did in the light sector. By contrast, the growth of gross output in both sectors was balanced in the SOE-led economy. This explains the increasing share of heavy sector GDP in total GDP since 1998 (figure 6.17). In particular, the share of value added to the real estate industry in GDP increased

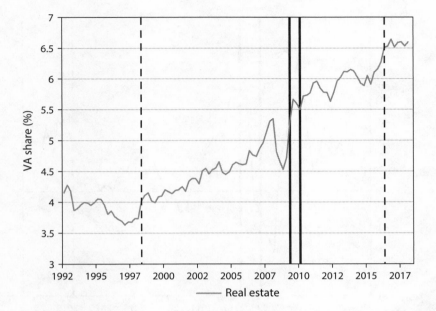

FIGURE 6.18. Share of value added (VA) to the real estate industry in total value added (GDP). *Sources:* CEIC and authors' calculation.

steadily (except for the global financial crisis) in the investment-driven economy (figure 6.18). As documented in Chen et al. (2018), most firms in the real estate industry are not SOEs.

The shift of a focus to invest in the heavy sector during the golden decade, from a focus to promote SOEs across all sectors in the SOE-led economy, resulted in more volatile PPI inflation than CPI inflation (table 6.2). In addition, growth in the real land (house) price was more volatile than inflation by an order of magnitude and on average much faster than (real) GDP growth (figure 6.19).

The trends and cycles in the investment-driven economy, especially during the golden decade, can be summarized as follows.

- Trends:
  - » (T1) A steady increase (decrease) of the ratio of aggregate investment (consumption) to GDP
  - » (T2) A declining share of income
  - » (T3) A steady increase in the ratio of medium to long-term (MLT) bank loans to short-term bank loans
  - » (T4) A steady increase in the ratio of gross output (and gross fixed assets) in the heavy sector to that in the light sector
- Cycles:
  - » (C1) No co-movement between aggregate investment and consumption
  - » (C2) No co-movement between aggregate investment and labor income
  - » (C3) A negative co-movement between MLT bank loans and short-term bank loans

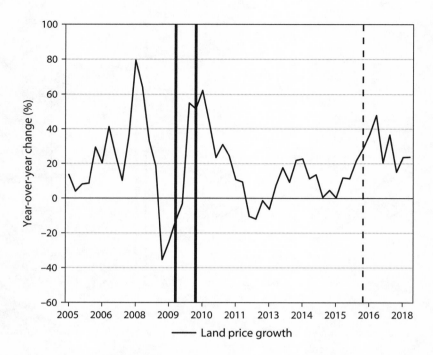

FIGURE 6.19. Annual growth in the land price. *Sources:* Wu et al. (2012) and authors' calculation.

Chang et al. (2015) develop a theoretical framework to explain these key facts of the investment-driven economy. The crucial difference between this model and that of Chen and Zha (2019) is that the government's funding through monetary/credit policy goes to the heavy sector as part of a shift of strategic emphasis to financing investment in that sector. Such a preferential credit reallocation caused resources to be reallocated toward the heavy sector as government net worth increased, which led to the upward trend of gross output in the heavy sector relative to that in the light sector, especially the real estate industry. Since the heavy sector had a higher investment rate than the light, the ratio of aggregate investment to aggregate output kept increasing during the golden decade. The preferential credit reallocation also made it costly to extend bank loans to the light sector. These costs, captured by the convex function of bank loans in the theoretical model, are one of the main explanations for the observed negative or insignificant correlation between investment and consumption.

Song et al. (2011, referred to herein as SSZ, after the three authors' names) provide a complementary explanation for the rapid growth during the golden decade. Their benchmark economy assumes one production sector in which less-productive SOEs enjoy preferential credits while productive POEs do not. Capital accumulation by POEs relies on their own savings. As a result, when POEs' capital stock increases, they demand more labor, which forces SOEs to downsize because of the competitive labor market. The capital reallocation from SOEs to POEs leads to an increase in allocative efficiency and therefore the aggregate TFP. As shown by Chen and Wen (2017), most of the increase in the share of private employment in total employment occurred between 1998 and 2004 (from

Table 6.5. Growth Accounting According to Long and Herrera (2016)

Growth (%)	1998–2008	2009–2010	2011–2015
GDP per worker	8.72	9.2	7.22
Due to capital	5.35	6.97	5.99
Due to TFP	3.38	2.23	1.22
Contribution by investment	61.3	75.8	83

Table 6.6. Growth Accounting According to Bai et al. (2006)

Growth (%)	1998–2008	2009–2010	2011–2015
GDP per worker	8.72	9.2	7.22
Due to capital	5.27	6.8	5.87
Due to TFP	3.45	2.4	1.35
Contribution by investment	60.5	73.9	81.3

15% to 50%), and this share kept increasing by another 10% between 2004 and 2011. Therefore, the SSZ model is crucial in understanding TFP growth during this period, which accounts for one-third of GDP growth (tables 6.3 and 6.4). The rest of GDP growth is accounted for by investment. Zilibotti (2017) regards all the years up to 2005 as an episode of "investment-led growth" and considers productivity growth to be a by-product of investment even in the absence of innovations or technical changes.

3.2.2. The 2009 Monetary Stimulus

During the phase of the investment-driven economy, the global financial crisis erupted in 2008. China's GDP growth (at a year-over-year rate) plummeted from 13.6% in 2007Q2 to 6.4% in 2009Q1. In November 2008, the State Council announced a plan to inject 4 trillion RMB of liquidity into the economy over the two-year period from 2009Q1 to 2010Q4. As it turned out, the monetary injection amounted to far larger than 4 trillion just within the first three quarters of 2009.

Overall, GDP growth jumped from 6.91% in 2008Q4 to 11.59% in 2009Q4 (figure 6.3) while aggregate investment grew by more than 20% during this period (figure 6.5). Growth in aggregate consumption growth, however, barely changed during this period. Chen et al. (2017) show that the monetary stimulus, represented mainly by a switch of monetary policy rule from the normal state to a more aggressive one, can explain 85% of the increase in GDP growth during the stimulus period.

In the investment-driven economy, moreover, investment played even a larger role in propelling economic growth both during and after the monetary stimulus period. Table 6.5 reports the growth accounting by breaking down the period of the investment-driven economy into three sub-periods: 1998–2008, 2009–2010, and 2011–2015. Across these three sub-periods, the contribution of investment increased from 61.3% to 75.8% and then to 83.0% (table 6.5) and from 60.5% to 73.9% and then to 81.3% (table 6.6).

Investment was mainly financed by massive credit injections engineered by loosening monetary policy (figure 6.1). Most of the increase in bank loans under the government's stimulus was channeled into fixed-asset investment, especially in the infrastructure sector. The land price bounced back immediately after the 2009 stimulus (figure 6.19), and the value added to the real estate not only bounced back but also kept increasing (figure 6.18). Such a monetary stimulus played a pivotal role in the recovery of GDP growth, but the asymmetric credit allocation during the golden decade was exacerbated during the stimulus period. The exacerbation can be seen in figure 6.16, as the share of MLT loans in total bank loans sprang up during the stimulus period. The ratio of total bank loans to GDP also sprang up during the stimulus period and kept increasing even after the stimulus was over (figure 6.20). Chen et al. (2017) show that the 2009 monetary stimulus produced an intertemporal tradeoff between short-run GDP growth and long-run indebtedness. In a similar spirit, Zilibotti (2017) argues that China's stimulus plan delayed innovations and created a tradeoff between fast short-run growth and sustainable long-run growth.

Bai et al. (2016) argue that an important part of financial stimulation was through an establishment of local government financing vehicles (LGFVs). Although local governments were legally prohibited from borrowing or running budget deficits, they circumvented the budget laws in 2009 and 2010 by creating off-balance-sheet companies, known as LGFVs, to finance investment in infrastructure and other commercial projects. According to Obstfeld (2016), LGFV borrowing as a percent of GDP increased from 16.3% in 2008 to 25.09% in 2010 (an increase of 8.79 percentage points), but this increase still paled in comparison to an increase of 31.58 percentage points in private sector borrowing as a percent of GDP during the same period.

3.2.3. The Post-Stimulus Episode, 2010–2015

To combat the rising inflation after the 2009 massive stimulus, the government implemented tightening monetary and credit policies to slow down investment in the heavy sector and thus to place economic growth on a sustainable path. GDP growth declined from 11.59% in 2009Q4 to less than 7% in 2015Q4. Yet the contribution of investment-to-GDP growth continued to increase (tables 6.5 and 6.6); investment in the heavy sector and upstream industries continued to play a major role (Bai et al., 2018). Although the value added to the heavy sector and upstream industries as the shares of GDP declined after the 2009 monetary stimulus, these shares still remained at an unsustainably high level, and bank credits continued to be channeled not merely to upstream industries but also to the heavy sector in general.

While monetary policy tightened after the 2009 stimulus, regulatory policy on shadow banking remained lax, which gave rise to the boom of shadow banking that fueled investment in real estate, construction, and other industries with excess capacity. The lack of coordination between monetary and regulatory policies gave non-state banks a strong incentive to avail themselves of the regulatory arbitrage to engage in shadow banking activities, especially in entrusted lending. As shown in figure 6.20, both off-balance-sheet financing and corporate bond financing have increased significantly since 2009. Consequently, the gap between bank loans and total social financing widened during and after the monetary stimulus (figure 6.21).

From 2009 to 2015, entrusted loans became the second largest financing source of loans after formal (traditional) bank loans. Entrusted lending is a loan made from one

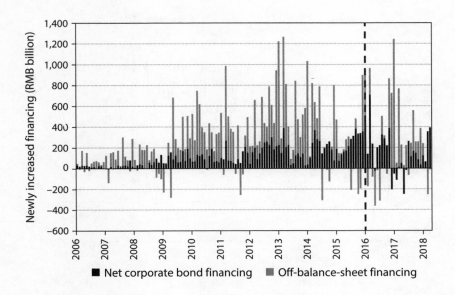

FIGURE 6.20. Nonbank financing in investment. *Sources:* CEIC and authors' calculation. *Note:* Off-balance-sheet financing is the sum of entrusted loans, trust loans, and bank acceptances.

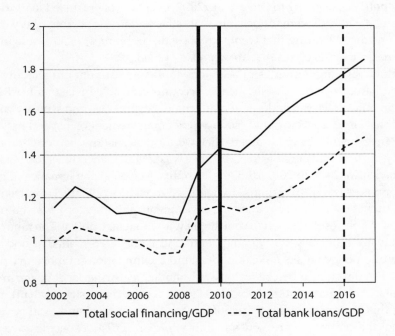

FIGURE 6.21. Ratios of total social financing and bank loans to GDP. *Sources:* CEIC and authors' calculation. *Note:* Total social financing is calculated as the sum of bank loans, entrusted loans, trusted loans, and bank acceptances.

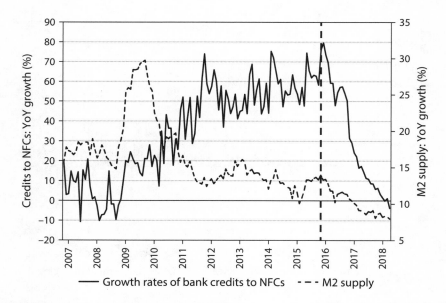

FIGURE 6.22. Growth rates of bank credits to NFCs and M2 supply. *Sources:* CEIC and authors' calculation.

nonfinancial firm to another nonfinancial firm. It was first facilitated by commercial banks off balance sheet but then brought onto the balance sheet to take advantage of lax regulatory policy. According to Chen et al. (2018), over 60% of entrusted loans during the period from 2009 to 2015 were funneled to real estate and its supporting heavy industries. As for the entrusted lending that went to real estate companies, 75.33% of loan volumes were channeled to enterprises that are *not* state owned.

As shadow banking activities blossomed, so did investments in shadow banking products on banks' balance sheets, such as account-receivable investment (ARI) and investments in NFCs. NFCs include asset management companies and security companies, companies that issue assets to banks (such as asset management plans) and use the funds to finance investments in risky assets that were often shadow banking products. As shown in figure 6.22, bank credits to NFCs have waxed and waned when monetary policy has tightened since 2009. In 2010–2015, these credits, as well as the issuance of municipal corporate bonds, "waxed" in response to tightened monetary policy.[12] The effectiveness of tightening monetary policy to reduce the investment rate, therefore, was hampered by other financial policies that failed to coordinate with monetary policy. The failure of coordination between monetary policy and other financial policies provided a good lesson for researchers and policymakers alike to understand the limitations of monetary policy.

Xiong (2018) develops a theoretical growth model, featuring local government GDP tournaments, to highlight another potential source for the rising shadow banking industry during this period: the agency frictions between the central and local governments arising from the central government's inability to distinguish a specific governor's administration ability from infrastructure investment in that governor's province. Consequently, the governor faces a tradeoff between debt and career. To advance his or her personal career, the governor takes on more debts to finance infrastructure investment

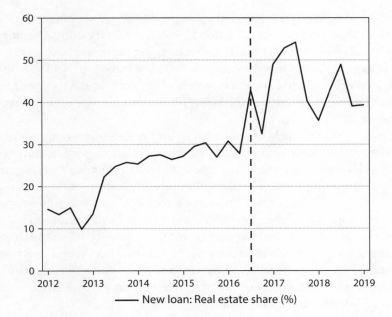

FIGURE 6.23. Loan concentration: The share of bank loans to real estate in total bank loans. *Sources:* CEIC and authors' calculation.

with an advantageous growth rate of regional productivity. But the governor has to face the high cost of paying the debts next period. This model implies that the governor's career development can lead to an overleverage of the local government and thereafter a booming shadow banking industry.

In the post-stimulus period, the real estate overstock problem persisted in small as well as medium-sized cities. Because of the overcapacity (low capacity utilization) in other heavy industries that support the real estate, many firms (especially large ones) became overleveraged. To reduce the overstock of real estate, credit policy for mortgage financing was loosened in 2014Q4–2016Q3, which created a boom of mortgage loans and an increasing concentration of bank loans to the real estate market (figure 6.23). The concentration in recent years has further raised systemic risks to the overall financial system.

In summary, the massive credit expansion during both the stimulus and post-stimulus episodes has led to rapid growth of the debt burden as a percent of GDP as well as to a widening gap between total social financing and aggregate bank loans. Both the rapid growth of shadow banking products and the increasing concentration of bank loans to the real estate industry have raised systemic risks to the entire financial system. For shadow banking products, systemic risks are associated with default risks to real estate companies and LGFVs.[13] For bank loans, systemic risks are associated with default risks to the household sector if the housing market were to collapse.

3.3. The New-Normal Economy, 2016–Present

As the debt-to-GDP ratio rose rapidly in the latter part of the investment-driven economy and has continued to rise in the new normal economy, the tension between robust GDP growth and financial stability has begun to build up. As a result, financial policies in the new normal economy are featured by strengthened regulations on shadow banking products as well as better coordination between monetary and regulatory policies under the MPA system. In this phase, two deleveraging processes have begun: financial deleveraging to guide banks to reduce shadow banking loans (e.g., bank credits to NFCs) and firm deleveraging to reduce corporate debts (e.g., ceasing the rollover of corporate debts). As can be seen from figure 6.22, both NFC credits and M2 supply have declined in tandem since 2016.[14]

The macroeconomic impacts of the financial and real deleveraging processes in the new normal economy need time to be fully assessed. Early evidence indicates that investment in both real estate and infrastructure, the two industries that were the largest beneficiaries of the rising shadow banking, has recently lost steam. Various regulations on shadow banking activities since 2017 have forced real estate developers to deleverage. The housing market and construction investment have begun to cool down. In 2018Q1, the premium rate in the land auction market was only 10%, far below the level of 30% during 2015–2017. Infrastructure investment has also slowed down since 2018, owing to a series of regulations meant to rectify local government financing guarantees.[15] The year-over-year growth rate of infrastructure investment fell since the second quarter of 2017 to 7.3% in the first half of 2018.

One unintended consequence of deleveraging is that POEs, especially the small and medium-sized ones, have had even a harder time to gain access to bank financing. During the deleveraging processes, the tightening of regulations on the shadow banking industry has led to defaults of unprofitable POEs, creating a tradeoff between cleansing effects and systemic risks as borrowing costs for healthy POEs have also increased. The mounting default risks, together with increasing deposit shortfalls under the financial deleveraging, have made banks more reluctant to lend to POEs, including even the healthy ones.[16] Since 2016, investment growth in the manufacturing industry has been continuously below GDP growth. And as GDP growth continues to slow down, the tension between that growth and financial stability challenges the government's determination for further deleveraging.

A deeper concern is the limited impact of deleveraging on SOEs in upstream industries, which have continued to receive preferential credits and remain unproductive and monopolistic. Implicit guarantees by local governments to such zombie firms make difficult the deleveraging of corporate debts. Figure 6.24 shows that in recent years, the share of newly issued bank loans to SOEs has increased steadily, while the share of bank loans to POEs has declined. To deal with this asymmetry between the treatments of SOEs and POEs, in 2016 the government introduced reforms to reduce the production of upstream industries in the heavy sector through administrative means. The production reduction resulted in an increase of PPI in the upstream firms, even while these unproductive and monopolistic firms continued to receive preferential credits. The increase of PPI, in turn, raised the costs to downstream industries, most of which belong to the light sector. It would inevitably exacerbate the credit and resource misallocations, putting further downward pressures on economic growth. As investment growth in the light sector has slowed in recent years, GDP growth has also slowed while the investment-to-GDP ratio has remained persistently high, over 42% as shown in figure 6.14.

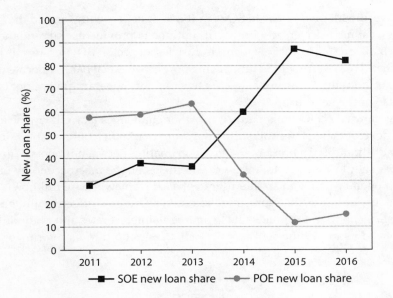

FIGURE 6.24. Share of newly issued bank loans to SOEs and POEs in total newly issued bank loans. *Sources:* CEIC and Chen and Zha (2019).

4. CONCLUSION

The preceding sections provide an overview of how regime shifts in the government's financial policies influenced the ways in which preferential credits were allocated to both SOEs and the heavy sector. The analysis highlights the role of the government in the structural changes of the economy. The regime's switching from a SOE-led economy to an investment-driven economy and then to the "new normal" economy has been a product of changes in the government's active financial policies.

Policy tools since 2016 have been adapted to assist a transition to the new normal economy. At the beginning of 2016, the government incorporated the MPA system to ensure an effective coordination between monetary and other financial policies. Other unifying rules on asset management across various financial sectors (e.g., formal banking and shadow banking) have been developed. Monetary policy has begun to experience a regime change as well: a transition from the quantity-based framework to an interest rate–based framework.[17] In addition to the conventional policy tools, the government has applied many unconventional tools such as standing lending facility (SLF), medium-term lending facility (MLF), and pledged supplementary lending (PSL) to assist this transition.

Such a transition, however, will not be smooth under China's institutional constraints. The GDP growth target still remains the foremost goal of monetary policy. According to the central government's Thirteenth Five-Year Plan (2016–2020), the GDP growth target as a lower bound will continue for the next five years. High GDP growth when vigorously pursued by the central government as the overriding policy goal puts a severe constraint on how the PBC conducts its monetary policy and on how tight regulatory policy should be. As long as the GDP growth target is in force, preferential credit policy with implicit government guarantees to SOEs in the SOE-led economy and to the heavy sector in the investment-driven economy will continue to provide useful guidance for how to allocate bank credits to various firms, industries, or sectors. Therefore, it is likely that the heavy hand of government in influencing how commercial banks allocate their loans will continue, making M2 growth an effective tool for monetary policy, not only in the past but also in the near future.

The new normal economy is marked by other challenges as well. Financial markets are in the development stage and still suffer from market frictions such as deposit rate ceilings and illiquidity in bond markets. Coordination between monetary and regulatory policies should continue to improve. The effects on the macroeconomy of a regime switch in monetary policy to an interest rate–based framework are unknown and difficult to measure at this point. Nor is much known about how effective will be the monetary transmission from the policy rate to interbank interest rates and eventually to bank lending rates. In sum, China will face new challenges both to its reforms on financial policies and to its policy impacts on the new normal economy.

NOTES

Tao Zha acknowledges research support from the Shanghai Advanced Institute of Finance at Shanghai Jong Tong University. This research is supported in part by the National Science Foundation Grant SES 1558486 through the NBER and by the National Natural Science Foundation of China Project Numbers 71473168, 71473169, and 71633003. The authors are grateful to Marlene Amstad, Pat Higgins, Tom Sargent, Guofeng Sun, and Wei Xiong for comments and suggestions, and to Yiqing Xiao for excellent research assistance. The views expressed herein are those of the authors and do not necessarily reflect the views of the Federal Reserve Bank of Atlanta, the Federal Reserve System, or the National Bureau of Economic Research.

1.   Most time series data used in this article and many other related data can be downloaded from https://www.frbatlanta.org/cqer/research/china-macroeconomy.aspx?panel=1 (the English version) or http://cmf.cafr.cn/ under 数据下载 (the Chinese version).

2.   During this phase, township and village enterprises (TVEs) experienced similar growth patterns and reforms as SOEs in the light sector. Also, they enjoyed local government guarantee of bank credit, despite a much smaller share of bank credit than that of SOEs.

3.   Chen et al. (2017) identify monetary stimulus as monetary policy switching to a more aggressive regime to combat the fall of GDP growth below its official target.

4.   In April 2018, the PBC and CBRC issued the joint notice "Guiding Opinions on Regulating Asset Management Business of Financial Institutions" to allow for flexibility in the redemption of asset management plan.

5.   Zhou (2007) calls such an incentive system for local governments the "promotion tournament," arguing that such a "tournament" is the key source of China's miraculous growth.

6.   The U.S. Bureau of Labor Statistics labels K/N "capital intensity." It is also often defined as "the ratio of capital services to hours worked in the production process" (see chart 2 on page 2 and page 10 of https://www.bls.gov/news.release/pdf/prod3.pdf). This chapter uses employment instead of hours because of the lack of Chinese data on the latter.

7.   See Brandt and Zhu (2007) for a comprehensive list of the laws and regulations enacted during this period.

8.   The decline of China's labor income share since the late 1990s is a robust fact, as confirmed by Bai and Qian (2009) and Qian and Zhu (2012), who have made data adjustments to take into account changes in the statistical coverage of labor compensations over time.

9.   According to Huang et al. (2015), between 1999 and 2007, labor-intensive firms increased their export shares while capital-intensive firms reduced their export share; at the same time, the capital intensity of export firms was reduced.

10. Examples of large and important POEs during the investment-driven phase include 华为 (communications), 联想 (information and technology), 吉利 (automobile), 万达 and 万科 (real estate).

11. See Liu (2005).

12. Chen et al. (2017) use province-level data to show that provinces experiencing an abnormally fast growth rate of bank loans in 2009 also experienced fast growth of municipal corporate bond issuances during 2012–2015.
13. Bai and Zhou (2018) find that the municipal corporate bond yields across provinces are negatively influenced by the value added to real estate (as a share of provincial GDP).
14. While the recent cooperation between monetary and regulatory policies has improved banks' balance-sheet standing, off-balance-sheet activities and corporate debts continue to be a serious problem. In 2017, for example, trust loans (a major part of off-balance-sheet banking) soared in response to the shrinking activities of on-balance-sheet investments (figure 6.21).
15. For example, the PBC, the Ministry of Finance, and four other government agencies issued a *Notice on Further Regulating Local Government's Debt Financing Behavior* in May 2017 for the purpose of rectifying local government's financing guarantees.
16. A similar situation occurred in the corporate bond market, as implied by the increasing credit spread.
17. See Ma and Guan (2018) for a detailed assessment of the transmission mechanism and the effectiveness of the reforms on the interest rate liberalization; see Liu et al. (2018) for a theoretical analysis.

REFERENCES

Bai, Chong-En, Chang-Tai Hsieh, and Yingyi Qian (2006). "The Return to Capital in China." Brookings Papers on Economic Activity, vol. 2: 61–101.

Bai, Chong-En, Chang-Tai Hsieh, and Zheng (Michale) Song (2016). "The Long Shadow of China's Fiscal Expansion." Brookings Papers on Economic Activity (Fall): 129–65.

Bai, Chong-En, Qing Liu, and Wen Yao (2018). "Skill Premium and Preferential Policy: The Case of China." Unpublished manuscript.

Bai, Chong-En, and Z. Qian (2009). "Factor Income Share in China: The Story Behind the Statistics." *Economic Research Journal* (in Chinese) 3: 27–41.

Bai, J., and Hao Zhou (2018). "The Funding Costs of Chinese Local Government Debt." Unpublished manuscript.

Brandt, Loren, and Xiaodong Zhu (2007). "China's Banking Sector and Economic Growth," in *China's Financial Transition at a Crossroads,* edited by Charles W Calomiris. New York: Columbia University Press.

Chang, Chun, Kaiji Chen, Daniel F. Waggoner, and Tao Zha (2015). "Trends and Cycles in China's Macroeconomy." *NBER Macroeconomics Annual* 30: 1–84.

Chen, Kaiji, Patrick Higgins, Daniel F. Waggoner, and Tao Zha (2017). "Impacts of Monetary Stimulus on Credit Allocation and the Macroeconomy: Evidence from China" (No. W22650). National Bureau of Economic Research.

Chen, Kaiji, Jue Ren, and Tao Zha (2018). "The Nexus of Monetary Policy and Shadow Banking in China." *American Economic Review* 108(12): 3891–3936.

Chen, Kaiji, and Yi Wen (2017). "The Great Housing Boom of China." *American Economic Journal: Macroeconomics* 9(2): 73–114.

Chen, Kaiji, and Tao Zha (2019). "Impacts of China's Credit Policy on the SOE-led and Investment-led Economies." Unpublished manuscript. https://sites.google.com/a/tzha.net/www/articles #CHINACREDITPOLICY

Chen, Z., C. Liu, and Z. He (2017). "The Financing of Local Government in China: Stimulus Loan Wanes and Shadow Banking Waxes." Unpublished manuscript.

Huang, Hanwei, Jiandong Ju, and Vivian Z. Yue (2015). "A Unified Model of Structural Adjustments and International Trade: Theory and Evidence from China." Unpublished manuscript.

Jiang, Shuxia, Jie Luo, and Junci Huang (2006). "Credit Concentration and Expansion, Soft Budget Constraints, and Systemic Credit Risks of Banks." *Journal of Financial Research* (in Chinese) 4: 40–48.

Lagakos, David (2018). "Accounting for Africa's Growth Miracle." Unpublished manuscript.

Liu, S. (2005). *Economic Cycle and Macro Regulation* (in Chinese). Beijing: Social Science Academy Press.

Liu, Zheng, Mark M. Spiegel, and Jingyi Zhang (2018). "Optimal Capital Account Liberalization in China." Unpublished manuscript.

Long, Zhiming, and Remy Herrera (2016). "Building Original Series of Physical Capital Stocks for China's Economy Methodological Problems, Proposals for Solutions and a New Database." *China Economic Review* 40: 33–53.

Ma, J., and T. Guan (eds.) (2018). *Interest Rate Liberalization and Reform of Monetary Policy Framework* (in Chinese). Beijing: China Finance Publishing House.

Obstfeld, M. (2016). "Comment: The Long Shadow of China's Fiscal Stimulus." Brookings Papers on Economic Activity, Fall, 166–72.

Qian, Z., and Xiaodong Zhu (2012). "Why Is the Labor Income Share So Low in China?" Unpublished presentation slides.

Song, Zheng, Kjetil Storesletten, and Fabrizio Zilibotti (2011). "Growing Like China." *American Economic Review*, February 101(1): 196–233.

Wu, Jing, Joseph Gyourko, and Yongheng Deng (2012). "Evaluating Conditions in Major Chinese Housing Markets." *Regional Science and Urban Economics* 42 (2): 531–45.

Xiong, Wei (2018). "The Mandarin Model of Growth." Unpublished manuscript.

Zhou, L. (2007). "Governing China's Local Officials: An Analysis of Promotion Tournament Model." *Economic Research Journal* (in Chinese) 7: 36–50.

Zilibotti, F. (2017). "Growing and Slowing Down Like China." *Journal of European Economic Association* 15(5): 943–88.

7

CHINA'S REAL ESTATE MARKET

Chang Liu and Wei Xiong

The real estate market is not only a key part of the Chinese economy but also an integral component of China's financial system. In 2017, housing sales totaled 13.37 trillion RMB, equivalent to 16.4% of China's GDP. The real estate market is also deeply connected to China's financial system through several important channels. First, housing holdings are the biggest component of Chinese households' asset portfolios, partly due to a lack of other investment vehicles for both households and firms in China's still underdeveloped financial markets. Second, China's local governments heavily rely on land sale revenues and use future land sale revenues as collateral to raise debt financing through Local Government Financing Platforms (LGFPs). Third, firms also rely on real estate assets as collateral to borrow, and since 2007, firms, especially well-capitalized ones, have engaged heavily in acquiring land for investment purposes. Finally, banks are heavily exposed to real estate risks through loans made to households, real estate developers, local governments, and firms that are either explicitly or implicitly backed by real estate assets.

Figure 7.1 provides an estimate made by the Deutsche Bank Report (2016) of the exposure of China's banking system to the real estate market. Through the third quarter of 2016, property-related loans totaled 55 trillion RMB, accounting for about 25% of China's banking assets. Among these loans, mortgage loans to households accounted for 17.9 trillion, loans to real estate developers accounted for 14.8 trillion (including 7 trillion in regular loans, 6.3 trillion in credit through shadow banking, and 1.5 trillion through domestic bond issuance), and loans collateralized by real estate assets to firms and local governments accounted for 22.2 trillion. This heavy real estate exposure of banks makes the real estate market systemically important in China's financial system.

Since the 1990s, the real estate market has experienced a dramatic and long-lasting boom across China. This boom has led to substantial concerns in both academic and policy circles—as shown, for example, in Wu et al. (2016), Chen and Wen (2017), Glaeser et al. (2017), and Song and Xiong (2018)—that the rising housing prices might have developed into a gigantic housing bubble, which could eventually burst and damage China's financial system and entire economy. Motivated by this concern, this chapter reviews the historical development of China's real estate market in section 1, describes the real

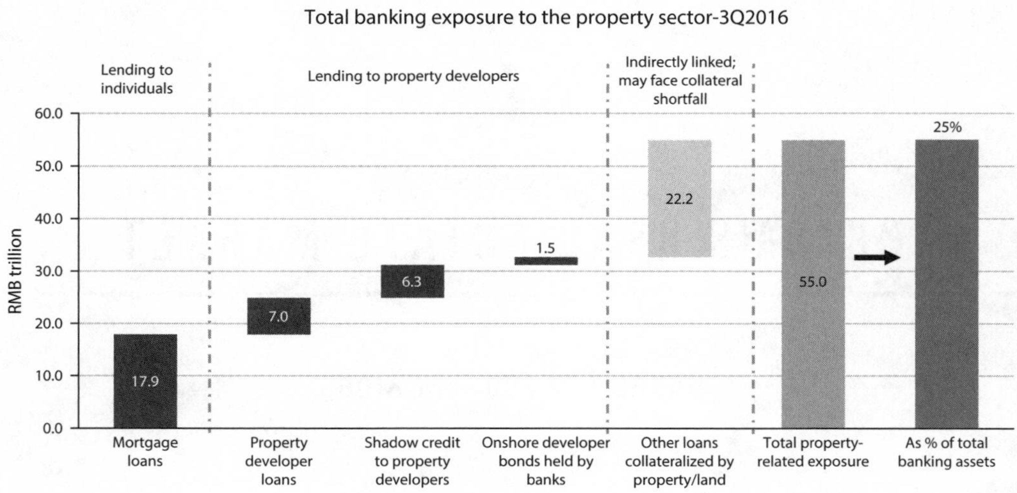

Total banking exposure to the property sector-3Q2016

FIGURE 7.1. Exposure of China's banking system to the real estate market. *Source:* Deutsche Bank Report (2016).

estate boom in section 2, discusses how the real estate market is linked to households in section 3, tells how it is linked to local governments in section 4, and shows how it is linked to firms in section 5. After these important aspects of China's real estate market have been covered, section 6 discusses why the authors do not expect a sudden nationwide real estate crash in China and concludes by highlighting several key factors regarding the sustainability of the market going forward.

1. DEVELOPMENT OF CHINA'S REAL ESTATE MARKET

The development of China's real estate market is deeply rooted in its great economic transition process. This section reviews several critical features of this development.

1.1. Housing Reforms

China experienced a series of market-oriented housing reforms in the 1990s. Housing reforms were initiated in 1994 when the government allowed state sector employees to purchase full or partial property rights to their current apartment units at subsidized prices, which essentially amounted to welfare for state employees. In 1998, the Chinese government abolished this welfare housing system when it targeted the real estate sector as a new engine of economic growth in response to the adverse effects generated by the 1997 Asian financial crisis. After this reform, Chinese citizens working for the government or government-related organizations could no longer purchase housing at discount, unleashing a flood of private housing demand.

The privatization of housing has had profound impacts on the Chinese economy. Wang (2011) finds that by allowing households to increase their housing consumption, the reform laid a solid foundation for subsequent increases in housing prices. Other studies suggest that the dramatic transformation of housing from state-owned to privately owned has stimulated entrepreneurship in China by alleviating credit constraints (Wang, 2012), and was associated with substantial increases in income inequality (Novokmet et al., 2018).

As an important impetus to the development of the private real estate market, in 1998 the People's Bank of China (PBC) outlined procedures for home buyers to obtain residential mortgages at subsidized interest rates. Moreover, between 1998 and 2002, the PBC lowered mortgage interest rate five times to stimulate private home purchases. By 2005, China had become the largest residential mortgage market in Asia. According to PBC reports, China's mortgage loans reached 17.9 trillion RMB in 2016, equivalent to 25% of the country's GDP that year. At the same time, the PBC also developed other policies to support the housing market, including broadening the scope of real estate loans and allowing presales by developers. Taken together, the abolishment of welfare housing distribution, along with the introduction of residential mortgage loans, stimulated the take-off of China's great housing boom.

1.2. Urbanization Process

China's urbanization process has traveled down a winding road. The country had an overpopulated and poor agrarian economy when Deng Xiaoping initiated the Opening-up Reform in 1978. To ensure a stable food supply and maintain adequate public services to urban citizens, China formerly had imposed strict regulations on rural-to-urban migration, known as the *hukou* system. This strict system not only distorted China's labor market but also dragged down the development of its housing market.

China's 10th Five-Year Plan, passed in 2001, set urbanization as a national strategy to stimulate demand and make the housing market a new engine of the country's economic growth. In accordance with this national strategy, the State Council issued a formal document that allowed free rural-to-urban migration for counties and small towns. The urban-rural divide in the *hukou* system ended in 2014 when the State Council completely abolished the urban and rural dual structure for labeling Chinese citizens' residence. Since then, citizens have been free to move to urban areas, except for a restricted number of large cities such as Beijing and Shanghai. Figure 7.2 shows the steady growth in the urbanization rate from 1990 to 2016. Interestingly, urbanization is still in progress, with more than 40% of Chinese citizens still living in rural areas at the end of 2016. By depicting the completion of new homes in each year, the figure also shows rapid increases in new home construction before 2012. Construction of new homes flattened out after 2012 and even dropped in 2015, indicating a slowdown in the construction boom.

In a recent study, Garriga et al. (2017) build a multisector, dynamic general-equilibrium model to study the rural-to-urban structural transformation in China's housing market. Their quantitative analysis suggests that the urbanization process accounts for about 80% of the growth in China's urban housing prices.

1.3. Ghost Towns

China's housing market development has been accompanied by a hotly debated phenomenon—the so-called ghost towns—as discussed by Shepard (2015) and Woodworth and Wallace (2017). One can often find newly constructed but mostly empty urban districts, usually in areas far away from traditional city centers. Well-known examples include Ordos in Inner Mongolia and Zhengdong New District in Henan Province. More generally, China's urbanization features a high vacancy rate in cities. According to data

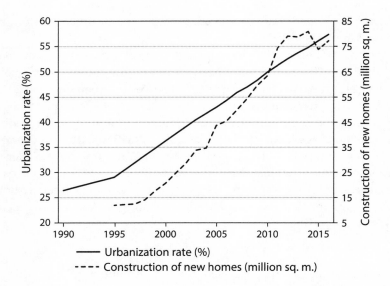

FIGURE 7.2. China's urbanization process. *Source:* China's National Bureau of Statistics.

constructed for 36 cities by Glaeser et al. (2017), the housing vacancy rate rose sharply after 2009 across first-, second-, third-, and even fourth-tier cities, as shown in figure 7.3.[1] This observation has led to serious concerns, given that a high vacancy rate is commonly regarded as an indicator of a potential housing bubble.

Note that the massive urbanization process naturally leads to a high vacancy rate in the early stages of developing a new district. It is common for local governments across China to develop new districts on empty land far away from city centers. A typical development process starts with the local government's outlining a master plan for commercial and residential properties to be built in the new district, along with supporting public infrastructure projects, such as roads, water and power plants, public schools, and hospitals. It may take several phases for a new district to become fully occupied and prosperous. In the first phase, the local government uses the master plan to attract developers to buy land and to build commercial and residential properties in the district. It may take one to five years for the property and infrastructure projects to gradually start up. In this phase, the local government also launches the infrastructure projects. Property buyers start to acquire housing units in this early phase, mostly driven by investment interests, and the occupancy rate for completed residential properties is low. In the second phase, which may be 6 to 10 years after the launch of the new district, most of the construction is completed and the occupancy rate gradually rises over time. It often helps if the local government moves some of its agencies and bureaus into the new district, which serves as a stimulus for commercial businesses, such as restaurants and shops, to move in with the state employees. It may take more than 10 years for the new district to become fully occupied. This marks the third phase—a period when commercial businesses are in full operation and living conditions in the district become comfortable. Only at this time do commercial businesses in the district become profitable and a secondary housing market becomes active.

As a result of this long development process, it is not surprising to see a high vacancy rate in the first and second phases of a new district. Nevertheless, several factors may

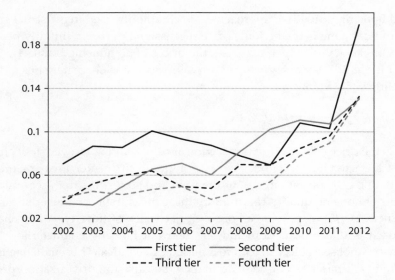

FIGURE 7.3. Vacancy rates for Chinese cities, 2001–2012. *Source:* Glaeser et al. (2017).

exacerbate the high vacancy rate and lead to ghost towns that remain unoccupied for prolonged periods. First, as will be discussed later, land sale revenues are an important source of local governments' fiscal budgets. This distinct institutional feature may incentivize local governments to overdevelop new districts and real estate projects. Second, as part of the national urbanization process, small cities have experienced an outflow of residents to first- and second-tier cities.

An extensive body of literature exists on what are called China's ghost towns. Woodworth and Wallace (2017) characterize some stylized facts. Zhang et al. (2016) relate high vacancy rates in Chinese cities to rising income inequality, measured by the income Gini index. Anglin et al. (2014) and Wang et al. (2018) show that the career concerns of local government officials, combined with China's land leasehold system and fiscal system, help to explain their outward development tendency (that is, their preference to build new urban districts). The decentralized spatial distribution of Chinese cities can also be partially attributed to the fast development of China's infrastructure system, including urban railroad and highway systems, as argued by Baum-Snow et al. (2017).

2. THE REAL ESTATE BOOM

Since the housing reforms that began in the 1990s, China has experienced a spectacular real estate boom that is still ongoing. This section discusses this boom.

2.1. Housing Prices

One cannot simply use prices from housing transactions from one month to another to compute housing-price appreciation in a city, because housing units transacted in two separate months are likely different and thus have different qualities. This feature makes housing transactions unlike trading of typical financial securities. As a result, it is important to construct a housing price index that adjusts for potential quality heterogeneity in transacted housing units. Two approaches are commonly used to construct such housing price indices. One is the hedonic price regression approach, initially proposed by Kain and Quigley (1970), which regresses the prices of all housing transactions that occurred at different times in a given city on all measurable characteristics of the transacted housing units as follows:

$$\ln P_{i,t} = \beta_0 + \sum_{s=1}^{T} \beta_s \cdot I\{s = t\} + \theta_c X_i + \epsilon_{it}$$

where $P_{i,t}$ is the price of a housing transaction at time t, and X_i is a vector of characteristics of the transacted housing unit, such as distance to city center, area amenities, availability of public transportation, size of the unit, and so forth. After accounting for the price effects of housing quality captured by these measurable characteristics, the time-effect coefficients $\{\beta_t\}_{t=0}^{T}$ provide a housing price index of the city. A key challenge to this approach is that failure to include all relevant housing characteristics, some of which may be unobservable, can lead to a biased price index. This challenge is particularly severe in China's nascent housing market, because the urbanization process has led to dramatic expansions of cities, making it extremely difficult to reliably measure housing quality.

In response to the challenges with the hedonic price regression approach, Case and Shiller (1987) have developed a second approach based on repeated sales of the same housing unit. As repeated sales share the identical housing quality, this approach does not require any direct measure of housing quality. A potential weakness of this approach, however, is that it needs a sufficient number of repeated housing transactions, which is again difficult for many Chinese cities, as repeated housing sales usually become more frequent only after the housing market matures.

In a recent study, Fang et al. (2016) develop a hybrid approach to account for the unique setting of China's nascent housing market. Specifically, they use housing transactions within the same housing communities. It has been common during China's urbanization process for a developer to build up a community with hundreds of apartment units in a number of high-rise buildings and then gradually sell these apartments over one to two years. These apartments share the same community amenities, which are usually difficult to measure, and differ only in their characteristics inside the community, such as size, number of rooms, floor level, and orientation, which are relatively easy to measure. Based on this observation, Fang et al. (2016) construct a housing price index for 120 cities in China by modifying the standard hedonic regression approach to include a community fixed effect, which controls for the community-level heterogeneity, together with a number of within-community characteristics:

$$\ln P_{i,j,t} = \beta_0 + \sum_{s=1}^{T} \beta_s \cdot I\{s = t\} + DP_j + \theta_c X_i + \epsilon_{it}$$

where $P_{i,j,t}$ is the price of housing transaction i in community j, DP_j is a set of community fixed effects, and X_i is a vector of characteristics of the transacted housing unit within community j. The time-effect coefficients $\{\beta_t\}_{t=0}^{T}$ again serve as a housing price index of the city. They estimate this regression by using a detailed mortgage data set from a major commercial bank for 120 Chinese cities for the period 2003 to 2013 with which they create a housing price index for each of these cities. A recent study by Chen et al. (2018b) uses a

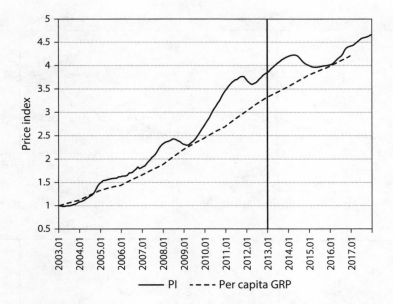

FIGURE 7.4. National average housing price index, 2003–2013. *Sources:* Fang et al. (2016) and NBS. *Note:* PI is weighted by urban population.

similar approach and employs a mortgage loan sample from a different major commercial bank to create a set of housing price indices for 70 cities after 2011.

China's National Bureau of Statistics (NBS) publishes housing price indices for 70 major cities. Before 2011, the NBS 70-city price indices show only small price appreciations across the country, in contrast to casual observations about housing transaction prices in these cities.[2] After 2011, the NBS adopted a new housing price construction approach, which adjusts for housing quality, according to a document released on the NBS website. Interestingly, Chen et al. (2018b) confirm that after 2011 the NBS 70-city index has become more reasonable in reflecting housing price fluctuations. To discuss China's housing boom, this chapter uses the housing price indices of Fang et al. (2016) to cover the period of 2003–2012 and uses the NBS 70-city index to cover the later period of 2013–2017.

Figure 7.4 depicts the monthly national average housing price indices (PI) from 2003 to 2017, which is weighted across cities based on urban population. The figure also shows a simple measure of households' purchasing power: per capita gross regional product (GRP), which is available up to 2016. The vertical line in the plot marks January 2013, which separates the two samples, with the housing price index from Fang et al. (2016) for the earlier period and the NBS 70-city index for the later period. The national housing price index level appreciated tremendously, reaching in 2017 a level about 4.5 times its 2003 level. Curiously, this tremendous housing price appreciation was nonetheless accompanied by similar growth in per capita GRP.

Figure 7.5 depicts in four separate panels the housing price indices for the four first-tier cities: Beijing, Shanghai, Guangzhou, and Shenzhen. In Panel A, the housing price index of Beijing experienced an enormous increase from an index level of 1 in 2003 to over 11 in 2017, an 11-fold increase in just 14 years. This increase is also substantially greater than the increase in per capita GRP of the city, which was about fourfold. As seen

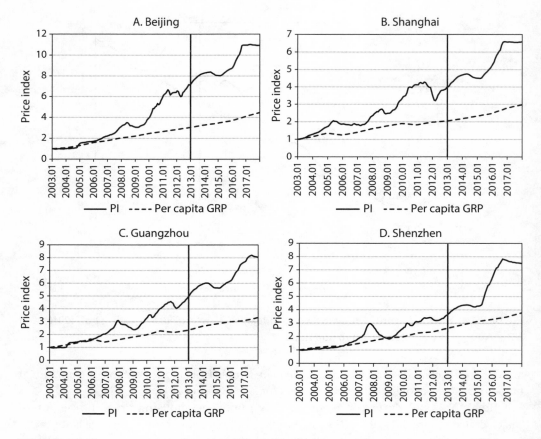

FIGURE 7.5. Housing price indices for China's first-tier cities. *Sources:* Fang et al. (2016) and NBS.

in Panel B, the housing price index of Shanghai registered a more modest, but neverthe-less enormous, increase of six times the initial level in the same period.

Panels C and D display the housing price indices for Guangzhou and Shenzhen, which are both located in the Pearl River Delta of Guangdong Province, one of the most vibrant manufacturing centers in the world. These two cities had similar housing price fluctuations in 2003–2017. While the overall price appreciation in this period is remark-able, both cities experienced multiple episodes of price adjustment, with the most-severe price adjustment occurring in 2007–2008. The 2008 world financial crisis had a great impact on the export industries in this region, and both cities suffered substantial hous-ing price drops in this period, with the housing price index of Shenzhen dropping by more than 30%.

Figure 7.5 also shows remarkable price increases across the four first-tier cities in 2015–2016, with the housing prices in Shenzhen almost doubled, before the prices in these cit-ies stabilized at their new levels in 2017 as a result of the government's effort to temper any further increases.

Figure 7.6 reports the average housing price indices for the second-tier cities and the third-tier cities in Panels A and B, respectively. Panel A shows that the second-tier cities,

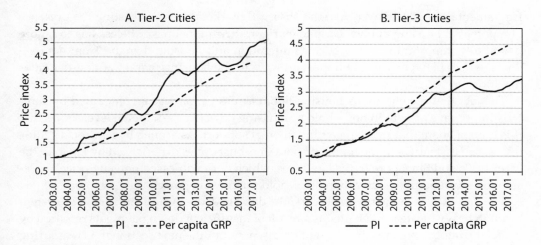

FIGURE 7.6. Housing price indices for China's second- and third-tier cities. *Sources:* Fang et al. (2016) and NBS. *Note:* PI is weighted by urban population.

which are typically provincial capitals and important commercial centers, had an enormous housing price appreciation of 400% from 2003 to 2017. This price appreciation, while more modest than that of the first-tier cities, is spectacular by any standard. Even more impressively, it was accompanied by neck-and-neck growth in the per capita GRP. Panel B shows that the third-tier cities, which are usually regional industrial or commercial centers, had a price appreciation of over 200% in the same period.[3] While this price appreciation is impressive, it actually lagged behind the growth of per capita GRP in these cities.

In sum, housing prices across China experienced tremendous appreciation from 2003 through 2017. These enormous price appreciations were accompanied by equally impressive growth in per capital GRP, except in a few first-tier cities.

2.2. Is There a Housing Bubble?

The world financial crisis in 2008 originated from the crash of the U.S. housing market. From 1996 to its housing market peak in 2006, the national housing price index in the United States, as measured by the Case-Shiller U.S. housing price index, grew by about 100%. In contrast, the national housing price index in China appreciated by an astonishing 250% from 2003 through 2013, and further appreciated after 2013. This tremendous housing price appreciation across China has led to a widely held concern that there might be a housing bubble occurring in the country—see Wu et al. (2016), Chen and Wen (2017), Glaeser et al. (2017), and Song and Xiong (2018).

This is a challenging issue because of the well-known difficulty of reliably measuring the fundamentals of a housing market, which are determined by complex dynamics of both supply and demand of housing in an uncertain macroeconomic environment. The rapid economic growth and urbanization process in China make assessment of its housing fundamentals even more challenging. To confront this challenge, Han et al. (2018) develop a general-equilibrium model based on dynamic rational expectations to quantify the fundamentals of Beijing's housing market. Founded on the balanced growth path of the model and using Hong Kong as a reference city, their analysis shows that the fundamentals are 30% lower than the observed market prices, suggesting the presence of a potential housing bubble. Despite its rigor, their model nevertheless has to ignore potentially important features, such as migration and housing demand from nonresidents, which play particularly important roles in the housing market of first-tier cities in China.

The fact that the enormous housing boom across China was accompanied by similarly impressive growth in household purchasing power at the national level shows that this is not a boom that lacks some fundamental support. As argued by Fang et al. (2016), this is also in contrast to the housing boom-and-bust cycles experienced by Japan in the early 1990s and Singapore in the late 1990s, which both witnessed housing price appreciations substantially greater than household purchasing power.

The recent U.S. housing crash directly damaged the American financial system through heavy mortgage defaults, as a result of insufficient down payments required by banks during the boom years. As will be discussed in the next section, it is reassuring that banks in China have imposed strict down payment requirements of over 30% on all mortgage loans, which protect banks against a sizable housing market meltdown of some 30% of mortgage loans. However, as will also be discussed, a key worry is that many households across China, especially low-income ones, have taken on substantial financial burdens to buy homes at up to 8 to 10 times their annual incomes. Their buying decisions cannot be explained by simple consumption motives, and instead build on expectations that high income growth will persist well into the future. Such expectations make China's housing market particularly vulnerable to a sudden nationwide economic slowdown, which could lead to dramatic corrections in household expectations about future income growth and housing price appreciation.

2.3. Land Prices

Land is a crucial input in housing development. In many other countries, such as the United States, land supply for housing in a city is determined by the landscape and local zoning restrictions. In contrast, land supply in Chinese cities is determined by land sales of local governments, as land is legally owned by the State and is controlled by local governments. For a long time after the establishment of the People's Republic of China in 1949, land transactions were actually prohibited. An important milestone occurred in 1988 when China amended its constitution to allow land transactions, which set the legal stage for privatization of housing. However, strictly speaking, the object of a land transaction is the "land usage right" of a land parcel for a period of time rather than its actual ownership.

China has rigid zoning restrictions to classify different land parcels for different uses, with industrial land logically for building industrial and manufacturing facilities, residential land for residential properties, and commercial land for commercial and business facilities. Under the current land law, industrial land can be leased for a term of 30 years, commercial land for 40 years, and residential land for 70 years. While the land law does not explicitly outline how land leases will be renewed, it is commonly presumed by the public that after a lease period expires, the property owner would be able to renew its land lease, possibly at a fee.

Similar to housing transactions, heterogeneity in land quality makes it difficult to compare prices in different land transactions. A recent study by Chen et al. (2018a) uses the

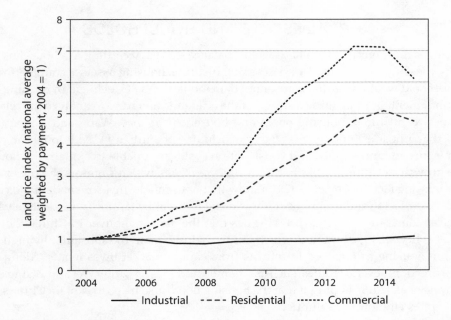

FIGURE 7.7. Land price index for different types of land sales in China. *Source:* Chen et al. (2018a).

standard hedonic price regression approach to construct a set of land price indices for 284 Chinese cities, based on information released by the Ministry of Land and Resources on all land transactions in these cities between 2004 and 2015. Their land price indices separate industrial, commercial, and residential land in each city.[4]

Figure 7.7 depicts the national land price indices for industrial land, commercial land, and residential land, which are weighted averages of the city level land price indices across the 284 cities used in Chen et al. (2018a). The plot shows that commercial land experienced enormous price appreciation, from a level of 1 in 2004 to over a level of 6.11 in 2015. Residential land had a more moderate, yet nevertheless dramatic appreciation, from a level of 1 to a level of about 4.75 over the same period. In contrast to the substantial price appreciation of residential and commercial land, the price of industrial land remained almost flat, from a level of 1 in 2004 to a level of about 1.5 in 2015. It is a common practice for local governments throughout China to offer industrial land at subsidized prices to support local industries. Since industrial enterprises can often obtain industrial land at low cost to start or expand their operations in a city, industrial land did not experience as much price appreciation as did commercial and residential land.

As will be discussed in section 4, the revenue from land sales is an important source of local governments' fiscal budgets. To the extent that local governments are local monopolies of land supply and heavily rely on land sale revenues for their own fiscal budgets, the markets for residential properties and commercial real estate are crucially tied to land sale policies and strategies of local governments. This is a special feature of China's real estate market.

3. REAL ESTATE AND HOUSEHOLDS

Housing is the largest item on households' balance sheets. According to a household survey by the China Economic Trend Research Institute, housing assets accounted for 66% of household wealth in 2016.[5] Household demand is also a key element in housing market fundamentals, motivating a strand of the academic literature to analyze the relationship between China's housing boom and household finance. Wang and Zhang (2014) show that a host of fundamental factors, including the urban *hukou* population, wage income, urban land supply, and construction costs, are unable to explain the housing price growth in Chinese cities between 2002 and 2008, which suggests the presence of other missing factors. Cao et al. (2018) show that households' investment demand can be this missing factor, and it is particularly relevant for wealthy families with relatively loose financial constraints. Zhang (2017) argues that the marginal buyer in China's housing market is liquidity constrained, which in turn helps explain the substantially higher returns in housing as opposed to returns from capital market investments. Along a reverse direction, several studies, such as Chamon and Prasad (2010), Wei and Zhang (2011) and Yang et al. (2018), highlight that the housing boom also helps to explain China's high saving rates and low consumption.

This section discusses the financial burdens faced by households, especially low-income households, in buying homes. Specifically, the concern is whether housing has been out of reach for typical households in China, which worries many commentators, and whether households purchase housing for pure consumption purposes. Understanding these issues helps to dissect the risks in China's real estate market from the household side.

Fang et al. (2016) analyze a sample of mortgage loans issued by a major commercial bank across 120 Chinese cities in 2003–2013. While wealthy households may not need mortgage loans to purchase homes, mortgages are necessary for many households, especially low-income ones. This section discusses several important observations uncovered by their study about home purchases of mortgage borrowers.

3.1. Down Payment

Householders' down payments are an important buffer that protects banks against the potential default risks of mortgage borrowers in the event of a future housing market meltdown. The analysis of Fang et al. (2016) shows that down payments in their mortgage sample had been consistently above 30% across first-, second-, and third-tier cities. They find that the average down payment ratio of mortgage loans made to the group with income in the lowest 10% of all mortgage borrowers was even slightly higher than that of the group with income in the middle quintile.

These high down payment levels are consistent with the strict mortgage policies imposed by the PBC on banks: One housing unit cannot be used as collateral for more than one mortgage loan. More important, mortgage policies require a minimum down payment of 30% on first mortgages. This minimum down payment requirement had changed over time from between 30% and 40%. The adjustment of the minimum down payment ratio has even become a powerful instrument for the central government to intervene in the housing market. Down payments on mortgages used to purchase second homes are even higher.

The high mortgage down payment levels in China stand in sharp contrast to the popular use of zero down payment loans and negative amortization loans during the U.S. housing bubble of 2000s,[6] and those high levels mitigate the risk of mortgage defaults in the event of a future housing market meltdown. Furthermore, mortgage loans in China are all recourse loans, which allow lenders to collect a borrower's other assets in the event of a mortgage default. These institutional arrangements make a U.S.-style subprime credit crisis less of a concern for China.

3.2. Income of Mortgage Borrowers

Fang et al. (2016) provide a detailed account of household income of mortgage borrowers in the bottom 10% and middle 10% of all mortgage borrowers in each year between 2003 and 2013 and across first-, second-, and third-tier cities in their sample. They find steady growth in the household income of these two groups of mortgage borrowers, consistent with the rapidly rising household income during this period in China. More interestingly, they also map the average income of the bottom-income group of mortgage borrowers into the income distribution constructed by the Urban Household Survey, which is available for all first- and second-tier cities. They find that despite rapid housing price appreciation across China, the position of the bottom-income group of mortgage borrowers in the income distribution of city residents remained below the 35th percentile in first-tier cities and below the 40th percentile in second-tier cities throughout 2003–2013. This suggests that the rapidly growing prices did not exclude households in the low-income fraction of the population from buying homes.

3.3. Price-to-Income Ratio of Mortgage Borrowers

The price-to-income ratio provides a convenient measure of the financial burdens endured by a household in acquiring a home. Figure 7.8 depicts the price-to-income ratio of mortgage borrowers in the bottom-income and middle-income subsamples from Fang et al. (2016). The financial burdens faced by the bottom-income group are particularly relevant. In this group, the price-to-income ratio started at a level slightly above 8 across the three tiers of cities in 2003. In first-tier cities, this ratio remained at around 8 before 2008 and then climbed to a peak of 10.7 in 2011 before dropping back to 9.2 in 2012. In second- and third-tier cities, this ratio was very similar and remained in a tight range around 8. It had a modest decline from a level slightly above 8 in 2003 to 7.2 in 2007 and then climbed back to a peak slightly below 9 in 2011 before dropping back to around 8 again in 2012.

The price-to-income ratio for the middle-income group was consistently lower than that for the bottom-income group. It was highest in the first-tier cities and lowest in the third-tier cities. Across the three tiers of cities, it had a similar pattern over time. In first-tier cities, it expanded from 5.6 in 2003 to 8.3 in 2011 before dropping back to 7.5 in 2012. In second-tier cities, it expanded from 5.7 in 2003 to 7.4 in 2010 before dropping back to 6.2 in 2012. In third-tier cities, it expanded from 5.0 in 2003 to 6.4 in 2010 before dropping back to 5.2 in 2012.

While the housing price appreciations in China are generally compatible with household income growth, figure 7.8 shows that home buyers nevertheless endure substantial financial burdens in buying homes. To clearly understand the financial burdens,

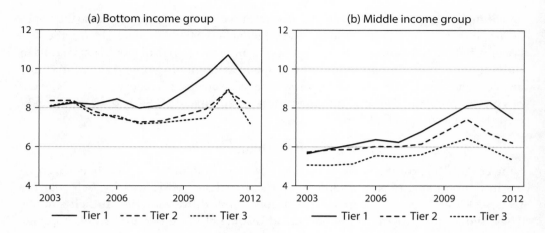

FIGURE 7.8. Price-to-income ratio of mortgage borrowers. *Source:* Fang et al. (2016).

let us consider a household that buys a home at eight times its annual income. A typical down payment of 40% implies that the household needs to save 3.2 years of its income before buying the home. In China, it is common for parents to pay the down payment for a young couple. In addition, the household needs a mortgage loan of 4.8 times its income. Even if the loan comes with a modest interest rate of 6% and a long maturity of 30 years, in each year the household would spend nearly 44.8% of its annual income to service the mortgage, including 28.8% to cover the interest payment and another 16% to pay down the loan at a linear schedule over 30 years.

Consumption motives alone cannot explain the willingness of these households to endure such financial burdens of buying homes. According to the data provided by the Housing Big Data Research Program of China's Social Science Academy, the annual rental yields of housing in Beijing and Shanghai were only 1.85% and 2.51% in July 2018,[7] which are even below the yield of China's one-year treasury bonds. In other words, renting homes is substantially cheaper than buying them.

What makes those bottom-income mortgage borrowers willing to endure the enormous financial burdens? Several factors may help explain their willingness. First, China has a substantially higher saving rate relative to developed countries. According to data released by China's National Bureau of Statistics, the ratio of aggregate savings by households and firms relative to the national GDP was approximately 35% in the 1980s and gradually grew to over 50% in the 2000s. Second, China's relatively underdeveloped financial markets offer few investment assets for households and firms to invest their savings. The stringent capital controls imposed by the central government also prevent them from investing their savings in global financial markets. As a result, housing is often used as an investment asset, not merely as a consumption good. Third, to make matters worse, the largely unbalanced gender ratio between boys and girls in China means that boys face substantial competition in the marriage market. Because homeownership serves as an important status symbol, the competition in the marriage market adds to demand for housing, as argued by Wei et al. (2012).

3.4. Housing Market Expectations

With housing as an investment asset, expectation plays an important role in driving households' willingness to pay 8 to 11 times their annual income to buy homes. Two compelling forces may have led to high expectations for housing price appreciation. First, after observing China's breakneck economic growth of 10% each year on average for 40 years, it was tempting to believe that the country's economy and household income would both continue to grow at a high rate, even if not as much as 10%, for a prolonged period. This kind of expectation would make the high housing prices appear more affordable. Suppose that a household expects its income to grow at an annual rate of 10% for five years. Then, its income would rise to 1.61 times the initial level, and an initial house price at eight times of its annual income would fall to below five times its income after five years. Such expectations make the housing market particular vulnerable to any sudden slowdown of the economy, which may knock down households' growth expectations, which in turn may lead to a substantial contraction in the price-to-income ratios that they are willing pay for homes.

Another force also may have contributed to households' housing expectations. Given the importance of the real estate sector in China's economy and the significant contribution of land sales to local governments' fiscal budgets, a crash in the housing market would damage the macro economy and perhaps even disable local governments. These severe consequences may have led to a perception that the central government would do whatever it could to avoid a housing market crash. In this sense, the housing market is "too important to fail" and enjoys implicit guarantees by the central government. In support of this perception, the central government has indeed used a broad set of instruments, as summarized by Fang et al. (2016), such as mortgage interest rates, mortgage down payment requirements, credit policies to real estate developers, and purchase restrictions on nonresidents, to implement countercyclical intervention policies in the housing market. Zhu (2016) argues that this perception of implicit government guarantees has strongly encouraged risk-seeking behaviors in the housing market.

4. REAL ESTATE AND LOCAL GOVERNMENTS

China's local governments are deeply engaged in the real estate market. On the one hand, they directly control land supply. On the other hand, land sale revenues serve as an important source for local governments to fund their fiscal budgets and local infrastructure projects. Furthermore, since the world financial crisis in 2008, local governments have commonly used the LGFP to raise debt, either implicitly or explicitly, by collateralizing land reserves and future land sale revenues. This section discusses the local governments' strong reliance on the real estate market.

4.1. Land Sales

Under the Chinese constitution, all land in China belongs to the State. In 1998, the 15th National Congress of the Communist Party of China passed a statutory bill granting local governments de jure ownership over land in their geographical jurisdictions. The Land Management Law passed in 1998 also authorizes local governments to sell usufruct rights over the land in their jurisdictions. Land transactions between local governments and

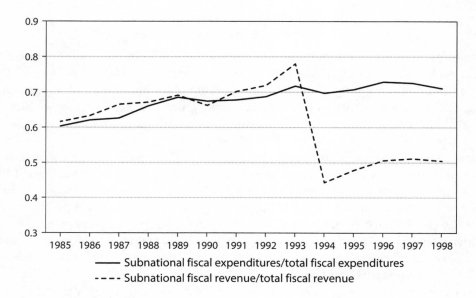

FIGURE 7.9. Shares of fiscal revenue and expenditures of subnational governments, 1985–1998. *Source:* Ministry of Finance, ed., *Public Finance Statistic Yearbook in Fifty Years of China.*

private buyers constitute the primary land market. Private buyers who obtain usufruct rights through a leasehold from local governments can also sell the leasehold to a third party in the secondary land market. However, compared to the primary land market, the size of the secondary land market only accounted for 3.75% of all land transactions in terms of payment from 2000 to 2015.

Two fiscal reforms in the 1990s enhanced local governments' reliance on land sale revenues: the Tax-sharing Reform in 1994 and the Budget Law enacted in 1995. Before 1994, China's intergovernmental financial relationship could be characterized as a "fiscal contracting system." In this system, the central government relied on local governments as its tax agencies and also gave them discretionary power over expenditures. Continuous declines of the total budgetary revenue as a fraction of GDP and the central government's share in the total budgetary expenditures eventually threatened the stability of China's macro economy. Zhu Rongji, the powerful Vice Premier at the time, strongly advocated the Tax-sharing Reform in 1994, which steered a greater share of the total budgetary revenue to the central government.

Figure 7.9 depicts the shares of subnational governments' budgetary revenue and expenditures from 1985 to 1998. There is a remarkable drop in the share of subnational governmental revenue after 1994, indicating that China's intergovernmental fiscal system moved into a new era with the central government taking a substantially greater share of the budgetary revenue. Although the central government provides intergovernmental transfers to remedy the gap between local governments' revenue and expenditures, the Tax-sharing Reform managed to extract a larger portion of fiscal revenue from local governments, especially from those rich provinces. Kung et al. (2013) and Han and Kung (2015) argue that the changing fiscal incentives might have caused local governments to shift their efforts from fostering industrial growth to

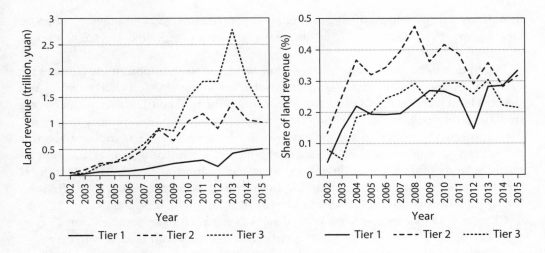

FIGURE 7.10. Land sale revenue for China's local government in 2002–2015. *Sources: China Municipal Statistical Yearbook* and *China National Land Resource Yearbook*, various years.

"urbanizing" China, for instance, by developing the real estate and construction sector.[8]

Another reason for local governments' deep engagement in the real estate market is the Budget Law enacted in 1995, which prohibited local governments from running budgetary deficits or obtaining external financing. This has been widely viewed as a critical step in confining the soft-budget constraint problem between local governments and the state-owned bank branches under their control. Facing these constraints, local governments managed to greatly expand their fiscal capacity after the late 1990s by relying on nonbudgetary funding sources such as land sales. Figure 7.10 depicts the revenue from land sales from 2002 to 2015 for three tiers of cities, with Panel A displaying the total land sale revenue and Panel B displaying its share in the local fiscal revenue. Total land sale revenue experienced rapid growth and reached a peak for the first- and second-tier cities in 2013. There is non-negligible heterogeneity in the share of land sale revenue in the total local fiscal revenue across cities, with this share particularly high for second-tier cities, which in some years reached over 40%.

Tying local government budgets to revenue from land sales is a novel mechanism design. Given the initial conditions of underdevelopment across Chinese cities in the early 1990s, local tax revenue was far from sufficient to fund large capital-intensive infrastructure projects as well as other local business developments. The great uncertainty also discouraged banks from funding such projects, even if local governments were allowed to directly raise debt financing. Like equity prices, land prices paid by buyers are determined not only by current business conditions in a city but also by their expectations of future conditions. Conditional on the fact that the local government is able to use its revenue from land sales to improve local infrastructure and business environments, land prices can be substantially higher than what is justified by current conditions, much like high-flying IPO prices for high-tech firms without any past earnings. As local governments need to regularly sell land to the public to fund their future budgets, they are incentivized to implement those promised infrastructure projects and thereby improve local business environments. Thus, this is an incentive-compatible design, much like staged VC financing.

In addition to its function as fiscal revenue, land is also an important instrument for local governments to attract prominent firms that will pursue projects in their cities and support local industrial policies. Land (especially industrial land) is often given out for free, as a land grant, or sold at a discount to promising firms in high-priority industries. As was discussed earlier, this is a key reason that industrial land has substantial lower prices than commercial land and residential land. Local governments may also supplement the land grant with an additional tax allowance or funding support. In return, local governments benefit from future tax revenues from these supported firms or from an improved business environment and industry structure in their regions.

Cheung (2008) views discounts in land sales as a main tool for local governments to compete for businesses. Discretion in giving such discounts can lead to both excessive competition and corruption. Several studies, such as Cai et al. (2013), Chen and Kung (2016), Cai et al. (2017), and Chen and Kung (2018), analyze corruption in China's land market. To restrict local governments' discretionary power in the land market, the central government stipulates the lowest price for industrial land and the lowest investment intensity for specific industries for different levels of cities and counties, generally according to their development levels and geographic locations. To restrain corruption, in 2002 the Ministry of Land and Resource issued the No. 11 regulation "Regulation on the Transaction Method of Leasehold Sale of Land by Local Government," which requires leasehold sales for commercial and residential developments to use open auctions. As a result of this regulation, the proportion of land transactions using open auctions, instead of case-by-case negotiations, rose from less than 20% in 2000 to over 90% in 2012.[9]

Finally, land sales by local governments are subject to a restrictive national quota constraint, which serves to protect necessary land for agricultural production at the national level as well as to discipline local governments' short-term incentives to overdevelop local real estate markets. The central government allocates the national quota across various regions, based on its macroeconomic policies and overall national development strategy. In recent years, China's Great Western Development Strategy has tilted more of the quota to central and western provinces, at the expense of eastern provinces. Liang et al. (2016) show that this shift in land supply has raised housing prices and wages in eastern provinces, which in turn has distorted the spatial distribution of China's economic activities.

4.2. Local Government Debt

Land and future land sale revenues also serve as key collaterals for local governments to raise debt financing. As was discussed above, China's Budget Law prohibited local governments from seeking debt financing. Bai et al. (2016) provide a detailed account of how this regulatory arrangement was changed in 2008. To backstop the potential spillover effects of the world financial crisis on China's export-driven economy, in 2008 China launched a massive fiscal stimulus program on the magnitude of 4 trillion RMB, equivalent to 12.5% of China's GDP. This stimulus program involved mostly infrastructure projects, which local governments implemented and financed. It was infeasible for local governments to fund this massive program through regular tax revenue or land sales in a short time period. Instead, the central government allowed local governments to create the LGFP to raise debt.[10]

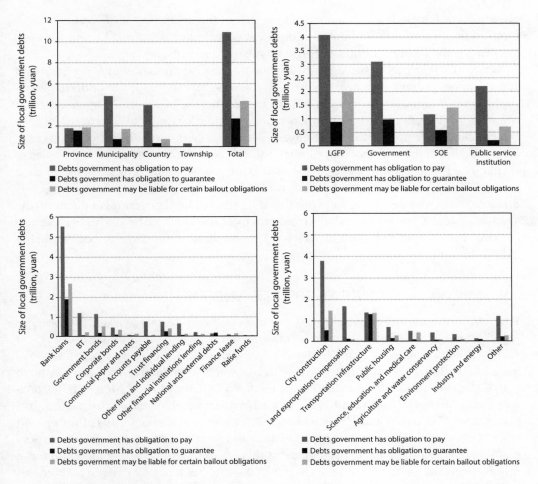

FIGURE 7.11. Size of local government debt by categories. *Source:* Audit Report on China's local debt.

The following chapter in this handbook, by Zhiwei Zhang and Yi Xiong, provides a detailed account of the arrangement of LGFP. Briefly speaking, in a typical arrangement to support a certain infrastructure project, a local government creates an LGFP and injects land reserves or future land sale revenues as capital into the LGFP, which in turn can apply for bank loans. In most cases, the LGFP also carries either explicit or implicit guarantees from the local government. These guarantees further mitigate any concern about credit risk. Local governments commonly use this arrangement at all administrative levels; this led to tremendous growth in debt taken on by local governments after 2008.

China's National Audit Office conducted a comprehensive audit of all local government debts at the end of June 2013. According to this audit, in that year the total volume of outstanding local government debt reached 10.89 trillion RMB, equivalent to 19.2% of China's national GDP. Among these debts, 37.23% used future land sale revenue as collateral. Figure 7.11 provides the distribution of local government debt across several dimensions. LGFP are the most important vehicles for local governments to raise debt, and governments have explicit obligations to pay 61% of the debts. Furthermore, bank loans were an important source of outstanding local government debt in 2013, and city construction is the most important purpose for raising the debts.

While LGFP helped to successfully implement the post-crisis stimulus program and fund many important infrastructure projects, their popularity has led to undesirable impacts on the financial system. Bai et al. (2016) argue that the LGPF arrangement reversed important progress made by China's previous economic reform to constrain the soft-budget-constraint problem of local governments. Furthermore, when the central government later tightened monetary policy to limit debt accumulation by local governments, LGFP had trouble rolling over their bank loans. Instead, this trouble pushed most LGFP debt financing into the shadow banking system, with higher borrowing costs and less transparency. Consistent with this migration of local government debt into the shadow system, Chen et al. (2017) find that provinces with an abnormally higher increase of bank loan growth in 2009 experienced more shadow banking activities during 2012–2015.

5. REAL ESTATE AND FIRMS

Firms in China are also heavily exposed to risks of the real estate market. Two or more key channels expose firms to the real estate market. First, real estate assets are the most widely used collateral for firms to borrow from banks. As shown by figure 7.1, banks have 22.2 trillion in outstanding loans with real estate as collateral, including loans to firms. Through this collateral channel, as modeled by Kiyotaki and Moore (1997), fluctuations in land price affect bank credit available to firms, which may in turn affect firm investment. Gan (2007) and Chaney et al. (2012) provide evidence of this effect of land price fluctuations on firm investment in Japan and the United States, respectively. Several recent studies have also been made of this effect in China. Wu et al. (2015) use a unique firm data set for 35 Chinese cities in 2003–2011 but find no evidence of increases in firm investment in response to land price increases. Chen et al. (2018a) employ a larger sample of firms in 284 prefectural cities in 2000–2015 and find some supportive evidence.

Another speculative channel exists through which firms actively seek real estate exposure during China's ongoing real estate boom. To discuss the speculative channel, this section builds on a recent study by Chen et al. (2018a), which analyzes the investment of a sample of nonfinancial and non–real estate firms publicly listed in China's A-share market. Figure 7.12 depicts the average investment of these firms in each year between 2000 and 2015. The annual investment is further decomposed into four components in the bars ranging from top to bottom: investment unrelated to land, investments to acquire residential land, commercial land, and industrial land. Firms' annual investment rapidly rose from about 100 million RMB in 2000 to the peak of nearly 1,500 million RMB in 2011, before dropping to approximately 1,200 million RMB in more recent years. While these firms spent nothing on land before 2007, they quickly expanded their land investments after 2007. At the peak years of 2010 and 2011, a firm spent on average roughly 500 million RMB on acquiring land; this was mostly commercial land rather than industrial land. In 2010, commercial land accounted for more than 30% of the firms' net

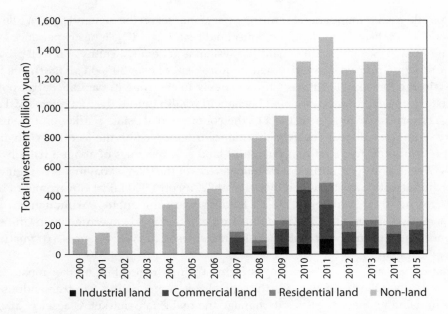

FIGURE 7.12. Investment of publicly listed firms in China. *Source:* Chen et al. (2018a).

investment. While the amount and the share of land investment dropped after 2011, they nevertheless remained substantial in 2012–2015.

As these firms cannot build industrial and manufacturing facilities on commercial and residential land, Chen et al. (2018a) argue that the investment of these firms on commercial and residential land represents a form of real estate speculation, induced by the higher capital returns from land price appreciation more than from the real economy during the real estate boom. Through a similar mechanism, both Li and Wu (2014) and Shi (2017) argue that the real estate boom in China has discouraged entrepreneurial activities.

6. CHALLENGES

The real estate market, being an integral part of China's financial system, has systemic importance to the Chinese economy. Real estate assets contribute the most to households' balance sheets and are the most important form of collateral that firms and local governments use to raise debt financing. Even more special in China, local governments control land supply through regular land sales and at the same time heavily rely on revenue from such sales to fund their own fiscal budgets and local infrastructure development. Furthermore, banks are heavily exposed to real estate through all sorts of loans, and either directly or indirectly connect to real estate.

Substantial concerns have been raised both inside and outside of China about the stability of the country's real estate market. While this chapter has discussed the market's various imperfections, it does not predict or expect a sudden, nationwide real estate crash. First, China's economic miracle over the last 40 years and the unfinished urbanization process laid a solid foundation for the real estate market on the demand side. While some households are heavily in debt, the household sector as a whole has experienced rapid income growth. Second, China's banking system is generally healthy and well protected by the strictly imposed down payment requirement of over 30% on all mortgage loans. Third, in the foreseeable future, China is likely to continue its capital control policies, which help to keep the accumulated household wealth within the real estate market. Finally, concern regarding the impact of the country's real estate market on the sustainability of policies of local government finance is tempered by the fact that with annual fiscal revenues of over 8 trillion yuan and land sale revenues of about 3 trillion yuan, local governments have sufficient cash flow to cover the interest payments of their debts. According to estimates provided by Bai et al. (2016) on 1,800 Local Government Financing Platforms, their total assets, mostly land reserves, amount to 70 trillion yuan, which is 50% more than their liability. It is thus unlikely that local governments in China will become illiquid or insolvent in the near future, unless China experiences a dramatic land price adjustment.

That being said, several challenges facing China's real estate market must also be discussed. Over the next few years, the central government will face a tremendous challenge in using its macro policies to manage the real estate market. Glaeser et al. (2017) discuss a delicate tradeoff: On the one hand, the Chinese government cannot afford to let the construction boom continue, because more homes are being built in "wrong places" with lower, rather than higher, household incomes and because such overconstruction will eventually lead to a housing bust. On the other hand, the government cannot stop the construction boom without slowing down the economy and causing distress to China's employment rates. While the authors of this chapter are not as pessimistic as Glaeser et al. (2017) about the inevitability of a housing bust in China, we are nevertheless sympathetic to the government's macroeconomic policy dilemma: how to temper the housing boom to maintain long-run stability while addressing the short-term pressure that would be caused to the overall economy by a slowdown of the real estate sector.

In the medium term, local governments need to find a more sustainable mechanism to fund local fiscal budgets. One possibility is property tax levied on real estate assets, as is common in many developed countries. In 2011, China conducted policy trials to levy a property tax on second homes in Shanghai and Chongqing. The central government hesitated to expand this property tax program to other cities because of resistance from homeowners as well as the fear that it might lead to a real estate crash and eventually threaten the stability of the country's financial system. With previously sold land leaseholds gradually reaching their maturities, the subsequent land renewal process provides a natural point for local governments to start collecting additional fees or taxes on real estate properties.

In the long run, China's real estate market faces a tremendous challenge from the rapid aging of its population. China started the "One-Child Policy" in the early 1980s. This policy has substantially changed the country's population structure by reducing the number of children born to each couple. Forty years after the start of this policy, China is beginning to see a serious aging problem throughout all the provinces. Figure 7.13 depicts China's working-age population, along with the old-age dependency ratio (i.e., the ratio of older people in the full population) from 1990 to 2016. China's working-age pop-

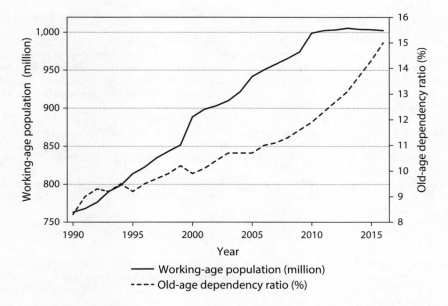

FIGURE 7.13. Structure change of China's demography. *Source:* China's Bureau of Statistics. *Note:* Working age is defined as 15–65 years old.

ulation reached to its peak in 2014 and has started to decline, while the old-age dependency ratio has substantially grown from 8.3% in 1990 to 15% in 2016. With this trajectory, China will inevitably become an "old" society. This aging population will put great pressure on the demand for housing in the long run, because houses currently owned by the older generation will be eventually transferred to the current younger generations, which are smaller in number. In 2016, the Chinese government officially replaced the One-Child Policy by a Two-Child Policy, which allows each couple to have two children. While this new policy will help to eventually improve the population structure, its effect is unlikely to be felt quickly enough to avoid the housing market pressure induced by the aging population.

NOTES

1. Cities in China are typically classified into four tiers, according to their administrative ranking and economic importance. The widely accepted first-tier cities are Beijing, Shanghai, Guangzhou, and Shenzhen. The second tier is generally composed of two autonomous municipalities (Tianjing and Chongqing), the capital cities of 24 provinces, and nine vital industrial and commercial centers. Lasha, the capital of Tibet, is typically excluded from the list owing to its special economic status. All cities in the first and second tiers are national (or at least regional) industrial or commercial centers.
2. By comparing their price indices with the NBS 70-city price indices, Fang et al. (2016) find that NBS's indices display substantial smaller price appreciations than their own during the period of 2003–2013.
3. Note that Panel B builds on two samples of third-tier cities. The sample before 2013 includes 85 third-tier cities from Fang et al. (2016), while the sample after 2013 includes the third-tier cities in the NBS 70-city housing price index.
4. See also Deng et al. (2012) for a study of land prices in China.

5.   Data source: *Survey Report on China's Household Wealth, 2017*, edited by China Economic Trend Research Institute of the Economic Daily.
6.   According to Mayer et al. (2009), during the U.S. housing bubble period of 2003–2006, households with poor credit (the subprime and Alt-A households) had commonly secured mortgages with a 5% or as little as 0% down payment to finance their home purchases. Some mortgages even allowed the borrowers to have negative amortization over time. When U.S. housing prices started to decline after 2006, these borrowers were more likely to default on their mortgage loans, exacerbating the housing market decline.
7.   For the data source, see the following: http://zfdsj.org/report/shownews.php?lang=cn&id=80.
8.   Zhang et al. (2017) also document that local governments' controls of residential land supply enlarged the impact of productivity shocks on housing prices.
9.   Data source: Annual Report of China's Land Resources, edited by the Ministry of Land and Resources, various years.
10.   Regarding debt financing by LGFP, Ang et al. (2016) find that real estate GDP is the most important determinant of the cross-section of excess yields of Chengtou bonds (i.e., bonds issued by LGFP to finance local infrastructure projects).

REFERENCES

Ang, A., J. Bai, and H. Zhou (2016). "The Great Wall of Debt: Real Estate, Political Risk, and Chinese Local Government Credit Spreads." Working paper, Tsinghua University.

Anglin, P. M., D. Dale-Johnson, Y. Gao, and G. Zhu (2014). "Patterns of Growth in Chinese Cities: Implications of the Land Lease." *Journal of Urban Economics* 83: 87–107.

Bai, C. E., C. T. Hsieh, and Z. M. Song (2016). "The Long Shadow of China's Fiscal Expansion." *Brookings Papers on Economic Activity* 2: 129–81.

Baum-Snow, N., L. Brandt, J. V. Henderson, M. A. Turner, and Q. Zhang (2017). "Roads, Railroads, and Decentralization of Chinese Cities." *Review of Economics and Statistics* 99(3): 435–48.

Cai, H., J. V. Henderson, and Q. Zhang (2013). "China's Land Market Auctions: Evidence of Corruption?" *Rand Journal of Economics* 44(3): 488–521.

Cai, H., Z. Wang, and Q. Zhang (2017). "To Build Above the Limit? Implementation of Land Use Regulations in Urban China." *Journal of Urban Economics* 98: 223–33.

Cao, Y., J. Chen, and Q. Zhang (2018). "Housing Investment in Urban China." *Journal of Comparative Economics* 46(1): 212–47.

Case, K. E., and R. J. Shiller (1987). "Prices of Single-Family Homes Since 1970: New Indexes for Four Cities." *New England Economic Review* 45–56.

Chamon, M., and E. Prasad (2010). "Why Are Saving Rates of Urban Households in China Rising?" *American Economic Journal: Macroeconomics* 2(1): 93–130.

Chaney, T., D. Sraer, and D. Thesmar (2012). "The Collateral Channel: How Real Estate Shocks Affect Corporate Investment." *American Economic Review* 102(6): 2381–2409.

Chen, T., and J. K. Kung (2016). "Do Land Revenue Windfalls Create a Political Resource Curse? Evidence from China." *Journal of Development Economics* 123: 86–106.

Chen T., and J. K. Kung (2018). "Busting the 'Princelings': The Campaign against Corruption in China's Primary Land Market." *Quarterly Journal of Economics* 134(1): 185–226.

Chen, Z., Z. He, and C. Liu (2017). "The Financing of Local Government in China: Stimulus Loan Wanes and Shadow Banking Waxes" (No. W23598). National Bureau of Economic Research.

Chen, T., L. Liu, W. Xiong, and L. A. Zhou (2018a). "Real Estate Boom and Misallocation of Capital in China." Working paper, Princeton University.

Chen, K., Q. Wang, T. Xu, T., and T. Zha (2018b). "Household Heterogeneity and the Transmission of Mortgage Policy in China: The Speculative Channel." Working paper.

Chen, K., and Y. Wen (2017). "The Great Housing Boom of China." *American Economic Journal: Macroeconomics* 9(2): 73–114.

Cheung, S. N. (2008). *The Economic System of China*. Hong Kong: Arcadia Press.

Deng, Y., J. Gyourko, and J. Wu (2012). "Should We Fear an Adverse Collateral Effect on Investment in China?" *NBER Reporter*, no. 4.

Deutsche Bank (2016). "Analyzing the Property Exposure." Market Research Report.

Fang, H., Q. Gu, W. Xiong, and L. A. Zhou (2016). "Demystifying the Chinese Housing Boom." *NBER Macroeconomics Annual* 30(1): 105–66.

Gan, J. (2007). "The Real Effects of Asset Market Bubbles: Loan- and Firm-Level Evidence of a Lending Channel." *Review of Financial Studies* 20(6): 1941–73.

Garriga, C., A. Hedlund, Y. Tang, and P. Wang (2017). "Rural-Urban Migration, Structural Transformation, and Housing Markets in China" (No. w23819). National Bureau of Economic Research.

Glaeser, E., W. Huang, Y. Ma, and A. Shleifer (2017). "A Real Estate Boom with Chinese Characteristics." *Journal of Economic Perspectives* 31(1): 93–116.

Han, B., L. Han, and G. Zhu (2018). "Housing Price and Fundamentals in a Transition Economy: The Case of the Beijing Market." *International Economic Review* 59(3): 1653–77.

Han, L., and J. K. Kung (2015). "Fiscal Incentives and Policy Choices of Local Governments: Evidence from China." *Journal of Development Economics* 116: 89–104.

Kain, J. F., and J. M. Quigley (1970). "Measuring the Value of Housing Quality." *Journal of the American Statistical Association* 65(330): 532–48.

Kiyotaki, N., and J. Moore (1997). "Credit Cycles." *Journal of Political Economy* 105(2): 211–48.

Kung, J., C. Xu, and F. Zhou (2013). "From Industrialization to Urbanization: The Social Consequences of Changing Fiscal Incentives on Local Governments' Behavior," in *Law and Economics with Chinese Characteristics: Institutions for Promoting Development in the Twenty-First Century*, edited by David Kennedy and Joseph E. Stiglitz. New York: Oxford University Press.

Li, L., and X. Wu (2014). "Housing Price and Entrepreneurship in China." *Journal of Comparative Economics* 42(2): 436–49.

Liang, W., M. Lu, and H. Zhang (2016). "Housing Prices Raise Wages: Estimating the Unexpected Effects of Land Supply Regulation in China." *Journal of Housing Economics* 33: 70–81.

Mayer, C., K. Pence, and S. M. Sherlund (2009). "The Rise in Mortgage Defaults." *Journal of Economic Perspectives* 23(1): 27–50.

Novokmet, F., T. Piketty, L. Yang, and G. Zucman (2018). "From Communism to Capitalism: Private Versus Public Property and Inequality in China and Russia." *AEA Papers and Proceedings* 108: 109–13.

Shepard, W. (2015). *Ghost Cities of China: The Story of Cities without People in the World's Most Populated Country*. London: Zed Books.

Shi, Y. (2017). "Real Estate Booms and Endogenous Productivity Growth." Working paper, Massachusetts Institute of Technology.

Song, Z., and W. Xiong (2018). "Risks in China's Financial System." *Annual Review of Financial Economics* 10: 261–86.

Wang, S. Y. (2011). "State Misallocation and Housing Prices: Theory and Evidence from China." *American Economic Review* 101(5): 2081–2107.

Wang, S. Y. (2012). "Credit Constraints, Job Mobility, and Entrepreneurship: Evidence from a Property Reform in China." *Review of Economics and Statistics* 94(2): 532–51.

Wang, Z., and Q. Zhang (2014). "Fundamental Factors in the Housing Markets of China." *Journal of Housing Economics* 25: 53–61.

Wang, Z., Q. Zhang, and L. A. Zhou (2018). "Career Incentives of City Leaders and Urban Spatial Expansion in China." Working paper, Peking University.

Wei, S. J., X. Zhang, and Y. Liu (2012). "Status Competition and Housing Prices" (No. w18000). National Bureau of Economic Research.

Wei, S. J., and X. Zhang (2011). "The Competitive Saving Motive: Evidence from Rising Sex Ratios and Savings Rates in China." *Journal of Political Economy* 119(3): 511–64.

Woodworth, M. D., and J. L. Wallace (2017). "Seeing Ghosts: Parsing China's 'Ghost City' Controversy." *Urban Geography* 38(8): 1270–81.

Wu, J., J. Gyourko, and Y. Deng (2015). "Real Estate Collateral Value and Investment: The Case of China." *Journal of Urban Economics* 86: 43–53.

Wu, J., J. Gyourko, and Y. Deng (2016). "Evaluating the Risk of Chinese Housing Markets: What We Know and What We Need to Know." *China Economic Review* 39: 91–114.

Yang, Z., Y. Fan, and L. Zhao (2018). "A Reexamination of Housing Price and Household Consumption in China: The Dual Role of Housing Consumption and Housing Investment." *Journal of Real Estate Finance and Economics* 56(3): 472–99.

Zhang, C., S. Jia, and R. Yang (2016). "Housing Affordability and Housing Vacancy in China: The Role of Income Inequality." *Journal of Housing Economics* 33: 4–14.

Zhang, J., J. Fan, and J. Mo (2017). "Government Intervention, Land Market, and Urban Development: Evidence from Chinese Cities." *Economic Inquiry* 55(1): 115–36.

Zhang, Y. (2017). "Liquidity Constraints, Transition Dynamics, and the Chinese Housing Return Premium." Working paper, Peking University.

Zhu, N. (2016). *China's Guaranteed Bubble: How Implicit Government Support Has Propelled China's Economy While Creating Systemic Risk*. New York: McGraw-Hill Education.

8

INFRASTRUCTURE FINANCING

Zhiwei Zhang and Yi Xiong

INTRODUCTION

Infrastructure is crucial for economic growth, particularly in developing countries. Improving infrastructure could raise productivity, stimulate trade and private investment, and ameliorate living standards. China's economic success in the past decades can be partly attributed to a sustained high level of investment in infrastructure. Aside from the role of the government, the financial sector also played a crucial role in mobilizing resources for infrastructure investment.

As this chapter will discuss, China's high level of infrastructure investment was achieved through a complex system of fiscal and financial arrangements. Quasi-fiscal entities such as local government financing vehicles (LGFVs) played an important role in leveraging financial resources for infrastructure investment. With these arrangements, local governments were able to mobilize resources far beyond budget constraints. However, this created a substantial amount of quasi-fiscal debt. The sustainability of these quasi-fiscal entities is a major macro problem that China faces today.

1. THE ROLE OF INFRASTRUCTURE INVESTMENT IN CHINA

China's infrastructure investment increased 20-fold between 2000 and 2017, according to statistics from the National Bureau of Statistics (NBS) (figure 8.1). Total infrastructure investment was RMB17.3trn in 2017, or 21% of GDP.[1] Improvement in infrastructure was evident: For example, total road length tripled from 1.7mn kilometers in 2000 to 4.7mn kilometers in 2017. Annual cement production quadrupled over the same period.

Infrastructure investment in China is usually government-led and serves two important yet distinct policy roles. The first role is promoting economic development. It is perhaps best illustrated by the famous slogan "Better Roads Lead to Richer Life," which has been popular among local officials since the 1980s.[2] Local governments are incentivized to maximize investment in infrastructure in order to boost growth, which is also, in part, owing to the close association between economic growth and government official promotions (Zhou, 2007).

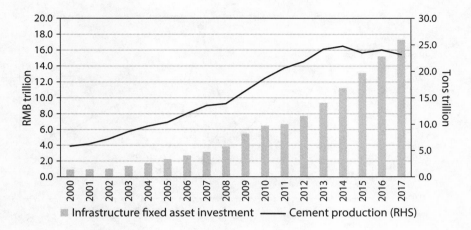

FIGURE 8.1. Infrastructure fixed asset investment. *Sources:* Authors' calculations, NBS, Wind database.

In its second role, infrastructure investment is also an important policy tool for managing economic cycles. During economic downturns, the central government has often resorted to infrastructure spending to support growth, such as the "4-trillion stimulus" mandated in 2009 in response to the global financial crisis. As discretionary capital spending with likely high fiscal multipliers and job creation, infrastructure investment is regarded as an effective countercyclical policy tool (figure 8.2).

As a result, infrastructure investment is an important policy tool for both central and local governments. Yet the government's direct spending on infrastructure is often constrained by the limited budgetary resources available. So, how did the government obtain financing for large-scale infrastructure investments?

2. FINANCIAL VEHICLES FOR INFRASTRUCTURE INVESTMENT

Infrastructure projects are largely carried out by the public sector, as they usually have high economic returns but much smaller financial returns to the investors themselves. Local governments are the main executioners of infrastructure projects in China. However, they face tight budgetary constraints: Government budgets allocated only about RMB2trn for infrastructure in 2017 (12% of total budgetary spending). Borrowings are largely constrained, as well; local government debt financing was not allowed before 2015, and even then was under tight national level borrowing limits from that year onward. Despite all the constraints, total infrastructure investment in China far exceeded government budgetary spending. In 2017, total infrastructure investment was RMB17trn.

How did this happen? The answer points to a large group of entities, as well as to their associated financial and institutional arrangements, on which local governments could leverage: the so-called local government financing vehicles (LGFVs). During the fiscal stimulus that followed the global financial crisis, LGFVs became active and since then have dominated local government infrastructure investment.

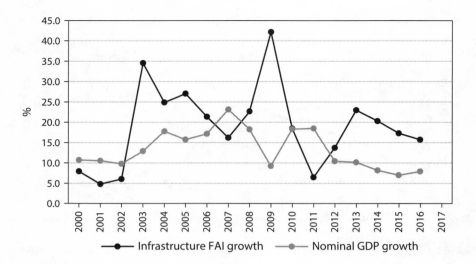

FIGURE 8.2. Infrastructure investment as a countercyclical policy tool. *Sources:* Authors' calculations, NBS, Wind database.

More recently, under new policy initiatives by the central government to regulate local government borrowing, two new types of financing arrangements have been created: public-private partnerships (PPPs), and local government special-purpose bonds.

2.1. Local Government Financing Vehicles (LGFVs)

2.1.1. What Are LGFVs?

LGFVs are local government-owned and government-controlled legal entities that carry out government investment projects. A large number of LGFVs take the form of "urban construction and investment companies," which are set up and run directly by local governments solely for the purpose of investing and financing infrastructure projects. They could take other forms, too, such as existing state-owned enterprises or their subsidiaries.

The first LGFVs were set up in the 1990s. Local governments needed to build infrastructure, but were banned from borrowing from banks and financial markets. To circumvent the legal constraint, local governments utilized LGFVs to borrow instead. LGFVs became active and widely used during the "4trn stimulus" period in 2009–2010. Local governments were pushed to build massive infrastructure projects to counter the shock from the global financial crisis, largely through LGFVs.

LGFVs are thus quasi-fiscal entities by nature, as they conduct government activities but lie outside the scope of government budgets and official branches of government. They usually satisfy most or all of the following characteristics:

1. They are majority- or solely-owned by the government.
2. Their managers and employees are supervised or hired by government officials. In some cases, they are operated directly by government officials.
3. They enter into contracts with local governments for building and operating infrastructure. Sometimes there is no clear contract, yet they directly report to local governments and carry out projects as instructed.

4. Part or all of their assets are public assets (such as land, roads, and public utilities) transferred to them by local governments.
5. They borrow from banks or financial markets with explicit or implicit guarantees from local governments.

2.1.2. LGFV Financing Structure

Starting capital for LGFVs usually came from local governments. To make sure LGFVs have sufficient startup capital, local governments usually transfer some of their public assets to them. Typical assets include (1) central government funding for infrastructure investment; (2) land usage rights; (3) public physical assets, such as roads, bridges, and buildings; (4) local government nontax revenues, such as utility fees; and (5) tax benefits.[3] These asset transfers not only help LGFVs to meet certain capital requirements for projects and borrowing but also provide them with collateral assets and income streams that they may borrow against.

Once sufficiently capitalized, LGFVs could obtain additional project financing through multiple channels. Bank loans are usually the most important source of financing, accounting for around 60% of LGFVs' total interest-bearing debt in 2017. LGFVs may borrow from national and regional commercial banks, most notably China Development Bank (CDB), which provides financing for government projects nationwide. LGFVs may obtain market financing by issuing corporate bonds or from the stock market. They may also get financing from the shadow banking system, or may obtain external financing from international financial institutions or Eurobond issuances. Where collateral assets were needed for certain financing, LGFVs could often use land as collateral assets. Borrowing could even be collateralized against future income streams from physical assets or government purchase agreements, or against government guarantees.

Access to financing significantly increased resources available for infrastructure investment. LGFVs are often highly leveraged, with debt-to-asset ratio at around 60% on average in 2017. Through LGFVs, local governments could often mobilize resources for infrastructure investment at multiples of their budgetary capital spending (net capital expenditure by LGFVs was RMB4trn in 2017, compared to budgetary infrastructure investment of about RMB2trn in the same year). LGFVs helped local governments maintain high levels of infrastructure investment, particularly from 2009 onward.

But massive government investment comes with its costs. LGFVs built up a large stock of quasi-fiscal debt, which is ultimately a burden for central and local governments.

2.1.3. LGFV Debt Level

Assessing LGFVs' debt stock is not straightforward. Aggregate statistics about LGFVs are not easily accessible. Neither NBS nor other government agencies compile or publish such statistics in a timely manner. Some statistics are, however, available from a few one-off surveys conducted by various government agencies. These include:

1. Two reports by the National Audit Office (NAO)[4] show total local government and government-guaranteed debt stock of RMB10.7trn as of end-2010, and RMB17.9trn as of end-June 2013. These debts include LGFV debt as well as debts of other government entities. NAO audited 6,576 LGFVs in 2010, and 7,170 in 2013.

2. The former China Banking Regulatory Commission (CBRC)[5] calculated that there were 10,468 LGFVs as of end-September 2011, with RMB9.1trn of outstanding bank loans. The CBRC continued to publish a list of LGFVs from time to time, but not their outstanding loans.

A Bottom-Up Approach Using Company-Level Data

An alternative way of understanding the operations of LGFVs is through a bottom-up approach, utilizing available information of individual LGFVs.[6]

Some 1,844 LGFVs issued bonds on the domestic financial market during the period 2009 through 2017. All these LGFVs with outstanding bonds are required to disclose financial information on a regular basis. The financial statements published by them have all been externally audited, and thus are comparable across LGFVs in the sample.

The sample does not include all LGFVs, however. If an LGFV has not issued any bond, its financial information would not be publicly available. Still, this LGFV sample is large enough to infer aggregate statistics of all LGFVs. Total interest-bearing debt of LGFVs in this sample was about RMB8.4trn in 2010, not far from the aggregate LGFV loans of RMB9.1trn reported by the CBRC in 2010.

LGFV Debt Still Growing, but Its Pace Slowed

LGFV debt continues to grow, although its pace has moderated (figure 8.3). Within the sample discussed in this section, interest-bearing LGFV debt grew by 13% to 15% per year in 2015–2017, compared to 21% on average in 2010–2014.

Based on the growth rates, we estimated that LGFV debt stock stood at RMB30trn as of end-2017. LGFV debt continued to increase as a share of GDP: It was at 36% of GDP in 2017, up from 31% in 2014. The pace of increase in LGFV debt-to-GDP ratio has slowed down; in previous years (2011–2014), debt was increasing by 4% to 5% of GDP on average each year. Loans remained the largest source of financing for LGFVs, although their share declined gradually to 60% in 2017 from 79% in 2010 (figure 8.4). Bond financing increased to 23% in 2017.

2.1.4. Can LGFVs Pay Their Debt?

Deteriorated Financials

The firm-level data from the aforementioned 1,844 LGFVs allows us to take a closer look at LGFVs' financial conditions. Almost all financial indicators have deteriorated in recent years.

Leverage continued to increase, despite the slowdown in debt growth. Median debt-to-asset ratio increased to 56% in 2016 from 49% in 2010. The ratio is 71% at the top decile; in other words, debt is more than double their equity.

Earnings have further deteriorated. The median LGFV's return on assets (ROA) dropped to merely 0.8% in 2016 from 1.1% in 2014 and 2.2% in 2010 (figure 8.5). Similarly, return on equity (ROE) fell below 2% in 2016. As such, LGFVs are among the most inefficient users of capital. Listed state-owned enterprises (SOEs) in comparable sectors, by contrast, had ROA and ROE at 2.5% and 6.3%, respectively, in 2016.

Cash flows also paint an alarming picture. The advantage of looking at cash flows is that they are less vulnerable to accounting manipulations, and they better capture companies' liquidity conditions. Between 2014 and 2016, about 70% of all LGFVs in the sam-

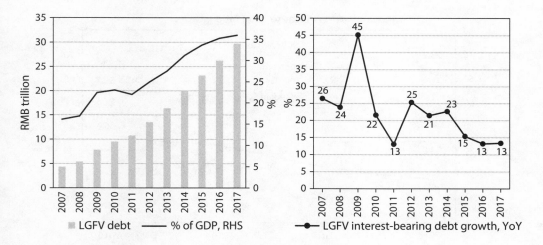

FIGURE 8.3. LGFV debt stock and growth. *Sources:* Authors' calculations, Wind database.

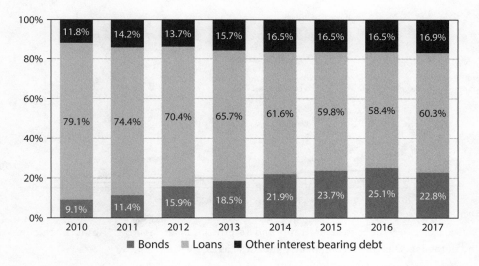

FIGURE 8.4. Composition of LGFV interest-bearing debt. *Sources:* Authors' calculations, Wind database.

ple ran negative free cash flows to the firm (FCFF). In addition, a divergence occurred in 2016 when the FCFF of the bottom quartile further deteriorated.

The important question remains whether LGFVs would be able to service their debt on their own; and, if not, how large the gap would be. The interest coverage ratio (ICR) approach can efficiently be used to measure LGFVs' capacity to repay. This is a common approach to measure debt-servicing capacity and potential NPLs. ICR is the ratio of corporate earnings to interest expense. An ICR ratio of less than 1 means that the firm's profit from regular operations is not sufficient to cover interest expenses on its debt; it is often regarded as a signal of debt distress, as the firm's debt would be unsustainable, absent any outside interventions.

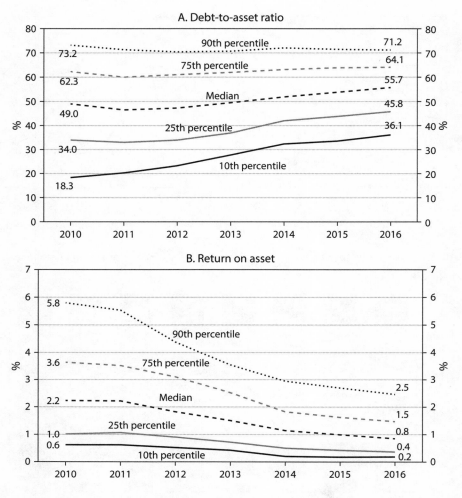

FIGURE 8.5. LGFV debt-to-asset ratio and return on asset. *Sources:* Authors' calculations, Wind database. Based on a balanced panel of 1,109 LGFVs.

We calculated three different ICRs:

- ICR1 = earnings / interest expenses
- ICR2 = earnings / adjusted interest expenses
- ICR3 = (earnings—subsidies) / adjusted interest expenses

Earnings: There are three candidates for measuring earnings: EBITDA, EBIT, and operating cash flow (OCF). A shortcoming of EBITDA is that it excludes the cost of depreciation and amortization. These costs can be large for LGFVs, and cannot be postponed indefinitely. In this regard, EBIT-based ICR is a better measure for debt-servicing capacity in the long run. Finally, OCF captures actual cash flow and is less subject to accounting manipulation, but it may underestimate earnings of long-term projects with front-loaded costs in their initial years. We choose EBIT-based ICR as our baseline, while we also calculated ICRs based on EBITDA and OCF as robustness checks for our results.

Adjusted interest expenses: LGFVs tend to capitalize a significant amount of interest expenses. This resulted in artificially low interest expenses in the income statement. The effective interest rate, calculated as the ratio of interest expense to interest-bearing debt, was well below market rates. LGFVs and listed SOEs should have similar credit-worthiness, yet the effective interest rate was much lower in LGFVs. Using the reported interest expense would significantly underestimate LGFVs' actual borrowing cost. Lacking the information to back out the amount of capitalized interest expenses, we applied the benchmark lending rate as a proxy. We set a 0.8x benchmark lending rate as the floor effective rate for all LGFVs in the sample, and we adjust up interest expenses accordingly.

Subsidies: Many LGFVs receive regular subsidies from the government. It is not, however, standard accounting practice to report government subsidies, and only a small portion of LGFVs do so. Using available observations, we found very strong correlation between subsidies and non-operating income: On average subsidies are about 88% of non-operating income, with a correlation coefficient at 0.98. To be conservative, we used 80% of non-operating income as a proxy for fiscal subsidies received by LGFVs. Our estimate shows that subsidies continued to increase as a share of earnings, and accounted for almost 30% of LGFV's EBITDA by 2016.

ICR1, the EBIT-based ICR before any adjustments, deteriorated across the board in recent years. For the median LGFV, earnings have fallen from 6.9x interest expense in 2010 to 2.2x in 2016 (figure 8.6, left panel). The figure also illustrates great disparity among LGFVs: While most LGFVs seem to have more than sufficient earnings to cover their interest expenses, the bottom 10% still have LCR ratios of less than 1 in 2016.

Interest coverage dropped dramatically for all LGFVs once capitalization of interest expenses are adjusted for (figure 8.6, middle panel). ICR2 was merely above 1 for the median LGFV in 2016. A total of 42% of the LGFVs lacked sufficient earnings to cover their interest payments that were falling due. While the aggressive capitalization of interest expenses helped paint a rosy picture on the accounting books, the reality is much more alarming.

If we subtract subsidies from LGFV earnings, ICR3 would be reduced further to 0.7x for the median LGFV. A total of 69% of LGFVs' ICR was below 1 in 2016. Furthermore, ICR was close to zero for the bottom 10% to 25% of the LGFVs, suggesting that they were not profitable at all once government subsidies are removed from their income (figure 8.6, right panel).

Which ICR best reflects the future debt-servicing capacity of LGFVs? It largely depends on future government policies. If LGFVs are to be fully regarded as commercial entities and would be cut off from subsidies, ICR3 would be the most accurate indicator. If the fiscal subsidies continue to increase at the same pace of LGFV debt, then ICR2 would be more accurate. The most likely scenario, in our view, is that subsidies will be continued at reduced, or even negative, growth rates. In this scenario, future interest coverage should be somewhere between ICR2 and ICR3.

Our interest coverage calculations also unveil huge disparities across LGFVs. One important determinant of such differences is geographical location (figure 8.7). Average interest expenses-adjusted ICR could range from 0.4 (Gansu) to 1.9 (Jilin) among different provinces. Once government subsidies are also excluded, only a few provinces still have their ICRs above 1—being mostly the richer provinces and huge cities such as Beijing,

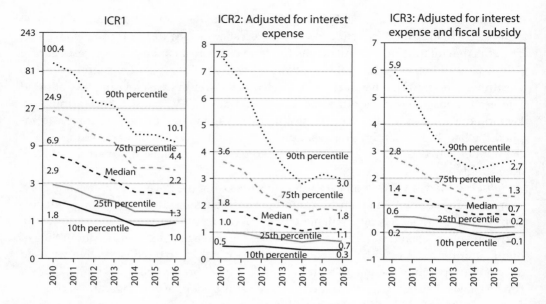

FIGURE 8.6. Distribution of EBIT-based interest coverage ratio. *Sources:* Authors' calculations, Wind database. Based on a balanced panel of 636 LGFVs.

Shanghai, Guangdong, and Fujian. On the other end of the spectrum, Heilongjiang stands out as having a negative ICR on average.

To sum up, LGFV debts are already at high levels and continue to increase. These debts are burdens not only for them but also for the general government. Most LGFVs are quasi-fiscal entities that are not financially sustainable on their own. Once the true borrowing cost and subsidies are taken into account, LGFV interest coverages are at alarmingly low levels. Without subsidies, most LGFVs do not have sufficient earnings to cover their true interest expenses. One may rightfully question whether LGFVs are sustainable on their own. It is likely that the LGFVs would demand further transfers from fiscal resources in the future.

2.1.5. Regulating LGFVs: Policies and Challenges

It is clear that LGFVs conducted substantial amounts of borrowing on local governments' behalf, which helped infrastructure investment but accumulated fiscal risks. Such risks have been on the government's radar screen for a long time. Indeed, a number of measures have been taken to address LGFV debt risks (figure 8.8):

- In June 2010, the central government issued its first policy document on LGFVs. The so-called document 19 tasked the Ministry of Finance, the central bank, and other ministries to take stock of existing LGFV debt and also to regulate LGFV future borrowing.
- The second round of tightening happened during late 2013–2014 with the issuance of NAO's auditing report on LGFVs, and the "document 43" policy that forbade LGFVs from borrowing with government guarantees.

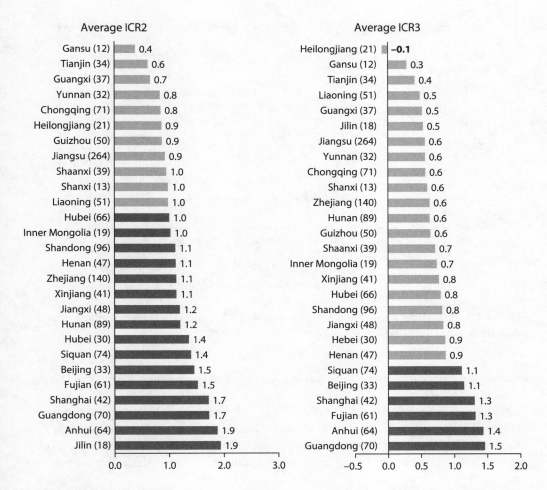

FIGURE 8.7. Average ICR by province, 2017. *Sources:* Authors' calculations, Wind database.

- The third round of tightening started in Q2 2017. A series of new policies was issued, mostly notably the "document 50" in April and the "document 87" in May 2017. These policies closed many loopholes that local governments formerly could use to borrow outside the budget, including through LGFVs.

Notwithstanding all the efforts, LGFV debt continued to pile up. The effectiveness of these policies was affected by a number of factors. One important factor is that conflicting policy goals have made implementation of such policies time-inconsistent. Infrastructure investment has an important role on both central and local governments' policy agendas. Local governments generally have a tendency to overborrow and overinvest, as GDP growth carries a heavy weight in their objective function. At normal times the central government may offset this tendency with tight policies and regulations. In economic downturns, however, the central government's policy focus will shift to maintaining macroeconomic and financial stability, and will have to rely on local governments to carry out fiscal stimulus, largely through infrastructure investment. As a result, policies

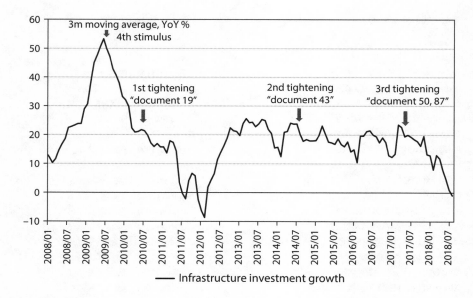

FIGURE 8.8. Infrastructure investment growth and LGFV policies. *Sources:* Authors' calculations, **NBS**, Wind database.

to constrain LGFV debt risks were not implemented in a consistent manner in the past decade.

Moreover, infrastructure investments have grown rapidly to become a main driver for growth. Any attempt to constrain LGFV borrowing would by itself lead to economic slowdown as infrastructure investment collapses. Past policy tightening often did not last long before running into another economic downturn and policy-easing cycle.

To make things worse, the financial sector has over time accumulated large exposure to LGFVs. LGFVs lack sufficient resources to pay off these debt, so they largely rely on local government subsidies and guarantees. When policies tighten on LGFVs, it becomes uncertain whether their debt will continue to be backed by governments. LGFVs, in turn, face higher borrowing costs and, in some cases, refinancing difficulties. Given the large size of LGFV debt, policy tightening on LGFVs also has financial stability implications.

To address these problems, the government attempted, first, to issue government debt to replace debt of LGFVs, so as to insulate the financial sector from LGFV debt risks and, second, to introduce alternative and better-regulated financial arrangements to replace LGFVs as creative new ways to finance infrastructure.

2.2. Replacing LGFVs: New Arrangements for Infrastructure Financing

In 2014, the State Council issued an important regulation on local government borrowing. The so-called document 43 banned LGFVs from issuing new debt on local governments' behalf. At the same time, it lifted the ban on local governments' direct borrowing, allowing them to issue bonds subject to debt ceilings and approval by the central government. Furthermore, it promoted the use of public-private partnerships (PPPs) as a new way to implement and finance public investment.

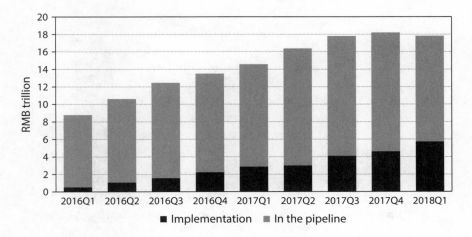

FIGURE 8.9. PPPs: under implementation and in pipeline. *Sources:* Authors' calculations, MOF, Wind database.

2.2.1. Public-Private Partnerships (PPPs)

Since 2014, China's government promoted PPPs as a new model for carrying out and financing public investment projects. The policy goal is to leverage on private enterprises and the financial sector to invest in infrastructure, while limiting the government's direct exposure to debt.

PPP projects are normally implemented by special-purpose vehicles (SPVs) that are set up and owned either solely by private partners or jointly with the government. The SPVs will sign contracts with the government on carrying out investment projects. In return it will receive future income streams either directly from the government or from the projects (e.g., road fees). The SPVs may then borrow from the financial sector, using these future revenue streams. In principle, the government should not be accountable for any debt of the SPVs.

PPPs grew rapidly. As of end-Q1 2018, about 3,500 PPP projects are under implementation, with total investment of RMB5.7trn. Another 9,000 projects totaling RMB12trn are in the pipeline and are under identification, preparation, or procurement (figure 8.9).

2.2.2. Local Government Special-Purpose Bonds

In the two decades after the 1994 Budget Law became effective, local governments were generally prohibited from issuing debt. The ban was lifted in 2014. With the 2014 revision of the Budget Law, local governments were permitted to issue bonds, subject to annual debt ceilings and approval by the central government. There are two types of government bonds: local government general bonds, which are used for financing of general budget deficits; and local government special-purpose bonds, which are used for financing of public capital spending outside the general budget. The central government manages local government bonds through setting both national and provincial debt ceilings in the annual budget.

The limit on new special-purpose bonds increased rapidly from RMB0.4trn in 2016 to 0.8trn in 2017, and further to 1.35trn in 2018 (figure 8.10). The increase was largely

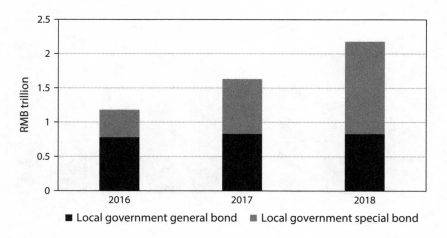

FIGURE 8.10. Limits on new local government bond issued. *Sources:* Authors' calculations, MOF.

intended to accommodate local government financing needs for infrastructure investment. A large share of proceeds from special-purpose bonds are used for infrastructure
investment such as land development and road construction. In contrast, the limit on
new local government general bonds has been stable in recent years and in line with
local government budget deficits.

3. FINANCING SOURCES OF INFRASTRUCTURE INVESTMENT

3.1. The Core Role of Land in Infrastructure Financing

There is no private landownership in China. The government sells the right of using
land to property developers, firms, and individuals. Land plays a unique and crucial role
in infrastructure financing.

First, land is the main source of local governments' extra-budgetary revenue
(figure 8.11). In 2017 local governments' extra-budgetary government funds revenue totaled RMB5.9trn, of which 5trn, or 90%, came from land sales. Local government budgetary revenue amounted to approximately 9.1trn in the same year. Unlike budgetary
revenue, which is mostly used for current spending, a significant share of land sales
revenue goes to government investment, setting aside funds spent on compensation to
previous land and housing owners.

Second, land is also frequently used as collateral for bank financing. Local governments may grant land usage rights to LGFVs as their principal assets. LGFVs may also
buy land from government land auctions. Regardless of how LGFVs acquired land, they
may subsequently use them as collateral to obtain bank financing.

It has largely been thanks to the continued appreciation of land and property prices
throughout China that local governments have managed to finance high levels of government capital spending. When land prices increase, not only does government land
sales revenue also increase, but the value of land assets owned by LGFVs appreciates as
well. LGFVs may then use those assets to obtain more bank financing.

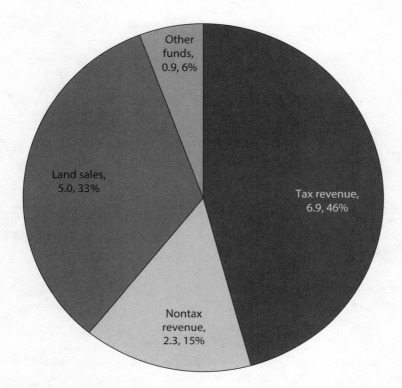

FIGURE 8.11. Local government revenue breakdown, 2017 (RMB trn). *Sources:* Authors' calculations, MOF, Wind database.

3.2. External Financing

In the 1980s and 1990s, external financing was an important source of financing for infrastructure investment throughout China. Total public and public-guaranteed external borrowing averaged 3% of GDP annually between 1986 and 1995 (figure 8.12). Both official creditors and private creditors provided large amounts of financing to China over this period.

As the largest official creditor to China, the World Bank Group committed USD $35bn of financing to China in the 1980s and 1990s; it committed another $24bn from 2000 onward. The Asian Development Bank was also an important creditor, providing a total of $37bn financing to China by end-2017. Its financing largely went to infrastructure sectors, such as transportation, urban development, water, energy, and agriculture. Private financing was also active in the 1980s and 1990s. Total public and public-guaranteed financing from private creditors reached $150bn over this period. In the 1990s, many road projects in China tapped into foreign financing, the costs of which were then paid off by road fees.

External financing over this period helped overcome two important constraints for investment: first, the relatively small and financially weak domestic banks in the 1980s and 1990s; and second, the lack of foreign exchange for imported inputs for investment—for example, FX reserves amounted to only USD $11bn, or 2.4 months of imports, in 1990.

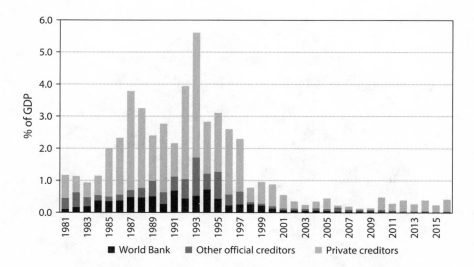

FIGURE 8.12. China: Public and public-guaranteed external borrowing. *Sources:* Authors' calculations, World Bank.

3.3. Bank Financing

External financing collapsed after the Asian financial crisis. China's total new public external borrowing dropped by 60% in 1998 from the previous year. Against this backdrop, new sources of financing for infrastructure investment were called for.

The gap was filled by the China Development Bank (CDB). The CDB was established by the central government in 1994 as a policy bank. Initially, it provided loans to national-level projects, such as the Three Gorges Dam project in 1994. In 1998, the CDB signed an RMB1.1bn, 10-year package loan with Wuhu Construction Investment Co. Ltd., a company owned by the Wuhu municipal government, to finance six local infrastructure investment projects. The loan carries a guarantee from that municipal government. This so-called Wuhu Model marks the first bank loan made to an LGFV to support local government infrastructure investment (Zhan, 2014).

Other local governments soon followed the "Wuhu Model." Chongqing, for example, set up no fewer than eight LGFVs in 2002. After establishing these, Chongqing's infrastructure investment grew threefold in the following five years, increasing from 80bn in 2001 to 247bn in 2006. CDB remains the main creditor to these LGFVs, accounting for about two-thirds of their total liabilities. Other commercial banks also provided loans to these LGFVs, although their financing terms (in maturity and interest rates) are generally stiffer than those of CDB loans (World Bank, 2010).

CDB's operations grew rapidly. Total assets of policy banks grew 20% per year between 2003 and 2016, reaching RMB23trn in 2016, of which 14.3trn were assets of the CDB itself (figure 8.13).

As a policy bank, the CDB does not take household deposits. Its main source of funding is the issuance of bonds on the interbank market. CDB issued its first bond in 1998, the same year it provided financing to Wuhu. Total CDB bond value outstanding was RMB8.4trn as of end-2017, which makes the CDB the biggest nonsovereign issuer on China's bond market.

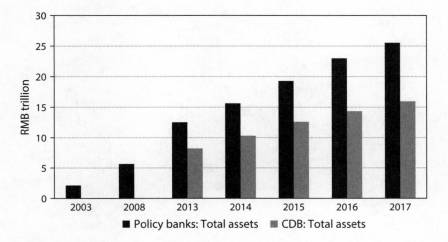

FIGURE 8.13. China: Total assets of policy banks. *Sources:* Authors' calculations, CBIRC, CDB, Wind database. *Note:* Policy banks include China Development Bank, China Exim Bank, and Agriculture Development Bank of China.

3.4. Market Financing

3.4.1. LGFV Bonds

Local government financing platforms started to issue bonds in the mid-2000s amid the rapid expansion of the interbank market. LGFV bonds, or *"cheng tou zhai,"* grew rapidly to become a sub-asset class on the domestic bond market. Total LGFV bonds stood at RMB7.1trn as of end-2017. Bond financing accounted for some 20% to 30% of LGFVs' interest-bearing debt.

Given LGFVs' nature as government financing platforms, they often lack sufficient assets or income inflows to repay all the debt. Their capacity to repay largely depends on local governments' continued support through asset and income transfers. The willingness of local governments to maintain their support to LGFVs may change over time, depending not only on financial factors such as local government fiscal revenue and expenditures as well as land market conditions, but also on policy factors such as overall fiscal policy stance and regulatory changes. Furthermore, LGFVs are not profit-maximizing market entities, and therefore they can be insensitive to financing costs. As a result, LGFV bond financing is often more costly than government financing, and LGFV bond prices can even be volatile at times (figure 8.14)

3.4.2. Local Government Bonds

In an attempt to regulate LGFV borrowing and reduce the effective borrowing costs of local governments, the 2014 revision to the Budget Law allowed local governments themselves to issue bonds. Meanwhile, the government initiated a large-scale bond swap program in 2014, allowing local governments to issue bonds to replace both the debt of LGFVs and other debt that was identified to be "government debt" in nature.

Local governments issued RMB14trn of bonds between 2014 and 2017. The majority of bonds issued over this period (11trn) were bonds for swapping out LGFV and other

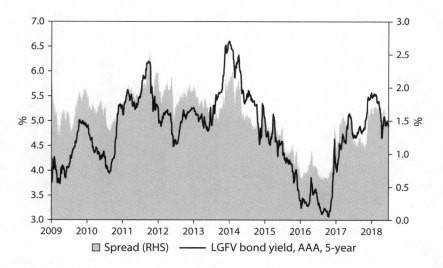

FIGURE 8.14. LGFV borrowing cost: LGFV bond yield and credit spread. *Sources:* Authors' calculations, Wind database.

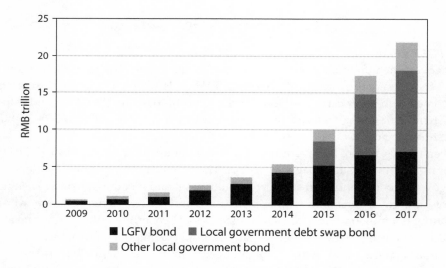

FIGURE 8.15. China: Local government bonds. *Sources:* Authors' calculations, Wind database.

government debt. The bond swap program came to an end in 2018. As swap-bond issuance declined, issuance of local government special-purpose bonds increased to 800bn in 2017 and to 1,350bn in 2018. These special-purpose bonds largely go to financing land development and infrastructure investment (figure 8.15).

3.4.3. Other Financing Sources
Aside from the bond market, local governments and LGFVs alike may obtain financing from a few other channels. A number of large LGFVs became public listed companies and tapped into financing from the equity market. LGFVs have also leveraged on the

shadow banking system. The asset pool of wealth management products may include a sizable amount of financing to LGFVs.

4. TOWARD A SUSTAINABLE REGIME OF INFRASTRUCTURE FINANCING

The Chinese government has been pushing hard for a change in its growth model. In the 19th Communist Party Plenum, held in October 2018, President Xi Jinping did not set a numerical growth target for China beyond 2020. Rather, he emphasized the importance of quality instead of speed of growth. He also highlighted the urgency to contain financial risks.

This change of policy has important implications for infrastructure financing:

- Less focus on growth means less dependence on infrastructure investment. Indeed, infrastructure investment growth has been falling since President Xi gave his speech at the 19th Party Plenum.
- More focus on financial risks means more scrutiny on project financing. In the past, investors assumed that LGFVs were guaranteed by the government. Indeed, the LGFV bonds have never defaulted so far. But this assumption is changing. The central government seems determined to remove implicit guarantees and to keep local government debt under control. It seems that LGFV bond default is inevitable. It is only a matter of time.

It is challenging to set up a new framework for infrastructure financing. First of all, infrastructure financing is really a fiscal issue. The rampant growth of LGFVs is clearly a problem, but it is the inevitable outcome of the conflict between high GDP growth targets and stringent fiscal arrangements. Therefore, the appropriate solution would require, first, either abolishing growth targets or making them more flexible, focusing instead on unemployment, inflation, and quality of growth; and second, reforming the fiscal system to make local governments' fiscal condition more sustainable. A sustainable macro and fiscal framework is a prerequisite for similarly sustainable infrastructure financing.

Moreover, the government needs to make local officials accountable for the debts they borrow. Local government debt grew rapidly because there was no accountability. Officials have the incentive to borrow as much as they can, boost growth, get promoted, and then leave the debt problem to their successors. President Xi said in mid-2017 that local officials should become accountable for the debt they borrow throughout their whole political career. It remains to be seen how the government will institutionalize such a requirement.

We believe that LGFV bond default would be good news for the financial market and China's economy in the long run. Without default, the LGFV bonds cause a moral hazard problem—investors buy the bonds and assume the risk is taken by government. The fiscal conditions of local governments vary tremendously, but their bonds have been treated similarly in the market, because investors assume they have the same credit quality—that is, the government will bail out these bonds if necessary, regardless of the fiscal health of individual bond issuers.

Another problem of LGFV bonds is that they crowd out private corporate bond issuance. LGFV bonds often paid high interest. The issuers were not sensitive to financing

costs because they assumed the government would provide subsidies to them if necessary. This led to an uneven playground for the private sector bond issuers. A healthy
financial market should help to allocate capital to firms based on financial returns and
risks. The rapid growth of LGFV bonds jeopardizes the functioning of the financial market. Therefore, we believe that default on LGFV bonds should help to resolve the moral
hazard problem and allow risks to be priced properly.

A related issue is that the government needs to resolve the stock of local government
debt, including LGFV liabilities. LGFV bonds are an important part of assets in the
shadow banking sector. A large number of wealth management products likely have
LGFV bonds as their underlying assets. While we think the government should allow
some defaults to happen, to make the new framework more credible requires delicate
maneuvers—for the regulators need to beware of triggering too many repercussions
throughout the financial system.

NOTES

1. Infrastructure investment is defined as, according to the NBS, fixed asset investment in trans-
    portation, electricity, gas, water, and public facilities sectors.
2. The positive effect of infrastructure on growth and productivity in China is confirmed by a num-
    ber of studies (e.g., Démurger, 2001; Fan and Zhang, 2004; Wan and Zhang, 2018).
3. World Bank (2010).
4. The NAO audits fiscal revenue and spending of central and local governments. It reports directly
    to the State Council. It was established in 1983.
5. The CBRC merged with the China Insurance Regulatory Commission in 2018 to become the
    China Banking and Insurance Regulatory Commission (CBIRC).
6. Deutsche Bank (2017).

REFERENCES

Démurger, Sylvie (2001). "Infrastructure Development and Economic Growth: An Explanation for Re-
gional Disparities in China?" *Journal of Comparative Economics*, 29(1): 95–117.
Deutsche Bank (2017). "Revisiting the LGFV Debt Issue." *China Fiscal Series*, November 6, 2017.
Fan, Shenggen, and Xiaobo Zhang (2004). "Infrastructure and Regional Economic Development in
Rural China." *China Economic Review*, 15(2): 203–14.
Jin, Hui, and Isabel Rial (2016). "Regulating Local Government Financing Vehicles and Public-Private
Partnerships in China." IMF Working Paper No. 16/187, September.
Wan, Guanghua, and Yan Zhang (2018). "The Direct and Indirect Effects of Infrastructure on Firm
Productivity: Evidence from Manufacturing in the People's Republic of China." *China Economic
Review*, 49(2): 143–53.
World Bank (2010). "The Urban Development Investment Corporations (UDICs) in Chongqing, China."
Washington, D.C.: World Bank.
Zhan Xialai (2014). "From 'Wuhu Model' to Comprehensive Pilot of New Urbanization: Innovative
Practice of Development Finance in the Process of Urbanization." Research on Development Fi-
nance, March.
Zhou, Li-an (2007). "Governing China's Local Officials: An Analysis of the Promotion Tournament
Model." *Economic Research Journal*, 2007(7): 36–50.

PART 4

ONGOING REFORMS

9

RMB INTERNATIONALIZATION

Past, Present, and Prospect

Kai Guo, Ningxin Jiang, Fan Qi, and Yue Zhao

INTRODUCTION

As an economic phenomenon that attracts much attention, the internationalization of the RMB has been going on for less than a decade and is still a work in progress. Given that the process might take decades, it is probably too early to properly review what has happened and its future prospects. Yet the RMB internationalization has its own characteristics. The first is its pace. Before 2009, RMB was seldom used outside China, except in several neighboring economies. By 2015, the International Monetary Fund (IMF) had recognized RMB as freely usable—widely used internationally and traded in the principal exchange markets, and had decided to include RMB in the special drawing rights (SDR) basket, something unthinkable in 2009. The second is its timing—that is, the process starting after the outburst of the 2008 global financial crisis, which is no coincidence. The third is that the authorities, in particular the People's Bank of China (PBC), have adopted a series of policy measures supporting RMB internationalization. While many of these measures were designed to meet market demand and eliminate unnecessary obstacles in using RMB, it is still noteworthy for a government to promote the internationalization of its currency through frequent adoption of measures and with clear objectives.

This chapter will briefly review the internationalization process of major currencies such as the U.S. dollar, the British pound, the euro, the Japanese yen, and several others. Then it provides an overview of the current state of RMB internationalization and describes how that has come about, in particular the efforts that the Chinese government has made in promoting it. Finally, the chapter will examine issues to be addressed going forward and describe the prospects for RMB internationalization.

Table 9.1. International Uses for a National Currency

	Private use	*Official use*
Unit of account	Trade invoicing and for financial transactions, commodities pricing	FX anchor and as a basis for expressing FX rates
Medium of exchange	Settlement, a vehicle currency	Intervention and balance of payment (BOP) financing
Store of value	Denominates asset values	FX reserves

Source: Kenen (1983).

1. CURRENCY INTERNATIONALIZATION: A HISTORICAL PERSPECTIVE

The term "currency internationalization" refers to the use of one currency beyond the border of the issuing country, including the use by nonresidents to purchase goods, services, and financial assets (Kenen, 2011). The international functions of a currency include three dimensions: unit of account, medium of exchange, and store of value (Kenen, 1983; see table 9.1). At present, major international reserve currencies include the dollar, euro, pound, and yen. In recent years, however, the international status of RMB has risen rapidly. In 2015, the IMF decided to include RMB into the SDR basket. Some see the RMB as the next major international reserve currency in the making. In this context, it is helpful to look at the internationalization path of other currencies and to learn from history.

1.1. Internationalization Process of Major Currencies

1.1.1. Pound Sterling

The United Kingdom was the first industrialized country, completing its industrial revolution in the 19th century. In 1850, Britain accounted for 30% of world industrial output and 21% of international trade, both ranking the first around the world (Mathias, 2001). The pound sterling was the invoicing currency in most international trade. In terms of its monetary system, the United Kingdom adopted the gold standard in 1844, in effect giving itself a gold-based monetary system with the British pound at the center. This further consolidated the pound's international status. After World War I and particularly after World War II, the status of the pound in global trade declined and its appeal as an international currency weakened accordingly (see figure 9.1). However, thanks to its sophisticated financial market and longstanding trading habits throughout the world, today the pound retains an important seat in the current international monetary system.

1.1.2. U.S. Dollar

The two world wars altered the political and economic landscape of the world and established the U.S. dominance in political, military, and economic arenas. Such dominance became the inherent driving force for dollar internationalization. Since the 1940s, dollar-denominated liquid assets and reserve assets exceeded those denominated in pounds.

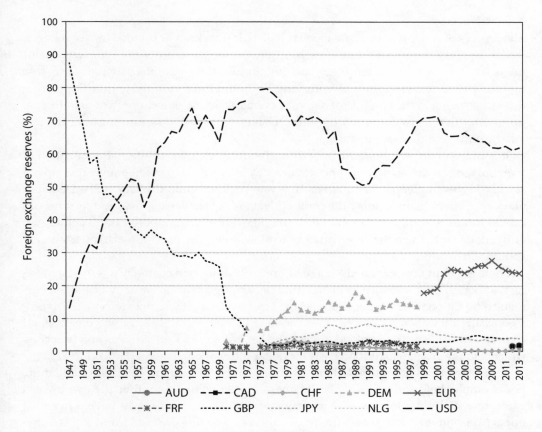

FIGURE 9.1. Currency composition of globally disclosed foreign exchange reserves, 1947–2013. *Source:* Eichengreen et al. (2016).

In the process of dollar internationalization, the creation of the Federal Reserve, the thriving of the U.S. financial market, and the establishment of both the Bretton Woods system and the Marshall Plan all played essential roles.

1.1.3. Euro

The euro is the most important invoicing and settlement currency besides the U.S. dollar. As an important outcome of regional currency cooperation, the euro not only serves as the settlement and invoicing currency in the eurozone area, but also plays a significant role in trade beyond the region. While the international use of the Deutsche mark and the French franc provided a foundation for euro internationalization, the weight of the eurozone in the world economy and trade as well as the creation of the European Central Bank buoyed the euro in its internationalization. Although concerns over eurozone member countries intensified in the wake of the 2011 European sovereign debt crisis, the eurozone economy has recovered with good momentum, and the international status of the euro has remained solid.

1.1.4. Yen

The process of yen internationalization is challenging and can be divided into two stages. In the first stage, from 1970 to the early 1990s, the Japanese economy grew rapidly, its financial markets were increasingly opening up, and the yen's international status rose rapidly. The second stage started from early 1990s and has continued to this day. During this stage, owing to the bursting of domestic bubbles and the slower progress of industrial upgrading, the international status of the yen has weakened, now ranking after the dollar, the euro, and the pound (Tetsuji, 2000).

It is noteworthy that governments differ in attitudes toward internationalization of their currencies. Some did not support currency internationalization or even put up obstacles. For example, out of concerns that internationalization would cause Deutsche mark appreciation, undermine the competitiveness of German exports, and lead to both capital inflow and high inflation, the German government hampered Iran's conversion of the dollar into the mark in an attempt to slow down the pace of mark internationalization (Eichengreen, 2011).

Some governments assumed a laissez-faire attitude toward currency internationalization, although a series of domestic institutional arrangements eventually facilitated currency internationalization. For example, the U.S. government was not always keen to promote dollar internationalization. However, in 1913 the Federal Reserve was created, and commercial banks started to lend abroad and set up overseas subsidiaries and branches, which laid the crucial institution basis for dollar internationalization (Frankel, 2012).

Some governments shifted their attitudes toward currency internationalization. For example, before the 1980s, the Japanese government was rather passive toward yen internationalization because its ministers worried that it might have a negative impact on domestic trade and financial markets. Starting from the mid-1980s, however, the Japanese government took initiatives to promote yen internationalization to mitigate exchange rate risk for domestic enterprises, facilitate the overseas development of Japanese financial institutions, and enhance Tokyo's status as international financial center (Takagi, 2009).

1.2. Potential Factors Affecting Currency Internationalization

The evolution of the international currencies suggests that fundamentals such as a given economy's size and trade network, the depth and liquidity of its financial markets, and the stability and convertibility of its currency are important determinants that support currency internationalization. No single factor determines successful internationalization; rather, the combination of the above factors as a whole determines where the currency internationalization is heading (IMF, 2011).

Fundamentally, the international status of a country's currency is underpinned by the size and strength of its economy. The dominant role of the British economy in the 19th century, and then of the United States since the 20th century, was matched by the dominant roles of the British pound and the U.S. dollar in the international monetary system. Moreover, large economic scale is supportive of creating deep and liquid financial markets, another key aspect of currency internationalization (Eichengreen and Flandreau, 2008; Genberg, 2009; Tavlas and Ozeki, 1992).

The global status of a currency is affected by demand-side and supply-side factors (IMF, 2011). From the demand side, the factors include:

Network effects: Historical experience shows that internationalization of currencies is supported by strong economic powers with wide international trade networks. Wide trade networks support the use of the currency as both a unit of account and a medium of exchange (Dwyer and James, 2003).

Invoicing practices: A number of factors influence actual trade invoicing behavior and determine the effective use of the currency in international trade. Trades among developed countries are more likely to be invoiced in the exporter's currency. By contrast, exports from developing to developed countries are often priced in the currency of the developed country. The country exporting specialized manufacturing products, such as high-tech products, usually has more bargaining power by invoicing in its own currency. Commodity exporters are less likely to invoice their trade in domestic currencies, and instead will adopt the global standard (Tavlas and Ozeki, 1992; Minikin and Lau, 2013).

Store of value: The macroeconomic and financial stability underlying a currency are key factors in determining a country's willingness to hold and transact in it. High GDP growth rates, as well as low and stable inflation, are key factors in determining the appeal of a currency. In this sense, crisis episodes could undermine efforts to internationalize domestic currencies, as was the case of Japan both after the banking crisis in the 1990s (Tetsuji, 2000; Takagi, 2009) and after the Asian financial crisis in 1997 when international willingness to hold the yen declined and its international status waned.

From the supply side, the ready access to assets denominated in a given currency will affect the degree to which a currency can assume an international role. Main supply-side factors include the following:

Depth of domestic financial market: Deep and liquid financial markets give both borrowers and investors access to a range of financial instruments, which is essential to allow hedging of currency and credit risks by international investors and which increases the currency's international appeal.

Role of offshore markets: Currency internationalization involves use of the currency by nonresidents, where offshore markets often play an important role. A well-developed offshore market not only could help promote currency internationalization but also could prompt the development of an onshore market. It should be remembered that offshore market development should always go in tandem with financial deepening onshore (He and McCauley, 2010).

Currency convertibility and capital account liberalization: Successful internationalization is generally associated with financial openness, allowing for a free flow of capital and contributing to the development of domestic financial markets (Eichengreen and Flandreau, 2008; Genberg, 2009). Importantly, limits on the convertibility of a currency in capital account transactions are likely to raise the costs of transactions denominated in the currency, and to further limit its international role as a store of value.

1.3. Pros and Cons of Currency Internationalization

The global use of a currency carries a set of benefits and risks for the issuing country. The benefits include:

- Opportunity to reduce transaction costs and exchange rate risks, with the option of settling payments in a domestic currency.

- Lower cost of funding than would otherwise be the case. According to some es-timates, the cost of funding in the United States is reduced by 50 to 60 basis points as a result of foreign demand for U.S. Treasuries (McKinsey Global Institute, 2009).
- Seignorage: Foreign countries must give up either real goods and services, or ownership of real capital stock, in order to add to their foreign reserves, which the issuing country prints with little cost (Frankel, 2012).

For some emerging market economies, including China, currency internationaliza-tion carries additional benefits. The global use of a currency enhances the confidence that international investors place in this currency, allows the issuing country to have more means to cope with a potential financial crisis by using domestic currency, and lowers the potential risks of currency mismatch or maturity mismatch (Eichengreen and Hausmann, 1999).

Meanwhile, currency internationalization involves a number of potential risks to monetary and financial stability. First, it may complicate monetary management (by reducing authorities' control over monetary aggregates as a result of increased offshore activities and offshore or onshore links, as well as reduced autonomy in setting domes-tic interest rates), and also strain the financial system's ability to adequately absorb capi-tal flows (owing to increased volatility of capital flow and susceptibility to surges and sudden stops). Currency and other financial markets that lack scale and depth could also become a source of systemic instability as a shift in portfolio allocation could result in destabilizing asset price swings (IMF, 2011).

Second, some governments fear that currency internationalization would lead to up-surges in the demand for their currencies, which would result in appreciation and hurt exporters' international competitiveness.

Third, currency internationalization brings a burden of responsibility. The monetary authority in the country of a leading international currency may be called on to take into account the effects of their actions on world markets, rather than being free to devote monetary policy solely to domestic objectives. Frankel (2012) argues that the Federal Re-serve probably cut interest rates more than it otherwise would have in the second half of 1982, and did so again in late 1998, in response to international debt problems in Latin America and elsewhere.

2. THE PROCESS OF RMB INTERNATIONALIZATION

2.1. Before the Global Financial Crisis: Limited Progress

2.1.1. Starting from Border Trade

RMB internationalization started from going regional at first, thanks to China's close trade ties with neighboring economies as well as its relative larger size compared to most of these economies. Ever since the reform and opening up, driven by the local trading needs, China has gradually lifted the restrictions on border trade. Since 1993, the People's Bank of China (PBC) has successively signed local currency settlement agreements on border trade with central banks of eight countries: Vietnam, Mongolia, Laos, Nepal, Rus-sia, Kyrgyzstan, North Korea, and Kazakhstan. After China became a member of the World Trade Organization (WTO), its border trade further expanded. Since the RMB was on an appreciation trend, the neighboring countries increasingly accepted RMB while

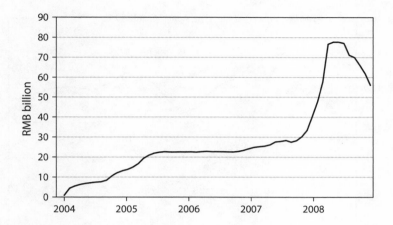

FIGURE 9.2. RMB deposits in Hong Kong SAR. *Source:* HKMA.

Chinese citizens were also willing to use RMB to reduce loss in currency exchanges. As a result, the demand for RMB as a payment currency in border trade gradually grew. However, RMB settlements in cross-border trade were uneven across different regions, and its overall volume was rather limited. As shown by incomplete data from the PBC, 80% of China–Vietnam border trade in Guangxi Province was settled with RMB while that of China–Russia border trade only stood at 0.1% in 2008. In 2006, the stock of RMB in Vietnam, Laos, and Myanmar approached RMB 7 billion.

2.1.2. Taking Advantage of the Special Roles of Hong Kong SAR and Macau SAR

Hong Kong SAR and Macau SAR (special administrative regions) are politically, economically, and geographically close to the Chinese mainland, so they have innate advantages in developing RMB business. Since the two regions have returned to China, their economic and trade ties with the mainland have grown stronger with frequent personnel flows that added to the popularity of RMB in the region, so RMB business was quickly developed. In 2003 and 2004, the RMB clearing banks in Hong Kong SAR and Macau SAR were appointed, respectively, to handle RMB deposit, exchange, remittance, and bank card operations for residents of the two regions, and RMB pools were gradually formed. To meet the investment demands of RMB holders in Hong Kong SAR, from 2007, China allowed domestic financial institutions to issue RMB bonds in Hong Kong SAR and expanded the scopes of issuers and issuing size. China Development Bank, HSBC (China), and Bank of East Asia (China) issued the first RMB bonds (also called "dim sum bonds") in Hong Kong SAR, contributing to its RMB market development. Notwithstanding the rapid growth of RMB business in Hong Kong SAR, the overall size was still limited where the balance of RMB deposits in Hong Kong SAR at end-2008 was only RMB 56.1 billion.

2.2. Post-Crisis Period: Significant Acceleration

2.2.1. Historic Opportunities Generated by the Crisis

Since the onset of the global financial crisis in 2008, some Asian economies have experienced huge shocks to their balance of payments (BOP) and foreign exchange markets. From the second half of 2008, economies such as those of South Korea, Singapore, Thailand, Philippines, Indonesia, India, and Hong Kong SAR started to experience BOP

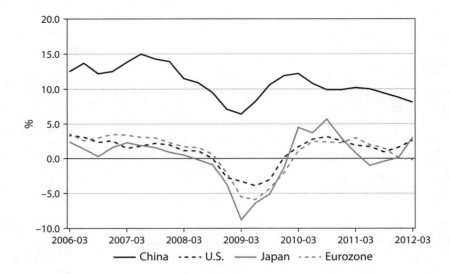

FIGURE 9.3. Quarterly GDP growth (YoY) for China, the United States, the eurozone, and Japan. *Source:* Wind database.

pressures. Against the volatility in the global financial market following the bankruptcy of Lehman Brothers, significant capital flowed back to the United States from the stock and bond markets in emerging economies because of acute risk aversion, worsening the BOPs in these economies. Volatility in Asian foreign exchange markets increased substantially, and their currencies depreciated to various degrees. Two particular examples were South Korea and India, which witnessed relatively large fluctuations of currencies, declines of foreign exchange reserves, and liquidity problems.

At the same time, the exchange rates of major international reserve currencies fluctuated significantly. After the outbreak of the crisis, the U.S. financial market and USD exchange rate experienced violent fluctuations. In the early stage of the crisis, with the most serious U.S. dollar shortage prevailing in the global financial markets, the United States signed swap agreements only with a few advanced economies. Still, the crisis eventually expanded to European countries and finally incurred a sovereign debt crisis in Europe. The economies and financial markets in the eurozone were heavily affected with huge fluctuations in the euro exchange rates.[1]

Although the crisis affected the Chinese economy and its financial markets to a certain extent, its financial system remained sound and the economy took hold and recovered quickly (see figure 9.3). Since China was a major trading partner to most countries and regions across the globe, its companies gained increasing recognition in using RMB for cross-border trade settlements, and the currency was acknowledged as a source of international liquidity by an increasing number of foreign central banks. In addition, foreign exchange reserves in China continued to grow rapidly, supporting a strong expectation for RMB appreciation in the foreign exchange market and propelling foreign investors to invest in the Chinese financial market. With all these favorable factors, the global demand of RMB rose rapidly, generating rare opportunities for RMB internationalization.

2.2.2. RMB Internationalization Progressed Rapidly

Facing a significant increase of international demand for RMB, China took the historic opportunity to promote the use of RMB in cross-border trade and investment, in line with the market demand and also with due respect for market disciplines. Since 2009, the Chinese government stepped up to gradually remove the existent institutional obstacles in the cross-border use of RMB. RMB internalization progressed rapidly in all aspects, ranging from trade settlement to investment settlement, from direct investment to security investment, and from the domestic market to the offshore markets. So far, it has broadly gone through three stages:

Stage 1: The RMB internationalization moved fast from 2009 to 2015. In this stage, multiple pilot programs of RMB cross-border use were launched and the institutional obstacles were removed step by step. The RMB internationalization experienced its "golden era" with rapid growths in the settlement amount of various transactions. This stage came to its peak when RMB was included into the SDR's currency basket.

Stage 2: The pace slowed down from 2015 to 2017. In this period, China faced severe capital outflows owing to the turbulence of financial markets in emerging market economies and the volatility of domestic financial market. The management on cross-border RMB transactions was tightened. As overseas investors perceived uncertainty over the trending of RMB and the economic and financial situation throughout China, some of the RMB cross-border operations were affected.

Stage 3: RMB internationalization steadily recovered after 2017. This occurred against a background of a steadily growing Chinese economy and financial markets. Moreover, administrative policies on capital flows were successively eased and supported the opening-up of Chinese financial markets. In March 2018, Bloomberg announced that it would add Chinese RMB-denominated government bonds and policy bank bonds to the Bloomberg Barclays Global Aggregate Index. In June, China's A shares were included in MSCI's Emerging Markets Index. All such measures were conducive to boosting confidence in RMB, thus promoting the capital allocation on relevant RMB assets.

The progress of RMB internationalization is summarized below along the lines of its functions as a unit of account, a medium of exchange, and a store of value:

1. RMB as a medium of exchange

First, cross-border RMB trade settlement. The pilot program for cross-border trade settlements in RMB in July 2009 marked a turning point in the path of the RMB as a medium of exchange. According to PBC statistics, the volume of such settlements under current account in 2009 only added up to RMB 2.56 billion; however, with the launch and expansion of the pilot program, the figure reached RMB 7.2 trillion in 2015, among which the RMB settlements for trade in goods stood at RMB 6.4 trillion, accounting for 22.6% of China's total cross-border trade in goods. From 2016 to 2017, the volume of RMB settlement of trade in goods edged down, while that of trade in services and other types of trade increased before later decreasing. Despite this, by 2017, the RMB was still the second most dominant currency in cross-border settlements in China (see figure 9.4).

Second, cross-border direct investment in RMB. PBC statistics indicated that, since the pilot program of RMB settlement on Foreign Direct Investment (FDI) was initiated in 2010, the volume of cross-border direct investment in RMB soared from RMB 28.03 billion in 2010 to RMB 2.3 trillion in 2015. In 2015, the volume of ODI-related RMB

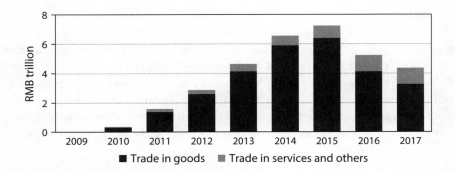

FIGURE 9.4. Annual RMB settlements of current accounts. *Source:* People's Bank of China.

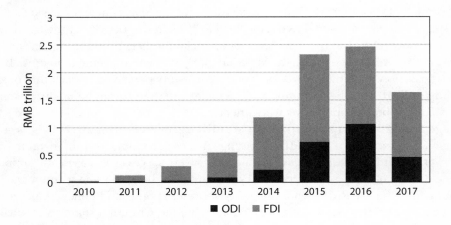

FIGURE 9.5. Annual RMB receipts and payments of cross-border direct investments. *Source:* People's Bank of China.

settlements amounted to RMB 736.17 billion, and that of FDI-related RMB settlements stood at RMB 1.59 trillion. From 2016 to 2017, affected by policy adjustments, the total RMB settlements of cross-border direct investments dropped dramatically, especially in 2017 (see figure 9.5).

Third, RMB-denominated international bonds. According to international bond statistics from the Bank for International Settlements (BIS), by end-March 2007, while the outstanding RMB-denominated international bonds totaled only equivalent to USD 895 million, it rose to USD 9.102 billion at end-March 2009. Since 2010, however, with the promotion of RMB cross-border settlements and the increasing offshore RMB pools, the outstanding RMB-denominated international bonds reached USD 125 billion by end of 2015 due to rapidly expanding issuance. Afterward, such bond issuances lowered to USD 103.2 billion by mid-2017. However, the latest data show that the bond issuance in Q1 2018 rebounded with outstanding bonds at USD 109.3 billion, up by USD 670 million from the end of 2017 (see figure 9.6)

Since 2015, PBC has actively encouraged foreign institutions to issue RMB-denominated bonds in the domestic interbank bond market (termed "Panda Bonds"), and the Panda

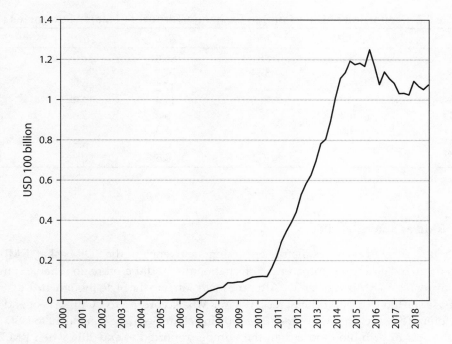

FIGURE 9.6. Outstanding RMB-denominated international bonds. *Source:* BIS.

bond market witnessed rapid growth. According to the National Association of Financial Market Institutional Investors, by end-May 2018, four types of foreign institutions (international development agencies, government organizations, financial institutions, and nonfinancial enterprises) registered bond issuance of RMB 433.71 billion in China with an actual issuance of RMB 163.96 billion. Also, the International Bank for Reconstruction and Development (IBRD) and Standard Chartered Bank issued SDR-denominated Mulan bonds of SDR 500 million and SDR 100 million, respectively, which are both settled in RMB.

Fourth, foreign exchange market transactions. According to the Triennial Central Bank Survey of Foreign Exchange and OTC Derivatives Markets by BIS, from 1998 to April 2007, the average daily turnover of RMB in global foreign exchange markets rose from virtually 0 to USD 15 billion, accounting for 0.5% of the total foreign exchange turnover (the total is 200%). By April 2016, the number grew to approximately USD 202 billion, accounting for 4.0% of the global turnover, but it is still of small size and proportion in the global foreign exchange compared to traditional international reserve currencies (see table 9.2).

Fifth, international payments in RMB. According to the latest data from SWIFT, as of the end of June 2018, RMB ranks fifth as a domestic and international payment currency in the world, with a share of 1.81%, smaller than the Japanese yen's 3.60% and the British pound's 7.44%, and far behind the shares of the dollar and euro, which are 39.35% and 33.97%, respectively. Yet, compared to its ranking two years ago, RMB has achieved progress and surpassed the Canadian dollar. If only international payments are considered, the RMB's ranking is eighth in the world, which stayed the same between June 2016 and June 2018 (see figure 9.7).

Table 9.2. Proportion of Daily Foreign Exchange Turnover of Major Currencies (%)

	2001	2004	2007	2010	2016
USD	89.9	88	85.6	84.9	87.6
EUR	37.9	37.4	37	39	31.4
JPY	23.5	20.8	17.2	19	21.6
GBP	13	16.5	14.9	12.9	12.8
AUD	4.3	6	6.6	7.6	6.9
CAD	4.5	4.2	4.3	5.3	5.1
CHF	6	6	6.8	6.3	4.8
CNY	0	0.1	0.5	0.9	4

Source: BIS.

2. RMB as a store of value

RMB in foreign reserves. Before becoming a currency in the SDR basket, RMB was not recognized as a reserve currency internationally, and therefore no reliable statistics were available on RMB as reserves. After the inclusion into the SDR, though, IMF's COFER database started to report official reserves in RMB. According to COFER, as of end-2017, total foreign reserves in RMB of COFER-reporting countries were equivalent to USD 122.8 billion, USD 32.02 billion more than the number reported at end-2016 when RMB was just included in the SDR basket, accounting for slightly more than 1% of total foreign reserves. Incomplete statistics of the PBC show that, as of the time of writing, more than 60 countries and regions have held RMB as part of their official reserves.[2]

Domestic RMB-denominated financial assets held by nonresidents. According to PBC statistics, 18 countries and regions have been granted a combined quota of RMB 1.74 trillion as RMB Qualified Foreign Institutional Investors (RQFII). As of end-2017, the outstanding domestic RMB-denominated stocks, bonds, loans, deposits, and other financial assets held by nonresidents amounted to RMB 4.29 trillion, for a year-on-year growth of 41.3%. Among these, holding of stocks was RMB 1.17 trillion, accounting for 2.1% of the total value of the A-share market; holding of bonds was RMB 1.2 trillion, or 1.9% of the total; holding of loans reached RMB 739 billion, or 0.6% of the outstanding RMB loans by financial institutions in China; holding of RMB deposits stood at RMB 1.17 trillion, or 0.7% of the total RMB deposits.

3. RMB as a unit of account

RMB internationalization in this area has been limited. Anecdotes suggest that trade invoicing in RMB has yet to become common practice, even within China. Some recent initiatives include the launch of a gold price quote in RMB by Shanghai Gold Exchange and the listing of RMB-denominated crude oil future contracts in Shanghai Futures Exchange. Also, China's BOP statistics are being reported both in USD and RMB, and in some cases also in SDR.

4. Offshore RMB market

Hong Kong SAR has always been the primary offshore RMB market. RMB deposits there rose from approximately RMB 54.3 billion in early 2009 to some RMB 1 trillion by end-2014. Since 2015, RMB deposits in Hong Kong started to decline. The lowest point

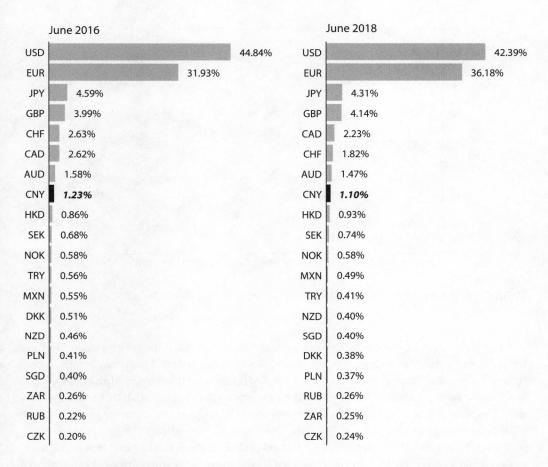

June 2016		June 2018	
USD	44.84%	USD	42.39%
EUR	31.93%	EUR	36.18%
JPY	4.59%	JPY	4.31%
GBP	3.99%	GBP	4.14%
CHF	2.63%	CAD	2.23%
CAD	2.62%	CHF	1.82%
AUD	1.58%	AUD	1.47%
CNY	*1.23%*	CNY	*1.10%*
HKD	0.86%	HKD	0.93%
SEK	0.68%	SEK	0.74%
NOK	0.58%	NOK	0.58%
TRY	0.56%	MXN	0.49%
MXN	0.55%	TRY	0.41%
DKK	0.51%	NZD	0.40%
NZD	0.46%	SGD	0.40%
PLN	0.41%	DKK	0.38%
SGD	0.40%	PLN	0.37%
ZAR	0.26%	RUB	0.26%
RUB	0.22%	ZAR	0.25%
CZK	0.20%	CZK	0.24%

FIGURE 9.7. RMB's ranking as an international payments currency. *Source:* SWIFT RMB Tracker, June 2018. *Notes:* Customer-initiated and institutional payments. Excluding payments within eurozone. Messages exchanged on SWIFT. Based on value.

was in March 2017, when they were only half of the 2014 peak. The figure recovered gradually afterward, reaching RMB 559.1 billion at end-2017 and RMB 584.5 billion by end-June 2018. By Q1 2018 deposits in the Taiwan Province of China, Singapore, and London stood at around RMB 310 billion, RMB 13.9 billion, and RMB 77.2 billion, respectively. Meanwhile, various indicators point to the recovery of offshore markets in 2018. For example, offshore RMB-dominated bond issuance amounted to RMB 57 billion in Q1 2018, growing nearly 50% year-on-year (see figure 9.8).

2.3. Facilitating Efforts by the Chinese Government on RMB Internationalization

The rapid advancement of RMB internationalization over the past decade would not have been possible without facilitating policies by the Chinese government, particularly the PBC, since 2009. A clear path can be identified in the efforts as the government moves to meet market demands by removing unnecessary administrative barriers and constructing a complete chain of RMB cross-border flows.

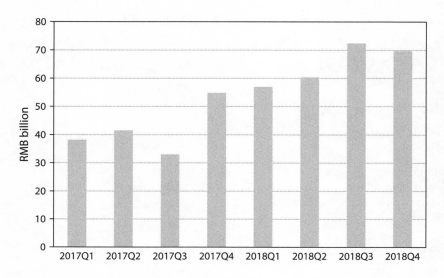

FIGURE 9.8. Offshore RMB-dominated bond issuance. *Source:* Bloomberg.

Originally, against the global financial crisis, China provided the much-needed liquidity support for many emerging market economies through bilateral currency swaps. Later, driven by market demands for cross-border RMB trade settlements, in July 2009 China launched a pilot program that ushered in a new era for accelerated RMB internationalization. Responding to RMB accumulation overseas, China gradually put in place relevant pilot programs of cross-border RMB direct investment and indirect investment channels, including Shanghai–Hong Kong Stock Connect and Shenzhen–Hong Kong Stock Connect, which generated additional opportunities for RMB to flow back into China. Then, after the trading volumes of cross-border RMB payment and settlement rose to considerable levels, China made further improvements in its financial infrastructure, such as in RMB settlement systems, so as to facilitate and smooth the cross-border flows of RMB.

2.3.1. Provide Liquidity Support through Currency Swaps

During the global financial crisis, China signed currency swap agreements with other economies to offer them emergency liquidity support so as to bolster market confidence and ensure financial stability in certain neighboring Asian countries and regions. From end-2008 to early-2009, the PBC reached bilateral currency swap agreements with the central banks or monetary authorities of South Korea, Hong Kong SAR, and Malaysia. To some extent, RMB started to play the role of a regional currency, effectively reducing the liquidity crunch in those economies.

After the crisis, more countries tried to engage in currency swaps with China, having two major objectives: to consolidate and develop their financial safety nets, and to facilitate trade and investment with China by providing liquidity support when needed. As of the end of 2018, the PBC has signed swap agreements with the central banks or monetary authorities of no fewer than 38 countries and regions, including South Korea, Hong Kong SAR, Argentina, Singapore, New Zealand, Turkey, Australia, the United Kingdom, Switzerland, Russia, and Canada. The overall amount of the agreements totaled roughly RMB 3.7 trillion.

Furthermore, bilateral currency swaps constitute one channel for China to offer emergent crisis assistance. Although most swap agreements would stay unused, their very existence sends a strong signal that is useful for boosting market confidence, reducing capital flight from the recipient country, and preventing the crisis from getting worse. Particularly after being included in the SDR basket, the RMB has been officially recognized as an international reserve currency, further enhancing the value of bilateral currency swaps. In recent years, the bilateral currency swap agreements with Mongolia, Egypt, Ukraine, Argentina, and other countries have all been considered part of BOP financing by the international community, as they have effectively mitigated economic and financial risks those countries have faced and have even helped lift some out of crisis.[3]

2.3.2. Facilitate Cross-Border RMB Use and Settlement in Line with Market Demands
The First Measure Is Cross-Border RMB Trade Settlement
Originally, far from being prevalent in cross-border transactions, the RMB was used only sporadically in border trade. In fact, China's own policy did not allow them to be used for trade settlements or other cross-border transactions. In July 2009, PBC and other relevant authorities jointly launched the pilot program of cross-border trade settlement in RMB, listing Shanghai and four cities of Guangdong Province—namely Guangzhou, Shenzhen, Zhuhai, and Dongguan—as the first-batch pilot areas. In June 2010 and August 2011, the pilot areas were further expanded to cover all domestic and foreign enterprises. After June 2012, the cross-border RMB trade settlement operations were conducted across the board, covering all current account items. After these policy initiatives, RMB won more and more recognition, and the volume of cross-border RMB settlement under current account soared.

The Second Channel Is Cross-Border RMB Direct Investment
After the pilot program of cross-border trade settlement in RMB was launched, the currency witnessed an increased acceptance overseas. In their efforts toward "going global," Chinese enterprises have shown a greater demand for the use of RMB, especially when it comes to outward direct investment (ODI). In addition, overseas enterprises demand more RMB to pay for equipment and service imported from China. After accumulating a certain amount of RMB through trade settlements, some overseas enterprises may choose to invest in China. Direct investment in RMB eliminates the exchange losses resulting from fluctuations in exchange rates, thus creating a win-win solution for both foreign and domestic firms. In this context, the PBC launched a pilot program on RMB settlement of FDI in 2010, and later RMB settlement of ODI and FDI was in full operation in 2011, expanding the use of RMB from current account to capital account. From 2012 to 2014, the PBC launched pilot programs of RMB loans for overseas projects; cross-border RMB cash pooling for multinational conglomerates; and other RMB operations in Qianhai, Kunshan, and the Shanghai Free Trade Zone, among others, thereby providing greater convenience for domestic as well as foreign firms when making cross-border investments in RMB.

The Third Channel Is Cross-Border RMB Security Investment
Having received RMB, foreign financial institutions, enterprises, and residents alike typically have the need to invest the received funds in RMB-denominated assets. Meanwhile, the growing wealth in China has led to increased demands on RMB financial products overseas from domestic financial institutions, enterprises, and residents. To

meet those investors' demand for RMB security investment, the Chinese government has actively expanded the two-way opening-up of the domestic financial market to enhance the interconnectivity between domestic and overseas financial markets, including the launch of the Shanghai–Hong Kong Connect, Shenzhen–Hong Kong Connect, and Bond Connect. Besides initiating the RMB Qualified Foreign Institutional Investors (RQFII) and RMB Qualified Domestic Institutional Investors (RQDII) schemes in 2011 and 2014, China also adopted a series of reform and opening-up measures in 2015 and 2016, and made available its interbank bond markets and foreign exchange markets to an increasing number of institutional investors, thus further enhancing RMB's functions in cross-border investment and hedging. In 2017, PBC announced a pilot program of an RMB overseas fund, allowing selected institutions to set up public or private RMB funds that invest in equities and debt instruments abroad.

The Fourth Channel Is Direct Bilateral Trading in Local Currencies

To meet the demands of economic entities for reducing currency exchange costs, the PBC also facilitated direct quote and trading between RMB and currencies of important trading partners as well as neighboring economies in the interbank foreign exchange market, in addition to the U.S. dollar. So far, the RMB has direct trading with 24 currencies, including those of Korea, Turkey, Russia, Japan, the eurozone, and the United Kingdom, as well as regional trading with currencies of Kazakhstan and Mongolia.

2.3.3. Improve Infrastructure for Cross-Border RMB Trading and Settlement

As a first step, the PBC established a network of RMB clearing banks

Whenever RMB is used, whether at home or abroad, the amount of RMB in the overseas market fluctuates, so clearing banks are needed to balance inflows and outflows in times of excess and lack of liquidity. In 2003 and 2004, the PBC designated RMB clearing banks in Hong Kong SAR and Macau SAR. After the global financial crisis was tempered down, with the rapid growth of cross-border use of RMB, an imperative need was seen for more clearing banks to facilitate cross-border RMB trading and settlement. In addition to neighboring countries and emerging economies, developed ones, including the United Kingdom, Germany, France, and Australia, also requested the establishment of RMB clearing bank arrangements. As of end-May 2018, the PBC has therefore established RMB clearing settlement arrangements in 24 countries and jurisdictions in Southeast Asia, Europe, the Middle East, North America, South America, Oceania, and Africa. These clearing banks have further facilitated trade and investment and have additionally provided support for cross-border RMB use and settlement.

As a More Permanent Solution, the PBC Is Building Up the RMB Cross-Border Interbank Payment System (CIPS) in Phases

To a certain extent, CIPS is an international payment system for RMB like the Clearing House Interbank Payment System (CHIPS) for the U.S. dollar in cross-border transactions. The PBC started to build Phase I of CIPS in 2012, aiming to integrate the channels and resources for cross-border RMB payment and settlement for greater efficiency. CIPS was formally launched in 2015. To adapt to the needs of the Bond Connect Program, Phase 2 of CIPS went into full operation in May 2018, supporting both real-time gross settlement (RTGS) and deferred net settlement (DNS) and covering the trading hours of the financial markets in every time zone. CIPS also connects to China's High Value Payment System (HVPS, similar to Fedwire in the United States) so that the RMB cross-border payment system connects to the RMB domestic payment and settlement system. According to the CIPS official website, as of end-June 2018, the CIPS had a total of 31 direct participants and 738 indirect participants and provided services to 2,395 financial institutions in 155 countries and jurisdictions.

2.3.4. Support Development of Offshore RMB Markets

From the above-mentioned data, it can be seen that the development of offshore RMB markets, especially that of Hong Kong, is an important part of RMB internationalization. This is largely owing to the natural advantages of Hong Kong SAR. The RMB business started early in Hong Kong SAR. After the RMB clearing bank was set up, cross-border RMB clearing and settlement became more convenient there. In the post-crisis period, based on its close economic and trade ties with the mainland and the local clearing bank, Hong Kong SAR attracted massive inflows of RMB funds, which led to the rapid development of offshore RMB businesses. To meet the rapidly expanding demand for RMB use in Hong Kong SAR, the mainland provided greater policy support, including support for the development of various RMB financial products in Hong Kong SAR, many of which were not available on the onshore market, thus promoting financial market interconnectivity and offering abundant RQFII quotas. As a result, the status of Hong Kong SAR as an offshore RMB market has been further enhanced.

After the crisis, countries and jurisdictions with relatively active RMB business, such as Singapore and London, also took measures to develop local offshore RMB markets. China actively strengthened bilateral financial cooperation to gradually remove the barrier to cross-border RMB flow, which facilitated the development of a number of offshore RMB markets. After years of development, the offshore RMB capital pool has expanded continuously, and a comprehensive system of offshore RMB financial products has been established, including RMB bonds, negotiable certificates of deposit (CDs), mutual funds, futures, and insurance products. Globally, Hong Kong SAR is the largest offshore RMB center, while offshore RMB businesses in other international financial centers such as London, Singapore, and Frankfurt have also witnessed rapid development. Together, they have formed what can be considered a global network of offshore RMB markets.

2.3.5. Inclusion of the RMB into the SDR Currency Basket

As China's economy has grown and the RMB's international status continuously improved, there has been an increasingly strong voice internationally advocating the inclusion of RMB in the SDR currency basket. In 2015, when the IMF was about to conduct its regular quinquennial review, the RMB internationalization was gaining momentum, presenting a historic opportunity for the RMB's inclusion in the basket.

To seize this opportunity, the PBC launched relevant studies and evaluations in the second half of 2014.[4] The following year, the PBC held intensive and in-depth exchanges and discussions with the IMF regarding the content of SDR review, standard and data, and operational issues relating to the free use of RMB, as well as relevant policy and technical issues. To follow up on the discussed issues, China made efforts jointly with the IMF on several important fronts: agreement on standards for SDR review was achieved and data gaps on measuring the degree of RMB's global use were filled. Meanwhile, China planned and pushed forward its financial reforms and opening-up measures so as to make RMB more freely usable.

In July 2015, the IMF staff submitted its preliminary SDR review report to its Executive Board.[5] The report on one hand recognized China's progress in financial sector reform, opening up and RMB internationalization, and on the other hand pointed out some technical issues, including the need to have a RMB/USD exchange rate quote in the foreign exchange markets of London (Bank of England), New York (Federal Reserve Bank of New York), and Frankfurt (the European Central Bank); the need to identify a market-determined representative RMB/USD rate; and the need to provide interest rate instruments to the IMF so it could set the SDR interest rate. These recommendations provided a clear direction for China's efforts over the next few months and indicated that RMB's inclusion in the SDR was in sight.

Afterward, following its domestic reform blueprint, China steadily promoted financial reform and opening-up and also resolved the operational issues indicated by the IMF. First, China opened up interbank markets and allowed foreign official institutions to have access to conduct asset allocation and risk hedging operations. Second, the Ministry of Finance started to issue three-month government bonds on a weekly basis, whose yield would be accepted by the IMF as the representative RMB interest rate. The China Foreign Exchange Trading System publishes reference exchange rates five times per trading day, and the one published at 4 P.M. is regarded as the representative RMB exchange rate. Third, China further facilitated RMB clearing and settlement arrangements for foreign institutions, including further clarification of rules for foreign central banks opening up RMB accounts with onshore commercial banks and also for the formal launch of CIPS (Phase I) in October 2015. Fourth, China worked to enhance data transparency. In November 2014, President Xi Jinping announced at the G20 Brisbane Summit that China would adopt the IMF's Special Data Dissemination Standards (SDDS). China formally joined the initiative in October 2015 and started to take part in the IMF's Coordinated Portfolio Investment Survey (CPIS), COFER, and the BIS's International Banking Statistics (IBS).

On November 30, 2015, the IMF Executive Board, in its final deliberation of the 2015 SDR review, recognized RMB as a freely usable currency and decided to include it in the SDR currency basket, to be effective October 1, 2016. Subsequently, the SDR currency basket was expanded to cover five currencies: U.S. dollar (USD), euro (EUR), RMB, Japanese yen (JPY), and British pound (GBP). The weight of RMB in the basket is 10.92%, while the weights of USD, EUR, JPY, and GBP are 41.73%, 30.93%, 8.33%, and 8.09%, respectively.

The inclusion of RMB into the SDR currency basket represents international recognition of China's progress in reform and opening up, it would promote the RMB internationalization process, and it would prompt China to become more deeply and widely integrated in the global economy. This would also increase the representativeness and attractiveness of the SDR and improve the international currency system. Meanwhile, this would also mean that the international community will hold China's financial institutional reform and opening-up to higher standards and require China to assume the responsibilities as an international currency-issuing country. Therefore, RMB also would need to shoulder the responsibilities of an international reserve currency and play its role in maintaining a stable global financial system.

3. INTERNATIONALIZATION OF THE RMB: CHALLENGES AND PROSPECTS

3.1. The To-Do List in RMB Internationalization

With its inclusion in the SDR currency basket, RMB has been recognized as a reserve currency. Yet, compared with major reserve currencies, the degree and quality of RMB internationalization remains limited. In fact, a truly international currency not only needs to serve as a settlement currency that is widely used in cross-border trade and investment, it also needs to be an investment currency for financial transactions, asset allocation, and store of value. The ultimate test is whether it is a "safe-haven currency" that investors turn to for safety during times of turmoil rather than turning against it (Prasad, 2017). From this perspective, there is still a long to-do list for true RMB internationalization.

At present, the technical tasks include the following:

First, there should be an easy and predictable regime of institutional arrangements, so that anyone using RMB can have stable and clear expectations about the currency's policy environment and convenience of usage, with no need to guess or face high uncertainties.

China has opened up a variety of channels for the inflows and outflows of capital, including a qualified foreign institutional investor (QFII) scheme, a qualified domestic institutional investor (QDII) scheme, an RMB qualified foreign institutional investor (RQFII) scheme, Shanghai–Hong Kong Stock Connect and Shenzhen–Hong Kong Stock Connect, and so on. Such channel arrangements are complicated and often inconvenient and offer low predictability in policy. It is necessary, therefore, to further liberalize capital accounts and establish additional facilitating institutional arrangements for capital account convertibility. To cope with sudden, large, disorderly capital flows, it is advisable to take transparent, market-based, and temporary capital flow management measures, instead of stringent and undifferentiated capital control measures through a one-size-fits-all administrative approach, which would greatly damage the confidence of investors.

China's exchange rate regime is being reformed. As it stands now, it is neither fixed nor clean floating. It is not even a managed floating regime in the traditional sense. In general, its current state will affect investors' expectations of the RMB exchange rate regime. Currency internationalization does not necessarily require a specific kind of exchange rate regime, be it fixed or floating. However, a floating regime seems a more natural choice for China, a large economy that needs a fairly free flow of capital and an independent monetary policy. Therefore, it could be expected to further enhance the flexibility of the RMB exchange rate to cope with larger capital flows and to play a better role of automatic stabilizer.

Going forward, the financial sector opening-up needs to proceed in tandem with the progress of exchange rate regime reform and capital account convertibility (Zhou, 2012) to allow investors to easily acquire, trade, and transfer RMB-denominated assets.

A second technical task that must be faced is the need to develop a mature capital market, increase the investor base, and enhance financial products, in particular developing a deep, broad, and liquid RMB bond market with a higher degree of openness. This is one of the most important tasks, as it is critical in transforming RMB from a settlement currency to an investment currency. China also needs to develop derivatives instruments so that international investors can hedge risks effectively.

The third technical task, in light of retaining capital control in China, is to improve offshore markets as an important path to provide RMB liquidity, investment, and financing channels to the international market. At present, the RMB offshore market is still small and not frequently used by enterprises. It is therefore necessary to further develop offshore products and improve their supporting infrastructure to make it easy for offshore participants to use RMB, which will in turn make transactions of RMB products commercially sustainable and will facilitate benign interaction and deeper integration between the offshore and onshore markets (Yi, 2017).

The fourth technical task is to promote the supporting infrastructure and institutional arrangements, such as advancing RMB transaction and settlement infrastructures, enhancing the capabilities of financial information processing and risk monitoring, and improving the crisis early-warning system and response mechanism (Lu and Li, 2016).

If the above technical issues can be solved properly, the status of RMB as a reserve currency will be greatly improved. But to make RMB a safe-haven currency and increase the appeal of RMB assets as safe assets pursued by investors during times of market turmoil, it is also necessary for China's institutional framework to win the confidence and trust of global investors. Prasad (2017) pointed out that a country seeking this status for its currency must have a solid institutional framework, including an independent judiciary, an open and democratic government, and robust public institutions, especially a credible central bank, so as to make sure its macro policies are accountable and property rights are protected. For example, the United States, the epicenter of the 2008 global financial crisis, was still able to issue bonds with low coupon rates after the outbreak of the financial crisis, precisely because investors trusted the U.S. system. Therefore, China should improve its institutional framework at a deeper level and gradually win the trust of foreign investors.

3.2. Outlook of RMB Internationalization and Its Impact on the International Monetary System

The size of China's economy, the pace of its growth, and the breadth of its participation in global trade and investment have laid a solid foundation for RMB internationalization and offer vast potential for it to become a major reserve currency. Among international currencies, RMB has a number of advantages, thanks to the size of the Chinese economy and its vast worldwide market. Moreover, unlike the euro, which is the single currency for a not yet fully integrated euro area, RMB is a sovereign currency and does not face the potential conflict between economic diversity and a single currency. With the progress of reform, opening-up, and financial market development, RMB's prospects of internationalization are promising. However, the process may be long and difficult, especially the critical transformation of RMB from a settlement currency to an investment currency, which requires deeper reform and more opening-up of the financial system. In addition, as a result of the network effect, a currency may not necessarily become a major international currency even after all the conditions are available. The eventual international status of RMB, therefore, will ultimately depend on how China tackles the above-mentioned challenges.

Barry Eichengreen (2011) has noted that the magnitude of the world economy means that more than one liquid market could eventually be established, to help reduce transaction costs. Technological revolution will also enhance competition in industries previously deemed natural monopolies. Thus, in the future, the world could see the coexistence of several international currencies. RMB internationalization is of great significance to the diversification of international monetary system and conducive to its stability and resilience. History has shown that reserve currency-issuing countries need to strike a balance between sufficient global liquidity and a stable value of the currency. Since the value of the U.S. dollar was decoupled from gold, the international monetary system's stability has been increasingly dependent on the monetary policy of the U.S. Federal Reserve. Overreliance on a single reserve currency has meant that the international currency system is inherently unstable, as reflected in the global financial crisis of 2008 (Zhou, 2012). After the financial crisis, the protracted monetary easing by advanced economies and the subsequent unwinding have aggravated financial market turbulence and created disorderly cross-border capital flow in both emerging markets and developing countries.

In the short term, it will be beneficial if the international community addresses the above deficiencies of the international monetary system by improving various layers of the global financial safety nets, and also by improving capital flows monitoring and management (IMF, 2011). In the long term, however, the root cause of such deficiencies can likely only be resolved by establishment of a diversified international reserve currency system. If the reserve currencies are adequately diversified and competitive among themselves, the elasticity of substitution of reserve currencies will grow. This will provide tighter restraints on the issuing countries and hold them more accountable in terms of macro financial policies, which will both improve economic policy coordination among countries and help ensure the stability of the international monetary system. The rising international status of RMB will help diversify the international monetary system. As a multipolar economic landscape emerges, the international monetary system will surely become more reasonable, balanced, and equal; will change the reserve currency landscape previously dominated by developed country currencies; will enhance the stability and resilience of the international monetary system; and will promote the sound development of the world economy and international finance.

In any event, RMB internationalization is still very much a work in progress, which will be subject to ups and downs. It is too early to draw any firm conclusions at this stage, so any forecast on how it may evolve is at best an educated guess. Whether RMB could become the next U.S. dollar or the euro, or share the fate of the Japanese yen, remains a great unknown. Only time will tell.

NOTES

The authors of this chapter work at the People's Bank of China. The views expressed in this chapter are theirs and do not necessarily reflect the views of the PBC. All errors remain their sole responsibility

1. See Zhou (2012).
2. See the 2018 RMB Internationalization Report, PBC, available at http://www.pbc.gov.cn /huobizhengceersi/214481/214511/214695/3635170/index.html.

3.   See IMF Staff Reports (2015, 2017a, 2017b, 2018).
4.   See People's Bank of China (2017)
5.   See https://www.imf.org/en/Publications/Policy-Papers/Issues/2016/12/31/Review-of-the
     -Method-of-Valuation-of-the-SDR-Initial-Considerations-PP4975.

REFERENCES

Dwyer, Gerald, and Lothian James (2003). "The Economics of International Monies." CRIF working paper series no. 10.

Eichengreen, Barry (2011). *Exorbitant Privilege: The Rise and Fall of the Dollar and the Future of the International Monetary System*. Oxfordshire, U.K.: Oxford University Press.

Eichengreen, Barry, Livia Chiţu, and Arnaud Mehl (2016). "Stability or Upheaval? The Currency Composition of International Reserves in the Long Run. *IMF Economic Review* 64.2: 354–80.

Eichengreen, Barry, and Marc Flandreau (2008). "The Rise and Fall of the Dollar, or When Did the Dollar Replace Sterling as the Leading International Currency?" (No. w14154). National Bureau of Economic Research.

Eichengreen, Barry, and Ricardo Hausmann (1999). "Exchange Rates and Financial Fragility" (No. w7418). National Bureau of Economic Research.

Eichengreen, Barry, Arnaud Mehl, and Livia Chiţu (2019). *How Global Currencies Work: Past, Present, and Future*. Princeton, N.J.: Princeton University Press.

Frankel, Jeffrey (2012). "Internationalization of the RMB and Historical Precedents." *Journal of Economic Integration* 27(3): 329–65.

Genberg, Hans (2009). "Currency Internationalization: Analytical and Policy Issues." Hong Kong SAR Institute for Monetary Research. Working paper 31, October.

He, Dong, and Robert McCauley (2010). "Offshore Markets for the Domestic Currency: Monetary and Financial Stability Issues." BIS Working Papers, No. 320, September.

IMF (2011). "Internationalization of Emerging Market Currencies: A Balance between Risks and Rewards." IMF Staff Discussion note.

IMF (2015). "Staff Report, Ukraine: Request for Extended Arrangement Under the Extended Fund Facility and Cancellation of Stand-By Arrangement." IMF Country Report no. 15/69.

IMF (2017a). "Staff Report, Arab Republic of Egypt: Request for Extended Arrangement Under the Extended Fund Facility." IMF Country Report no. 17/17.

IMF (2017b). "Staff Report, Mongolia: 2017 Article IV Consultation and Request for an Extended Arrangement Under the Extended Fund Facility." IMF Country Report no. 17/140.

IMF (2018). "Staff Report, Argentina: Request for Stand-By Arrangement." IMF Country Report no. 18/219.

Kenen, Peter (1983). "The Role of the Dollar as an International Reserve Currency." Occasional Papers no. 13, Group of Thirty.

Kenen, Peter (2011). "Currency Internationalization: An Overview." BIS Papers 61.1, 1–10. www.bis.org.

Lu, Lei, and Hongjin Li (2016). "RMB Internationalization and Reform of International Monetary System After RMB Is Included in SDR Basket: A Money Function and Reserve Currency Supply and Demand Perspectives." *International Economic Review*, 3: 41–53.

Mathias, Peter (2001) *The First Industrial Nation: The Economic History of Britain 1700–1914*. London: Routledge.

McKinsey Global Institute (2009). "An Exorbitant Privilege? Implications of Reserve Currencies for Competitiveness." Discussion paper, December.

Minikin, Robert, and Kelvin Lau (2013). *The Offshore RENMINBI: The Rise of the Chinese Currency and Its Global Future*. Singapore: John Wiley and Sons.

Ministry of Finance, Japan (1999). "Internationalization of the Yen for the 21st Century." Japanese Ministry of Financial Council on Foreign Exchange and Other Transactions, April.

People's Bank of China (2017). *The Journey Towards SDR's Inclusion of Renminbi*. Beijing: China Financial Publishing House.

People's Bank of China (2018). *Report on RMB Internationalization*. Beijing: China Financial Publishing House.

Prasad, Eswar (2017). *Gaining Currency: The Rise of the Renminbi*. Oxfordshire: Oxford University Press.

Takagi, Shinji (2009). "Internationalizing the Yen, 1984–2000: Unfinished Agenda or Mission Impossible?" Paper presented at the BoK-BIS Seminar on Currency Internationalization: Lessons from the Global Financial Crisis and Prospects for the Future in Asia and the Pacific, Seoul, March 19.

Tavlas, George, and Yuzur Ozeki (1992). "The Internationalization of Currencies: An Appraisal of the Japanese Yen." IMF Occasional Paper 90.

Tetsuji, Murase (2000). "The Internationalization of the Yen: Essential Issues Overlooked." Asia Pacific Economic Papers 307, Australia National University.

Yi, Gang (2017). "Four Pillars of RMB Internationalization." Speech prepared for 2017 Annual Meeting of China Finance 40 Forum.

Zhou, Xiaochuan (2012). *The Global Financial Crisis: Observations, Analysis and Countermeasures.* Beijing: China Financial Publishing House.

Zhu, Ning (2016). *China's Guaranteed Bubble: How Implicit Government Support Has Propelled China's Economy While Creating Systemic Risk.* Beijing: CITIC Press.

10

CHINA'S CAPITAL ACCOUNT LIBERALIZATION

A Ruby Jubilee and Beyond

Yanliang Miao and Tuo Deng

1. INTRODUCTION

China started opening its capital account[1] four decades ago with the inception of a Reform and Opening-up movement. In 1993, a plan was announced to reach full capital account convertibility by 2000. After a quarter century of twists and turns, this ambitious plan has yet to materialize. Certain types of flows, such as foreign direct investment (FDI), have become freer to come and go. For others, more stringent regulations apply. In stark contrast with the quick and smooth liberalization of the current account, fully convertible since 1996, China's path toward a convertible capital account has been slower and bumpier. This path has centered on and been shaped by three contentious and recurring debates.

First, how open is China's capital account and how much more needs to be done? A commonly used data source is the International Monetary Fund's *Annual Report on Exchange Arrangements and Exchange Restrictions* (AREAER), which records the statutory regimes of exchange rate and trade for IMF members. Based on AREAER, international observers tend to hold a "glass-half-empty" view that few types of capital can freely flow across the border. For example, Schipke (2016) argued that 43 out of 53 types of AREAER-defined capital transactions remain subject to some control. In contrast, China's policymakers prefer the "glass-half-full" alternative that nearly all types of capital transactions are at least partially convertible. For example, PBC (2017) emphasized that 37 out of 40 types of AREAER-defined capital transactions are at least partially convertible.[2] From

Note: "Liberalization" is a misnomer. China's official documents have used the terms capital account "convertibility" and "opening-up" since the 3rd Plenary Session of the 14th Communist Party of China's Central Committee in 1993, but have never used "liberalization." As will be shown, China has been opening up its capital account to make it increasingly convertible. A laissez-faire capital account, as hinted by the word "liberalization," does not seem to square with China's intention. Nevertheless, the authors interchangeably use "liberalization" with "opening" and "convertibility" to conform to the literature.

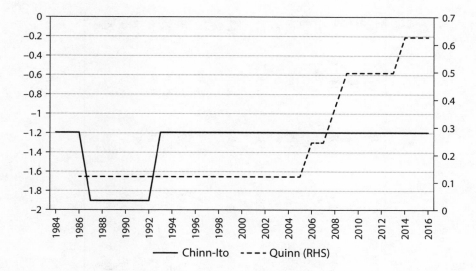

FIGURE 10.1. De jure capital account openness, Chinn-Ito vs. Quinn. *Sources:* Chinn and Ito (2006); CF40 (2017).

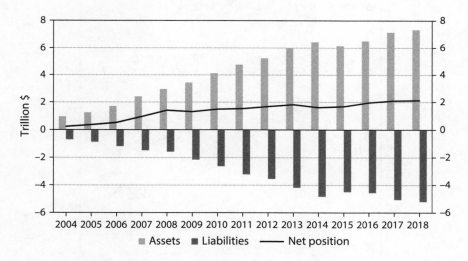

FIGURE 10.2. China's international investment position. *Source:* IMF.

AREAER records, the academic literature has derived various measures of de jure capital account openness, with mixed results. The Chinn-Ito index,[3] a popular measure, has a value of –1.20 for China, compared with +0.3 for emerging market economies (EMEs), and +2.36 for advanced economies. This makes China the 104th of 182 sampled economies in terms of openness. Perhaps more surprisingly, China's Chinn-Ito index value has been *un-changed* since 1993, at odds with the Quinn index,[4] which exhibits an improving trend for China since 2005 (figure 10.1). Yet, as of 2016, China's openness still trails an average EME. In comparison, China's de facto openness has undoubtedly improved. From 2004 to 2017, the country's external assets and liabilities have expanded more than sevenfold (figure 10.2)

Table 10.1. China's International Investment Position (billion $)

	2008	2009	2010	2011	2012	2013	2014	2015	2016	2017	2018
Net position	1494	1491	1688	1526	1675	1809	1603	1673	1950	2101	2146
Assets	2957	3437	4119	4735	5213	5986	6438	6156	6507	7149	7405
FDI	186	246	317	425	532	660	883	1096	1357	1809	1982
Portfolio	253	243	257	204	241	259	263	261	367	492	498
Equity	21	55	63	86	130	153	161	162	215	298	270
Debt	231	188	194	118	111	105	101	99	152	195	228
Other investment	552	495	630	850	1053	1187	1394	1389	1680	1606	1750
Reserve assets	1966	2453	2914	3256	3388	3880	3899	3406	3098	3236	3168
FX reserves	1946	2399	2847	3181	3312	3821	3843	3330	3011	3140	3073
Liabilities	1463	1946	2431	3209	3538	4177	4836	4483	4557	5048	5259
FDI	916	1315	1570	1907	2068	2331	2599	2696	2755	2726	2827
Portfolio	168	190	224	411	528	573	796	817	811	1099	1096
Equity	151	175	206	374	453	485	651	597	580	762	684
Debt	17	15	18	37	74	89	145	220	232	337	412
Other investment	380	442	637	891	943	1272	1440	964	984	1220	1329

Source: SAFE.

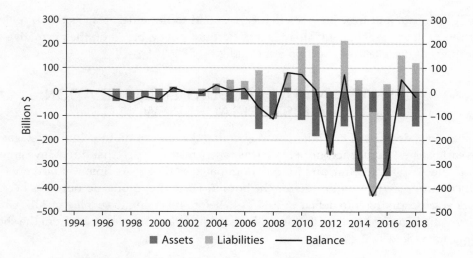

FIGURE 10.3. China's capital account: Other investments. *Source:* SAFE.

while its capital account becomes increasingly volatile (table 10.1). In particular, the other investment (lending-related) component has swung sharply from mildly positive in 2013 to sharply negative in 2014–2016, then back to mildly positive in 2017 (figure 10.3). It suggests that China's capital account has become increasingly porous.

In the second recurring debate, the question is how committed is China to opening its capital account? Despite policymakers' vocal commitment, observers remain skeptical. One critique holds that China has deliberately slowed liberalization down. By resisting inflows, China keeps renminbi (RMB) undervalued to boost export (Jeanne et al., 2011, chapter 2). Another critique popular among market participants asserts that China's tightening of capital controls in 2015 and 2016 has revealed its lack of commitment (Wharton, 2016). A related but more sympathetic view notes that financial stability concerns prevent China's capital account from becoming more convertible. According to this view, greater convertibility invites greater capital flow volatility, which stretches China's fragile financial system (Yu, 2017) and complicates its macroeconomic policymaking (Zhou 2017).

Third in the recurring debate, the question arises whether China is ready to open up further, and if so, how. Many observers recommend a cautious approach, either because (a) many preconditions for safe opening-up have yet to be realized (Lardy and Douglass, 2011; Yu, 2015), or (b) hastily opening up against an unfriendly external backdrop may impair macroeconomic and financial stability (Zhang, 2015). A more optimistic view disagrees, arguing that China's increasingly robust financial system helps to limit the downside (Sheng et al., 2012). Even China's policymakers have swung back and forth, from optimistic in the early 2010s,[5] to cautious and risk-focusing in 2015 and 2016,[6] and to cautiously optimistic since 2017.[7]

This chapter reviews China's capital account openness through the lens of these three debates. Section 2 provides a detailed chronology and presents evidence that China's capital account convertibility has substantially improved over the last four decades, although the progress has been neither uniform nor completed. Section 3 takes stock of the "good, bad, and ugly" lessons that correspond to these debates. Section 4 reviews the recent developments of China's capital account policy, based on the normative implications of these lessons. Section 5 concludes.

2. CHINA'S CAPITAL ACCOUNT LIBERALIZATION: A HISTORICAL REVIEW

China's four decades of capital account liberalization can be divided into six stages. In the early stages, capital account policy was rather restrictive, so that direct investments dominated capital account, and inflows dominated outflows. As time went by, non-FDI gained more freedom to flow across the border. Therefore, capital account has become more volatile, diving into deficit in 2014–2016 before reversing to surplus in 2017. China has greatly benefited from FDI inflows, but also suffered in recent years from the short-term capital flow swings.

2.1. First Welcome to Capital Inflows: 1979–1991

The promulgation of the Joint Ventures Law[8] in 1979 marked China's first step to open up its capital account. In the same year, China established four Special Economic Zones (Shenzhen, Zhuhai, Xiamen, and Shantou) on its southeast coast as pilot destinations for foreign investment, offering tax incentives and managerial autonomy. Since then, other provincial and local governments followed suit. In response to the broadening of preferential treatments, China's FDI grew steadily, albeit unspectacularly, until the early 1990s. About 70% of total FDI inflows came from Hong Kong and Taiwan, which are geographically and culturally tied to the mainland, while capital from advanced economies remained cautious. Interestingly, despite Chinese authority's preference for FDI, it was other investment (lending-related) that contributed the most to capital inflows in this period (figure 10.4).

2.2. FDI Expansion and Setback of Early Ambition: 1992–1997

The year 1992 marked an inflection point in China's modern history. Deng Xiaoping's Southern Tour in the spring irreversibly reoriented China's national priority toward Reform and Opening-up, the very plan he architected in late 1978. Since then, foreign capital became increasingly confident in venturing into China. FDI inflows surged by ten-fold from $4.4 billion in 1991 to $44 billion in 1997, comfortably dwarfing portfolio and other investment inflows as the main contributor to capital account surplus (figure 10.4). In addition, the source of FDI inflows became more diversified: An increasing share of FDI came from major developed economies such as the United States, Europe, and Japan.

More dramatic changes took place in exchange rate and current account. At the beginning of 1994, the People's Bank of China (PBC) abolished the dual-tracked[9] exchange rates in favor of a single, market-based managed floating exchange rate regime. RMB was devalued by 33% against the dollar to 8.7:1 (later 8.28:1). The lower value of RMB boosted China's current account to surplus, ending its fluctuation around zero since the early 1980s. In 1996, China made its current account fully convertible, greatly reducing the cost of trade. Thanks to strong FDI inflows and sizable current account surplus, China's FX reserves quickly rose from its trough of $18.8 billion in mid-1993 to $120.9 billion in mid-1997, a nearly six-fold increase in four years (figure 10.5).

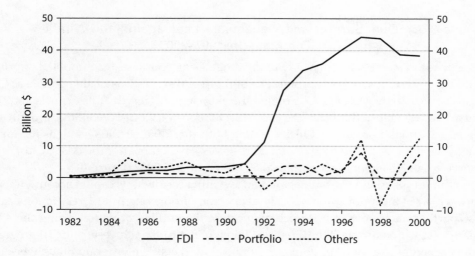

FIGURE 10.4. Capital inflows by type, 1982–2000. *Source:* SAFE.

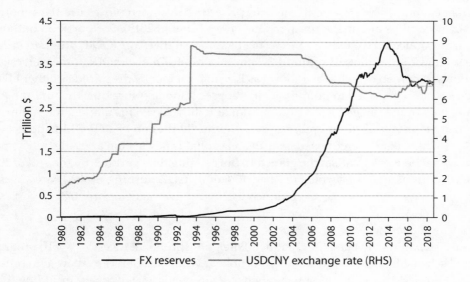

FIGURE 10.5. China's FX reserves and USDCNY exchange rate. *Source:* SAFE.

As an integral part of the socialist market economy proposed by the 14th Communist Party of China's National Congress in 1992, China released an ambitious plan in 1993 to reach full capital account liberalization by 2000. Unfortunately, the plan was suspended as the 1997 Asian financial crisis (AFC) broke out. Thanks to China's relatively abundant FX reserves and not-yet-lifted capital outflow controls, RMB's peg against the dollar remained intact. But the crisis clearly demonstrated the destructive power of fickle capital flows, forcing policymakers to think twice before liberalizing portfolio and other investment flows.

2.3. Dual Surplus and Piecemeal, "Lean against the Wind" Opening-Up: 1997–2007

In response to the crisis, China, like many other Asian countries, had doubled efforts in building up reserves as a precaution. The buildup of reserves was made possible as China's accession to the WTO in 2001 fueled the exponential growth of its exports and current account surplus. Moreover, the export sector boosted China's economic growth and helped to attract more inward FDI, creating both the "dual surplus" and, as its mirror image, the rapid accumulation of official reserves. Five years after the crisis, China's FX reserves doubled again to more than $250 billion in mid-2002 (figure 10.5).

As the fear of crisis eventually faded away, China resumed its capital account liberalization plan in a cautious manner. The relaxation of portfolio inflow restrictions came first, partly because of the still-fresh memory of the outflow pressure during the AFC. In late 2002, China unveiled the Qualified Foreign Institutional Investors (QFII) program, granting access to a range of domestic financial markets. The program quickly became popular as global investors diversified into China.

The rising concerns about "hot money" inflows, overaccumulation of reserves, and looming inflation pushed policymakers to relax capital outflow restrictions. For ODI, China began to encourage domestic enterprises to "go abroad" to secure the supply of key commodities and move up the value chain (Zhang, 2015). For portfolio outflows, China introduced the Qualified Domestic Institutional Investors (QDII) program in 2006 (see section 2.3.1 for details of the Q Schemes). Despite ODI and QDII, however, capital outflows remained dwarfed by inflows as FDI and hot money disguised as either FDI or trade surplus continued to pour in. RMB's appreciation pressure quickly built up. As a result, the PBC de-pegged RMB from the dollar in July 2005. This marked the beginning of a truly managed floating exchange rate regime. By the end of 2007, RMB appreciated by 13%. China also strengthened controls on capital inflows. However, the policy measures were too weak to offset the giant and burgeoning dual surplus. By the end of 2007, China's current account surplus reached 10% of its GDP, pushing up its FX reserves to $1.5 trillion—an astonishing six-fold increase in just five years (figure 10.5).

2.3.1. The Q Schemes

In late 2002, China unveiled the Qualified Foreign Institutional Investors (QFII) program, its first scheme-based liberalization for portfolio investment. QFIIs are allowed to convert their FX into RMB and to invest in a range of RMB-denominated assets, including the A shares.[10] The popularity of QFII was evidenced by its rapidly expanding approved quota, from $1.7 billion by the end of 2003 to $10 billion in January 2007, exhausting the maximum quota then allowed. In the next decade, maximum QFII quota was raised several times, from $10 billion to $30 billion in 2007, $80 billion in 2012, and $150 billion since 2015. By August 2018, total approved QFII quota had reached $100 billion (figure 10.6).

China introduced the Qualified Domestic Institutional Investors (QDII) program in 2006. This was the first scheme-based liberalization for domestic institutional investors to access 11 overseas financial markets.[11] Total approved QDII quota started at $10 billion in 2006, then quickly quintupled to $50 billion by the end of 2007, then to $90 billion since 2015. By June 2018, total approved QDII quota had reached $103 billion (figure 10.6). Initially, QDIIs could only invest in fixed-income securities. A year later in 2007, they were

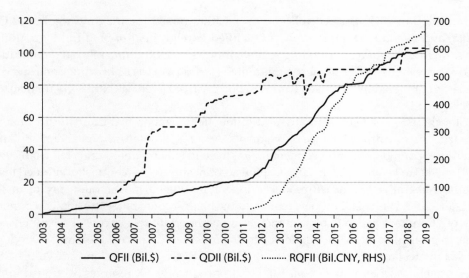

FIGURE 10.6. Approved quotas of Q schemes. *Source:* SAFE.

granted access to equities. Over time, QDIIs were allowed to invest in broader sets of assets, and to more flexibly manage asset allocations.

The Renminbi Qualified Foreign Institutional Investors (RQFII) program was introduced in 2011. RQFIIs are allowed to invest in China's domestic markets using their offshore RMB holdings (as opposed to foreign currency) directly. In the early days, only Hong Kong (HK) subsidiaries of domestic financial institutions could apply for RQFIIs. Later, RQFII expanded to global asset managers' HK offices. By the end of 2013, total approved RQFII quota amounted to 157 billion RMB. It then quickly surpassed 300 billion RMB in 2015, and 600 billion RMB in late 2017. By August 2018, the total approved RQFII quota had reached 627 billion RMB (figure 10.6).

2.4. Liberalization and Carry Trade: 2008–2013

China rushed out a plethora of expansionary policies to shelter its economy from the global financial crisis (GFC) shockwave. Since mid-2008, China re-pegged RMB to the dollar at 6.8 for two years to provide relief for its hard-hit export sector, and also briefly tightened capital outflow controls to stabilize domestic financial conditions. In 2009, China announced the controversial "four trillion RMB" stimulus package to make up for the depressed external demand. Domestic investment demand rebounded sharply, especially in infrastructure and real estate. China's banking system, however, was unable to satisfy the spiking demand for funds. Chinese enterprises therefore sought financing elsewhere, including previously tightly regulated borrowing from overseas.[12] In the meantime, major global central banks slashed policy rates to or near the zero lower bound and carried out massive quantitative easing (QE) programs. Once the overseas borrowing restrictions were relaxed, the strong domestic demand and excess global liquidity created a perfect storm of capital pouring into China.

The country then relaxed many capital inflow regulations to accommodate for the stimulus-driven financing needs. For FDI, the registration procedures were substantially streamlined in 2012. For portfolio inflows, China raised the maximum allowed QFII quota, and introduced the Renminbi Qualified Foreign Institutional Investors (RQFII) program in 2011. For other (lending-related) inflows, in 2010 China relaxed qualifications on overseas loans under domestic guarantee (*"neibao waidai"*), allowing domestic companies, guaranteed by domestic banks, to borrow from overseas banks via their subsidiaries abroad.

Global crisis, domestic stimulus, and inflow liberalization had dramatically changed the structure of China's balance of payments. As a result of falling global demand and a stimulus-driven domestic investment boom, the current account surplus fell from 10% of GDP in 2007 to less than 2% in 2011. Capital account surplus, by contrast, continued to rise as inflow liberalization measures kicked in, dominating current account surplus in 2010, 2011, and 2013. While FDI inflows remained the biggest contributor to capital account *surplus*, other inflows began to play an increasingly important role in capital account *fluctuations*. In particular, the lax regulation of cross-border lending, the wide China–Developed Market interest rate spread, and the resumption of RMB's appreciation since 2010, had invited sizable short-term *carry trade* inflows. Consequently, FX reserves continued to rise, reaching an unprecedented $3.8 trillion at the end of 2013 (figure 10.5). But unlike FDI, carry trade inflows are much more volatile and short-term in nature; they may take profit and withdraw at any moment. It turned out that the carry trade inflows from 2010 to 2013 had sowed the seed of a sharp reversal in the not-so-distant future.

2.5. Liberalization Met Carry Trade Reversal: 2013–2016

Since 2013, China's capital account management has undergone a paradigm shift. A "negative list" approach initially gained favor. Instead of relying on ex-ante review and approval, regulators refocused on ex-post monitoring and regulation for an expanding set of cross-border transactions, especially outflows. A number of factors contributed to the shift. Cyclically, China had become increasingly concerned about "hot money" inflows and overaccumulation of reserves, therefore more willing to relax outflow controls. Structurally, China encouraged more companies to invest abroad, especially to the "Belt and Road" countries. In addition, RMB's accelerated internationalization called for broadening its global usage, hence relaxing controls.

As a result, capital account liberalization moved up a gear. For direct investments, China replaced many application-for-approval procedures with registration, and further streamlined the procedures. By mid-2015, both FDI and ODI had become "almost fully" convertible (Guo, 2018). For portfolio flows, China expanded the existing QFII, QDII, and RQFII programs, and established a number of new schemes. In late 2014, China unveiled the Shanghai–Hong Kong Stock Connect, allowing both institutional and individual investors to participate in the two markets with greater ease (see section 2.5.1 for details of the Stock Connects, or C Schemes).

These opening-up measures facilitated an unprecedented sharp rise in capital outflows. China's capital account (excluding errors and omissions) turned from a $343 billion surplus in 2013 to a $434 billion deficit in 2015, and a $416 billion deficit in 2016. China's ODI tripled from $72.9 billion in 2013 to $216.4 billion in 2016. In the meantime, portfolio investment outflows jumped from $5.3 billion to $103 billion. Part of the rise in outflows reflected the long-desired diversification of Chinese households and businesses toward global assets.

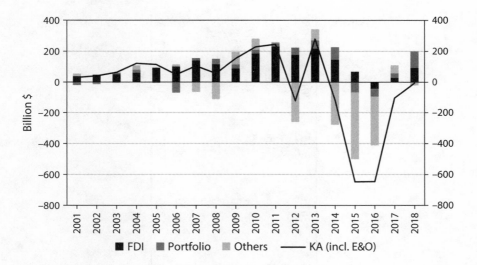

FIGURE 10.7. Capital account balance by type. *Source:* SAFE.

However, the rest of the outflows were much less benign. On top of ODI and portfolio outflows, other investment positions collapsed from a $72 billion surplus in 2013 to a $434 billion deficit in 2015, and a $317 billion deficit in 2016. In addition, the net errors and omissions deficit more than tripled from $62.9 billion to $229 billion. These indicators strongly suggested that many of the outflows were highly speculative in nature (figure 10.7).

Indeed, the carry trade inflows built up since the GFC had unwound their positions and quickly withdrawn from China, generating the sudden reversal. Five years after the crisis, the U.S. economy had gradually recovered. In 2014, the Federal Reserve concluded its QE3 program, and hinted about hiking the federal funds rate later. This led to a sharp appreciation of the dollar against the deflation-mired euro and yen. RMB, however, maintained its peg against the dollar roughly unchanged at 6.15 to 1. Gradually, RMB became overvalued. From 2013 to 2015, China's economy slowed as rising labor costs and strong RMB reduced its export competitiveness, and as the debt-fueled stimulus package ran out of steam. The burst of the stock bubble in mid-2015 stoked more worries of a hard landing. The carry trade unwound, RMB depreciated, and FX reserves turned south (see section 2.5.2), ending up in the greatest capital reversal in history (table 10.2).

2.5.1. The C Schemes
In late 2014, China unveiled the Shanghai–Hong Kong Stock Connect. This bidirectional scheme allowed domestic investors, both institutional and individual, to participate in Hong Kong's equity market, and global investors to take advantage of mainland's A shares. The total southbound quota was set at 250 billion RMB, with a daily quota of 10.5 billion. The corresponding northbound quota was 300 billion RMB in total, and 13 billion RMB for each day. Unlike the QFII, QDII, and RQFII programs, investors participating in the Stock Connect are not subject to individual quota limits, hence finding it more convenient.

A similar Shenzhen–Hong Kong Stock Connect was introduced in late 2016. In addition, the Mutual Recognition of Funds program, introduced in mid-2015, allowed funds

Table 10.2. The Great Capital Reversal (billion $)

	2008	2009	2010	2011	2012	2013	2014	2015	2016	2017	2018
Current account	421	243	238	136	215	148	236	304	202	195	25
(in % GDP)	9.2	4.8	3.9	1.8	2.5	1.5	2.3	2.8	1.8	1.6	0.2
Capital account	37	195	282	260	−36	343	−51	−434	−416	110	173
(in % GDP)	0.8	3.8	4.6	3.4	−0.4	3.6	−0.5	−4.0	−3.7	0.9	1.2
Net errors and omission	19	−41	−53	−14	−87	−63	−67	−213	−229	−213	−179
Δ Reserve assets	480	400	472	388	97	431	118	−343	−444	92	19
FX reserves	1946	2399	2847	3181	3312	3821	3843	3330	3011	3140	3073

Source: SAFE.

based in Hong Kong to be distributed to mainland investors, and vice versa, up to 300 billion RMB in each direction.

2.5.2. The August 11 Exchange Rate Reform

On August 11, 2015, the PBC unexpectedly announced RMB's new "central parity" exchange rate mechanism, and devalued RMB by nearly 2% against the U.S. dollar. While it stressed that the new mechanism better aligned the daily opening exchange rate of RMB to the previous day's closing price, hence allowing it to be more market-determined, the 2% devaluation was negatively perceived as a sign of rapid deterioration of China's economic fundamentals. The unwinding of carry trade position exacerbated. Chinese authorities responded with stricter enforcement of existing capital controls and macroprudential tools, such as the 20% FX risk reserve requirement, and even intervened in the FX market from time to time. These measures prevented RMB from a free fall, and gradually curbed the excessive outflows, but at a huge cost. In a mere 18 months, China's FX reserves had shrunk from $4 trillion in mid-2014 to $3 trillion by end-2016.

A sizable portion of the unwinding was a result of Chinese companies' accelerated repayment of overseas debt (Miao and Rao, 2016). It showed up as a sharp reversal of China's other investment liabilities, from positive $214 billion in 2013 to negative $351 billion in 2015. During the early years, these companies (many of them highly leveraged real estate developers) exploited China's liberalized overseas debt regulation and borrowed more dollar debt than they needed, to take advantage of the low interest rate as well as to bet on further appreciation of RMB. Once RMB began to fall, however, the dollar debt suddenly became hugely expensive, forcing these companies to deleverage. The deleveraging then triggered the classic vicious cycle of depreciation, forced deleveraging, and even more depreciation (Korinek and Mendoza, 2014). Anecdotal evidence also pointed to heightened capital flights, possibly disguised as fake imports that therefore would show up as big negative numbers in errors and omissions.

2.6. Economic Rebound and Resumption of Liberalization: Since 2017

China's economy rebounded since mid-2016, thanks to the supply-side structural reform and a solid recovery of global demand. The rebound morphed into a globally synchronized acceleration in 2017. Against this backdrop, RMB started its rebound around the beginning of 2017, appreciating by more than 6% against the dollar by the end of the year. Carry trade flowed back to China. In 2017, other investment liabilities rebounded from the negative $351 billion trough in 2015 to a positive $151 billion. The errors and omissions deficit remained large at $221.9 billion, but had stabilized. As a result, China's FX reserves slowly rebounded to $3.1 trillion by end-2017.

As the economy stabilized and markets calmed down, China relaxed the enforcement of capital controls, and resumed its concerted efforts to opening up (see section 2.6.1). In April 2018, President Xi Jinping emphasized in Boao that China is firmly committed to opening up further. For inward FDI, China initiated new opening-up measures and reduced investment restrictions. For the existing QFII, QDII, and RQFII schemes, China expanded the quotas, and made them more flexible. For the Stock Connects, China increased the limits for the two existing ones, and prepared to launch a new Shanghai–London Stock Connect. China had also resumed its liberalization for alternative investments.

2.6.1. Recent Opening-Up Measures

In April 2018, China resumed the Qualified Domestic Limited Partners (QDLP) and Qualified Domestic Investment Enterprise (QDIE) pilot programs after more than two years of hiatus. Under these programs, global asset managers can issue funds in China to invest in overseas alternative projects. While these pilot programs are quite small ($5 billion quota each), and are limited to Shanghai (QDLP) and Shenzhen (QDIE), a new overseas asset class has become accessible.

On May 1, 2018, China quadrupled the daily quotas of Shanghai–Hong Kong and Shenzhen–Hong Kong Stock Connects to 52 billion RMB northbound and 42 billion RMB southbound. The increase of daily quotas will cater to global investors' increasing demand for A shares because of their inclusion into the MSCI EM Index since June 1, 2018. In addition, the new Shanghai–London Stock Connect was said to be "ready to go" and expected to be launched later in the year.

On June 12, 2018, China rescinded the 20% cap on monthly repatriations for QFIIs, and removed the three-month lock-up periods for QFIIs and RQFIIs, allowing them to more easily withdraw from domestic financial markets. In addition, China also allowed QFIIs and RQFIIs to hedge their FX risks onshore.

On June 28, 2018, the National Development and Reform Commission (NDRC) and the Ministry of Commerce (MOFCOM) released the 2018 version of the Special Administrative Measures on Access to Foreign Investment, commonly known as the "negative list." Effective July 28, 2018, the negative list introduced new opening-up measures in 22 industries spanning agricultural, manufacturing, and services sectors, and also reduced the total number of special administrative measures (restrictions) from 63 to 48. In particular, the negative list detailed timetables for opening up financial services by 2021 and automobile manufacturing by 2022.

2.7. How Much Has China Actually Opened Its Capital Account?

The chronology shows that China has come a long way in opening up its capital account. But why is China's Chinn-Ito index unchanged since 1993? The main issue is AREAER's binary nature. It tracks the existence of restrictions, but is less accurate in capturing how strictly they are enforced. Only major policy shifts can change AREAER's values. But China has opened up its capital account gradually. For most types of capital transactions, restrictions are relaxed rather than removed. This explains why most Chinese officials hold a glass-half-full view of China's de jure openness. The Quinn index, by contrast, is designed to capture the enforcement of capital controls. However, the intensity or effectiveness of controls are by definition difficult to measure with precision. Given the divergence between the Chinn-Ito and Quinn indices, as well as the high measurement errors associated with the Quinn index, one reasonable conclusion is that it is difficult to evaluate China's capital account openness based solely on de jure indices.

A less controversial alternative is de facto openness, which measures an economy's financial integration into global markets. The standard metric for aggregate de facto openness is an economy's external assets and liabilities as a percent of GDP, based on its international investment positions (IIP). Yet there are other metrics that better capture the details. China's IIP indisputably confirms its rising de facto capital account openness. From 2004 to 2017, both external assets and liabilities had more than *sextupled*. In 2017, China's external assets and liabilities stood at 57.6% and 42.5% of its GDP, respectively.

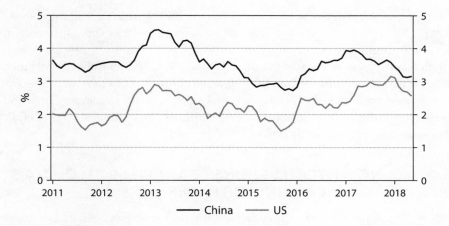

FIGURE 10.8. China and U.S. 10-year government bond yields. *Sources:* Chinabond, Federal Reserve Board.

These ratios imply that China's capital account is more open than other EMEs such as India, but less open than advanced economies.

The composition of China's IIP also points to rising de facto openness. On the asset side, 71% of China's external assets were reserves in 2009. By 2017, reserves' share declined to 47%. As long desired,[13] China's external assets are increasingly owned by the private sector. On the liability side, FDI consistently dominated external liabilities (55% to 60%) due to China's preference for stable long-term funding, but portfolio investments' share increased from 9% in 2004 to 20% in 2017. Relatedly, since non-FDI flows are more volatile than FDI, the rising capital account variability reflects China's increasing acceptance of non-FDI flows.

The co-movement of domestic and foreign long-term bond yields suggests that improving market integration across the border is occurring, hence rising de facto openness. Since 2012, the correlation between China and U.S. 10-year government bond yields has been high at 0.7 (figure 10.8), while the correlation between one-year government bond yields is much lower at 0.14 (not shown). Although monetary policies in China and the United States obviously diverge, their long-term bond *premiums* strongly co-move. This is consistent with the rising global footprint in China's interbank bond markets, the third largest in the world.[14] As of August 2018, China's outstanding central government debt amounted to 13.6 trillion RMB, 8% of which (1.03 trillion RMB) was held by overseas institutions. China's continued expansion of portfolio inflow schemes (QFII, RQFII, and Bond Connect), as well as global bond indices' inclusion,[15] have both led to increasing global interest in the country's government bonds.

However, global investors remained cautious about participating in China's credit and equity markets. As of June 2018, global investors hold merely 0.4% of the country's credit bonds and 2% of A-shares' capitalization. Despite the increasingly accessible schemes, multiple structural issues continued to plague China's financial system, such as weak regulation and corporate governance, lack of reliable credit ratings, and heavy government intervention, plus certain trading frictions.[16] These issues, among others, have prevented China's credit bonds and equities from being included in major global indices, discouraging a global appetite for them. Consequently, China's credit and equity markets are highly speculative; its credit spreads and equity indices exhibit little resemblance to those of their global counterparts.

A logical conclusion is that China's capital account has become substantially more convertible. However, opening-up has been slow and bumpy, especially for non-FDI flows. On a number of occasions, the country's capital account policy has swung back and forth between restricting inflows and restricting outflows. Nevertheless, the overall trend points clearly to an increasingly open capital account.

3. TAKING STOCK: LESSONS LEARNED FROM CHINA'S OPENING-UP EXPERIENCE

Judging by the result, China's capital account liberalization has been mostly successful. In four decades, China has attracted $3.1 trillion of foreign direct investment; its external assets and liabilities have grown from virtually nil to $7 trillion and $5.5 trillion, respectively. It has withstood the shockwaves of the Asian and the global financial crises. Like other EMEs, however, China has suffered its own setbacks, such as the capital flow reversal from 2015 to 2016. Many lessons, good, bad, and "ugly," can be drawn from China's experience, and they speak to the three debates about China's capital account liberalization outlined at the beginning of this chapter.

3.1. The Good: Sequencing and Gradualism

China liberalized direct investments before opening its door to portfolio and other investment flows. Both literature and experience have favored FDI as the best type of capital inflows. Not only does it help form new plants and create new jobs, but it also brings in technology and managerial know-how. Moreover, FDI is long-term and stable, posing lower financial risks than other types of capital flows. The right sequencing of opening-up has enabled China to reap the benefits of FDI while keeping at bay the dangers of fickle capital flows, at least before the mid-2010s. As of 2017, FDI still dominated portfolio and other investment liabilities in size.

Opening-up is not once and for all, even for FDIs. In the early 1980s, China's market economy was in its infancy, and the government had limited experience in managing it. A premature opening-up to capital inflows, even to growth-enhancing FDIs, could have led to inefficient investment booms. Instead, China conducted pilot programs first, establishing 4 Special Economic Zones in 1979, then another 14 Economic and Technology Development Zones in 1984. Foreign capital received more preferential treatment and operational autonomy in these special zones. It was only after the success of these pilot programs that China decided to fully embrace FDI. Since 1986, China has allowed foreign capital to receive tax benefits, regardless of location.[17] While it is difficult to analyze the counterfactual scenarios, the volatile growth and inflation that occurred in the 1980s suggested that an unchecked "FDI boom" would likely exacerbate China's economic overheating.

So, China opened up to portfolio investments even more cautiously. Relying on schemes, regulators decide which investors and how much portfolio capital to flow in and out. Participation in QFII was initially restricted to long-term investors such as central banks and sovereign wealth funds. Only after QFII's initial popularity and success did regulators broaden it to include more institutional investors, and to relax various restrictions such as maximum individual quotas, minimum holding periods, and repatriation rules. However, short-term speculators still faced tight restrictions for accessing China's financial assets. QDII and RQFII have been following similar steps to expand. After successfully launching these "Q schemes," China unveiled the Stock and Bond Connects. These "C schemes" are more flexible in that both institutional and retail investors have access to them, subject to no individual quotas. On top of the open-market "Q schemes," the launch of QDLP and QDIE expanded the investable asset classes to riskier private equities and debts. Both QDLP and QDIE started with small quotas to control risk.

The good lesson is that China has picked the right sequence of opening up, and has proceeded gradually. By adding small but incremental opening-up steps, China has substantially improved capital account convertibility without straining its developing financial system.

3.2. The Bad: Unevenly Paced Capital Flow Management Reform

Despite the variety of increasingly accessible portfolio investment schemes, skepticism remains about China's actual commitment to capital account liberalization. The skepticism was particularly strong during the capital flow reversal from 2015 to 2016, as the tightening outflow controls stoked fears that, once conditions turned south, China would shy away from its stated goal of liberalization (Wharton, 2016).

This skepticism stands in stark contrast with China's capital flow management (CFM) reform since 2009. The reform marked a philosophical change as well as a material modernization of CFM (Yi, 2014). The outdated, interventionist approach was replaced by a market-oriented, business-friendly alternative. The lengthy and opaque ex-ante review and approval process for many types of capital transactions was abolished, giving way to more streamlined and transparent ex-post monitoring and analysis. The positive (can-do) lists were superseded by negative (cannot-do) lists, expanding the set of allowed transactions. The State Administration of Foreign Exchange (SAFE) has been following the new regulatory philosophy until today and intends to adhere to it going forward.

Given the CFM reform that pointed firmly at opening up further, why did the skepticism remain? The slow development and implementation of a countercyclical macroprudential framework is to blame. The CFM reform had focused mostly on modernizing *microlevel* regulations; the *macroprudential* measures that prevent the buildup of carry trade inflows ex ante were underdeveloped until 2016.[18] The relaxation of microlevel regulations led to a rapid expansion of non-FDI carry trade inflows, making China's capital account increasingly volatile since the global financial crisis.[19] To smooth the capital account, regulators had followed a "lean against the wind" approach. Ill equipped with macroprudential measures, however, they had to resort to traditional administrative controls and discretion to micromanage the flows ex post. Whenever inflow pressure builds up, they shore up inflow controls and lift outflow restrictions (for example, by encouraging companies to invest abroad in the years before the GFC). Conversely, when outflow pressure dominates, they do the opposite (for example, relaxing entry barriers for foreign investors, and tightening review of overseas investments, including ODI in 2015 and 2016). Being administrative and micro means that these controls were inevitably more ad hoc and less transparent, leaving an impression that regulators treated capital flows discriminatively, depending on type, direction, or timing. In particular, the tightening of controls in 2015 and 2016 was apparently at odds with policymakers' vocal support for opening-up further, therefore fueling the skepticism about China's commitment to further liberalization.

The bad lesson, then, is that the CFM reform, while showing major progress in regulatory relief at the microlevel, had been slow in developing and implementing the macroprudential framework. Consequently, regulators were constrained to rely on administrative and discretionary controls as imperfect substitutes in response to carry trade swings. To restore market confidence in their commitment, complementing the modernized microlevel regulations with macroprudential measures is essential (section 4.2).

3.3. The "Ugly": Lack of Coordination between Capital Account Liberalization and Other Reforms

It is clear from the chronology that China *accelerated* its capital account opening-up during the first few years since the GFC. From 2008 to 2013, overseas borrowing restrictions were substantially relaxed. As the tide turned since 2014, however, China was seen reversing course and tightening its capital controls. So, why did an acceleration of opening-up end in a tightening of controls?

The problem lies not in capital account opening-up per se, but rather in China's distorted domestic financial system and its inflexible exchange rate regime. The country's domestic interest rates were heavily controlled and distorted. Deposit rates were repressed to ensure a low cost of funding for banks. The bank loan rates, while low, were not available for all. Some firms, particularly SOEs, could secure cheap credit easily and roll them over forever. Other firms, particularly private enterprises, could only borrow at premium rates or not at all (Song et al., 2011). As a result, interest rate differential between home and abroad widened at the margin. It widened further after the GFC, as major global central banks cut policy rates to the zero lower bound and then carried out QE programs to suppress long-term bond yields. When China relaxed overseas borrowing, in part to accommodate the stimulus-driven demand for funds, the wide interest rate gap led to strong appreciation expectations for RMB, and then to sharp carry trade inflows.

A large fraction of the carry trade inflows turned out to be overseas borrowing by domestic enterprises. From 2008 to 2014, corporate overseas borrowing totaled $1.1 trillion (figure 10.9), contributing to the rise of FX reserves that peaked at $4 trillion in mid-2014 (Miao et al., 2015). In addition to satisfying their own financing needs, domestic enterprises were often involved in shadow banking activities, lending out their overborrowed funds to other domestic borrowers for extra profit (Huang et al., 2018).

Exchange rate inflexibility amplified the carry trade flows. If the exchange rate floats freely, then speculative inflows will quickly push up the domestic currency, reduce profit opportunity, and discourage further inflows. Under China's inflexible exchange rate regime, however, profit opportunity lasted much longer, invited greater inflows, and put stronger appreciation pressure on the RMB. Thanks to this positive feedback, domestic borrowers, meaning shadow bankers in disguise, profited not only from the distorted interest differential, but also from the RMB's continued appreciation. However, when the carry trade inevitably unwound, the same positive feedback bit in the opposite direction, forcing the shadow banks to repay their debts, thereby generating

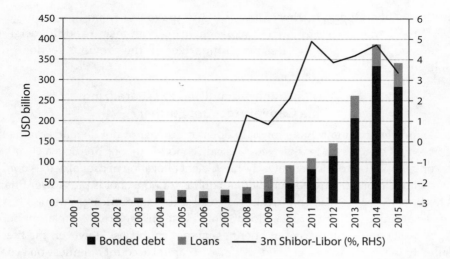

FIGURE 10.9. Corporate overseas debt and loan issuance and interest rate differential. *Source:* Miao and Rao (2016).

enormous capital outflow pressure in 2015 and 2016 and adding to the pessimism about the RMB.

Therefore, the exchange rate reform since August 11, 2015, was in fact long overdue.[20] With greater exchange rate flexibility, China could ex ante dampen the carry trade inflows and slow down the accumulation of FX reserves. Ex post, China could let RMB fall, without having to incur the heavy loss of FX reserves as the carry trade unwound. China's loss exposes the shortcomings of an inflexible exchange rate regime, under which the only noncontrol option for counterbalancing capital flows is to adjust FX reserves. An important asymmetry is noted: A country can accumulate FX reserves with no upper bound, but cannot run it down below zero. Under an inflexible exchange rate regime, this asymmetry creates a vicious cycle in which investors view FX reserves as the barometer of financial strength (Miao, 2018): Worries about depreciation cause the FX reserves to fall, which in turn makes investors even more worried that the central bank may run out of ammunition, in turn causing the FX reserves to drop even more quickly.

The "ugly" lesson, therefore, is that China accelerated liberalizing its capital account at a time when reforms to its financial system and exchange rate mechanism lagged behind. Capital account opening-up in isolation ended in volatile capital flow swings that ultimately *delay* and not speed the progress toward convertibility. To avoid making the same mistake, coordinating opening-up with financial reforms and flexible exchange rates will be critical (section 4.3).

4. GOING FORWARD: CONTINUING CAPITAL ACCOUNT LIBERALIZATION

Since outflow pressure eased in 2017, policymakers have brought back the halted capital account liberalization, focusing on non-FDI flows. Both global history and China's own setbacks in 2015 and 2016 have shown that non-FDI flows can be tricky. So, why is China committed to liberalizing further? How will it improve its capital flow management? How will the country open up further while ensuring both macro and financial stability? The good, bad, and "ugly" lessons summarized in the previous section provide possible answers.

4.1. Why Is China Committed to Liberalizing Its Capital Account Further?

As the "good" lesson above has shown, to open up further or not depends on the tradeoff between its benefits and risks. Neoclassical economic theory predicts a clear benefit that an open capital account facilitates more-efficient allocation of capital across borders—in other words, more globally diversified portfolios for households plus lower financing costs for businesses. Yet the empirical evidence for this theoretical prediction has been mixed. The academic literature has documented a strong positive correlation between GDP per capita and capital account openness across countries. However, the literature has failed to identify a robust effect of a *change* in capital account openness on economic *growth* (Jeanne et al., 2011, chapter 3; Wei, 2018). Even worse, open capital accounts tend to pose significant risks to EMEs, including sudden stops, capital flights, currency crises, and rising inequality (Furceri and Loungani, 2015). China's own capital reversal experience seems to echo these empirical findings (section 2.4).

If the benefit-risk tradeoff seems uncertain, why then is China committed to liberalizing its capital account further? One possible reason is that it aims to become an advanced economy, and therefore views an open capital account as an end in itself. After all, the positive correlation between openness and level of income cannot be ignored. In particular, convertible capital accounts seem to offer much better benefit-risk tradeoffs for advanced economies than for EMEs. To explain the difference, the literature points to a "threshold effect," in which for economies above a certain threshold (income per capita, financial depth, institutional quality, labor market flexibility, infrastructure, and so on) their capital flows are less likely to wreak havoc and more likely to boost growth (Kose et al., 2009 Jeanne et al., 2011, chapter 4; Wei, 2018). As China's economy continues to develop, the benefit-risk tradeoff may become more favorable over time (Prasad and Rajan, 2008). Perhaps for this reason, China has not shunned away from opening up its capital account.

Even if the direct, neoclassical benefit is ambiguous, capital account liberalization may bring indirect, "collateral" benefits (Kose et al., 2009). For China, an important collateral benefit is to improve financial sector openness and promote financial reforms. China has been the largest trading country since 2013, but its financial sector has been less open. Global financial institutions remained minor participants in China's financial market (section 2.7). With little foreign competition, domestic financial institutions have limited incentives to improve products and services, to strengthen risk management, or to enhance accountability and governance. Financial laws and regulations are more likely twisted and lenient to excessive leveraging and risk-taking. Critical financial reforms are more difficult to implement and more easily rolled back.

Capital account opening-up may serve as a commitment device to financial reforms. Foreign financial institutions, once gaining access to China's financial markets, are very difficult to weed out. Their competition will force domestic financial practice and regulations to catch up with global standards (Schoenmaker, 2013; Obstfeld, 2015). For example, the introduction of strategic investors to China's state-owned banks in the mid-

2000s had improved their capital adequacy, competitiveness, and resilience. With stronger financial discipline, excess corporate and local government debts are less likely to build up and more likely to be contained. The shadow banking system can become more transparent and pose fewer risks to financial stability.

Yet another collateral benefit is to accommodate RMB's internationalization. An internationally accepted RMB will better facilitate China's trade and investment with global partners. RMB's inclusion into the SDR basket in 2015 was a key milestone. But it still has a long way to go before becoming a major currency. In fact, its share in global transactions *declined* from 2014 to 2017.[21] Both the carry trade reversal and the tightening of controls may have contributed to the decline. Looking forward, greater capital account convertibility will lift the demand for RMB in cross-border transactions, helping it recoup the lost ground and expand.

In short, improving capital account convertibility is an end in itself, and provides substantial collateral benefits. By proceeding carefully and cautiously, as the good lesson has shown, reaping these benefits is possible. The associated risks, while high, should be dealt with by coordinating financial and exchange rate reforms (section 4.3). This explains why policymakers have relaxed the enforcement of regulations and released new steps to open up further when outflow pressure eased after 2017 (section 2.6).

4.2. How Will China Improve Its Capital Flow Management?

Opening-up will likely lead to significant increases in both the volume and the volatility of capital flows. Bayoumi and Ohnsorge (2013) estimated that, following capital account liberalization, China's gross foreign assets may increase by 15% to 25% of GDP, and foreign-held Chinese assets may rise by 2% to 10% of GDP. As a result, China's financial system will become more exposed to external financial shocks. Neither floating exchange rates (Obstfeld, 2015; Obstfeld and Taylor, 2017) nor monetary policy (Jorda et al., 2018) can fully offset these shocks, making capital flow management (CFM) indispensable. In light of the "bad" lesson (section 3.2), some policymakers have emphasized upgrading CFM to accommodate the more-liberalized cross-border movement of capital (Yi, 2018). Only in this way can China more effectively safeguard its financial system (Pan, 2018).

The upgraded CFM framework builds on and distinguishes between two pillars: macroprudential and microprudential. Both pillars differ in their objective, scope, and tools. The *microprudential* pillar aims to ensure the authenticity and legality of *individual* transactions. It impartially treats inflows and outflows, FDI, portfolio and other flows, and it enforces the rules with the same rigor regardless of financial ebbs and flows. In addition, it strengthens the once-porous enforcement against underground banking and other illegal transactions.

The *macroprudential* pillar, by contrast, aims to safeguard overall financial stability. It is *targeted*, focusing on the volatile short-term flows that pose the greatest threat to financial stability. It is also *countercyclical*, aiming to stabilize flows over time. In practice, regulators have established monitoring and early warning systems for short-term flows, have improved their risk assessments, and have also developed new policy tools to lower capital flow volatility, such as risk reserve requirements for FX derivatives.[22] The rationale is that corporates' FX forward position tends to be procyclical, forcing counterparty banks to buy FX in spot markets. Macroprudential regulation complements FX reserves in taming procyclical flows and herding behavior. As FX reserves can serve as lenders of last resort, domestic borrowers may feel less worried about repaying their foreign debts and about their borrowings' impact on overall financial stability. This moral hazard problem leads to overborrowing similar to the spirit of Bianchi (2011). By internalizing this negative pecuniary externality, macroprudential regulation reduces the incentive to overborrow (Acharya and Krishnamurthy, 2018). Macroprudential regulation, then, is especially important before the RMB exchange rate becomes sufficiently flexible (section 3.3).

Strengthening the macroprudential pillar should not be misinterpreted as imposing capital controls. The two differ in a number of important dimensions. On the one hand, macroprudential regulation focuses on reducing systemic financial risk; it restricts domestic borrowing, regardless of the source of credit's being domestic or foreign. Capital control, on the other hand, restricts the transaction between residents and nonresidents (Korinek and Sandri, 2016). Macroprudential regulation is price-based and nondiscriminative, aiming to safeguard financial stability ex ante. Capital control is more discretionary, attempting to mitigate the crisis fallouts ex post (Jeanne et al., 2011, chapter 2). Macroprudential regulation is a standing facility, like a fence, while capital control is a backstop, used only during emergencies.

This dual-pillared approach is a major upgrade from discriminative and time-inconsistent past practice. If implemented as planned, it should help to restore market confidence in China's capital account liberalization, discourage regulatory arbitrage and capital flights, and facilitate a steady growth of two-way capital flows.

4.3. How Will China Open Up Its Capital Account Further?

Judging by the "ugly" lesson, it can be risky to open up the capital account when the domestic financial system is distorted and the exchange rate remains inflexible. But, given the complexities of financial and exchange rate reforms as well as the collateral benefits of capital account liberalization (section 4.1), analysts wonder how and when China can possibly choreograph its myriad of reforms. Several views can be adduced.

The *preconditions* view argues that a safe capital account liberalization relies on the fulfillment of many preconditions, including stable macroeconomic fundamentals, a sound banking system, and developed financial markets (Fischer, 1998). Lardy and Douglass (2011) concluded that because of its weak banking system, underdeveloped financial markets, and lack of a market-determined exchange rate, China was not ready to make its capital account convertible. Yu (2017) emphasized that because of regulatory loopholes, a sudden liberalization would lead to massive capital flights.

The *sequencing* view holds that policymakers should design and follow an optimal sequence of reforms. McKinnon (1991) argued that the optimal sequencing is to liberalize domestic trade and finance first, followed by exchange rate flexibility, and lastly by capital account liberalization. As a negative example, Mexico's experience after its debt crisis in the 1980s showed that pushing forward capital account liberalization simultaneously with many other reforms induced sharp carry trade inflows and exacerbated macroeconomic imbalances that ultimately led to the 1994 "Peso Crisis." For China, some have argued that exchange rate reform should precede interest rate and capital account liberalizations (CF40, 2015).

The *stability* view warns that reform and opening-up may become destabilizing in the near term. In particular, lifting controls and regulations all at once may give rise to spikes in exchange rate volatility, and also to sharp cross-border flow swings, thus threatening both financial and macroeconomic stability. The stability view prescribes slowing down the reform.

All three views have merits, yet they are also limited. The argument against the preconditions view is that some preconditions cannot realize before the intended reforms. For example, during the exchange rate reform debates in 1993, the preconditions view argued that exchange rate reform had to satisfy three preconditions: strong exports, sufficient FX reserves, and experienced macroeconomic management. But, absent exchange rate reform, China would continue to suffer from a lack of export competitiveness, experience a shortage of FX reserves, and not be able to learn about modern macroeconomic management simply by "doing." The decision to push forward exchange rate reforms in 1993 before the preconditions were met turned out to be hugely successful. One possible reason was that the reform sent a strong signal and boosted market confidence, so that it had less resistance (Zhou, 2017).

The argument against the sequencing view is that situations are often complex and fast-changing, and disagreements among policymakers tend to erect political hurdles. While economists can sometimes deduce from economic principles an optimal sequence of reforms, political interests often make the problem so complex that no optimal sequencing can be found. For example, if multiple regulators disagree on either the preconditions or the sequencing, each of them would have an incentive to wait and free-ride on others' efforts, so that the reform will likely end up in shirking or even deadlock (Zhou, 2017). Empirically, both successful and failed opening-up attempts can be found, no matter how the reforms are sequenced.

The argument against the stability view is that short-term stability may come at the price of destabilization in the long run. Without reforming the distortions, economies will remain susceptible to external shocks. Even worse, to leave the problems unsolved is effectively to let them grow, eating into the policy rooms and damaging tools for the future.

In practice, China's policymakers have favored a "troika" approach, by coordinating exchange rate, capital account liberalization, and financial reforms (Zhou, 2017; Yi, 2018; Xu, 2018). This approach has built in both gradualism and opportunism. Instead of preconditions or sequencing, it focuses on pushing the lagging reforms forward to catch up on other reforms, so that over time, all reforms are marching ahead. More favorable domestic and external conditions will allow policymakers to push the reforms faster, while adverse shocks may slow them down. This approach is less prone to rollbacks, so policymakers have suggested using the "ratchet effect" (i.e., irreversibility) of opening-up as a commitment device for financial and exchange rate reforms (Zhou, 2017).

For the other two items of the troika, China's interest rate liberalization seems to have been completed. In October 2015, the People's Bank of China lifted its control of bank loan and deposit rates. However, they were still informally subject to the PBC's window guidance and capped by what was called the banking industry's "self-discipline." Therefore, China's interest rates remained dual-tracked: fully liberalized bond rates versus underliberalized bank rates. Because banks remain the dominant source of financing in China today, the capped bank rates lead to inefficient allocation of capital, distort the equilibrium exchange rate, and encourage speculative carry trades. As the troika approach suggests, more flexible exchange rates and more-open capital accounts necessitate a more-liberalized interest rate. In April 2018, PBC Governor Yi Gang talked about unifying the dual-tracked interest rate system and allowing banks more autonomy in rate-setting.[23] This marked a further step toward market determination of interest rates.

China has made significant progress in liberalizing its exchange rate *mechanism*. On August 11, 2015, it reformed the RMB-dollar central parity to more closely align with the closing price on the previous trading day. In December 2015, it linked the exchange value of RMB to a basket of currencies and introduced the China Foreign Exchange Trading System (CFETS) RMB index. The countercyclical factor, inserted into the central parity and temporarily introduced in mid-2017, had been neutralized by early 2018 and reintroduced in August 2018. After these reforms, the RMB exchange rate has become increasingly flexible. As the troika approach suggests, the exchange rate is closer to equilibrium only if the interest rate is less distorted and the capital account is more open, thereby allowing more-efficient elimination of arbitrage opportunities and better price discovery. What China has yet to develop is an active, deep, and liquid *FX market*. China's FX market is still tightly regulated, with limited participation, products, and hedging tools. However, the country's eventual convergence toward clean floating rests on interest parity, which holds better only if China's FX market deepens, with a greater number of sophisticated and contrarian investors, a wider range of tradeable products, more-efficient hedging tools, lower trading costs, and fewer trading restrictions.

4.4. How Do These Measures Add Up?

An open capital account never operates in isolation. Instead, it is tightly connected to monetary independence and to exchange rate flexibility, so as to form an "Impossible Trinity." So, how do a more opened capital account, an upgraded capital flow management framework, and a more flexible exchange rate add up?

China's path of capital account liberalization and related financial reforms is best illustrated on the Impossible Trinity triangle (figure 10.10). Each point in the triangle represents a combination of capital account openness, exchange rate flexibility, and monetary autonomy. The classical "Trilemma" dictates that no country can simultaneously enjoy monetary autonomy, a stable exchange rate, and a convertible capital account—hence the set of all feasible options that form a triangle. China started Reform and Opening-up at the southwest corner (B), when it had a closed capital account and inflexible exchange rate yet enjoyed high monetary autonomy. Over time, the country increased exchange rate flexibility and partially liberalized its capital account, though, as the Trilemma dictates, it lost some of its monetary autonomy. In the triangle, China has moved northeast toward the center (O).[24]

Most advanced economies are near the southeast corner (A'), where they enjoy monetary autonomy and open capital account, but allow exchange rate to be flexibly determined by the market. A' also best serves China's long-term interests. A more-liberalized capital account reduces autonomy, making a flexible exchange rate essential (Obstfeld, 2015). However, as the literature and experience have both demonstrated, it is optimal to maintain a certain amount of capital flow management. Therefore, the optimal destination is slightly to the left of A' at A, where economies keep monetary autonomy, maintain an almost fully convertible (though not laissez-faire) capital account, and let the exchange rate float (Miao and Tan, 2018).

Many paths lead toward A (figure 10.11). Policymakers may choose either (a) a path that *tightens* the capital account before relaxing it, or (b) one that keeps capital account

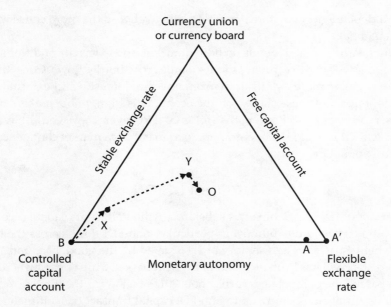

FIGURE 10.10. China's path on the "Impossible Trinity." *Source:* Miao and Tan (2018).

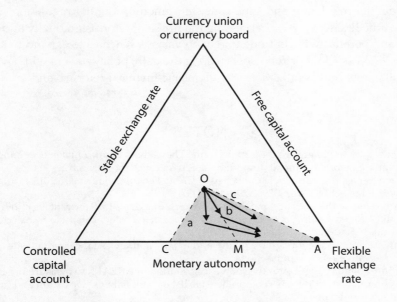

FIGURE 10.11. Alternative reform paths toward A. *Source:* Miao and Tan (2018).

openness unchanged for a while, or (c) one that pushes capital account opening-up along the path. From (a) to (c), capital account liberalization is increasingly aggressive, at the cost of more slowly achieving monetary autonomy. Therefore, the choice depends on policymakers' preference with regard to monetary independence. If domestic and global business cycles align, policymakers may prefer (c) the path that more quickly achieves capital account convertibility because monetary independence is less binding. However, if domestic and global business cycles differ significantly, the need to maintain monetary independence may force policymakers to choose the more conservative path (b) or even path (a).

The path toward A also depends on both domestic and external conditions. Opening up more aggressively (path c) invites more-volatile cross-border flows. Consequently, the economy may suffer more significantly from adverse domestic and external shocks. If the potential impact of these shocks on the economy is high, policymakers may prefer more conservative approaches—paths (b) or (a). However, they would have to better communicate their intention of opening-up, so as to enhance market confidence and thus avoid costly capital flow swings.

5. CONCLUSION

Over the past four decades, China has substantially liberalized its capital account. However, the path has been quite bumpy. In particular, non-FDI flows across the border are still somewhat restricted. The way forward is shaped by the good, bad, and "ugly" lessons learned. As RMB has been included in the SDR basket, China's capital account opening-up has passed the point of no return (Zhou, 2017). Following the three principles[25] (Yi, 2018), China commits to opening up to non-FDI capital transactions, ultimately reaching full capital account convertibility. Accordingly, China can be expected to further upgrade its capital flow management framework, which builds on dual pillars: countercyclical macroprudential regulation and time-consistent microprudential regulation. To reduce the risks, China likely proceeds harnessing the troika of reforms gradually and opportunistically, and perhaps will continue to rely on various schemes to expand in an orderly fashion the cross-border portfolio flows. Along the path, policymakers will have to coordinate capital account liberalization with domestic financial reforms, and to make RMB more flexible.

NOTES

The views expressed here are the authors' only. The authors thank Zhiwen Jiao, Yang Hao, and Yuyan Tan for helpful comments and Lizhong Liu for excellent research assistance. This chapter is derived in part from an article published in China Economic Journal in 2019, available online at https://doi.org/10.1080/17538963.2019.1670472.

1.	The term refers to the sales and purchases of assets. In today's IMF terminology, in this chapter they will be called *financial account*, whereas *capital account* refers mostly to transfers, gifts, and foreign aid.
2.	The only exceptions are foreigners' equity and money market issuance in domestic markets, as well as derivative-related transactions.
3.	The Chinn-Ito index aggregates the source information in AREAER to measure the existence of capital account restrictions on a comprehensive list of capital flows. See Chinn and Ito (2006) for methodological details.
4.	The Quinn index is also based on AREAER. Different from Chinn-Ito, the Quinn index better captures the enforcement of restrictions, even if they are unchanged on paper. See Quinn (1997) for details.
5.	PBC's annual work conference in early 2013 proposed studying the Qualified Domestic Individual Investors (QDII2) program, which for the first time would allow wealthy individuals in select cities to invest directly in developed financial markets and real estates. The 3rd Plenary Meeting of the 18th CPC Central Committee in late 2013 also proposed accelerating RMB's convertibility in capital account transactions.
6.	See section 2 for more details.
7.	In May 2017, SAFE Administrator Pan Gongsheng expressed that the pace of capital account liberalization should be consistent with a country's economic development, financial market and financial stability, and external conditions.

8. Formally, the Law of the People's Republic of China on Chinese-Foreign Joint Ventures. The law was approved in 1979, and revised twice in 1990 and 2001. This law has been replaced by the new Foreign Investment Law, passed in March 2019.

9. From 1981 to 1993, China maintained both an official exchange rate and a swap-based exchange rate. The former was set artificially high to support key imports, while the latter was more freely negotiated between importers, exporters, and foreign-invested enterprises to reflect market supply and demand.

10. Before QFII was introduced, foreign investors could only buy B shares of Chinese companies in mainland China's financial market. B shares are quoted in foreign currency (U.S. dollar for Shanghai-listed companies, HK dollar for Shenzhen-listed).

11. Comprising the United States, United Kingdom, Japan, Korea, Singapore, Australia, Luxembourg, Germany, Canada, Malaysia, and Hong Kong.

12. Another key supplement to bank credit was shadow banking. See Zhu (2018) for a review of China's shadow banking system that emerged after the stimulus package.

13. The policy slogans are "let the people hold the foreign assets" (*cang hui yu min*) for households and "go abroad" (*zou chu qu*) for businesses.

14. In a series of reforms, China has removed quota limits for foreign investors in the interbank bond market—first in central banks and sovereign wealth funds (in 2015), then in general QFIIs (in 2016). Since 2012 China's bond market has become the third largest in the world (next only to those of the United States and Japan). As of June 2018, the total bond market size is 75.8 trillion RMB.

15. In March 2018, Bloomberg announced its inclusion of China's central government and policy bank bonds into the Bloomberg-Barclays Global Aggregate Index, starting in April 2019. J.P. Morgan and FT-Russell have also signaled an interest in including China's governments in their bond indices.

16. Examples are the ±10% daily price change limits and the lack of short-selling mechanisms.

17. China removed FDI's tax benefits in 2008.

18. The macroprudential measures were finalized in mid-2016 (Guo, 2018).

19. Lack of exchange rate flexibility also contributed to the volatile carry trade flows. See section 3.3.

20. Prasad (2016) criticized that the timing was bad owing to the stock market crash in mid-2015, and opined that the PBC had failed to timely convey its intentions to market participants, causing confusion and widespread panic that triggered heavy sell-offs of RMB following the reform.

21. According to SWIFT, only 1.5% of global transactions used RMB in 2017, 0.6 percentage points lower than in 2014. By the end of 2017, more than 60 countries and regional economies had included RMB in their FX reserves, for a total amount equivalent to $122.8 billion, or 1.23% of all FX reserves.

22. As part of its macroprudential framework, the PBC implemented the 20% risk reserve requirement for FX derivatives in October 2015, suspended it in September 2017, and reinstated it in August 2018.

23. "Governor Yi Gang's Q&A on Monetary Policy Normalization at the 2018 Boao Asia Forum." http://www.pbc.gov.cn/goutongjiaoliu/113456/113469/3518129/index.html.

24. The paths B–X, X–Y, and Y–O correspond to China's key exchange rate reforms in 1994, 2005, and 2015, respectively. From 1994 to 2005, RMB was pegged to the dollar after brief fluctuations, while capital account slowly opened up (B–X). From 2005 to 2015, RMB gradually appreciated against the dollar, while capital account convertibility improved (X–Y). From 2015 on, exchange rate had become more flexible, while capital account openness largely stayed unchanged (Y–O).

25. The three principles are pre-establishment national treatment and negative lists for foreign institutions, coordinating capital account opening-up with financial and exchange rate reforms, and matching the degree of opening-up with regulatory capabilities.

REFERENCES

Acharya, Viral V., and Arvind Krishnamurthy (2018). "Capital Flow Management with Multiple Instruments." (No.w24443). National Bureau of Economic Research.

Bayoumi, Tamim, and Franziska Ohnsorge (2013). "Do Inflows or Outflows Dominate? Global Implications of Capital Account Liberalization in China." IMF Working Paper No. /13/189, August 28.

Bianchi, Javier (2011). "Overborrowing and Systemic Externalities in the Business Cycle." *American Economic Review* 101(7): 3400–26.

CF40 (2015). "Interest Rate Liberalization in China's Economic Development and Reform." China Financial Reform Report. Beijing: China Finance Press.

CF40 (2017). *China's Financial Opening-up: The Second Half.* Beijing: CITIC Press.

Chinn, Menzie D., and Hiro Ito (2006). "What Matters for Financial Development? Capital Controls, Institutions, and Interactions." *Journal of Development Economics* 81(1): 163–92.

Fischer, Stanley (1998). "Capital Account Liberalization and the Role of the IMF," in *Should the IMF Pursue Capital Account Convertibility?*, edited by Peter Kenen. Princeton Essay in International Finance, No. 207. Princeton, NJ: Princeton University.

Furceri, Davide, and Prakash Loungani (2015). "Capital Account Liberalization and Inequality." IMF Working Paper No. 15/243, November.

Guo, Song (2018). "Capital Account Liberalization on Its New Journey." *China Forex*, 2018(9): 31–34.

Huang, Yi, Ugo Panizza, and Richard Portes (2018). "Corporate Foreign Bond Issuance and Interfirm Loans in China" (No. w24513). National Bureau of Economic Research.

Jeanne, Olivier, Arvind Subramanian, and John Williamson (2011). *Who Needs to Open the Capital Account?* New York: Columbia University Press.

Jorda, Oscar, Moritz Schularick, Alan M. Taylor, and Felix Ward (2018). "Global Financial Cycles and Risk Premiums." Federal Reserve Bank of San Francisco working paper 2018-05.

Korinek, Anton, and Enrique G. Mendoza (2014). "From Sudden Stop to Fisherian Deflation: Quantitative Theory and Policy Implications." *Annual Review of Economics* 2014(6): 299–332.

Korinek, Anton, and Damiano Sandri (2016). Capital Controls or Macroprudential Regulation? *Journal of International Economics* 99(Supplement 1): S27–S42.

Kose, M. Ayhan, Eswar S. Prasad, Kenneth Rogoff, and Shang-Jin Wei (2009). "Financial Globalization: A Reappraisal." *IMF Staff Papers* 56(1): 8–62.

Kose, M. Ayhan, Eswar S. Prasad, and Ashley D. Taylor (2009). "Thresholds in the Process of International Financial Integration." Brookings Institution Global Economy and Development Working Paper 35, May 19.

Lardy, Nicholas, and Patrick Douglass (2011). "Capital Account Liberalization and the Role of the Renminbi." Peterson Institute for International Economics working paper, 2011-6.

McKinnon, Robert (1991). *The Order of Economic Liberalization*. Baltimore, MD: Johns Hopkins University Press.

Miao, Yanliang (2018). "Understanding the Rise and Fall of FX Reserves." Mimeo.

Miao, Yanling, and Tuo Deng (2019). "China's Capital Account Liberalization: A Ruby Jubilee and Beyond." *China Economic Journal* 12(3): 245–71.

Miao, Yanliang, and Can Rao (2016). "How Much Have Chinese Companies Borrowed from Abroad? An Update." *New Finance Review* 2016(4): 24–39.

Miao, Yanliang, and Yuyan Tan (2018). "From Saha to Paramita: How Can RMB Exchange Rate Achieve Clean Floating?" Mimeo.

Miao, Yanliang, Yu Zhang, and Xinyong He (2015). "How Much Have Chinese Companies Borrowed from Abroad?" *New Finance Review* 2015(2): 92–105.

Obstfeld, Maurice (2015). "Trilemmas and Tradeoffs: Living with Financial Globalization," in Claudio Raddatz, Diego Saravia, and Jaume Ventura (eds.), *Global Liquidity, Spillovers to Emerging Markets and Policy Responses*. Central Bank of Chile.

Obstfeld, Maurice, and Alan M. Taylor (2017). "International Monetary Relations: Taking Finance Seriously." *Journal of Economic Perspectives* 31(3): 3–28.

Pan, Gongsheng (2018). "Further Pushing Forward the Balanced Approach of Foreign Exchange Management, and Better Serving the Comprehensive Opening-Up." *Caixin*, February 7.

PBC (2017). "2017 RMB Internationalization Report." People's Bank of China.

Prasad, Eswar S. (2016). *Gaining Currency*. Oxfordshire, U.K.: Oxford University Press.

Prasad, Eswar S., and Raghuram G. Rajan (2008). "A Pragmatic Approach to Capital Account Liberalization," *Journal of Economic Perspectives* 22(3): 149–72.

Quinn, Dennis (1997). "The Correlates of Change in International Financial Regulation." *American Political Science Review* 91(3): 531–51.

Schipke, Alfred (2016). "Capital Account Liberalization and China's Effect on Global Capital Flows." Reserve Bank of Australia Conference Volume, 163–72. https://www.rba.gov.au/publications/confs/2016/pdf/rba-conference-volume-2016-schipke.pdf.

Schoenmaker, Dirk (2013). *Governance of International Banking: The Financial Trilemma*. Oxfordshire, U.K.: Oxford University Press.

Sheng, Songcheng, Nuojin Xu, Xiandong Yan, and Weiliang Zhu (2012). "The Conditions Are Ready for China to Accelerate Capital Account Liberalization." *China Finance*. 2012(5): 14–17.

Song, Zheng, Kjetil Storesletten, and Fabrizio Zillibotti (2011). "Growing Like China." *American Economic Review* 101(1): 196–233.

Wei, Shang-Jin (2018). "Managing Financial Globalization: A Guide for Developing Countries Based on the Recent Literature." ADBI Working Paper 804. Tokyo: Asian Development Bank Institute.

Wharton (blog) (2016). "China's Currency Test: Can It Get Capital Controls Right?" Knowledge@Wharton, February 17. http://knowledge.wharton.upenn.edu/article/chinas-currency-test-can-it-get-capital-controls-right/

Xu, Zhong (2018). "Face Up to Further Opening-Up of the Financial Industry." *Economic Daily*, March 29, 2018.

Yi, Gang (2014). "The Historical Change in FX Management." *China Finance* 2014(19): 15–18.

Yi, Gang (2018). "Opening Up the Financial Industry to Lift Its International Competitiveness." Speech prepared for 2018 Boao Asia Forum Annual Meeting at Boao, China, April 11.

Yu, Yongding (2015). *The Final Shield: Debates on Capital Account Liberalization and RMB Internationalization*. Beijing: Oriental Press.

Yu, Yongding (2017). "Why China's Capital Account Liberalization Has Stalled." Project Syndicate, October 31. https://www.project-syndicate.org/commentary/china-capital-account-liberalization-on-hold-by-yu-yongding-2017-10

Zhang, Ming (2015). "The Liberalization of Capital Account in China: Retrospect and Prospect." in Joseph E. Stiglitz and Refet S. Gurkaynak (eds.), *Taming Capital Flows: Capital Account Management in an Era of Globalization*. Basingstoke: Palgrave Macmillan.

Zhou, Xiaochuan (2017). "Exchange Rate Reform Should Grasp Its Opportunity Window." *Caijing*, October 9.

Zhu, Xiaodong (2018). "The Varying Shadow of China's Banking System." Working paper 605, Department of Economics, University of Toronto.

PART 5

STOCK MARKET

11

THE DEVELOPMENT OF THE CHINESE STOCK MARKET

Franklin Allen, Jun "QJ" Qian, Chenyu Shan, and Julie Lei Zhu

1. HISTORY OF THE CHINESE STOCK MARKET

1.1. Establishment of Stock Exchanges

The domestic Chinese stock market (the "A-share" market) started in 1990 with the establishment of two independently operated domestic stock exchanges: the Shanghai Stock Exchange (SSE hereafter) was founded on November 26 and began operating on December 19, and the Shenzhen Stock Exchange (SZSE) was established on December 1, 1990. A greater number of larger firms and state-owned enterprises (SOEs) have been listed on the SSE as compared to the SZSE. As of the end of 2018, the total market capitalization of the two exchanges stood at $6.3 trillion, the second largest stock market in the world at the time, trailing only the U.S. equity markets.[1]

Products from four broad categories are traded in the exchanges: stocks, fixed-income securities/bonds, funds, and derivatives. Fixed-income securities include publicly issued bonds, privately placed bonds, and asset-backed securities, among others. Funds include exchange-traded funds (ETFs), listed open-ended funds (LOFs), structured funds, and closed-end funds. Only a small number of financial derivatives are traded in the A-share market. One publicly traded stock option is the ETF50, with both calls and puts written on the SSE50 Index, an exchange-traded funds that includes some 50 actively traded stocks in the SSE. However, no options on *individual* stocks are traded. Figure 11.1 shows the transaction amounts of the four types of financial products in the Chinese markets (stocks, bonds, funds, and futures) over the period of 1999–2018.

The Chinese stock market issues two types of stocks: A-share and B-share stocks. The A-share stocks are denominated in RMB yuan and issued to domestic investors (as well as to qualified foreign institutional investors, QFII). B-share stocks are quoted in U.S. or HK dollars and issued to offshore investors. These stocks became available to domestic investors with foreign currency accounts in 2001. According to statistics published in May 2018, the total market capitalizations for A shares and B shares were RMB 32.0 trillion

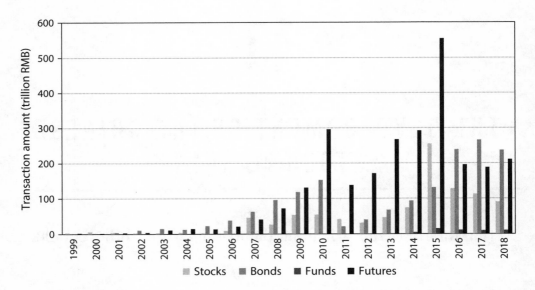

FIGURE 11.1. Transaction amounts of financial products in China's securities market. *Source:* National Bureau of Statistics.

and 87.2 billion, and the market capitalizations for *traded* A shares and B shares were RMB 27.2 trillion and 87.2 billion, respectively.[2] Thus, the B-share market accounts for only 0.27% of the entire A-share market in terms of capitalization.[3]

While the A-share market is still dominated by retail investors in terms of trading, institutional investors have increased their presence in it over the past few years. For example, total trading volume in the SSE was RMB 101 trillion for 2017, 81.6% of which was by retail investors, a decline of 4% from 2016 (Gao et al., 2018). The percentage of SSE's market cap held by retail investors has been declining over the years, and it was about 21% at the end of 2017, while (domestic) institutional investors' holdings made up over three-quarters of the total market cap.

1.2. Evolution of A-Share Listed Firms

The number of listed firms in mainland China has grown rapidly since the market's inception. There were only 10 publicly listed firms in mainland China in 1990, 8 of which were listed in SSE and 2 in SZSE; the total market cap was RMB 104.8 billion measured as of 1992. As shown in figure 11.2, by the end of 2018 the number of listed firms in the two exchanges reached 3,584, of which 99 also issued B-share stocks. The total market capitalization increased to RMB 43.5 trillion measured as of the end of 2018, an increase of 415 times relative to the level of 1992.[4]

One of the stated purposes of establishing the stock market, perhaps unique to the landscape of the Chinese economy back in 1990, was to promote the (partial) privatization of SOEs by helping them raise funds through markets. During most of the 1990s, the stock market was dominated by SOEs and collectively owned firms. As more privately owned firms entered the stock market, the percentage of listed SOEs declined over the years, from 56.4% in 2000 to 37.9% in 2014 (Allen et al. 2019).

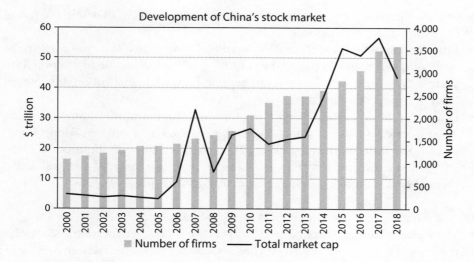

FIGURE 11.2. Number of firms listed in China's stock market and its total market capitalization. *Source:* National Bureau of Statistics annual data (http://data.stats.gov.cn/easyquery.htm?cn=C01).

1.3. Stock Market Regulations

Both exchanges (SSE and SZSE) are nonprofit organizations regulated by the China Securities Regulatory Commission (CSRC). Subordinated to the State Council, CSRC has set up 36 securities regulatory bureaus over the country. In addition, the Securities Association of China (SAC), which was established on August 28, 1991, exercises self-disciplinary administration within the securities industry. The Security Laws, which regulate the issuance and trading of stocks in China, were passed by the National People's Congress on December 29, 1998.

The Chinese stock market has experienced multiple rounds of reforms over the past 30 years. The following reforms are considered to have had significant impacts on the stock market development and investors:

- Restrictions of price limit (1996): to mitigate extreme stock price movement, the SSE and SZSE require that except for newly listed stocks, the price change of the other stocks within one trading day must be within the range of –10% to +10%.
- The Split-Share Reform (2005–2006): the Chinese government recognized that the predominance of nontradeable shares in the stock market was a major problem for its further development, so it implemented this reform to float a large fraction of the nontradeable shares during 2005–2007.
- Introduction of margin trading, including leveraged trades and short-selling (2010) to improve market liquidity and price discovery.
- Introduction of financial derivatives, such as stock index futures and government bond futures (2010), and the ETF50 options (2010), to enhance hedging and risk management.
- Establishment of the Small-and-Medium sized Enterprises Board (the SME Board) and the Growth Enterprises Board (GME board): the goal is to establish a multilayer stock market to create more listing opportunities for high-tech,

innovative firms that cannot meet the listing standards in the main board but have high growth potential.

- Introduction of QFII (2002) to allow qualified foreign investors to invest in the A-share market, and to permit both QDII (qualified domestic institutional investors, 2006) and RQFII (renminbi qualified domestic institutional investors, 2011) to enter global markets.
- Launch of the Shanghai–Hong Kong Connect (2014) and the Shenzhen–Hong Kong Connect (2016):[5] to allow investors in Shanghai/Shenzhen (Hong Kong) to trade stocks listed in Hong Kong (Shanghai/Shenzhen), to improve the interconnection between the A-share market with the Hong Kong market, and to further open the domestic stock market to foreign investors.

One of the most important reforms is the Split-Share Reform of 2005–2006 led by the CSRC. By virtue of heritage, around two-thirds of the shares in the Chinese stock market were nontradeable shares before 2005. These nontradeable shares were mainly held by various state agencies, institutions, or SOEs. The existence of large amount of such shares led to severe incentive problems and conflicts between large shareholders and minority shareholders. With their controlling position in most listed firms, the incentive of the controlling state shareholders to improve firm performance is rather limited, resulting in both corporate governance problems and inefficient resource allocation in the stock market. Under these circumstances, the State Council issued "Opinions on promoting the reform, opening up and stable development of the capital market" on January 31, 2004, which explicitly requires "actively and steadily solving the split-share problem." Once the nontradeable shares are converted to tradeable shares, the owners of the nontradeable shares can "cash out" their investment at market prices; large amounts of nontradeable shares floated to the market following the reform could have a large price impact on the stocks. These factors imply that nontradeable shareholders need to compensate tradeable shareholders during the conversion process (Li et al., 2011). By the end of 2016, 1,301, or 97% of the listed firms have completed the split-share reform.

Liao et al. (2014) find that the expectation of privatization quickly boosted SOE output, profits, and employment, but did not change their operating efficiency or corporate governance. The reform improved SOE corporate governance only after substantial changes in their ownership structure. Their results suggest that stimulating incumbent management's incentive with expectation of privatization also have positive effects. Liao et al. (2011) examine a short window around share lockup expirations in the split-share reform. They find that the abnormal stock returns are positively correlated with firm information transparency and post-reform performance improvement.

An important issue in the split-share reform is the pricing of nontradeable shares. As discussed above, to make their shares tradeable, holders of nontradeable shares compensated holders of tradeable shares. Li et al. (2011) find that the compensation ratio is positively associated with both the gain in risk sharing and the price impact of more shares' coming on the market as a result of the reform, but negatively associated with firm performance. They also show that the risk-sharing effect is stronger for nondiversified, nontradeable shareholders than for diversified nontradeable shareholders, which is consistent with the risk-sharing hypothesis.

2. INSTITUTIONAL FEATURES OF THE MARKET

2.1. The Initial Public Offering (IPO)

The initial public offering mechanism in China is administration-based—that is, a firm's IPO must be approved by the regulatory authority CSRC. To publicly issue stocks, the issuing firm is required first to find a sponsor or underwriter (e.g., a securities firm) to be responsible for the underwriting process, and then to submit its IPO application to CSRC. In deciding whether to approve the application, the CSRC can consult the local government where the firm's headquarter is located. The issuing firm and the sponsor are required to publish the prospectus and the recommendation letter on the CSRC website. After examining the quality of the issuing firm and the qualifications of the sponsor, the CSRC proceeds to decide whether to approve an IPO application. The CSRC can terminate an application if the issuing firm fails to meet the listing requirements, or if the issuing firm or sponsor is found to have false records or made misleading statements in either the prospectus or the recommendation letter.

The CSRC sets a series of requirements on the listing firm's information disclosure, operation, accounting quality, and usage of proceeds raised from stock issuance. In particular, to enter the stock market the issuing firm must clear high hurdles on earnings and cash flows. For example, when the firm submits its IPO application, it must have generated positive earnings in the past three consecutive years, and the accumulated earnings must exceed RMB 30 million; the firm also needs either to have accumulated cash flows of no less than RMB 50 million in the past three years or to have achieved a cumulative operating income of more than RMB 300 million. Moreover, the minimum capital stock has to be no less than RMB 30 million before the IPO.[6]

The CSRC has been contemplating reforming the IPO mechanism, from the current administration-based process to a registration/market-based process. The CSRC issued "Opinions on further promoting the reform of the IPO system" on November 30, 2013, in which it outlines the new, information-disclosure-centered supervision philosophy. This is considered as an important step toward a market-based IPO process, as it emphasizes information transparency as situated at the center of the approval process. Under the new regime, the regulatory authority will no longer judge the quality of the issuing firm as measured by the accounting and financial metrics; instead, the focus will be shifted to ensuring the quality of the issuing firm's information disclosure. Therefore, the proposed new IPO mechanism does not imply loosening listing standards; rather, it places more emphasis on the ex ante review of compliance and ex post enforcement of information disclosure.

Under the new IPO mechanism, especially with the accounting and financial performance hurdles removed, observers would expect more firms from new and growth industries but without current steady cash flows to conduct IPOs. At the same time, investors will have to expend more efforts in evaluating the quality and prospects of IPOs, rather than relying on the regulators' approval as quality assurance. Reforming the IPO process has been proven to be a complex and challenging task. The new IPO mechanism was first proposed in 2013 to the third Plenary Session of the 18th CPC Central Committee. It was also mentioned in the annual government work report in 2015. However, it was not included in the revisions of the Securities Law or mentioned in the annual government work report in either 2016 or 2017.

Following a speech by President Xi Jinping during the opening ceremony of the inaugural China Import Expo in November 2018 in Shanghai, the CSRC announced in early 2019 that the SSE will initiate a pilot program using a "registration system" similar to those used in Hong Kong, the United Kingdom, and the United States, to select and list firms from a set of technology and new industries. This pilot "Science and Technology Innovation Board" (the SSE STAR Market) was formally launched on June 14, 2019, during the annual Lujiazui Forum, and includes strict and swift implementation of the delisting procedure of poor-performing firms. Once this pilot program becomes fully functional, the registration system will be extended to other segments of the A-share market.[7]

2.2. The Delisting Process

The "special treatment" (ST) process was introduced to the Chinese A-share market on April 22, 1998. Firms that experience losses for two consecutive years would receive the ST status. Firms that experience losses for three consecutive years would receive warnings for delisting, and the trading of their stocks would be suspended. A firm can have its ST status removed if it has improved its performance and met a set of requirements: It must show that it has restored its normal operation and achieved both positive earnings and positive shareholder equity in the most recent fiscal year; earnings per share must be no less than RMB 1 yuan, for example. Allen et al. (2019) studied A-share firms for the period of 2000–2014 and found that 527 of 2,872 firms received the "ST" status; many jettison the label ST title after reemerging from restructuring, while 82 were *permanent* ST firms—meaning they could maintain the ST status until the end of 2014.[8]

A stock delisting can be voluntary or involuntary. A voluntary delisting can result from a listed firm's being privatized. When such a firm is acquired or merged into a new company, the firm applies for a voluntary delisting from the exchange. An involuntary delisting usually happens when the firm violates regulations or cannot meet the minimum financial requirements set by the exchange. The CSRC specifies that a firm's listing status would be suspended if the firm experiences negative earnings in three consecutive years; more severely, it would be delisted if the loss continues in the subsequent six months. On March 21, 2016, ST Boyuan was delisted, and it is regarded as the first case of forced delisting owing to repeated violations of regulations as well as fraudulent behavior, including misreporting earnings.

However, firms are rarely delisted in the A-share market. Allen et al. (2019) document that only around 20 stocks (or 1%) were delisted from the market every year over the period 2000–2014, and fewer than 10 were delisted because of poor performance. These percentages are far below those in other large markets. For example, from 2000 to 2014, the average percentages of delisted firms in the United States and Brazil were 33% and 13%, respectively.

To improve the efficiency of the delisting process, CSRC published "Opinions on reforming, improving and strictly implementing delisting of listed firms" on October 14, 2014. The proposed reform focuses on the following:

- Improving information disclosure
- Completing and clarifying the delisting standard

- Strengthening the enforcement of the delisting process, especially for firms that experience earnings losses for extended periods and for so-called zombie firms
- Strengthening the decision-making role and responsibility of stock exchanges in enforcing the delisting process

Conceivably, more firms would be delisted from the exchanges when the delisting mechanisms become better enforced. Firms that cannot meet the IPO standards may seek opportunities for "backdoor listings" through asset injection into or restructuring ST firms, which give rise to related-party transactions and other forms of "rent-seeking" behavior. With more efficient delisting mechanisms, it would be more difficult and costly to speculate on the "shell" value of ST firms or to seek backdoor listings, thus mitigating the widespread rent-seeking problem related to ST firms in the A-share market.

2.3. Trading Mechanisms and Regulations

The Chinese stock market implements in the A-share market the so-called T+1 trading rule, which forbids investors from selling the stock on the same day as they buy it.[9] Instead, they can start selling the stock they purchased on "day T" from day T+1 and onward. The purpose of implementing the T+1 trading rule is to reduce speculative trading and stabilize the stock market. Meanwhile, the "T+0" rule is applied to the invested capital—that is, investors are allowed to use their funds from stock sales for purchase on the same day. Stocks are traded according to the Trading Rules of Shanghai (Shenzhen) Stock Exchange.

Both exchanges set daily price change limits to be 10%, meaning that the maximum price change within one trading day cannot exceed the range −10% to +10% of the closing price in the prior trading day.[10] The trading rules specify the circumstances in which the price change limit does not apply—for instance, on the first trading day of an IPO of a stock or closed-end fund, or on the first trading day when a stock's trading is resumed after trading suspension. The daily price change rule also applies to the B-share market.[11]

The stock exchanges have issued a series of rules and regulations to prohibit insider trading. Two major rules are trading suspension and trading account lockup. Specifically, the stock exchange has the right to suspend stock trading when stock prices or trading behavior are detected to be "abnormal." A typical case that can trigger suspension is when the three-day cumulative price increase or decrease reaches +20% or −20%.[12] A suspension will also be triggered if the turnover (trading volume or market capitalization of traded stock measured as of the day) reaches or exceeds 80%.

The stock exchange also has the right to lock up or set restrictions on a trading account if insider trading is detected for this account. Insider trading is difficult to detect in any exchange around the world. Nevertheless, the Chinese stock exchanges set rules to prohibit certain trading behavior that is likely to be associated with trading on insider information. For instance, a stock account would be locked up if it buys more than 500,000 shares that are on the warning board (such as ST stocks), or if it submits a larger amount of buying or selling orders without a trading purpose. Market manipulation is also prohibited in the Chinese stock market. The stock exchange would lock up or put restrictions on a trading account of a securities firm if the account is found to trade against its publicly recommended security analysis or security trading strategy. Rules also prohibit producing or spreading fraudulent information that can influence security prices or mislead other investors.[13]

2.4. Stocks Listed and Traded on Various Boards

The A-share market is composed of the Main-board Market (主板市场), Second-board Market (二板市场), and Third-board Market (三板市场). The Main-board is also named First-board Market, which is the primary market for stock trading with strict listing requirements as discussed above. Established in 2009, the Second-board Market of the SZSE is also named the Growth Enterprise Market (GEM) in China, similar to Nasdaq in the United States and to the Alternative Investment Market (AIM) in the United Kingdom. In China, the main rationale for establishing this market is to provide additional opportunities for small and growth firms to publicly issue stocks. For example, the Second-board Market sets the minimum equity capital to be RMB 20 million, lower than the minimum of RMB 30 million set by the main board. The Second-board Market also has lower requirements on earnings and cash flows for firms: (1) they must generate positive earnings for two consecutive years, and the cumulative earnings over the two years must be no less than RMB 10 million; (2) they must generate positive earnings in the most recent year, and the earnings in the most recent year must be no less than RMB 5 million; (3) the operating income must be no less than RMB 50 million in the most recent year; and (4) the operating income growth must be no less than 30% in the recent two consecutive years. Firms that meet either set of requirements are considered to be eligible to be listed in the GEM.

There is another tier in the A-share market, the so-called the Small-and-Medium Enterprise (SME) Board. It was launched in 2004 as a subordination to the SZSE. Stocks with market capitalization of traded shares less than RMB 100 million can choose to be listed in the SME Board, which sets lower listing standards than the main board but higher listing standards than the Growth Enterprise Market (GEM) Board. Because most listed firms in the SME Board also meet the listing requirements of the GEM Board, the former board is believed to have accomplished its role in the transition to the latter board. Figure 11.3 shows the number of firms listed on the main board, the GEM Board, and the SME Board for the period 2000–2018.

The Third-board Market was established in 2001 as an alternative trading venue for both firms unqualified to be listed in the main board and those delisted from it. The old Third-board Market was an over-the-counter market dominated by low-quality stocks with little liquidity. In 2006, a new shares transfer system was set up in the Zhongguancun Science Park in Beijing, named the "New Third-board Market (新三板)" or "New over-the-counter (OTC) Market," intended to provide a pilot trading platform for transfer of shares of unlisted private firms. The operating body of the New Third-board Market is the National Equities Exchange and Quotations, the third national securities exchange established after the SSE and SZSE. At the time of writing, firms quoted on the New Third-board Market are not limited to high-tech unlisted firms in the Zhongguancun area, but are extended to all private unlisted firms throughout the country.

By the end of 2019, 8,953 firms were listed on the New Third-board Market, a decline of 2,677 from 2017, when the figure peaked at 11,630. The market experienced exponential growth in 2016. The number of newly listed firms in that year almost doubled that in 2015. The growth rate slowed down in 2017. The main purpose of establishing the New

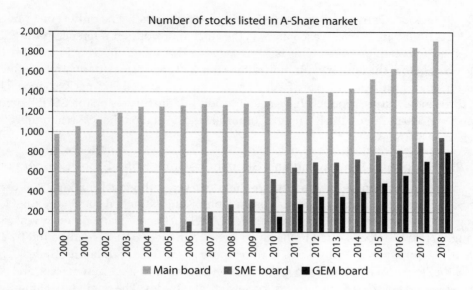

FIGURE 11.3. Number of firms listed in the Main Board, the GEM Board, and the SME Board. *Source:* CSMAR.

Third-board Market is to facilitate trading of shares of high-growth, innovative small firms. Unlike the main board, the New Third-board Market does not set minimum requirements on the firm's operating performance. Any firm that has been in operation for at least two years and meets the requirement of legitimate operation, corporate structure, and appropriate information disclosure can be quoted on the market. Qualified investors are allowed to participate in the New Third-board Market.[14]

The main challenge for the New Third-board Market is its lack of liquidity. Since there is no public sale of stocks (as is the case for an IPO), information disclosure requirements are much lower in the New Third-board. Insufficient information disclosure by the firms can then lead to lack of investor participation and adverse selection of firms. One motive for investors to participate in this market is that they expect that some firms can be "transferred" to the main board, making it easier and less costly to conduct an IPO in the main board directly via transferring from the Third Board. However, such "transferring to the main board" has not materialized yet; in fact, firms are subject to the same set of listing standards regardless of whether they have been quoted in the New Third-board Market.

2.5. Stock Market Products

A variety of products in addition to stocks are traded on the stock exchanges. They include equity funds, warrants, and stock and index options. Both open-end funds and closed-end funds are traded on the exchanges. ETFs dominate the market in terms of trading volume.[15] These are open-end funds whose returns closely track those of the underlying stock indices: The fund assets are usually composed of the same stocks that comprise the underlying index, and their weights also mimic those of the underlying index. ETFs are typically managed by asset management companies. Investors can buy or sell shares of ETFs in the secondary market, and can also subscribe or redeem the shares.

Few stock derivatives are available in the A-share market. The only type of option products traded in the stock exchanges is the stock index option referencing the SSE50 index (the SSE50 ETF option). This is a European option that is delivered on a specified date on or before the option expiration date. Another type of stock derivative product is the stock index futures, which are traded on the China Financial Futures Exchange. Thus far, three index future products have been introduced: the futures on the CSI (Shanghai-Shenzhen) 300 index, on the IC (Index China) 500 index, and on the SSE (Shanghai Stock Exchange) 50 index.

2.6. Shanghai–Hong Kong and Shenzhen–Hong Kong Stock Connects

As an important step to integrate the A-share market with global markets, CSRC and the Securities and Futures Commission in Hong Kong launched the Shanghai–Hong Kong Stock Connect Program on November 17, 2014. This program allows investors in Shanghai to trade stocks listed in the Hong Kong Exchange (HKEX, southbound trades), and allows investors in Hong Kong to trade those in the SSE (northbound trades). Trading of the stocks follows rules and regulations of the *local* exchange and market, and each market uses its own clearing houses for settling the trades. The Shanghai–Hong Kong Connect mainly covers index component stocks with large market caps listed in the SSE and HKEX.[16] Individual investors from mainland China are required to have a minimum of RMB 500,000 in their accounts to qualify for the southbound trades. Since its inception, the total trading volume through the Connect has amounted to RMB 7.8 trillion, 4.3 trillion of which is for SSE-listed stocks while the rest is the trading volume of the Hong Kong stocks.

The Shenzhen–Hong Kong Connect Program was launched on December 5, 2016. Different from the Shanghai–Hong Kong Connect, which covers large-capitalized stocks, the Shenzhen–Hong Kong Connect Program covers smaller stocks. Specifically, this program covers components of the SZSE Constituent Index with market capitalization of no less than RMB 6 billion and components of the SME Price index. Investors who trade through the stock connect programs also enjoy some tax breaks. For example, individual investors in Shanghai who invested in stocks listed in Hong Kong via the Shanghai–Hong Kong Connect were exempted from capital gains tax during the three-year period of November 17, 2014, to November 16, 2017. Both institutional and individual investors in Hong Kong who invested in A-share stocks were exempted from the capital gain tax since November 17, 2014.

Evidence of "regulatory arbitrage" using the connect programs also emerged. In the context of tightened regulations on leveraging, some investors in mainland China have been seeking ways to "lever up" their positions. Certain stockbrokers and private equity funds would raise debt financing in Hong Kong (at a lower cost as compared to that in the mainland market) and then invest in A-share stocks under the two connect programs, with the leverage levels of the positions sometimes exceeding the regulatory maximum set by CSRC.

2.7. Chinese Firms Listed in Hong Kong and Overseas Markets

Hong Kong has a long history of stock trading, dating back to the 19th century. Hong Kong Exchanges and Clearing Limited ("Hong Kong Exchange" for short, or HKEX) is the only institution in Hong Kong that operates the stock market. It was formed in 2000 by merging three companies: the Stock Exchange of Hong Kong Limited, the Hong Kong Future Exchange Limited, and the Hong Kong Securities Clearing Company. Hong Kong SAR Government is the largest shareholder of the HKEX. As of May 2018, 2,201 firms were listed on the HKEX, with a total market capitalization amounting to HK$35 trillion.

Many more products are actively traded in the HKEX than in the A-share market. Besides traditional securities like stocks and bonds, other securities including ETFs, Real Estate Investment Trusts (REITs), and structured products such as derivative warrants and callable bull/bear contracts are also traded. Debt securities are included in the basket of products, too. Derivatives include equity index futures and options, single stock options, foreign exchange futures, interest rate futures, and commodity futures, among others.

Compared with the A-share market, the accounting and financial requirements for listing are lower at the HKEX. For example, to be listed in the Main Board of HKEX, a firm needs to meet a set of profit and market capitalization tests. The profit test specifies that a new applicant has to generate a minimum profit of HK$20 million in the most recent fiscal year, and to have aggregated a minimum profit of HK$30 million in the past two consecutive years.[17] The listing standards set by the Growth Enterprises Market (GEM) Board are even lower. It only requires that firms to be listed must have generated cash flow from operation of at least HK$30 million for the two fiscal years preceding the IPO; there is no further "profit test" to pass through as set in the Main Board listing rule.[18]

To attract even more growth firms from mainland China and elsewhere, in April 2018 HKEX announced its amendments to the main board listing rules. They include allowing: (1) listings of biotech companies that do not meet any of the Main Board financial eligibility tests; and (2) listings of companies with weighted voting right structures (or allowing the use of "dual-class" shares with different voting rights).[19]

The high, performance-based listing hurdles in the A-share market partly explain the rationale of some large Chinese tech firms' choosing to list in external markets: examples include Alibaba's listing in NYSE, Tencent's listing in HK, and Baidu's listing in Nasdaq. The second largest online retailer in China behind Alibaba, JD.com was listed on Nasdaq in May 2014 and raised $1.78 billion in the IPO. According to CSRC requirements, had the company applied for an IPO in the A-share market, it would have had to show profits in each of the three years 2011, 2012, and 2013; a small loss in 2012 actually rendered it impossible for the firm to be listed in the A-share market.

Many Chinese firms seek listing in Hong Kong as well as in other overseas markets to raise funds globally and also to avoid the stringent listing requirements in the A-share market. According to statistics released by the HKEX, as of May 2018 there were 1,076 firms from mainland China listed in Hong Kong: 254 out of those 1,076 firms were "H shares" (SOEs headquartered in mainland China), 164 were "Red Chip" stocks (Chinese SOEs established in Hong Kong), and 658 were mainland private enterprises.[20]

Chinese firms can be listed in overseas market through direct listing or indirect listing. Direct listing refers to an IPO. Chinese firms seeking a direct listing in overseas stock exchanges need to first submit an application to the CSRC for approval. The CSRC then sets a series of requirements that the firm has to meet.[21] Indirect listing often refers to "reverse mergers," which are typically completed through mergers and acquisitions with currently listed firms. These transactions are generally cheaper and quicker to complete as compared to traditional IPOs, but the amount of capital raised is often smaller. For a Chinese firm to be listed in the U.S. market through a reverse merger, it must first register with China's State Administration of Foreign Exchange (SAFE), and then it must arrange to be acquired by a foreign-based entity (typically based in the Cayman Islands or other offshore locales). Once these Chinese firms clear these hurdles and legally enter the U.S. market through reverse mergers, they expose themselves to U.S. listing regulations as well as the scrutiny of institutional investors, including activists and short-sellers.

Since 2000, hundreds of Chinese firms have gone public on the various U.S. stock exchanges, with many doing so through reverse mergers. Given fewer listing and information disclosure requirements associated with reverse mergers, these transactions may eventually lead to adverse selection and governance problems. For example, in recent years a number of Chinese firms have been accused of committing accounting fraud. Despite the negative publicity generated by various public anecdotes, the overall quality of the Chinese reverse mergers as an investment vehicle remains an open empirical question. In this regard, Lee et al. (2015) studied a sample of 146 Chinese firms listed in the United States through reverse mergers and found no evidence that they were more problematic than similar firms trading on the same exchange. In fact, they noted that the Chinese firms outperformed other firms also entering the U.S. market through reverse mergers in the long run, in terms of both stock returns and operating performance.

3. PERFORMANCE OF THE MARKETS AND LISTED FIRMS

3.1. Main Characteristics of the Chinese Stock Market

The Chinese stock market is dominated by individual investors in terms of trading and is characterized by high turnover ratios. According to 2017 statistics shown in table 11.1, SSE and SZSE exhibited turnover ratios of 161.60% and 264.54%, respectively, far exceeding those of the world's other large stock exchanges.

Another feature of the Chinese stock market is its high volatility. Qiao et al. (2018) compare stock return volatilities of A-share and other large stock markets in the world for the period 2000–2017. As shown in table 11.2, the average annual return volatility during this period was approximately 29% for the A-share market, approximately two times that of the U.S. market. For most of the years, the return volatilities in the A-share market were also higher than those in other developed markets like Japan's, and higher than other large emerging markets like India's. Note that stocks listed in the Indian and Brazilian stock exchanges experienced much higher returns in the past decades than the A-share market.[22] Hu et al. (2018) provide an overview of China's capital market, documenting that the rolling-window standard deviations of stock returns were relatively large from 1997 to 1998 and were low from 2001 to 2005. As shown in figure 11.4, return volatility increased again after 2006 and peaked in 2009, followed by a steady decline afterward until the first half of 2015, and then switched to an upward trend since the market turmoil in the second half of 2015.

Table 11.1. Largest Stock Exchanges in the World, 2017

Ranking	Exchange	Market cap ($mil)	Turnover (%)
1	NYSE	22,081,367.01	60.00
2	Nasdaq – U.S.	10,039,335.64	116.79
3	Japan Exchange Group	6,222,834.71	103.94
4	LSE Group	5,611,031.74	67.19
5	Shanghai Stock Exchange	5,084,357.76	161.60
6	Euronext	4,393,016.14	47.96
7	Hong Kong Exchanges and Clearing	4,350,500.69	49.18
8	Shenzhen Stock Exchange	3,617,883.45	264.54
9	TMX Group	2,367,131.58	56.64
10	National Stock Exchange of India	2,351,463.85	51.01
11	BSE Limited	2,331,568.12	7.46
12	Deutsche Börse AG	2,262,233.41	67.25

Source: Allen et al. (2019).

Table 11.2. Return Volatilities of Stocks Listed in Large Markets

	Brazil	China	India	United States
Mean	0.11	0.09	0.14	0.05
StDev	0.36	0.29	0.23	0.15
Skew	−0.11	0.19	−0.22	−0.58
Kurt	3.49	5.22	4.85	4.23

Source: Qiao et al. (2018).

Notes: Numbers in this table are extracted from table 2 of Qiao et al. (2018). Mean and StDev (standardized deviation) values are annualized; skewness (Skew) and kurtosis (Kurt), are estimated from monthly stock market returns for Brazil, China, India, and the United States, January 2000–October 2017.

Bekaert et al. (2017) examine the price-to-earnings (P/E) ratio of stocks listed in the A-share market and in United States, and find that the price earnings ratio has mostly been significantly higher in China than in the United States (see figure 11.5). They explore several factors that may contribute to their cross-sector and time-series variation, including financial openness, financial development, growth prospects, and the investor base. They conclude that all three channels contribute to the valuation differentials, the most important explanatory variables being foreign capital access, retail investors' speculative motives, state ownership, and financial development.

Like other emerging markets, stocks listed in the A-share market also demonstrate high synchronicity. Morck et al. (2000) document that over 80% of stocks in the A-share market often move in the same direction in a given week. The stock price synchronicity is not a result of co-movement in firm fundamentals, they find, but rather is explained by weak property rights protection. When a government's property protection is weak, stock prices are more likely to be affected by political-related reasons or "noise trading," rather than being affected by firm fundamentals. The same authors, Morck et al. (2013),

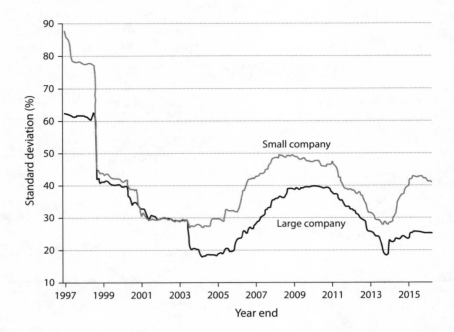

FIGURE 11.4. Return volatilities of firms listed on China's stock market. *Source:* Hu et al. (2018). *Notes:* This figure presents the rolling window volatility for both large and small companies. At the end of each year, from 1997 to 2015, the authors sorted all A-share stocks listed on the main boards of the Shanghai Stock Exchange and the Shenzhen Stock Exchange into 10 equally populated groups or deciles, according to their floating market values. The Large Company Portfolio and the Small Company Portfolio are the first decile and the last decile, respectively.

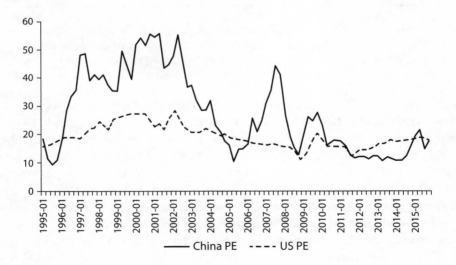

FIGURE 11.5. Time-series of PE ratios for Datastream indices, 1995Q1–2015Q4. *Source:* Bekaert et al. (2017). *Notes:* This figure plots the time-series of earnings yield (EY) for China A shares and U.S. firms in our sample from 1995 to 2015. We calculated firm-level earnings at quarter t as the trailing annualized net income by summing up net income from quarter t-5 to quarter t-1. Negative values of firm earnings are set as zero before being aggregated into sector or market level. Total market value is calculated as the summation of all the stocks' prices multiplied by common shares outstanding at the end of each quarter. EY is total earnings divided by total market value.

updated the data and analyses to 2010, and continued to find higher synchronicity in emerging markets. China had the highest synchronicity measured by the average R-squared in 1995–2010 among the 45 countries worldwide covered in their sample. Brunnermeier et al. (2017) argue that this high co-movement can be driven by investors' speculation of government intervention policies in the Chinese stock market. Gul et al. (2010) provided ownership-related explanations for stock price synchronicity. They documented that synchronicity is a concave function of ownership, and that synchronicity is higher when the largest shareholder is government related.

How have the stocks listed in the A-share market been performing, and how is its performance compared with other markets? Allen et al. (2019) examine the buy-and-hold returns of major stock index and returns of individual stocks listed in each country. Figure 11.6 shows the performance of the Shanghai Stock Exchange (SSE) Composite index and the stock indices of other large countries from 1992 to 2018. For each country, the authors adjust the nominal indices in local currencies with year-end CPIs to real terms. The inflation-adjusted indices are normalized to one at the end of 1992, and cumulated until the end of 2018. The cumulative SSE index return over the period 1992–2018 is substantially lower than that of other emerging countries like Brazil and India, and also lower than that of the United States. The SSE index only outperformed Japan's Nikkei index.[23] As shown in figure 11.6, the SSE index had negative real returns during most of the 1990s. One reason is that inflation during the period was very high, with the CPI reaching 27% in 1994.

Several researchers have explored how the Fama-French factor model applies to the Chinese stock market. Hu et al. (2019) find a significant size effect in the cross-section of returns in the Chinese stock market. A zero-cost small size–minus–big size (SMB) portfolio earns an average premium of 0.61% per month, statistically significant at the 1% level. They also find that a similar zero-cost value portfolio (high B/M–minus–low B/M, HML) does not generate significant premium. Overall, they find that SMB represents the strongest factor in explaining the cross-section of Chinese stock returns, while the market factor and the value factor have no significant explanatory power. Liu et al. (2019) construct size and value factors in China. They exclude the smallest 30% of firms from constructing the size factors, and argue that the smallest group of firms are potential shells in the reverse mergers; therefore, returns of the smallest firms are highly correlated with the average stock return performance of reverse mergers. They construct the value factor based on the earnings-price ratio. Overall, they show that their three-factor model dominates a model formed by replicating the Fama and French (1993) procedure in China.

Chen et al. (2010) examine stock return predictability in China. They find that only five firm-specific variables predict returns in the Chinese market. Tests on U.S. stock returns show that having more predictors can explain cross-sectional stock return variation. Less heterogeneously distributed return distribution in China and less informative stock prices may explain their finding. The reaction of stock prices in the Chinese stock market is found to be speedier after certain events in recent years. Carpenter et al. (2018) investigate the efficiency of the Chinese stock market in reacting to reforms and regulation changes. They determine that stock prices in China have become as informative about future firm profits as they were in the United States since 2000s. They document a positive correlation between stock price informativeness and corporate investment

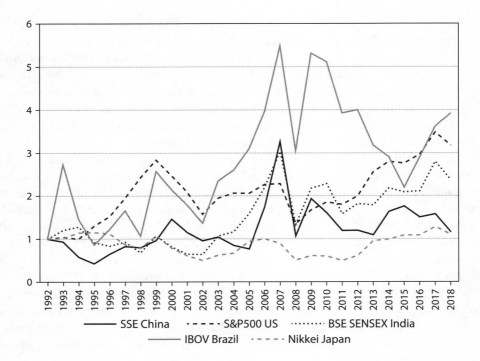

FIGURE 11.6. Buy-and-hold returns of stock indices in large stock markets. *Source:* Allen et al.
(2019). *Notes:* The figure plots the cumulative returns of the stock indices in large countries from
1992 to 2018. Annual index return data is collected from Bloomberg. The nominal returns are in
local currencies and adjusted for local inflation, measured by the year-end CPI. The SSE index
was launched on July 15, 1991. The constituents are all stocks listed on the Shanghai Stock Exchange, including A shares and B shares. The constituents are weighted by the total market
value of all outstanding shares. The S&P 500 index is calculated based on the 500 large companies that have common stocks listed in NYSE or NASDAQ. The components are weighted by
the market value of their floating shares (shares that are readily available for trading). SENSEX
is a free-float market-weighted stock market index of the 30 largest and most actively traded
stocks listed on the Bombay Stock Exchange. IBOV (IBOVESPA) is a stock market index of
about 60 stocks that are traded on B3 (Brasil Bolsa Balcão S.A. in full), a major stock exchange
located in São Paulo, Brazil. The Nikkei Index was founded in 1950 and is composed of 225 blue-
chip companies traded on the Tokyo Stock Exchange. It is a price-weighted index of which the
constituent stocks are ranked by share price rather than by market capitalization.

efficiency. In addition, they find evidence that the Chinese stock market offers global
investors high average monthly returns and low correlation with other global stock
markets. Although it is possible to have "efficient and rational" reactions toward firm
news in the cross-section, the levels of pricing and valuation could still be wrong. As
shown by Allen et al. (2019), the A-share market has underperformed other large markets since its inception, especially during the post-2000 period.

Overall, extant studies find that the performance of stocks listed in mainland China's
stock market has been disappointing. Returns of stocks listed in the A-share market underperform not only stocks listed in large developed markets (United States and Japan)

and emerging markets (India and Brazil), but even underperform other Chinese firms listed in external markets (Hong Kong and United States, among others).

3.2. Performance of A-Share Listed Firms

Allen et al. (2019) explore reasons for the underperformance of the Chinese stock market. One reason for the poor performance of China's A-share market is that corporate investment yields low returns. They measure investment returns by net cash flows, or EBITDA–Change in Working Capital–Income Taxes–Capital Expenditure. They compare the scale of investment and net cash flows of firms listed in China with those listed externally and listed firms from other large countries. As figure 11.7 shows, firms listed in the A-share market have by far the largest scale in investment (capital expenditure scaled by total assets) among the group of large countries. Domestic listed firms also consistently invest more than their counterparts listed externally. Allen et al. (2019) then compare the value-weighted average (with year-end book assets as the weight) net cash flows generated by Chinese firms with that generated by firms listed in other countries. A-share firms have lower net cash flows than those of listed firms from India and Brazil in most of the years. Starting in 2007, Chinese firms actually have the lowest level of net cash flows among the five large countries, and even lower than that of Chinese firms listed externally. The results suggest that A-share listed firms have high investment level but low investment efficiency.[24]

Overall, Allen et al. (2019) find that A-share listed firms underperform three groups of firms in terms of stock return performance, investment efficiency and net cash flows: (1) firms listed in other large countries such as the United States, India, Brazil, and Japan; (2) Chinese firms listed in external markets such as Hong Kong and the United States; and (3) Chinese firms that stay private (never publicly listed in the A-share market). These results indicate that domestically listed firms are *not* necessarily the best-performing ones in their respective industry.

Why, then, are good firms not "selected" to be listed in the A-share market? One strand of the literature argues that the poor performance of Chinese listed firms is related to financial packaging incentives in the pre-IPO period. Aharony et al. (2000) and Allen et al. (2019), among others, document that Chinese firms have high profitability in the years leading to an IPO. However, their profitable measures suddenly drop by about half in the year of the IPO. This observation could be related to the high listing standards in the A-share market, which requires that firms show positive earnings for consecutive years before listing. To meet the standards, firms seeking an IPO may attempt to increase their credit sales to achieve high earnings at the expense of sacrificing long-term growth opportunities.

An extensive strand of the literature finds that tunneling presents a serious problem in many emerging markets, including China. Firms listed in the Chinese stock market are found to be involved in related-party transactions, which also results in the low cash flows of A-share listed firms. Jiang et al. (2010), using data for firms listed in Shanghai and Shenzhen stock exchanges for the period 1996–2006, found that Chinese listed companies transfer funds out of the firm by issuing long-term intercorporate loans, which loans are typically made to parties related to the controlling shareholder. Cheung et al. (2006) examined a sample of connected transactions between Hong Kong listed firms and their controlling shareholders. They documented that firms announcing connected transac-

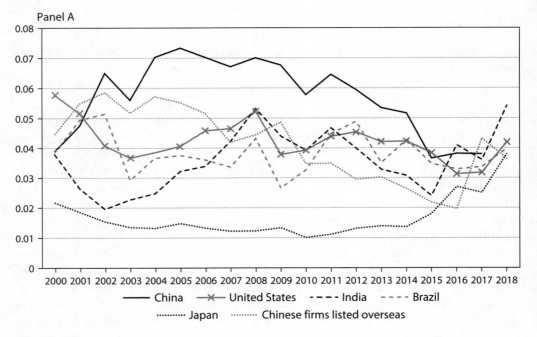

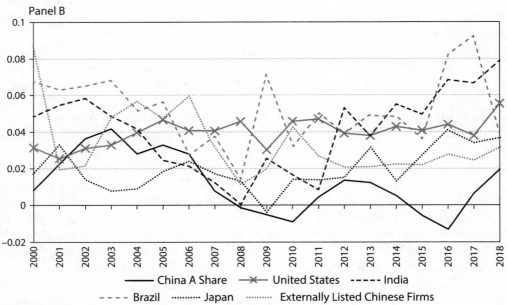

FIGURE 11.7. Investment of firms listed in China and other large countries: 2000–2018. *Source:* Allen et al. (2019). *Notes:* This figure plots the average investment and net cash flows of A-share listed firms, firms listed in other large countries, and externally listed Chinese firms by year. Panel A plots the average investment of listed firms. Investment is measured by capital expenditure in year t scaled by the book assets in year t. Panel B plots the average net cash flows of listed firms. Net Cash Flow is calculated as (EBITDA –Change in Working Capital –Income Taxes –Capital Expenditure)/Total Assets. Both the investment and cash flow measures are (weighted) averaged across firms with the year-end total assets as the weight. The sample is restricted to firms that have nonmissing data on EBITDA, capital expenditure, working capital, income taxes, and book assets. The number of unique firms that enter the plot for China, United States, India, Brazil, Japan, and Chinese firms listed externally is 3695, 10529, 3708, 321, 4183, and 1487, respectively.

FIGURE 11.8. Shanghai Stock Exchange Index: The 2007–2008 market rise and collapse, and the 2015 market crash. *Source:* CSMAR. *Note:* This figure plots the time-series of the Shanghai Stock Exchange index by month. Numbers used for the plot are raw numbers of the index, not adjusted for inflation.

tions earn significant negative excess returns. This study provides details about ways through which expropriation of minority shareholders takes place in firms with concentrated ownership. Allen et al. (2019) examine poor corporate governance in the form of tunneling by firms' controlling shareholders, which is part of the explanation for low levels of net cash flows of Chinese A-share firms. They follow the literature and measure tunneling activities by the direction and amount of related-party transactions. They find that more outflows of funds and assets through related-party transactions are associated with lower stock returns, operating cash flows, and net cash flows in the next period.

To summarize, results from this subsection suggest that low investment efficiency together with weak corporate governance in the form of tunneling by controlling shareholders can explain why firms in the Chinese A-share market have lower net cash flows than firms listed in other large countries as well as Chinese firms listed externally.

4. CRISES AND FURTHER REFORMS

This section discusses two market crashes in the A-share market: the 2007–2008 market rise and collapse, and the 2015 market bubble and crash. These two are similar in that a quick price run-up occurred (even doubled or tripled within one year) before the collapse, and the market index reached its highest level since market inception in 1990. On May 30, 2007, and after, the Shanghai Stock Exchange (SSE) index dropped over 20% within one week. From mid-2007 to 2008, the SSE index rose from 3,821 to over 6,124 as of October 16, 2007, then clipped off and bottomed at 1,664 in 2008. The other market crash in the A-share market occurred in June 2015. From mid-June to early July of that year, the SSE index plunged by 32% (Huang et al. 2016). Figure 11.8 plots the monthly SSE index from the end of 1992 to the end of 2018, with the two market crashes in 2007–2008 and 2015 marked by the vertical lines.

4.1. The 2007–2008 Market Rise and Crash

4.1.1. Timeline

- 5/29/2007, midnight: The Ministry of Finance announced that the stamp duty will be raised from 0.1% to 0.3%.
- 5/30/2007: the SSE Index dropped by 281.83 points, or 6.5%; the SZSE Index dropped by 829.45, or 6.2%. The B-share index in both the Shanghai and Shenzhen stock exchanges dropped by over 9%. Prices of more than 2,000 stocks declined within the day. Some 500 stocks saw their price drop hit the daily price change limit (10%).[25] The May 30 market collapse was largely interpreted by the public as a negative market reaction to the stamp tax increase on stock trading. Cai et al. (2018) find that stamp tax increases (on stock trading) caused speculative frenzy to migrate from the stock market to the warrant market.
- 5/31/2007: The A-share stock index slightly rebounded. However, the number of stocks that saw a price increase far exceeded the number of stocks that saw a decrease: 237 stocks' prices went up; 612 stocks' price went down, of which 170 of them saw their price drop hit the daily price change limit.
- 6/1/2007: The majority of A-share stocks see a price drop. The A-share index dropped significantly before closing. The SSE Composite Index declined by 2.65%. The Shenzhen Component Index declined by 3.95%. More than 600 stocks' price drop hit the limit.
- 6/4/2007: On "Black Monday," the SSE Composite Index declined by 8.26%. More than 700 stocks' price drop hit the limit. The three major securities newspapers commented, dryly, that increasing the stamp tax was not intended to suppress the stock market.

4.1.2. Valuation Deviating from Economic and Corporate Fundamentals

An important feature of the Chinese stock market is that it remains largely isolated from the global markets. Shan et al. (2018) document that stock returns in the A-share market typically have low correlations with those of the global markets. They find that frequent government interventions, disconnection with the real economy, and low foreign ownership can explain the potential diversification benefits of China's stock market for international investors.

One widely accepted reason for China's stock market crash in 2007 is that stock prices deviated too much from fundamentals, helping to precipitate the crash. Indeed, the market index increased by 80% from the beginning of 2007 to April 2007. Loose monetary policy in the period 2005–2007 provided sufficient liquidity to the market and resulted in credit expansion, allowing firms to invest more. Meanwhile, the low interest rate environment shifted money flow from the debt market to the stock market. From a behavioral perspective, high investor sentiment after the split-share reform completion also likely contributed to the rapid rise of stock prices in the first half of 2007. The average P/E of A-share stocks measured at the end of 2007 was 35, or roughly double that of the

U.S. market. The average P/E figure would have been even higher if the peak prices on May 29, 2017, were used.

After the 2007 stock market crash, the Chinese government was strongly criticized for its intervention of the market. Its decision to raise the stamp tax was believed to be unwise (from an ex post point of view). Yet stock prices' deviating from the fundamentals was probably the main reason for the crash; the bubble would ultimately have burst anyway, when some negative news hit the market.

The dramatic boom in the Chinese stock market between 2005 to 2007 pushed most of the "put" warrants written on the stocks deep out of the money. Xiong and Yu (2011) employ the warrant market setting to examine a set of bubble theories. Their findings support bubble theory predictions on short-sale constraints and the heterogeneous beliefs on the part of investors. For example, they confirmed the prediction that the size of a price bubble is positively related to trading volume and return volatility. The more investors disagree about future price movement, the more intensively they trade with each other, and the more they are willing to pay for the resale option. When asset return is more volatile, investors also tend to disagree more, which in turn makes the bubble larger.

4.2. The 2015 Market Bubble and Crash

During this more-recent episode, the Chinese stock market dropped by 38% from mid-June to mid-August, 2015. The following section studies the evolution of the market and reasons for that crash.

4.2.1. Timeline (June 15–August 26, 2015)
First Round of Crash

During the week of June 15–19, the SSE Composite Index, the Shenzhen Component Index, and the GEM Board Index dropped by 13.32%, 13.11%, and 14.99%, respectively. June 26 was a "Black Friday," during which more than 2,000 stocks' price drop hit the daily price change limit. On June 27, China's central bank, the People's Bank of China (PBC) announced a 0.25% decrease in the base interest rate. On June 29, around 1,500 stocks' price drop hit the limit, while the SSE Index recovered by 5% to 4,200 points the very next day. On July 2, the CSRC announced its plan to inspect market manipulation. From June 15 to July 3, the SSE Index, the Shenzhen Component Index, and the GEM Board Index dropped by 28.64%, 32.34%, and 33.19%, respectively.

On July 4, the State Council called together the PBC, CSRC, China Banking Regulatory Commission (CBRC), China Insurance Regulatory Commission (CIRC), Ministry of Finance, and officials of large SOEs to discuss possible ways to save the stock market. On July 5, CSRC announced that the PBC would take a variety of measures to provide liquidity to China Securities and Financial Ltd. (CSF)—the key player in the rescue. On July 6, the SSE Composite Index rose by 2.4%, while the CIC 500 Index dropped by 9%. More than 1,000 stocks experienced a price run-up at opening but a quick reverse afterward, and the price drop finally hit the limit at closing. On July 7, the majority of the stocks listed on the GEM Board dropped by 10%, with over 50% of the stocks suspending trading. The next day, the SSE Index dropped by 5.9%, and 1,300 stocks' drop hit the limit while more than 1,400 stocks went into trading suspension. The A-share market then recovered over the coming days. On July 9, the SSE Index recovered by 5.76%, closing at 3,700; more than 1,000 A-share stocks' price increases hit the price limit (up 10%). On July 10, the SSE Index rose by 4.54%, and more than 1,300 stocks' price increase hit the price limit.

Second Round of Crash

During August 18–26, the SSE Composite Index dropped by 25% to below 3,000 points. Thus far, the SSE Composite Index had shed 38% of its value from June 12 to August 24. Yet another "Black Monday" came on August 24, when the SSE Composite Index dropped by 8%. That same day, global stock markets also went down, and commodity prices and most Asian currencies hit new lows, occasioned by the stock market plunges and other factors. The market experienced another day of sharp losses on the SSE Composite Index, which dropped by 7.6% on August 25. The second round of rescue started on August 26 and ended on September 25. The SSE Index finally stabilized at around 3,000 points.

4.2.2. Government Interventions and the "National Team" in 2015

Starting in late June of 2015, the Chinese government took a series of actions to rescue its stock market. What follows is a summary of the interventions.[26]

Starting on June 27, the People's Bank of China (PBC), the central bank, cut interest rates and trimmed banks' required reserve ratios, which was widely interpreted mainly as a step to support the slumping stock market. In early July, after the market closed, the Shanghai and Shenzhen stock exchanges announced plans to lower securities transaction fees by 30% percent from August. The CSRC announced relaxation of rules on margin trading, thus lowering the threshold for individual investors to trade on margins and also expanding brokerages' funding channels. The CSRC also announced it would set up a team to look into illegal manipulation and investigate cases if needed. On July 4, China Financial Futures Exchange (CFFEX) suspended 19 accounts from short-selling for one month.

The most notable intervention that occurred was the establishment of a so-called national team that entered the stock market strictly to buy shares. On July 4, China's top 21 securities brokerages pledged to invest at least RMB 120 billion (US $19 billion) collectively to help stabilize the market.[27] They also promised not to sell their own stocks when the SSE Composite Index dipped below 4,500 points. On very next day, the state-owned investment company China Central Huijin Investment Ltd (CCH) said it had recently purchased ETFs to support the market and would continue to do so. The growing number of state agents and brokerages as well as other entities drawn into the market rescue effort were soon dubbed "the national team." The CSRC announced that the PBC would inject liquidity directly to the state-backed margin finance company to stabilize the tumbling stock market. On July 8, Chinese regulators came out with another series of support statements and measures, in particular raising margin requirements for short positions taken against the small-cap CSI500 Index, and making it easier for insurers to buy blue chips. As a result of the massive state-sponsored rescue effort, the China "national team" owned a total of 6% of the A-share stock market. CSF was the main conduit for the injection of government funds. It owned 742 different stocks at the end of September, up from only 2 stocks at the end of June.[28]

Meanwhile, the Chinese regulatory authorities prohibited large shareholders from selling their shares. On July 8, 2015, the regulators imposed a lockup on shareholders' owning 5% or more of their companies, prohibiting them from selling for six months. Fear of the locked-up shares' perhaps flooding the market the following January 2016 (when the initial lockup period would expire), among other factors, in fact triggered another steep decline in stock prices that January. The Chinese government then extended the lockup.[29]

As part of its rescue plan, Chinese regulators then looked into illegal trading activities. On July 31, regulators stated that it had frozen 24 stock trading accounts for suspected trading irregularities. Meanwhile, China had asked financial institutions in Singapore and Hong Kong for stock trading records, thereby widening its pursuit of investors shorting Chinese stocks.

During the second round of the market crash in August, China announced on August 23 that it would allow pension funds managed by local governments to invest in the stock market for the first time. In that month, the PBC cuts interest rates and the required reserve ratios (for banks) for the second time in two months, ratcheting up support for the stumbling economy as well as the plunging stock market. Regulators and police started cracking down on suspected violators of stock dealing rules and fabricators of false trading information, the latest in a slew of steps meant to clean up the market amid wild price gyrations.

4.2.3. The Circuit Breaker

On December 4, 2015, the SSE and the SZSE, along with China Financial Futures Exchange, launched a circuit breaker, which restricts a stock's order price to be within a given range whenever the stock price drop hits a prespecified limit. That circuit breaker set two limits, at 5% and 7%, on the CSI300 index. The circuit breaker became effective on January 1, 2016. Chen et al. (2018) document the timeline of the circuit breaker's being triggered in the A-share market. On January 4, the first trading day after the circuit breaker was triggered, both thresholds were reached, and it took only 7 minutes from the reopening of the markets following the 15-minute halt for the index to reach the 7% threshold. Both circuit breakers were triggered again on January 7, when the entire trading session lasted for only 30 minutes.

An initial purpose of designing the circuit breaker is to stabilize stock prices and protect small investors. However, the January 2016 mechanism did not work as expected and instead exacerbated the losses and market uncertainty.[30] Investors were found to be exploiting this mechanism by rushing to sell before the index went down enough to trigger the trading halt. Realizing the problems in the circuit breaker, the CSRC announced it would suspend the mechanism on January 7, only four days after initiating it.[31]

According to Chen et al. (2018), a U.S. circuit breaker, whose threshold was based on the DJIA (Dow Jones Industrial Average) Index, was triggered only once—on October 27, 1997. At 2:36 P.M. that day, a 350-point (4.54%) decline in the DJIA led to a 30-minute trading halt on stocks, equity options, and index futures. After trading resumed 30 minutes later, prices fell rapidly again and led to an early market closure for that day. The market stabilized the very next day.

Analysts have explored how circuit breakers affect a market, and, more importantly, how their success or failure can be assessed. Greenwood and Stein (1991) developed theoretical models to illustrate how imperfections in transactional mechanism can lead to a market crash. They argued that, when properly designed and implemented, circuit breakers may help to overcome informational problems and improve the market's ability to absorb large volume shocks. Lauterbach and Ben-Zion (1993) studied the behavior of a small stock market that encountered circuit breakers during the October 1987 crash. They found that circuit breakers reduced both the next-day opening order imbalance and the initial price loss; however, the breakers had no effect on the long-run response. Subrahmanyam (1994) showed that the announcement of an impending circuit breaker may affect investors' decisions before the triggering of the breaker and thus cause a "magnet effect," in which the probability of hitting the trigger price increases as the stock price approaches it.

On a related note, other early studies, including Kim and Rhee (1997), studied the impact of price limits on the stock market. Price limit supporters advocate that a price limit reduces stock price volatilities, while price limit critics claim that the limits cause higher volatility levels. Kim and Rhee examined the Tokyo Stock Exchange price limit system and concluded that the overall effects of price limits can be negative. Kim and Park (2010) derived a model to show that price limits may in fact deter arbitrage activities, and provided empirical evidence consistent with this hypothesis. Chen et al. (2019) use account-level data from the SZSE to show that daily price limits lead to destabilizing market behavior.

Chen et al. (2018) develop an intertemporal equilibrium model to study how the introduction of a downside circuit breaker affects investors' trading behavior and the equilibrium price dynamics overall. They find that a downside breaker tends to lower the stock price and increase its volatility. Owing to this increased volatility, the circuit breaker's own presence actually raises the likelihood of reaching its triggering price and thus increases the probability of hitting that triggering price as the stock price approaches it.

4.2.4. What Drove the 2015 Stock Market Crash?

Academic researchers and practitioners alike have for years explored various reasons that might explain China's stock market crash of 2015. Margin trading and leverage-induced fire sale are found to be one dominant drive. Bian et al. (2017) use account-level data that covers margin investors' borrowing and trading activities. They find that margin investors heavily sell their holdings when their account-level leverage approaches their maximum leverage limits. Their proprietary data covers two types of margin accounts: brokerage-financed and shadow-financed margin accounts. While the brokerage-financed margin system allows retail investors to obtain credit from his or her own brokerage firm (which of course is tightly regulated), the shadow-financed margin system falls in a regulatory gray area. Both margin trading systems grew rapidly in popularity in early 2015. The average leverages measured as asset/equity of brokerage/shadow-financed margin accounts were 6.62 and 1.43, respectively. They find that investors are much more likely to sell assets if the proximity to the Pingcang Line (or forced sale level) is close and when leverage is also high, and they concluded that the relation is stronger when the market is down rather than up. They also find that the government announcement aimed at curbing excessive leverage may have intensified leverage-induced selling in the short run, triggering marketwide crashes.

Overall, Bian et al. (2017) conclude that unregulated and highly leveraged shadow-financed brokerage accounts contribute more to the market crash, relative to regulated brokerage accounts.

Some market analysts have debated whether index future trading even contributed to the 2015 market crash. Statistics show that the trading volume of index futures amounted to RMB 37 trillion during January–August 2015, far exceeding the trading volume of index futures after the "national team" stepped in to rescue the market that July. The trading volume of index futures during August–December 2015 was estimated to be merely RMB 370 billion.

However, the positive correlation between index future trading and stock price drop does not imply any causality. Many researchers believe that causality is actually reversed—that is, it was not that short-selling index futures caused the stock price declines, but that the large trading volume in the index futures signaled a large fluctuation in the stock market. One argument supporting this view is that the index futures' trading volume is not large enough to have a material impact on the stock market index. Moreover, in July 2015, the China Financial Futures Exchange proclaimed that most institutional investors, including security brokerages, fund companies, insurance companies, trust companies, QFIIs, and RQFIIs, used index futures mainly for hedging purposes. The long and short positions almost canceled each other out in the index futures market, it was said, and as a result the so-called naked position does not actually exist in the Chinese index futures market.

4.3. Remaining Issues and Future Reforms

4.3.1. The Effectiveness of Government Intervention

Based on the above discussion, it can be seen that the Chinese government intervened in its stock market in different ways from that in the United States. Veronesi and Zingales (2010) analyzed the costs and benefits of the U.S. government's intervention (the so-called Paulson's Plan, after the Secretary of the Treasury) during the nation's 2008 financial crisis. As noted by Huang et al. (2016), the U.S. government provided a $125 billion preferred equity infusion to the country's nine largest commercial banks, along with a three-year government guarantee on new unsecured bank debt issues; this contrasts with how the Chinese government directly purchased shares of A-share listed firms during its 2015 market crash.

Starting on July 6, 2015, the so-called national team consisting of the CSF and CCH directly purchased stocks of more than 1,000 firms. Huang et al. (2016) estimate the economic benefits and costs of the government's purchases of stocks from July 1 to September 30, 2015. According to their analysis, after subtracting the estimated costs to taxpayers, those government purchases increased the value of the rescued firms to a range as high as RMB 2.5 to 3.4 trillion, for a net benefit of about 4% to 6% of Chinese GDP. They find the value creation comes from three major sources. First, the government purchase increased the demand for shares and thereby raised investors' confidence. Second, the government purchase reduced default probabilities of the rescued firms and thus increased their debt value. Third, the government purchase improved rescued firms' liquidity.

Both pros and cons can be stated with regard to government intervention in the market. Pastor and Veronesi (2012) note that a government tends to change its policy after performance downturns in the private sector. Stock prices fall at the announcement of policy changes, on average. They posit that policy changes increase volatility, risk premia, and correlations among stocks. Brunnermeier et al. (2017) develop a conceptual framework to analyze government intervention through direct trading against "noise" traders in asset markets. They find that the political process itself introduces unintended noise into the market and becomes an additional asset pricing factor. The new pricing factor can attract speculation by investors, who may choose to acquire private information about the government's noise and, as a result, be distracted from acquiring information about fundamentals. In doing so, investors' speculation about that noise can worsen the information efficiency of the asset price. This speculation reinforces the impact of noise in the government's policy on asset prices. Their model derives a "government-centric" equilibrium in which investors tend to trade alongside the government against the noise traders. The implications of their model capture important observations about China's financial markets, including that speculations about government policies play a central role in driving market dynamics and that market participants tend to pay greater attention to government policies than to economic fundamentals.

How effective was the government intervention in the A-share market during the 2015 market crash? Ghysels and Liu (2017) focus on the downside risks, using the 1% and 5% conditional percentile of the equity index returns. They conclude that the government share purchase actions in 2015 were effective at alleviating downside risks in the A-share market. As discussed above, Huang et al. (2016) conclude that the national team rescue has both benefits and costs. On one hand, they find that government intervention during the market crash increased the rescued firms' value. On the other hand, the long-run costs of government intervention are of concern. The massive stock purchases by the government prevented market discovery of stock prices, leading to price deviation from fundamentals. Its trial-and-error approach may have created more uncertainty in the market, which in turn may exacerbate market volatility. The rescue may also have created a moral hazard problem on the side of the firms.

4.3.2. Shadow Margin Lending and Margin Trading

The 2015 stock market crash featured a substantial amount of margin lending and margin trading. It is widely believed that excessive leverage taken by unregulated shadow-financed margin accounts and the subsequent fire sales by the deleveraging process were the main driving forces of the Chinese stock market's collapse. As discussed earlier, Bian et al. (2017) provide empirical evidence supporting this notion.

Bian et al. (2019) emphasized that margin trading can make investors vulnerable to temporary fluctuations in security value and funding conditions, since a levered investor may be forced to liquidate her positions if her portfolio value falls below some predetermined level. Employing the account-level trading data, Bian et al. examine the effect of margin-induced trading on stock prices during the 2015 market turmoil in the A-share market. They find that individual margin traders have a strong tendency to scale down their holdings after experiencing negative portfolio shocks. In market downturns, returns of stocks help forecast future returns of stocks that share common margin-investor ownership with the stocks in question, and as a result they help forecast the latter's future returns. They conclude that idiosyncratic, adverse shocks to individual stocks can be amplified and transmitted to other securities through a deleveraging channel.

4.3.3. Bank Loans Using Stocks as Collateral

One important product that connects the Chinese stock market and Chinese banks is stock pledge loans, as when shareholders of listed firms use stocks as collateral to obtain bank loans. Almost all listed firms in the A-share market have this type of loans. Stock pledge loans may amplify downward pressure on the stock market and spread the risks to the banking sector in the following way: When stock prices fall below the "Ping Cang Xian" (price at which the bank forces the borrower to sell the stock), stocks will undergo forced sales in the market, leading to a further drop in stock prices of the firm and other firms as well. A further drop in stock prices will result in even more forced sales, leading to a downward spiral. Forced stock sales also result in more losses by banks, and to widespread forced sales that would occur when there is a marketwide downturn, in which case the total amount of NPLs in the banking sector will also rise.

Li et al. (2019) provide empirical evidence for these hypotheses. At the end of 2016, they find that the largest shareholder of a listed firm pledges a greater fraction of his stock holdings in exchange for credit when the firm is in a growth industry, more financially constrained, less profitable, and not majority owned by the government. The 2017 performance of firms with high levels of stock-pledged loans was not significantly different from those with low levels of such loans. During the bear market of 2018, however, highly pledged firms faced greater stock crash risk, owing in part to "forced sales" of pledged stock, had worse stock returns and a higher likelihood of default, and turned in a worse operating performance. A "contagion" effect can also result from the selling of one high-pledged stock to another.

Using a policy shock in 2013 that allowed securities companies to provide stock-pledged loans to listed firms, Li et al. (2019) find that obtaining these loans relaxed firms' financial constraints and improved firm performance during 2013–2014. However, this lending channel imposes substantial risk on the firms during stock market downturns, while concentrated selling of pledged stock can impose a systemic risk on the market itself.

Similar episodes occurred in the United States during the 2008–2009 financial crisis, and also in Japan after its real estate bubble burst. In both cases the market value of assets tied to the real estate sectors plunged, leading to forced sales of assets by financial institutions holding large amounts of "toxic" assets (in the United States in 2009) or even pushing some firms into financial distress because of the loss of collateral value (in Japan, when firms used real estate assets as collateral). One key is how to price (collateral) assets during times of market failure. Abandoning "mark-to-market" pricing (when prices reflect "fire-sale" prices) and using pricing models based on historic and current information are viable solutions.

5. CONCLUSION

The Chinese stock market has been developing rapidly since the establishment of the Shanghai and Shenzhen stock exchanges in 1990. Market size, in terms of total market capitalization, was the third largest in the world as of October 2018. With the inclusion of the Hong Kong Exchange, in which many Chinese firms are listed, the country's stock market is the second largest, behind only the U.S. equity markets. This chapter's review of the history of that market, and the extensive research on it, reveals a number of problems and strongly indicates that further reforms are needed. It seems fair to conclude that further development of the stock market will be one of the key tasks of the Chinese financial system over the next decade.

The IPO process first needs to be reformed and transitioned from an administration process to a registration and market-based process. The new process will encourage the listing of a greater number of privately owned firms in growth industries. The delisting process needs to be strengthened to ensure an effective exit mechanism for poor-performing firms. More products, especially derivatives (including options on individual stocks), need to be introduced in the market. These products will provide additional tools to help sophisticated institutional investors hedge their risks and improve their long-term performance. This, in turn, will help develop the delegated-asset-management industry in which finance professionals manage a greater fraction of households' capital and assets.

All the available research indicates that the role of government in the stock market should be primarily as an effective regulator and enforcer of the law. Government needs to be crystal clear about its goals in the market and willing to interfere only when market forces fail. Finally, corporate governance needs to be further strengthened, because tunneling by controlling shareholders remains a serious threat to both the performance of listed firms and returns to minority shareholders. Further opening up the A-share market to global investors, especially long-term institutional investors, will help grow the market.

NOTES

The authors thank Marlene Amstad, Wei Xiong, and participants in the conference on China's financial system at Chinese University of Hong Kong, Shenzhen for their helpful comments.

1. The Chinese A-share market dropped more than 20% in 2018, given all the adverse news about the economy and problems with the listed firms. As of October 10 of that year, the total market cap of the A-share market (stocks listed on SSE and SZSE) had fallen below that of the Japanese stock market and ranked third in the world. With the addition of stocks from the Hong Kong Exchange, however, that would still place the greater China stock market second in the world.
2. For more details, see http://www.sse.com.cn/market/stockdata/overview/monthly/.
3. The stock prices in the A-share and B-share markets for the same firm are not identical. Mei et al. (2009) found that the A-B share premium is positively related to A-share turnover, suggesting that speculative motives on the part of A-share investors generated a speculative component in A-share price. This finding is consistent with theories that analyzed the effects of short-sale constraints and also with heterogeneous beliefs about stock prices and trading volumes.
4. For more details, see http://data.stats.gov.cn/easyquery.htm?cn=C01.
5. The Shanghai–London Stock Connect was launched in June 2019, intended to follow different trading mechanisms as compared to both the Shanghai–Hong Kong and the Shenzhen–Hong Kong connect.
6. For more details, see CSRC, "Administrative Measures for Initial Public Offering and Listing." http://www.csrc.gov.cn/pub/newsite/flb/flfg/bmgz/fxl/201012/t20101231_189708.html.
7. For more details about the relevant regulations and rules of the SSE STAR Market, go to http://www.csrc.gov.cn/pub/zjhpublic/zjh/201901/P020190130725847011706.pdf.
8. To shed the ST title, a firm must meet at least three accounting requirements: (1) positive earnings for the current fiscal year; (2) positive net asset per share; and (3) positive earnings per share. Other "soft" requirements include that a firm have no accounting errors or fraud statements and no negative views by auditors on the financial report, and so on. If a ST firm did not meet these requirements set by CSRC, it would retain its ST status.
9. See Item 106 of the Securities Laws: The T+1 trading rule became effective on January 1, 1995, for the A-share market, and in December 2001 for the B-share market.

10. This set of Trading Rules of SSE became effective on July 1, 2006; the latest set of Trading Rules of SZSE became effective on November 30, 2001.

11. To be precise, the B-share market is subject to the T+0 and T+3 rules—that is, B share investors are allowed to sell the stocks they buy on the same day (T+0), but delivery of stocks and funds is completed on the fourth day after the trading day (T+3).

12. For ST firms, a trading suspension will be triggered if a three-day cumulative price increase or decrease reaches +15% or –15%, according to the trading rule launched by the SSE in 2006 (http://biz.sse.com.cn/ps/zhs/fwzc/flfgk_szsywgz.shtml). The trading rule of SSE specifies other circumstances for abnormal price movement.

13. For more details, see http://www.sse.com.cn/lawandrules/sserules/trading/universal/c/c_20150906_3976423.shtml.

14. Individual investors are allowed to participate in the New Third-board Market but need to meet a set of requirements, including financial assets (including bank deposits, stocks, fund shares, wealth management products, insurance products, futures, and other derivatives) under the investor's name averaged in the previous 10 days must total at least 5 million RMB yuan; the investor must have at least two years' experience in trading stocks, funds, or futures.

15. See, for example, http://www.sse.com.cn/market/funddata/overview/yearly/.

16. The covered stocks in the A-share market include the component stocks of the SSE180 index, SSE380 index, and stocks cross listed in both the Shanghai and Hong Kong markets ("A+H stock"). The covered stocks in the Hong Kong market include component stocks of the Hang Seng Composite Large Stock Index and the Hang Seng Composite Medium Stock Index, plus stocks cross listed in the Shanghai and Hong Kong markets.

17. For more details, see "Disclaimer for the Consolidated Main Board Listing Rules." http://en-rules.hkex.com.hk/net_file_store/new_rulebooks/c/o/consol_mb.pdf.

18. See http://en-rules.hkex.com.hk/net_file_store/new_rulebooks/c/o/consol_gem.pdf. The market capitalization test requires that the market capitalization of equity securities in the hands of the public must be at least HK$45 million.

19. See "Amendments to Main Board Listing Rules." http://en-rules.hkex.com.hk/net_file_store/new_rulebooks/u/p/Update_119_Attachment_1.pdf.

20. "H-share" firms are Chinese state-owned firms registered in mainland China; "Red Chip" firms are also Chinese-concept firms but are registered in Hong Kong or other overseas regions. "Red Chip" firms are usually "window companies" set up by China's central government or local governments. They often have significant state ownership and conduct major operations and business on the mainland. "Mainland private enterprises" are Chinese firms that are headquartered or registered in mainland China and that are ultimately controlled by nongovernment entities.

21. For instance, the applicant firm must have minimum net assets of RMB 400 million; a minimum after-tax net income of RMB 60 million in the preceding year; and minimum total proceeds to be raised in overseas market of US$50 million.

22. The next subsection will discuss and compare stock returns of A shares and other countries.

23. Note that the A-share stock market stays at almost the same level in 2017 as in 2014, partly because the China "national team," composed of China Securities Finance Corp, Central Huijin Investment, the State Administration of Foreign Exchange (SAFE), along with other government rescue funds entered the market to buy shares in June 2015. They owned 742 different stocks at the end of September 2015. The intervention succeeded in shoring up the A-share stock prices. See Gabriel Wildau, "China's 'National Team' Owns 6% of Stock Market," *Financial Times*, November 26, 2015. Although it is reported that the "national team" sold part of its holdings in 2018 Q1, it maintained the majority of its holdings, which is estimated at $210 billion. See Emma Dunkley, "China's 'National Team' Sells $28bn of Stock Holdings in First Quarter," *Financial Times*, May 28, 2018.

24. With granular data on within group capital transfers, Chen et al. (2016) document that while private groups allocate more capital to units with better investment opportunities, state-owned groups sometimes do the opposite, possibly following nonprofit maximization goals.

25. On the same day, the total number of stock accounts in China's stock market hit and exceeded 100 million for the first time.

26. For more details, see Reuters, "Timeline of China's Attempts to Prevent Stock Market Meltdown," August 28, 2015.

27. The names of the 21 securities firms can be found here: http://finance.sina.com.cn/stock/quanshang/qsyj/20151203/092323919396.shtml.

28. For more details, see Wildau, "China's 'National Team' Owns 6% of Stock Market."

29. For more details on the government's intervention in the stock market, see Huang et al. (2016).
30. For more information, see Lingling Wei, "China's Security Regulator to Suspend New 'Circuit Breaker' Mechanism," *Wall Street Journal*, January 7, 2016.
31. For more information, see Salidjanova (2016).

REFERENCES

Aharony, Joseph, Chi-Wen J. Lee, and T. J. Wong (2000). "Financial Packaging of IPO Firms in China." *Journal of Accounting Research* 38(1): 103–26.

Allen, Franklin, Jun Qian, Chenyu Shan, and Lei Zhu (2019). "Dissecting the Long-Term Performance of Chinese Stock Market." Working paper, Fudan University.

Bekaert, Geert, Zhaojing Chen, and Xiaoyan Zhang (2017). "The China Equity Valuation Premium." Working paper, Columbia University, Purdue University, and Tsinghua University.

Bian, Jiangze, Zhiguo He, Kelly Shue, and Hao Zhou (2017). "Leveraged-Induced Fire Sales and Stock Market Crashes." Working paper, University of Chicago and NBER.

Bian, Jiangze, Zhi Da, Dong Lou, and Hao Zhou (2019). "Leverage Network and Market Contagion." Working paper, University of International Business and Economics, University of Notre Dame, London School of Economics and CEPR, PBC School of Finance, and Tsinghua University.

Brunnermeier, Markus, Michael Sockin, and Wei Xiong (2017). "China's Model of Managing the Financial System." Working paper, Princeton University.

Cai, Jinghan, Jibao He, Wenxi Jiang, and Wei Xiong (2018). "The Whack-a-Mole Games: Tobin Taxes and Trading Frenzy." Working paper, University of Scranton, Shenzhen Stock Exchange, CUHK Business School, The Chinese University of Hong Kong, Princeton University, and the NBER.

Carpenter, Jennifer, Fangzhou Lu, and Robert Whitelaw (2018). "The Real Value of China's Stock Market." Working paper, New York University.

Chen, Donghua, Dequan Jiang, Alexander Ljungqvist, Haitian Lu, and Mingming Zhou (2016). "State Capitalism vs. Private Enterprise." Working paper, New York University and NBER.

Chen, Ting, Zhenyu Gao, Jibao He, Wenxi Jiang, and Wei Xiong (2019). "Daily Price Limits and Destructive Market Behaviour." *Journal of Econometrics* 208(1): 249–64.

Chen, Xuanjuan, Kenneth Kim, Tong Yao, and Tong Yu (2010). "On the Predictability of Chinese Stock Returns." *Pacific-Basin Finance Journal* 18(4): 403–25.

Chen, Hui, Anton Petukov, and Jiang Wang (2018). "The Dark Side of Circuit Breakers." Working paper, Massachusetts Institute of Technology.

Cheung, Yan-Leung, Raghavendra P. Rau, and Aris Stouraitis (2006). "Tunneling, Propping and Expropriation Evidence from Connected Party Transactions in Hong Kong." *Journal of Financial Economics* 82(2): 343–86.

Fama, Eugene, and Kenneth French (1993). "Common risk factors in the returns on stocks and bonds." *Journal of Financial Economics* 33, 3–56.

Gao, Huasheng, Donghui Shi, and Bin Zhao (2018). "Does Good Luck Make People Overconfident? Evidence from a Natural Experiment in China." Working paper, Fudan University.

Ghysels, Eric, and Hanwei Liu (2017). "Has the Downside Risk in the Chinese Stock Market Fundamentally Changed?" Working paper, University of North Carolina, Chapel Hill.

Greenwood, Bruce, and Jeremy Stein (1991). "Transactional Risk, Market Crashes, and the Role of Circuit Breakers." *Journal of Business* 64(4): 443–62.

Gul, Ferdinand, Jeong-Bon Kim, and Annie Qiu (2010). "Ownership Concentration, Foreign Shareholding, Audit Quality, and Stock Price Synchronicity: Evidence from China." *Journal of Financial Economics* 95(3): 425–42.

Hu, Grace X., Can Chen, Yuan Shao, and Jiang Wang (2019). "Fama-French in China: Size and Value Factors in Chinese Stock Returns." *International Review of Finance* 19(1): 3–44.

Hu, Grace X., Jun Pan, and Jiang Wang (2018). "Chinese Capital Market: An Empirical Overview" (w24346). National Bureau of Economic Research.

Huang, Yi, Jianjun Miao, and Pengfei Wang (2016). "Saving China's Stock Market." Working paper, Boston University and Hong Kong University of Science and Technology.

Jiang, Guohua, Charles Lee, and Heng Yue (2010). "Tunneling through Intercorporate Loans: The China Experience." *Journal of Financial Economics* 98(1): 1–20.

Kim, Kenneth, and Ghon Rhee (1997). "Price Limit Performance: Evidence from the Tokyo Stock Exchange." *Journal of Finance* 52(2): 885–901.

Kim, Kenneth, and Jungso Park (2010). "Why Do Price Limits Exist in Stock Markets? A Manipulation-based Explanation." *European Financial Management* 16(2): 296–318.

Lauterbach, Beni, and Uri Ben-Zion (1993). "Stock Market Crashes and the Performance of Circuit Breakers: Empirical Evidence." *Journal of Finance* 48(5): 1909–25.

Lee, Charles M. C., Kevin K. Li, and Ran Zhang (2015). "Shall Games: The Long Term Performance of Chinese Reverse Merger Firms." *Accounting Review* 90(4): 1547–89.

Li, Feng, Jun Qian, Haofei Wang, and Lei Zhu (2019). "Stock Pledged Loans, Capital Markets, and Firm Performance: The Good, the Bad and the Ugly." Working paper, Fudan University.

Li, Kai, Tan Wang, Yan-Leung Cheung, and Ping Jiang (2011). "Privatization and Risk Sharing: Evidence from the Split Share Structure Reform in China." *Review of Financial Studies* 24(7): 2499–2525.

Liao, Li, Bibo Liu, and Hao Wang (2011). "Information Discovery in Share Lockups: Evidence from the Split-share Structure Reform in China." *Financial Management* 40(4): 1001–27.

Liao, Li, Bibo Liu, and Hao Wang (2014). "China's Secondary Privatization: Perspectives from the Split-share Structure Reform." *Journal of Financial Economics* 113(3): 500–18.

Liu, Jianan, Robert F. Stambaugh, and Yu Yuan (2019). "Size and Value in China." *Journal of Financial Economics* 134: 48–69.

Mei, Jianping, Jose Scheinkman, and Wei Xiong (2009). "Speculative Trading and Stock Prices: Evidence from Chinese A-B Shares Premia." *Annals of Economics and Finance* 10(2): 225–55.

Morck, Randall, Bernard Yang, and Wayne Yu (2000). "The Information Content of Stock Markets: Why Do Emerging Markets Have Synchronous Stock Price Movements?" *Journal of Financial Economics* 58(1–2): 215–60.

Morck, Randall, Bernard Yang, and Wayne Yu (2013). "R-squared and the Economy" (w19017). National Bureau of Economic Research.

Packer, Frank, and Mark Spiegel (2016). "China's IPO Activity and Equity Market Volatility." *FRBSF Economic Letter*, 2016–18. June 6.

Pastor, Lubos, and Pietro Veronesi (2012). "Uncertainty about Government Policy and Stock Prices." *Journal of Finance* 67(4): 1219–64.

Qiao, Fang, Lai Xu, Xiaoyan Zhang, and Hao Zhou (2018). "Variance Risk Premiums in Emerging Markets." Working paper, PBC School of Finance and Syracuse University.

Salidjanova, Nargiza (2016). "China's Stock Market Meltdown Shakes the World, Again." U.S.-China Economic and Security Review Commission Issue Brief, January 14.

Shan, Chenyu, Yongjun Tang, Sarah Qian Wang, and Chang Zhang (2018). "The Diversification Benefits and Policy Risks of Accessing China's Stock Market." Working paper, Shanghai University of Finance and Economics, University of Hong Kong, and Warwick University.

Subrahmanyam, Avanidhar (1994). "Circuit Breakers and Market Volatility: A Theoretical Perspective." *Journal of Finance* 49(1): 237–54.

Veronesi, Pietro, and Luigi Zingales (2010). "Paulson's Gift." *Journal of Financial Economics* 97(3): 339–68.

Xiong, Wei, and Jialin Yu (2011). "The Chinese Warrants Bubble." *American Economic Review* 101(6): 2723–53.

12

CORPORATE GOVERNANCE IN CHINA

Cong Wang

1. INTRODUCTION

1.1. Agency Problems in Chinese Firms

Corporate governance is the system of rules and mechanisms by which a company is directed and controlled, with the aim of mitigating conflicts of interests between principals and agents. Two types of agency problems often arise. The classic one—the Type I agency problem—described decades ago by Berle and Means (1932) and Jensen and Meckling (1976), is caused by the separation of ownership and control. In a typical large public corporation with diffused ownership structure, management owns little ownership but effectively controls the decision-making process in the company. Shareholders, who are the actual owners of the corporation, delegate decision-making to management owing to their lack of sufficient information or expertise. Consequently, conflicts develop as managers (agents) and shareholders (principals) have different goals. Self-interested managers tend to value high levels of private-benefit consumption, excessive remuneration and perks, and less-intensive work, all of which are achieved usually at the expense of shareholders. Much of the corporate governance literature is devoted to study various governance mechanisms to mitigate the conflicts of interests between managers and shareholders.

A different type of agency problem—the Type II agency problem—emerges when a company has a controlling shareholder that may use its controlling power to extract private benefits at the expense of minority shareholders. Existing studies have shown that such concentrated ownership structure is prevalent in both developed and developing economies (La Porta et al., 1999; Claessens et al., 2002). The conflicts of interest between the controlling and the minority shareholders are intensified when the controlling shareholders' voting power is enhanced through special ownership arrangements such as pyramidal, cross-holdings, and dual-class structures. These special ownership structures can result in a significant wedge between controlling owners' voting rights and cash flow rights. As controlling shareholders have disproportionally more voting rights than cash flow rights, they only bear a smaller proportion of the financial consequences of their self-dealing behaviors. At the same time, the enhanced control increases their ability to fend off any potential threat from outside the firm that could jeopardize their private-benefit consumption and continued employment at the company.

This chapter provides an overview of corporate governance in China. The current section mainly describes the feature of ownership structures in Chinese listed firms and explains which type of agency problems dominates in the country. Section 2 and section 3 review various corporate governance mechanisms currently available in China and details their effectiveness in mitigating agency problems, with the former section focusing on internal governance mechanisms and the latter section covering external governance controls. Section 4 concludes.

While the ownership structure of most public firms in the United States is widely dispersed, listed companies in China have a high concentration of ownership. Table 12.1 presents the summary statistics of the percentage of ownership held by controlling owners in each year during the period between 2003 and 2015. The sample comprises 22,645 firm-year observations, with ownership information available in the China Stock Market & Accounting Research (CSMAR) Corporate Governance database. The table provides statistics separately for state-owned enterprises (SOEs) and non-state-owned enterprises (non-SOEs). A SOE is a company whose ultimate owner is the state, represented by an agency known as the State-owned Assets Supervision and Administration Commission (SASAC). SASAC's headquarters is in Beijing, overseeing the central government-controlled SOEs. It also has branches in several provinces, cities, or counties to supervise the local government-controlled SOEs. Table 12.1 shows that controlling shareholders own significant portions of shares in both SOEs and non-SOEs. The average of percentage of shares held by the controlling shareholder is never below 30% during the sample period, giving rise to the Type II problem: the expropriation of minority shareholders by large controlling owners.

According to China's company law, corporations throughout the country need to follow the "one-share, one-vote" rule and therefore are not allowed to issue multiple classes of shares with unequal voting rights. However, controlling owners of mainland-listed companies can achieve excessive voting rights by setting up chains of control, or the so-called pyramidal structures. Figure 12.1 provides such an example. Dan Dong Xintai Electric Co., an electrical equipment maker, went public in 2014 on the ChiNext board, a Nasdaq-style board for growth enterprises on the Shenzhen Stock Exchange. The figure shows the company's ownership chain. At the bottom of the chain is the listed corporation, Dan Dong Xintai Electric Co. (hereafter "Xintai Electric"). The company's controlling shareholder, a Mr. Wen Deyi, owns 77.35% of Liaoning Xintai, a nonlisted shell that holds 26.59% of the listed company's shares. Wen's cash flow rights in the listed firm are calculated as the product of the ownership stakes along the chain, or 20.57% (=77.35% * 26.59%). His control rights, however, are 26.59%, as is determined by the weakest link along the control chain. This pyramidal structure gives Wen about 6% control rights in excess of his cash flow rights, and such discrepancy creates incentives for him to pursue self-dealing activities at the expense of minority shareholders.

In 2015, one year after the company's IPO, the China Securities Regulatory Commission (CSRC) started an investigation into Xintai Electric with regard to possible manipulation of financial data in its IPO application. In 2017, the company was convicted of

Table 12.1. Percentage of Ownership Held by the Controlling Owner

Panel A: SOEs

Year	N	Mean	Standard deviation	P10	P25	Median	P75	P90
2003	677	46.74	16.48	25.00	33.36	47.31	59.68	67.57
2004	904	46.05	16.57	24.31	31.48	46.62	59.63	67.57
2005	881	44.53	16.18	23.62	30.18	44.65	57.95	65.81
2006	877	39.75	15.71	19.82	27.45	39.04	51.51	60.08
2007	899	39.16	15.73	19.43	26.61	38.74	50.50	60.01
2008	914	39.12	15.62	18.86	26.58	38.92	50.74	59.81
2009	919	39.87	16.02	19.19	27.46	39.28	51.45	61.04
2010	962	39.73	15.87	19.68	26.91	39.37	51.51	61.06
2011	965	39.74	16.06	19.36	26.78	39.27	51.33	61.36
2012	969	40.00	15.99	19.86	27.00	39.37	51.64	61.49
2013	961	40.05	15.96	20.00	27.26	39.34	51.73	61.51
2014	959	39.93	15.82	20.07	27.19	39.46	51.33	61.42
2015	992	39.07	15.54	20.08	26.59	37.82	50.25	60.19

Panel B: non-SOEs

Year	N	Mean	Standard deviation	P10	P25	Median	P75	P90
2003	108	31.08	12.61	16.53	23.75	28.97	36.13	52.34
2004	317	32.38	12.85	18.62	24.58	29.01	39.94	52.50
2005	343	31.52	12.31	18.12	23.86	28.88	37.41	51.92
2006	417	30.59	12.92	17.80	21.74	27.40	36.91	49.66
2007	504	31.95	14.09	16.90	21.84	29.19	41.01	51.62
2008	546	32.49	14.42	16.54	21.95	29.49	41.86	52.28
2009	674	33.23	15.28	16.39	22.10	29.90	42.49	53.66
2010	971	34.40	15.69	16.97	22.56	31.39	44.46	55.06
2011	1206	33.79	14.66	16.48	22.77	31.29	43.16	53.82
2012	1300	34.00	14.62	17.04	22.67	31.56	43.23	54.55
2013	1332	33.84	14.80	16.65	22.57	31.46	42.93	54.08
2014	1437	33.12	14.33	16.38	22.17	31.14	42.01	52.36
2015	1611	32.02	13.64	15.72	21.45	30.29	40.91	50.36

Source: CSMAR Corporate Governance database.

Notes: This table presents the summary statistics of the percentage of shares held by a firm's controlling shareholder. Figures are percentage points.

FIGURE 12.1. The pyramidal structure of Dan Dong Xintai Electric Co. *Note*: This figure presents the pyramidal structure of a company that went public in 2014 and was forced to delist in 2017 for falsifying financial data.

falsifying financial data and forced to delist from the stock exchange, becoming the first company to be banned from the ChiNext board. The investigation of CSRC shows that in order to get listed, Xintai Electric wrote off large balances of receivables at the end of each accounting period via external loans or forged bank bills, and then wrote back the receivables after the beginning of the next accounting period.[1] The company had been using the practice in the IPO application process and continued to do so after going public. It turns out that a large portion of the company's receivables consisted of the so-called fund occupation by the controlling owner, Wen. These types of fund occupation often have another name, "intercorporate loans"—which means money transferred from the listed company to the controlling shareholder. In fiscal year 2014 alone, 63.88 million RMB was tunneled out of the listed company and transferred to Wen in the form of intercorporate loans. Jiang et al. (2010) study the intercorporate loans in listed firms in China and find that a large portion of these loans do not accrue interest, that sometimes even the principal is never paid back, and therefore such loans are widely used by controlling owners to tunnel money out of the listed corporations in China.

The expropriation of minority shareholders by controlling shareholders is particularly prevalent in non-SOEs, because the controlling owner directly benefits from these tunneling activities. For SOEs, SASAC controls the appointment of SOEs' senior managers, who are usually government bureaucrats. Since the appointed managers act as agents for SASAC and cannot directly benefit from the wealth transfer from the listed corporation to the controlling owner, the Type II agency problem in SOEs is not as severe as in non-SOEs. Figure 12.2 presents the annual distribution of the wedge between controlling shareholders' voting rights and cash flow rights. The wedge is higher in non-SOEs than in SOEs, consistent with the argument that the controlling owner's incentive to expropriate minority shareholders is higher in non-SOEs. By contrast, since senior managers in SOEs rarely own significant portions of their listed companies' shares, the classic Type I agency problem also exists in SOEs in the form of shirking as well as excessive consumption of perks.

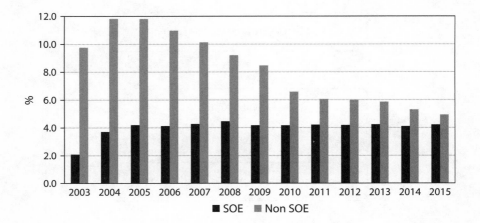

FIGURE 12.2. The divergence between controlling shareholders' voting rights and cash flow rights. *Note:* This figure shows the wedge between controlling owners' voting rights and cash flow rights (in percentage points). Controlling shareholders' cash flow rights are calculated as the product of the ownership stakes along the control chain, while voting rights are determined by the weakest link along the chain.

1.2. Two-Tier Share Structure and the Split-Share Reform

The misalignment of interests between controlling shareholders and minority shareholders was aggravated by the two-tier share structure that existed in China until 2007. Since the beginning of the mainland stock markets in early 1990s, domestic A shares were divided into tradable shares and nontradeable shares. Nontradeable shares were typically held by controlling owners, while tradable shares were held by outside minority shareholders. Although the two types of shares carry the same voting and cash flow rights, nontradeable shareholders are not allowed to sell their shares on stock exchanges and therefore cannot realize any gains from stock price increases. As a result, entrenched controlling shareholders have greater incentives to tunnel resources out of the listed corporations under the two-tier share structure. Realizing that such structure exacerbates the agency conflicts between controlling owners and minority shareholders, regulatory authorities started a reform in 2005 that required all domestic-listed firms to convert their nontradeable shares into tradable ones.[2] By the end of 2007, almost all mainland-listed firms had completed the conversion.

Research on the split-share reform suggests that the reform brought substantial changes to the control of shareholders' incentives and also mitigated the conflicts of interest between controlling owners and minority shareholders. For example, Lin (2009) documents a significant decline in tunneling activities by controlling shareholders after the reform. Chen et al. (2012) find that cash holdings of affected firms declined following the reform, especially for poorly governed firms. The increased alignment of interests is also supported by the sudden decline in the controlling shareholder's excess control rights for non-SOEs following the split-share structure reform (see figure 12.2). This trend is consistent with the notion that as the reform allows controlling shareholders to realize gains from stock price appreciation, their interests become more aligned with those of shareholders and hence they have less incentive to hold disproportionally higher voting rights than cash flow rights.

Still, controlling owners hold more than 30% of shares in listed corporations. This high concentration of ownership inevitably causes conflicts of interest between controlling owners and minority shareholders. The following sections review various governance mechanisms currently available in China and discuss whether these governance designs can curb the agency issues.

2. INTERNAL CORPORATE GOVERNANCE MECHANISMS

This section reviews the internal corporate governance mechanisms: the boards of directors and the design of managerial compensation.

2.1. Boards of Directors

2.1.1. Board Structure and Functions
The board of directors is an integral element of a firm's corporate governance system and performs the dual role of monitoring and advising senior management. Under the Company Law of the PRC, a listed company must adopt a two-tiered board structure that consists of a board of directors and a supervisory board. The number of directors sitting on the board must be at least 5 and no more than 19, and the supervisory board must have at least 3 members. While employee representation is not required on the board of directors, one-third of the members on the supervisory board must be employee representatives.

The tasks of a corporate board in China include guiding corporate strategies, reviewing annual financial budgets, monitoring and evaluating performance of managers, hiring and firing top management, and overseeing major investment plans. In performing these functions, directors are obligated to be loyal and diligent, so as to safeguard the overall interests of both the company and, in particular, the interests of minority shareholders. The supervisory board primarily carries out the function of monitoring the performance of directors and senior managers, and therefore its members cannot be a director or senior executive of the company. The supervisory board has the power to dismiss a director or a senior manager in the case of violation of laws, regulations, and articles of association or in the event of a resolution adopted at the shareholders' meeting. Other than company employees, members of a supervisory board often include an official from the company's internal Party Committee. Therefore, it is believed that the supervisory board is a way for the Party to exert political influence.

2.1.2. Independent Directors
A typical board in the United States consists of three types of directors—employee directors, "gray" directors, and independent directors. Gray directors are those who have business, financial, familial, or interlocking relationships that could compromise their ability or their incentives to perform board oversight duties in the best interests of shareholders (e.g., former employees of the company or persons who provide it with financial, legal, and advisory services). Independent directors are those who do not have such conflicts of interest and, therefore, are believed to play a critical role in monitoring management. In China, the concept of independent directors first appeared in 2001 when CSRC issued a

Table 12.2. Summary Statistics of Board Size and the Number of
Independent Directors

Year	N	Average board size	Average number of independent directors	Median board size	Median number of independent directors
2003	1278	9.9	3.2	9	3
2004	1367	9.7	3.3	9	3
2005	1368	9.6	3.3	9	3
2006	1443	9.4	3.3	9	3
2007	1534	9.4	3.3	9	3
2008	1576	9.3	3.3	9	3
2009	1760	9.2	3.3	9	3
2010	2106	9.1	3.3	9	3
2011	2347	9.0	3.3	9	3
2012	2492	9.0	3.3	9	3
2013	2536	8.9	3.3	9	3
2014	2652	8.7	3.2	9	3
2015	2841	8.6	3.2	9	3
2016	3135	8.6	3.2	9	3

Source: CSMAR Corporate Governance database.

new rule requiring listed firms to have one-third of the board made up of independent directors by June 30, 2003 ("The Guidelines for Introducing Independent Directors to the Board of Directors of Listed Companies"). CSRC's definition of independent directors is largely in line with that used in the United States, except that an independent director in China cannot be a significant shareholder who either owns more than 1% of shares of the listed company or is related to a shareholder who holds more than 5% of the shares. As a result, representatives of the company's major shareholders cannot be independent directors. This is consistent with the main objective of corporate governance in China—protecting the interests of minority shareholders.

Tables 12.2 and 12.3 present summary statistics of board composition measures, including board size, the number of independent directors, and the percentage of independent directors. The data is obtained from CSMAR's Corporate Governance database, covering all listed firms in China from 2003 to 2016. The median firm has nine directors on the board, at least one-third of whom must be independent. The percentage of independent directors has a very small standard deviation, suggesting that there is little variation across firms. The statistics for different percentiles also show that a large portion of listed firms have exactly one-third of their board members also being independent directors. This implies that most listed firms in China structure their boards in a way to simply comply with the regulation, thus raising potential concerns over the effectiveness of a board's monitoring function.

2.1.3. Director Terms and Election

A director in a Chinese listed company can serve up to two consecutive terms on the board, each of which runs for three years. Therefore, only directors whose first terms are expiring stand up for reelection each year, rather than all at once. This is similar to

Table 12.3. Summary Statistics of the Percentage of Independent Directors

Year	N	Standard deviation	Mean	P10	P25	Median	P75	P90
2003	1278	5.91	32.90	25.00	33.33	33.33	36.36	37.50
2004	1367	5.02	34.31	28.57	33.33	33.33	36.36	40.00
2005	1368	4.61	34.81	33.33	33.33	33.33	36.36	40.00
2006	1443	4.70	35.24	33.33	33.33	33.33	36.36	42.86
2007	1534	4.88	35.89	33.33	33.33	33.33	37.50	42.86
2008	1576	5.24	36.19	33.33	33.33	33.33	37.50	42.86
2009	1760	5.21	36.46	33.33	33.33	33.33	38.46	42.86
2010	2106	5.35	36.67	33.33	33.33	33.33	38.89	42.86
2011	2347	5.51	36.92	33.33	33.33	33.33	40.00	42.86
2012	2492	5.48	37.03	33.33	33.33	33.33	40.00	42.86
2013	2536	5.52	37.35	33.33	33.33	33.33	42.86	42.86
2014	2652	5.44	37.29	33.33	33.33	33.33	42.86	42.86
2015	2841	5.67	37.68	33.33	33.33	36.36	42.86	42.86
2016	3135	5.48	37.51	33.33	33.33	35.71	42.86	42.86

Source: CSMAR Corporate Governance database.

the staggered board arrangement in the United States that typically divides directors on a board into three classes serving staggered terms, with one class of directors up for reelection in each annual shareholder meeting. Most studies on staggered boards in the United States point to the conclusion that a staggered board is a powerful anti-takeover device and thus can protect both management and directors from the discipline of the market for corporate control and shareholder influence (Bebchuk and Cohen, 2005).

To increase the chance for minority shareholders to elect a director, the Governance Code in China stipulates that a cumulative voting system be used in director elections. In a cumulative voting arrangement, the number of votes available to a shareholder is equal to the number of shares she holds, multiplied by the number of directors to be elected. The shareholder can cast all her votes for a single candidate and thus can have a larger impact on director election than in a traditional voting system.

2.1.4. Board Committees

Although not a statutory requirement, it is a common practice for listed firms to establish specialized committees on the board. The code of Corporate Governance recommends that a listed company set up the following four board committees: an audit committee, a nomination committee, a compensation committee, and a corporate strategy committee. The first three committees must be chaired by independent directors and have the majority of committee members being independent. At least one independent director on the audit committee needs to be an accounting expert, such as a certified public accountant, a senior accounting professor, or the like.

Although corporate boards in China share some features of Western corporate boards, such as having specialized subcommittees and a minimum percentage of independent directors, there are several reasons to question whether boards in China can effectively monitor senior managers, who are often under the control of large shareholders. First, since independent directors rarely make up more than half of the board, they can hardly succeed in blocking a managerial decision that may hurt shareholder value. Second, independent directors cannot be a significant shareholder of the company in which they serve as directors and therefore do not have enough incentives to stand up to management or to controlling shareholders and thereby to safeguard minority shareholders' interests. Empirical analysis of independent director voting behavior supports this argument. In 2004, CSRC mandated that public-traded firms in China disclose how directors vote on proposals sponsored by management or controlling shareholders. The CSMAR Corporate Governance database records this information. According to its data, among the nearly 300,000 proposals submitted to boards of directors of all public firms during the period between 2004 and 2016, dissenting or abstention votes from independent directors only existed in 513 proposals—less than 1% of all the proposals that were voted on.[3]

A third reason is that independent directors in China may not have the capability to perform their monitoring duty, owing to lack of expertise or work experience in the firm's industry. Using a sample of U.S. public firms, Wang et al. (2015) show that it is critical for independent directors to possess experiences from and expertise about the industries of the firms they serve when performing their monitoring function. However, instead of recruiting industry experts to the boardroom, listed firms in China tend to hire independent directors with academic or legal backgrounds. The CSMAR Corporate Governance database also collects information on directors' backgrounds disclosed in companies' annual reports. Figure 12.3 presents the distribution of independent directors'

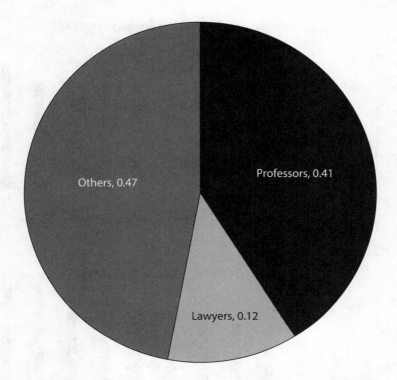

Figure 12.3. The distribution of independent directors' backgrounds. *Source*: Directors' background information based on 2016 annual reports of all listed firms in China, obtained from CSMAR's Corporate Governance database.

primary professions for fiscal year 2016. For that year, 41% of all independent directors sitting on the boards of public firms were professors and 12% were lawyers. These two type of directors alone account for more than 50% of all independent directors.[4]

2.2. Executive Compensation

An effective managerial compensation plan is usually considered an internal governance mechanism to properly motivate the agents in control and also to reduce agency problems. The disclosure of executive compensation is regulated by CSRC through its "Guidelines on contents and formats of information disclosure of annual report for listed companies." Guidelines issued before 2005 only required firms to disclose the sum of total compensation for the three highest-paid top executives. Guidelines revised in 2005 required firms to disclose the total compensation of each individual senior manager, director on the board, and member of the supervisory board from 2006 onward. Below are some descriptions of executive compensation in Chinese listed firms. The information is obtained from the CSMAR Corporate Governance database.

2.2.1. Cash Compensation

Figure 12.4 shows the mean and median cash compensation (including salary and bonus) paid to the chairs of boards for SOEs and non-SOEs during the period between 2006 and 2017. Note that the compensation of the board chair is used here, not the CEO's, because

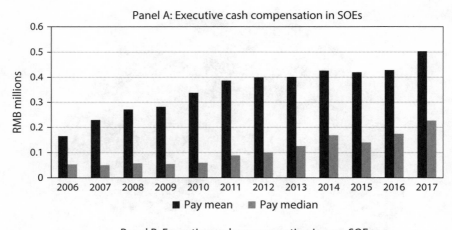

Panel A: Executive cash compensation in SOEs

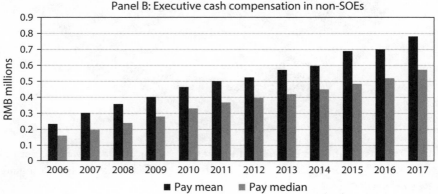

Panel B: Executive cash compensation in non-SOEs

FIGURE 12.4. The mean and median of executive cash compensation. *Source*: CSMAR Corporate Governance database.

unlike CEOs in U.S. companies, in China an executive holding the title of "CEO" is often not the top manager in charge of a company's day-to-day operations. Instead, the board chair in China has more power than the CEO and is the actual decision-maker in a company's daily operations. Figure 12.4 suggests that on average, the top manager pay in non-SOEs is higher than in SOEs. For example, in 2017, the average pay for board chairs of SOEs is about 530,000 RMB, while the average pay for board chairs in non-SOEs is around 700,000 RMB. Controlling for other determinants of executive pay, Gu et al. (2010) also document that executive compensation at SOEs, especially those under strong government control (defined as SOEs with fewer layers along the state-control chain), is significantly lower than at non-SOEs. This result is not surprising, because the process of setting executive pay in SOEs lies under government intervention and is subject to political pursuits of such values as social harmony and equality. SASAC is the authority that oversees SOEs and is responsible for appointing SOE top executives as well as approving executive compensation.

It also appears from the figure that the top executive pay at non-SOEs has been consistently increasing during the sample period, while the pay at SOEs reached its peak in 2014 and then declined slightly in 2015. This is the result of a new rule passed in early

2015 to cut executive pay in both central government-controlled SOEs and state-owned financial institutions. The new rule mandates that top executive pay in these companies be no more than 600,000 RMB annually. This was not the first time that the government restricted pay of SOE managers. In 2009, the government announced a plan to impose a ceiling on the ratio of top executive pay to average employee compensation among SOEs. Bae et al. (2018) use the 2009 setting and study the effect of restricting executive pay. They find that the pay restriction led to significant pay cuts in SOEs and that, following those cuts, top managers simply increased their consumption of perks and tunneling activities. Pay-performance sensitivities in these firms also decline. Their evidence suggests that restricting executive pay produces unintended consequences and creates incentives for managers to engage in more self-dealing activities.

2.2.2. Pay-Performance Sensitivity and Equity-Based Compensation

Several studies examine the pay-performance sensitivity in China's publicly traded firms and reveal how state control affects the relation between pay and performance. Using executive compensation data for the relatively early period of 2001–2005, Conyon and He (2011) show that change in executive pay in Chinese listed firms is positively correlated with change in performance, measured either by return on assets (ROA) or by shareholder return. They further document that pay-performance sensitivity is stronger in non-SOEs than in SOEs. Gu et al. (2010) also find that the relation between pay and performance is stronger in privately controlled non-SOEs when compared to companies that are under more direct state control. One possible explanation for the lower pay-performance sensitivity in SOEs is that their ultimate owner, meaning the government, has its own goals of creating more jobs and maintaining social stability, which sometimes have direct conflicts with maximizing firm profitability and shareholder wealth (Bai et al., 2006).

The compensation data used in Conyon and He (2011) and Gu et al. (2010) do not cover equity-based pay such as restricted stocks and stock options. Equity-based compensation was not permitted in China before 2005. In that year, however, CSRC introduced a series of new rules to allow listed firms that had completed the split-share reform to adopt equity-based incentive plans. Chen et al. (2017) conduct event studies of the announcements of these new rules and find that the market reactions were significantly positive for firms that were expected to adopt equity-based compensation plans following the passage of the regulations. Panel A of figure 12.5 presents the annual percentage of all listed firms that adopted equity-based compensation plans during the period between 2006 and 2017. Only about 2% of listed firms adopted equity-based compensation plans in 2006, the first year following the passage of the new rules. The percentage rose steadily during the sample period and reached the highest level of 22% in 2017. The percentage of adopters among non-SOEs is much higher than among SOEs. For example, in 2017, 33.2% non-SOEs adopted equity-based pay schemes, while the number for SOEs is only 5.9%.

Panel B of figure 12.5 shows the newly granted shares as a percentage of total outstanding shares for both SOEs and non-SOEs. Again, it appears that SOEs are more conservative in granting equity to top managers: The percentage of shares newly granted to top executives is higher in non-SOEs than in SOEs for almost all the years during the sample period. Conyon and He (2011) also find that state-controlled firms in China provide fewer equity incentives to managers than do privately controlled firms. These empirical findings are contrary to what theories predict. Since top managers in SOEs are

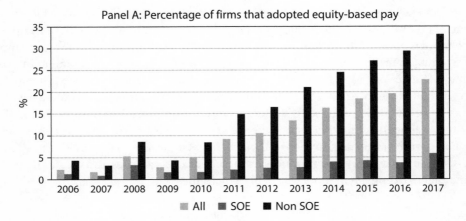

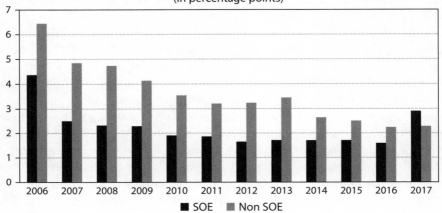

FIGURE 12.5. Equity-based compensation: Comparison between SOEs and non-SOEs. *Source*: CSMAR Corporate Governance database. *Note:* Panel A of this figure presents the percentage of public companies that adopted equity-based compensation plans. Panel B shows the newly granted shares as the percentage of outstanding shares for those firms that adopted equity-based compensation plans.

agents appointed by the controlling shareholder, or SASAC, more equity incentives are needed to mitigate the classic principal-agent conflicts. The fact that SOEs are less aggressive in offering equity-based pay to their top managers is likely driven by SASAC's political objectives of maintaining social stability and equality.

3. EXTERNAL CORPORATE GOVERNANCE MECHANISMS

3.1. The Market for Corporate Control

In addition to internal governance mechanisms, external governance mechanisms such as the market for corporate control also play an important role in disciplining self-dealing managers as well as insiders. By replacing poorly performing and inefficient managers,

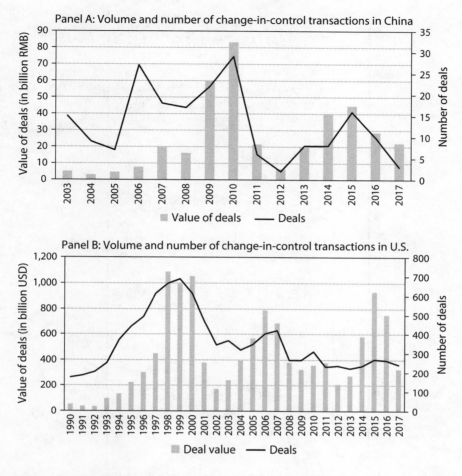

FIGURE 12.6. The market for corporate control in China vs. the United States. *Source:* Information on China obtained from Wind database; information on the United States obtained from Thomson Reuter SDC Mergers and Acquisitions database.

a hostile takeover can perform an ex post settling-up function and provide managers with the proper incentives to maximize both firm value and shareholder wealth (Jensen, 1986); Mitchell and Lehn, 1990).

Figure 12.6 displays the number and volume of acquisitions targeting listed firms in China and the United States. The information on China's change-in-control transactions is obtained from WIND, while the data for change-in-control transactions in the United States is obtained from Thomson Reuters' SDC Mergers and Acquisitions database. Compared to the United States, China lacks an active market for corporate control. The number of transactions that result in change-in-control in a public corporation in China is below 35 in each of the years for the period between 2003 and 2017, accounting for less than 1% of all listed companies. The absence of an active takeover market in China is not surprising, since most listed firms have a concentrated ownership structure that gives the controlling owner enough power to forestall any hostile attempts to gain control of the company.

Table 12.4. Summary Statistics of Ownership Percentage Held by Institutional Investors

Year	N	Mean	Standard deviation	P10	P25	Median	P75	P90
2003	930	7.30	14.28	0.16	0.72	2.45	6.25	16.60
2004	969	8.80	15.00	0.33	1.08	3.12	9.05	23.64
2005	975	9.24	14.56	0.40	1.19	4.00	10.25	22.80
2006	1078	9.41	13.13	0.60	1.59	4.62	11.60	22.18
2007	1166	9.69	12.75	0.53	1.52	5.47	12.76	21.84
2008	1134	9.57	12.67	0.68	1.76	5.35	12.10	21.56
2009	1375	8.37	11.41	0.48	1.48	4.95	10.35	18.60
2010	1753	8.00	10.49	0.60	1.86	5.04	9.83	16.80
2011	2051	7.08	9.75	0.54	1.48	4.29	8.87	14.75
2012	2174	6.36	9.59	0.44	1.08	3.28	7.66	13.99
2013	2045	6.94	9.90	0.46	1.30	3.91	8.56	15.14
2014	2360	6.54	9.18	0.58	1.54	3.74	8.04	13.99
2015	2615	6.40	8.57	0.67	1.82	4.25	7.72	12.36
2016	2781	6.63	8.60	0.67	1.93	4.38	8.01	13.54
2017	2847	6.08	8.35	0.53	1.56	3.66	7.44	12.88

Source: CSMAR Corporate Governance database.

Note: Figures are percentage points.

Table 12.5. Percentage of Ownership Held by Different Types of
Institutional Investors in 2017

Types of institutional investors	Mean	Median
Security fund	1.49	0.54
Insurance company	0.50	0.00
QFII	0.22	0.00
Trust	1.97	0.41
Banks	0.04	0.00
Finance company	0.02	0.00
Nonfinance company	1.20	0.00

Source: CSMAR Corporate Governance database.
Note: Figures are percentage points.

3.2. Institutional Investors and Shareholder Activism

Another important external governance mechanism is the monitoring from institutional shareholders. Institutional shareholders can engage in costly monitoring activities to influence a firm's corporate governance. For example, large institutional investors can replace incumbent board members through proxy fights, push companies to adopt better governance practices through shareholder proposals, and raise their voice against excessive CEO pay. Table 12.4 presents the summary statistics of the percentage of ownership held by institutional shareholders by year for the period between 2003 and 2017. The data is also available in CSMAR's Corporate Governance database. It appears that institutional investors in China on average hold a small percentage of shares of listed firms. For example, in 2017, the last year of the sample period, the average stake held by institutional investors is only 6%, and the median is 3.7%. The low level of ownership raises the question as to whether institutional investors in China have sufficient incentives and capability to play an effective monitoring role.

Chen et al. (2007) use U.S. data to investigate which types of institutional investors in the United States have better incentives and ability to monitor. They conclude that institutions that have long-term investment horizons and have no business relationship with the companies in which they invest tend to be better monitors. In contrast, "gray institutional investors," defined as institutional investors with an existing or potential business relationship with the invested firms, may be less active monitors. These gray institutional investors typically include banks, trust companies, and insurance firms. Table 12.5 provides a breakdown of the ownership by various types of institutions in China in 2017. Stakes held by gray institutional investors account for a large portion of the average intuitional ownership in a listed firm (about 40%), further casting doubt on the effectiveness of the monitoring role that institutional investors play in China.

Compared to the U.S. market, in which institutional investors play a dominant role, China's stock market is dominated by individual investors. Individual investors in China tend to be more short-term focused and trade more frequently than their counterparts in the rest of the world. Figure 12.7 presents the stock market turnover ratios across different countries in 2017. The turnover ratio (in percentage points) is defined as the number of shares traded over the year, divided by the total number of shares outstanding. Not surprisingly, China has the highest turnover ratio—almost 200%—which implies that

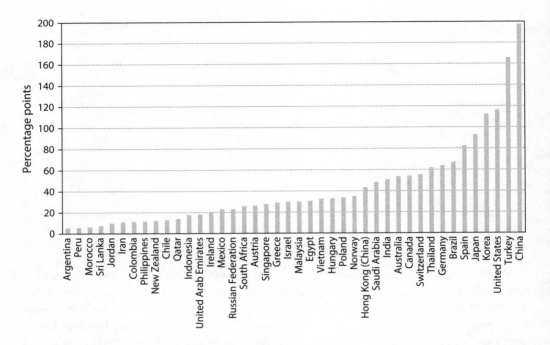

FIGURE 12.7. Stock market turnover ratio across different countries in 2017 (percent). *Source:* World Bank. *Note:* The turnover ratio is defined as the number of shares traded over the year, divided by the total number of shares outstanding.

the average investor in that country holds the invested shares for only six months. Given their short-term investment horizons, investors in China, especially individual investors, may not pay much attention to firms' corporate governance practices and may not even bother to exercise their rights to vote on governance-related issues. A recent study by Institutional Shareholder Services (ISS) compares voting behaviors of China's domestic investors to those of investors in more developed markets, including the United States, the United Kingdom, France, and Hong Kong (Frank et al., 2014). The study finds that China A-share markets have the lowest level of shareholder participation in corporate voting. The average voter-turnout rate in mainland-listed firms is only about 55%, significantly lower than the turnout rate of 85% in the United States. Although shareholder participation rate is low, the approval rate for management-sponsored or controlling-shareholder-sponsored proposals in China is over 99%—the highest among all the markets studied in the report—suggesting that minority shareholders in China rarely vote against management or the controlling shareholders.

3.3. Regulatory Monitoring

While China generally lacks an active takeover market and activist shareholders, its regulatory agencies play a large role in exerting one important external governance mechanism to protect minority shareholders' interests. The key regulatory body in China, the China Securities Regulatory Commission (CSRC), was officially established in 1998 as the main supervisory agency for the country's stock markets. The two stock

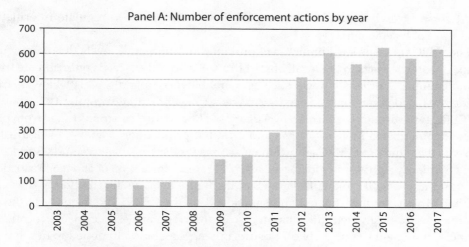

Panel A: Number of enforcement actions by year

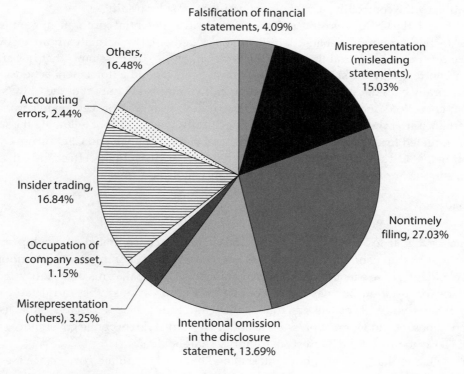

Panel B: Distribution of types of enforcement actions

FIGURE 12.8. CSRC enforcement actions. *Source:* CSMAR Corporate Governance database.

exchanges, Shanghai Stock Exchange and Shenzhen Stock Exchange, although established in 1990, are under CSRC's direct control. For example, the commission is in charge of the appointment of the two stock exchanges' presidents and vice presidents. The CSRC has issued a number of rules to regulate the governance practices of listed firms, with the aim of preventing fraud and protecting the interests of minority shareholders.

The two stock exchanges also promulgate their listing rules to regulate information disclosure of listed companies.

The CSRC operates local branches at provincial or municipal levels that pay regular or special on-site visits to the locally listed firms. It also collects leads on corporate fraud from a number of other channels, such as shareholder complaints, whistleblowers from inside the listed company, and media reports. Once a potential irregularity is spotted, the CSRC typically starts a formal investigation. The eventual sanctions range from public condemnation to monetary fines and criminal prosecution. Panel A of figure 12.8 presents the number of CSRC enforcement actions for the period between 2003 and 2017. Their frequency significantly increased after 2008, reaching a level of about 600 sanctions per year between 2012 and 2017. Panel B of the figure lists the distribution of the types of frauds that were investigated and sanctioned by the CSRC. The majority of the enforcement actions targeted information disclosure irregularities, such as falsification of financial statements, nontimely disclosure, misrepresentation intended to manipulate stock prices, and intentional omission in disclosure. Cases also arose against fund occupation by the controlling shareholder and illegal insider trading.

Although the CSRC was quite active in investigating potential corporate misconducts and sanctioning frauds, debate continues about whether it can actually improve governance practices among public firms. One criticism of the commission is that it is effectively controlled by the state and hence its investigations and enforcement actions may be politically biased. Chen et al. (2005) empirically examine the impact of the CSRC's enforcement actions and find that the targeted firms experience improvement in corporate governance after the enforcement actions. Specifically, they show that following the sanctions, targeted firms have a higher probability of auditor change and CEO turnover, indicating that CSRC's regulatory monitoring does have a disciplinary effect and can contribute to the improvement of governance quality in listed firms.

4. CONCLUSIONS

China's public listed corporations are characterized by concentrated ownership structures that lead to conflicts of interest between controlling shareholders and minority shareholders. These agency conflicts are manifested in several forms of minority shareholder expropriation, such as intercorporate loans and various types of related party transactions. Since China lacks an independent and well-developed legal system, listed corporations feel under great pressure to adopt Western-style corporate governance standards so as to protect the interests of minority shareholders.

This chapter has reviewed both internal and external corporate governance mechanisms in the country and provided stylized facts about these governance practices. Although many of the internal governance concepts and standards are modeled after governance codes in Western countries, questions still arise concerning the true effectiveness of the current governance practices in China. For example, most of the boards of directors of China's listed companies are structured to merely fulfill regulatory requirements, with no variations of duties to meet with company-specific monitoring demands. The design of managerial compensation in SOEs is also subject to political influences and constraints and therefore may not provide adequate incentives to senior managers and insiders. Among external governance mechanisms, market-oriented approaches such as shareholder activism and the market for corporate control are still dysfunctional, owing to short-term-focused investors and ownership concentration. In the near term, regulatory reforms and monitoring activities, including the CSRC's investigations and enforcement actions, are expected to play a more important role in China's corporate governance system. At the same time, it is also necessary to explore alternative solutions other than Western-style practices that may not always apply to China's governance problems.

NOTES

1. China currently has an approval-based IPO system, in which maintaining a large balance of receivables often reduces an IPO's chance of obtaining the CSRC's approval.
2. To make their shares freely tradable on stock exchanges, holders of nontradable shares were required to compensate holders of tradable shares, typically in the form of cash or bonus stocks.
3. In Chinese culture, people tend to avoid direct confrontation and instead adopt an indirect approach toward conflicts. Therefore, an abstention is a way for directors in China to, in effect, express their disagreement with top managers; this is usually considered to have a similar effect as voting "no."
4. Giannetti et al. (2015) studied the backgrounds of both executive and non-executive directors on the boards of Chinese listed companies. They found that directors with foreign experience contribute positively to firm valuation, profitability, and governance quality, suggesting that such directors can bring better management and governance practices to local Chinese firms.

REFERENCES

Bae, Kee-Hong, Zhaoran Gong, and Wilson H. S. Tong (2018). "Restricting CEO Pay Backfires: Evidence from China." Working paper, York University.

Bai, Chong-En, Jiangyong Lu, and Zhigang Tao (2006). "The Multitask Theory of State Enterprise Reform: Empirical Evidence from China." *American Economic Review* 96(2): 353–57.

Bebchuk, Lucian A., and Alma Cohen (2005). "The Costs of Entrenched Boards." *Journal of Financial Economics* 78(2): 409–33.

Berle, Adolph A., and Gardiner C. Means (1932). *The Modern Corporation and Private Property.* New York: Macmillan.

Chen, Gongmeng, Michael Firth, Ning Gao, and Oliver Rui (2005). "Is China's Securities Regulatory Agency a Toothless Tiger? Evidence from Enforcement Actions." *Journal of Accounting and Public Policy* 24(6): 451–88.

Chen, Qi, Xiao Chen, Katherine Schipper, Yongxin Xu, and Jian Xue (2012). "The Sensitivity of Corporate Cash Holdings to Corporate Governance." *Review of Financial Studies* 25(12): 3610–44.

Chen, Xia, Jarrad Harford, and Kai Li (2007). "Monitoring: Which Institutions Matter?" *Journal of Financial Economics* 86(2): 279–305.

Chen, Yanyan, Bin Ke, and Na Liu (2017). "Does Allowing Publicly Listed Firms to Adopt Equity-Based Compensation Increase Shareholder Value? Evidence from China." Working paper, National University of Singapore.

Claessens, Stijn, Simeon Djankov, Joseph P. H. Fan, and Larry H. P. Lang (2002). "Disentangling the Incentive and Entrenchment Effects of Large Shareholdings." *Journal of Finance* 57(6): 81–112.

Conyon, Martin J., and Lerong He (2011). "Executive Compensation and Corporate Governance in China." *Journal of Corporate Finance* 17(4): 1158–75.

Frank, Jun, Rui Deng, and Faye Mo (2014). "Investor Stewardship: An Examination of Voting and Engagement Activities in China." ISS report. www.issgovernance.com.

Giannetti, Mariassunta, Guanmin Liao, and Xiaoyun Yu (2015). "The Brain Gain of Corporate Boards: Evidence from China." *Journal of Finance* 70(4): 1629–82.

Gu, Zhaoyang, Kun Wang, and Xing Xiao (2010). "Government Control and Executive Compensation: Evidence from China." Working paper, Chinese University of Hong Kong.

Jensen, Michael C. (1986). "Agency Costs of Free Cash Flow, Corporate Finance, and Takeovers." *American Economic Review* 76(2): 323–29.

Jensen, Michael C., and William H. Meckling (1976). "Theory of the Firm: Managerial Behavior, Agency Costs, and Ownership Structure." *Journal of Financial Economics* 3(4): 305–60.

Jiang, Guohua, Charles M. C. Lee, and Heng Yue (2010). "Tunnelling through Intercorporate Loans: The China Experience." *Journal of Financial Economics* 98(1): 1–20.

La Porta, Rafael, Florencio Lopez-De-Silanes, and Andrei Shleifer (1999). "Corporate Ownership Around the World." *Journal of Finance* 54(2): 471–517.

Lin, Huidan (2009). "Essays on Empirical Corporate Finance and Corporate Governance." Working paper, Columbia University.

Mitchell, Mark L., and Kenneth Lehn (1990). "Do Bad Bidders Become Good Targets?" *Journal of Political Economy* 98(2): 372–98.

Wang, Cong, Fei Xie, and Min Zhu (2015). "Industry Expertise of Independent Directors and Board Monitoring." *Journal of Financial and Quantitative Analysis* 50(5): 929–62.

13

THE ACCOUNTING SYSTEM IN CHINA

Tianyu Zhang

1. INTRODUCTION

Accounting information, which reflects the financial situation of the reporting entity as well as the economic performance of a jurisdiction, plays an important role in economic systems. The availability of high-quality accounting information will improve investment efficiency within a firm (Biddle and Hilary, 2006), protect minority shareholders from expropriation by insiders (Ball et al., 2003), and thus set the foundation for a well-functioning financial system. The quality of accounting information relies on an accounting system, which incorporates accounting standards. How well the accounting system is enforced is shaped by the institutions and the derived incentives of stakeholders in such institutions (Ball et al., 2003; Piotroski and Wong, 2012). The role of the market in an economy determines how important the accounting information should be in the jurisdiction. In a planning economy, economic activities are merely executed according to economic plans made by the government, leaving limited room for using accounting information to guide resource allocation. Formerly, accounting information was used mainly to reflect the status and safety of state capital, without giving much consideration to market-based transactions. However, with the launching of economic reform within China since 1978, the situation changed, especially after the emergence of the capital market.

The evolution of the Chinese accounting system was a process of harmonization with international accounting standards. The reform of the accounting system was launched initially to cater to the demand from firms with foreign ownership after the introduction of the open-door policy in the early 1980s. The first set of accounting standards was designed in accordance with the framework of international accounting standards. In the 1990s, the accounting system evolved further, induced by the growing development of the economy and the capital market. On November 8, 2005, the Ministry of Finance (MOF) and the International Accounting Standards Board (IASB) signed a memorandum declaring that China's accounting standards had substantially converged to the International Financial Reporting Standards (IFRS), marking a milestone in the reform China's accounting system. After that, the system achieved further recognition throughout the international business community, which included Hong Kong and the European Union, by means of cooperation between the Chinese government and IASB.

The dynamics of China's accounting system over the past few decades deserves a comprehensive review. By understanding its history, information users will gain a deeper understanding of how accounting information is generated and thus be able to reconcile the differences between current and historic accounting information. They will also gain insights into the differences that exist between China's accounting system and international standards. This review does not intend to explain China's accounting history in exhaustive detail. Instead, it will focus on a discussion of the driving forces behind key reforms in the accounting system, the changes and consequences induced by those reforms, and the implementation of the accounting system in practice.

This chapter is organized as follows: section 2 will introduce the legislative framework of China's accounting system; section 3 will review the system's evolution; section 4 will provide evidence on the impact imposed on financial reporting through convergence with the IFRS; section 5 will briefly review the evolution of auditing standards in the country; and section 6 will conclude this chapter.

2. LEGISLATIVE FRAMEWORK OF THE CHINESE ACCOUNTING SYSTEM

Accounting standards are professional rules guiding accounting practices to ensure the quality of accounting information. Thus, the standard setters in most common-law countries normally exist as professional bodies, rather than as political agents. For example, the IASB, the standard setter for IFRS, consists of an independent group of experts with an appropriate mix of recent practical experience in setting accounting standards; preparing, auditing, or using financial reports; and supporting accounting education.[1] The Financial Accounting Standards Board (FASB) describes itself as an "independent, private sector, not-for-profit organization that establishes financial accounting and reporting standards for public and private companies and not-for-profit organizations."[2] As a private professional body, the standard setters cannot authorize the implementation of accounting standards among reporting entities, since the true authority comes from the regulator or government adopting the standards.

However, in China, the accounting system is established by a government agent that is automatically granted the legal authority to implement accounting standards among reporting entities. In addition, the legal status of the accounting system is explicitly recognized by Accounting Law, which guarantees the implementation of the system. Thus, before discussing the evolution of the accounting system, this section will describe the legislative framework of the system, which includes four levels of laws or rules issued by various regulatory bodies. Figure 13.1 illustrates the composition of the current accounting system.[3]

At the top of the Chinese accounting system stands Accounting Law, which is promulgated by the highest legislative body in China, the National People's Congress. It sets up the legal foundation for the country's accounting system. The law was first issued in 1985 and revised twice—in 1992 and 1999, respectively. Accounting Law is the superior rule of the accounting system, and no conflicts with it are allowed in the accounting sys-

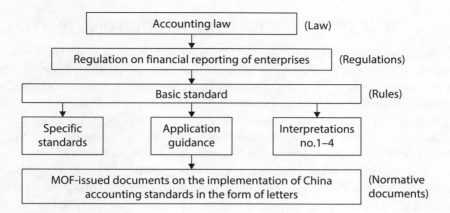

FIGURE 13.1. Legislative framework of China's accounting system. *Source:* Modified from Otto (2011).

tem. The system's legal status also implies that violation of that system in China can be dealt with through legal procedures.

The second level of the system consists of the administrative regulations issued by the Council of State in the form of orders from the prime minster. These orders are known as the Regulations on Financial Accounting Reports of Enterprises. The regulations are applicable to all types of enterprises that prepare external financial reports. As stated in the first article of the regulation, the objective is to "control financial scandal and guarantee the truthfulness and fairness of accounting information."

The third level of the system is Accounting Standards for Business Enterprises (ASBEs), a series of rules issued by the MOF to guide accounting practices throughout the country. The ASBEs have three components: basic standards, specific standards, and interpretations of accounting standards. Accounting standards in China are regarded as part of the legal system and thus are mandatorily adopted. Companies violating accounting rules are regarded as illegal, which strengthens the enforcement of the standards in China (Liu, 2007).

The fourth level of the system includes normative documents issued by the MOF in implementing the ASBEs, such as Implementation Guidance for ASBEs, which was issued in 2010. It provides further direction and interpretations for implementing the accounting standards adopted in 2006.

Related to the implementation of the accounting system, two other regulatory bodies are worth mentioning. The China Securities Regulatory Commission (CSRC) is not directly involved in setting up accounting rules, but it plays a very important role in implementing the accounting system. In the capital market, CSRC regulates information disclosure, especially accounting information, by listed companies. The manipulation of accounting information by bending accounting standards will be punished by the CSRC; such punitive measures ensure the implementation of the accounting system in the capital market. The China Institute of Certified Public Accountants (CICPA) sets up the China Standards for Certified Public Accountants, which are professional standards for auditing practices. The quality of audit, which is determined by the auditing standards, is another important factor for the effective implementation of the accounting system.

3. EVOLUTION OF THE CHINESE ACCOUNTING SYSTEM

The evolution of the accounting system in China was driven by the demand for accounting information that originated from the emergence of new business transactions. Before the economic reform, the system had achieved some development, such as borrowing experience from the Soviet Union, but it was later dismantled during the Cultural Revolution. In that stage, economic development gave way to the political agenda. Business management and accounting practices thus were considered inconsistent and even conflicting with the Cultural Revolution. Accounting during this era lost both scientific support and its human capital foundation because accounting education was abandoned for some 10 years in China's universities. A typical example capturing the situation of accounting practices during this period was called "accounting without books," meaning that the key elements of accountants and ledgers had been abandoned. All told, this indicated that the accounting system did not function properly. This chapter will not review the accounting system before the economic reform launched in 1978, but will elucidate the evolution of the accounting system after that.

3.1. Before 1992: Emergence of the Market-Oriented Accounting System

With the progress of economic reform, a demand emerged for accounting information from newly restored business operations. However, even the accounting model borrowed from the Soviet Union had been abandoned. Thus, the priority was to restore an accounting system that could accommodate the demand for accounting information about business activities in state-owned enterprises. Given the dominance of state-owned industrial enterprises in the economy, as well as the segmentation of accounting by business sectors, the first restored accounting system was the Accounting System in State-Owned Industrial Enterprises–Accounts and Financial Statements, issued by the MOF in 1980, which was a revised version of the accounting system issued in 1973. State-owned enterprises (SOEs) were not considered economic entities independent from the state, and thus the original accounting system's key function was to record the interflow of capital between enterprises and the state, as well as to document how enterprises were implementing the goals of state economic planning. As reform delved further, more decision power over the operation was transferred from the state to the management of the enterprises. The state ceased to exert direct administration over state-owned enterprises but still withheld key power over important decisions, such as financing decisions and personnel appointments. A contract responsibility system emerged among SOEs in the late 1980s, a direct consequence of which was that enterprises were transformed from simply cost centers in implementing instructions from the state into profit centers. Commercial activities and interrelationship between enterprises and the state became complicated, leading to revisions of the accounting system that took place in 1985 and 1989, respectively. Major changes in the accounting system during those years included: (1) the account for specific funds for specific purposes, which had been introduced to implement state economic planning, was abolished; (2) new accounts, such as bank loans and corporate funds, were presented in a balance sheet instead of a government funds account; and (3) intangible assets, such as trademarks, patents, and goodwill, were allowed to be recognized on the balance sheets of joint ventures and other business combinations. In this stage, discretions in accounting recognition and treatment were gradually introduced into China's accounting system.

The promulgation of the Accounting Law in 1985, the first law in accounting history since the country's foundation in 1949, marked a milestone in the evolution of the Chinese accounting system. It set up a legal foundation for the accounting profession, ensuring discipline in the profession, enforcement over accounting frauds, and protection for accounting practitioners. The law also played a key role in restoring order in accounting practice from a situation in which accounting fraud thrived and even ignorance of accounting rules in management was prevalent. The legal authority of the accounting system was recognized by the Accounting Law, which had profound implications for the further development of the accounting profession.

Foreign investment in China in the early 1980s was a powerful market force that pushed the adoption of an accounting system catering to a market economy. With the open-door policy, more and more foreign-owned firms, in the form of joint ventures or wholly foreign-owned entities, were established in China. The foreign-owned firms differed significantly from state-owned enterprises. Typically, the foreign-owned enterprises are independent economic entities possessing a legal identity. Their operation should therefore be separate from that of the firm's owners. Those owners, of course, were engaged in profit sharing as well as risk taking. However, the existing accounting system serving state-owned enterprises still could not accommodate such a market-based relationship between owners and foreign-owned firms. Thus, the "Accounting Regulation for Joint Ventures Using Chinese and Foreign Capital" was promulgated in 1985 to fill the gap. It was regarded as a step representing the establishment of the modern Chinese accounting system, and it aimed to fully comply with international accounting rules. A significant change brought about by this regulation was the adoption of the accounting equation, Assets = Liability + Equity, to replace the fund-based system, in which the accounting equation was in a format of Capital Occupied = Capital Sources.[4] Joint ventures were thereafter required to prepare a balance sheet, an income statement, and a cash flow statement and then to submit them to the Chinese government—exactly the financial reporting framework that developed markets had adopted.

In the 1980s the Council of State also issued two other regulations, the Tentative Regulation on the Depreciation of Fixed Assets for State-Owned Enterprises, and the Regulation on Cost Management of State-Owned Enterprises, to regulate accounting practices in recognizing depreciation expenses and cost calculation. These changes were intended to provide more-accurate estimations of expenses or costs in the entity, compared with situations in which the depreciation rate was determined by a government agent and the cost recognition guidelines were missing.

Overall, throughout this stage, the accounting system was integrating market factors into its framework.

3.2. Between 1992 and 2006: Harmonization with International Accounting Standards

After years of pilot experiments until the early 1990s, the shareholding system was gaining recognition as the legitimate organizational form for modern enterprises. The official objective of economic reform was to develop the socialist market economy, starting in 1992. Yet the accounting system designed for state-owned enterprises operating in the planning economy could not provide the accounting information required by various stakeholders, beyond the state, in the newly emerged shareholding entities. Thus, the

MOF, together with the National Economy Restructuring Commission, issued the Accounting System for Experimental Enterprises with the Shareholding System in May 1992, which launched a new era of accounting reforms. This was the first trial of the Chinese accounting system to follow the regularity that had been established in international accounting practice concerning domestic firms, regardless of their business sectors.

The Accounting Standards for Business Enterprises (ASBEs), which were as important as the Accounting Law, were issued in November 1992. It became the first set of formal accounting standards in China's accounting history, paving the way for the establishment of new accounting standards and simultaneously reforming the accounting system throughout the market economy (Ge, 1993). With their application to all companies, regardless of their sectors, the ASBEs ended the period of fragmentation in accounting practice by ownership type or operating sectors. The new general principle accomplished a complete shift from the traditional, fund-based accounting system to a market-oriented one.

Compared to the regulations in the past accounting system, the ASBEs in 1992 featured the following changes (Fu, 2015):

1. They established a conceptual framework and a general principle for a financial accounting system in China. The former accounting system had focused on the accounts setup and their function, as well as on the data sources for financial statements, which was more like a working manual for accountants. The purpose of the old accounting system was to establish the rules followed in accounting practices, leaving little discretion for management judgment. Even though the Accounting System for Joint Ventures had tried to include a fundamental explanation and general principles for management's discretion, they were incomplete and unsystematic. In addition, the application scope was limited strictly to joint ventures. However, the conceptual framework and general principles of ASBEs were applicable to all companies, regardless of their affiliated sectors.

2. The accounting equation was widely adopted. In the planning economy, the capital of companies came from the state or from state-owned banks, making it meaningless to differentiate between the interests of creditors and shareholders. Thus, the accounting equation was expressed as "Capital Occupied = Capital Sources." However, modern enterprises had some autonomy in operating, financing, and investment decisions, implying a separation between management and owners. The interest of various stakeholders should be well recognized and recorded, especially for creditors and equity holders. Thus, the ASBEs adopted the internationally used accounting equation of "Assets = Equity + Liability." The information presented according to this equation was more relevant for information users to help them understand a company's capital structure and liquidity.

3. Internationally recognized accounting methods were also adopted in ASBEs. For example, the allowance method is allowed to recognize bad debt expenses, and the accelerated depreciation method is also allowed.

4. The international financial reporting system was adopted in ASBEs. Traditionally, three statements—a balance statement of capital, an income statement, and

a cost statement—were reported to government agencies. The ASBEs adopted the international financial reporting system, requiring companies to present three statements—a balance sheet, an income statement, and a statement of changes in financial position shared with external information users. The cost statement can be kept within the company without disclosure to outsiders, for confidentiality purposes.

5. The ASBEs unified the accounting system across different sectors.
6. The ASBEs also guaranteed the maintenance of initial investments from shareholders. For example, a net loss resulting from the disposal of assets was recognized as losses through the income statement, rather than directly as a write-off against the owner's equity as in the traditional accounting system.

However, significant gaps still existed between ASBEs and international accounting standards. For example, the conceptual framework was not explicitly stated, the main information function remained oriented toward the state, the "substance over form" principle was not implemented, limited discretion was allowed for management judgment, and conservative accounting was insufficiently implemented.

While the ASBEs had set up the general principles for accounting treatment, they lacked either specification or a detailed explanation of accounting treatment for business transactions. Following traditional practices, companies still sought detailed rules or instructions that could be executed in their respective accounting practices. In response, the MOF issued specific accounting systems for no fewer than 13 industries, among which the Accounting System for Industrial Enterprises was most representative. For example, based on the general guidelines from ABSEs, that system provided detailed explanations for industries setting up accounts or preparing financial statements.

In 1992, in addition to the industry-specific accounting system, the MOF also launched a project for drafting specific accounting standards, including some for measuring, recording, and disclosure. The intention was to align accounting practices in China with those employed in the international market. The specific accounting standards focused on accounting treatment of specific transactions or disclosure. By 1996, the MOF had drafted over 30 accounting standards, which were to be implemented starting the next year. Only 10 additional standards were issued from 1997 to 2001. The specific accounting standards were not widely issued in the 1990s because accounting practitioners did not view it as necessary to adopt these standards, thinking that the ASBEs, with the assistance of industry-specific accounting systems, were sufficient for their business. Such a response from accounting practitioners themselves led to a switch in mindset of the MOF with regard to setting up the specific accounting standards. Such standards would be issued on an ad hoc basis as the demand arose in the market. For example, the first specific accounting standard for "Disclosure of Related Parties and Related Party Transactions" was issued in 1997 on the unraveling of a financial scandal uncovered on the part of Qiong Minyuan, a listed company from Hainan Province charged with engaging in aggressive related-party transactions. Subsequent to that event, a series of specific accounting standards, such as the standards for the "Statement of Cash Flow," "Debt Restructuring," "Revenue," and "Construction Contract," were issued in response to market demand.

The Accounting System for Experimental Enterprises with the Shareholding System, issued in 1992, fell far behind market development, which included such events as the establishment of a new legal system for corporations, taxation reform, the foreign exchange system, and the emergence of new transactions beyond the coverage of the old accounting system, in the later 1990s. Thus, the MOF issued the Accounting System for Enterprises of the Shareholding System in 1998. The new system had aggregated the achievement in accounting reform over the past previous years, pushing China's accounting system into greater alignment with international practices. The system featured the first adoption of several widely accepted international accounting practices. For example, it required that accounting treatment be strictly separated from taxation regulation. Article 7 stated: "When there is conflict between the accounting treatment required in this system with taxation regulation, the company should follow the requirements of this system, and pay tax according to the taxation regulation." Related to revenue, the original accounting system would have allowed revenue recognition on a "realization" basis, while the new system also required an additional condition of evidence for the transfer of risk and returns related to ownership.

To make China's accounting system even more comprehensive, the MOF issued the Accounting System for Business Enterprises, effective January 1, 2001, and applicable to shareholding enterprises. Its objective was to unify the accounting systems applied to firms from various industries and with contrasting ownership structure and organization form. As an aggregation of almost all the preexisting accounting rules, together with international accounting practices, the new accounting system was significantly different from its predecessors in at least five respects. First, the accounting elements, including assets, liabilities, equity, revenue, cost, and profit, were redefined in the new accounting system, based on changes in economic conditions, while the accounting elements defined in the ABSEs in 1992 did not touch their economic nature. Second, the principle of "substance over form" was first introduced and the object of accounting was revised. Information users were then equally ranked. Third, the conservatism principle was emphasized in the new accounting system to guarantee the quality of reported assets. Fourth, specific regulations for accounting treatment for new transactions were added or revised to accommodate the economic consequences of these transactions in the reporting system. And, fifth, the financial reporting required under the new accounting system included balance sheet, income statement, cash flow statement, allowance for assets, statement of profit distribution, statement of change in owner's equity, segment report, and several others.

The Accounting Law was revised for a second time in 1999, and two years later the Council of State issued a Regulation for Financial Reporting in Business Enterprises with the intention of suppressing financial scandals.

3.3. After 2006: Convergence to IFRS

Each step taken in China's accounting reform made its accounting practices far more aligned with international routines. However, accounting information prepared according to Chinese accounting standards was still not fully comparable with that prepared according to International Financial Reporting Standards (IFRS). As a consequence, Chinese firms would bear substantial costs in doing business in the global market owing to the incomparability of financial reporting. Therefore, Chinese firms had to switch to financial reporting prepared according to the accounting standards accepted by the destination market when they went overseas for financing or investment. After joining the World Trade Organization (WTO), many antidumping cases were raised against China. An aggrieved country could ignore Chinese accounting data to establish the cost of production but would need to rely on data known as "constructed value," based on accounting information from third-party exporters or producers (Ramanna et al., 2013). Thus, the Chinese government had an incentive to further align its accounting standards with those widely adopted in the international business community.

The convergence to IFRS would both increase the credibility of Chinese companies' financial statements and also reduce the companies' associated costs in the international market. Thus, the MOF issued a set of both new and revised Accounting Standards for Business Enterprises (called "new ASBEs") in 2006, which became effective on January 1, 2007, among listed companies. The new ABSEs consisted of basic standards, which were the revised version of accounting standards for business enterprises in 1992, including 38 specific standards, 22 of which were newly promulgated and 16 were revised versions of the existing standards, application guidance, and interpretations. Table 13.1 presents the complete list of accounting standards in China in comparison with that of IFRS. As of February 15, 2006, the International Accounting Standards Board (IASB) officially recognized that the China Accounting Standards had substantially converged to IFRS.

After analyzing the differences between the new ASBEs and the Hong Kong Financial Reporting Standards (HKFRS), the China Accounting Standards Boards and the Hong Kong Institute of Certified Public Accountants made a joint statement on December 6, 2007, that the new Chinese ASBEs and HKFRS were equivalent to each other. This was a meaningful step for the internationalization of China's accounting standards. Accordingly, mainland firms listed on the Hong Kong Stock Exchange could choose either China accounting standards or HKFRs for their financial reporting.[5] In a similar spirit, the European Union accepted the financial reports of Chinese companies prepared according to Chinese Accounting Standards without further adjustment after 2009, implying its recognition of the equivalence of Chinese Accounting Standards in European Union countries. The MOF continued to seek further recognition of new ASBEs in the international community, including countries such as Japan, Australia, and South Korea.

Converging with the IFRS, the new ABSEs had brought fundamental changes to the Generally Accepted Accounting Principles in China. The global accounting firm of Ernst & Young (2006a) featured a list of significant impacts imposed on financial reporting by the new ABSEs, including: (1) the introduction of fair value measurement; (2) the introduction of accounting standards and detailed guidelines for both business combinations and consolidated financial statements; (3) previously off-balance-sheet items were then required to be recorded in the balance sheet; (4) the introduction of new standards for specialized industries (e.g., financial institutions, insurance companies, and the like); (5) the introduction of new standards on "Impairment of Assets," specifying that impairment loss could not be reversed in future accounting periods; and (6) the introduction of stricter, more detailed disclosure requirements in line with IFRS.

Nevertheless, discrepancies still existed between the new ABSEs and IFRS, which defined the adoption of the new ABSEs as a convergence to IFRS, rather than a full adoption of IFRS (Ernst & Young, 2006b; Liu, 2007). They included the following.

Table 13.1. Comparison Between China Accounting Standards for
Business Enterprises and International Financial Reporting Standards

China accounting standards		International financial reporting standards	
ASBE 1	Inventories	IAS 2	Inventories
ASBE 2	Long-term equity investments	IAS 27	Consolidated and separate financial statements
		IAS 28	Investments in associates and joint ventures
		IAS 29	Financial reporting in hyperinflationary economies
ASBE 3	Investment property	IAS 40	Investment property
ASBE 4	Fixed assets	IAS 16	Property, plant, and equipment
ASBE 5	Biological assets	IAS 41	Agriculture
ASBE 6	Intangible assets	IAS 38	Intangible assets
ASBE 7	Exchange of nonmonetary assets	IAS16	Property, plant, and equipment
		IAS 38	Intangible assets
		IAS 40	Investment property
ASBE 8	Impairment of assets	IAS 36	Impairment of assets
ASBE 9	Employee benefits	IAS 19	Employee benefits
ASBE 10	Enterprise pension funds	IAS 26	Accounting and reporting by retirement benefit plans
ASBE 11	Share-based payments	IFRS 2	Share-based payments
ASBE 12	Debt restructurings	IAS 39	Financial instruments: recognition and measurement
ASBE 13	Contingencies	IAS 37	Provisions, contingent liabilities, and contingent assets
ASBE 14	Revenue	IAS 18	Revenue
ASBE 15	Construction contracts	IAS 11	Construction contracts

(*continued*)

Table 13.1. (continued)

China accounting standards		International financial reporting standards	
ASBE 34	Earnings per share	IAS 33	Earnings per share
ASBE 35	Segment reporting	IFRS 8	Operating segments
ASBE 36	Related party disclosure	IAS 24	Related party disclosure
ASBE 37	Financial instruments: Presentation and disclosure	IFRS 7	Financial instruments: Disclosures
		IAS 32	Financial instruments: Presentation
ASBE 38	First adoption of accounting standards for business enterprises	IFRS 1	First-time adoption of international financial reporting standards
ASBE 39	Fair value measurement	IFRS 13	Fair value measurement
ASBE 40	Joint arrangement	IFRS 11	Joint arrangement
ASBE 41	Disclosure of interest in other entities	IFRS 12	Disclosure of interest in other entities
		IFRS 5	Non-current assets held for sale and ceased
		IAS 29	Financial reporting in hyperinflationary economies

Source: Ministry of Finance.
Note: ASBE = Accounting Standards for Business Enterprise; IAS = International Accounting Standards; IFRS = International Financial Reporting Standards.

1. In China, state-controlled enterprises played an important role in the economy. According to IFRS, state-controlled entities were no longer exempted from the disclosure of related parties. If ASBEs also adopted the same requirements as IFRS, each SOE would disclose all the other SOEs as its related parties, which was impossible. Thus, the ASBEs defined related parties through a direct investment relationship, rather than through the identity as an SOE. The IASB allowed partial exemption for China in applying this requirement.

2. The reversal of impairment loss for long-term assets was allowed in IFRS but disallowed in ABSEs. The IASB allowed this treatment in China's ASBEs with reference to similar practices in U.S. accounting standards.

3. According to ASBEs, the fair value measurement was not applied as widely as in IFRS. Without an active market to provide reliable information about fair value, the reliability of accounting information would be challenged if fair value measurement was widely adopted. Thus, ASBEs only allowed fair value measurement for several scenarios, such as investment properties, debt restructuring, and biological assets.

4. For a business combination, ASBEs allowed the pooling interest method under common control. However, IFRS only allowed the acquisition method, without considering a combination under common control.

5. IFRS's accounting standard called "Non-current assets held for sale and discontinued operation" specified the accounting treatment for assets held for sale and discontinued operation. However, the corresponding specification was included in standards for fixed assets rather than in a separate standard.

6. In IFRS, "Employee Benefit" and "Accounting and Reporting by Retirement Benefit Plans" both specified the accounting treatment for defined contribution plans and as well as defined benefit plans. However, the latter plans did not exist in China. Thus, ASBEs only had accounting treatment for pensions, which was similar to the defined contribution plan in "Enterprises Pension Funds."

7. The accounting standard for financial reporting in hyperinflationary economies was not included in the ASBEs because it was regarded as unnecessary, given the low likelihood of hyperinflation. However, following a suggestion from the IASB, the accounting adjustment was provided in the standard for foreign currency exchange in ASBEs.

8. Several standards in IFRS were rearranged in ASBEs. The IFRS's "Financial Instruments: Recognition and Measurement" was decomposed in ASBEs as "Financial Instruments: Recognition and Measurement," "Transfer of Financial Assets," and "Hedging." "Insurance Contract" in IFRS was decomposed as "Direct Insurance Contract" and "Indirect Insurance Contract" in ASBEs. "Separate and Consolidated Financial Statement" and "Investment in Associate and Joint Ventures" in IFRS were combined as "Long-Term Investment" in ASBEs.

This elaborate convergence process continued long after new ASBEs were issued in 2006. The scope of applying new ASBEs also expanded. It was initially adopted among listed companies starting January 1, 2007, and would be applied to Central Government–controlled firms, unlisted financial banks and insurance companies, and some state-owned enterprises starting in 2008. Based on the Roadmap of Continuous Convergence of Chinese Accounting Standards for Business Enterprises to International Financial Reporting Standards, which the MOF released MOF in 2010, the ABSEs would revise and improve in accordance with the revision and improvement in IFRS for "continuous convergence." In 2017, the MOF issued exposure draft statements applying to several specific standards: "Revenue," "Non-current assets held for sale and discontinued operation," "Disclosure of Financial Instrument," and "Interpretations for Accounting Standards 9–12," among others. This implied a further convergence to IFRS.

At long last, after many years of reform, China had established a relatively complete and comprehensive accounting system with substantial convergence to IFRS. New accounting issues would, of course, emerge in China's transitional economy over time. But under the current agreement, the Chinese government will collaborate with the IASB to tackle these issues. The specificity in country-level institutions might have made the full adoption of IFRS in China difficult. Still, the substantial convergence to international standards as well as recognition by other economies would ease the disclosure of Chinese firms in the international market, which would, in turn, facilitate greater international trade.

4. IMPACT OF THE CONVERGENCE TO IFRS ON FINANCIAL REPORTING IN CHINA

4.1. Direct Impact on Financial Reporting

With the adoption of new ASBEs, the financial reporting of Chinese firms would shift toward international practices, and the reported accounting information would be changed accordingly. The MOF comprehensively reviewed the impact imposed by the adoption of new accounting standards on the financial report in 2007. According to ASBE No. 38, the First-Time Adoption of Accounting Standards for Business Enterprises, the reporting entities were required to provide a reconciliation of differences in the starting balance of shareholders' equity occasioned by the new and replaced standards. The starting balance of total shareholders' equity in 2007, according to the new ASBEs, amounted to RMB4,562 billion for 1,557 listed companies, according to their annual reports disclosed by April 30, 2008; the ending balance of total shareholders' equity of these same firms in 2006, reported according to the old ASBEs, amounted to RMB4,148.66 billion. Without counting the difference induced by minority interests,[6] shareholder equity thereby achieved an increase of RMB100.26 billion, equivalent to a growth rate of 2.42%. A detailed comparison is presented in table 13.2. "Financial assets at fair value through profit and loss and available-for-sale financial assets" induced the largest increase in shareholder equity of RMB79.504 billion (1.92%), involving 454 firms. "Differences in long-term equity investment" led to a decrease of RMB16.078 billion (–0.39%), involving 737 firms. This report by the MOF concluded that "although large adjustments were made to some items in the transition from the old to new standards, the total amount after offsetting remained largely unaffected, so the transition was smooth."

The IFRS was fully adopted in Hong Kong in 2005. Thus, firms dually listed on the Hong Kong Stock Exchange and the Shenzhen or Shanghai Stock Exchange were expected to present their financial reports in Hong Kong according to HKFRS, but in China according to its ASBEs. The difference in reported profit under the two standards

Table 13.2. Impact of New Accounting Standards for Business Enterprises

	Items	Number of firms	Amount	%*
a	Shareholders' equity on December 31, 2016 (old standards)	1,557	41,486.64	–
1	Differences in long-term equity investment	737	–160.78	–0.0039
2	Investment properties to be measured in fair value model	14	39.29	0.0009
3	Accrued depreciation for previous years for estimated assets, decommissioning expenses, etc.	6	–25.77	–0.0006
4	Termination benefits quali-fied for the recognition criteria of provisions	149	–114.39	–0.0028
5	Share-based payment	8	–5.64	–0.0001
6	Restructuring obligations qualified for the recognition criteria of provisions	4	–1.26	0
7	Business combination	166	335.81	0.0081
8	Financial assets at fair value through profit or loss and available-for-sale financial assets	454	795.04	0.0192
9	Financial liability at fair value through profit and loss	11	–0.37	0
10	Equity increased by separa-tion of financial instruments	19	–6.56	–0.0002
11	Derivative financial instruments	31	–4.83	–0.0001
12	Income tax	1,360	–1.43	0
13	Minority interest	1,267	3,136.18	0.0756
14	Special retrospective adjust-ment to listed companies with B or H shares	14	–5.03	–0.0001
15	Others	616	158.59	0.0038
b	Total adjustment	–	4,138.85	0.0998
c	Net increase in shareholders' equity	–	1,002.67	2.42%**
d	Shareholders' equity on January 1, 2017 (new standards)	1,557	45,625.49	–

Source: Ministry of Finance.
Notes: Currency unit: 100 million; *Item % = adjustment amount of item/shareholders' equity under old accounting standards; **Change rate of shareholders' equity = (shareholders' equity under new standards-minority interest) / shareholders' equity under old accounting standards.

should be reconciled and disclosed in the annual report. Thus, the analysis of the trend in the difference between reported earnings under the two standards would provide evidence for how effectively the China accounting standards had converged with the IFRS. Through analysis of the financial reports of listed companies by the Ministry of Finance (2011), the reported profit in 2010, according to the HKFRS, of 66 listed companies with both A and H shares was RMB1,081 billion, while it was RMB1,078 billion according to China's accounting standards—a difference of 0.33%. Tracing back, the difference was 4.69% in 2007, 2.39% in 2008, and 0.64% in 2009, which clearly showed a declining trend. Specifically, 32 out of 66 firms with both A and H shares in 2010 reported exactly the same accounting profit under the two accounting standards. The evidence also implied a successful convergence of China's accounting standards to IFRS in practice.

4.2. Impact on Earnings Quality

A set of high-quality accounting standards is a necessary infrastructure to enable the generation and dissemination of fair and relevant information about reporting entities, thus facilitating the efficiency of both resource allocation and market development. In addition to the series of reform measures aimed at improving the corporate transparency of accounting standards, the Chinese government has also tried to improve corporate governance, strengthen legal protections, and develop market institutions. Thus, it acknowledges that good reporting standards and regulations are strong guarantees of the quality of accounting information. The distribution of earnings and the timeliness of loss recognition are widely used in the accounting field to measure earnings quality. Figure 13.2, Panel A, presents the distribution of ROE, which is earnings scaled by owner's equity for all listed firms between 2001 and 2006. It can clearly be observed that there two cutoff points, 0% and 6%, followed by a bigger cluster of firms as in Liu (2007), which was based on earlier data. Many fewer firms are distributed among the range of negative earnings, a different situation than that in the United States (Burgstahler and Dichev, 1997). The underlying reason is that these cutoff points are used as a benchmark in bright-line regulations, such as for seasonal equity financing, as well as for delisting by the CSRC. Listed companies will try by all possible means to satisfy the regulatory requirements, and will even distort accounting information from reflecting the firm's real situation (Piotroski and Wong, 2012). Panel C of the figure presents the timeliness of loss recognition compared with several developed countries (Piotroski and Wong, 2012). This indicates significantly lower timeliness in recognizing negative information in reported earnings, which may lead to the further misallocation of economic resources. The question arises: Can convergence to IFRS make significant changes to such earnings quality in general? Plotting the distributions of ROE between 2007 and 2016, which is a period after the convergence to IFRS, Panel B of figure 13.2 still shows an absence of firms' reporting losses. However, the other cutoff point, 6%, does not induce the clustering of firms in distribution, because the specific regulatory requirement for seasonal offerings referring to this benchmark was abandoned. Comparing Panels A and B in the figure, it is not obvious that the IFRS have significantly increased earnings quality.

The IFRS are featured with their wide application of fair value measurement and recognition. Reflecting the most updated value of fundamentals of a given reporting

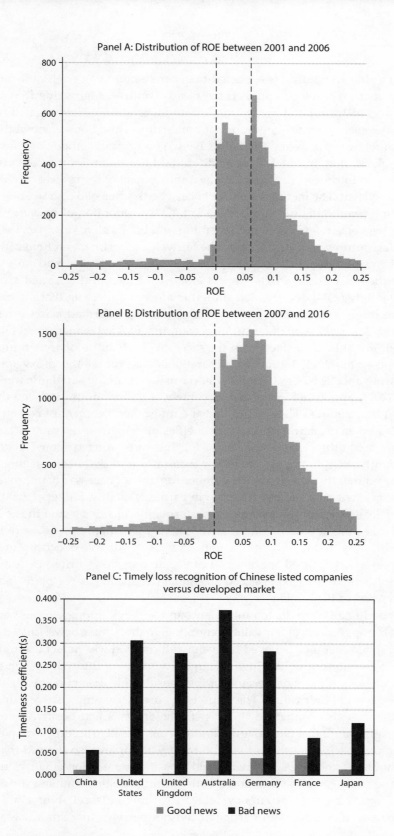

FIGURE 13.2. Properties of earnings. *Sources:* Panels A and B are from the author's data. Panel C is taken from Piotroski and Wong (2012)

entity, fair value accounting is expected to generate more value-relevant information. The evidence from developed markets has clearly confirmed fair value accounting's superiority over historical cost accounting. Qu and Zhang (2015) investigated the change in value relevance of accounting information, earnings, and book value in the Chinese capital market over a 20-year period after 1990. With typical methodology for value relevance analysis, they reached three findings: (1) the value relevance of earnings and book value had improved, as a result of the improvement of the market mechanism and accounting system. The incremental relevance of book value had also steadily increased since the inception of China's capital market. (2) The adoption of new ASBEs in 2006 improved the value relevance of both earnings and book value. However, the impact of fair value accounting was very trivial. The fair value adjustment on financial assets for trading financial assets held to maturity and available for sale had no explanatory power for the stock price.[7] (3) The impact of fair value accounting varied across industries. Elshandidy (2014) documented similar evidence supporting that the convergence to IFRS has improved the value relevance of accounting information in China.

However, the application of fair value accounting allowed management more discretion, which might be associated with the sacrifice of reliability of accounting information. Zhang et al. (2013) found that discretionary accruals—the proxy for earnings management—increased significantly after the new accounting standards were adopted. Wu et al. (2014) investigated information content in the earnings disclosed during several accounting periods. They found that the information content of concurrent earnings, measured as the earnings response coefficient, remained the same after adoption of the new accounting standards, while the future earning response coefficient increased significantly, implying less timely information in disclosed earnings. The evidence showed that the new accounting standards did not necessarily improve earnings quality. Consistent with the deterioration in earnings quality, Ball et al. (2003) found a significant decline in pay-for-accounting-performance sensitivity after the new accounting standards were adopted. Central government–owned enterprises were influenced more significantly by the new ASBEs, and, as a result, the role of accounting information in contracts decreased more significantly among these firms. In contrast, local government-owned firms experienced no similar decline in pay-for-performance sensitivity, according to their evidence.

Xiao and Hu (2017) conducted interviews and surveys among various stakeholders regarding the application of fair value accounting. In those interviews, financial analysts in general stated that they believed fair value information was in fact useful in making investment decisions or delivering investment advice. Yet the analysts felt concerned about earnings manipulation because of the considerable discretion available to management measuring "fair value." The response from a large sample survey among financial analysts has also confirmed this belief. The analysts had positive feedback with economic significance that fair value accounting contributed to accuracy, frequency, timeliness, and the specificity level of their forecasts. The survey also showed that financial analysts, auditors, and CFOs in general held a positive perception of fair value accounting, because of its capacity to improve both earnings quality and specific accounting characteristics, such as transparency, relevance, timeliness, reliability, and comparability. However, the auditors in particular did not perceive that fair value accounting would increase the conservatism of accounting to the same extent that the financial analysts and CFOs did. Still, all the respondents perceived that the adoption of fair value accounting had made a positive impact on reporting entities, such as increasing their efficiency of internal decision-making. Thus, this evidence from the field confirmed the findings through archival analysis, which had reached mixed conclusions on the impact of the convergence to IFRS.

4.3. Limitations of Applying IFRS in China

Xiao and Hu (2017) looked specifically into the implementation of fair value measurement via the new accounting standards by reading carefully through the annual reports of a sample of listed companies from 2007 to 2011. They concluded that "the quantity of FV (fair value)-disclosure was very small and the quality was very low. Almost no company disclosed the FV-related information the CASs (China Accounting Standards) require in the footnotes, e.g., what methods are used to measure the FV, and how." They also surveyed some 200 auditors about their clients' attitudes about the adoption of fair value in the new accounting standards. They found that a minimal 12.76% of their clients were positive about fair value adoption, while 44% and 43% of their clients had either negative or neutral perceptions toward it.

The effectiveness of implementing new accounting rules relies heavily on the institutional environment. Ball et al. (2003) investigated the earnings quality of four Eastern Asian countries—Hong Kong (city), Malaysia, Singapore, and Thailand—all of which have adopted widely accepted, high-quality accounting standards. However, owing to the lack of incentives on the part of insiders within reporting entities to provide information to outsiders, the reported earnings were still associated with low quality in practice. In China, He et al. (2012) argued that the institutions of the country's emerging market were simply incompatible with fair value accounting. They documented evidence that fair value accounting, such as securities available for sale, was typically utilized by insiders for earnings management when the underlying incentive to meet a certain earnings threshold emerged. In China's emerging market, most companies are still state-controlled after listing; the capital market remains heavily subject to government regulation; market institutions are weak; property rights are not well protected; and the local auditors lack independence (Piotroski and Wong, 2012). Given these institutional constraints, the positive value of IFRS may not be fully executed in China, even after local rules converge with international practice.

The application of new accounting standards was also challenged by technical difficulties. Through a survey taken among auditors, CFOs, and financial analysts, Xiao and Hu (2017) found that the leading challenge to the implementation of fair value accounting was difficulty in obtaining the required fair value in a less developed and less active market. They found a second barrier to be imperfect accounting standards, along with insufficient guidance on applying fair value in the current accounting standards. Other difficulties recognized in the field include an imperfect supporting system and facilities, a lack of fair value–related technical knowledge among accountants, low professional competence of the external auditor, and so forth. Thus, to make high-quality accounting standards work, the institutional arrangement should also be brought into line with proper incentives to apply those standards.

5. EVOLUTION OF THE AUDITING SYSTEM

The auditing profession, as the gatekeeper for accounting information, serves as an important factor in implementing accounting standards effectively. Harmonizing accounting standards throughout China with those of accepted international practices has created a similar demand for the audit profession throughout the country. In 1993, the "Law for Certified Public Accountants" was approved by the National People's Congress, thereby establishing a legal foundation for the accounting profession. It promulgated, among other items, certification for accountants, their business scope, the organization of audit firms, the establishment of the China Institute of Certified Public Accountants, and litigation obligations in the profession. However, the law's chief objective was to discipline the management of the professional accounting industry without any intention of specifying how audit work should be executed in the field. Regulatory bodies in the profession were also segmented then, because of the coexistence of the China Institute of Certified Public Accountants and the China Institute of Certified Auditors before 1995, which resulted in conflicts within the regulations and even undermined the credibility of the profession. That same year, as a significant improvement in the profession, the two regulatory bodies were consolidated into one, the China Institute of Certified Public Accountants (CICPA), as the single professional regulatory body under the supervision of the Ministry of Finance and the National Department of Audit. The CICPA then took responsibility for setting professional standards, which did not exist yet but in theory were in great demand to guide the profession's fieldwork.

The first batch of independent auditing standards drafted by the CICPA was issued by the Ministry of Finance in 1995 and became effective at the beginning of the next year. The standards included one basic standard and seven specific standards, as well as an announcement for asset appraisal. The issuance of independent audit standards was a milestone in the development of professional accounting in China. After it issued the first batch of auditing standards, the Ministry of Finance issued another five batches up through April 2003. Thus, the complete professional audit system was established with the inclusion of 48 standards-related items in it.

However, it developed that the audit quality was not satisfactory, even with the comprehensive audit standards. A series of notorious financial scandals had emerged in the China capital market, which undermined investor confidence in the accounting profession and heightened the risks for auditors. For example, Yin Guangxia and Lan Tian, two publicly listed companies, were found to have engaged aggressively in manipulating reported earnings in 2001 and 2002. The scandals resulted in tremendous losses to investors, leading to a demand for assurance about earnings reported by management. In step with the convergence of Chinese accounting standards with the IFRS, the auditing profession, led by the CICPA, also took the initiative in converging the domestic auditing standards to international audit standards. Following the international practice, the MOF Finance issued new Independent Auditing Standards, which on February 15, 2006, were renamed Standards for Certified Public Accountants. The new audit standards featured higher requirements for risk-oriented audits, alignment with international auditing practices, and protection for the benefit of public stakeholders. The CICPA continued to revise and update the country's auditing standards, in coordination with the International

Auditing and Assurance Standards Board (IAASB). On November 10, 2010, the CICPA and IAASB jointly announced that full convergence had been achieved, which implied recognition of China's new auditing regulations by the international community (Gillis, 2014).

This convergence has greatly helped Chinese accounting firms expand their international business. For example, following the mutual recognition of accounting standards between mainland China and Hong Kong, the financial reports of mainland firms listed in Hong Kong and audited by mainland auditors according to China's auditing standards have been accepted since 2010.

6. CONCLUSION

The Chinese accounting system has experienced ground-breaking changes during recent decades, in step with economic reforms intended to accommodate a demand for better accounting information in the market. The change rode a trend of harmonization with international accounting practices and in 2006 was recognized by the International Accounting Standards Board as a substantial convergence to IFRS. The convergence is still in progress to extend to other economies given the recognition received from Hong Kong in 2007 and the European Union in 2008. However, owing to the institutional environment, the implementation of newly adopted accounting standards still demands further improvement, in spite of the accounting profession's transition to a new era throughout China.

NOTES

1. See the IFRS website at https://www.ifrs.org/groups/international-accounting-standards-board/.
2. See the FASB website at https://www.fasb.org/facts/.
3. This is the structure of the accounting system as it stood after 2006; it may vary in future as a result of the introduction of new rules within the level.
4. The main purpose was to accurately reflect the flow of funds between state-owned enterprises and the state itself.
5. By the end of 2017, only 14% (55) of mainland firms listed on the Hong Kong Stock Exchange applied ASBEs in preparing their financial reports.
6. The change in shareholders' equity induced by "minority interest" should not be considered, since this item was presented separately from owners' equity in the old standards but included in that equity in the new standards.
7. The explanatory of earnings and book value over firm value increased from 29.3% in the pre-adoption period (2001–2006) to 48.2% in the post-adoption period (2007–2010).

REFERENCES

Ball, Ray, Ashok Robin, and Joanna S. Wu (2003). "Incentives Versus Standards: Properties of Accounting Income in Four East Asian Countries." *Journal of Accounting and Economics* 36(1–3): 235–70.

Biddle, Gary, and Gilles Hilary (2006). "Accounting Quality and Firm-level Capital Investment." *Accounting Review* 81(5): 963–82.

Burgstahler, David, and Ilia Dichev (1997). "Earnings Management to Avoid Earnings Decreases and Losses." *Journal of Accounting and Economics* 24(1): 99–126.

Ding, Yuan, and Xijia Su (2008). "Implementation of IFRS in a Regulated Market." *Journal of Accounting and Public Policy* 27(6): 474–79.

Elshandidy, Tamer (2014). "Value Relevance of Accounting Information: Evidence from an Emerging Market." *Advances in Accounting*, incorporating *Advances in International Accounting* 30(1): 1766.

Ernst & Young (2006a). "China Boardroom Briefing: New Standard, New Era—Special Edition on the New Chinese Accounting Standards," no. 1, issue 1: March.

Ernst & Young (2006b). "China Boardroom Briefing: Comparison of the New Chinese Accounting Standards with Current PRC GAAP—Special Edition on the New Chinese Accounting Standards," no. 2, issue 3: June.

Fu, Lei (2015). *A History of China's Accounting System from 1949* (in Chinese). Shanghai: Lixin Accounting Publishing House.

Ge, Jiashu (1993). "The Characteristics of Accounting Standards for Business Enterprises in China." *Accounting Research* (in Chinese). Vol 1.

Gillis, Paul L. (2014). *The Big Four and Development of the Accounting Profession in China.* Bingley, UK: Emerald Group Publishing.

He, Xianjie, T. J. Wong, and Danqing Young (2012). "Challenges for Implementation of Fair Value Accounting in Emerging Markets: Evidence from China." *Contemporary Accounting Research* 29(2): 538–62.

IFRS Foundation (2017). "IFRS Application Around the World Jurisdictional Profile: People's Republic of China." Research report, IFRS Foundation.

Liu, Qiao, and Zhou Lu (2007). "Corporate Governance and Earnings Management in the Chinese Listed Companies: A Tunneling Perspective." *Journal of Corporate Finance* 13(5): 881–906.

Liu, Yuting (2007). "China Accounting Standards: Framework, Convergence and Equivalence." *Accounting Research* (in Chinese) 3: 2–8.

Ministry of Finance (2008). "Analysis Report on the Implementation of New Accounting Standards by Chinese Listed Companies in 2007." Beijing: Press of Economic Science.

Ministry of Finance (2011). "Analysis Report on the Implementation of New Accounting Standards by Chinese Listed Companies in 2010.", Beijing: Press of Economic Science.

Otto, Jens Peter (2011). "Applying New China Accounting Standards by Foreign Investment Enterprises." PricewaterhouseCoopers.

Piotroski, Joseph, and T. J. Wong (2012). "Institutions and the Information Environment of Chinese Listed Firms," in *Capitalizing China*, edited by Joseph Fan and Randall Morck. Chicago and London: University of Chicago Press.

Qu, Xiaohui, and Guohua Zhang (2015). "Value Relevance of Earnings and Book Value Over the Institutional Transition in China: The Suitability of Fair Value Accounting in This Emerging Market." *International Journal of Accounting* 50(2): 195–223.

Ramanna, Karthik, G. A. Donovan, and Nancy H. Dai (2013). "IFRS in China." Harvard Business School Case 110-037. Boston: Harvard Business School Publishing.

Wu, Grace Shu-hsing, Shu-hsing Li, and Steve Lin (2014). "The Effect of Harmonization and Convergence with IFRS on the Timeliness of Earnings Reported under Chinese GAAP." *Journal of Contemporary Accounting and Economics* 10(2): 148–59.

Xiao, Jason Zezhong, and Guoqiang Hu (2017). "Fair Value Accounting in China: Implementation and Usefulness." London: Chartered Accountants' Trustee Limited.

Ye, Bin, Yubo Li, and Hongqi Yuan (2016). "The Substantial Convergence of Chinese Accounting Standards with IFRS and the Managerial Pay-for-Performance Sensitivity of Publicly Listed Chinese Firms." *Journal of Accounting and Public Policy* 35(6): 567–91.

Zhang, Yuyang, Konari Uchida, and Hua Bu (2013). "How Do Accounting Standards and Insiders' Incentives Affect Earnings Management? Evidence from China." *Emerging Markets Review* 16: 78–99.

PART 6

ASSET MANAGEMENT

14

INVESTMENT FUNDS IN CHINA

Wenxi Jiang

1. INTRODUCTION

On March 27, 1998, the very first two investment funds, Jintai Fund and Kaiyuan Fund, were issued to the public in China. Both were closed-end mutual funds solely investing in domestic stocks. The date came approximately eight years after the inception of the country's stock market, at a time when retail investors who had previously only owned stocks directly were exhibiting an extremely high demand for professional investment services. Both funds set their initial issuance at 2 billion yuan, yet the subscription climbed to over 161.6 billion, implying an oversubscription of 40 times. The frenzy in closed-end funds continued in the following year, when dozens of new funds were issued, again with substantial oversubscription.

Like most advancements in the development of China's financial market, the birth of mutual funds was both spurred and facilitated by the government's deregulation. In November of 1997, the government passed "Interim Measures on the Management of Securities Investment Funds," which legalized the closed-end mutual fund business for the first time.[1] The interim measures of 1997 specified the legal responsibilities of fund managers, custodians, and trustees, as well as disclosure requirements and regulatory measures governing investor protection. Further in October 2000, "Interim Measures on Open-end Securities Investment Funds" was passed to allow open-end mutual funds to begin doing business. The first open-end fund, Huaan Creative, was then issued on September 21, 2001, with total net assets (TNA) of 5 billion yuan at inception.

In 2003, legislation in China combined the two interim measures into the Securities Investment Fund Law (called the Fund Law 2003 hereafter) and formalized regulations of mutual funds. The regulatory principles and measures that China adopted were quite similar to the practice in the United States. With the passage of Fund Law 2003, the mutual fund industry in China stepped into a fast-growing track: The number of mutual funds has increased from 46 in 2001 to 4,395 in 2017, while total net assets grew 58.9 billion to 12.9 trillion yuan, implying an annual growth rate of over 40% (figure 14.1).

360

CHAPTER 14

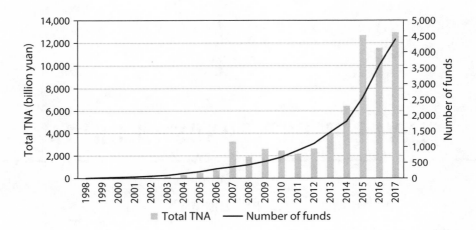

FIGURE 14.1. Total TNA and number of funds from 1998 to 2017. *Source:* Author's calculation, based on CSMAR data.

With its rapid development over 20 years, China's mutual fund market today offers a wide variety of products. Funds not only invest in Chinese stocks but also provide exposure to additional asset classes, such as bonds and money markets, as well as to nondomestic markets. The market size of passive index funds, exchange-traded products, and structured mutual funds has experienced a disproportionately high growth in recent years, offering many more options to fund investors.

As an effort to further liberalize the market, China's legislation amended Securities Investment Fund Law yet again in 2013 (hereafter called Fund Law 2013) to legalize the business of private fund management. Similar to regulations in the United States, private funds in China became subject to fewer investment restrictions and disclosure requirements but can only sell to qualified institutions and high-net-wealth individuals. The deregulation, again, matched the strong demand for alternative investments from wealthier households in China: The total TNA of hedge funds reached 1.72 trillion yuan at the end of 2017, or approximately 13% of the size of public mutual funds. Taken together with private equity and venture capital funds, all types of private funds are now managing over 12 trillion yuan of assets. There is no doubt that private funds have today become an important component of China's investment fund industry.

This chapter presents a set of stylized facts about the country's investment fund industry, with an emphasis on mutual funds. These facts derive from data analyses following the standard methodology in mutual fund literature, complemented with statistics from various sources and comparisons between Chinese and U.S. markets. Overall, China's fund market has its unique features and calls for more research to be better understood. The key characteristics can be summarized as follows:

1. Despite its fast growth, the mutual fund sector remains relatively small compared to the size of the asset market overall. In the stock market, for example, mutual funds in total own only 3% to 4% of the market capitalization, while

retail investors hold more than 40%. By comparison, U.S. mutual funds own approximately 30% of the stock market.

2. Similar to the global trend, China's passive index funds and exchange-traded products grow increasingly larger, compared to active funds (16.5% market share in 2017 versus 1.2% in 2004).

3. The country's mutual funds charge a high level of fees, for both active and passive funds. As of 2017, the average expense ratio of active and passive mutual funds was 1.2% and 0.8% per year, respectively. By comparison, the expense ratio for U.S. funds was approximately 0.8% for active funds and lower than 0.2% for passive index funds.

4. Active managed mutual funds' return net of fees does *not* appear to underperform either the market or risk-adjusted benchmark. This finding is different from the situation in the United States, where active funds' net return underperforms. Preliminary and anecdotal evidence suggests that Chinese mutual funds may have made profits from insider trading or pump-and-dump strategies against retail investors.

5. No evidence is available for persistent performance of Chinese mutual fund managers. That is, we do not find that fund managers who perform well in the past tend to outperform subsequently.

6. The majority of mutual fund investors are retail with a short horizon: only 9.2% of investors hold mutual funds more than five years, while 43.1% invest for less than a year (the average of U.S. investors is seven years). Chinese mutual fund investors exhibit a strong tendency for chasing past-outperforming funds.

7. Chinese households on average allocated only 3.8% of their savings in mutual funds in 2017 but invested more than 80% of them in bank deposit and wealth management products.

8. The private fund sector, which includes hedge funds, private equity funds, and venture capital funds, has grown as large as the mutual fund sector (with total net assets [TNAs] of 12.7 trillion yuan in 2018). Detailed and high-quality data (e.g., bias-free self-reports) is yet to be available to the public or academic researchers.

In the rest of this chapter, first the mutual fund database from CSMAR is introduced in section 2. The next section reviews the development of China's mutual fund industry over the past 20 years. Section 4 analyzes mutual fund expense, section 5 performance, and section 6 mutual fund investors. Finally, section 7 describes the development of private funds.

2. CSMAR CHINA FUND MARKET RESEARCH DATABASE

Unless otherwise specified, the mutual fund data used in this chapter comes from the CSMAR China Fund Market Research Database (CFM). The database covers all types of mutual funds, including both closed- and open-end, from 1998 to today. The user guide of CFM does not make explicitly clear whether its data is free of "survivorship bias"; rather, it claims that the data's coverage is complete. When the number of funds in CFM is compared with that reported in statistical yearbooks by the National Bureau of Statistics of China from 2000 to 2016, the numbers in the two sources are very close, suggesting that survivorship biases should not be a concern.

The source of CFM is mostly as required by regulatory disclosures. CFM data are comprehensive and include basic fund information, fund performance, quarterly portfolio holding, clientele, fund managers' bio and experience, and so on. The total content is roughly comparable to the combination of the CRSP mutual fund database, Thomson Reuters holding data, and Morningstar mutual fund data. CFM also contains some data that is not available in U.S. databases, such as detailed clientele information at the share-class level.

CFM's construction and structure are highly similar to that of datasets often used for research on U.S. mutual funds. Some information in it is reported at the fund share class level and some at the fund level. CFM provides a link table between fund identifier (*fundid*) and share class identifier (*fundclassid*). In the following paragraphs, the construction of key variables used in the analysis is introduced, with a focus on differences from standard U.S. datasets.

Mutual funds in China are required to report the net asset value (NAV) of fund shares on a daily basis, yet they report the number of fund shares outstanding only every quarter. Thus, fund size, meaning total net assets (TNA), is only available quarterly and is calculated by multiplying quarter-end NAV by the number of fund shares outstanding. All funds use the calendar-quarter end in China.

Researchers also need to calculate mutual fund returns from daily NAVs. CFM provides a variable, called *AccumulativeNAV*, which is adjusted for historical fund payouts and splits, making it comparable over time. CFM calculates the monthly, weekly, and even daily growth rate of *AccumulativeNAV*, that is, *ReturnAccumulativeNAV*, using it as a measure of fund returns (denoted as *FundRet*). Note that, since it is based on NAV changes, *FundRet* is net of expenses, which is the return that investors achieve. *FundRet* is at the share class level, and the fund-level return equals the value-weighted average of *FundRet* by the most recent quarter-end TNA of share classes.

Calculating the gross fund return in China is a bit different from the way it is done in the U.S. market. Unlike the latter case, funds' expense ratio may not be the same across share classes in the former. Thus, 1/12 of the annual expense ratio is added back to the monthly share class *FundRet*, and the average to the fund level is taken. The gross fund return is denoted as *GrossFundRet*.

CFM provides detailed information on expenses and loads at the share-class level. The total *Expense* ratio is calculated as the sum of management fee, custodian fee, and sales fee. Then, the value-weighted average of share class *Expense* to the fund level weighted by TNA is taken. *Load* is defined as the simple average of load rates in the fund's load schedule, after which the value-weighted average across share classes is calculated to obtain fund-level *Load*.

CFM contains funds' clientele information, such as number of holders, composition of fund investors (e.g., retail versus institution), and so on. The information is at the share class level. As for basic information about the fund, CFM includes inception date, closed- or open-end, fund category (i.e., equity, hybrid, fixed income, money market, and others), as well as a number of indicators of fund type, such as exchange-traded fund

Table 14.1. Number and Total TNA of Chinese Mutual Funds

Year	Total TNA (billion yuan)	No. of funds	Average fund's TNA	No. of fund companies	Average company's TNA
1998	6.46	3	2.15	3	2.15
1999	40.36	18	2.24	9	4.48
2000	70.55	31	2.28	10	7.06
2001	58.91	46	1.28	14	4.21
2002	88.30	69	1.28	17	5.19
2003	138.36	97	1.43	24	5.77
2004	296.85	154	1.93	37	8.02
2005	459.27	211	2.18	47	9.77
2006	722.60	300	2.41	52	13.90
2007	3260.34	362	9.01	57	57.20
2008	1920.65	432	4.45	59	32.55
2009	2606.92	535	4.87	60	43.45
2010	2464.07	672	3.67	60	41.07
2011	2176.88	886	2.46	64	34.01
2012	2645.75	1106	2.39	70	37.80
2013	4055.65	1463	2.77	74	54.81
2014	6455.51	1811	3.56	93	69.41
2015	12695.86	2579	4.92	103	123.26
2016	11555.20	3580	3.23	111	104.10
2017	12934.98	4395	2.94	119	108.70

Source: Author's calculation based on CSMAR data.

(ETF), listed open-end fund (LOF), index fund, structured fund, qualified domestic institutional investor (QDII), and so on.

3. THE DEVELOPMENT OF THE MUTUAL FUND INDUSTRY

3.1. Total Size

The last 20 years have witnessed the fast growth of China's mutual fund industry. Table 14.1 presents summary statistics of the number of funds and total TNA by each year from 1998 to 2017. As of the end of the latter year, the total number of mutual funds was 4,395, with total TNA of 12.9 trillion yuan. While the average growth rate was about 40% per year, the total assets experienced sharp drops in some years. For example, following the stock market bubble bust in 2007, the total TNA decreased from 3.2 trillion to 1.9 trillion the next year, owing to large losses and investor redemption. One interesting pattern is that the average fund size does not change significantly over time: Through the years, the average fund TNA ranges between 2 and 4 billion yuan.

Observers may think that, given its sharp increase in total size, China's mutual fund sector is increasingly important to the asset market. Yet this is not the case. Figure 14.2 shows the fraction of stock market capitalization owned by mutual funds. The fraction peaked at 7.45% in 2007 and decreased to 3.21% in 2017. This is not surprising, given that the total capitalization of the stock market, include both the Shanghai and Shenzhen

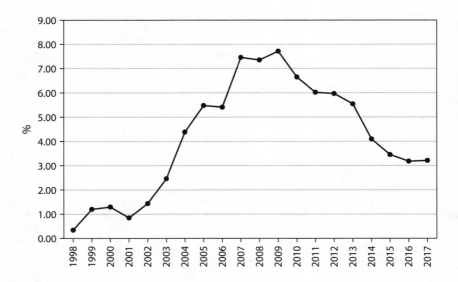

FIGURE 14.2. Fraction of total stock market capitalization owned by mutual funds. *Source:* Author's calculation, based on CSMAR data.

stock exchanges, expanded even faster from about 2 trillion yuan in 2000 to 56.5 trillion in 2017. By comparison, in the U.S. stock market, mutual fund ownership has stayed at approximately 30% in recent years. In this sense, Chinese mutual funds can be seen as playing a less influential role in the stock market.

3.2. Mutual Fund Management Company

In 1998, China had a total of three mutual fund companies. Like the case in other markets, mutual fund management companies in the country usually serve as the general partner of a mutual fund. In business operations, by contrast, a mutual fund company selects its fund manager and provides support such as marketing, compliance, data, and technical infrastructure, to individual funds. As of 2017, the number of mutual fund companies stood at 119. Also in that year, the average size of fund companies increased significantly, from 2 billion yuan in 1998 to 109 billion.

Figure 14.3 lists the market share of China's largest 10 mutual fund companies. In total, those companies held 57% of the total mutual fund TNA in 2017. The largest two are China Universal Asset Management Co., with a 16% market share, and Tianhong Asset Management Co., with a 13% market share.

Over the market's 20-year development, while dozens of mutual fund companies have entered the market, the larger ones have typically gained an advantage in competition because of their economy of scale. Large fund companies can hire better fund managers, offer more diversified products to attract investors, and run daily operations in a more cost-effective way. Figure 14.4 plots the market share of China's largest 10% of mutual fund companies over the sample years. It clearly shows that large fund companies own increasingly more market share, from approximately 10% in 2000 to more than 60% in 2017. It will be more difficult for small companies to survive in the future, and they are even likely to be merged with larger players in the market.

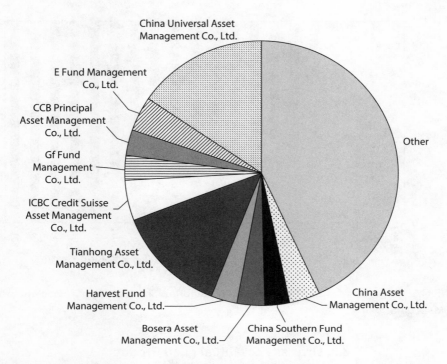

FIGURE 14.3. Market share of China's 10 largest mutual fund companies as of 2017. *Source:* Author's calculation, based on CSMAR data.

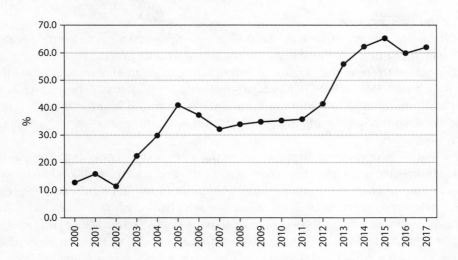

FIGURE 14.4. Market share of China's top 10% fund companies from 2000 to 2017. *Source:* Author's calculation, based on CSMAR data.

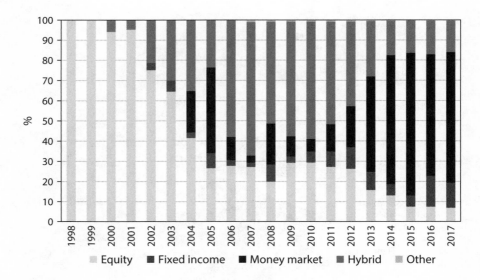

FIGURE 14.5. Market composition by mutual fund categories. *Source:* Author's calculation, based on CSMAR data.

3.3. Diversity of Mutual Fund Products

China's mutual fund industry began with two closed-end equity funds, but after its 20-year development, the market now offers investors a wide range of fund products for their consideration. This section reviews these trends in detail.

3.3.1. Fund Category by Asset Class

Over the years, mutual funds that invested in non-equity assets have become available to investors: The first fixed income fund was issued in 2002, and the first money market fund appeared the next year. Figure 14.5 shows the composition of mutual fund categories in each year. Before 2003, equity funds made up the majority of the market, but hybrid funds later became the largest in about 2007. In the period 2013 through 2017, money market mutual funds grew rapidly, yet equity funds shrank to less than 10% of the mutual fund market.

Chinese investors apparently benefit from the increased diversity. For example, fixed income funds give retail investors access to corporate and government bond markets that an individual can hardly invest in directly. Also, money market funds, because of their larger scale, can negotiate a higher interest rate with banks, which in turn lets fund investors earn higher returns than simple retail bank deposits. In addition, mutual funds provide liquidity transformation: Fund shares are liquid claims that can be purchased or redeemed on a daily basis. By comparison, some financial assets, such as corporate bonds, are relatively illiquid.

3.3.2. Nondomestic Investment: QDII

Mutual funds often extend their investment to overseas assets through the qualified domestic institutional investor program (QDII). Because of capital controls, Chinese investors have limited choices if they want to diversify to nondomestic assets. The QDII program,

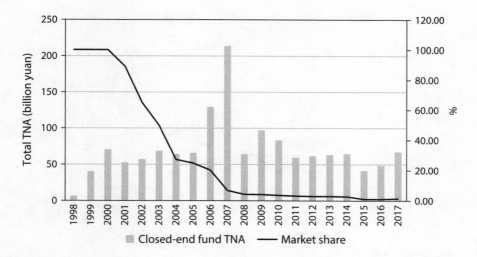

FIGURE 14.6. Total TNA and market share of closed-end mutual funds. *Source:* Author's calculation, based on CSMAR data.

which started in 2007, is one of the first few channels that allowed investors to do so. At the end of that year, the total issuance of QDII funds was 107.9 billion yuan, or 3.43% of the size of all mutual funds (excluding money market funds). Although the majority consisted of equity funds, some QDII funds also invest in foreign bonds, real estate, and futures. That said, the growth of total size of QDII funds has been relatively modest: At the end of 2017, the total TNA decreased to 92.9 billion yuan, for a 2.0% market share. The lower-than-expected development of QDII funds has possibly been due to their high fees (e.g., an expense ratio close to 2% per year). That slow development is also possibly a result of the recent inception of the Hong Kong–Shanghai/Shenzhen Connect program, which allows domestic investors to directly trade stocks in the Hong Kong stock market.

3.3.3. Extinction of Closed-End Funds

The majority of mutual funds in the Chinese market shift from closed-end to open-end. In the early years, before open-end mutual funds were legalized in 2001, all mutual funds were closed-end. Since 2001, open-end mutual funds have become more popular. Figure 14.6 plots the total TNA and market share of closed-end funds. It shows that the total market size equals the TNA by all mutual funds, excluding money market funds. Closed-end funds are clearly disappearing: Starting from 2008, their market share has been lower than 5% and even decreased to only 1.5% in 2017. It is widely believed that the key reason for this is the illiquidity of closed-end fund shares, making investors less willing to trade and leading to severe discounts for share prices. The closed-end fund discount on average is more than 10% in China, compared to 4.87% in the United States, and the discount gets even larger during a bear market.[2] Yet some media reports point out that closed-end funds deliver superior long-term performance, because their managers are not bothered by short-term fund flows compared to open-end funds. More systematic evidence is needed to support this point, however.

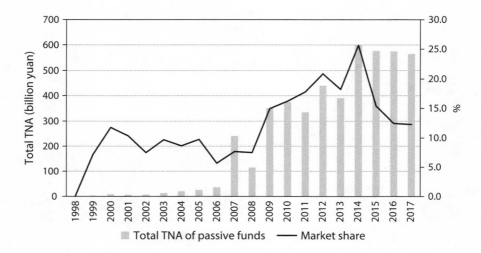

FIGURE 14.7. Total TNA and market share of passive index funds. *Source:* Author's calculation, based on CSMAR data.

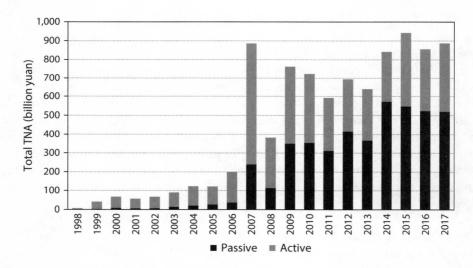

FIGURE 14.8. Passive versus active equity funds. *Source:* Author's calculation, based on CSMAR data.

3.3.4. Passive Index Funds

Similar to most developed markets, China has experienced rapid growth in its passive index mutual funds in recent years. Figure 14.7 plots the total TNA of passive mutual funds and shows the market share of all funds' TNA (excluding money market funds). The market share peaked at 25% in 2014 but decreased to about 12% in 2017.

In particular, for equity funds, since 2011 passive funds have become the majority. As shown in figure 14.8, at the end of 2017, the total TNA managed by passive funds totaled 519.9 billion yuan, while the number for active funds was 367.9 billion. Most index funds track the major stock market indices, such as Shanghai 50 and CSI 300. The largest index

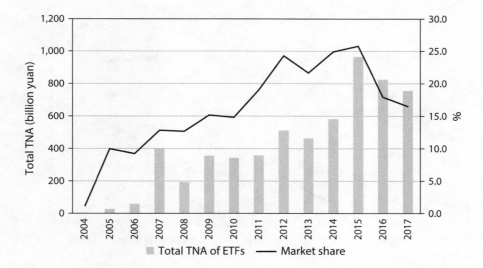

FIGURE 14.9. Total TNA and market share of exchange-traded mutual fund products. *Source:* Author's calculation, based on CSMAR data.

fund as of June 2017 was Shanghai 50 Exchanged-traded Index Fund, issued by China Asset Management Co., with total TNA of 30 billion yuan.

3.3.5. Exchange-Traded Products

Another related pattern is the rise of exchange-traded products. In China, there are two main types of mutual funds of this kind: Listed Open-End Fund (LOF) and Exchange-Traded Funds (ETF). Both are actually exchange-traded open-end funds; the subtle difference is that in the exchange market, LOF investors buy or sell fund shares with the fund itself, while, in contrast, the ETF traders transact with other ETF investors. For both LOF and ETF, investors can purchase or redeem with the fund directly outside the exchange. In this sense, an arbitrary mechanism (albeit with some frictions) permits investors to buy and sell across the two markets, so that the price of fund shares does not deviate much from their net asset value.

Because LOF and ETF are of good liquidity, meaning that investors can trade anytime the market is open, and also, unlike closed-end funds, because the price of LOF and ETF generally equals net asset value, more and more investors have started trading in those products. Figure 14.9 shows that the total TNA of LOF and ETF totaled over 700 billion yuan in 2017, or 16.5% of the market, growing from 2.7 billion and 1.2%, respectively, in 2004.

3.3.6. Structured Products

The first structured fund product in China was issued in 2009. The most popular mutual fund product of this kind today is the AB fund. It splits the payoffs of a regular mutual fund (i.e., a parent fund) into two separate products: a dividend-based product (A) and an appreciation-based product (B). Holders of A funds receive dividends, at a prespecified rate of the principal fund investment. The dividend rate normally equals the base interest rate plus a premium of 2% to 3%. Investors in B funds, by contrast, have a

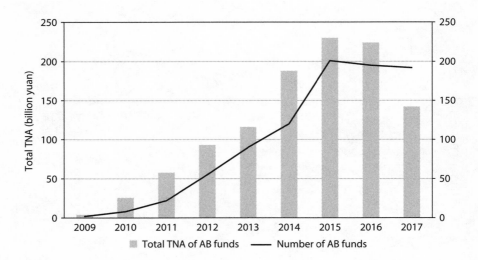

FIGURE 14.10. Total TNA and number of AB funds. *Source:* Author's calculation, based on CSMAR data.

residual claim on the underlying assets after the funds pay off their A investors. In this sense, B funds are leveraged and financed by A fund investors. Given this setting, the AB fund is a financial innovation that facilitates lending among fund investors with different risk appetites: The A funds attract conservative investors, while more speculative traders tend to buy B funds.

AB funds quickly became popular among Chinese investors. The number of AB funds peaked in 2015 at a total of roughly 200, with TNA of over 230 billion yuan. According to Gao et al. (2020), more than 7% of active individual investors in China are investing in the AB fund as of 2015. The authors find that the B fund has been particularly popular among extrapolative investors who were leverage constrained during the bubble circle of 2014–2015. However, the AB fund market has since cooled down after: The total size of AB funds decreased to 142 billion yuan in 2017 (figure 14.10).

Similar products (e.g., primes and scores) emerged in the United States in 1980s but disappeared after a few years. One possible reason for today's popularity of AB funds in China is retail investors' tendency to speculate and a high cost/hurdle to obtain leverage. The unique setting of AB funds is ideal for studying interactions between pessimists (that is, an A fund buyer, the lender) and optimists (B fund buyer, the borrower).

4. FEES AND OTHER COSTS OF INVESTING MUTUAL FUNDS

The cost of buying mutual funds comes from two parts: expense and load. In China, expenses consist of three components: management fee, custodian fee, and sales fee. Revenue from management fees and sales fees goes to the fund company. The sales fee is similar to the 12b-1 fee in the United States, and funds are supposed to use it strictly for marketing and sales. The custodian fee will be paid solely to custodian banks. Management and custodian fees are usually the same for share classes of the same fund, although sales fees can be different. As mentioned earlier, the *Expense* ratio is defined as

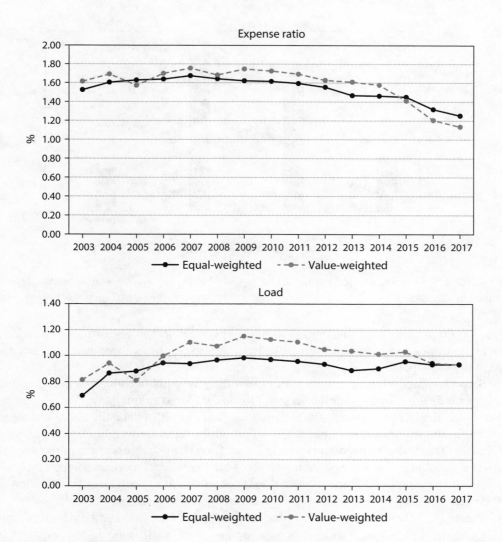

FIGURE 14.11. Average expense ratio and load (%) of mutual funds by year. *Source:* Author's calculation, based on CSMAR data.

the sum of management fee, custodian fee, and sales fee, and the value-weighted average of share class *Expense* to the fund level weighted by share class TNA is taken.

Like the case in the United States, loads in China are paid to fund distributors, such as banks and brokerage firms. Loads may be charged at purchase and/or at redemption. When and how much the load is charged normally vary with fund share classes. For the same share class, the load rate may sometimes differ, depending on the investors' purchase amount or the holding period. *Load* is defined as the simple average of load rates in the fund's load schedule. In this sense, the estimated *Load* may be a "noisy" proxy for the actual load that investors pay.

Figure 14.11 plots the average *Expense* and *Load* of actively managed mutual funds in the market (excluding money market funds), when equal-weighted and value-weighted by fund TNA. First, market watchers can find that the expense ratio has started to

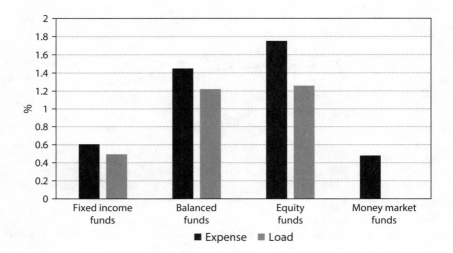

FIGURE 14.12. Expense and load (%) as of 2017 by fund category. *Source:* Author's calculation, based on **CSMAR** data.

decrease in recent years; the average annual expense ratio was above 1.5% before 2014 but has dropped to around 1.2% in 2017. By comparison, the average load does not exhibit the same pattern.

Second, value-weighted average is not lower than the equal-weighted, suggesting that larger funds are charging similar fees and loads compared to smaller funds. The literature finds the opposite case in the U.S. market: Based on 2018 data, the equal-weighted average expense ratio of equity funds is 1.42%, while the value-weighted average drops to 0.55%. This is due to economy of scale: Large funds can charge a lower rate of fees to cover the cost of operation, and such lower fees can help attract more investors. The finding in China suggests that the competition is not sufficient to push large funds to lower their fees.

Figure 14.12 shows the value-weighted average of fund *Expense* and *Load* by fund category at the end of 2017. The level of expense and load is still very high, compared to more developed markets such as that in the United States. For example, equity funds' average expense ratio is 1.75% with a load of 1.26%. Given that the median holding years total 2 (more discussion on this in section 6), the total cost for investors is estimated as 1.75% + 1.26%/2 = 2.38% per year.

This is a very high level of costs compared to the United States market. According to the statistics by the Investment Company Institute (2019), the value-weighted average expense ratio of active managed equity funds was 0.79% in 2017, while 85% of mutual fund investments were in zero-load fund shares. Therefore, the total cost in the United States is estimated to be between 0.80% to 0.85% per year, which is much smaller than the number in China. The high level of fees is also true for passive index funds in China. Figure 14.13 shows that both expense and load are 0.8% per year. By comparison, the value-weighted average of index fund expense ratio is estimated to range from 8 to 20 basis points in the United States.

This finding suggests that the entire mutual fund industry in China is not running as efficiently as the United States market. The high level of fees can be the result of high

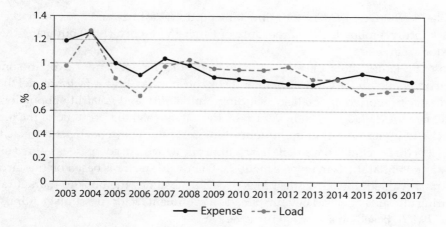

FIGURE 14.13. Expense and load (%) of passive index funds. *Source:* Author's calculation, based on CSMAR data.

costs of running the business. Also, since large fund companies are increasingly dominating the market, the competition among fund companies may not function well to bring down the expense. No matter what drives it, the high cost often discourages fund investors from participating or even detours them to other financial assets.

5. MUTUAL FUND PERFORMANCE

This section examines whether mutual funds in China actually generate superior performance, focusing on active, open-end equity funds from 2003 to 2016. The sample includes 305 unique funds and 14,892 fund-month observations. The methodology, explained in detail below, follows the mutual fund literature on the United States market.

5.1. Risk-Adjusted Fund Return

First, the market-adjusted fund return is calculated as *FundRet* minus the floating-cap-weighted average return of all stocks (denoted as *MKT*). In addition, following the method of Carhart (1997), three models are adopted to make the risk adjustment to fund performance: Capital Asset Pricing Model (CAPM), Fama-French 3-factor model (FF3), and China 4-factor model (CH4) as examined in Liu et al. (2019). Specifically, fund performances relative to the CAPM, FF3, and CH4 are estimated and modeled as

$$r_{it} = \alpha_i + \beta_i MKTRF_{it} + e_{it}$$

$$r_{it} = \alpha_i + \beta_i MKTRF_{it} + s_i SMB_{it} + h_i HML_{it} + e_{it}$$

$$r_{it} = \alpha_i + \beta_i MKTRF_{it}^{CH4} + s_i SMB_{it}^{CH4} + v_i VMG_{it} + p_i PMO_{it} + e_{it}$$

where r_{it} is the return on a portfolio of mutual funds in excess of a risk-free rate, which is proxied by a one-year deposit interest rate in China. $MKTRF_{it}$ is the excess return on the floating-cap-weighted portfolio of all stocks. SMB_{it} and HML_{it} are returns on value-weighted, zero-investment, factor-mimicking portfolios for size and book-to-market ratio in stock returns, following the procedure of Fama and French (1993) but using the Chinese stock market data.

Liu et al. (2019) show that the China-version FF3 model cannot explain some reported anomalies in the Chinese market. They construct a China 4-factor model that can explain most reported anomalies, including profitability and volatility anomalies. The market factor, $MKTRF_{it}^{CH4}$, is the return on the value-weighted portfolio of the top 70% of stocks, in excess of the one-year deposit interest rate. They construct the size factor (SMB_{it}^{CH4}) that excludes the smallest 30% of firms, which are companies valued significantly as potential shells in reverse mergers. Their value factor is based on the earnings-price ratio (value minus growth, VMG_{it}), which subsumes the book-to-market ratio in capturing all value effects. They further add a sentiment factor (pessimistic minus optimistic, PMO_{it}) based on abnormal turnover.[3]

First, the average return of all equity funds is examined, with a focus on net fund returns, as they are the return that investors achieve. Table 14.2 presents the regressions of the above-mentioned factor models; t-statistics, reported in parentheses, are based on Newey-West standard errors with a lag of 11 months. In columns 1 through 4, the left-hand-side variable is the value-weighted average of $FundRet$ (in percent). According to column 1, actively managed equity funds outperform the market by 52 basis points per month, but it is not statistically significant. After adjusting fund returns with CAPM or FF3 model in columns 2 and 3, respectively, funds' alpha increases to 82 to 96 basis points per month and is significant (with t-statistics around 2). Note that funds' loading on the market factor is approximately 0.66, suggesting that mutual funds' exposure to systematic risk is lower than that of the market. The loading on HML in column 3 indicates funds tilt their holdings toward growth stocks.

When the CH4 model is applied in column 4, funds' alpha decreases to 37 basis points per month and becomes insignificant. This finding indicates that CH4 factors can better capture some mutual funds' strategies. By contrast, CAMP and FF3 models are possibly mis-specified for the Chinese market: It can be seen that fund returns are positively correlated with CH4 size and value factors but are negatively correlated with the FF3 counterparts. Further, the loading on the sentiment factor is positive (with a t-statistic of 1.4), implying that funds are trading against retail investors. The estimates in column 4 suggest that mutual fund overweight on small, value, and low abnormal turnover stocks, though these estimates are statistically insignificant. Columns 5 through 8 use equal-weighted fund returns, and the pattern is generally similar. When using the CH4 factor model, analysts find that equal-weighted fund returns exhibit an alpha of 37.7 basis points that is significant at a 10% level, or 4.5% per annum.

The takeaway from the analysis here is that active equity mutual funds in China do *not* significantly underperform the market or other risk-adjusted benchmarks. This is clear from the fact that in all the specifications in table 14.2, the point estimates of alpha are positive. Whether Chinese mutual funds significantly outperform depends on which risk model is used. Importantly, this pattern is different from the finding in the United States. According to Chen et al. (2004), actively managed mutual funds significantly underperform the market by approximately 1% per year, after taking into account expenses.

So the question arises: *Why* do Chinese mutual funds exhibit better performance than U.S. funds? Although more systematic research is needed to find a definitive answer,

Table 14.2. Mutual Fund Performance and Factor Loadings

%	Value weighted				Equal weighted			
	Market adj. (1)	CAPM (2)	FF3 (3)	CH4 (4)	Market adj. (5)	CAPM (6)	FF3 (7)	CH4 (8)
α	0.519	0.819**	0.959**	0.371	0.328	0.676***	0.746**	0.377*
	(0.93)	(2.12)	(1.98)	(0.93)	(0.75)	(3.07)	(2.57)	(1.73)
MKTRF		0.669***	0.661***	0.737***		0.616***	0.607***	0.663***
		(9.52)	(8.99)	(9.09)		(11.33)	(11.2)	(12.66)
SMB			−0.077	0.037			−0.021	0.075
			(−0.53)	(0.52)			(−0.26)	(1.35)
HML			−0.446*				−0.350**	
			(−1.85)				(−2.43)	
VMG				0.086				0.049
				(0.55)				(0.51)
PMO				0.27				0.156
				(1.43)				(1.42)
N	168	168	168	168	168	168	168	168
Adj. R2	–	0.37	0.39	0.39	–	0.65	0.68	0.69

Source: Author's calculation based on CSMAR data.

Note: *, **, and *** indicate significance levels of 10%, 5%, and 1%, respectively.

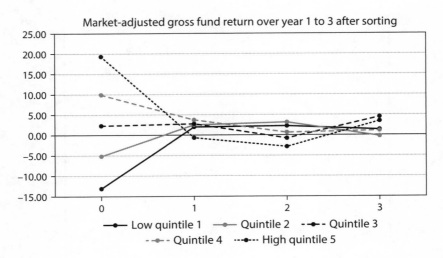

FIGURE 14.14. Fund performance persistence. *Source:* Author's calculation, based on CSMAR data.

several studies provide some insights by uncovering evidence that mutual funds in fact often make profits from front-running retail investors. Gu et al. (2013), for example, find that mutual fund managers, by coordinating with analysts who issue inflated "strong buy" recommendations, pump the stock price up and then dump the stocks to trend-chasing retail investors. Hansman et al. (2018) exploit the staggered deregulation on margin trading from 2011 to 2015 and find that mutual funds increase their holdings on stocks likely to qualify for margin trading before the implementation date, and then sell to margin traders (mostly retail) afterward at higher prices.

Those findings are consistent with many anecdotal reports in China's media that mutual funds often conduct pump-and-dump strategies of various kinds. This type of strategy is plausibly profitable, given that mutual funds only own a small fraction of the stock market (approximately 3% to 7% as shown above) and are mostly trading against retail investors, who are strongly trend-chasing and hold more than 40% of the market. It would be interesting to see more research on how mutual funds trade and generate returns in China.

5.2. Performance Persistence

Another classic question in mutual fund literature is examined: Can outperforming funds continue to outperform in the future? Following Carhart (1997), all mutual funds are sorted into quintiles based on market-adjusted gross fund returns at the end of every year. Gross return is used to eliminate the effect of expense, which is a persistent component in fund performance, and is adjusted by market return (results are similar when using other benchmarks). Then, the (equal-weighted) average performance of funds is tracked in each quintile over one to three years. If some funds do have persistent superior performance relative to other funds, outperformers at the sorting year (year 0) should exhibit high returns in subsequent years.

The results are presented in figure 14.14. It can be noted that after the sorting year, fund performance across the five groups converges from the first year. That is, mutual

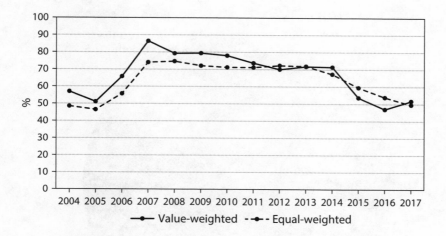

FIGURE 14.15. Fraction of mutual fund assets owned by retail investors. *Source:* Author's calculation, based on **CSMAR** data.

funds in China do *not* exhibit persistence in superior performance. This pattern is consistent with the findings in the United States.

6. MUTUAL FUND INVESTORS

According to the annual report by the Asset Management Association of China (AMAC, 2017), as of the end of 2016, the total number of active mutual fund investors was 269,546,000, which is approximately one-fifth of China's total population. At the fund level, retail investors comprise the main clientele of mutual funds. Figure 14.15 plots the average fraction of mutual fund assets from retail investors. The fraction is shown to be close to 90% in 2007, then decreases approximately 50% in recent years. Institutional investors invest more in mutual funds now.

To better understand the characteristics of mutual fund investors, AMAC conducted a survey in 2017 on more than 76,000 investors. Some survey findings are interesting and well worth discussing.[4] First, the majority of mutual fund investors are middle-income households: 87.1% of them have after-tax income of below 150,000 yuan per year; 28.4% investors have annual income of below 50,000 yuan. The average per capita disposable income in China was 25,974 yuan in 2017. Some 44% of mutual fund investors own financial assets of less than 100,000 yuan.

The second finding is that Chinese households tend to invest a small proportion of their savings in mutual funds (only 3.8%); the breakdown is 65.8% in bank deposits, 14.6% in wealth management products, and 15.9% in stock market (direct own).[5] By comparison, U.S. investors allocate more financial assets to mutual funds. A survey by the Investment Company Institute (2019) shows that 44.5% of U.S. households owned mutual funds in mid-2017, and among them 65% held more than half of their financial assets in mutual funds.

The third interesting finding is that investors in China are of short horizon. Only 9.2% of them hold mutual funds for more than five years, while 43.1% invest less than a year; see figure 14.16. This is much shorter than that of U.S. investors, whose average horizon

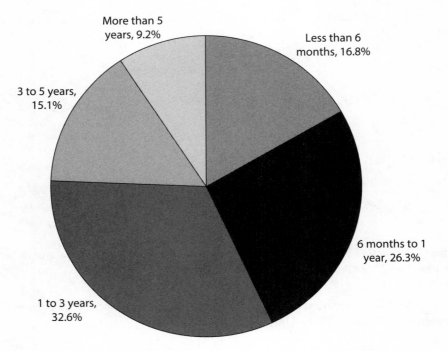

FIGURE 14.16. Investment horizon of Chinese mutual fund investors. *Source:* Reproduced from Annual Report of Securities Investment Fund Industry 2016 (in Chinese, AMAC 2017), 201.

in mutual fund investment is believed to be seven years, as cited in the literature. For U.S. mutual fund investors, 93% of their fund investment is in savings for retirement (Investment Company Institute, 2019), suggesting a very long investment horizon.

Those statistics suggest that Chinese mutual fund investors do not consider mutual funds as their main and long-term investment vehicle that can help preserve and increase the value of their savings. Their trading behaviors with mutual funds are similar to what can be observed among stock investors, who typically have short-term investments.

To examine this point with systematic data analysis, the flow-to-performance sensitivity test is conducted using the Chinese data, following Chevalier and Ellison (1997). Quarterly fund net flow are calculated as

$$NetFlow_q = \frac{TNA_q + TNA_{q-1}(1 + FundRet_q)}{TNA_{q-1}}$$

Then, $NetFlow_{q+1}$ are regressed on fund performance rank and a set of controls, X, at quarter q, as specified below:

$$NetFlow_{i,q+1} = c + f\left(PerfRank_{i,q}\right) + X_{i,q} + e_{i,q}$$

where performance rank, $PerfRank_{i,q}$, is sorted based on market-adjusted fund return over the past four quarters and ranges from -10 to 10. The nonparametric function, $f(.)$, is allowed to fit the data. The set of control variables includes fund size, fund company size,

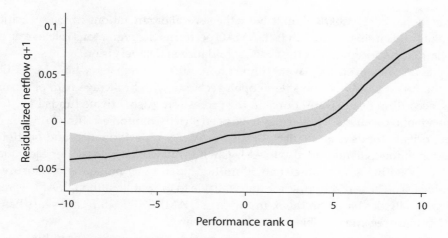

FIGURE 14.17. Mutual fund flow to performance sensitivity. *Source:* Author's calculation, based on CSMAR data.

fund age, expense ratio, load, dummies of fund category, and year-quarter fixed effects. $NetFlow_{q+1}$ is winsorzied at 2.5% and 97.5% level by quarter.

Figure 14.17 presents the fitted function of *NetFlow* on performance rank with 95% confidence intervals. The pattern illustrates that fund investors in China are strongly chasing past winners. Especially notable is that extreme outperformers receive disproportionally more inflows than the outflow from poorly performing funds; the flow-to-performance relationship is convex. This finding is similar to what is seen in the U.S. market.

7. NEW DEVELOPMENT: PRIVATE FUND

In 2013, new legislation in China made substantial amendments to the Securities Investment Fund Law (Fund Law 2013) and also legalized the operation of private funds. In general, private funds are not publicly sold in the country and are subject to fewer regulatory constraints in trading and disclosure requirements than are mutual funds. Before the amendment of the Fund Law, private funds could be organized under the Trust Law, but since the regulatory framework of the Trust Law was not specifically designed for investment funds, measures on investor protection were not established. To fill the gap, several industry pioneers developed the Sunshine Private Fund Program, a self-regulated scheme to improve transparency and investor protection. One of its main functions was to bring independent banks and brokerage firms together as, in effect, the custodian between investors and fund managers, so as to better secure investors' assets.

The Fund Law 2013 formalizes the legal definition of private funds in China and clarifies the regulatory requirements for managing a private fund. In general, the regulatory measures follow the practice in the United States under the Dodd–Frank Act. According to the written law, albeit it is not mandatory, private funds are strongly advised to register with the main regulator, Asset Management Association of China (AMAC). According to its website, AMAC is "a national, industry-oriented, and nonprofit social organization incorporated voluntarily by the several organizations in the securities investment funds industry." But in fact, AMAC performs the regulator's role in exercising compliance operations, under the CSRC's guidance and supervision.

In practice, however, all private funds are required to register with AMAC. Otherwise, the funds would not be able to open accounts with brokerage firm or custodian banks, according to a private source in the profession. Also, private funds have to hire independent custodians. These rules have been strictly reinforced since 2015. Once registered, private funds need to disclose fund NAV, TNA, performance, and portfolio information to their clients and also to AMAC within 10 working days after each quarter-end. Funds with TNA of more than 50 million yuan must make the disclosure on a monthly basis. Those disclosures are not available to the public, although AMAC reports summary statistics based on them. In this sense, AMAC data in recent years has been selection-bias-free and suitable for academic research.

Private funds in China are not allowed to market their shares to the public, and they can only sell to qualified purchasers. To qualify as purchasers, individual investors need to own more than 3 million yuan in financial assets and have an annual income of greater than a half million, while institutional investors and corporations should have net assets of over 10 million yuan. The minimum investment requirement is set to be 1 million yuan. A limit is set on the number of investors to a fund: Depending on the fund's legal organization, the limit varies between 50 and 200.

Private funds in China are offered in three main categories. The first category, whose official name translates as "private securities investment fund," is equivalent to "hedge fund" in the U.S. market. These funds mainly trade in the secondary market of various financial assets, including stocks, bonds, and futures; they may also take leverage or use complex financial instrument to implement their strategies. The second category is private equity funds (PE), which invest mostly in equities of private firms. The third type of fund is the venture capital fund (VC), which invests in the ownership of startup firms.

According to AMAC's reports, the private fund sector has grown tremendously fast since the Fund Law was imposed in 2013. Figure 14.18 shows the total number of funds and TNA by fund categories. Since now all private funds have to register with AMAC, the statistics should be highly accurate. The number of private funds can be seen to have increased from 7,514 in 2014 to 74,642 in 2018—an approximately 10-times increase over only five years. The TNA managed by private funds rose from 2.05 trillion in 2014 to 12.7 trillion in 2018, close to the current size of the mutual fund sector. Such remarkable growth highlights the strong demand from China's increasingly more numerous high-net-wealth households that wish to invest in riskier projects as well as to diversify their investments among alternative asset classes.

Although the total size of the country's private funds is already large, the average TNA managed by private funds is much smaller than mutual funds. Hedge funds and PE funds are two major categories in terms of the number of funds. Nonetheless, PE funds' TNA consists of more than 60% of the private fund sector, while the figure for hedge funds is 16.8%.

To date, few studies have fully examined this emerging yet fast-growing sector in China. Many questions are worth asking and answering. For example, can Chinese hedge

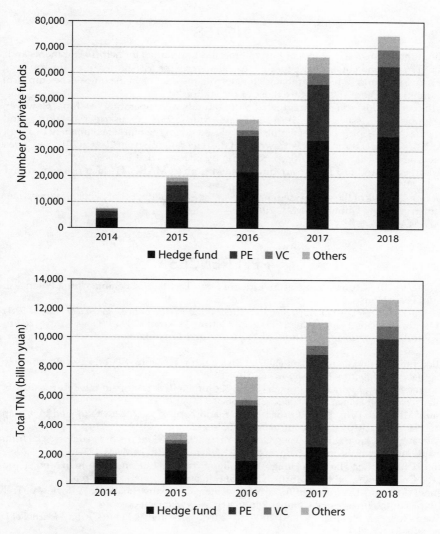

FIGURE 14.18. Number and total TNA (billion yuan) of private funds by category. *Source:* Author's calculation, based on CSMAR data.

fund managers actually outperform? What are the role and impact of PE funds in companies' IPO process? What is the normal behavior of private fund investors? One of the main obstacles to resolving these questions is the lack of high-quality data about private funds (AMAC possesses the data but does not make it publicly available). Several online platforms voluntarily report private funds' performance and other information, in order to attract potential investors. One widely used platform of the kind is Simuwang .com, which covers more than 86,000 funds, but like the self-reported hedge fund databases in the United States (such as TASS), Simuwang.com's reported data com is subject to potential selection bias and must be used with caution.

NOTES

The author thanks the editors of this volume and Ron Kaniel for helpful comments and discussion; Tieze Li and Hulai Zhang for their excellent research assistance; and Cameron Peng, Jialan Liu, Yu Yuan, and Robert Stambaugh for sharing the data used in some of the empirical analyses in this chapter. All errors are those of the author.

1. In the early 1990s, several unregulated mutual funds were operating in China. However, owing to problematic issues such as related-party transaction, excessive risk-taking, and Ponzi schemes, the People's Bank of China (PBC) closed down the market completely in May 1993.
2. Statistics of the U.S. market are drawn from the data ranging from 2009 to 2019. See "Closed-end funds—Historical premium/discount chart" by Invesco Trust Units.
3. Risk-free rate and FF3 factors are downloaded from CSMAR. CH4 factors are provided by Liu et al. (2019).
4. For more details of the survey, see chapter 8 of the Annual Report of Securities Investment Fund Industry 2016 (in Chinese; AMAC 2017).
5. See AMAC (2017), 8.

REFERENCES

AMAC (2017). "2016 China Securities Investment Fund Fact Book." Beijing: China Finance and Economics Press House.

Carhart, Mark M. (1997). "On Persistence in Mutual Fund Performance." *Journal of Finance* 52(1): 57–82.

Chen, Joseph, Harrison Hong, Ming Huang, and Jeffrey D. Kubik (2004). "Does Fund Size Erode Mutual Fund Performance?: The Role of Liquidity and Organization." *American Economic Review* 94(5): 1276–1302.

Chevalier, Judith, and Glenn Ellison (1997). "Risk Taking by Mutual Funds as a Response to Incentives." *Journal of Political Economy* 105(6): 1167–1200.

Fama, Eugene F., and Kenneth R. French (1993). "Common Risk Factors in the Returns on Stocks and Bonds." *Journal of Financial Economics* 33: 3–56.

Gao, Paul, Allen Hu, Peter Kelly, Cameron Peng, and Ning Zhu (2020). "Exploited by Complexity," March 14. SSRN: https://ssrn.com/abstract=3554402.

Gu, Zhaoyang, Zengquan Li, and Yong George Yang (2013). "Monitors or Predators: The Influence of Institutional Investors on Sell-Side Analysts." *Accounting Review* 88(1): 137–69.

Hansman, Christopher, Harrison Hong, Wenxi Jiang, Yu-Jane Liu, and Juan-Juan Meng (2018). "Riding the Credit Boom." (No. w24586). National Bureau of Economic Research.

Investment Company Institute (2019). "2019 Investment Company Fact Book: A Review of Trends and Activities in the Investment Company Industry." www.icifactbook.org.

Liu, Jianan, Robert F. Stambaugh, and Yu Yuan (2019). "Size and Value in China." *Journal of Financial Economics* 131(1): 48–69.

15

CHINA'S VENTURE CAPITAL MARKET

Zhaojun Huang and Xuan Tian

1. OVERVIEW OF CHINA'S VENTURE CAPITAL MARKET

The past 10 years have been a period of unprecedented success for both China's emerging industries and the venture capital (VC) market behind them. According to the latest report by PitchBook, China now has the second largest VC market in the world in terms of deal value.[1] According to a report by Zero2IPO Research, one of the leading VC/PE research institutions in China, the country's VC investment reached 211.8 billion RMB in 2018, and the number of megadeals has been increasing dramatically since 2014.[2] While the rapid growth in recent years is largely driven by domestic VCs, the whole market was dominated by experienced foreign VCs in the 1990s and early 2000s. The rapid expansion of the overall VC market does not necessarily mean the market is matured, though. On the contrary, some unique features and cautionary notes are worth sounding.

The primary focus of this chapter is on drawing together the descriptive observations and statistics that illustrate the general picture of China's VC market. With this focus in mind, a few limitations with regard to this chapter must initially be mentioned.

First, the chapter will not center on the academic research that sheds light on China's venture capital market. The main reason is the limited number of academic papers that specifically focus on this market, compared to the fruitful literature exploring VCs in the United States. It is hoped that the stylized facts in this chapter can trigger additional related academic studies in the near future. Second, while the chapter will discuss certain important government policies related to China's VC market, it will not focus on the detailed policies or legal rules associated with raising venture funds or making investment decisions in the country. Third, the chapter will instead focus specifically on venture capital, defined as "professionally managed, dedicated pools of capital focusing on equity or equity-linked investments in privately held and high growth companies," following Gompers and Lerner (2001).

It is worth mentioning that the boundary of venture capital and private equity (PE) firms is blurry in China. Even though venture capital is only a special type of private equity that mainly focuses on early-stage investment in the United States, in China the

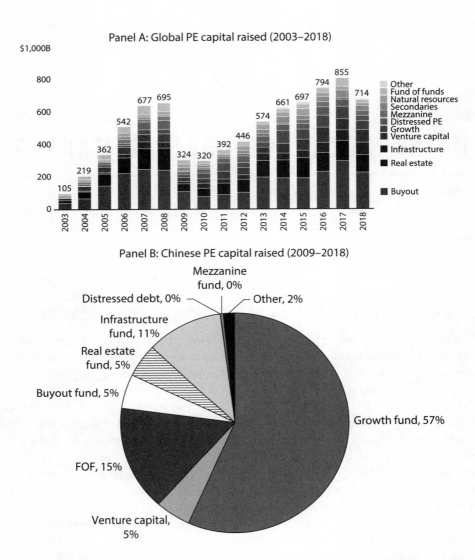

FIGURE 15.1. Global VC and global PE. *Sources:* U.S.: Bain & Company, 2019, Global Private Equity Report. China: www.pedata.cn. *Notes:* Panel A includes funds in the global PE market with final close and represents the year in which funds held their final close. Panel B includes all funds with final close 2009–2018 by PE firms investing in China.

two terms are often used interchangeably, due largely to the overlapping investment strategies used by Chinese venture capital and private equity firms. Figure 15.1 highlights the types of funds managed by global PE firms and Chinese PE firms—that is, PE firms that stay active in China. For global PEs, buyout funds account for the most important part and largely exceed the amount of venture capital funds and growth funds. By contrast, in China, growth funds contributed 57% of the overall amount of capital that has been successfully raised by Chinese PE firms from 2009 to 2018, which, however, are used for neither buyout deals nor merger-and-acquisition (M&A) deals, two typical strategies conducted by global PEs.

In addition, VC as well as PE firms have mixed investment portfolios that range from early stages to later ones. Comparisons of Chinese VC activities and U.S. ones will be given later, but readers should be aware of this difference at the outset when China's VC market is described. In particular, we follow the classification of PEdata (www.pedata .cn) to identify VC firms that are active in China's market. This is a comprehensive database on China's VC market provided by Zero2IPO Research and is widely used by both Chinese academia and practitioners. With a few exceptions, most of the analyses are based on the data between 2009 and 2018, due to the relatively low data quality for early years.[3]

2. AT A GLANCE: THE BRIEF HISTORY OF CHINA'S VENTURE CAPITAL INDUSTRY

In the mid-1980s, Chinese VC firms were initially set up to meet the government's desire to revitalize the high-tech industry. With the majority of domestic VCs being backed mainly by the government, these initial attempts, however, proved to be far from satisfactory because of their owners' lack of experience and, more important, by the lack of exit channels. Many early attempts ended at about the time of the bankruptcy of China New Technology Start-up Investment Company, the first domestic VC firm in the country, in 1998. That same year, however, the government endorsed the so-called "Proposal No.1," aimed at officially expanding China's VC industry.[4] The proposal was widely accepted as the turning point of China's VC market, thus triggering the first boom for domestic VCs around 2000. As shown in figure 15.2, no fewer than 277 domestic VC firms were founded between 2000 and 2001, exceeding the total number of such firms founded in the previous decade.

A second contribution of the proposal was that it raised a plan to build a "Chinese Nasdaq." It was thought that the lack of exit channels faced by domestic VCs would be largely resolved once the plan got implemented. Therefore, the boom in 2001 also largely resulted from the expectation that the plan would soon be deployed. When the expectation was not satisfied as the plan was suspended, the domestic VC market soon cooled down. For quite a long time thereafter, foreign VC firms were the main players in China's VC market. They had witnessed and even boosted the abrupt rise of the IT industry in the country in the early 2000s.

Another turning point for domestic venture capitalists came in 2005 when the Chinese government implemented the split-share structure reform to further privatize the stock market, thus opening up a door for domestic VCs to exit through initial public offerings (IPOs) in mainland China. While two-thirds of the domestically listed A shares were not publicly tradeable at that time, the reform mandatorily converted all nontradeable shares to tradeable ones, subject to shareholders' approval and with appropriate compensation negotiated. Figure 15.2 shows that the number of newly established domestic VC firms reached its height in 2006 compared to that of the past 15 years. Ever since then, China has been building its domestic VC industry in what is considered its first "golden period."

Activities in China's venture industry increased dramatically in 2009 when the ChiNext Board was launched on October 30. The new board has provided an alternative for domestic VC firms to exit through IPOs in mainland China that would otherwise

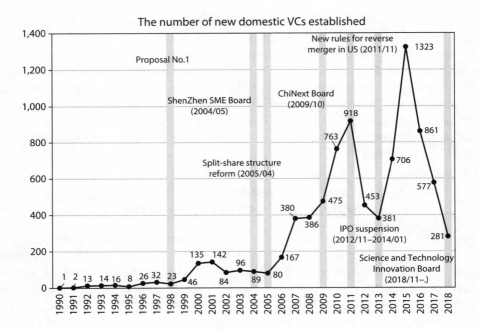

FIGURE 15.2. New domestic VC firms. *Source:* www.pedata.cn.

have to rely heavily on the U.S. and Hong Kong markets. The number of IPOs on the A-share market hits a record in 2010 when approximately 30% of the newly listed firms were backed by VC/PE firms. That year, the return generated from IPOs accounted for approximately 94% of the overall return of exit deals for domestic VCs.

As shown in figure 15.2, some 918 new domestic VCs were founded in 2011 alone, setting a new record for China's market. Those young venture capitalists all seemed to be ready to make a sensation until their wholehearted enthusiasm was soon dampened by unexpected economic turmoil from both at home and abroad. In the United States, the trend to short-sell China-concept firms led to a large number of delisting cases in 2012 as cross-listed Chinese firms battled against a perception of being either weak or tainted with fraud. In November 2011, the U.S. Securities Exchange Commission (SEC) strengthened its regulations for all reverse merger (RM) deals, making it harder for domestic VCs to exit through that channel. In China, a bearish A-share market triggered a long IPO suspension implemented by the China Securities Regulatory Commission (CSRC) that extended from November 2, 2012, to January 17, 2014. Lacking good exit alternatives, China's VC market has encountered a new round of torture. In 2013, the main exit choice for domestic VCs was M&A; IPOs contributed less than 20% of the overall returns. For VCs that exited through IPOs at that time, the entire IPO deals went to the Hong Kong Main Board. Figure 15.2 highlights the bearish VC market in China as the number of newly established domestic VCs drops sharply and China's VC market witnesses a plunge in overall deal amounts and volumes, as will be revealed in later sections of this chapter.

With 1,323 new domestic VC firms founded in 2015, Chinese venture capitalists enjoyed another unprecedented period in history. What made them even prouder was that they were the "wave riders" this time. In particular, 97% of the money raised was directed to domestic VCs in 2017, which contributed 81% of overall investment in that year. Meanwhile, the markets for both the general partner (GP) and the limited partner (LP) become more professional. The span was characterized by the departures of experienced fund managers from foreign VCs to build their own domestic VC firms, plus a split of generalized VCs into smaller, professional ones. Stricter regulations were also implemented by the Chinese government, to be discussed in later sections.

Growing jitters about an economic downturn and various uncertain situations recently have affected the decision-making processes for both GPs and LPs, ranging from due diligence to exit planning. 2018 was not a fruitful year for the Chinese VC market, since the number of newly established VC firms reached its lowest level in a decade, alongside rates of overall investment and fundraising coming in a smidgen lower than in previous years. For anyone who wonders how long the weak times can last, that is hard to predict without mentioning the launch of the Science and Technology Innovation Board in the Shanghai Stock Exchange Market, or the "STAR Market," as announced directly by President Xi Jinping. More than providing just another alternative exit method, the new board makes revolutionary changes in the IPO process and also establishes multiple measures to better facilitate the IPO of innovative firms. Those changes are aiming at making the capital market more suitable for emerging firms to seek financial support and foster innovative ideas. And of course, the new board also provides further opportunities for venture capitalists to play important roles in the country's economy.

The following sections examine China's VC industry as it has continued to raise capital, make deals, and exit at a historic pace. Also to be discussed are alternative forms of traditional VC investments in China, such as corporate venture capital (CVC) and government-guided funds. The chapter concludes with a brief discussion of the recent regulatory environment for the industry.

3. FUNDRAISING

Given their sustained enthusiasm about China's economy, a stampede of limited partners (LPs) have tapped into this large and growing market, continuously flooding it with fresh capital. Figure 15.3 shows the percentage of capital raised by VC funds in China's market, relative to the total amount of capital raised in the global VC market between 2009 and 2018. In particular, China's VC market raised around $4.2 billion in 2009, drawing a share of 19% of the overall amount raised in the global VC market. The influx of capital constantly propelled the growth of the market for a few years, reaching a peak of 42% in 2011 before the market cooled down in 2013. Contrary to the flourishing VC market in the United States, approximately $4.9 billion was directed to China's VC industry in 2013, an amount that was much lower than the $34 billion raised in the U.S. during the same stretch. The second "golden period" started soon afterward, when China's VC market expanded dramatically in 2017 as it raised approximately $18 billion in a single year. However, the boom did not last long since the market cooled down again in 2018 and attracted even less capital in the first quarter of 2019.

3.1. The Growth of RMB Funds

Since 2005, China's local currency funds, or renmimbi (RMB) funds, have gained popularity in terms of both deal value and deal count, mainly as a result of the expansion of domestic capital VCs.

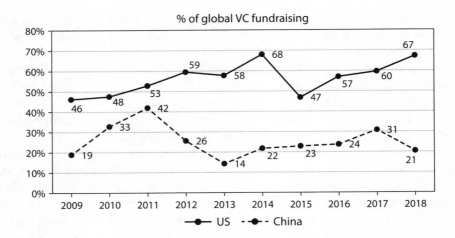

FIGURE 15.3. Fundraising in China's VC market. *Sources:* United States and global: National Venture Capital Association (NVCA) 2019 Yearbook. China: www.pedata.cn. *Notes:* The figure reports the percentage of closed VC funds in China's VC market over that in the global VC market in terms of raised amount. For Chinese data, all the VC funds raised between 2009 and 2018 are included, while those that are liquidated, withdrawn, or still raising are excluded. The fund amount is calculated at the fund closing year.

Figure 15.4 illustrates the growth of RMB funds over the past two decades. Since the market was dominated by foreign VC firms in the early 2000s, fundraising then was conducted in foreign currency, and the majority of the funds were raised in U.S. dollars. RMB funds started to gain popularity in 2005, reaching a peak only three years later when they accounted for 85% of all the fundraising in terms of deal number. However, the amount raised by RMB funds remained small and made up only 35% of the total raised amount at that time. The situation began to change with the expansion of domestic VC firms, buttressed by the launch of the ChiNext Board and the ebullient equity market thereafter. In 2017, RMB funds accounted for a whopping 98.6% of the total number of funds and 92% of the total raised amount in China's VC market.

Although the majority of foreign VC firms have invested primarily with U.S. dollars, they raise RMB funds occasionally. In 2010, RMB funds ate up approximately 15% of the overall amount of capital raised by foreign VC firms. The taste for RMB funds at that time was partially a result of favorable regulations by the Chinese government. The trend, however, disappeared shortly afterward, and today the majority of foreign capital funds are still U.S. dollar–denominated.

3.2. Who Are the LPs?

In the 1980s and 1990s, domestic VC funds were almost entirely backed by the Chinese government. The situation changed gradually with the development of China's limited partner (LP) market. China permits several types of LPs, including traditional financial institutions, such as VC/PE investment institutions, fund-of-funds (FOFs), investment companies, banks, and trusts. Since 2008 social security funds and insurance funds have been allowed to participate in the VC market. There are also nonfinancial corporates,

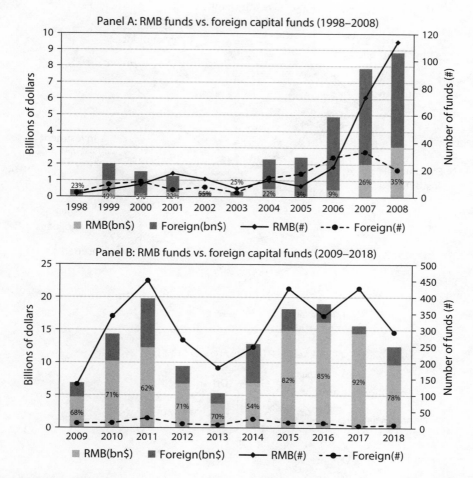

FIGURE 15.4. RMB funds vs. foreign currency funds. *Source:* www.pedata.cn. *Notes:* The figure reports the share of RMB funds and foreign currency funds of all closed VC funds in China's VC market. The columns represent the total amount raised eventually. The graph lines represent the number of RMB (foreign currency) funds. All the numbers are calculated at the fund initiating year.

which represent approximately 16% of the LP market, as well as other types of nonprofit organizations such as university endowments and local governments.

A comparison of the compositions of LPs between the United States and China highlights some interesting features of major participants in the latter's VC market. Among all, unlike in the former, an important role played by wealthy families and individual LPs cannot be ignored. As shown in Panel B of figure 15.5, wealthy families and individuals represent 57% of the market share in China's LP market in terms of fund count. The same group of LPs accounts for less than 2% in the U.S. market. By contrast, institutional LPs play the most important role in the U.S. market, as shown in the figure's Panel A.

Figure 15.6 illustrates the dynamic change of LP composition between 2000 and 2018 in China's VC market. It can be noted that the importance of wealthy individual investors

Panel A: LP investor types in the United States

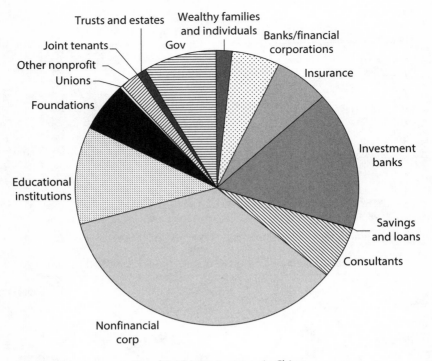

Panel B: LP investor types in China

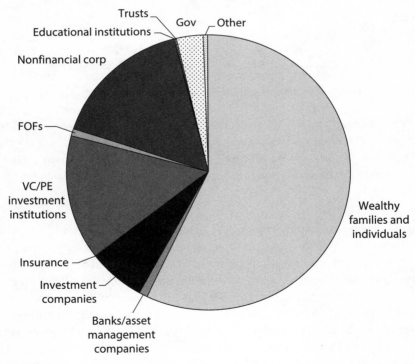

FIGURE 15.5. Limited partner types (number). *Sources:* United States: VentureXpert database, SDC platform. China: www.pedata.cn. *Notes:* Panel A reports all the LPs that are located in the United States and in the VentureXpert database. Panel B reports China's LPs covered by PEdata. Included are all LPs that invested in VC funds of domestic capital and joint capital firms between 2009 and 2018.

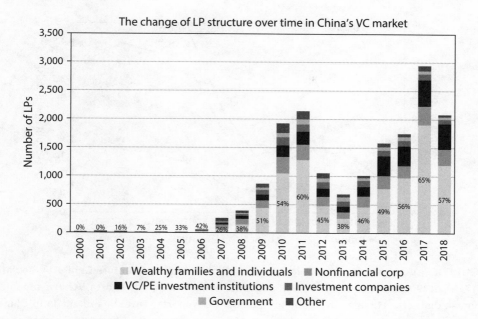

FIGURE 15.6. Individual limited partners (number). *Source:* www.pedata.cn. *Notes:* Included are all LPs that invest in domestic or joint capital VC firms. Percentages represent shares of wealthy families and individual LPs compared to the total number of LPs in the fundraising year.

is more cyclical, matching the boom-and-bust trends of the market. In particular, more than 50% or 60%, respectively, of the LPs are represented by wealthy families and individuals during the boom period such as 2011 and 2017, but their market share plunged dramatically in the downturn such as in 2012 and 2013.

One limitation of this analysis is that the LP composition cannot be described simply by their investment number. For example, it might be useful to know who these wealthy families and individuals are, in terms of their investment amount, experience, and background. Anecdotal evidence suggests that some such investors are founders or successors of certain family firms and some are experienced professionals. Due largely to the data limitations, this section has to stay silent about the possible influence this group may have on the stability of China's VC market.

4. INVESTMENT

Venture capital has been playing an important role in China's economy. It provides capital to promising startup companies that might otherwise be impossible to attract financing. Such firms are often in their early stages and invest heavily in exploring new technology or products. As a result, they are easily financially constrained but have high levels of uncertainty and are lacking tangible assets that can be used as collateral for debt financing.

Chinese startup companies have been attracting an increasing amount of VC investments in recent years. As shown in figure 15.7, two investment booms have occurred in China's VC market since 2009 regarding both deal value and deal count. The first one

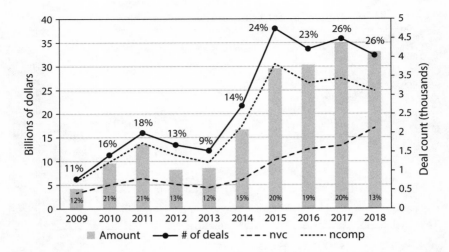

FIGURE 15.7. VC investments in China. *Sources:* Global: National Venture Capital Association (NVCA), 2019 Yearbook. China:www.pedata.cn. *Notes:* The figure reports VC investments in Chinese districts. The amount is the total amount of reported investments made to Chinese startup companies in a year. Percentages on the bar represent the shares of Chinese investment in the global VC market. Deal count is the number of deals financed by VC firms in a year. Percentages on the line represent shares of Chinese investment in the global VC market in terms of deal count.

was around 2011 when the market obtained 21% of total global VC investments and 18% of the deal counts in that year, while the second one was around 2017 when China received 20% of total global VC investments and 26% of the deal counts. In 2015, there were 3,817 Chinese startup companies that received investments from some 1,284 VCs. While the number of active VC firms is increasing monotonically, the number of VC-backed startup companies and the VC deal volume remain at similar levels in recent years. In terms of geographical locations, Beijing, Shanghai, Guangdong, Jiangsu, and Zhejiang have been attracting most of the VC investment since 2000. Beijing alone received approximately 30% of the investment in 2018.

4.1. The Dominance of Domestic VCs

China's VC industry not only is increasingly attracting the attention of foreign capitalists but also has exhibited an impressive surge in investments by domestic VCs who replace foreign VCs in dominating the market.

The activities of foreign VCs in China date back to the early 1990s. With many of them invested as fortune seekers in this big virgin market, several have stayed and remained active ever since. Chinese entrepreneurs can never be too familiar with foreign VCs, such as Sequoia Capital and IDG Capital (which used to be called IDGVC).[5] Those names have continually appeared in some fascinating entrepreneurial myths, such as the success of Alibaba, Baidu, and so on, which most entrepreneurs admire. Both VCs have invested in over a thousand projects in China over the years, with an average successful exit rate of approximately 10%. By contrast, joint capital (i.e., VC firms that are jointly held by both domestic and foreign capital) is not a very popular format in China, and the reasons to form a joint capital venture vary. J.P. Morgan (China) Venture Capital, US-Tsing Capital, and Shenzhen Innovation Softbank VC are some examples.

Figure 15.8, Panel A, illustrates the investment of both foreign capital and joint capital that have been active in China's VC market in recent years. While both investment value and deal flow have risen sharply since 2014, China-based investment has become an increasingly smaller portion since 2011. In particular, 93% of the investment was directed to China in 2009. But the portion plunged to around 38% in 2015 and reached a historically low point of 33% the next year.

While the current investment cycle has gone upward, the industry has benefited primarily from the record-breaking growth of domestic investors. Figure 15.8, Panel B, highlights the trend. Consistent with the previous analysis, the contribution of domestic capital was increasing dramatically and consistently with the proportion creeping from 42% in 2009 all the way up to 81% in 2017 before it came in slightly lower in 2018. Unlike their foreign capital peers, over 97% of the investments of domestic capitals are concentrated in Chinese startups in terms of both deal count and deal value.

4.2. Investment Stage

Tools used by VC firms to alleviate information asymmetry are pre-investment intensive scrutiny and post-investment monitoring. Staged capital infusion mechanism, as one example of such monitoring, has been proved to be an effective monitoring method (Sahlman, 1990; Gompers, 1995; Tian, 2011; Liu and Tian, 2019) and been widely used in the industry. In China, the secular penetration of VC investments is thorough. Fresh capital floods into the startup companies at the seed-round or angel-round, all the way up to the pre-IPO round or even the post-IPO round, with most of the investment concentrated in the early stages. Figure 15.9 compares the investment rounds of Chinese VC firms against those of American VC firms in terms of deal count. While angel- and seed-stage startups attract more frequent investment in the U.S. VC market, Chinese VCs are more likely to invest in relatively later-stage startups at all times. However, exactly the opposite results are found when their investment amounts are analyzed. According to the 2019 yearbook of the National Venture Capital Association (NVAC), approximately 63% of funds in the U.S. VC market was swallowed by late-stage investment in 2018. This number is sound, given that only 5.7% of funds in the U.S. VC market was directed to angel- or seed-stage startups. Nevertheless, in China's VC market, early-stage investment remains the majority. Considering the amount of money invested, 58% of investments were directed to early-stage startups while 38% were eaten up by late-stage startups, with the rest (4% to 5%) flooding into the seed- or angel stages in 2018.

One implication from the inconsistency between the deal value and deal count is that U.S. VC firms are probably more cautious when they choose to invest in seed- or angel-stage startups. As a result, investments are more frequently made with a small amount each time.

4.3. Incubation Period

With a few exceptions, Chinese general partners (GPs) are clearly "impatient" and in no mood to hang on to projects any longer than they have to. Figure 15.10, Panel A, shows the distribution of incubation periods for VCs that are active in the Chinese market. The

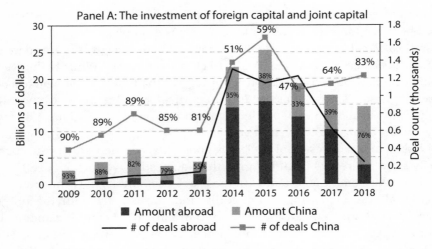

Panel A: The investment of foreign capital and joint capital

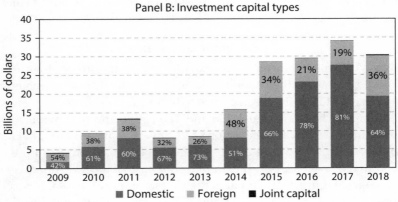

Panel B: Investment capital types

FIGURE 15.8. Investments: Foreign capital vs. domestic capital. *Source:* www.pedata.cn. *Notes:* Panel A reports the distribution of the invested district chosen by foreign capital and joint capital that are active in China. Amount China is the total reported amount of money invested in China; Amount abroad is the total reported amount of money invested outside China. The number of deals for China is the total deals made to Chinese firms, while the number of deals abroad is the total deals made to foreign firms. The percentage numbers on the line represent the portion of the number of deals made to China over the total number. The numbers on the bar represent the percentage of the reported amount of money invested in China over the total amount. Panel B reports the capital type for active VCs in China. The numbers on the bar represent the share of the overall investments of domestic (foreign) VCs over the total investment made to China. Deals with missing capital types are excluded from this figure.

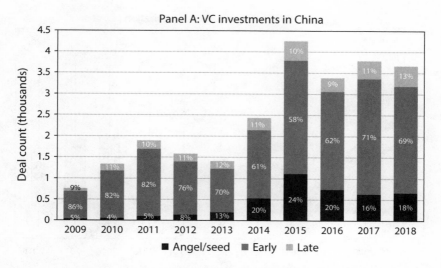

Panel A: VC investments in China

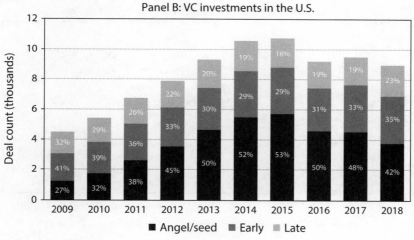

Panel B: VC investments in the U.S.

FIGURE 15.9. Investment stage. *Sources:* Global: National Venture Capital Association (NVCA), 2019 Yearbook; China: www.pedata.cn. *Notes:* Panel A and Panel B report VC deal count of China and the United States between 2009 and 2018. Following PitchBook (data provider for NVCA Yearbook), Angel/Seed represents the investments make to angel- or seed-stage start-ups. Early stage refers to investments made to round pre-A, A, A+, B, and B+ startups; late stage refers to round C, D, and later rounds. "PIPE," "Strategic Investment," and "Neeq Private Placement" investments are excluded.

median incubation period, defined as the median number of months between the initial investment date and the exit date, was 26 months in 2009. The right-skewed distribution also suggests that many deals have clustered at the region in which firms get even shorter financing support from VCs. The incubation period crept up to around 38 months in 2010 but edged down slowly to 44 months in 2018 from a peak of 55 months in 2016. In 6 out of 10 years, China's VC market observed "quick flips" in which half the domestic GPs get in and out of an investment within only 3 years. The incubation period for

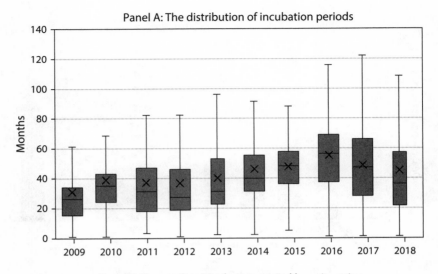

Panel A: The distribution of incubation periods

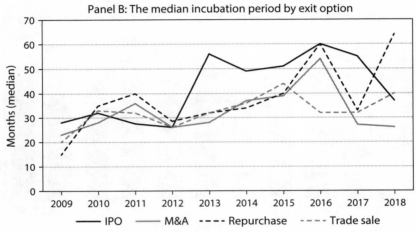

Panel B: The median incubation period by exit option

IPO ——— M&A ——— Repurchase ---- Trade sale - - - -

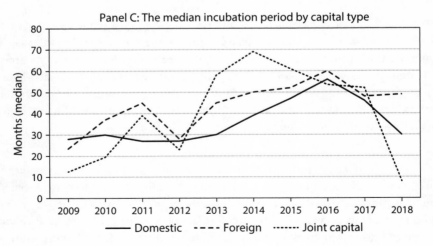

Panel C: The median incubation period by capital type

Domestic ——— Foreign ---- Joint capital ······

Chinese VCs is well below that of the U.S. VCs. According to a report from PitchBook in 2017, the median time to exit is 8.2 years for an IPO and 5 years for acquisitions or buy-outs in the United States.

Figure 15.10, Panel B, reports the median incubation period for VCs with different exit options. The short time interval for IPO exits is likely to be the main driver for the difference in incubation periods between the United States and China. In particular, the incubation period for IPO exits was the shortest among all the other exit channels between 2010 to 2012, ranging from 26 to 32 months, before it later turned longer. However, even when the incubation period for IPO exits reached a peak in 2016, the approximately five-year length is still much shorter, compared with that of the United States. This is less an issue for M&A exits. When the incubation period for M&A exits reached a peak in 2016, half of the VCs hold their portfolio firms for more than 4.3 years, almost matching that of the United States in 2017.

The urgency to sell may reflect a number of factors. First, it is possible that lacking good exit alternatives in the early years may trigger the VCs' propensity to exit earlier than later so as to get a better return. This argument is likely to partially explain the up-going trend in the incubation period in recent years when VCs have found it easier to exit in mainland China. A comparison between foreign and domestic capital could help us better understand the mechanism if we assume foreign capital firms—U.S. capital firms in particular—have better access to the U.S. market or other international stock markets and thus should have a longer incubation period. Figure 15.10, Panel C, reports the median incubation period for domestic VC, foreign VC, and joint VC firms that are active in China's market. It shows that for most of the time, foreign VC firms hold a startup longer than do domestic VC firms. Moreover, the incubation period for joint VC firms is more cyclical. They may hold a startup longer in good times but sell it faster when the market is getting weak.

A second possibility is that the cyclical change in VCs' incubation periods may reflect their concerns about economic weakness. In particular, a piled-up weakness in the economy may make it harder to sell later. As a consequence, many VC firms feel willing to sell anything that is not actually tied down. This may partially explain why the incubation period is more right-skewed during bad times than in booms, as shown in figure 15.10, Panel A.

FIGURE 15.10. (facing page) Investment incubation period. *Source:* www.pedata.cn. *Notes:* Panel A reports the number of months between the initial investment date and the exit date. The box graph captures the minimum, 25%, median, 75%, and the maximum of the distribution from the bottom to the top, respectively. "X" represents the mean of the distribution. The data contains all the reported exit deals in China's VC market between 2009 and 2018. Excluded are initial investments that belong to "Neeq Private Placement," "PIPE," or "Strategic Investment," and also deals with negative investment length and deals with unreported initial investment date. The statistical software was permitted to drop outliers when generating the figure in Panel A. Panel B further excludes deals with unreported exit options. Panel C further excludes deals made by VCs with unreported capital types. The year is the exit year for the deal.

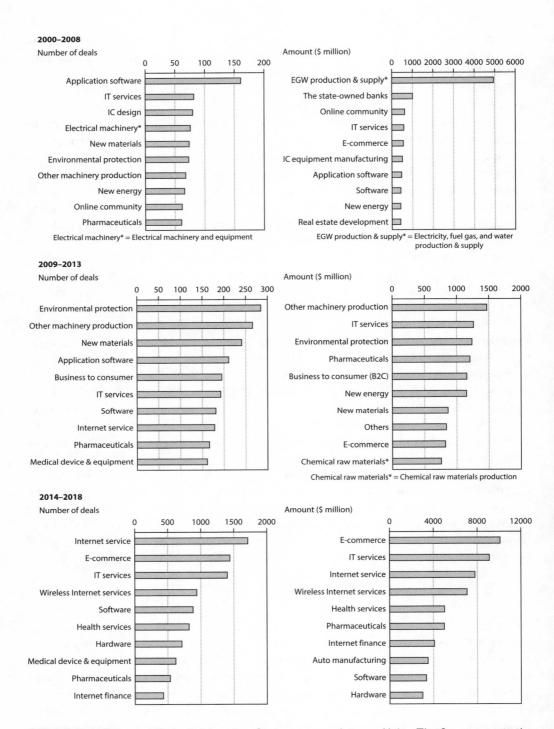

2000–2008

Number of deals

Application software	
IT services	
IC design	
Electrical machinery*	
New materials	
Environmental protection	
Other machinery production	
New energy	
Online community	
Pharmaceuticals	

Scale: 0, 50, 100, 150, 200

Electrical machinery* = Electrical machinery and equipment

Amount ($ million)

EGW production & supply*	
The state-owned banks	
Online community	
IT services	
E-commerce	
IC equipment manufacturing	
Application software	
Software	
New energy	
Real estate development	

Scale: 0, 1000, 2000, 3000, 4000, 5000, 6000

EGW production & supply* = Electricity, fuel gas, and water production & supply

2009–2013

Number of deals

Environmental protection	
Other machinery production	
New materials	
Application software	
Business to consumer	
IT services	
Software	
Internet service	
Pharmaceuticals	
Medical device & equipment	

Scale: 0, 50, 100, 150, 200, 250, 300

Amount ($ million)

Other machinery production	
IT services	
Environmental protection	
Pharmaceuticals	
Business to consumer (B2C)	
New energy	
New materials	
Others	
E-commerce	
Chemical raw materials*	

Scale: 0, 500, 1000, 1500, 2000

Chemical raw materials* = Chemical raw materials production

2014–2018

Number of deals

Internet service	
E-commerce	
IT services	
Wireless Internet services	
Software	
Health services	
Hardware	
Medical device & equipment	
Pharmaceuticals	
Internet finance	

Scale: 0, 500, 1000, 1500, 2000

Amount ($ million)

E-commerce	
IT services	
Internet service	
Wireless Internet services	
Health services	
Pharmaceuticals	
Internet finance	
Auto manufacturing	
Software	
Hardware	

Scale: 0, 4000, 8000, 12000

FIGURE 15.11. Chinese VC deals by sector. *Source:* www.pedata.cn. *Notes:* The figure reports the top 10 industries attracting the most VC investments made to Chinese districts between 2009 and 2018. The number (amount) is the summation of the total number of deals (total reported amount) in a given period. Industry classifications follow the definitions used by Zero2IPO reports.

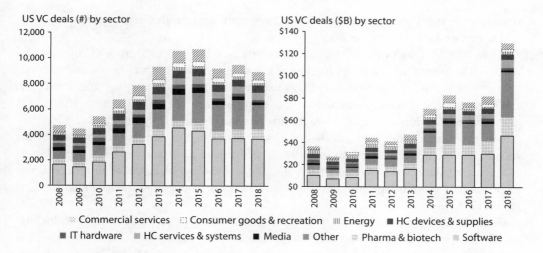

FIGURE 15.12. U.S. VC deals by sector. *Source:* https://pitchbook.com/news/articles/18-charts -to-illustrate-us-vc-in-2018. *Notes:* According to the 2019 NVAC Yearbook, "Other" industry groups include: commercial products, commercial transportation, other business products and services, consumer durables, consumer nondurables, services (nonfinancial), transportation, other consumer products and services, utilities, other energy, capital markets/institutions, commercial banks, insurance, other financial services, other healthcare, IT services, other information technology, agriculture, chemicals and gases, construction (non-wood), containers and packaging, forestry, metals, minerals and mining, textiles, and other materials.

Other mechanisms may also drive the difference in incubation periods between Chinese VCs and foreign VCs, apart from the macro-level market structure. For example, the different composition of LPs, discussed in the previous section, may play an important role here. Furthermore, the differences in culture and management structure are worth exploring as well, which this chapter will leave for future studies.

4.4. Industry

Chinese venture capitalists never seem to lack a desire to seek out emerging opportunities. Their shared tastes and predictions of where the economy might go are captured largely by the most popular startups and sectors in which they invest. With China's economy having expanded dramatically over the past few years, investors' tastes change at tremendous speed. Figure 15.11 explores the top-10 most popular sectors for Chinese VCs during the past decade, then figure 15.12 further compares the trend with that of U.S. VC firms.

From 2000 to 2008, foreign VC firms were the main player in China's VC market, while the development of domestic VCs was severely constrained by incomplete LP markets and limited exit options. With the dot-com bubble fresh in their memories, VCs were focusing their diligence on more traditional sectors while still trying hard to explore the IT-related sectors in the emerging Chinese market. As for deal count, application software and IT services attracted the most frequent investments from the VC industry, although at relatively low amounts. What really caught investors' attention during this stretch were traditional sectors, such as the supply and production of electricity, gas, and water, and state-owned banks.

From 2009 to 2013, domestic VCs grew at a tremendous pace. China's VC market has waxed and waned with the fluctuation of the stock market both at home and abroad. While the majority of the investment was used to feed the machinery production sector, capital was more diversely distributed into other sectors, such as pharmaceuticals and new materials. Environmental protection received the most frequent capital injections during that period, followed by other machinery-production sectors and the new materials sector. Meanwhile, IT-related sectors were increasingly attracting more capital from VC investors, which include the IT service sector and the e-commerce sector that retained its popularity from the previous round, and emerging interests in the Business to Consumer (B2C) sector.

Some 15 Chinese firms successfully launched their IPOs on Nasdaq in 2014, including the e-commerce giant Alibaba Group, JD.com, Jumei.com, and so on. The high investment return immediately attracted ravenous investors who fed the industry with gargantuan sums of money shortly afterward. From e-commerce and IT service to Internet service and wireless Internet service, Chinese Internet and technology firms—or these "service" sectors—have attracted most of the investment from China's VC industry, which since 2014 has become the brand of the period.

The preference of U.S. venture capitalists seems to be more consistent. Figure 15.12 presents the sectors invested by U.S. VC firms. In the past 10 years, software, pharmaceuticals, and biotech sectors have continued to eat up the money as U.S. VC investors constantly feed the businesses with enormous sums of capital and are eager to keep on doing so. The fruitful products and innovation that emerge from these sectors then permeate into other sectors, motivating the development of the market.

Maybe it is too soon, though, to conclude that Chinese venture capitalists are episodic. A close look at figure 15.11 gives new insights indicating that IT and e-commerce have continued to rank in the top-10 most popular sectors being supported by Chinese VC firms over the past 20 years. The question is how these developments can be transferred to other sectors and can, in turn, support the new development of the economy and thereby improve the well-being of everyone in China.

4.5. VC Syndication

VC syndication is common in the United States VC market, with rationales and consequences being discussed extensively by academic researchers. Syndication provides VC investors with the benefit of diversification (e.g., Wilson, 1968) and allows them to learn a "second option" from each other (e.g., Casamatta and Haritchabalet, 2007; Cestone et al., 2006). The combination of complementary management skills and expertise from different VC partners in the syndication creates value for entrepreneurial firms and leads to a more successful exit (e.g., Brander et al., 2002; Tian, 2012; Tian et al., 2016; Bayar et al., 2019).

Syndication is not popular with Chinese VC firms, though. As shown in figure 15.13, Panel A, approximately 80% of the deals in China are conducted by a single VC firm at a time, a trend that has been consistent since 2009 before changing slightly in 2018. The average number of VCs in a deal ranges from 1.2 to 1.4 and rose slightly in 2018. Comparatively, in the United States, 70% of the investments are backed by VC syndicates (Tian, 2012).

For syndicated deals in China, figure 15.13, Panel B, highlights the syndication strategies. While almost half the syndicated deals are backed by the cooperation between

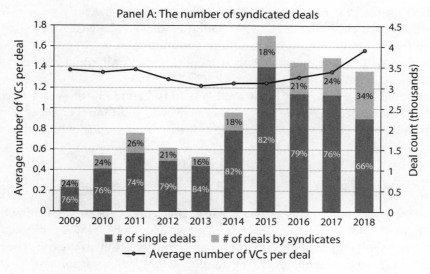

Panel A: The number of syndicated deals

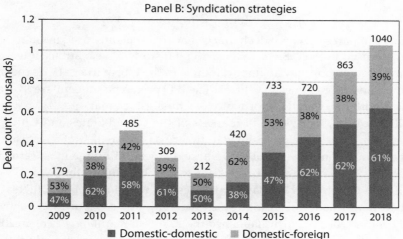

Panel B: Syndication strategies

FIGURE 15.13. VC syndication in China. *Source:* www.pedata.cn. *Note:* The figure reports the syndication of VC investments in China. Panel A contains all reported investments made to Chinese startups. Excluded are deals with unreported company names, VC names, or investment dates. # of single deals refers to the number of deals with only one VC investor at the particular round of financing, while # of deals by syndicates refer to the number of deals with at least two different VC investors. Panel B focuses only on syndicated financing deals. Deals with unreported VC capital types are further dropped. Domestic-Domestic refers to the number of deals made by VC syndications between domestic VCs only. Domestic-Foreign refers to the number of deals jointly invested by both domestic VCs and foreign VCs.

domestic VCs, the preference bounced around somewhat in the early years before the trend started to be clear after 2014. In particular, syndication between domestic VCs rebounded from a low of 38% in 2014 to 62% in 2016 and 2017.

Bayar et al. (2019) show that single investment is always preferred by VC generalists. This may be one of the explanations for what is observed in China's VC market. If this argument holds, more VC syndicates are likely to be created in the years to come as Chinese VC firms become more specialized. However, substantial changes may need more time, because cultivating cooperative culture cannot be achieved within a short period.

5. EXIT

Empirical analyses on the U.S. VC market (e.g., Black and Gilson, 1998) show that the growth of its VC industry largely depends on the development of the IPO market, which in turn determines how likely VC investors can exit successfully in the end. The history of China's VC market provides another example backing up this argument.

5.1. Exit Channels

Figures 15.14 compares various exit channels that are frequently used in China's VC market with those used in the U.S. VC market over a historic 10-year stretch. Overall, while mergers and acquisitions play an important role in the U.S. market, IPO is the more preferred exit pathway for Chinese VC firms. The IPO preference of Chinese VC capitalists is associated with the overall performance of China's stock market.

From 2009 to 2010, the two giant markets of the United States and China seem to have behaved in exactly the opposite way, in terms of the exit strategies used by their VCs. When acquisitions ate up the U.S. market by generating the most returns for investors, China's active investors turned out to rely heavily on IPO exits. The preference for IPO in China has been largely buttressed by the launch of ChiNext and the overall good performance of China's stock market by then. Figure 15.15 shows that a total of 349 entrepreneurial firms launched their IPOs in mainland China in 2010, while 31% of them were backed by VCs. In the same year, IPO exits accounted for 94% of the overall exit value for domestic VCs and accounted for 69% of the value for foreign VCs in China.

By contrast, the preference changed dramatically in 2012 and 2013. While IPOs accounted for more than 60% or even 70% of the total exit value in the United States due to the unprecedented stock market performance of the U.S. market in that period, Chinese VC investors almost gave up the IPO channel entirely. This resulted from the bearish stock performance for Chinese firms in both the home market and the market abroad, combined with the IPO suspension policy implemented by China's CSRC. Figure 15.15 shows that with zero IPOs launched in mainland China in 2013 (hence no bar shown for that year), the IPO market was "hot" in the United States with a total of 339 firms going public and 87 of them being VC-backed IPOs.

The year 2014 delivered another solid performance in the U.S. IPO market. With a total of 384 IPOs launched, 33% of them were backed by VC investors. Regarding foreign capital in China, IPOs accounted for 99% of the exit value in that year and produced unprecedented distribution for these investors. Nevertheless, China's IPO market was "cold"

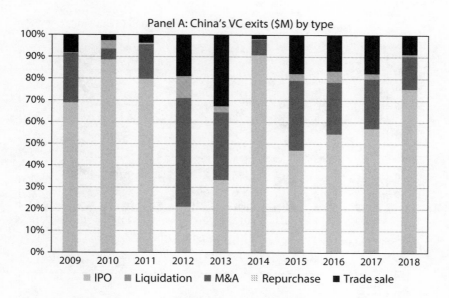

Panel A: China's VC exits ($M) by type

IPO   Liquidation   M&A   Repurchase   Trade sale

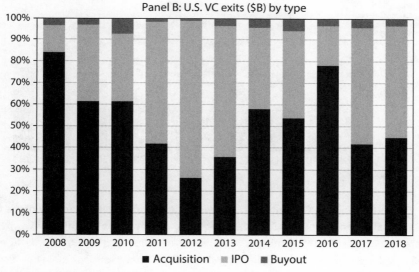

Panel B: U.S. VC exits ($B) by type

Acquisition   IPO   Buyout

FIGURE 15.14. Exit channels. *Sources:* United States: https://pitchbook.com/news/articles/18-charts -to-illustrate-us-vc-in-2018; China:www.pedata.cn. *Note:* The figure reports the portion of several exit methods in the overall exit return amount. Panel A includes all the exit deals in China that are reported in PEdata and with nonmissing return amount (millions of dollars). Panel B comes from Pitchbook's website.

at the same time, making M&As the first-ranking exit channel for domestic VC investors that had limited access to foreign IPO markets. A relatively small number of IPOs occurred in mainland China, less than half of them being VC-backed.

From 2015 to 2018, IPOs maintained their dominant role as the most-used exit channel in China's VC market for both domestic and foreign capital, while U.S. exit deals were bouncing back and forth between IPOs and M&As.

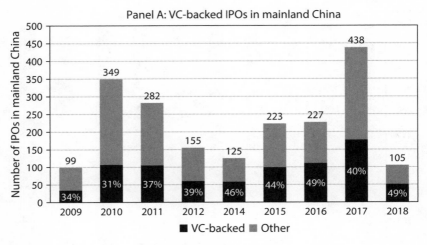

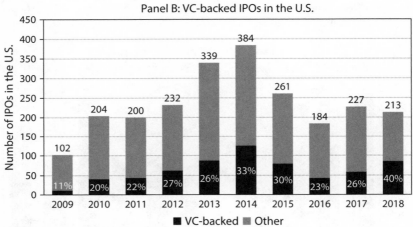

FIGURE 15.15. VC-backed IPOs (number). *Sources:* United States: 2019 Yearbook of the National Venture Capital Association(NVCA) (data provided by PitchBook); China: www.pedata.cn, Wind database. *Notes:* Panel A reports the number of IPOs on the four boards in mainland China—Shanghai Stock Exchange main board, Shenzhen Stock Exchange main board, ChiNext, and Shenzhen SME board. Almost no IPO was launched at the Shenzhen Stock Exchange main board during the time span. VC-backed IPO is defined as IPOs with at least one VC exit at the IPO year. Panel B reports the number of IPOs in the United States.

Figure 15.15 illustrates the number of VC-backed IPOs for both China and the United States from 2009 to 2018. With few exceptions, VC-backed IPOs account for a larger portion in China than that in the United States. On average, 40% of the IPO firms were VC-backed in China during the 10-year time interval while the portion was only 27% in the United States.

Figure 15.16 highlights the different preferences of domestic and foreign capital VCs in their choices of exit channels. It shows that IPOs accounted for more than half the exit value for both domestic and foreign capital VC firms in China. In the extreme case, IPOs

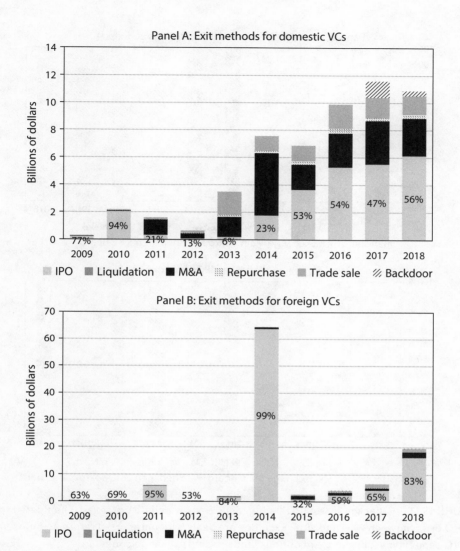

FIGURE 15.16. China's VC market: Exit channels for domestic and foreign capital. *Source:* www .pedata.cn. *Note:* The figure reports exit channels for domestic VCs and foreign VCs in China's VC market. The figure contains all the exit deals between 2009 and 2018, while excluding deals with unreported return amount, missing VC capital types, and missing exit options.

accounted for 99% of the unprecedented distribution gained by foreign investors in 2014, which is almost 10 times the overall exit value for domestic VCs at the same time. Although M&As and trade sales remain important exit options for domestic capital, they are less important for foreign capital firms than the contribution of IPO exits. One possible reason could be that foreign capital firms get more access to the international IPO markets but face greater information asymmetry in M&As and trade sales in China's market. The next section takes a closer look at IPO exits in terms of their listing decisions.

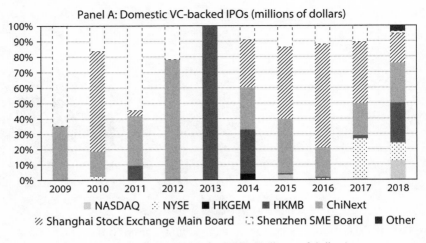

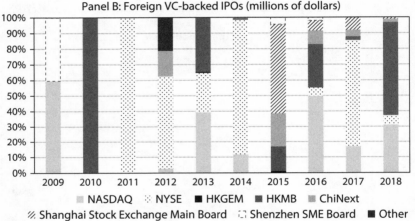

FIGURE 15.17. VC-backed IPOs: IPO listing. *Source:* www.pedata.cn. *Notes:* The figure reports all IPO exits between 2009 and 2018. Excluded are deals with unreported return amounts, missing VC capital types, missing exit options, and missing exchange codes.

5.2. IPO Exits

VC-backed IPOs are listed on various stock exchanges, and the listing location is partially associated with whether they are backed by domestic VCs or foreign VCs. As shown in figure 15.17, most domestic VC-backed IPOs are launched in mainland China. By contrast, most foreign VC-backed IPOs are listed in either Hong Kong or the United States.

In particular, the Shanghai Stock Exchange (SSE) contributed the largest portion of IPOs returns for domestic VCs in 2010, 2015, and 2016. The exchange was established in 1990 as the first stock exchange in mainland China. By the end of 2018, there have been 1,450 firms listed on the exchange, with approximately 27 trillion RMB market value in total. Overall, the Shanghai Stock Exchange has 40% of the IPO exits for domestic VCs and is the most popular stock exchange for IPO listings that are backed by domestic capital VCs.

The Shenzhen Small and Medium Enterprise (SME) Board, which was established in 2004, is another alternative for IPO exits in mainland China. Differing from the main board, the SME Board has lower standards for IPOs and is set up to support small and medium-sized firms in the country. By the end of 2018, the board had 922 listed firms with a market value of about 7 trillion RMB. While the board accounted for 28.4% of IPO exits for domestic capital before 2013, its contribution was diminishing after that as its importance was gradually replaced by a newly launched board for growth enterprises.

The plan to establish the ChiNext Board was initiated in 1998 but the implementation was postponed until 2009. Shortly after its opening, ChiNext began continuously attracting IPOs of growth enterprises and has come to play an important role in IPO exits backed by domestic VC firms. In particular, in 2012 ChiNext represented 78% of all domestic VCs' IPO exit value. As of 2018, there were 739 firms listed in the market, whose value reached approximately 4 trillion RMB. Over the past decade, ChiNext has contributed approximately 24% of the overall IPO exit value for domestic capital. Domestic VCs never conceal their enthusiasm toward it, despite its late arrival.

For domestic VCs that exited through IPOs in 2013, 100% of the IPOs were listed on the Hong Kong Main Board, owing to IPO suspension in mainland China. While the Hong Kong Growth Enterprise Market (GEM) may be more friendly for growth firms, given its relatively lower listing standards, the Hong Kong Main Board contributes more in terms of exit value for both domestic and foreign capital VCs. Approximately 33% of IPOs backed by domestic VCs chose to list on the Hong Kong Exchange in 2014, a number that fell to 26% in 2018.

For foreign capital VCs, the Hong Kong Stock Exchange ranks the third most popular destination for their IPO exits, as it has contributed 12.5% of all the overall IPO exit value during the past 10 years. The exchanges that rank first (NYSE) and second (Nasdaq) cover approximately a total of 85% of the exit value. In particular, while 16% is directed to Nasdaq, 69% is obtained by the NYSE. Regarding their listings made in mainland China, ChiNext is the most popular listing place, which accounts for 1.3% of the exit value, followed by the Shanghai Stock Exchange with about 1%.

Domestic capital has recently been increasingly interested in foreign stock exchanges. In particular, figure 15.17 shows that NYSE and Nasdaq accounted, respectively, for 27% and 24% of the IPO exit value for domestic capital VCs in 2017 and 2018.

5.3. Exit Returns

The past 10 years have been a period of unprecedented success for Chinese VC firms. Figure 15.18, Panel A, illustrates the average internal rate of return (IRR) for all Chinese-based investments closed in the given years. The distribution is shown to be strictly positive for all types of VCs in China. While domestic capital obtained higher returns before 2013, foreign VCs have been catching up quickly in recent years and have even exceeded domestic capital to become the most profitable ones in China's market.

Figure 15.18, Panels B and C, illustrate the most valuable exit channels for domestic and foreign capital VCs. The figures show that with few exceptions, IPOs provide the best return for both domestic and foreign capital, although the return gets lower after 2015 and ranks the lowest compared with the returns of other types of exits in recent years.

One possible reason is that China's VC market is becoming far more competitive than it was in the past. With more cash flooding into the market and investors' increasing preferences for IPO exits, general partners are clearly hungry to do more deals and spare no effort to search for the most profitable ones. However, when they identify promising projects, they consistently encounter aggressive competitors who are willing to push the

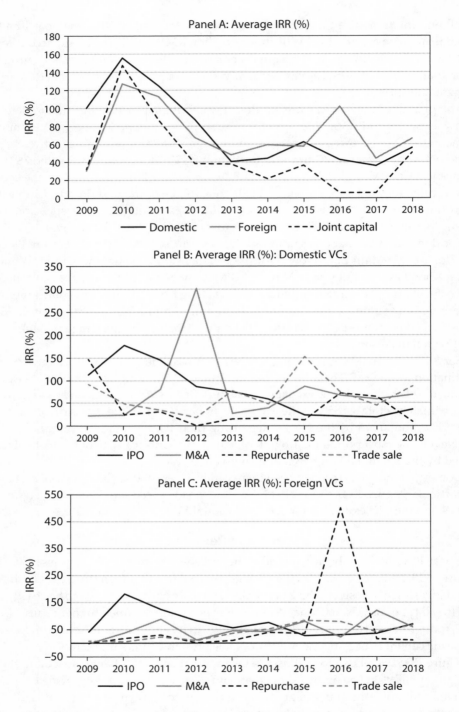

FIGURE 15.18. Average internal rate of return (IRR). *Source:* www.pedata.cn. *Notes:* The figure reports the average annualized IRR for VC investments in Chinese firms. The returns are further separated by capital types of VC firms and their exit channels. Specifically, the average IRR is taken for all exit deals in the year. Excluded are deals with nonreported IRRs, extremely high or low IRRs, missing VC capital types, and deals with missing exit dates.

project valuation (and price) even higher, ending up with a relatively lower return on average.

6. ALTERNATIVE FORMS OF VC INVESTMENTS

In addition to traditional VC firms discussed above, alternative forms of VC investments have different organizational structures and varying investment objectives. This section discusses two alternative forms to traditional VC firms, namely, corporate venture capital (CVC) firms and government-guided funds.

6.1. Corporate Venture Capital (CVC)

6.1.1. Overview

One special type of VC firms that strategically invest in startups on behalf of their parent companies are called corporate venture capital (CVC) firms. They are typically a subsidiary of an industrial firm or a fund that is jointly set up by the parent firm along with a traditional VC firm. These organizational forms are frequently used by U.S. companies to extend their product lines as well as to conduct research and development (R&D) externally. Unlike traditional VC firms whose investment goals are to maximize financial returns, CVC firms' investment goals are quite multidimensional. Besides financial returns, their investment goals include obtaining new techniques, acquiring new products, recruiting new talent, and establishing connections with promising industries. Overall, strategic concerns instead of financial returns are the main goals of CVC investment. The important roles that CVCs play both in nurturing technological innovations within startup companies in which they invest, and in fostering their own innovations, have been explored by both academic researchers (e.g., Chemmanur et al., 2014; Dushnitsky and Lenox, 2006) and practitioners.

While such an organizational form is an age-old invention in the United States, few CVC funds were established in China until 1998. Over the years, the country's CVC investments have grown dramatically and become an increasingly important part of its VC market.

Figure 15.19 highlights the development of CVCs in both China and the United States from 2009 to 2018. While CVC investors have remained an important source of capital for startups in the U.S. market, China's CVCs are still in a relatively early stage while catching up at a tremendous pace in recent years. Regarding the deal count, U.S. CVC investments have shown great resilience and been strong overall for years. By contrast, the growth of China's CVCs is worth considering. The share of CVC-backed deals in China jumped from 5% in 2009 all the way up to a peak of 16% in 2014 and has dropped slightly afterward. The growth in deal value is sounder, having risen from 1% of the VC/PE industry in 2009 to a high of 23% in 2015. While the investment amount of CVCs has kept rising thereafter, the growth was slower compared to the whole VC/PE market, ending up with a slightly lower proportion in 2016 and 2017.

6.1.2. Baidu, Alibaba, and Tencent

Establishing CVC subsidiaries has become increasingly popular with the tech titans of China when they have extended their platforms into virtually all IT-related sectors in recent years. Like the FAMGA (Facebook, Apple, Microsoft, Google, and Amazon) in the

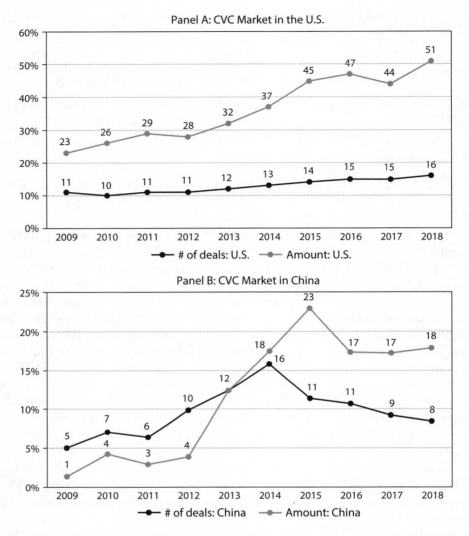

FIGURE 15.19. CVC investment. *Sources:* United States: National Venture Capital Association (NVCA), 2019 Yearbook; China: www.pedata.cn. *Notes:* The figure reports CVC investments in China and the United States. The number in Panel A represents the portion of U.S. CVC investments to the overall VC investments regarding the deal value and deal count in the year. The number in Panel B represents the portion of Chinese CVC investments to the overall VC/PE investments regarding the deal value and deal count in the year.

United States, China's set of IT giants are known as BAT, which stands for Baidu, Alibaba, and Tencent. Each of them started with singular business objectives in the early 2000s. Baidu used to be a search engine like Google, Tencent a messaging app, and Alibaba an e-commerce marketplace similar to Amazon. With the rapid expansion of earning customers' favor for mobile technology and all-things-Internet, the BAT companies are expanding their platforms pervasively to address their millions of customers' needs. Most expansion attempts are achieved by the strategic investments of their CVC subsid-

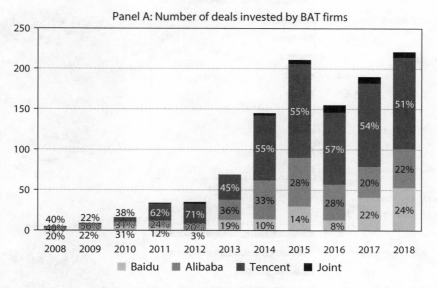

Panel A: Number of deals invested by BAT firms

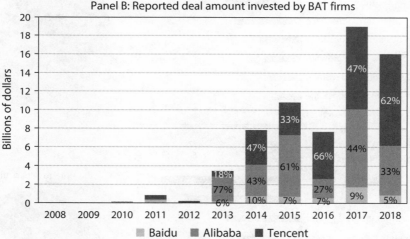

Panel B: Reported deal amount invested by BAT firms

FIGURE 15.20. BAT-backed investments. *Source:* www.pedata.cn. *Notes:* The figure reports all deals invested by CVCs of Baidu, Alibaba, and Tencent. Excluded are deals with unreported investment date. Panel B further excludes deals with unknown investment amount.

iaries. According to PitchBook's report, 19 out of 71 Chinese "unicorns" have received financing from BAT firms or are even controlled by them. According to the 2019 "unicorn" list published by CB Insights, Tencent and Alibaba rank the top 10 investors around the world for the number of "unicorns" they invested in. Their CVCs have outperformed most independent VC firms in this regard.

Figure 15.20 highlights the investments made by BAT's CVC vehicles between 2008 and 2018. Overall, both investment value and deal count have been increasing dramatically over those years. As shown in Panel A, Tencent has kept its dominant role in terms of owning the largest number of deals since 2011. This, however, is not always the case

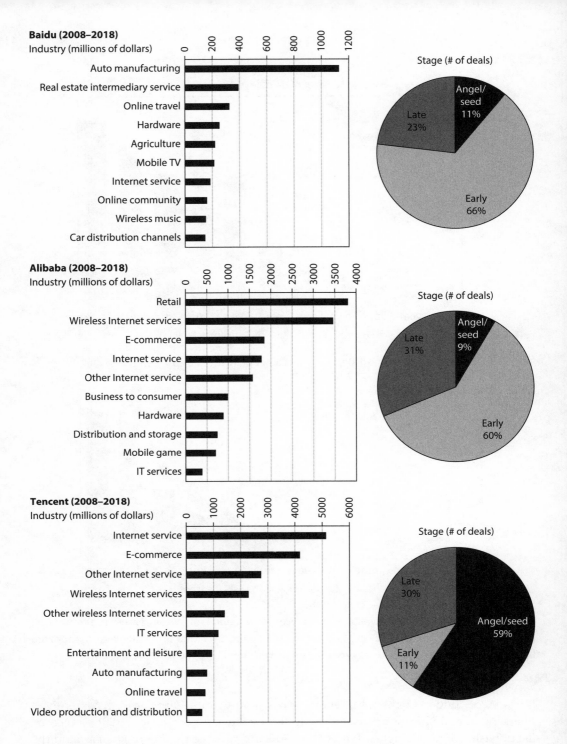

Baidu (2008–2018)
Industry (millions of dollars)

| Auto manufacturing |
| Real estate intermediary service |
| Online travel |
| Hardware |
| Agriculture |
| Mobile TV |
| Internet service |
| Online community |
| Wireless music |
| Car distribution channels |

Stage (# of deals)
- Angel/seed 11%
- Late 23%
- Early 66%

Alibaba (2008–2018)
Industry (millions of dollars)

| Retail |
| Wireless Internet services |
| E-commerce |
| Internet service |
| Other Internet service |
| Business to consumer |
| Hardware |
| Distribution and storage |
| Mobile game |
| IT services |

Stage (# of deals)
- Angel/seed 9%
- Late 31%
- Early 60%

Tencent (2008–2018)
Industry (millions of dollars)

| Internet service |
| E-commerce |
| Other Internet service |
| Wireless Internet services |
| Other wireless Internet services |
| IT services |
| Entertainment and leisure |
| Auto manufacturing |
| Online travel |
| Video production and distribution |

Stage (# of deals)
- Late 30%
- Angel/seed 59%
- Early 11%

FIGURE 15.21. CVC investments of BAT: industry and stage. *Source:* www.pedata.cn. *Notes:* The left column reports the top 10 industries attracting the most investment from CVCs of the BAT firms between 2008 and 2018. The right column shows how these investments are distributed into various stages. Angel/Seed represents the investments made to angel- or seed-stage startups. Early refers to investments made to round pre-A, A, A+, B, and B+ startups. Later refers to rounds C, D, and later rounds. Excluded are "PIPE," "Strategic Investment," "Neeq Private Placement," and "Other." Deals with unreported amounts are excluded from the left column. Deals with unreported financing rounds are excluded from the right column.

regarding the investment amount. In particular, while Tencent's investment value ranked at the top six times over the past 11 years, Alibaba ate up approximately 70% of the investments made by the BAT trio in 2009, 2013, and 2015; Baidu accounted for 65% of the overall amount in 2010. In addition, the number of joint deals reached a peak in 2016 and remained solid in 2017 and 2018, suggesting that the BAT members are somehow prone to cooperation.

A closer analysis of their CVC investment strategies suggests that the members share different tastes in sector selections as well as investment stage choices.

Figure 15.21 highlights the top 10 sectors that are heavily invested by CVCs of BAT between 2008 and 2018. Baidu, which used to be a search engine, has since centered its investments on auto manufacturing and its other related services, such as online travel, while also exploring additional IT-related services such as mobile TV and wireless music delivery. Alibaba, while focusing mostly on business-to-consumer (B2C)- and business-to-business (B2B)-related services, has been extending its attention to wider platforms, such as mobile games and other Internet services and tools. For years, Tencent has grown from a messaging app to a comprehensive platform for social interaction, online payment, entertainment, and news, among other things; its CVC investments have focused on Internet and IT services as well as the entertainment and video production sectors.

The pie charts in figure 15.21 show how the members' investments are distributed into various investment stages. On average, approximately 65% of the money has been directed to late-stage startups for the past 11 years. Nevertheless, the number of deals gives us new insights into CVC investment strategies. Tencent, in particular, has backed up 361 angel- or seed-stage deals, which accounts for 59% of its overall venture investment during the period—a much higher proportion than any other investments conducted by traditional VC firms as discussed earlier.

6.2. Government-Guided Funds

Another type of special VC funds needing to be discussed is government-guided funds in China. Fully established and funded by the Chinese government, by their very name government-guided funds are set to attract investments of social capital from various financial institutions to meet the country's needs. According to the report by the China Financial Research Center (CCFR) of Tsinghua University, a total of 2,041 national government-guided funds have been established in China since 2000, with a total of 3.7 trillion RMB raised during the same span.

The number of these funds has been increasing explosively since 2014, largely having benefited from the government's desire to make full use of its fiscal reserves. As shown in figure 15.22, the number of such funds grew from 68 in 2013 all the way up to a peak of 533 funds in 2016, before coming in a bit lower in recent years.

Importantly, government-guided funds are *not* purely profit-driven. With a limited amount of money funded mainly by the government, the purpose of such funds is to enjoy the leverage amplification effect by guiding and attracting more money from the market to special sectors, cities, or certain investment stages. As a result, these funds always invest in VC firms or newly established VC funds in the form of fund-of-funds (FOFs). Figure 15.22 illustrates the deal count of VCs with direct or indirect involvement of government-guided funds. The number has continued to increase over the

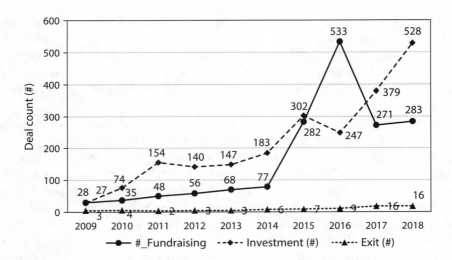

FIGURE 15.22. Government-guided funds in China (number). *Source:* www.pedata.cn. *Notes:* The figure reports government-guided funds in China in terms of the number of funds raised, deal count, and the number of exits between 2009 and 2018. All VC deals with direct or indirect involvement of government-guided funds are included in the deal count. All government-guided funds raised between 2009 and 2018 are included for fundraising.

past ten years, even though fewer government-guided funds were founded in 2017 and 2018.

Figure 15.23 highlights the investment industries and investment stages of such VCs. Tastes in investment have been consistent over time. In particular, while a large portion of the investments was eaten up by telecom equipment, IT services, and machinery production sectors before 2014, these sectors have remained their attractiveness in recent years. For the past 10 years, in general most of the investments have been made in the IT services, as shown in figure 15.23, Panel A.

During the same time span, government-guided funds directed massive amounts of social capital to further support startup companies in early- or seed-stages. In particular, as shown in figure 15.23, Panel B, 78% of the deals were made to early-stage startup companies, and round A investments alone account for 52% of them.

7. REGULATION

This section will take a bird's-eye view of how the regulatory environment has changed in the venture capital and private equity industries in China.

7.1. Regulatory Authority

The definition of a "VC business" and the filing requirements for one were first clearly stated in the "Interim Measures on the Administration of Venture Capital Investment Enterprises," approved by the State Council on September 7, 2005. However, what failed to be defined was who or what should be responsible for regulating the VC industry. For quite a long time, the industry had been scrutinized under all relevant authorities,

Panel A: Top-10 sectors ($M, 2009–2018)

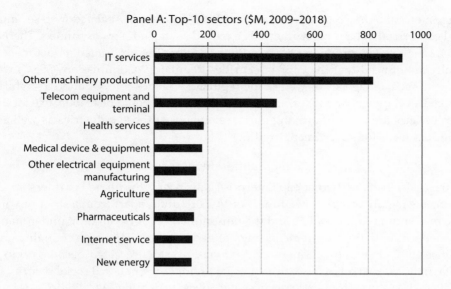

Panel B: Investment stages (# of deals, 2009–2018)

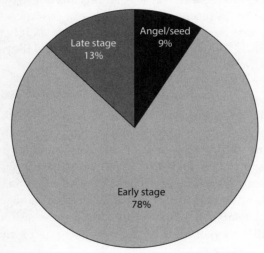

FIGURE 15.23. Investment of government-guided funds. *Source:* www.pedata.cn. *Notes:* The figure reports the investments made by VCs with the involvement of government-guided funds. Angel/Seed represents the investments make to angel- or seed-stage startups. Early refers to investments made to round pre-A, A, A+, B, and B+. Later refers to rounds C, D, and later rounds. Excluded are "PIPE," "Strategic Investment," "Neeq Private Placement," and "Other" as well as deals with unknown investment-round information.

and a somewhat blurry boundary of responsibility has been associated with several potential concerns that have been gradually exposed as the industry expanded. Therefore, in 2014, the State Commission Office of Public Sectors Reform issued a document that officially announced that the China Securities Regulatory Commission (CSRC) would be the enforcement agency as well as the regulatory agency for VCs and PEs, while the National Development and Reform Commission (NDRC) would be responsible for drawing up policies aimed at improving the development of those industries as well as for setting standards for government funding.

7.2. Qualified Investors

With the revision of the Partnership Enterprise Law in 2007, the limited partnership structure became legally accepted in China. For VC/PE funds, apart from a strict restriction on the maximum number of LPs and the minimum level of the amount under management for each fund, the requirements on qualified investors have been changing gradually since 2007. On one hand, more institutional investors received permission to participate in the VC market in the early years. For example, the national social security fund and several insurance funds got permission to invest in qualified VC/PE projects in 2008 and 2010, respectively. On the other hand, regulations on being a qualified investor have become increasingly strict in recent years. As only one instance, the currently implemented "New Regulations on Asset Management" set up a higher standard for qualified individual investors in terms of their personal wealth and the minimum investment amount, so as to improve the market's overall stability.[6]

7.3. Registration and Disclosure

The filing requirements for Chinese VC firms were initiated in 2005. Since then, registration and disclosure requirements have been gradually improving.

The "Interim Measures for the Supervision and Administration of Privately Offered Investment Funds," as implemented by the CSRC on August 21, 2014, clarified the definition of VC/PE funds and meanwhile established the information disclosure system for all registered VC/PE funds. On February 5, 2016, the Asset Management Association of China further specified detailed registration and disclosure requirements for such funds and reiterated the qualification of fund managers in its updated announcements.

8. WHAT'S NEXT?

While the good times are rolling, some bells of worry are tolling. The year 2019 (when this chapter was written) probably was not a good start for China's VC market, in view of less money being raised, invested, and distributed back to investors than in previous years. Concurrently, the ongoing United States–China trade disputes, persistent worries about IT industry overpricing, volatile financial markets, Brexit anxieties, and the ever-present threat of a slowing-down global economy all have triggered uncertainty that greatly concerns most venture capitalists.

Nevertheless, numerous opportunities beckon beyond the span of recent years. Fundamental shifts in the world's economic and political structures that have been triggered by the technology explosion are likely to drive long-term opportunities for China's VC market, which plays an indispensable role in financing and cultivating small and medium-sized promising entrepreneurial firms to reach maturity. This ongoing movement will surely have seismic impacts for both dealmakers and the investors behind them. Meanwhile, the launching of the Science and Technology Innovation Board in the Shanghai Stock Exchange and the implementation of a registration-based IPO system will markedly expand exit channels for VCs, which, in turn, may boost both fundraising and investment opportunities. In addition, a gradually improved regulation system and an increasingly diversifying market structure will lay a solid foundation for the healthy development of China's VC industry.

All in all, it seems evident that Chinese venture capitalists have been perversely striding forward and sticking to their mission of supporting the country's innovative minds over the past 20 years. Perhaps this is indeed the beginning of what comes next in the story of China's VC industry.

NOTES

Author Xuan Tian acknowledges financial support from the National Natural Science Foundation of China (Grants No.71825002, 71790591, and 91746301) and Beijing Outstanding Young Scientist Program (BJJWZYJH01201910003014).

1. PitchBook press releases, March 19, 2019.
2. Zero2IPO Research is owned by Zero2IPO Group, a pioneer in China's entrepreneurship and investment industry that manages 30 billion RMB of assets. Its reports and rankings are widely viewed as vital references for Chinese VC/PE firms.
3. The data was downloaded in May 2019, thus reflecting the information at that time. A robustness check conducted in March 2020 suggested that the trends and findings mentioned in the chapter still hold, even though the database is continuously updated when information becomes available in later years.
4. "Proposal No. 1" was initially raised in the 1st Session of the Ninth Chinese People's Political Consultative (CPPC) Conference in 1998 by the then-Chairman of the China Democratic National Construction Association (CDNCA), Cheng Siwei. It proposed to establish the country's VC market in three steps, including the establishment of VC firms and VC funds and the setting up of channels for VC investments and exits that may include a plan to build a "Chinese Nasdaq."
5. Sequoia Capital ranks first for both its fundraising and its investment record in the "2018 Top 50 VCs in China" as analyzed by the Zero2IPO Group. It is followed by IDG Capital, which ranks second in overall performance. https://pe.pedaily.cn/201812/438595.shtml.
6. According to the "New Regulation on Asset Management" (2018 version), qualified individual investors are those who must have at least two years' investment experience and meet one of three requirements: having total assets of at least 5 million RMB, or having net assets of 3 million RMB, or receiving an average annual income of at least 400,000 RMB each year for the past three years. Qualified legal entities must have at least 10 million RMB net assets for the most recent year. By comparison, in the past, qualified individual investors only needed at least 3 million RMB in total assets or an average annual income of at least 500,000 RMB over the previous three years; no investment experience is required, and there are no restrictions on the legal entities' net assets for the most recent year or a previous year. Detailed requirements are still under modification after the chapter was written.

REFERENCES

Bain & Company (2019). Global Private Equity Report. https://www.bain.com/contentassets/875a49 e26e9c4775942ec5b86084df0a/bain_report_private_equity_report_2019.pdf.

Bayar, O., T. Chemmanur, and X. Tian (2019). "Peer Monitoring, Syndication, and the Dynamics of Venture Capitalist Interactions." *Journal of Financial and Quantitative Analysis*, forthcoming.

Black, B., and R. Gilson (1998). "Venture Capital and the Structure of Capital Markets: Banks Versus Stock Markets." *Journal of Financial Economics* 47(3): 243–77.

Bowden, A. (2017). "VC Investing Still Strong Even as Median Time to Exit Reaches 8.2 Years." https://venturebeat.com/2017/05/19/vc-investing-still-strong-even-as-median-time-to-exit-reaches-8-2-years/.

Brander, J., R. Amit, and W. Antweiler (2002). "Venture Capital Syndication: Improved Venture Selection vs. Value-Added Hypothesis." *Journal of Economics & Management Strategy* 11(3): 422–52.

Casamatta, C., and C. Haritchabalet (2007). "Experience, Screening and Syndication in Venture Capital Investments." *Journal of Financial Intermediation* 16(3): 368–96.

Cestone, G., J. Lerner, and L. White (2006). "The Design of Syndicates in Venture Capital." Working paper, Harvard Business School.

Chemmanur, T. J., E. Loutskina, and X. Tian (2014). "Corporate Venture Capital, Value Creation, and Innovation." *Review of Financial Studies* 27(8): 2434–73.

China Financial Research Center (CCFR) and MyFP (2018). "Government-Guided Funds Report."

Dushnitsky, G., and M. Lenox (2006). "When Does Corporate Venture Capital Investment Create Firm Value?" *Journal of Business Venturing* 21(6): 753–72.

Gompers, P. (1995). "Optimal Investment, Monitoring, and the Staging of Venture Capital." *Journal of Finance* 50(5): 1461–89.

Gompers, P., and J. Lerner (2001). "The Venture Capital Revolution." *Journal of Economic Perspectives* 15(2): 145–68.

Liu, B., and X. Tian (2019). "Do Venture Capital Investors Learn from Public Markets?" Working paper, Tsinghua University.

National Venture Capital Association (2019). Yearbook. https://nvca.org/wp-content/uploads/2019/08/NVCA-2019-Yearbook.pdf.

PitchBook (2019). "Analyst Note: Venture Capital in China." March 15. https://pitchbook.com/news/reports/1q-2019-pitchbook-analyst-note-venture-capital-in-china.

Sahlman, W.A. (1990). "The Structure and Governance of Venture Capital Organizations." *Journal of Financial Economics* 27(2): 473–524.

Tian, X. (2011). "The Causes and Consequences of Venture Capital Stage Financing." *Journal of Financial Economics* 101(1): 132–59.

Tian, X. (2012). "The Role of Venture Capital Syndication in Value Creation for Entrepreneurial Firms." *Review of Finance* 16(1): 245–83.

Tian, X., G. Udell, and X. Yu (2016). "Disciplining Delegated Monitors: When Venture Capitalists Fail to Prevent Fraud by Their IPO Firms." *Journal of Accounting and Economics* 61(2–3): 526–44.

Wilson, R. (1968). "The Theory of Syndicates." *Econometrica* 36(1): 110–32.

PART 7

PENSION SYSTEM

16

THE CHINESE PENSION SYSTEM

Hanming Fang and Jin Feng

1. INTRODUCTION

The Chinese pension system is multilayered. The first layer consists of several public pension schemes, some of them mandatory (Basic Old Age Insurance and Public Employee Pension) and some voluntary (Urban Resident Pension and New Rural Resident Pension). These public pension schemes aim to provide basic social security to all residents when they reach old age, regardless of whether they were employed. The second layer consists of employer-sponsored annuity programs, which employers voluntarily provide as a supplement to the public pension schemes. The third layer consists of household savings–based annuity insurance policies. The public pension schemes of the first layer receive substantial direct fiscal subsidies from the government, while all schemes or products regardless of layer receive tax preferences.

As of the end of 2017, Chinese public pension schemes had more than 915 million participants (accounting for 65.8% of the total population), and the total public pension expenditure was 4,032 billion RMB, about 5% of China's GDP. Unlike the broad coverage of the first layer, participation in the second layer is much more limited; only about 80,000 firms, accounting for less than 0.5% of all the firms in China, offered employer-sponsored annuity programs to 23.3 million employees in 2017.[1] The third layer is still in its infancy.

The remainder of this chapter is structured as follows. Section 2 offers a detailed overview of the three layers of China's pension system. The development of China's pension system and the problems it faces are discussed in sections 3 and 4, respectively. Section 5 presents some ideas for future reforms. Section 6 concludes.

2. CHINA'S MULTILAYERED PENSION SYSTEM

2.1. Public Pension Schemes

China's public pension system is on track to achieve universal coverage. Until 2015, the system encompassed four schemes that were intended to cover the entire eligible population. The first two schemes were for *employed* workers in firms and in the government

Table 16.1. Public Pension Schemes in China

Scheme	Basic Old Age Insurance system (BOAI)	Public Employee Pension (PEP)	Resident pension (unified in 2014)	
			2011 Urban Resident Pension Scheme (URP)	2009 New Rural Resident Pension Scheme (NRP)
Establishment	Established in 1951; Current practices finalized in 1997	Established in 1953; Practices finalized in 1978; Merged into BOAI in 2015		
Participants	Urban employees in enterprises	Urban employees in public sectors	Urban non-employed 16 years or above	Rural residents 16 years or above
Contribution	Pay-as-you-go: 20% of payroll (depending on locality) Individual accounts: 8% of individual wage	No contribution required	Individual accounts: government subsidy +individual contribution	Individual accounts: government subsidy +individual contribution
Benefit	Social pooling: Minimum 15 years of contribution. 1-year accrual rate 1%; 35% based on 35 years of contribution Individual accounts: Replacement ratio: 24.2% Total replacement ratio from both: 59.2%	Average replacement ratio: 80%–90%	Basic Pension+ Individual account Pension	Basic Pension+ Individual account Pension
Mandatory	Yes	Yes	No	No

Source: Authors' calculations.

sector, respectively, while the latter two schemes were for *non-employed* individuals in rural and urban areas.

- Basic Old Age Insurance (BOAI, 城镇职工基本养老保险): For employees in for-profit enterprises, including for-profit public enterprises, and in all other private sectors
- Public Employee Pension (PEP, 机关事业单位养老保险): For civil servants and employees in nonprofit government institutions, such as schools and cultural and health facilities
- Urban Resident Pension (URP, 城镇居民养老保险): For urban residents aged 16 and older without a formal nonagricultural job
- New Rural Resident Pension (NRP, 新型农村养老保险): For rural residents aged 16 and older without a formal nonagricultural job

At the beginning of 2014, China's State Council announced that the URP and NRP were to be merged into a uniform Resident Pension system (城乡居民养老保险). Also, in 2015, the PEP was merged into BOAI, making BOAI the uniform program for all employees in urban sectors. As of the end of 2017, BOAI had 402.9 million participants, of which about 37 million were public sector employees. The Resident Pension scheme had 512.6 million participants.

The public pension system's four schemes—BOAI, PEP, URP, and NRP—aim to cover various groups of the population and workforce, and therefore they vary in their contribution and benefit rules. The existence of two different systems for employees (BOAI and PEP) and the fact that non-employed individuals fall into different schemes depending on their residency status (urban or rural) help explain the vast inequalities in the country's pension system. Table 16.1 summarizes the key features of the four pension schemes.

These schemes were established by the State Council and are regulated by China's Ministry of Human Resources and Social Security (MOHRSS). However, local governments are responsible for managing these schemes. Thus, a second source of the serious inequalities in the generosity of public pension schemes across different locations is their fragmented nature. This feature also leads to portability challenges when individuals change their employment to a different public pension administrative region. Section 4 addresses such inequality issues in detail.

2.1.1. Basic Old Age Insurance (BOAI)

BOAI is the most important public pension scheme. Established in 1951 for urban employees of enterprises, it was reformed into a multipillar system in 1997. The first pillar of BOAI is a compulsory scheme with both defined contribution and defined benefit features. On the contribution side, employers are required to contribute 20% of the wages paid to their workforce. The maximum wage level subject to the contribution requirement is 300% of the local average wage, and the minimum wage level subject to the requirement is 60% of the local average wage.[2] On the benefit side, employees with a contribution history of 15 or more years are entitled to the pension benefits, and the replacement ratio (pension benefit as a percentage of preretirement wage) depends on the number of years of contribution as well as the individual's wage relative to the local average wage. For example, a retiree whose preretirement wage was equal to the local average wage will, in the first year of retirement, have a pension replacement ratio of

35% after 35 years of contribution; pension benefits in later years will be adjusted according to inflation rate and local wage growth rate, although there is no clear rule.

The second pillar of BOAI is the individual account pension, which has a contribution rate of 8% of wages. The individual account is notional, and individuals do not have the authority to make any allocation decisions regarding how contributions to it are managed. In 2005, the MOHRSS published a target replacement ratio of 59.2% (relative to the local average wage) for a person who worked for 35 years, with 35% from the pooling account (basic pension) and 24.2% from the individual account.[3]

The BOAI retirement eligibility age is 50 for female blue-collar workers, 55 for female white-collar workers, and 60 for males.

2.1.2. Public Employee Pension (PEP)

PEP was established in 1953 for civil servants and employees in the nonprofit public sector. PEP system expenditure is included in both the central and local governments' fiscal budgets. It is more generous than the other schemes, and one notable feature is that it does not require any contribution from public employees. Such employees have an average pension replacement ratio of 80% to 90% of preretirement wages. When PEP was merged into BOAI in 2015, the contribution and benefit rules for public employees were switched to those of BOAI. There is a transition arrangement between the two schemes. For those who retired before the 2015 reform, pension benefits are unchanged; for those who entered the public sector after that year, the BOAI system applies; and for those who were already in PEP but not yet retired in 2015, a transitional arrangement is available for financing individual accounts, as there had been no contributions to individual accounts before the reform. The PEP retirement eligibility age is 55 for females and 60 for males.

2.1.3. New Rural Resident Pension (NRP) and Urban Resident Pension (URP)

The NRP was established in 2009 to cover rural residents, and the URP was established in 2011 to cover urban non-employed residents. The NRP and URP are voluntary schemes funded in conjunction with government subsidies. Individual contributions are put into individual accounts. In addition, because the amount of contributions depends on local economic conditions, clear variations exist across regions as well as between urban and rural residents. For example, as of 2019, the participants in Shanghai can choose their amount of annual contribution in a range of 500 to 5,300 RMB, while the range is 100 to 2,000 RMB in Chongqin, and 1,200 to 2,520 RMB in Nanjing. Benefits consist of two parts: a basic pension and the individual account pension. Participants with a contribution history of 15 or more years are entitled to receive a basic pension on reaching 60 years of age (at a benefit level of 55 RMB per month in most regions when the scheme was introduced). The basic pension is funded entirely by the central government in the middle and western provinces, owing to the low fiscal capacity of local governments, while in the eastern provinces it is funded equally by the central and local governments. Local governments have the autonomy to raise basic pension benefits in line with local economic conditions, but they are responsible for outstanding financial obligations. The replacement ratio is about 20% (nationwide average) of rural per capita net income. At the beginning of 2014, the State Council announced that the two schemes would be merged into a uniform Resident Pension system. The pension eligibility age for the NRP and URP is 60 years for both males and females.

The Social Insurance Law enacted in 2011 stipulates that rural migrant workers are entitled to the same treatment given to urban workers. However, among both employers and migrant workers, compliance with the policy is poor.

2.2. Enterprise Annuity and Occupational Annuity

The employer-sponsored pension system (Enterprise Annuity, or EA; 企业年金) was introduced in 1991. The EA system has grown considerably in the ensuing years, but it is still an underdeveloped market in terms of the number of participants, the number of providers (enterprises), and the pension assets. As of 2017, the EA system had 23.3 million participants, representing only about 5.8% of the number of BOAI participants. The number of enterprises providing EA was 80,400, about 0.35% of total enterprises. Total assets stood at about 1,288 billion RMB at the end of 2017, roughly 1.5% of GDP.

Enterprises offering pension plans tend to be large state-owned enterprises (SOE) or monopolistic companies in, for example, the railway, electricity, and communication industries (Cai and Cheng, 2014; Impavido et al., 2009). Employers are increasingly offering defined contribution (DC) plans in which they are not responsible for how pension money is invested and do not guarantee a certain benefit. Most employers, however, cannot afford pension plans and have little incentive to offer them. Legislation and regulations have played key roles in the development of pension plans; the central government issued two regulations in 2004 on the EA system and the management of pension funds. In addition, since 2014, contributions and investment returns from both employers and employees have been tax exempt; favorable tax treatment was not in place before 2014.

As part of the 2015 reform of the PEP, public sector employers are required to provide an occupational annuity (职业年金) as a complement to benefits. Employers contribute 8% of employees' wages, while employees contribute an additional 4%, with tax preferences applied. Occupational annuity differs from EA in that the individual accounts are partly notional, because government employers' contribution for civil servants is notional, and also because some self-financed public sectors cannot afford the contribution. The contribution of employees is fully funded in the accounts. Implementation of the occupational pension is still in the initial stage, with little publicly available information about the extent of coverage.

2.3. Private Annuity Insurance

As of 2014, 69 insurers in China are involved in the commercial annuity business through a variety of products. Annuity insurance has grown rapidly, with an average annual growth rate of 16.9% between 2001 and 2014. In 2014, annuity insurance income totaled 282.2 billion RMB (increasing more than 77.2% year-over-year). There were 69.433 million in-force policies covering 100 million people, providing protection amounting to 1.4 trillion RMB.[4] Until 2018, no tax preference was available for commercial annuity insurance. However, it should be noted that many of these annuity insurance products are sold as wealth management products and are not intended to be kept in force for long durations; such products are thus unlikely to serve the genuine purpose of pension income.

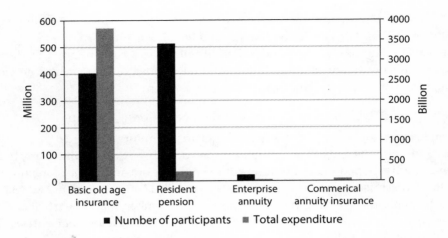

FIGURE 16.1. Comparison of the various pension schemes in China. *Sources:* MOHRSS; China's Statistical Yearbook of the Insurance Industry (2017).

At the beginning of 2018, a pilot policy was issued to provide individual income tax-deferred annuity insurance products in Shanghai, Fujian Province, and the Suzhou Industrial Park. The model incorporates income tax deductions for individual premiums and does not tax investment returns, but benefits are subject to income taxation when received by individuals who reach the eligible age. However, the maximum premium that can receive a tax deduction is limited to 6% of one's taxable income, or 12,000 RMB, whichever is lower. Tax preferences are also given for annuity benefits, with 25% of the annuity free from income taxation.

Figure 16.1 shows the number of participants and total pension benefits of each program and layer. The Resident Pension program covers the greatest number of people, while BOAI accounts for the lion's share of benefits. The pension programs of the second and third layers are quite marginal in comparison.

3. DEVELOPMENT OF CHINA'S PUBLIC PENSION SYSTEM

China's public pension system has gone through four phases. The first phase began in 1951, when "labor insurance" was introduced as an unfunded, employer-sponsored pension program that covered employees of both SOEs and collectively owned enterprises. A separate pension system was also available for public (civil service) employees—the Public Employee Pension (PEP)—although the rural population had no formal old-age social security.

The second phase lasted from the mid-1980s to the early 1990s. After the marketization of the economy and the various reforms of SOEs, the enterprise-based pension system was viewed as hindering fair competition and the mobility of labor. The pooling of pensions at the municipal or county level was introduced, but the system remained pay-as-you-go (PAYG), financed by enterprises.

The third phase lasted from the early 1990s to the late 2000s. In 1997, China adopted a three-pillar pension system for urban employees to deal with population aging and SOEs' growing pension burden. The new system was called Basic Old Age Insurance

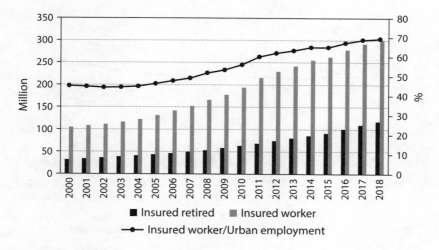

FIGURE 16.2. Number of participants in the BOAI system. *Source:* MOHRSS.

(BOAI). The first pillar was the PAYG system, financed by employers; the second pillar was the notional individual account, financed by employees' contributions; and the third pillar was voluntary retirement savings.

The fourth phase, which began in 2009, can be characterized by the expansion of pension system coverage to non-SOE firms. To achieve universal coverage, the New Rural Resident Pension (NRP) scheme was established in that year to cover rural residents, and the Urban Resident Pension (URP) scheme was established two years later to cover urban non-employed residents. The Social Insurance Law enacted in 2011 stipulates that rural migrant workers are to be given the same treatment as that given to urban workers.

3.1. Coverage and Dependency Ratio

The BOAI system has steadily increased its coverage in recent decades (figure 16.2). The number of participants (workers) as a percentage of total urban employees increased from 45.1% in 2000 to 69.3% in 2018.

The in-system dependency ratio in BOAI increased from 18.6% in 1990 to 32.5% in 2010 and 39.2% in 2018. In other words, it has gone from 5.4 workers supporting a retiree to fewer than three workers. This is mainly attributable to the shift in the age distribution of the Chinese population. The old-age dependency ratio—elderly (60+ years)/working age (15–59 years)—has risen over time (figure 16.3). From 1950 to 2010, the number of people over 60 increased threefold to 240 million, rising from 7.5% of the total population in 1950 to 17.2% in 2010. The proportion of 65-year-olds and above has risen from 4.5% in 1950 to 8.2% in 2010. Meanwhile, the proportion of people in the 15–59 age group has risen from 58.3% in 1950 to 68.2% in 2010, while the proportion in the 15–64 age group has risen from 61.3% to 72.4%. The fact that both the "aged" group and the "working age" group have seen their population shares increase reflects the rapid decline in China's fertility rate; the population share of the 0–14 age group declined from 34.2% to 19.5%.

As noted in section 2.2, the NRP and URP programs were merged into a unified Resident Pension scheme in 2014. The number of pensioners increased from 89.2 million to

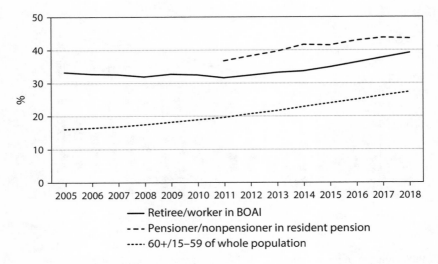

FIGURE 16.3. Dependency ratio in the pension system and demographic change. *Sources:* Participant data is from MOHRSS; population structure data is from the China Statistical Yearbook, various years.

152.7 million. The dependency ratio within the Resident Pension scheme stood at 43% in 2016, much higher than that of the BOAI system.

To summarize, the in-system dependency ratio of China's Basic Old Age Insurance system is about 38%, much higher than the population-wide dependency ratio of 27.4% in 2018. The in-system dependency ratio of the Resident Pension scheme was 43.6% in 2018.

3.2. Contributions and Benefits

3.2.1. China Has One of the Highest Statutory Pension Contribution Rates in the World, at 28% before 2019

The contribution rate of BOAI is among the highest in the world, even higher than the rates seen in Sweden, the United States, and France (table 16.2).

China enacted the Social Insurance Law in 2011 to help enforce the regulations that require employers to pay contributions for their employees. Since then, compliance among private firms has improved. However, it has led to a heavier burden on employers, with their social insurance and housing fund contributions reaching more than 40% of employees' wages. To lessen the burden, in 2016 the State Council decided to lower the contribution rates for employers. For BOAI, if the local contribution rate is higher than 20%, it should be reduced to 20%. In provinces with contribution rates of 20% and a pension fund balance sufficient to cover at least nine months of expenditure, the contribution rate can be further reduced by one percentage point, to 19%. In May of 2019, the government cut the employer's contribution rate to 16%, so the total contribution rate of employer and employee is 24%.

3.2.2. The Average Replacement Ratio Has Declined Steadily and Stood at 46% in 2018

Pension benefits were generous before the reform in the mid-1990s, at about 75% to 90% of a worker's pre-retirement wages. The reform of the late 1990s reduced the replacement ratio of pensions for enterprise workers, particularly for younger workers (Feng et al.,

Table 16.2. Cross-Country Comparison of Contribution Rates

Country	Employer	Employee	Total
Canada	5	5	9.9
France	6.8	9.9	16.7
Germany	10	10	19.9
Sweden	7	11.9	18.9
United Kingdom	11	12.8	23.8
United States	6.2	6.2	12.4
Japan	7.7	7.7	15.4
Korean	4.5	4.5	9
Hungary	1.5	24	25.5
Czech Republic	6.5	21.5	28
Chile	–	18.8	18.8
Brazil	7.7	20	27.7
China	16	8	24

Sources: HDNSP Pensions Database of the World Bank.

2011). According to the reform framework, those who had retired before 1997 (referred to somewhat ungraciously as the "old" workers) remained in the original PAYG system; those who entered the labor market in or after 1997 (the "new" workers) came under the new three-pillar pension system; and those who started work before 1997 and have since retired or will retire after 1997 (the "middle" workers) were covered by a transitional plan, which reduced the replacement ratio gradually over cohorts. Another reform in 2005 set the target replacement ratio (first-year pension benefit after retirement/ local average wage) at 59.2% for a worker who had worked for 35 years and earned wages equal to the local average wage.

The average replacement ratio—that is, pension benefits per pensioner as a percentage of the average wage of workers—has declined steadily over the last decade in China (figure 16.4). This is the combined result of the transitional arrangement, wage differences across cohorts and the different growth rates of wages and pension benefits.

The mandatory retirement age is the same in the BOAI and PEP programs. For men, it is age 60. For women, it is age 55 for white-collar employees (i.e., civil servants, professionals, administrative staff in enterprises, and the like) and age 50 for blue-collar employees. Only a small fraction of women work in white-collar jobs or the public sector and hence qualify for the higher retirement age; Chinese urban household survey data from the National Bureau of Statistics shows that about 7% of women employees are eligible for the higher retirement age of 55 years. In urban China, reaching retirement age means one must retire from one's current job and start receiving public pension benefits. After that, the individual can stay in the labor market informally without losing pension benefits, although the opportunity to find a job declines dramatically. The current retirement age policy was established at the beginning of the 1950s, when life expectancy at birth was about 43 years. An increase to the retirement age is likely to happen, given population aging. Section 5.3 will discuss a reform proposal to raise the retirement age.

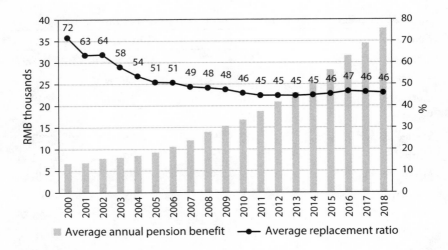

FIGURE 16.4. Average pension benefit and replacement ratio. *Sources:* Pension data is from MOHRSS; wage data is from the China Statistical Yearbook, various years.

To summarize, the current retirement ages are 60 for men, 50 for women who work in blue-collar jobs, and 55 for women who work in white-collar jobs; about 93% of women are required to retire at age 50.

3.3. Revenue, Expenditure, and Government Subsidy

3.3.1. BOAI Runs a Fiscal Deficit in Some Provinces in the Absence of Government Subsidies

The BOAI pension fund has maintained an annual surplus for many years. In 2018, the fund's revenue was 5.50 trillion RMB and its expenditure was 4.76 trillion RMB (figure 16.5). The BOAI fund's surplus is mainly attributable to the steady expansion of coverage, with the increase in participants far exceeding the increase in retirees. Furthermore, BOAI also receives government subsidies, which accounted for 16.7% of total revenue in 2015 (figure 16.6). If these subsidies were subtracted from the accounting, BOAI funds in 14 provinces (including Shanghai, Jiangsu, Hubei, and Hunan) would likely be in a deficit, and BOAI accounts would have reported a total deficit in 2010, possibly as large as 67.9 billion RMB, instead of the surplus that was observed.

3.3.2. Three-Quarters of Revenue in Resident Pension from Government Subsidy

In the Resident Pension system, revenue was 330.4 billion RMB at the end of 2017, of which about 25% came from individual contributions and the rest from national and subnational government subsidies. Expenses totaled 237.2 billion RMB. The system has an accumulated surplus of 631.8 billion RMB, mostly from the accumulated balance of individual accounts belonging to younger cohorts.[5] In the future, when more residents start receiving pension benefits, the individual account surplus will be reduced.

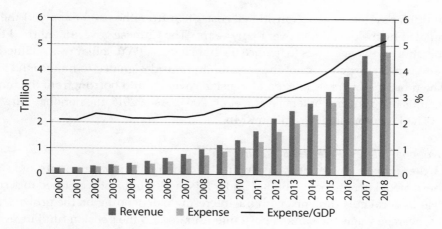

FIGURE 16.5. Revenue and expenses of the BOAI system. *Sources:* Revenue and expense data is from MOHRSS; GDP data is from the China Statistical Yearbook, various years.

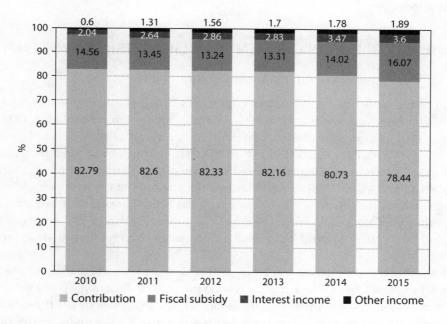

FIGURE 16.6. Sources of revenue in the BOAI system. *Source:* Zheng (2016).

3.4. Notional Individual Account

3.4.1. From Fully Funded to Notional Account

Individual accounts in BOAI were designed to be fully funded. However, many provinces have been using the funds in individual accounts to support the PAYG pillar, which renders the accounts essentially notional. The use of the individual account balance was necessitated by the transitional costs of the 1997 public pension reform, which established the multipillar system. These transitional costs stem from the need to pay off the debt accumulated by the old system over many years.[6] The Chinese government tried to use a combination of two methods to finance the transition. A PAYG pillar was retained, and about seven percentage points of the contribution was designated to finance the transition. The other method was to expand pension coverage and borrow from the individual accounts of younger workers (Wang et al., 2004). As of 2016, the notional individual accounts had accumulated 3.6 trillion RMB.[7]

3.4.2. Notional Interest Rate was 8.31% in 2016

In 2013, the Chinese government gave up fully funded individual accounts and started to follow a model of notional accounts. Under this model, interest is credited to accounts each year by local governments, with the interest rate depending on the growth rate of the local average wage, the bank deposit interest rate, and the pension fund investment rate. Before 2016, notional interest rates were less than 4% in most provinces. In 2016, however, MOHRSS published a high unified-interest rate of 8.31%. This incredible high rate maintained at 7.12% in 2017 and 8.29% in 2018, much higher than the return of most financial products.

4. PROBLEMS IN CURRENT PUBLIC PENSION SYSTEM

4.1. Financial Sustainability

Similar to the tendency in many other countries, China's pension system will have to face the challenges of a dwindling labor force and a rapidly aging population. Owing to rapid aging, the share of the Chinese population over 65 years of age will double between 2010 and 2030, from 8.4% in 2010 to 16.8% in 2030. This is much more rapid than the pace of aging in the world as a whole, where the share of population over 65 will increase from 7.8% to 11.6% from 2010 to 2030.[8] Meanwhile, the present Chinese pension system is barely maintaining its financial balance with the help of government subsidies. The fiscal subsidy for the public system stood at 800 billion RMB as of 2017, or about 1% of GDP, and this is likely to exhibit a dramatic increase if no reforms are made in the near future.

Table 16.3 shows simulation results regarding the future fiscal balances of the BOAI scheme. Feng and Chen (2016) explicate related population dynamics. There are several assumptions under the simulations. In scenario 1, the assumptions are the following. First, the urbanization process is expected to continue in China, with its share reaching 70% in 2030. Second, no change will occur either in BOAI contribution and benefit rules or in the program's retirement age. It is also assumed that all contributions due can be collected. Third, benefits are indexed; specifically, they grow after retirement in line with the average rate of real wage growth rate and future inflation. The growth rate assumptions for wages and GDP are World Bank projections (World Bank, 2012), where the annual growth rate of GDP is 8.6% during 2011–2015, 7.0% during 2016–2020, 5.9% during 2021–2025, and 5% during 2026–2030.

In scenario 1, the coverage rate remains unchanged at 80% for local employees and 20% for migrant workers. In scenario 2, the coverage of migrant workers expands gradually from 20% in 2010 to 60% in 2050. Each simulation is an estimation of the national

Table 16.3. Simulations for Future Fiscal Balances of
Basic Old Age Insurance System

	2020 (%)	2025 (%)	2030 (%)	2035 (%)
Scenario 1				
Balance as a percentage of current GDP	−0.40	−1.25	−2.15	−2.60
Accumulated deficit to current GDP	1.77	−2.27	−11.17	−23.37
Scenario 2				
Balance as a percentage of current GDP	−0.08	−0.61	−1.11	−1.09
Accumulated deficit to current GDP	3.19	1.68	−2.86	−8.38

Sources: Simulation results by authors.
Notes: Policy rules of BOAI remain unchanged. In scenario 1, it covers 80% for local employees and 20% for migrant workers. In scenario 2, coverage of migrant workers expands gradually to 60% from 2010 to 2050.

average level. In scenario 1, a clearly increasing trend is observed in the number of pensioners over time, while the number of contributors is declining. The annual deficit as a percentage of GDP will be 2.15% in 2030. The accumulated deficit in 2030 will be 23.37% of GDP. It is obvious, therefore, that the current arrangement of BOAI is unsustainable.

In scenario 2, increasing BOAI coverage among migrant workers improves the potential deficit situation. The annual deficit as a percentage of GDP will be 1.11% in 2030, while the accumulated deficit will be 2.86% of GDP. Expanding coverage of BOAI among migrant workers will lead to a slower increase in the deficit, although it does not offer a complete solution.

A report published in May 2019 predicts more-pessimistic results that the balance of BOAI will be exhausted in 2035, even with government subsidy.[9] The situation is similar to that of the social security system in the United States, where a recent report by the U.S. Treasury Department predicts that the trust fund account of the U.S. social security system will be exhausted in 2035.[10]

For the Resident Pension scheme, the initial pension benefit is rather low (representing less than 20% of the average income per capita), and so the scheme has not yet caused significant financial burden on local governments. However, the Resident Pension scheme relies more on ad hoc governmental support than on sound actuarial principles. The balance between fund revenues and expenditure has not received much attention at the current stage.

4.2. Participation Incentives

Social insurance contribution evasion is a prevalent phenomenon in China. In 2015, 70% of firms paid less than the prescribed levels of social insurance contributions (Zheng, 2016).

Several reasons can be suggested for the low participation incentives. First, as has already been noted in section 3.2.1, the contribution rate in China is higher than in most other countries. The social insurance contribution rate for employers ranges from 24% to

28% (BOAI: 16%; Health insurance: 6% to 10%; Unemployment insurance: 1%; Injury insurance: 0.5%; Maternity insurance: 0.5%); employees contribute 10.5% of their own wages (BOAI: 8%; Health insurance: 2%; Unemployment insurance: 0.5%). The wage levels subject to the contribution requirement range from a lower bound of 60% of the local average wage to an upper bound of three times the local average wage. Employers can evade contributions by not formally registering employees at local government bureaus; hiring temporary employees or family members; postponing social insurance contribution payments; and shrinking reported nominal wages to reduce contributions (Nyland et al., 2010).

Second, some employees are simply not willing to join the insurance programs. Those in the low-income group face unstable employment and, hence, high uncertainty about their eligibility for future benefits. Young people have high current consumption demand, and the high contribution rate reduces their consumption. Thus, incentives abound for employers and employees to collude so as to default on pension contributions (Nyland et al., 2011).

Third, local governments do not punish defaults on contribution payments with the kind of severity that would be needed to deter cheating. Those governments normally focus on targets related to economic growth and adopt preferential policies to reduce employers' tax and contribution burdens. They are therefore quite lax in enforcing social insurance contribution requirements.

The Resident Pension scheme carries both positive and negative incentives for participation. The most obvious positive incentive is the heavy government subsidy. For example, those who are already 60 years old at the time the program starts will automatically receive basic pension benefits without paying any premiums. However, the lack of sufficient returns on individual contributions to pension accounts creates a negative incentive. This is the most important factor that determines younger people's willingness to participate in the scheme. Currently, the fund's rate of return is claimed to be the one-year term deposit interest rate. Although very secure, such a low rate virtually guarantees a low individual account balance at retirement and thus weakens participation incentives for rural workers (Lei et al., 2014; Dorfman et al., 2013). As a result, participants tend to choose the lowest premium standard and the shortest contribution period and therefore will only be eligible for cash transfers under the basic pension.

An empirical investigation using micro data verifies these disincentive phenomena. Lei et al. (2014), employing CHARLS (China Health and Retirement Longitudinal Studies) data from 2011, found that individuals prefer shorter periods of participation and choose the lowest level of premiums. There is an age gradient of enrollment rates; the enrollment rates generally increase with age, even though they are generally low among all age groups. Numerous surveys on the NRP find similar evidence that the enrollment was observed only from age 45, leaving 15 years of contribution to meet the eligibility.

4.3. Regional Disparity and Inequality

As has been emphasized, China's public pension systems are managed by local governments. In the BOAI system, some provinces pool their funds at the provincial level, although most provinces pool funds at the city or even county levels. While the statutory rules of contributions and benefits are determined by the central government, the actual contribution rates are different across regions. Wage inequalities also help explain the disparities in the amount of contributions and benefits. Workers in municipalities and

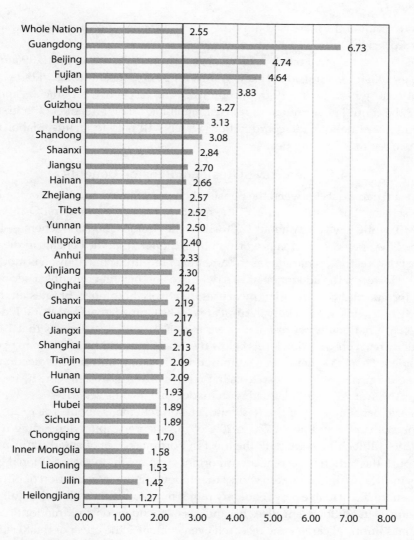

FIGURE 16.7. Regional disparity in the support ratio (number of contributors/number of retirees), 2018. *Source:* MOHRSS.

East Coast provinces earn much higher incomes than those in the inland provinces. When workers move from one city to another to get a better job, their pension plans remain tied to their original city of employment. This creates serious inequality issues and problems with labor mobility.

Along with disparities in regional economic development, demographic structures are also becoming greatly differentiated across provinces (figure 16.7). In those provinces with better job opportunities, the demographic structure becomes more favorable as younger workers are attracted. For example, in Guangdong Province, about nine workers support one retiree. Eastern regions like Beijing, Fujian, and Shandong also have more-favorable demographics than other provinces. Shanghai's population aging remains severe as a result of the increased life expectancy, although it continues to attract young migrant workers.

To balance the payment burdens on local governments, China in July 2019 announced plans to establish a central adjustment system for basic pension funds in BOAI. The adjustment fund will draw a certain portion from the respective provincial capital pool, enabling the central government to redistribute it later. This was likely the first significant step toward nationwide coordination, which will help to facilitate labor mobility and reduce regional inequalities.

4.4. Adequacy of Resident Pension Benefits

A significant gap exists between the pension benefits of BOAI and those of the Resident Pension scheme. For example, in 2017, the monthly average pension in BOAI was about 2,870 RMB, while it was only about 127 RMB in the Resident Pension scheme—less than 5% of the BOAI pension level. It is worth noting, though, that the benefits in the two systems are not directly comparable, as the amount of required contribution is much higher in BOAI. However, the adequacy of Resident Pension benefits remains a serious problem. By income and consumption measures, relatively high poverty rates are recorded for elderly households, especially in rural areas. The China Urban and Rural Elderly Survey in 2006, a nationally representative sample of the elderly, suggests that 19% of the rural elderly had consumption levels below the official poverty line (Dorfman et al., 2013). The Resident Pension scheme was supposed to provide a universal protection floor to alleviate old-age poverty, yet, despite its impressive progress in achieving near-universal coverage, the system is still plagued with inadequate income security.

The basic pension level of the Resident Pension scheme is about 10% to 25% of consumption per capita and about 7% to 20% of income per capita, depending on the region. While adult children remain the most important source of elderly care and financial support, the NRP has become an important supplement to the traditional eldercare patterns in rural China. Research shows that following the introduction of NRP, enrollees were more likely to live independently rather than co-reside with their adult children in rural areas. In addition, enrollees became less dependent on children for financial resources and informal care. Some research even evaluates the effect of the Resident Pension scheme on family transfers, with results indicating a degree of the crowding-out effect on family transfers (Chen et al., 2017).

4.5. Fiscal Risks

As population aging continues to unfold, subsidies to the BOAI and Resident Pension schemes will play an increasingly key role in financing social security expenditure in the future. The share of BOAI subsidies of total government fiscal expenditure remained steady at around 2% in the last decade, while the share of social insurance expenditure in total fiscal expenditure was about 10%. In the future, central and local fiscal subsidies will inevitably be key sources of financing for the pension system.

Concerns are growing over China's fiscal risks, particularly concerning the contingent liabilities of local governments in recent years (Table 16.4).[11] A slowdown in economic growth, an aging population, and high financial repression are all factors that can contribute to fiscal position deterioration. Among emerging economies, China's public sector balance sheet is one of the more indebted. Hemming (2012) pointed out that contingent liabilities are one of the reasons for the lower government debt ratios in emerging

Table 16.4. Total Government Debt, 2015–2017

Debt (percent of GDP)	2015	2016	2017	2018
Official government debt	15.47	16.15	16.29	16.33
Local government debt	21.42	20.65	19.96	20.07
Ministry of Railways liabilities	5.94	6.34	6.03	5.69
Total government debt	42.83	43.14	42.29	42.10

Sources: Ministry of Finance of China; National Audit Office.

Asian countries, China being a notable example. Various contingent liabilities in China have the potential to raise the total debt ratio to as high as 113%. The risks posed by contingent liabilities will challenge the sustainability of the entire fiscal system when growth slows down.[12]

5. FUTURE REFORMS

5.1. Exploring More Ways to Finance the Pension System

5.1.1. National Social Security Fund (NSSF)

The National Social Security Fund (NSSF) of China was established in 2000 as a strategic reserve fund to cope with future pension needs. The NSSF is financed in four ways: (1) funds allocated from the central government's budget; (2) capital and equity assets derived from the sale of shares of SOEs, which are required to remit 10% of their IPO funds to the NSSF; (3) other methods approved by the State Council, such as state lottery license fees and funds obtained through a securities repurchase program; and (4) investment returns. Total NSSF assets have increased rapidly from 781 billion RMB to 1.83 trillion RMB in 2017.

The NSSF can invest in a broad set of instruments, subject to certain restrictions on allocation. According to the "Temporary Regulations on the National Social Security Fund Investment Management" ("全国社会保障基金投资管理暂行办法") issued in 2001, NSSF assets can be invested in the following three broad categories: (1) bank deposits and treasury bonds (no less than 50% of total assets, with bank deposits accounting for no less than 10%); (2) corporate bonds (企业债) and financial bonds (金融债) (no more than 10% of total assets); and (3) securities investment fund (证券投资基金) and stocks (股票) (no more than 40% of total assets). Table 16.5 shows annual rates of return for the NSSF from 2010 through 2018. Between 2001 and 2012, the NSSF achieved an average annual rate of return of more than 8%, outpacing inflation, which stood at around 4%. However, it should be noted that the NSSF invests nearly 40% of the fund in the Chinese stock market, and therefore fluctuations in investment returns are likely to be correlated with the volatility of the domestic stock market. The fund is now allowing investments in private equity and foreign equity, and it is beginning to invest in both emerging and European markets.

5.1.2. Dividend from SOE

As of 2017, China's SOEs have assets valued at 52 trillion RMB.[13] SOE profits as a share of China's GDP were about 3.85% in 2014 and 3.5% in 2017.[14] SOEs were also exempted from paying dividends through much of the 1990s and 2000s, which gave them an advantage over competitors by keeping their cost of capital low. At the same time, it also

Table 16.5. National Social Security Fund Assets and Investment Return Rate

	2010	2011	2012	2013	2014	2015	2016	2017	2018
Assets (billion RMB)	781	773	893	991	1241	1508	1604	1830	2235
Investment return (%)	4.23	0.84	7.01	6.20	11.69	15.19	1.73	9.68	7.82

Source: NSSF Board of Managers.

reduced government revenue that could have been spent on pensions, education, and other social services. This changed in 2007, when the State Council mandated that central SOEs must begin paying dividends at a rate of 10% in highly profitable industries, 5% in industries where SOEs were less profitable, and 0% for protected firms like military armaments manufacturers. In 2011, the rates were increased by five percentage points across the board to 15%, 10%, and 5% percent, respectively. In 2016, SOEs in China made a net profit of 2.3 trillion RMB, of which 216 billion RMB, or about 9.4%, was remitted to central and local governments.

The World Bank (2012) noted that Chinese SOEs are far outside the international norm when it comes to dividend payout ratios. The average dividend payout for mature and established industrial firms in the United States is 50% to 60%. SOEs in Demark, Norway, Finland, and Sweden set multiyear payout targets ranging from 33% to 67% of earnings. In contrast, Chinese SOEs listed in Hong Kong pay an average dividend of only 23%. Thus, even the top rate of 15% set by the State Council is still low, relative to what Chinese SOEs themselves pay shareholders in Hong Kong.

China will moderately boost the ratio of dividends paid out by SOEs by increasing the number of centrally and locally administered SOEs that are required to pay dividends to the State. The central government has regarded SOE dividends as a key building block in funding the social security system. Further reform also calls for changes in how SOE dividends are managed. In the past, these funds were not included in the general budget to pay for public expenditure. Now, it has been decided that the Ministry of Finance will collect the dividends and place them into a "State Capital Management Budget."

Hypothetically, an increase in SOEs' dividend payout rate to 20% can translate to an extra 145 billion RMB, based on SOEs' total net profit of 2.9 trillion RMB in 2017. These additional funds can be used to finance the BOAI pension deficit.

5.2. Improving Productivity

The key to sustaining the pension system lies in the enhancement of labor productivity. If productivity is rising, the wealth created by the younger generation can, in effect, support a larger group of old people. With growing output (and thereby also income), the PAYG system remains in balance without the need for either a reduction in pensions or an increase in contributions. An increase in output is possibly the best solution for funded schemes, as it will help control inflation in the goods market and deflation in the asset market.

Table 16.6 reports the World Bank's (2012) estimates of China's labor productivity growth through 2030. Here, labor productivity is measured by the amount of real GDP produced by an employee. While China's labor productivity growth rate is expected to

Table 16.6. Projected Labor Productivity Growth, 1995–2030

	1995–2010 (%)	2011–2015 (%)	2016–2020 (%)	2021–2025 (%)	2026–2030 (%)
GDP annual growth	9.9	8.6	7	5.9	5
Labor growth	0.9	0.3	−0.2	−0.2	−0.4
Labor productivity growth	8.9	8.3	7.1	6.2	5.5
Share of employment in agriculture	38.1	30	23.7	18.2	12.5
Share of employment in service	34.1	42	47.6	52.9	59

Source: The World Bank and Development Research Center of the State Council, "China 2030: Building a Modern, Harmonious, and Creative High-Income Society." Washington, DC: The World Bank, 2013.

drop in tandem with the GDP growth rate, it will still continue to grow at a relatively high level of approximately 5.5% annually from 2026 to 2030. Improving labor productivity will thus both increase the amount of effective labor and offset the negative influence of population aging.

Of course, increases in future productivity depend on certain crucial factors, the first being the quality of the labor force. The educational level of China's labor force has been rising. The average years of schooling received by workers as of the 1964 census was only 2.34 years; this figure increased to 9.07 years in 2010. Enrollment in higher education increased from 45.7 per 10,000 individuals in 1995 to 218.8 in 2010. Since China is faced with an aging population, expanding its investment in human capital is likely an effective strategy to raise productivity. The second crucial factor is that any change in labor productivity also hinges on economic restructuring. Labor productivity in the agricultural sector is typically lower than that in nonagricultural sectors. Policies that facilitate the mobility of labor will thus play a crucial part in ensuring a rise in labor productivity.

5.3. Raising the Retirement Age

A common policy recommendation for pension reform is to raise the retirement age. This is often considered an obvious remedy for the fiscal problems the pension system may face because of China's currently low retirement ages (see section 3.2).

Proponents of raising the retirement age all implicitly assume that elderly workers would still be able to find employment if their retirement were to be delayed. In recent research, Fang and Zhang (2018) question this assumption. They provide evidence that Chinese workers' productivity has been growing at a more rapid rate, about 6.13% per annum, than that of their counterparts in developed economies (at about 1.5% per annum). This rapid growth in productivity across cohorts, coupled with the behavioral tendency of higher pay for more senior workers relative to their junior counterparts, may make firms unwilling to hire elderly workers when the retirement age is delayed. Because of the rapid productivity growth in China, it stands to reason that the productivity of the elderly falls behind that of the young, so a competitive labor market should require that the old be paid much less than the young. However, Fang and Zhang (2018) argue that many factors, such as traditional respect for seniority in Chinese society and especially in SOEs, as well as perhaps the fair wage hypothesis, would require the wage level for the elderly to be close to that for the young. The resulting "wage compression" would imply that a reform to delay the retirement age would not automatically guarantee a demand for elderly labor. The analysis of Fang and Zhang (2018) thus calls for more-extensive labor training for the elderly before reforms that delay pension eligibility can be implemented

5.4. Unlocking Housing Wealth for Retirement

The homeownership rate in China is about 89.68%, according to the China Household Finance Survey (CHFS), with the rate being 85.49% in urban areas and 92.60% in rural areas. Chinese homeownership is substantially higher than the world average of 63% as well as the rates in the United States (65%) and Japan (60%). Moreover, housing wealth accounts for a much higher fraction (74%, according to CHFS) of household wealth in China than in other countries. For example, housing wealth accounts for about 40% of household wealth in the United States. Older households typically hold an even larger proportion of their wealth in residential housing. Home equity release-products such as reverse mortgages allow older homeowners to liquidate and consume home equity without relocating. Theoretical studies document welfare gains of reverse mortgages in life-cycle models (see, e.g., Davidoff, 2009; Cocco and Lopes, 2014; Hanewald et al., 2016; Nakajima and Telyukova, 2017).

In 2014, the Chinese government started a two-year pilot program to introduce reverse mortgages throughout the country. The insurer Happy Life Insurance was commissioned to offer reverse mortgages in Beijing, Shanghai, Guangzhou, and Wuhan starting from July 1, 2014. In 2016, the program was extended to mid-2018 and also expanded to a larger number of cities (Wee, 2016). The product is sold under the name "幸福房来宝老年人住房反向抵押养老保险" XYZ, which is usually translated as the "house for pension" program (Merton and Lai, 2016). However, the piloted reverse mortgage proved to be unpopular in China. Up to the end of July 2017, only the minuscule number of 65 households had participated in the program nationwide. News reports list several factors underlying the low demand, including children's disapproval of their parents' mortgaging their homes in return for a monthly pension, legal and regulatory concerns, and high mortgage rates charged by providers that consider the product too risky (Merton and Lai 2016; Asia Insurance Review, 2017).

How can the disappointing results from the pilot study be interpreted? Could the lack of demand be a result of the poor design of the reverse mortgage? Could it have resulted from parents' incorrect expectations of how their children would react to their using home equity to finance retirement? Are there alternative designs of the reverse mortgage contracts that may be more suitable for the Chinese market? What is the potential of home equity release products in financing the retirement of Chinese elderly? These and other questions must be answered. In recent work, Bateman et al. (2020) conduct and analyze two online surveys on the demand for reverse mortgage products in China. They test a flexible product design that overcomes the shortcomings of the above-mentioned unsuccessful reverse mortgage product that the Happy Life Insurance company recently piloted in the country. The key innovation of their study is the product design and product description. Their hypothetical product allows borrowers to choose the level of debt as well as the type of payment that best suits their retirement needs. Possible payment types include a lump sum, lifetime fixed regular payments, or flexible payments. In addition, their product explicitly allows the borrowers' heirs to settle the outstanding debt and keep the property at the end of the contract, if they so prefer. Their product description also takes special care to address potential consumers' concerns about how the house sales will be conducted, whether rental is permitted, how a loss of the property will be handled, and other matters. Their hypothetical product has a simpler debt structure and lower fees than the reverse mortgage offered by Happy Life Insurance. In addition, they make sure to test the subjects' understanding of their reverse mortgage product. They find that older homeowners aged 45–69 years are attracted to this new reverse mortgage product, and that their adult children aged 20–49 years would likely recommend such a reverse mortgage product to them. In addition, they find that participants mainly want to use reverse mortgage payments to live more comfortably in retirement and to pay for better medical treatment and aged care services. They also identify individual covariates influencing the interest in the reverse mortgage product and the use of the product payments. These results provide a new evidence base for the development of China's reverse mortgage market.

6. CONCLUSION

This chapter provides a detailed review of the three layers of China's pension system, and discusses the development of the system and the problems facing it. It also presents several ideas for future reforms in the Chinese pension system.

As the Chinese population ages, reforming and improving the pension system is of utmost importance. The system should be based on social insurance schemes, which provide a basic level of old-age support for all Chinese retirees, supplemented by private insurance products such as private annuity or reverse mortgage products. In all these areas, many issues remain open to study. For example, on the social insurance side, what is the standard consumption insurance/behavioral moral hazard tradeoff in China? What is the efficiency cost of China's fragmented social insurance system? What are the fiscal implications for the pension system if the country's growth slows down further? On the private insurance side, what are the product characteristics for annuity or reverse mortgage products that may appeal to the general Chinese population? Where are the gaps in the supply of resources needed to meet the rising demand for long-term elderly care? How would the need to care for parents affect the mobility and efficiency of the Chinese labor market? These and many other significant questions must be addressed.

NOTES

We acknowledge the financial support from the National Natural Science Foundation of China (Project number 71974036), Ministry of Education of People's Republic of China (Project number 17JZD028).

1. Data in this section is from the Ministry of Human Resources and Social Security (MOHRSS) of China.
2. "Local" could mean the provincial, city, or even county level, depending on the administrative region of the public pension fund.

3. Self-employed people or workers in informal sectors may participate in BOAI voluntarily. The contribution is 20% of the local average wage, of which 8% is recorded in the individual account. The benefit rule is the same as that for workers in the formal sectors.
4. China Insurance Industry Association, "Annual Report of the Chinese Insurance Market 2015." Beijing: Economic Science Press.
5. See Information from Statistics of MOHRSS at http://www.mohrss.gov.cn/SYrlzyhshbzb/zwgk/szrs/tjgb/201805/W020180521567611022649.pdf.
6. Transition cost arises from the financing gap created when expenditure to pensioners and future retirees must continue even though part of the contributions has been diverted to funded individual accounts (Wang et al., 2004).
7. Zheng Bingwen, "China Pension Report 2016" (in Chinese). Economic Management Press, 2016, Beijing.
8. See UN World Population Prospects 2019 at https://population.un.org/wpp/Download/Standard/Population/.
9. "An Actuarial Report for China's Pension System, 2019–2050," http://www.sohu.com/a/308165702_99956025.
10. "2019 Social Security and Medicare Trustees Report," https://home.treasury.gov/news/press-releases/sm665.
11. Contingent liabilities are liabilities that may be incurred by an entity, depending on the outcome of future events.
12. If growth slows down, then nonperforming loans and other liabilities are likely to rise. When they increase to an extent that leads to a financial crisis, the government may have to inject capital into the financial sector.
13. Data from State-Owned Assets Supervision and Administration Commission (SASAC) of the State Council of China athttp://www.sasac.gov.cn. The SOEs included in the statistics are all SOEs administered by central and local governments, except for financial SOEs.
14. SASAC released only the net profits of central SOEs before 2014.

REFERENCES

Asia Insurance Review (2017). "China: Reverse Mortgage Scheme Struggles to Take Off." *Asia Insurance Review*, August 2017. https://www.asiainsurancereview.com/News/View-NewsLetter-Article/id/40150/type/eDaily/China-Reverse-mortgage-scheme-struggles-to-take-off.
Bateman, Hazel, Hanming Fang, Katja Hanewald, and Shang Wu (2020). "Is There a Demand for Reverse Mortgages in China? Evidence from Two Online Surveys." *Journal of Economic Behavior & Organization* 169(1): 19–37.
Cai, Y., and Y. Cheng (2014). "Pension Reform in China: Challenges and Opportunities." *Journal of Economic Surveys* 28(4): 636–51.
Chen, X., K. Eggleston, and A. Sun (2017). "The Impact of Social Pensions on Intergenerational Relationships: Comparative Evidence from China." *Journal of the Economics of Aging* 12: 225–35.
Cocco, J. F., and P. Lopes (2014). "Reverse Mortgage Design." Technical report, London Business School.
Davidoff, T. (2009). "Housing, Health, and Annuities." *Journal of Risk and Insurance* 76(1): 31–52.
Dorfman, M., R. Holzmann, P. O'Keefe, D. Wang, Y. Sin, and R. Hinz (2013). *China's Pension System: A Vision*. Washington, DC: World Bank.
Fang, Hanming, and Yi Zhang (2018). "Growing Pains in the Chinese Social Security System." Working paper, University of Pennsylvania.
Feng, Jin, and Qin Chen (2016). "Public Pension System and Fiscal Policy Response in China" in *Age Related Pension Expenditure and Fiscal Space: Modelling Techniques and Case Studies from East Asia*, edited by Mukul G. Asher and Fauziah Zen. New York: Routledge.
Feng, J., L. He, and H. Sato (2011). "Public Pension and Household Saving: Evidence from Urban China." *Journal of Comparative Economics* 39(4): 470–85.
Hanewald, K., T. Post, and M. Sherris (2016). "Portfolio Choice in Retirement—What Is the Optimal Home Equity Release Product?" *Journal of Risk and Insurance* 83(2): 421–46.
Hemming, R. (2012). "Public Debt Sustainability and Hidden Liabilities in the People's Republic of China," in *Public Debt Sustainability in Developing Asia*, edited by B. Ferrarini, R. Jha, and A. Ramayandi. London and New York, NY: Routledge.
Impavido, G., Y. W. Hu, and X. Li (2009). "Governance and Fund Management in the Chinese Pension System." IMF Working Papers, 09/246, November.

Lei, X., C. Zhang, and Y. Zhao (2014). "Incentive Problems in China's New Rural Pension Program." *Research in Labor Economics* 37: 181–201.

Merton, R., and R. N. Lai (2016). "On an Efficient Design of Reverse Mortgages: A Possible Solution for Aging Asian Populations." Available at SSRN: https://ssrn.com/abstract=3075087.

Nakajima, M., and I. A. Telyukova (2017). "Reverse Mortgage Loans: A Quantitative Analysis." *Journal of Finance* 72(2): 911–50.

Nyland, C., R. Smyth, and C. J. Zhu (2010). "What Determines the Extent to Which Employers Will Comply with Their Social Security Obligations? Evidence from Chinese Firm-level Data." Social Policy & Administration 40(2): 196–214.

Nyland, C., S. B. Thomson, and C. J. Zhu (2011). "Employer Attitudes Towards Social Insurance Compliance in Shanghai, China." *International Social Security Review* 64(4): 73–98.

Wang, Y., D. Xu, Z. Wang, and F. Zhai (2004). "Options and Impact of China's Pension Reform: A Computable General Equilibrium Analysis." *Journal of Comparative Economics* 32(1): 105–27.

Wee, S.-L. (2016). "China's 'Godfather of Real Estate' Pitches Reverse Mortgages to Skeptical Elders." *New York Times*, December 26, 2016.

World Bank (2012). "China 2030: Building a Modern, Harmonious, and Creative High-Income Society." http://www.worldbank.org/content/dam/Worldbank/document/China-2030-complete.pdf.

Zheng, B. (2016). *China Pension Report 2016* (in Chinese). Beijing: Economic Management Press.

PART 8

NEW DEVELOPMENTS

17

FINTECH DEVELOPMENT

Bohui Zhang

1. OVERVIEW OF FINTECH DEVELOPMENT IN CHINA: FROM AN INTERNATIONAL PERSPECTIVE

Defined as the application of new technologies to financial services, "fintech" is a shortcut for the term "financial technology" that comprises various aspects. Conventional examples of fintech applications include mobile banking, peer-to-peer lending, crowdfunding, robo-advisors, cryptocurrency, and the like. In China, one particularly important application of fintech lies in financial inclusion, so this chapter will primarily focus on this field. Owing to many technological advances, especially the use of smartphones, tech giants such as Tencent and Ant Financial have provided hundreds of millions of consumers with convenient and smart payment methods as well as innovative savings and loan products. These emerging fintech businesses are also reshaping the way Chinese consumers pay, borrow, and invest, thereby generating new revenue and profits.

1.1. Fintech Development

Over the past several years, China has emerged as a leader in the fintech industry. The leading role of China in the fintech sector is reflected in three aspects: fintech adoption rates, fintech companies, and fintech hubs. Although taking a leading role, fintech development in China still faces many unsolved problems, such as unserved small to medium-sized enterprises (SMEs) and unbanked populations (ING 2016).

1.2. Fintech Adoption Rates

As a center of global fintech innovation, China leads the world with a fintech adoption rate[1] of 87% (figure 17.1; Ernst and Young, 2019) while global average fintech adoption rate is 64%. Following China, the top four fintech adoption countries in the world are India, Russia, South Africa, and Colombia.

With regard to SMEs' use of fintech services (shown in table 17.1), according to EY's survey (Ernst & Young, 2019), China remains the leading country in fintech adoption rate in most segments except the insurance industry. Among those segments, the adoption rates of banking and payments, financial management, financing are 92%, 91%, and 89%,

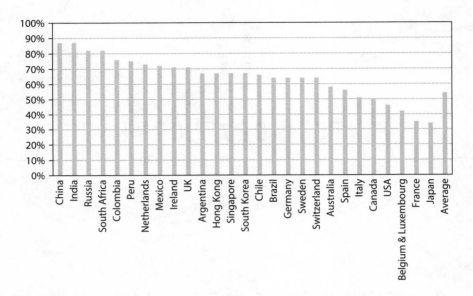

FIGURE 17.1. Fintech adoption rates across 27 markets. *Source:* Ernst & Young, 2019, FinTech Adoption Index. *Notes:* Ernst & Young did a survey in 2019 by interviewing more than 27,000 consumers in 27 markets. Fintech adoption rate is defined by fintech adopters as a percentage of the digitally active population in each market. A fintech user is a respondent who reported using one or more fintech services.

Table 17.1. Comparison of Five Markets with the SMEs' Fintech Adoption for Each Fintech Category

	Banking and payments (%)	Financial management (%)	Financing (%)	Insurance (%)
China	92	91	89	62
Mexico	49	36	31	23
South Africa	47	43	34	26
United Kingdom	41	37	34	24
United States	52	49	41	31

Source: EY, 2019, FinTech Adoption Index.
Note: The figures show the percentage of SMEs that have used at least one service in the respective category.

respectively, which are significantly higher than those of the following countries in the table. Nevertheless, regulatory concerns underlie the high fintech adoption rate. For example, large number of P2P platforms, meaning China's fintech credit market main players, defaulted or became problematic around 2016 after a period of high growth (Claessens et al., 2018).

While plenty of reasons were offered for China's rapid financial development in science and technology, the following factors are still worthy of note. First, the country's

Table 17.2. Top 10 Fintech Companies Worldwide

Rank	Company	Country	Year founded
1	Ant Financial	China	2004
2	JD Finance	China	2013
3	Grab	Singapore	2012
4	Du Xiaoman Financial	China	2015
5	SoFi	United States	2011
6	Oscar Health	United States	2013
7	Nubank	Brazil	2013
8	Robinhood	United States	2013
9	Atom Bank	United Kingdom	2014
10	Lufax Holding	China	2011

Source: KPMG, Fintech100 Leading Global Fintech Innovators, 2018.
Note: The Fintech100 list is determined based on data across a range of dimensions, including the following factors: Average annual capital raised; rate of recent capital raising; geographic diversity; sectoral diversity; and degree of product, service, and business model innovation.

mature digital infrastructure is a solid foundation for the rapid rise in fintech, with the Internet and mobile technologies effectively driving private consumption. Moreover, the government's guidance in and encouragement of the innovation of fintech enterprises have also provided it with unique opportunities for transforming fintech on a global scale. Chinese regulators are committed to developing appropriate regulatory standards and frameworks, which also shows the government's faith in and determination to promote digital finance and financial reform.

1.3. Fintech Companies

Over the past three years, China has continued to dominate the fintech landscape. Chinese fintech companies accounted for four of the top five fintech companies in 2016. In 2017, the top three fintech companies in the world were all from China. Four of the top 10 fintech companies in 2018 are giants in Chinese retail, insurance, and the Internet (see table 17.2), including Ant Financial (蚂蚁金服), JD Digits (京东数科), Du Xiaoman Financial (度小满金融), and Lufax Holding (陆金所). These companies represent the highest level of fintech companies in the world and demonstrate China's leadership position in the industry. For the past three years, China and the United States have each accounted for nearly half of the world's top 10 fintech companies (KPMG, 2018).

Moreover, the number of users and products of China's fintech giants is growing at an alarming rate. Ant Financial, for example, has increased funding for its Yu'ebao platform, to expand the company's consumer base. Tencent Holdings recently invested $180 million in the Brazilian fintech giant Nubank. In addition, driven by the prospect of overseas markets, many Chinese fintech companies are accelerating their overseas expansion. This allows the country's consumers to use their third-party payment tools in brick-and-mortar retail stores in 28 other countries and regions.

Table 17.3. Global Fintech Hubs

City	Rank	City	Rank	City	Rank
Beijing	1	Singapore	11	São Paolo	21
San Francisco	2	Berlin	12	Paris	22
New York	3	Atlanta	13	Seoul	23
London	4	Tokyo	14	Los Angeles	24
Shanghai	5	Stockholm	15	Guangzhou	25
Shenzhen	6	Bangalore	16	Mumbai	26
Hangzhou	7	Boston	17	Dublin	27
Chicago	8	Toronto	18	Nanjing	28
Sydney	9	Tel Aviv	19	Zurich	29
Hong Kong	10	Seattle	20	Amsterdam	30

Source: Zhejiang University, Academy of Internet Finance; Cambridge Centre for Alternative Finance (CCAF); Zhejiang Association of Internet Finance (ZAIF); and TongBanJie Financial Technology Group (2018). "The Future of Finance Is Emerging: New Hubs, New Landscapes." Global Fintech Hub Report.

1.4. Fintech Hubs

China's cities are abuzz with the rush to build fintech hubs. Table 17.3 shows that four of the world's top seven fintech hubs are in China. They are spread among Beijing, Shanghai, Hangzhou, and Shenzhen.

These cities are concentrated in the Beijing–Tianjin–Hebei region, the Yangtze river delta, and the Guangdong–Hong Kong–Macao Greater Bay Area. These regions are home to a number of fintech unicorns such as Ant Financial and JD Digits (formerly known as "JD Finance"), providing a core driver for fintech development. In addition, the Chinese people's embrace and tolerance of fintech have provided a continuous impetus for the country's rapid development of a fintech center. Furthermore, Beijing ranks first in the fintech industry as well as in the total number of fintech companies worldwide, and ranks second in total financing. In addition, as the only developing country in the top 10 worldwide, China has five cities in the top 10 and seven in the top 30. Among the top 10 cities, three are in the United States and only one in the United Kingdom. Moreover, from the perspective of what may be called the fintech ecosystem, there are three leading cities: New York, San Francisco, and London. New York is driven by traditional finance, San Francisco by technological innovation, and London by regulatory innovation. Beijing, Shanghai, Shenzhen, and Hangzhou have the top fintech ecology in the world. China's intensive recent development of the economic and financial environments, a strong innovation atmosphere, and significant government support have provided fertile ground for fintech's development.

2. DRIVING FACTORS OF FINTECH DEVELOPMENT

2.1. Financial Inclusion

The term "financial inclusion" has been highlighted by the World Bank since the early 2000s and is defined as the availability and equality of people's opportunities to access financial services. Ironically, financial inclusion is relative to financial exclusion, and the popularity of the latter term in recent years indicates that a significant group of individuals, firms, and institutions still lack opportunities to access financial services in their respective economies. The academic literature suggests that the extent of financial inclusion affects the efficiency of resource allocation, costs of capital, informal credit markets, and formal financial institutions (e.g., Beck et al., 2011; Beck et al., 2008; Levine, 2005; Klapper et al., 2006; Demirgüç-Kunt et al., 2008).

Like other emerging markets, China encounters both challenges and opportunities in the development of its country's financial inclusion. The country's SMEs form the backbone of its economy, comprising 90% of all, according to a speech by Gang Yi, president of the People's Bank of China, at the 10th Lujiazui Forum in 2018. In 2013, China's SMEs contributed to more than 60% of the country's national income and 80% of its urban employment (OECD, 2016). These firms have also contributed largely to China's economic system reform. Despite the importance of SMEs in China, 58% of those SMEs are financially constricted, and the size of the finance gap they have to deal with totals 17% of GDP. There are 11 million SMEs in China, accounting for 56% of all SMEs in developing countries, and 44 million microenterprises, representing 31% of all microenterprises in developing countries (World Bank Group, 2017).

China's financial institutions and markets are greatly underdeveloped. In general, the overall unsatisfied financing demand of Chinese corporations and SMEs' uneven access to credit remain the most important two issues to deal with.

According to World Bank Group researchers,[2] more than half of China's corporations are constrained from obtaining credit. The research divides the degree of corporate credit constraints into four discrete dimensions: "not credit constrained," "maybe credit constrained," "partially credit constrained," and "fully credit constrained." Based on this classification and the enterprise credit conditions, the survey shows that 29% of enterprises are fully credit constrained, 18% may be credit constrained, and 7% are partially credit constrained. Constraints on credits for Chinese companies remain a pressing issue (Kuntchev et al., 2012).

Among China's corporations with constrained financing, SMEs are more constrained from obtaining credit (see figure 17.2). The threshold of obtaining credit for small firms in China is higher and the chances of obtaining credit are smaller, as confirmed by World Bank Group's Enterprise Surveys. While SMEs' financing demand has been continually increasing in recent years, SMEs still can hardly obtain formal credit from banks and often can only turn to alternative channels (Tsai, 2015). The lack of appropriate financing sources has frequently caused financing difficulties for SMEs in China (Jiang et al., 2014).

Chinese households are also faced with an uneven distribution of credit resources (see table 17.4). Households in rural areas have a higher demand for loans. A relatively smaller proportion of households are able to obtain bank loans, while others have to rely on private lending (CHFS, 2015).

Nevertheless, the high fintech adoption rates and digital technology associated with fintech innovation in China have greatly promoted financial inclusiveness in recent years. The rapid development of financial services such as mobile payments and online lending makes it more accessible, affordable, and sustainable for both individuals and SMEs to be financed. According to the Peking University Digital Financial Inclusion Index of China (Guo et al., 2019), the overall situation of China's digital finance has improved from the lower tier in 2011 to the upper middle tier in 2017 (see figure 17.3). Also, the geographic

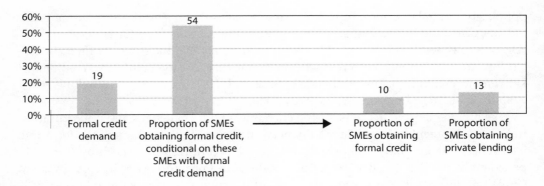

FIGURE 17.2. Credit for small and micro enterprises, 2015. *Source:* Survey and Research Centre for China Household Finance, 2015, "Credit for Small and Micro Enterprises."

Table 17.4. China Household Finance, 2015

	Bank loan demand (%)	Proportion of households obtaining bank loans (%)	Proportion of households using private lending (%)
China	33.70	55.50	36.50
Urban	29.80	63.80	30.20
Rural	41.60	43.60	49.10

Source: Survey and Research Centre for China Household Finance, 2015, Household Credit.

inequality with regard to digital finance has been addressed, to some extent, with the gap between developed areas and developing areas narrowing.

2.2. Traditional Financial Institutions and Markets

Banks evaluate large firms' credit ratings and operating performance based on firms' financial statements. However, SMEs cannot provide sufficient information for banks to determinate their default rates. Moreover, banks need to use traditional methods and tedious procedures to assess a firm's creditworthiness. The assessment period normally lasts for weeks or months. Therefore, relatively speaking, it is costly for banks to issue loans to SMEs.

Compared with that of large firms, the financing of SMEs has several disadvantages. First, SMEs suffer high default risk, and bank loans are often used for investments in high-risk projects (Beck et al., 2011). Second, bank loans normally involve collaterals, while pledging collateral goes beyond SMEs' capabilities. Finally, SMEs suffer relatively high information asymmetry (Hanedar et al, 2014; Lin and Sun, 2005).

Since the traditional indicators used to measure financial development do not take into account the complexity and multifaceted nature of financial development, the deficiencies are revealed. Therefore, the International Monetary Fund has launched a new index to measure financial development, which covers a wide range of areas and has a sound evaluative system (figure 17.4) (IMF, 2016).

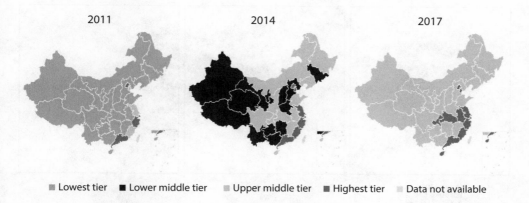

FIGURE 17.3. China digital inclusive finance index, 2011–2017. *Source:* Institute of Digital Finance, Peking University, 2019. *Note:* For each year, regions are separated into four colored tiers covering 80% to 100%, 70% to 80%, 60% to 70%, and below 60%, respectively, of the maximum index value. The convergence of shades of black and gray represents a reduction of digital finance inequality.

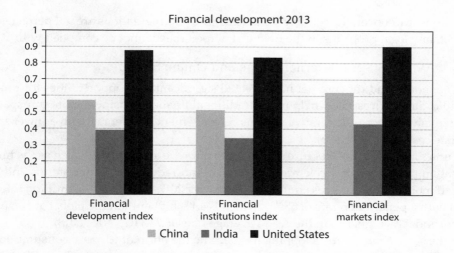

FIGURE 17.4. Financial development, 2013. *Source:* IMF, "Introducing a New Board-based Index of Financial Development," Working Paper No. 16/5, 2016.

The main reasons for China's lagging financial development are as follows. First, the financial structure is not perfect. The unbalanced development of bank financial structure and nonbank financial institutions has restricted the overall development of China's financial market. Second, compared with that of developed countries, China's financial instrument innovation is still very backward and few balanced options are available for investors, thus increasing their risk and making them lose confidence in the market. In addition, China's financial innovation relies heavily on the government, a reality that reduces the financial efficiency and weakens the international competitiveness of financial

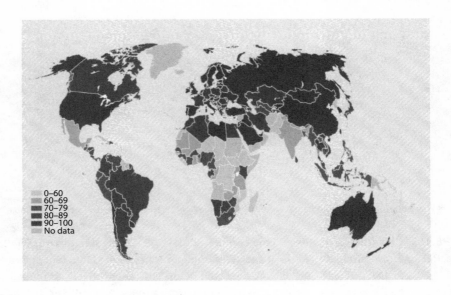

FIGURE 17.5. Mobile phone ownership around the world: Percent of adults with a mobile phone, 2017. *Source:* Gallup World Poll, 2017.

innovation. Moreover, the country's financial laws and regulations are not perfect, leading to many legal problems in the financial market that cannot be complied with.

2.3. Internet Usage and Online Shopping

Mobile phones and the Internet have created significant new opportunities for providing financial services. They help make traditional financial business more transparent, more involved, more cooperative, and more convenient to operate, with a lower intermediate cost (see figure 17.5).

China's Internet infrastructure continues to improve and upgrade, even as the implementation of policies of accelerating the speed and reducing fees has significantly increased mobile Internet access traffic. By December 2017, China had 772 million Internet users with a penetration rate of 55.8%, which is 4.1% higher than the global average rate (51.7%) and 9.1% higher than the Asian average rate (46.7%) (CNNIC, 2018).

At the same time, online shopping has become the norm of Chinese consumption in which more and more consumers every month are participating (see figure 17.6). New entrants can even offer installment loans via the Internet, and the transaction scale of the online retail market covers an increasing proportion of total retail sales of consumer goods.

Another important concept is termed "Internet plus." Generally speaking, printed or broadcast impressions of "Internet+" mean "Internet+various traditional industries." However, this is not simply the combination of the two but instead the deep integration of the Internet and traditional industries by using information communication technology and the wider Internet platform to create a new development ecology.

Internet usage and online shopping promote fintech development in China. With the increasing use of the Internet, customers can conduct various financial transactions online and also take advantage of more-simplified transaction processes such as risk pric-

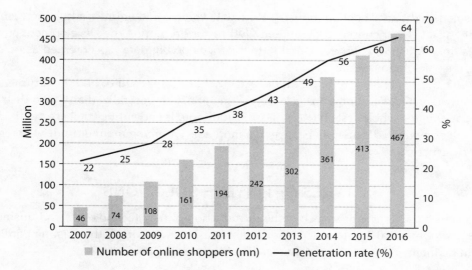

FIGURE 17.6. Number of online shoppers and penetration rate in China from 2007 to 2016. *Sources:* Wind database, Macquarie Research, November 2017.

ing and maturity matching. In addition, online shopping provides huge data for the development of fintech as well as promotes risk assessment and risk control mechanisms for it. For example, fintech companies make use of the seamless connection of Alibaba, Taobao, Alipay, and other e-commerce platforms to set up data models of customers' transaction data, behavioral data, and credit input. They also use third-party cross-verification to accurately identify customers' credit rating and to conduct risk pricing and management of their products.

2.4. Credit Bureau and Big Data

The concept of "social credit" first appeared in the 2003 Report of the Third Plenum of the 16th Central Committee, which highlighted the importance of social credit as well as introduced a system to evaluate social credit. However, the "social credit system" mentioned that year was in fact quite different from that in wide use at present. In 2003 the Credit Reference Centre of the People's Bank of China (PBC) was responsible for issuing individual credit reports that assist lenders such as banks to make decisions (Kostka, 2019).

China's State Council initiated a Social Credit System (SCS) plan in 2014, intending to establish a credit system that incorporates data from both the government and private sectors such as firms. The plan was titled "State Council Notice concerning Issuance of the Planning Outline for the Construction of a Social Credit System (2014–2020)". Before the official initiation of the SCS, however, the first step toward a national SCS had already been taken by state media. In 2013, the Supreme People's Court began a blacklist of debtors, accumulating roughly 32,000 names.

In January 2015, the PBC issued the "Notice on Preparing for Personal credit Investigation" (关于做好个人征信业务准备工作的通知), which informed eight enterprises,[3] including Sesame Credit (芝麻信用) and Tencent Credit (腾讯征信), of preparations being made for personal credit investigations, marking the first step toward the marketization of the personal credit investigation industry. With data volume and online trading increasing, China's State Council issued the Action Outline for Promoting the Development of Big Data on August 31, 2015. Since that date the focus on big data has emerged as one of China's chief national strategies.

With the establishment of credit bureaus that are composed of both governmental organizations and corporations, a large volume of data is centralized and then distributed within the whole system (Kostka, 2019). Individuals and entities that are monitored as well as evaluated generally behave in a more self-enforcing manner under the regulatory structure.

3. TYPES OF FINTECH SOLUTIONS

The key characteristic of fintech is the introduction of new technologies and business models to financial services. This movement is expected to break the existing equilibrium maintained by incumbent financial institutions and markets.

3.1. Payment

As the world's largest card payment organization ahead of Visa and Mastercard, Union-Pay is China's state-run credit and debit card network, which was launched in March 2002. For daily transactions, UnionPay provides all kinds of bank card services. However, in recent years, UnionPay's market share has gradually been challenged by Ant Financial's Alipay and Tencent's WePay.

Figure 17.7 shows the change in the market share of Alipay, WeChat Pay, and Union-Pay from 2011 to 2018. Alipay and WeChat are highly competitive and have occupied the majority of the market share by 2018. UnionPay has a smaller market share under the squeeze of the two giants.

Alipay refers to the payment tool owned by Alibaba, which is a leading third-party payment platform in China. Alipay is an intermediary between users and commercial banks that facilitates the flow of money and information between them. Alipay's business model not only includes online consumption payment but also expands offline payment services through scanning payment, including catering, supermarkets, convenience stores, taxis, public transportation, and the like.

WeChat payment is the payment function integrated with the WeChat platform. WeChat users can complete a fast payment process through their mobile phones. At present, WeChat payment has realized card payment, code scanning payment, public account payment, and app payment, satisfying different payment scenarios of both users and merchants. The WeChat payment background is supported by Tencent's big data, massive data, and cloud computing, which can determine in a timely fashion whether the user's payment behavior is at risk (Qu et al., 2015).

In addition, WeChat is a platform for so-called Mini programs (i.e., applications that do not need to be downloaded and installed). The application connects users with developers and service providers in the WeChat platform through mini programs. These applets are sub-applications that can be launched within WeChat without requiring users to download individual programs. Moreover, the more users that WeChat acquires, the greater the number of developers and service providers it attracts and the faster its ecosystem will grow.

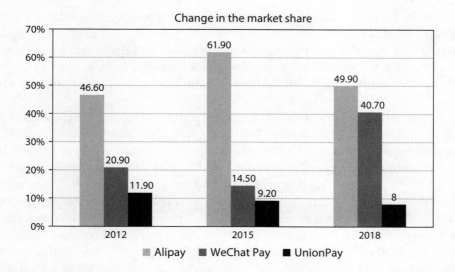

FIGURE 17.7. Market shares of Alipay, WeChat Pay, and UnionPay. *Sources:* EnfoDesk, 2018; China mobile payment market Annual Report.

QR (Quick Response) codes are more complex in appearance than barcodes but contain more content. Therefore, they also show the following advantages: As they contain more information and a wide range of coding, QR codes can introduce encryption measures. There are two common patterns of scanning code. First, the merchants generate the product-related QR codes according to the rules. After the users scan the codes, the client initiates a request toward the designated address of the merchants. In response to this request, the merchant system completes the order, obtains the prepayment information, and returns it. And then the client completes the payment. Second, after the user places an order, the merchant system obtains the prepayment information and generates the QR code for the user to complete the payment.

3.2. Credit Scoring

The growth of Internet finance provides accessible information for fintech companies to evaluate their customers' creditworthiness. These data of individual customers include several categories, such as credit history, fulfillment capacity, personal information, user's preference, and preferred social network.

These individual customers' credit scores can be calculated based on either linear or nonlinear econometric models.

Sesame Credit is a brand of credit scoring system developed by Ant Financial. Consumers can access credit scores in a variety of ways, and Ant Financial will increase loans to highly rated customers.

Sesame Credit is the most representative enterprise in China's Internet financial personal credit system. It collects and processes huge personal data, relying on big data technology and cloud computing technology. In addition, not only is it based on traditional financial data, but it also cooperates seamlessly with public institutions such as the Public Security Bureau to establish a comprehensive personal credit database. Such a credit evaluation method can enable lenders to make more accurate judgments about their loan users' repayment ability.

Alibaba established its online bank, named MYbank, in 2015. MYbank's large stakeholders use the Internet platform to provide online financial services at its e-commerce platforms. It has no physical subsidiaries and does not provide traditional financial services.

According to the statistics of eMarketer.com, e-commerce sales in China reached $1.53 trillion in 2018. Alibaba's Taobao and Tmall account for 58% and JD accounts for 16% of the total amount of e-commerce sales. These large sales volumes deliver important information about customers and online vendors. Based on such a vast scale of data from various Alibaba platforms, such as operating conditions, sales, payments, past credit behaviors, and historical default, MYbank generates a credit score to assess the overall credibility of a merchant and to provide "3-1-0" online lending. This loan service can be characterized by a three-minute application process, one-second loan granting, and the whole process finished with zero manual intervention. Normally, qualified online merchants receive a credit line including loan rate, max loan amount (up to one million RMB), maturity (six months to one year), and loan contract.

3.3. Investment

After the brutal growth over the past few years, domestic Internet financial platforms have gradually formed an oligopoly, among which Yu'ebao, Tencent's Licaitong, and Lufax have formed a tripartite confrontation.

Licaitong has obvious advantages among a number of money market funds. It has a higher interest rate than demand deposit, greater liquidity than ordinary money fund, ready access, and high market acceptance. It is the core pillar of Tencent's financial system. Tencent's Licaitong has more than 800 million users of WeChat, and the number of users grew by 60 million over the past three years alone.

Yu'ebao is a value-added service launched by Alipay. For users, the application of Yu'ebao can gain not only a higher income but also increase the flexibility of funding and realize the functions of transfer and online shopping at any time. The funds transferred to Yu'ebao can be withdrawn in two ways, namely (T+1) and (T+2). The difference lies in the time need for determining the shares after the transferred amount. There is no strict limit on the number of funds transferred, with a minimum amount of 1 yuan and an unlimited maximum amount. Moreover, the funds transferred to Yu'ebao are also very convenient to use. They can be withdrawn at any time. The maximum amount of withdrawal is about 10 times greater than that of a bank's demand deposits in the same period. The emergence of Yu'ebao not only has had positive influences on China's financial industry but has also been faced with challenges. First, compared with private banks, Yu'ebao charges a lower interest rate for loans, thus reducing the loan interest required by small companies. Second, the success of Yu'ebao prompts commercial banks to launch similar services more quickly, improve their service quality, and narrow the gap. Furthermore, Yu'ebao has a great impact on commercial banks' deposit-taking business and the sale of financial products on a commission basis. As a consequence, many people have abandoned the deposit services and wealth management products provided by traditional banks, reducing the banks' interests and profits. Finally, the launch of Yu'ebao not only affects commercial banks but also has a significant impact on the fund industry.

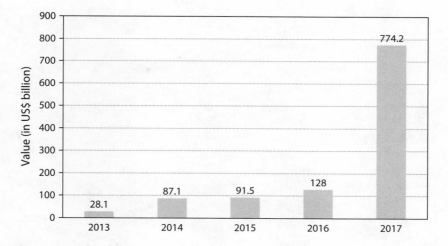

FIGURE 17.8. Yu'ebao's assets under management. *Source:* Tianhong Yu'ebao annual report, 2013–2018.

Users can use Yu'ebao to buy wealth management products directly, pointing out the way for other fund companies. From 2013 to 2017, the assets under the management of Yu'ebao increased phenomenally from 28.1 billion RMB to 774.2 billion RMB (see figure 17.8).

Tencent's Licaitong is a platform on which Tencent cooperates with many financial institutions to provide diversified wealth management services for users. On the platform, as providers of financial products, financial institutions are responsible for the structural design and asset operation of financial products. They provide users with services such as account opening, account registration, product purchase, income distribution, product withdrawal, and share inquiry. When real-name users open WeChat Lucky Money, they can apply for Licaitong's monetary fund; they receive money in a red envelope and can increase the value of the money with one click. By February 2019, the total number of users of Tencent's Licaitong had exceeded 150 million with asset holdings having exceeded 500 billion RMB. Compared with Yu'ebao, Tencent's Licaitong sells funds with higher yields. However, the experience of using funds through Licaitong is not as flexible as that of Yu'ebao. For example, the funds in Yu'ebao can be directly used for consumption and transfer, while Licaitong lacks these two functions. From 2017 to 2018, the assets under the management of Licaitong increased from 300 billion RMB to 600 billion RMB (figure 17.9).

Lufax, which belongs to Ping'an Group, is a financial asset trading information service platform. It was registered in Shanghai in September 2011 and headquartered in Shanghai Lujiazui, an international financial center. Lufax's online investment and financing platform was officially launched in March 2012. By the end of October 2016, it had acquired more than 26 million registered users. It is committed to combining financial development with Internet technology innovation to establish a reliable risk control system and also to provide investment and financing services for enterprises and individuals. Compared with Yu'ebao, the yield of wealth management products of Lufax is higher. However, Lufax's funding liquidity is lower than that of Yu'ebao. For example,

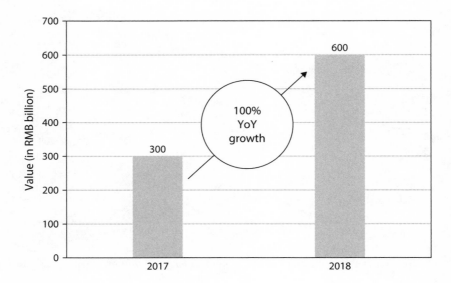

FIGURE 17.9. Assets under management on Licaitong. *Sources:* Tencent financial reports, Walk-the Chat Analysis.

the funds in Yu'ebao can be redeemed at any time, but Lufax has a certain redemption limit. For investors in Lufax, the investment cannot be canceled. If investors are in urgent need of funds, they may transfer their loan creditor's rights to other investors so as to recover part of the funds.

3.4. Peer-to-Peer Lending

A new type of financial service, peer-to-peer (P2P) lending, has come into being that matches borrowers with lenders. China's P2P market has experienced substantial growth since 2007. Peer-to-peer lending arises as an important financing channel for SMEs and individuals alike, as well as an alternative investment channel for households (figure 17.10).

The P2P lending market size in China reached its peak in 2017 with the trading volume amounting to 2.8 trillion RMB and declined to 1.79 trillion RMB in 2018 (Frost & Sullivan, 2018). As a supplement to the traditional financial market, the majority of the customers of P2P lending are SMEs and individuals whose credit demands are usually met with some difficulty by formal financial intermediaries. A large portion of P2P lending is short-term funding with a duration of less than one year. Although the interest rate of P2P lending is almost twice that of the benchmark lending rate (figure 17.11), P2P lending still reduces the financing costs of borrowers who can only turn to private lending without P2P platforms.

Overall, P2P lending development throughout China has gone through several phases. In 2007, such lending was initiated in China with the establishment of the first P2P platform, ppdai (拍拍贷). At that time, the P2P platform's business model was simply to match borrows with lenders. Since 2012, the role of P2P lending platforms has changed, as they started to be involved in the lending process by providing a guarantee for principal and interest and even made a commitment of "rigid redemption" to borrowers. From 2014 to 2016, the trading volume of P2P lending increased by almost 8.4 times.

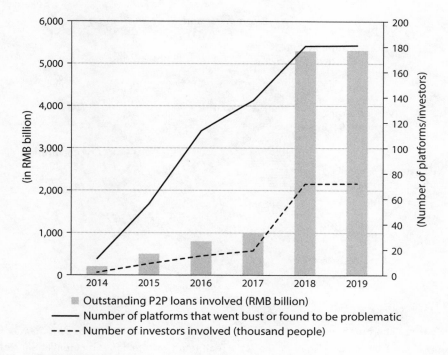

FIGURE 17.10. The P2P lending market in China. *Source:* WDZJ.com

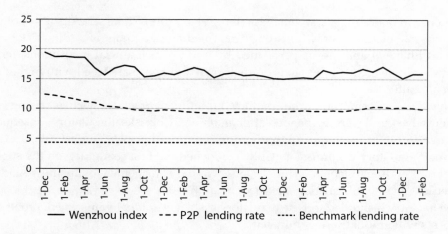

FIGURE 17.11. China P2P lending interest rate. *Sources:* Bloomberg, WDZJ.com, and People's Bank of China. *Notes:* The Wenzhou Index, released by the Wenzhou Municipal Government Finance Office, measures private lending cost.

Risks emerged with the quick expansion of the P2P lending market. Lacking risk management and operation experience, numerous P2P lending platforms became problematic, experiencing surging default rates. Some financial scholars have found that platforms without SOE affiliation tend to be less trustworthy and have a higher probability of failure, possibly due to the lack of governmental implicit guarantees as well as relevant

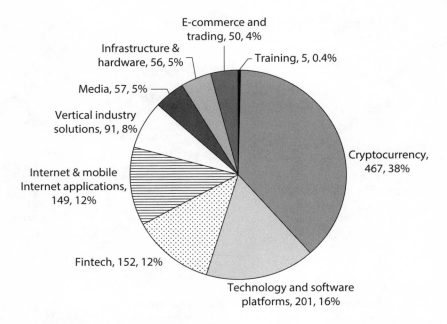

FIGURE 17.12. The number of blockchain enterprises by industry (worldwide). *Source:* China Academy of Information and Communications Technology, white paper on blockchain, 2018.

experience in operating a loan business (Jiang et al., 2019). Some scholars also point out that since P2P platforms only function as intermediaries, without providing risk evaluation and financial analysis as performed by traditional financial institutions, lenders have to make investment decisions on their own and hence are faced with higher risks (Xu et al., 2015).

Some P2P platforms have even conducted fraudulent practices, such as raising funds for themselves, and were suspended after an outbreak of risks. Regulators subsequently tightened regulatory policy and introduced relevant legislation. In August 2016, the China Banking Regulatory Commission (CBRC) launched the first regulation on the supervision of P2P lending, titled "Interim Measures for the Management of Business Activities of Internet Lending Information Intermediaries" (网络借贷信息中介机构业务活动管理暂行办法). As the industry reshuffles and the regulatory system is gradually improved, problematic platforms will gradually be eliminated.

3.5. Blockchain

Blockchain provides a trusted channel for information and value transfer and exchange by incorporating point-to-point networks, cryptography, consensus mechanisms, intelligent contracts, and other technologies. Blockchain combines cutting-edge technologies such as cloud computing and big data and is now deeply integrated with other fields, including finance, medical care, and justice. Global blockchain companies are actively exploring business applications to segmented fields.

Until July 2018 the number of active blockchain companies in the world totaled 1,242, and the number of Chinese blockchain companies ranked second, following the United

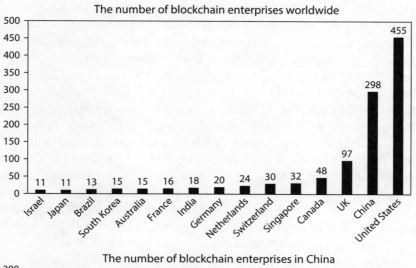

The number of blockchain enterprises worldwide

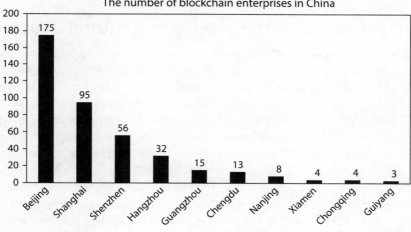

The number of blockchain enterprises in China

FIGURE 17.13. Number of blockchain enterprises worldwide and in China. *Source:* China Academy of Information and Communications Technology, white paper on blockchain, 2018.

States with 298 companies (China Academy, 2018). Currently, blockchain companies are mainly engaged in cryptocurrency (38%), technology and software platform (16%), financial technology (12%), and Internet and mobile Internet applications (12%) (figure 17.12). Beijing leads China with 175 blockchain companies, which account for more than half of the country's total. It is followed by Shanghai and Shenzhen, with 95 and 56 blockchain companies, respectively (figure 17.13).

Chinese blockchain companies focus on both the innovation and application of blockchain technology. Among these companies, the most famous one is Bitmain, which facilitates bitcoin mining and which filed for IPO in 2018 in Hong Kong. It designs application-specific integrated circuit (ASIC) chips for bitcoin mining. In 2018, Bitmain had 11 mining farms operating in China and had become one of the largest ASIC designers in the world. It even reported profits that year.

Meanwhile, some companies also focus on developing blockchain infrastructure. Take Sinochain, for example, a company that has the underlying technology of blockchain with independent intellectual property rights. Sinochain extensively applied blockchain to several projects in various fields, including food tracing, poverty alleviation, big data storage, government financial subsidy storage, digital contract service, and blockchain e-commerce sharing promotion.

Meanwhile, Initial Coin Offering (ICO) has become a new financing channel. Globally speaking, blockchain startup financing (non-ICO) totaled $4.81 billion from 2009 to 2018, and ICO accumulated financing reached $18.09 billion between 2014 and 2018. China, however, strictly restricts blockchain financing. In September 2017, ICO was banned. In 2018, the China Banking Regulatory Commission, the Ministry of Public Security, and five other ministries issued a document named "Risk tips on preventing illegal fund raising in the name of virtual currency and Blockchain" (关于防范以"虚拟货币""区块链"名义进行非法集资的风险提示), aiming at "regulating the currency, encouraging the chain" (规范币，鼓励链), and promoting the orderly and benign development of blockchain in China.

4. THE IMPACT OF FINTECH ON FINANCIAL INSTITUTIONS

The development of fintech in China is dynamic and can be characterized as a result of joint efforts by the two types of fintech drivers, or companies: disruptors and incumbents. Disruptors are IT companies, such as Alibaba, Tencent, Baidu, and JD, which apply big data, AI, blockchain, and Internet of Things (IoT) techniques to financial services. By contrast, incumbents are banks, insurance companies, brokerage companies, and asset management firms, which make changes in their traditional business models and methods in response to the competition pressure from these disruptors.

4.1. Banks

The banking sector, which accounts for 80% of China's financial assets, plays a significant role in the country's credit markets. China's banking system consists of the central bank, regulators, self-regulatory agencies, and banking and financial institutions. The latter two play different roles, but they are both vital.

The fintech investments of Chinese commercial banks has surged in recent years.

Table 17.5 shows the strategic cooperation between the "big four" banks and fintech companies. These banks have cooperated with Alibaba, Ant Financial, Baidu, JD, and Tencent in financial technology, financial products, and other fields.

Today, the challenge faced by most banks comes not only from fintech companies but also from the extent to which banks use fintech. It is urgent for banks, therefore, to develop adequate financial technology. Some fintech strategies adopted by the banking industry can be classified into the following three categories

4.1.1. Internal R&D

Internal research and development (R&D) refers to the development of innovative financial technologies and products promoted by banks through the existing department of information technology or the establishment of fintech subsidiaries. First the internal R&D of banks generally take the form of setting up fintech subsidiaries. Since the establishment of China Industrial Bank (CIB) fintech (兴业数金) in December 2015, the big "Six

Table 17.5. Strategic Cooperation between the Big Four
Banks and Fintech Companies

Time (year/ month)	Bank	Fintech companies	Cooperation content
2017.3	China Construction Bank	Alibaba, Ant Financial	Online and offline business cooperation, electronic payment, and business cooperation
2017.6	Agricultural Bank of China	Baidu	In-depth cooperation in fintech and financial products
2017.6	Industrial and Commercial Bank of China	JD Finance (now known as "JD Digits")	Fintech, retail banking, consumer finance, corporate credit, campus ecology, and asset management
2017.9	Bank of China	Tencent	Cloud computing, big data, blockchain, and artificial intelligence

Banks" of China (Industrial and Commercial Bank of China, Agricultural Bank of China, Bank of China, China Construction Bank, Postal Savings Bank of China, Bank of Communications) have set up fintech subsidiaries, which can be divided into three categories according to their business purposes. The second is exporting fintech solutions. For example, CIB fintech has reached 311 contracted banks; connected to 43,600 outlets; and served small and medium-sized banks, nonbanking institutions, governmental and public service institutions, and industrial Internet participants. The third category mainly refers to technical services provided for the group's internal financial business. For example, the main function of China Everbright Bank (CEB) (光大银行) is to incubate new products, services, models, and business forms and to improve the group's overall information technology level.

At present, internal R&D is mainly applicable to large commercial banks. Small and medium-sized banks do not have the ability to develop technologies, talents, and resources independently.

4.1.2. Investment and Acquisition

Investment and acquisition refer to the concept that banks invest their own capital in fintech companies to establish partnerships and serve as external fintech R&D bases to shorten the time of technology R&D and application. In April 2016, the China banking regulatory commission, the Ministry of Science and Technology, and the People's Bank of China jointly issued a "Guidance on supporting banking financial institutions to increase innovation efforts and carry out pilot projects for joint lending by sci-tech and innovation enterprises" (关于支持银行业金融机构加大创新力度开展科创企业投贷联动试点的指导意见). Banks thereafter have been allowed to set up subsidiaries to engage in equity investment in scientific and technological innovation and entrepreneurship, which also creates opportunities for commercial banks to develop fintech.

At present, investment and acquisition of Chinese banks are still in the pilot phase and not being done on a large scale. However, foreign banks such as Goldman Sachs have invested in 29 fintech companies since 2016 with a wide range of investment types, including big data analysis, credit investigation, insurance, financial management, and lending.

4.1.3. Cooperation

The cooperation between banks and fintech companies includes strategic alliances to build joint laboratories and even joint subsidiaries to permit banks to purchase services from fintech companies.

At present, the cooperation mode of joint laboratory construction and the subsidiary establishment is still in the stage of trial and exploration. Because of the weak landing ability of applications, the main approach adopted by Chinese banks is the purchase of services from fintech companies. According to PWC's 2017 China overview of global fintech survey, 48% of financial institutions in China now purchase services from fintech companies, and 68% of them will increase their cooperation with fintech companies over the next three to five years. For example, Baidu exported the development of its technical ability to the Bank of Nanjing, helping that bank expand its customer services, and so on.

4.2. Insurance Companies

Fintech has also been reshaping the Chinese insurance industry. Since China joined the WTO, the development of China's insurance industry has been accelerating. Major institutions in the industry include China's insurance regulatory commission, the Insurance Association of China (IAC), and various insurance companies. The insurance industry today is playing an increasingly important role in promoting the country's economic development.

The fintech applications to the insurance industry are being led by several Chinese insurance giants, such as Ping An Insurance and Taikang Insurance. The innovations in insurance services focus on underwriting, purchasing, activation, and claims processing. For underwriting, big data and AI technologies realize risk selection and pricing based on customers' individual preference. For purchasing, insurance services are combined with other types of products and sold to customers via non-insurance platforms. Moreover, flexible insurance products are provided for heterogeneous consumers.

Fintech strategies adopted by insurance companies can be classified into two categories: technology enhancement and technology spillovers.

4.2.1. Technology Enhancement

Insurance companies utilize big data and AI technologies to improve their product quality, customer services, and claim management. For example, Ping An Insurance Technology has penetrated into every aspect of insurer Ping An's business and is changing it. About 90% of traffic accidents can be handled in a streamlined manner by applying technologies such as artificial intelligence. Ping An established various service models in its claims database, which included the cost of each car part if purchased in different cities, related labor costs, and even fraud. The goal is to create an intelligent and efficient system for processing auto insurance claims. With this system, drivers can shoot and then upload accident photos, after which an artificial intelligence module can analyze the extent of damage and determine responsibility easily and quickly without waiting for traffic police.

4.2.2. Technology Spillovers

Insurance companies can use fintech to extend the application of technology from the insurance sector to other sectors. Companies have long been actively seeking to integrate with the "big health" industry, especially since the integration with large insurance companies in the medical industry has been quite effective.

For example, Ping An is selling its facial recognition technology to the travel industry. Zhongan Insurance is also broadening the application of scientific and technological channels. In 2017, it sold dozens of its technological innovations to hundreds of customers in numerous industries, generating $6.4 million in sales. And Sunshine Insurance Group established the first hospital led by insurance capital management "Sunshine Union."

4.3. Asset Management Firms

Robo-advisors increasingly becoming popular as a result of the provision of low-cost and automated services for customers. For example, Rossi and Utkus (2020) indicate that robo-advisors increase investors' holdings of low-cost indexed mutual funds, expand their international diversification, and improve their overall risk-adjusted performance. Moreover, robo-advisors provide investors with customized wealth management solutions, which once were only available for wealthy investors. These benefits of robo-advisors are inducing more and more Chinese fund companies to invest in the application of AI to asset management.

China's robo-advisors started in 2016, and their assets under management may exceed 5 trillion yuan by 2020. Robo-advising has been included in the regulatory system in China since 2018. As pointed out by "Guiding Opinions on Regulating the Asset Management Business of Financial Institutions "(《关于规范金融机构资产管理业务的指导意见》), financial institutions must obtain investment consultant qualification to carry out robo-advising with artificial intelligence technology; also, nonfinancial institutions cannot operate beyond a certain scope or carry out asset management business in disguise with the aid of robo-advising.

Robo-advisor strategies adopted by Chinese fund companies can be classified into two categories:

1. The full-robo-advisor model: This means that the asset allocation recommendation is completely made by the artificial intelligence algorithm of the robot investment advisor, which only conducts necessary and limited intervention or does not intervene at all. The model is mainly applied to portfolio construction and transaction execution. Most of these companies started business with emerging Internet platform investment companies, such as Betterment, Wealthfront, SIGFIG, and so on.
2. The semi-robo-advisor model: This model's asset allocation plan is suggested by the robot investment advisor only as a reference. The final investment proposal must be manually examined and processed before it can be adopted by users who have more interaction with traditional investment advisors.

From the perspective of industrial development, the semi-robo-advisor model is currently in the leading position, because it relies on the resources of the platform and customer channels of traditional financial institutions. However, with the development of technology, the full-robo-advisor model will likely become mainstream in the future.

For example, the Industrial and Commercial Bank of China has applied its latest AI technology to its wealth management business. The company's new "robo-advisor" service will allow computer programs to offer investment advice to retail investors through its mobile banking platform, becoming the first one of China's "big four" state-owned banks to promptly unleash the potential of a hot new service increasingly being adopted by the global banking industry.

5. FINTECH CITIES

The development of fintech in China includes emerging business forms, such as Internet banking, Internet securities, and Internet insurance. These forms range in territory from the Beijing-Tianjin-Hebei region and the Yangtze river delta region to the Guangdong-Hong Kong-Macao Greater Bay Area. At present, Beijing, Shanghai, Shenzhen, Hangzhou, and several other cities are world-class financial technology hubs.

5.1. Shenzhen

5.1.1. Key Fintech Companies
Shenzhen, a city with a history of only 40 years, has become China's economic center due to its rapid development. The city today hosts eight top-50 fintech companies, including the first Internet bank, Webank; and the first overseas-listed online broker, Futu Securities, which ranks third in the country (Zhejiang University et al., 2018).

Webank is the first private Internet bank in China, having been initiated and established by Tencent and other well-known enterprises. In December 2014, Webank obtained the financial license issued by Shenzhen Banking Regulatory Bureau.

Futu Securities is a licensed corporation approved by the Securities and Futures Commission of Hong Kong and is a participant of the Hong Kong Stock Exchange, mainly by providing online securities brokerage services.

5.1.2. Local Advantages and Disadvantages of Fintech Development
Shenzhen is home to a large number of technology enterprises represented by Huawei and Tencent. Because it hosts the national financial trading center of the Shenzhen Stock Exchange, Shenzhen has established its status as a financial center. Its accumulation of enterprises dealing with finance and technology will be the driving force of the city's development of fintech.

As a bridge between the mainland and Hong Kong, Shenzhen will benefit from the development of the Guangdong-Hong Kong-Macao Greater Bay Area, encouraged by the government. Shenzhen can more easily attract talent, capital, and technology. It can also learn from Hong Kong's experience in fintech regulation.

In contrast, despite Shenzhen's efforts to develop its education industry, its limited number of universities and research institutions may hinder the rapid development of fintech, in the face of a growing demand for talent. For Shenzhen, the issues of how to clearly position itself in the Guangdong-Hong Kong-Macao Greater Bay Area and to find appropriate roles in both competing and cooperating with other cities will pose both opportunities and challenges.

5.2. Hangzhou

5.2.1. Key Fintech Companies

Hangzhou is the forerunner of China's fintech enterprises because it owns the industry giant Ant Financial. It has a total of three of the top-50 fintech companies in China, ranking in fourth position in the country. Ant Financial, which started as Alipay, is committed to building an open and shared credit system and financial service platform, mainly by providing inclusive financial services to consumers as well as small or micro-enterprises.

5.2.2. Local Advantages and Disadvantages of Fintech Development

Hangzhou's financial adoption rate amounts to 91.5%, which is the highest in the country (Zhejiang University, et al., 2018). Its comprehensive fintech infrastructure gives it an extra advantage for industry development. In addition, Hangzhou is home to leading global digital economy companies such as Hikvision and Dahua. Hikvision is an intelligent IoT solution and a big-data service provider with video as its core. Dahua focuses on video as well, and provides video-centric smart IoT solution and service. The city's good entrepreneurial atmosphere and increasing international influence will both boost Hangzhou's future development of fintech.

Compared with Beijing, Shanghai, and Shenzhen, Hangzhou lacks the advantage of being an international or regional financial center. Its overall size and the limited depth of the fintech industry therefore remain to be developed. As a pioneer in fintech, Hangzhou may have to explore a unique development path.

5.3. Beijing

5.3.1. Key Fintech Companies

As the capital of China as well as the political, economic, and cultural center of the country, Beijing has become a world-class city for fintech. It hosts the greatest number among the leading 50 fintech companies in the country, totaling 21, which included JD Digits ("京东数科") and Yirendai ("宜人贷").

JD Digits, formerly known as JD Finance, focuses on the three cutting-edge technologies of the era—namely data technology, AI, and IoT. It leads the city in the fields of digital finance, digital city, and digital agriculture.

Yirendai was launched by Creditease to provide credit loan consulting services and professional online wealth management services. Yirendai was China's first fintech listed company, trading on the New York Stock Exchange.

5.3.2. Local Advantages and Disadvantages of Fintech Development

Beijing's chief advantages lie in its rich educational and scientific resources. While its GDP ranks second in the country, after only Shanghai, its R&D investment as a proportion of GDP was the highest in 2017 with a rate of 5.4%. Beijing has more than 30 "Double First-Rate" (双一流) universities, including world-class institutions such as Tsinghua

University and Peking University. Beijing also is home to a large number of entrepreneurial incubators and innovative laboratory clusters.

The city also serves many financial regulatory agencies, including China's banking
and insurance regulatory commission and its securities regulatory commission. Since
Beijing may have a stricter regulatory environment than other cities, it is a challenge for
it to balance fintech's innovations and their associated risks. Beijing also needs to promote the coordinated development of fintech in the Beijing–Tianjin–Hebei region.

5.4. Shanghai

5.4.1. Key Fintech Companies

As China's international financial center, Shanghai is home to numerous fintech companies, including Lufax and Zhongan Insurance, the latter of which is the country's first
online insurance company. Shanghai has 14 fintech companies that are ranked among
the top 50 in China, putting the city second in the country in that ranking. (Zhejiang
University, et al., 2018)

Lufax, a member of the Pingan Group, was established with the support of the Shanghai municipal government to provide financial asset transaction-related services as well
as investment and financing advisory services.

Zhongan Insurance was the very first Internet insurance company in China. It gained
a listing on the main board of the Hong Kong Stock Exchange in 2017 and has developed its business entirely through the Internet.

5.4.2. Local Advantages and Disadvantages of Fintech Development

Shanghai's GDP has long ranked in the first position in the country. Its strong economic
strength provides fertile soil for the development of a variety of fintech enterprises. In
addition, financial trading centers such as the Shanghai Stock Exchange and free trade
zones to be built in the future will also greatly boost fintech's development. In terms of
scientific research, Shanghai also enjoys a considerable advantage, with its 7 national
leading institutions of higher learning and 17 special research institutions.

In recent years, Shanghai's profound financial background was a powerful impetus
for its fintech development. How to transform from only finance to fintech, and how to
better combine science and technology with the world of finance, will be future challenges for the city.

6. FINTECH AND POLICIES

6.1. Law and Regulations

Throughout the world, the rapid rise and development of fintech has brought severe challenges to many financial regulatory departments. The current regulatory system in
most countries cannot yet effectively incorporate big data, machine learning, artificial
intelligence, and other technologies, not to mention corresponding innovative services
and products. A given country's regulatory system has a great impact on the growth and
operations of fintech companies, whether consumers or other financial institutions. Regulators need to prevent and control risks with reasonable regulatory costs in a fintech-

Table 17.6. Selected Features of Dedicated Fintech Credit Policy Frameworks

Jurisdiction	Tax incentives	Regulations[a]	Licensing / authorization[a]	Investor protections[a]	Risk management requirements[a]
Australia	—	—	—	—	—
Brazil	—	✓	✓	✓	—
Canada	—	—	—	—	—
Chile	—	—	—	—	—
China	✓	✓	✓	✓	✓
Estonia	—	—	—	✓	—
Finland	—	✓	✓	—	—
France	✓	✓	✓	✓	✓
Germany	—	—	—	—	—
Japan	✓	—	—	—	—
Korea	—	—	—	—	—
Mexico	—	✓	✓	—	✓
Netherlands	—	—	—	✓	—
New Zealand	—	✓	✓	—	✓
Singapore	—	—	—	—	—
Spain	—	✓	✓	—	✓
Switzerland[b]	—	✓	✓	✓	✓
United Kingdom	✓	✓	✓	✓	✓
United States	—	—	—	—	—

Source: Committee on the Global Finance System (CGFS) and the Financial Stability Board (2017), "FinTech Credit: Market Structures, Business Models, and Financial Stability Implications" (www.bis .org); national authorities.

[a] Specific rules for fintech credit that are separate from preexisting rules for other financial intermediaries.

[b] New rules effective from 2019.

booming background. Each party in the system has a unique role. Successful regulations require integrating each participant into a regulatory framework with broader dynamics. Effective financial regulations can benefit the whole system, helping enterprises identify and manage risks, promoting effective competition in the market, and protecting the rights and interests of consumers (table 17.6).

The regulatory patterns followed by various countries reflect their specific levels of regulatory rigor and focus. Regulators that prefer to promote fintech will encourage innovations in a risk-controlled environment through measures such as limited licensing, exemptions, and regulatory "sandboxes."

The regulatory sandbox model has been adopted in the United Kingdom, and exists in many different forms in other countries. It allows for the protection of consumer rights and for testing of new products and services within a specific scope. The regulatory authorities will then monitor and evaluate the corresponding risks and decide whether to promote or restrict the tested products and services. A regulatory sandbox can effectively reduce restrictions on innovative financial products, making fintech's various innovations more flexible. Specific rules of the regulatory sandbox vary from country to country, according to the maturity of its financial system, the structure of its existing regulatory system, and its overall tolerance of risk.

Fintech was formally incorporated into China's regulatory framework in 2015. The People's Bank of China, the Ministry of Industry and Information Technology, and eight other government agencies jointly published the "Guidance on Promoting the Sound Development of Internet Finance" (《关于促进互联网金融健康发展的指导意见》).

In 2016, under the framework guidance of the "Guiding Opinions," various regulatory agencies began special rectification work on Internet financial risks, focusing on the governance of areas such as P2P online lending, blockchain, and third-party payment.

For P2P lending, "Interim Measures for the Management of P2P Network Lending Business" (《P2P网络借贷业务管理暂行办法》) was enacted on August 17, 2016, by the CBRC with the cooperation of Ministry of Industry and Information Technology, the Ministry of Public Security, and the Internet Information Technology Office.

For blockchain, the People's Bank of China and six other government agencies jointly issued a guidance that immediately banned fundraising through the offering of tokens and required that all cryptocurrency exchanges be closed by the end of September 2017.

For third-party payment, the People's Bank of China published "Notice on Regulations of Innovative Payment Business" (《关于规范支付创新业务的通知》) in December 2017 to further strengthen the management of payment business, improve payment innovation, and promote the sustained and healthy development of the payment service market.

In 2017, fintech regulations entered a new stage of elaboration when regulatory authorities introduced relevant policies such as online lending industry supervision and payment industry supervision. From 2016 to 2017, the China banking regulatory commission had taken the lead to build a network of lending industry under "One Measure" and "Three Guidelines" principles, which include the "Online Lending Information Intermediary Business Management Interim Measures" (《网络借贷信息中介机构业务活动管理暂行办法》), " Online Lending Information Intermediary Institutions for the Record Registration Management Guidelines" (《网络借贷信息中介机构备案登记管理指引》), "Online Lending Funds Depository Business Guide" (《网络借贷资金存管业务指引》), and the "Online Lending Information Intermediaries Information Disclosure Guideline." Moreover, the fintech committee of the People's Bank of China was established in May 2017 to strengthen research planning and coordination of fintech work.

Regulators have also noted the importance of privacy and data protection and therefore have begun to closely monitor the behavior of market participants. The regulations in China related to personal data protection are scattered among the Criminal Law, the Tort Law, the Cyber Security Law, the Rules on Protection of Personal Data of Telecommunications and Internet Users, and other laws and regulations.

6.2. Regulatory Risks

On the one hand, fintech has to date played an important role in promoting innovation-driven development, broadening the availability of finance, and improving the efficiency of the financial system. On the other hand, it also poses new challenges for regulators. Fintech regulation must deal with serious problems of balancing between improving financial efficiency and both preventing and controlling financial risks.

6.2.1. Information Risk

As a first concern, some institutions have a weak awareness of how to protect personal information. When carrying out business, they often exchange customer information with each other as business resources, leading to inadvertent and sometimes damaging information disclosure. Taking Internet payment as an example, some people use fake QR codes, public WiFi, phishing websites, Trojan horses, and other means to commit online fraud. These risks and losses loom larger and will be harder to manage than those of traditional financial payments.

Second, although P2P online lending can easily match lenders with borrowers, it cannot completely solve the problem of evaluating credit level and borrowers' repayment ability. In general, P2P online lending by itself cannot complete credit risk assessment and solve the problem of asymmetric information between lenders and borrowers, or seek out hidden dangers of large-scale network loan defaults.

Third, certain emerging fintech business models are active in various jurisdictions in which they might increase uncertainty. As one example, bitcoin is based on a platform of distributed ledger technology (DLT), where users can join or quit at any time. The point-to-point trading characteristics of blockchain technology and its good encryption protection greatly increase both the difficulty and the cost of information tracing for regulators. In addition, bitcoin transaction data cannot be decrypted or even traced, and it can readily be used for illegal activities such as money laundering.

6.2.2. Regulatory Challenges

Fintech may challenge the traditional risk management mechanism of existing forms of financial regulation throughout China. As fintech evolves rapidly, one of the questions faced by regulators is how a centralized institution like it can handle decentralized data. At the same time, certain financial technologies make traditional risk management methods ineffective. For example, a blockchain transaction is a form of immediate clearing, which greatly raises the speed of risk spread and simultaneously poses new challenges to the financial safety net composed of financial supervision, a deposit insurance system, and a lender of last resort of central bank.

6.2.3. Systemic Risk

One of the advantages of intelligent investment consulting is its ability to customize the portfolio of risk assets through algorithms and models so as to grasp forward-looking risks more accurately and make investment decisions that are more reasonable and more scientific. In fact, intelligent investment services offered by different platform operators are based on several successful model algorithms, which may in turn lead to similar recommendations and transactions. This approach may result in a degree of consistency in expectations and operations. The market's pump-and-dump mechanism possibly may further trigger the vulnerability of the system.

NOTES

1. Ernst & Young has done a survey by interviewing more than 27,000 consumers in 27 markets in 2019. Most fintech adopters define the fintech adoption rate as a percentage of the digitally active population in each market.
2. World Bank Group Enterprise Surveys.
3. The eight companies are Zhima Credit (芝麻信用管理有限公司), Tecent Credit (腾讯征信有限公司), Qianhai Credit (深圳前海征信中心股份有限公司), PY Credit (鹏元征信有限公司), CCX Credit (中诚信征信有限公司), INTELLI Credit (中智诚征信有限公司), Kaola Credit (拉卡拉信用管理有限公司), Sinoway Credit (北京华道征信有限公司), respectively.

REFERENCES

Beck, T., A. Demirgüç-Kunt, and M. S. M. Pería (2011). "Bank Financing for SMEs: Evidence across Countries and Bank Ownership Types." *Journal of Financial Services Research* 39(1–2): 35–54.

Beck, T., A. Demirgüç-Kunt, L. Laeven, and R. Levine. (2008). "Finance, Firm Size, and Growth." *Journal of Money, Credit and Banking*, 40(7): 1379–1405.

Brunnermeier, Markus, Michael Sockin, and Wei Xiong (2017). "China's Gradualistic Economic Approach and Financial Markets." *American Economic Review Papers & Proceedings* 107(5): 608–13.

CHFS (China Household Finance Survey) (2015). "Credit for Small and Micro Enterprises." Survey and Research Centre for China Household Finance, Southwestern University of Finance and Economics, Chengdu.

China Academy of Information and Communications Technology (2018). White paper on Blockchain.

Claessens, S., J. Frost, G. Turner, and F. Zhu (2018). "Fintech Credit Markets around the World: Size, Drivers and Policy Issues." *BIS Quarterly Review*, September, Bank of International Settlements.

CNNIC (2018). "The 41st Statistical Report on China's Internet Development: Toward Universal Financial Inclusion in China—Models, Challenges, and Global Lessons." World Bank Group and People's Bank of China. http://www.cac.gov.cn/2018-01/31/c_1122347026.htm.

Demirgüç-Kunt, A., and R. Levine (2008). "Finance, Financial Sector Policies, and Long-Run Growth." Policy Research Working Paper; No. 4469. Washington, DC: The World Bank.

Ernst and Young (2019). "EY Global FinTech Adoption Index." https://www.ey.com/en_us/ey-global-fintech-adoption-index/.

Frost & Sullivan (2018). "China's P2P Lending Industry Market Research Report." http://www.frostchina.com/wp-content/uploads/2019/05/P2Pjiedai.pdf.

Guo, Feng, Jingyi Wang, Fang Wang, Tao Kong, Xun Zhang, and Zhiyun Cheng (2019). "Measuring China's Digital Financial Inclusion: Index Compilation and Spatial Characteristics." Working paper, Institute of Digital Finance, Peking University.

Hanedar, E. Y., E. Broccardo, and R. Bazzana (2014). "Collateral Requirements of SMEs: The Evidence from Less-Developed Countries." *Journal of Banking & Finance* 38: 106–21.

IMF (2016). "Introducing a New Board-based Index of Financial Development," Working Paper No. 16/5, January.

ING Economics Department (2016). "The Fintech Index." https://www.ing.nl/media/ING_EBZ_fintech-index-report_tcm162-116078.pdf.

Jiang, Jinglin, Li Liao, Zhengwei Wang, and Xiaoyan Zhang (2019). "Government Affiliation and Fintech Industry: The Peer-to-Peer Lending Platforms in China." Available at SSRN: https://ssrn.com/abstract=3116516 or http://dx.doi.org/10.2139/ssrn.3116516.

Jiang, Juanjuan, Zhiming Li, and Chanyan Lin (2014). "Financing Difficulties of SMEs from Its Financing Sources in China." *Journal of Service Science and Management* 7(3): 196–200.

Klapper L., L. Laeven, and R. Rajan (2006). "Entry Regulation as a Barrier to Entrepreneurship." *Journal of Financial Economics*, 82(3): 591–629.

Kostka, Genia (2019). "China's Social Credit Systems and Public Opinion: Explaining High Levels of Approval." *New Media and Society* 21(7): 1565–93.

KPMG (2018). "Fintech100 Leading Global Fintech Innovators." https://home.kpmg/xx/en/home/insights/2018/10/2018-fintech-100-the-worlds-leading-fintech-innovators-fs.html.

Kuntchev, V., R. Ramalho, J. R. Meza, and J. S. Yang (2012). "What Have We Learned from the Enterprise Surveys Regarding Access to Finance by SMEs?" Washington, DC: World Bank.

Levine, Ross (2005). "Finance and Growth: Theory and Evidence," in *Handbook of Economic Growth*, volume 1, edited by Philippe Aghion and Steven Durlauf, 865–934. Netherlands: Elsevier.

Lin, Yifu, and Xifang Sun (2005). "Information, Informal Finance and SME Financing." *Economic Research Journal*, 7: 35–44.

Liu, C., J. Lu, and C. S. Yu (2018). "Examining WeChat Social Commerce Continuance Intention and Use of Incorporating Personality Traits." *ICBDT '18:* Proceedings of 2018 International Conference on Big Data Technologies. New York: Association for Computing Machinery (ACM), 115–19.

OECD (2016). *Financing SMEs and Entrepreneurs 2016: An OECD Scoreboard*. Paris: OECD Publishing.

Plantin, J. C., and G. de Seta (2019). "WeChat as Infrastructure: The Techno-Nationalist Shaping of Chinese Digital Platforms." *Chinese Journal of Communication* 12(3): 1–17.

Qu, Y., W. Rong, Y. Ouyang, et al. (2015). "Social Aware Mobile Payment Service Popularity Analysis: The Case of WeChat Payment in China." Asia-Pacific Services Computing Conference. Springer, Cham: 289–99.

Rossi, A. G., and S. Utkus (2020). "Who Benefits from Robo-advising? Evidence from Machine Learning." Available at SSRN: http://dx.doi.org/10.2139/ssrn.3552671.

Svirydzenka, K. (2015). "Introducing a New Broad-based Index of Financial Development." Washington, DC: International Monetary Fund.

Tsai, Kellee S. (2015). "Financing Small and Medium Enterprises in China: Recent Trends and Prospects beyond Shadow Banking." HKUST IEMS Working paper no. 2015-24.

World Bank Group (2017). "Enterprise Surveys." http://www.enterprisesurveys.org.

Xu J.J., Y. Lu, and M. Chau (2015). "P2P Lending Fraud Detection: A Big Data Approach," in Intelligence and Security Informatics: Intelligence and Security Informatics. PAISI 2015. *Lecture Notes in Computer Science*, vol. 9074, edited by M. Chau, G. Wang, and H. Chen. Cham: Springer.

Zhejiang University, Academy of Internet Finance; Cambridge Centre for Alternative Finance (CCAF); Zhejiang Association of Internet Finance (ZAIF); and TongBanJie Financial Technology Group (2018). "The Future of Finance Is Emerging: New Hubs, New Landscapes." Global Fintech Hub Report. https://www.jbs.cam.ac.uk/fileadmin/user_upload/research/centres/alternative-finance/downloads/2018-ccaf-global-fintech-hub-report-eng.pdf.

EDITORS AND CONTRIBUTORS

EDITORS

MARLENE AMSTAD is economics and finance professor at the Chinese University of Hong Kong, Shenzhen and co-director of its FinTech Center at the Shenzhen Finance Institute. She is senior fellow at the Kennedy School at Harvard University and serves as vice chair at the Swiss Financial Market Supervisory Authority. A former deputy director and head of investment strategy and financial market analysis at the Swiss National Bank, Amstad worked at the Bank for International Settlements, the Federal Reserve Bank of New York, Credit Suisse, and the Swiss Economic Institute. She served as senior adviser to the major Asian central banks and coordinated their Asian Bond Fund initiative. Her research focus is money, banking, and Chinese financial markets. She is the coeditor of *Central Bank Digital Currency and Fintech in Asia* with the Asian Development Bank, and created the "Fed New York staff underlying inflation gauge (UIG)." She was awarded research fellowships and visiting positions by Bank of Japan, Bank of Finland, and Princeton University, and received her Ph.D. in econometrics from the University of St. Gallen.

GUOFENG SUN is the director general of the Monetary Policy Department of People's Bank of China, an adjunct professor at Tsinghua University, a member of China's Foreign Exchange Committee, and a member of China Finance 40 Forum. He was director general of the Research Institute of the PBC and previously worked in the PBC's Monetary Policy department, where he served as deputy director of Open Market Operations, director of Foreign Exchange Operations, and deputy director General of the Monetary Policy department. He designed and implemented the RMB Exchange Rate Regime reforms in 2005–2015. Dr. Sun was a visiting professor in the Economics Department of Princeton University, a visiting fellow at the Bank for International Settlements, and a visiting fellow at Stanford University. He won the 2018 Sun Yefang Financial Award, the most prestigious financial research award in China. He is the author of *Reforms in China's Monetary Policy* and *Financial Reforms in Modern China*. He received his Ph.D. in economics from the Chinese Academy of Social Sciences.

WEI XIONG is the Trumbull-Adams Professor of Finance and Professor of Economics in the Department of Economics and Bendheim Center for Finance, Princeton University; as well as Academic Dean of the School of Management and Economics at The Chinese University of Hong Kong, Shenzhen; and academic director of Shenzhen Finance Institute. He is also co-editor of the *Journal of Finance* (the flagship journal of American Finance Association), and research associate at the National Bureau of Economic Research. His academic work covers a wide range of topics related to capital market imperfections and behavioral finance. His current interests focus on understanding China's financial system and the Chinese economy. He has received various awards, including the Smith Breeden Award (first prize) for the best noncorporate finance paper published in the *Journal of Finance* in 2012; the 2013 NASDAQ OMX Award for the best asset pricing paper presented in Western Finance Association Meetings; the inaugural Sun Yefang Financial Award in 2014; and the China Economics Prize in 2018. He received his Ph.D. in finance from Duke University.

CONTRIBUTORS

FRANKLIN ALLEN has been professor and director of the Brevan Howard Centre at Imperial College London since 2014. He was at the Wharton School, University of Pennsylvania, from 1980 to 2016 and is Emeritus. He has been editor of the *Review of Financial Studies* and the *Review of Finance*, president of the American Finance Association, and the Western Finance Association. He is a Fellow of the Econometric Society and the British Academy. His doctorate is from Oxford University.

KAIJI CHEN is currently a tenured associate professor at Emory University and senior research fellow of the Federal Reserve Bank of Atlanta. His main research fields are macroeconomics and financial economics. He has published in several top economic journals, such as *American Economic Review, NBER Macroeconomic Annual, American Economic Journal: Macroeconomy*, and *Journal of Monetary Economics*. His paper "The Great Housing Boom of China," was awarded the third Sun Yefang Financial Innovation Award in 2018.

TUO DENG has been an economist at the State Administration of Foreign Exchange Investment Center (SAFEIC) since 2015. At the center he specializes in the U.S. economy, providing in-depth views on U.S. growth, inflation, monetary policy, and more. He has also participated in several research programs on China's macroeconomic policy. He holds a B.A. in finance from Peking University and a Ph.D. in economics from University of Rochester.

HANMING FANG is the Class of 1965 Term Professor of Economics and a professor of health care management at the University of Pennsylvania, and dean of the School of Entrepreneurship and Management at ShanghaiTech University. He is a Fellow of the Econometric Society and a research associate of the National Bureau of Economic Research. He was a co-editor of the *Journal of Public Economics* and the *International Economic Review*, and is currently a senior editor of the *Journal of Risk and Insurance*.

JIN FENG is professor of economics at Fudan University, chair of its Department of Public Economics, and vice director of its Employment and Social Security Research Center. She was selected into the "Program for New Century Excellent Talents" by China's Ministry of Education. Her research interests focus on social security reforms, health care, and elderly care in China. She has had papers published in the *Journal of Economic Behavior and Organization, World Development, Journal of Comparative Economics, Feminist Economics*, and top Chinese journals.

TINGTING GE received her Ph.D. from the National School of Development at Peking University. She served as a part-time economist in IMF's Resident Representative Office for China in 2018–2019 and was selected for the 2019 Fund Internship Program. She was a visiting scholar at Cornell University in 2017–2018. Her research field covers monetary economics, international finance, and macroeconomics, while her current research focuses on leverage, financial risk, and fintech.

KAI GUO is deputy director-general of the Monetary Policy Department of the People's Bank of China. His main responsibilities include central bank lending and foreign exchange issues. He holds a Ph.D. in economics from Harvard University and worked as an economist at the IMF before joining the PBC. His research interests include the Chinese economy and international finance.

XIAOBEI HE is project head for macrofinance research at the Center for Finance and Development at the National Institute for Financial Research, Tsinghua University. Xiaobei holds a Ph.D. in economics from Goethe University in Frankfurt, a master's degree in economics from the Hong Kong University of Science and Technology, and a bachelor's degree in engineering from Tongji University.

ZHIGUO HE serves as the Fuji Bank and Heller Professor of Finance, director of the Becker Friedman Institute China, and co-director of the Fama-Miller Center at the University of Chicago. He is a research associate at NBER, the Special-Term Alibaba Foundation Professor at Tsinghua University, and a member of the Academic Committee of Luohan Academy. His most recent research includes financial institutions' role in the 2008 global financial crisis, Chinese financial markets, and economic issues on cryptocurrency and blockchain.

YIPING HUANG is the Jin Guang Chair Professor of Economics and deputy dean of the National School of Development and director of the Institute of Digital Finance at Peking University. In October 2018, he was appointed by the International Monetary Fund's managing director to be a member of the External Advisory Group on Surveillance. He served as a member of the Monetary Policy Committee at the People's Bank of China during 2015–2018.

ZHAOJUN HUANG is a research associate at the PBC School of Finance and the National Institute of Financial Research of Tsinghua University. Her research centers on entrepreneurial financing, corporate innovation, and general topics on firm investments and financing. Her current research focuses on innovation and fintech.

NINGXIN JIANG joined the People's Bank of China in 2017 and has worked in the International Department. She got her M.A. in finance from Peking University in 2017. Her main academic interests include financial sector opening-up and currency internationalization issues.

WENXI JIANG is an assistant professor of finance at the Chinese University of Hong Kong. He obtained a Ph.D. in financial economics from Yale University. His research focuses on behavioral finance, institutional investor, and climate finance. He conducts several projects on the behavior of Chinese investors and its implications for market efficiency, financial stability, and regulatory policies. His works are published in top economics and finance journals, including *Journal of Econometrics, Journal of Finance,* and *Review of Financial Studies.*

CHANG LIU is a postdoctoral research associate at the Paul and Marcia Wythes Center on Contemporary China at Princeton University, which is associated with the School of

Economics and Management at the Chinese University of Hong Kong, Shenzhen. His research interests center on public finance, the political economy, and the development economy, with a regional focus on China.

JUN MA is director of the Center for Finance and Development at Tsinghua National Institute of Financial Research, and a member of the Monetary Policy Committee of the People's Bank of China, where he previously served as chief economist of the Research Bureau. He held various positions at Deutsche Bank, including managing director, chief economist for Greater China, and head of China and Hong Kong Strategy. He worked at the International Monetary Fund and World Bank and was a research fellow at the Development Research Center of China's State Council.

YANLIANG MIAO is chief economist at China's State Administration of Foreign Exchange Investment Center, where he shapes macro views for the world's largest reserve manager. He is also an adjunct professor at Peking University's National School of Development. Previously, he served as senior advisor to the Administrator of SAFE while rebuilding its research group. He was an economist with the IMF from 2008 to 2013. He holds a Ph.D. from Princeton University's Woodrow Wilson School.

FAN QI joined the People's Bank of China in 2010 and has worked in the Research Bureau and the International Department. She got her Ph.D. in economics in 2016 from the Chinese Academy of Social Sciences. Her main academic interests include international monetary system reform and sovereign debt issues.

JUN "QJ" QIAN is professor of finance and executive dean at the Fanhai International School of Finance, Fudan University. He was a tenured finance professor at Boston College before returning to China. He received his Ph.D. from the University of Pennsylvania in 2000. His research interests span corporate finance, financial institutions, and capital markets. He also studies financial systems in emerging economies, including China, India, and Africa, and researches their relationship with economic growth in these countries.

CHENYU SHAN is associate professor of finance at the School of Finance, Shanghai University of Finance and Economics (SUFE). She was a visiting assistant professor at the Shanghai Advanced Institute of Finance before joining SUFE. She earned a Ph.D. in finance at the University of Hong Kong in 2013. She served as a Fulbright visiting scholar at the Wharton School. Her research focuses on credit default swaps, credit markets, corporate finance, banking, and Chinese financial markets.

XUAN TIAN is JD Capital Chair Professor of Finance at the PBC School of Finance, Tsinghua University. His research focuses on corporate finance, venture capital, corporate innovation, and IPOs. More than 20 of his papers have been published in leading academic journals, two of which, including one single-authored paper, were awarded the Jensen Prize of the *Journal of Financial Economics*. Before joining Tsinghua, he was a tenured professor of finance at the Kelley School of Business at Indiana University.

CHU WANG is a master student of the National School of Development at Peking University. His research interests cover monetary policy and fintech. He co-authored a report on the risk and surveillance of internet finance, as part of a project for the Financial Research Center at the Counselors' Office of State Council.

CONG WANG'S research interests include corporate governance as well as mergers and acquisitions. He has published papers in globally leading finance and accounting journals such as *Journal of Finance, Review of Financial Studies, Journal of Accounting and Economics*, and *Journal of Financial and Quantitative Analysis*. He has taught at CUHK, CEIBS, and CUHK (Shenzhen). His work has received a fair amount of recognition. One of his publications won the 2015 Emerald Citations of Excellence Award.

TAO WANG is head of Asia Economic Research and Chief Economist for China at the UBS Investment Bank. Her research on China covers monetary policy, financial sector reform, exchange rate and capital flows, local government debt, trade, the property bubble, and demographic shifts. Before joining UBS, she worked briefly at Bank of America and BP plc, and she was a senior economist at the International Monetary Fund. She received her Ph.D. degree in economics from New York University and a B.A. from Renmin University of China in Beijing.

YI XIONG is Chief Economist for China at Deutsche Bank. He was an economist at the International Monetary Fund from 2009 to 2017, working on China, including at the organization's Resident Representative Office in China from 2009 to 2010, and assisting China's G20 Presidency in 2015–2016—as well as on a broad range of countries in the Asia Pacific, Europe, and Africa. He has a Ph.D. e in economics and a B.S. degree from Peking University in Beijing.

TAO ZHA is executive director of the Center for Quantitative Economic Research at the Federal Reserve Bank of Atlanta, the Samuel Candler Dobbs Professor of Economics at Emory University, and a research associate at the National Bureau of Economic Research. He is an elected Fellow of the Econometric Society. He has published numerous articles and served on editorial boards of various academic journals.

BOHUI ZHANG is Presidential Chair Professor and executive associate dean of the School of Management and Economics at the Chinese University of Hong Kong, Shenzhen. He is also the director of the Center for FinTech and Social Finance at Shenzhen Finance Institute. Previously, he served as professor of finance at the Business School at University of New South Wales, Sydney, Australia. He studies the role of information intermediaries on capital markets, Chinese and foreign capital markets, and fintech.

TIANYU ZHANG is a professor in the School of Accountancy at the Chinese University of Hong Kong, and director of the Centre of Institutions and Capital Market, Shenzhen Finance Institute. His research focuses on political institutions and governance in China's emerging market.

ZHIWEI ZHANG is the president and chief economist at Pinpoint Asset Management. Before joining Pinpoint in 2019, he worked at Deutsche Bank, Nomura Securities, China International Capital Corporation, Hong Kong Monetary Authority, International Monetary Fund, and the Bank of Canada. He has published widely in academic journals, including the *Quarterly Journal of Economics, the Review of Economics and Statistics, and China Economic Review*. He has a Ph.D. in economics from the University of California, San Diego.

YUE ZHAO is currently an advisor in the Office of Excursive Director for China at International Monetary Fund. She received her Ph.D. in economics from Peking University in 2014. From 2012–2013, she was a visiting scholar at Columbia Business School. She worked in the international department at People's Bank of China from 2014 to 2018. She is also a young economist in the China Finance 40 Forum.

JULIE LEI ZHU is associate professor of Accounting, with tenure, at the Fanhai International School of Finance, Fudan University. She received her Ph.D. from Columbia University in 2009. Her research interests span many subjects and topics of empirical accounting and financial economics, with a focus on the impact of financial statements and other aspects of the accounting system, as well as regulations and enforcement on firms' activities, market efficiency, and the overall economy.

INDEX

Page numbers in *italics* refer to figures and tables.